Netherlands Yearbook of International Law

NETHERLANDS YEARBOOK OF INTERNATIONAL LAW

published jointly with the
Netherlands International Law Review
and under the auspices of the
Stichting T.M.C. Asser Instituut,
Institute for Private and Public
International Law,
International Commercial Arbitration
and European Law,
The Hague

VOLUME XXXI
2000

T·M·C·ASSER PRESS

Under the combined subscription arrangements this volume of the Yearbook is linked to Volume 47 of the Netherlands International Law Review. Orders or requests for further information should be sent to: T.M.C. Asser Press, c/o Kluwer Law International, P.O. Box 85889, 2508 CN The Hague, The Netherlands.

All correspondence with regard to the contents of the Yearbook should be addressed to the Managing Editor, T.M.C. Asser Instituut, P.O. Box 30461, 2500 GL, The Hague, The Netherlands, e-mail NYIL@asser.nl.

See page X for General Information for authors.

Library of Congress Catalog Card Number 72-623109
ISBN 978-90-6704-143-0
ISSN 0167-6768

T.M.C. Asser Instituut - Institute for Private and Public International Law, International Commercial Arbitration and European Law

Institute Address: R.J. Schimmelpennincklaan 20-22, The Hague, The Netherlands; Mailing Address: P.O. Box 30461, 2500 GL The Hague, The Netherlands; Tel.: (31-70)3420300; Fax: (31-70)3420359; Internet: www.asser.nl.
Over thirty years, the T.M.C. Asser Institute has developed into a leading scientific research institute in the field of international law. It covers private international law, public international law, including international humanitarian law, the law of the European Union, the law of international commercial arbitration and increasingly, also, international economic law and the law of international commerce.
Conducting scientific research, either fundamental or applied, in the aforementioned domains, is the main activity of the Institute. In addition, the Institute organizes congresses and postgraduate courses, undertakes contract-research and operates its own publishing house.
Because of its inter-university background, the Institute often cooperates with Dutch law faculties as well as with various national and foreign institutions. The Institute organizes *Asser College Europe*, a project in cooperation with East and Central European countries whereby research and educational projects are organized and implemented.

TABLE OF CONTENTS

ABBREVIATIONS

Aanh. Hand. I/II	Aanhangsel tot het Verslag der Handelingen van de Eerste/ Tweede Kamer der Staten Generaal
AB	Administratiefrechtelijke Beslissingen
AB kort	Administratiefrechtelijke Beslissingen kort
AFDI	Annuaire français de droit international
AJIL	American Journal of International Law
Am. Univ. JIL & P	American University Journal of International Law & Policy
Australian YBIL	Australian Yearbook of International Law
Bijl. Hand. I/II	Bijlagen bij het Verslag der Handelingen van de Eerste/ Tweede Kamer der Staten-Generaal
Boston Univ. ILJ	Boston University International Law Journal
BYIL	British Yearbook of International Law
Cambridge LJ	Cambridge Law Journal
Case Western Reserve JIL	Case Western Reserve Journal of International Law
CLMR	Common Market Law Reports
CMLRev.	Common Market Law Review
Cmnd	United Kingdom Command Papers
Colorado JEL&P	Colorado Journal of Environmental Law & Policy
ECR	European Court Reports
EJIL	European Journal of International Law
ELR	European Law Review
ETS	European Treaty Series
FYBIL	Finnish Yearbook of International Law
GV	Gids Vreemdelingenrecht
Hand. I/II	Verslag der Handelingen van de Eerste/Tweede Kamer der Staten-Generaal
Harvard ILJ	Harvard International Law Journal
Hastings I&CLR	Hastings International & Comparative Law Review
ICJ Rep.	International Court of Justice, Reports of Judgments, Advisory Opinions and Orders
ICLQ	International & Comparative Law Quarterly
ILC Rep.	International Law Commission Reports
ILC Yearbook	Yearbook of the International Law Commission
ILM	International Legal Materials
ILR	International Law Review
JAR	Jurisprudentie Arbeidsrecht
JM	Jurisprudentie Milieurecht
JV	Justitiële Verkenningen
KG	Kort Geding
Leiden JIL	Leiden Journal of International Law
Melbourne JIL	Melbourne Journal of International Law
MR	Migrantenrecht
M&R	Milieu & Recht
Michigan JIL	Michigan Journal of International Law
Michigan LR	Michgan Law Review

MR	Migrantenrecht
MRT	Militair Rechtelijk Tijdschrift
NAV	Nieuwsbrief Asiel-en Vluchtenlingenrecht
NILR	Netherlands International Law Review
NIPR	Nederlands International Privaatrecht
NJ	Nederlandse Jurisprudentie
NJB	Nederlands Juristenblad
NYIL	Netherlands Yearbook of International Law
OJ	Offcial Journal of the European Communities
PCIJ Rep.	Permanent Court of International Justice, Reports
PCIJ Ser. A/B	Permanent Court of International Justice
RdC	Recuiel des Cours
RECIEL	Review of European Community and International Environmental Law
RIAA	Reports of International Arbitral Awards
RGDIP	Revue Générale de droit international public
RV	Rechtspraak Vreemdelingenrecht
RvdW	Rechtspraak van de Week
San Diego LR	San Diego Law Review
Stb.	Staatsblad van het Koninkrijk der Nederlanden
Stc.	Staatscourant
Suffolk Transn. LR	Suffolk Transnational Law Review
Trb.	Tractatenblad van het Koninkrijk der Nederlanden
Tulane JIL	Tulane Journal of International Law
UKTS	United Kingdom Treaty Series
UN Doc.	United Nations Documents
UNTS	United Nations Treaty Series
Vanderbilt JIL	Vanderbilt Journal of International Law
Virginia JIL	Virginia Journal of International Law
Yale JIL	Yale Journal of International Law
YbIEL	Yearbook International Environmental Law
YbILC	Yearbook International Law Commission
YIEL	Yearbook of International Environmental Law
YEL	Yearbook of European Law
YUN	Yearbook of the United Nations
YIHL	Yearbook of International Humanitarian Law
ZaöRV	Zeitschrift für ausländisches öffentliches Recht und Völkerrecht

GENERAL INFORMATION FOR AUTHORS

1. **Copyright and embargo** Copyright is exclusively reserved to the author(s). Acceptance of the Editors' offer to publish implies, however, that authors agree to an embargo on publication elsewhere, either in English or another language, for a period of two years following the year of publication of the Yearbook containing the article in question. Articles should not be currently under consideration elsewhere.

2. **Fees** Authors will not receive a fee, but will be represented with a copy of the Yearbook containing their article, together with 25 off-prints free of charge. Any additional copies of the Yearbook and/or off-prints can be ordered and will be charged.

3. **Editorial policy** All papers are refereed. The Board of Editors reserves the right to suggest modifications and/or additions to the paper submitted, and further reserves the right to reject, or to revoke acceptance or to withhold publication of any paper.

4. **Language** Authors are requested to submit their paper in English. Papers accepted for publication may, at the discretion of the Editors, be linguistically revised.

5. **Proofs** The author will receive proofs for correction. Corrections should be kept to a minimum. The only corrections which should normally be necessary are those relating to type-set errors or those which take account of important material or references not previously available, or subsequent developments of notes. Substantial modifications to the text or footnotes will not be permitted, except in consultation with and with the consent of the Editors.

6. **Typing** The manuscript should be typed, double-spaced with wide margins, on one side of standard A4 paper. Two copies of the paper should be submitted, and one retained by the author. Pages must be consecutively numbered. The text should be divided into chapters and each chapter may be divided into sections and subsections.

Authors should carefully check for errors before submitting. Authors are responsible for accuracy of quotations, for supplying complete and correct references, and for obtaining permission where needed to cite another author's material. Authors will be asked to provide a diskette containing the final version of their paper following acceptance for publication. The author is responsible for ensuring that the final hard copy and diskette version of the manuscript are identical.

The maximum length should be 450 words per page, 35 pages, including footnotes for a full article and 20 pages, for a case note. The first page should contain: full title of the article, author(s) full name(s), affiliation, address, telephone and fax and e-mail address.

For house-style please refer to the most recent NYIL.

ARTICLES

GENERAL INTERNATIONAL LAW IN THE EUROPEAN COURT OF JUSTICE: FROM HYPOTHESIS TO REALITY?*

Olufemi Elias**

** Visiting Lecturer, King's College, University of London. I am grateful to Olga Thomas and Caroline Meunier. Responsibility for the views expressed here is mine.

1. INTRODUCTION

There is a considerable amount of literature on the place within the European Community legal order of international agreements concluded by the European Community as well as those concluded by the Member States,[1] and this includes the case-law of the European Court of Justice (hereafter 'the Court')[2] on the matter. Similarly, much has been written on the relationship between European Community law and the legal systems of the Member States and on the relationship between international law and national legal systems. In contrast, the place of non-treaty international law within the Community legal order has not been the subject of such extensive analysis,

1. See e.g., E.-U. Petersmann, 'Application of the GATT by the Court of Justice of the European Communities', 13 *CMLRev.* (1983) p. 397; T. Hartley, 'International Agreements and the Community Legal System: Some Recent Developments', 8 *ELRev.* (1983) p. 383; G. Bebr, 'Agreements Concluded by the Community and their Possible Direct Effect: from International Fruit Company to Kupferberg', 20 *CMLRev.* (1983) p. 35; E.L.M. Völker, 'The Direct Effect of International Agreements in the Community's Legal Order', *1 Legal Issues of European Integration* (1983) p. 131; J. Bourgeois, 'Effects of International Agreements on European Community Law: Are The Dice Cast?', 82 *Michigan LR* (1984) p. 1250; J. Rideau, 'Les accords internationaux dans la jurisprudence de la Cour de Justice des Communautés européennes: Réflexions sur les relations entre les ordres juridiques international, communautaire et nationaux', 94 *RGDIP* (1990) p. 289; I. Cheyne, 'International Agreements and the European Community Legal System', 18 *ELRev.* (1994) p. 581; L. Hancher, 'Constitutionalism, the Community Court and International Law', 25 *NYIL* (1994) p. 259; P. J. Kuyper, 'The Community and State Succession in Respect of Treaties', in D. Curtin and T. Heukels, eds., *Institutional Dynamics of European Integration: Essays in Honour of H. G. Schermers* (Dordrecht, Martinus Nijhoff 1994) Vol. II, p. 640; J.M. Grimes, 'Conflicts Between EC Law and International Treaty Obligations: A Case Study on the German Telecommunications Dispute', 35 *Harvard ILJ* (1994) p. 535; C. Kaddous, 'L'arrêt *France* c. *Commission* de 1994 (accord concurrence) et le contrôle de la légalite des accords externes en vertu de l'art. 173 CE: la difficile réconciliation de l'orthodoxie communautaire avec l'orthodoxie internationale', *Cahiers de droit Européen* (1996) p. 613; P. Eeckhout, 'The Domestic Legal Status of the GATT: Interconnecting Legal Systems', *CMLRev.* (1997) p. 11; J. Klabbers, 'Re-inventing the Law of Treaties: The Contribution of the EC Courts', 30 *NYIL* (1999) p. 45; M. Hilf, F. G. Jacobs and E.-U. Petersmann, eds, *The European Community and GATT* (Deventer, Kluwer 1986); I. Macleod, I. Hendry and S. Hyett, *The External Relations of the European Communities: A Manual of Law and Practice* (Oxford, Clarendon 1996) Chs. 4, 5 and 9; D. McGoldrick, *International Relations Law of the European Union* (London, Longman 1997) Ch. 7; K. Lenaerts and P. van Nuffel, *Constitutional Law of the European Union* (London, Sweet & Maxwell 1999) pp. 550-561.

2. This term, as used hereafter, includes both the Court of Justice and the Court of First Instance as described in Arts. 220, 221 and 225, formerly Arts. 164, 165 and 168a respectively, of the consolidated version of the Treaty Establishing the European Communities (hereafter 'the EC Treaty'). Following the changes made in the Maastricht Treaty (1992), the jurisdiction of the Court was limited to matters arising out of the EC Treaty. Despite the Treaty of Amsterdam conferring jurisdiction on the Court over European Union decisions on police and judicial co-operation in criminal matters, the Court still deals mostly with the law relating to the EC Treaty. Therefore the reference in this paper will be to European Community law rather than European Union Law.

whether in the literature or in the case-law of the Court.[3] It is the treatment by the Court of this kind of international law that is the subject of this paper.[4]

It is perhaps to be expected that the discussion of role of non-treaty international law within the European Community legal order has not been extensive. It was possible for the parties to the original EC Treaty to establish a system under which rules of general international law (at least those of the character *jus dispositivum*) would not apply; in fact, the point of establishing a new legal regime by means of a treaty is to derogate from the general law, so it could be expected that rules of general international law could play no more than a limited role within that regime. As will be seen in section 2 below, the Court emphasized in its early jurisprudence that the Community legal order was different from the international legal order, possibly with the aim of ensuring the exclusion of certain methods in general international law which would not be conducive to the achievements of the ends of European integration.[5] There was thus reason not to suppose that general public international law would play a significant role in the Community legal order. It was written that, considering its nature as a dynamic 'law of integration', in contrast to the 'static' nature of both international

3. There are a few significant exceptions, but even those often involve greater consideration of treaties than general international law. See e.g., J. van Panhuys, 'Conflicts between the Law of the European Communities and Other Rules of International Law', 3 *CMLR* (1965/66) p. 420; K. Meessen, 'The Application of Rules of Public International Law Within Community Law', 13 *CMLRev.* (1976) p. 485; H. Schermers, 'Community Law and International Law', 12 *CMLRev.* (1975) p. 77; H. Schermers and D. Waelbroeck, *Judicial Protection in the European Communities*, 5th edn. (Deventer, Kluwer Law and Taxation Publishers 1992) pp. 100-107; Lenaerts and van Nuffel, loc. cit. n. 1, at pp. 561-564.

4. The term 'general international law', has been the subject of criticism; see e.g., P. Weil, 'Towards Relative Normativity in International Law', 77 *AJIL* (1983) p. 413. In this paper it is used to refer to international law other than treaty rules, and it includes includes customary law, judicial decisions, rules of *jus cogens* and resolutions of organs of the United Nations.
General principles of law, either within the meaning of Art. 38(1)(c) of the Statute of the International Court of Justice or as applied in the jurisprudence of the Court, are not treated separately in this paper, for two reasons. Firstly, the application of general principles by the Court derives not from international law but from 'the constitutional traditions' of the Member States of the Community and from the 'inspiration' provided by international treaties to which the Member States are parties, notably the European Convention on Human Rights. For discussion of the Court's treatment of general principles, see e.g., Lenaerts and van Nuffel, loc. cit. n. 1, at pp. 534-550. Secondly, the distinction between general principles of law in international law (to the extent that they form a distinct category of international law), and customary international law may be difficult to draw; see O. Elias and C. Lim, 'General Principles, 'Soft' Law and the Identification of International Law', 28 *NYIL* (1997) p. 3.

5. T.C. Hartley, *Constitutional Problems of the European Union* (Oxford, 1999) Ch. 7, especially at pp. 136-137: 'Three reasons may be suggested: first, the Court probably regarded international law as a weak and ineffective system, and wanted to distance Community law from it so that it would be possible to develop doctrines, such as direct effect and supremacy, that would make Community law more effective than international law had ever been; secondly, it wanted to avoid having to apply rules of international law in proceedings before it; thirdly, it thought that the methods of 'interpretation' [that it has applied] could be more easily put into practice if Community law were not regarded as part of international law'. For a rather passionate description of the superiority of community law over international law, see P. Pescatore, 'International Law and Community Law: A Comparative Analysis', 7 *CMLRev.* (1970) p. 167.

law and the constitutional law of federal states, 'rules of international law ... are only applicable insofar as they happen to coincide with principles of Community Law, which means that they hardly are of any help in solving legal problems.'[6]

The distinction to be drawn, then, is between the role of public international law as a source of law governing legal relations within the Community on the one hand, and legal relations between the Community and third states on the other. In the latter context, general international law can be expected to have more relevance, given that such third parties are not bound by the EC Treaty, so that the relations between such third parties would be regulated primarily by international law. And, over the years, the relations between the Community and third states has become increasingly varied and complex.[7] As will be seen in section 3 below, the cases in which questions of general international law have been examined at some length by the Court have all involved, to greater or lesser extent, relations with third parties.

This paper will examine the treatment of general international law by the Court in its earlier case-law and then in more recent cases. The Court's handling of international law will be examined critically, in order to see whether the way the Court has treated international law is a necessary consequence of the Court's institutional position within the Community legal order.

2. THE EARLY CASE-LAW OF THE COURT

It was written in 1976 that, apart from 'some early innocent references to international law', the Court 'avoided open references to international law'.[8] These observations are supported by some of the Court's seminal judgments in the earlier years of the Community's existence. The Court made it clear that the Community legal order was not merely a part of the international legal system, and it clearly intended to distinguish the EC Treaty from other treaties. In *Van Gend en Loos*,[9] it stated that 'the Community constitutes a new legal order of international law, for the benefit of which states have limited their sovereign rights, albeit within limited fields, and the subjects of

---

6. Meessen, loc. cit. n. 3. See also van Panhuys, loc. cit. n. 3, at pp. 424-426.

7. Meessen, loc. cit. n. 3, at p. 486.

8. Meessen, loc. cit. n. 3. For example, the Court has applied the principle that a Member State may not plead its internal law as an excuse for failure to comply with its obligations under the EC Treaty, see e.g., *Commission* v. *Belgium* (the *Wood* case), case 77/69 [1970] *ECR* 243, in which the Belgian government had argued that its failure to adapt its national law that imposed a tax on imported wood contrary to a provision of Community law was due to in ability to get a newly elected parliament to bring the law into line with Community law. No reference was made to the well-established principle of international law to the same effect, which was codified in Art. 27 of the Vienna Convention on the Law of Treaties (1969).

9. Case 26/62 [1963] *ECR* 1.

which comprise not only Member States but also their nationals'.[10] Even stronger was the statement in *Costa* v. *ENEL*[11] that '[b]y contrast with international treaties, the EEC Treaty has created its own legal system which on the entry into force of the Treaty, became an integral part of the legal system of the Member States and which their courts are bound to apply.'[12] In the context of such insistence on distinguishing between Community law and international law, it is not surprising that the role to be played by international law would be a limited one. In the *Dairy Products* case, it had been argued that under international law, failure by one party to fulfil her obligations under a contract released the other from the obligation to fulfil their part. The Court ruled that the alleged rule of international law as well as the related principle of self-help were not applicable to the EC Treaty; 'the EEC Treaty establishes a new legal order which regulates the powers, rights and duties of the subjects to whom it applies as well as the necessary procedure for determining and adjudicating upon any possible violation.'[13]

These observations on the relative lack of importance to be attributed to international law within the Community legal order are borne out when one considers more closely some of the cases often considered to demonstrate the importance attached to international law by the Court. One case is the often-cited *Third International Fruit Company* case.[14] Unlike previous cases before it, this case involved the obligations of the Community, and this is one of the reasons why considerable significance has been attached to it. For present purposes, the pertinent issue in the case was whether certain EEC Regulations that prohibited quantitative restrictions on imports were void as they were in conflict with the provisions of the GATT. The Court, in expressing its view that the Community was bound by international law, ruled that it was under a duty to examine the validity of acts of the Community in the light of rules of international law. The Court however would test the validity of a Community law with a

10. Ibid., at p. 12. The case also serves as an example of those cases involving an 'innocent reference' to international law. It had been argued before the Court that, in international law, treaty provisions were not self-executing in domestic legal orders to the extent that individuals could rely on those provisions before national courts, unless such a result was intended by the parties. In a ruling confirming the teleological approach adopted by the Court in its interpretation of the EC Treaty, the Court rejected that submission stating that it was necessary to consider 'the spirit, general scheme and wording of those provisions' in order to determine their effect. On this, it has been written that this conclusion is hardly disquieting for an international lawyer; see Schermers, loc. cit. n. 3, at pp. 78-79. This is so given that there are no non-derogable rules on the direct effect of international law (treaty provisions) in national legal orders. It is well-known that practice on the status of international law within national legal systems varies from jurisdiction to jurisdiction. See e.g., Sir R. Jennings and A. Watts, *Oppenheim's International Law*, 9th edn., Vol. 1 (London, Longman 1999) pp. 54-81

11. Case 6/64 [1964] ECR 585.

12. Ibid., at p. 593.

13. *Commission* v. *Belgium and Luxembourg*, cases 90-91/63 [1964] *ECR* 1217, at pp. 1232-1232. On this, Schermers, loc. cit. n. 3, at pp. 78-79, wrote that 'this reasoning seems in conformity with international law. The same would apply to any other international community which has its own procedure for determining and adjudicating upon violations against its rules.'

14. Joined cases 21-24/72 [1972] *ECR* 1219.

provision of international law only if two conditions exist; firstly, if the rule was 'binding on the Community', and secondly, if the rule is capable of creating rights of which interested parties may avail themselves in a (national) court of law. The first condition is uncontroversial (since rules that do not bind a subject of the law, in this case the Community, do not invalidate its acts), and seems to accord primacy to international law.[15]

Regarding the second condition, in contrast, it has been argued that, on the basis of the ruling in this case, an act of the Community would be found to be invalid for incompatibility with a rule of international law only if the rule of international law in question is one that can be invoked in a (national) court. The point is that there are many rules of international law that may stipulate clear and self-executing obligations for Member States of the Community but which may nevertheless not be invoked in a court of law for a variety of reasons, depending on the rules governing the reception of international law into the relevant national legal system. It could be that even where an act of the Community conflicts with a rule of *jus cogens*, the Court would not test its validity if the rule of international law could not be invoked in a court of law.[16] It would appear that the Court's treatment of international law in this case is not as significant as it might have appeared, and is limited to a general statement that Community law may be subject to international certain limited circumstances. While it is the case that under a specific legal regime, it should be expected that the parties intend to circumscribe the application of international law in their relations under that regime, the second condition imposed by the Court would seem to exclude a considerable amount of international law.[17]

A similar conclusion can be drawn in respect of another case that is widely regarded as demonstrating the Court's use of international law as a source of law (or more accurately as a source of interpretation of Community law)[18], namely the *Van Duyn* v. *Home Office*[19] case. It will be recalled that one of the issues in that case was the consideration that the restriction on entry into the United Kingdom imposed upon the Dutch plaintiff did not apply to British nationals seeking to take up the kind of employment with the same organization as that sought by the plaintiff. The Court stated that 'it is a principle of international law, which the EEC cannot be assumed to disregard in the relations between Member States, that a State is precluded from refusing its own nationals the right of entry or residence.' This case would appear to indicate reference to international law by the Court to support its preferred interpretation of a provision of the Treaty. The significance of this case has however been questioned. It has been pointed out that the Court 'neither goes on to adduce evidence of the exis-

---

15. As will be seen later, the significance of this case is not diminished for present purposes because the international law in question was a treaty rule, as the Court has applied this first condition in cases involving customary international law; see the discussion of *Racke* v. *Hauptzollamt Mainz* case in section 3.2.3 below.

16. Schermers, loc. cit. n. 3, at pp. 80-81.

17. See section 3.2.3 below.

18. See e.g., Schermers, loc. cit. n. 3, at p. 79.

19. Case 41/74 [1974] *ECR* 1337.

tence of such a rule nor to re-open a number of questions on the relationships between international law and Community law that were left unanswered by the earlier judgment of 1972 in the *International Fruit Co. and Others* v. *Produktschap voor Groenten en Fruit case*'.[20] Even stronger is the dismissal of the significance of this case as having involved a 'rather ill-conceived allusion' to 'an alleged principle of international law'.[21] What is clear is that it is correct to note that the Court did not enter into any remotely rigorous consideration of the bases for the principle of international law to which it referred in this case, and for that it may be rightly criticized.[22] There is support for the view that the Court did not take international law seriously in these cases.

In the context of the distinction drawn earlier between intra-Community relations on the one hand and relations between the Community and third parties on the other, one area of law that could prove instructive for present purposes is the field of extraterritorial jurisdiction, as that involves, in a direct way, relations with third parties. In the *Dyestuffs*[23] case, the Commission had served a statement of complaint by post to the headquarters of the defendant companies in Switzerland, thereby violating the territorial integrity of Switzerland according to principles of international law. The Advocate-General had expressly stated that the Community had violated rules of international law, and that jurisdiction should be founded only upon direct and immediate, reasonably forseeable and substantial effect.[24] The Court was not as explicit about the compatibility of the Community act with international law in its judgment. Instead, it found that the Community had jurisdiction on the basis that the defendant undertakings that had concluded restrictive agreements to fix the price of dyestuffs had corporate subsidiaries that were based within the Community. In international law terms, it would appear that jurisdiction here was based on the territorial principle, as the Court had stated that, by 'making use of its power to control its subsidiaries, established in the Community, the applicant was able to ensure that its decision was implemented on the market.'[25] This difficulty is compounded by the fact that the Court did not treat the case in terms of international law, and while on one analysis the Court may be considered to be contributing to international law, its reluctance to

20. K. Simmonds, '*Van Duyn v Home Office*: The Direct Effectiveness of Directives', 24 *ICLQ* (1975) p. 419, at p. 437.

21. Meessen, loc. cit. n. 3, at pp. 485-486.

22. It should be noted that the same criticism is often made of other courts and tribunals applying international law. See e.g., the criticism by Sir Humphrey Waldock of the ruling by the International Court of Justice in the *Anglo-Norwegian Fisheries* case (*ICJ Rep.* (1951) p. 116) 28 *BYIL* (1951) and that of the same Court in the *Military and Paramilitary Activities in and against Nicaragua* (*ICJ Rep.* (1986) p. 14) by M. H. Mendelson, 'The *Nicaragua* case and Customary International Law', 26 *Coexistence* (1989) p. 85. This observation does not, however, diminish the truth of the proposition in the text above.

23. *ICI* v. *Commission*, case 48/69 [1972] *ECR* 619.

24. See para. 57 of his Opinion.

25. See para. 130 of the judgment.

base its judgment explicitly on that law is noteworthy.[26] In the *Wood Pulp* case,[27] the Court went even further and decided that the selling of products at co-ordinated prices by foreign enterprises to customers within the Community was a sufficient basis to found the Community's jurisdiction, even where the foreign companies had no 'presence', even in the form of subsidiaries or agents, in the territory of the Community. This is similar to the controversial 'effects doctrine'[28] in international law, but the Court's only real reference to international law consisted of the questionable statement that 'the Community' s jurisdiction to apply its competition rules to such conduct is covered by the territoriality principle as universally recognized in public international law.'[29] In reality, the judgment turned on the interpretations of the conditions for the application of Article 85 of the EC Treaty, which prohibits various forms of anti-competitive conduct by undertakings or groups of undertakings.[30]

Thus, it can be concluded that in the cases considered thus far, the Court's treatment of international is remarkable only in its brevity. Even in the cases involving third parties, the Court has refrained from basing its judgments explicitly or extensively on general international law. Apart from the often-noted laconic nature of the Court's pronouncements even when general international law is not involved,[31] the circumstances of the Community as a whole, with its express goal of economic and social integration, would have played a major role. On the basis of this brief overview, the Court could hardly be mistaken for a court that applied general international law.[32]

---

26. See also *Béguelin Import Co* v. *SACL Import Export*, case 22/71 [1971] *ECR* 949; *Walrave* v. *Union Cycliste Internationale*, case 36/74 [1974] *ECR* 1405, at p. 1420, where the Court held that 'a rule of Community law was applicable to legal relationships if 'the place where they take effect' is within the territory of the Community'.

27. *Åhlström Osakehtiö* v. *Commission*, Joined cases 89, 104, 114, 116 & 125-129/85 [1988] *ECR* 5193. For discussion of this case, see D.G.F. Lange and J.B. Sadange, '*The Wood Pulp* decision and its implications for the scope of EC competion law', 26 *CMLRev.* (1989) p. 137; F.A. Mann, 38 *ICLQ* (1989) p. 375; C. Vedder, 'A Survey of Principal Decisions of the European Court of Justice Pertaining to International Law', 1/2 *EJIL* (1990) pp. 365-377.

28. On the effects doctrine in international law, see Jennings and Watts, loc. cit. n. 10, at pp. 466-478.

29. At para. 18, p. 5243.

30. Vedder, loc. cit. n. 27, at p. 370, states that 'The Court does not differentiate between the fulfilment of the conditions of Article 85 and the applicability of that rule under international law, the former being only the prerequisite of the latter. It does not clearly separate [sic] between the elements of an infringement of Article 85 under Community law and the question whether or not Article 85 applies to undertakings based outside the Community's territory. The Court is obviously of the understanding that 'effects' fall under the territorial jurisdiction because they are already a part of Article 85 of the Treaty, which it simply then applies.' Thus the question of whether or not the Community has jurisdiction under international law is reduced to the mere application of Article 85 of the treaty.

31. See e.g., P. Craig and G. de Burca, *EU Law: Text, Cases and Materials*, 2nd edn. (Oxford, Oxford University Press 1998) at p. 86.

32. See R. Plender, 'The European Court as an International Tribunal', *Cambridge LJ* (1983) p. 279.

3. TAKING GENERAL INTERNATIONAL LAW SERIOUSLY

In contrast, more recently, the Court has had to deal with general international law more directly and more frequently.[33] The discussion in this section will focus on cases decided by the Court in the last decade in which questions involving a number of different areas of general international law have arisen squarely for consideration by the Court, as distinct from those cases in which there have been merely 'innocent references to international law'. All the cases considered in this section involved relations with third parties, as distinct from purely intra-Community matters.[34] The extent to which the Court's treatment of general international law in these more recent cases differs from the approach considered in the previous section can then be considered.

3.1 **The interpretation of Community legislation**

Perhaps the clearest statement of the applicability of customary international law in the relations of the Community is *Poulsen and Diva Corporation*.[35] That case involved a regulation adopted in the context of the conservation of fishery resources, that prohibited the transport and storage on vessels of salmon caught in certain areas not under the sovereignty or jurisdiction of Member States. The issue was whether the regulation applied to all Community nationals regardless of the facts that the fishing vessel in this case was registered in a non-member country and that some members of the crew were not nationals of members states. The ship fished for salmon in an area outside the jurisdiction of the Community and was forced to berth at a Danish port with a cargo of salmon on board, where, following inspection by Danish officials, criminal proceedings were brought against a national of a Member State for breach of the prohibition contained in the regulation. In its response to a request for a preliminary ruling from the Danish court, the Court stated that:

> 'As a preliminary point, it must be observed, first, that the European Community must respect international law in the exercise of its powers and that, consequently, [the regulation] must be interpreted, and its scope limited, in the light of the relevant rules of the law of the sea.'[36]

The real significance of this case for present purposes lies in the way the Court handled the sources of the relevant customary law of the sea. In contrast to the position as discussed in section 2 above, the Court stated expressly that it had to take account of the 1958 Geneva Conventions on the Territorial Sea and the Contiguous zone, the High Seas and on Fishing and Conservation of the Living Resources of the High Seas

33. See e.g., MacGoldrick, loc. cit. n. 1, at Chapter 10.
34. See text accompanying n. 7 above.
35. *Anklagemyndigheden* v. *Paulson and Diva Navigation*, case C-286/90 [1992] *ECR* I-6019)
36. Ibid., at p. 6052, para. 9.

'in so far as they codify general rules recognized by international custom.' The Court again took account of the 1982 United Nations Convention on the Law of the Sea, stating that, at that time, 'it had not entered into force, but many of its provisions are considered to express the current state of customary international maritime law'. The Court proceeded to consider the aim of the prohibition contained in the regulation in question, and concluded that, as provided for in Article 6 of the 1958 Convention on the High Seas, Article 118 of the 1982 Convention and the Convention for the Conservation of Salmon in the North Atlantic (to which the European Community is a party), it recognized the interest of coastal states in the living resources of the high seas adjacent to the waters within their jurisdiction. The Court then stated that the prohibition contained in the regulation 'must be interpreted so as to give it the greatest practical effect, *within the limits of international law*'.[37]

Even more significant is the reliance placed by the Court on the jurisprudence of the International Court of Justice as a basis for deriving the applicable law, both in terms of the substance of the rules and in terms of the method of arriving at those rules. It referred to the *Gulf of Maine* case[38], the *Libya/Malta Continental Shelf* case[39] and the merits stage of the *Nicaragua/United States* case,[40] which confirmed the customary law status of the relevant rules in these conventions. The Court's reference to specific pronouncements on the often delicate question of the relationship between customary international law and treaty law is unusual, considering that the Court ultimately defined the scope of Community law by reference to international law in its judgment.

The Court proceeded to affirm that pursuant to the rules codified in Articles 5 and 6 of the 1958 Geneva Convention on the High Seas and Articles 91 and 92 of the 1982 Convention, a vessel has only the nationality of the state in which it is registered, and where that state is a non-Member State, that vessel cannot be considered to be flying the flag of a Member State even if it has a genuine link with that Member State.[41] The

---

37. Ibid., at p. 6053, para. 11 (emphasis added).

38. There the International Court of Justice stated there that certain provisions of the Convention on the continental shelf and the exclusive economic zone may 'nevertheless be regarded as consonant with the general international law on the question'; *ICJ Rep.* (1984) p. 246, at p. 294, para. 94.

39. The International Court stated that '... it cannot be denied that the 1982 Convention is of major importance, having been adopted by the overwhelming majority of States; hence it is clearly the duty of the Court, even independently of the references made to the Convention by the Parties, to consider in what degree any of its provisions are binding upon the Parties as a rule of customary international law; *ICJ Rep.* (1985) p. 30, para. 27.

40. 'The Court has no doubt that these prescriptions of treaty-law merely respond to firmly established and longstanding tenets of customary international law'; *ICJ Rep.* (1986) p. 111, para. 212.

41. At paras. 12-16, p. 6054. In relation to the question whether the regulation could be applied to members of the crew on the grounds that they were national of a Member State regardless of the country of registration of the vessel, the Court did not make any explicit reference to rules of international law. In contrast, the Advocate-General referred to Art. 14 of the 1958 Convention on Fishing and Conservation of the Living Resources of the High Seas, and also to the judgment in the *North-West Atlantic Fisheries* case, XI *UNRIAA* (1910) p. 167 et seq. as authority for the proposition that the nationality of the crew, as distinct from the nationality of the vessel, was irrelevant.

Court also drew a distinction between the powers of a coastal state over activities on the high seas which are beyond the jurisdiction of a coastal state and those within its inland waters and ports, which are subject to the unlimited jurisdiction of that coastal state. However, with respect to the exclusive economic zone and the territorial sea, the Court ruled that it is within the coastal state's powers to adopt rules classifying as illegal the transport and storage of salmon in the latter areas, but that:

> 'although the territorial sea falls under the sovereignty of the coastal State, the latter must respect the right of innocent passage through it of vessels flying the flag of other States (Arts. 14 to 23 of the Geneva Convention on the territorial Sea and Contiguous Zone of 29 April 1958; Articles 17 to 23 of the United Nations Convention on the Law of the Sea). As far as the exclusive economic zone is concerned, the coastal State must in exercising its powers observe in particular freedom of navigation (see Art. 58(1) of the United nations Convention on the Law of the Sea).'[42]

Accordingly, the regulation could be applied to the vessel in question only in the inland waters of the coastal (member) state.

The final pertinent ruling in this case related to the question whether Community law contained rules concerning compliance with the prohibition contained in the regulation as regards vessels registered in non-member states that have entered a port of a Member State in situations of distress. The Court ruled first that there was no Community law on this matter, and that the question did not concern the determination of the sphere of application of Community legislation, but rather 'the implementation of that legislation by the authorities of Member States.' The Court then held that, in those circumstances, it is for the national court to determine, 'in accordance with international law', the legal consequences flowing from such a situation.[43] This ruling indicates that the Court considers international law binding, albeit in the absence of any pertinent Community legislation, on the Member States.[44]

The case thus underlines the important role to be accorded to customary international in the interpretation of provisions of Community law thereafter, as illustrated in the subsequent cases considered below.[45]

42. Ibid., at paras. 25-26, p. 6056.

43. Ibid., at paras. 35-39, pp. 6058-6059.

44. See section 4 below on the significance of the procedure for preliminary rulings under Art. 234 (formerly Art. 177) of the EC Treaty (through which this and other cases considered in this section came before the Court) as far as the Court's treatment of international law is concerned.

45. See also, on the law of the sea, *The Queen* v. *The Secretary of State for Transport, ex parte Factortame Ltd and Others*, case 221/89 [1991] *ECR* I-3905, paras. 15-17, at pp. 3963-3964, and more recently, *Commission* v. *Greece*, case 62/96 [1997] *ECR* I-6725, at para. 22. For other cases in which the Court has taken account of rules of written and non-written international law, as well as decisions of international organizations, in interpreting community law, see e.g., *Bakels* v. *Oberfinanzdirektion München*, case 14/70 [1970] *ECR* 1001, paras. 6-11 at pp. 1008-1009; *Interfood* v. *Hauptzollamt Hamburg*, case 92/71 [1972] *ECR* 231, para. 6 at p. 242; *Nederlandse Spoorwagen* v. *Inspecteur der Invoerrechten en Accijnzen*, case 38/75 [1975] *ECR* 1439, at p. 1451; *Enka* v. *Inspecteur der Invoerrechten en Accijnzen*, case 38/77

3.2 The customary international law of treaties

The Court has dealt at some length with various aspects of the customary international law of treaties in a number of important cases.[46]

3.2.1 *Interpretation of treaties*

In the *Anastasiou*[47] case, the question referred to the Court for a preliminary ruling by the High Court of Justice was whether British authorities were acting in breach of Community law in accepting imports of citrus fruits and potatoes that originated from the Turkish Republic of Northern Cyprus, where the products in question were not accompanied by the certificates, required under Community law, of origin and plant health issued by the authorities of the Republic of Cyprus. The requirement of certificates dated back to the 1972 Association Agreement (and a Protocol of 1977) between the Community and the Republic of Cyprus. The Turkish Republic of Northern Cyprus had not been recognized by any of the Member States of the Community.[48] The Court found that the acceptance of certificates not issued by the Republic of Cyprus would constitute a denial of the object and purpose of the system set up by the Agreement.

In response to the argument put forward by the Commission and the United Kingdom that the application of the preferential arrangements pursuant to the Agreement for products from the southern part of Cyprus but not the northern part would be discriminatory contrary to the terms of the agreement,[49] the Court referred to the rules on the interpretation of treaties as codified in Article 31 of the Vienna Convention on

---

[1977] *ECR* 2203, paras. 24-29 at pp. 2214-2215; *Beer Purity* case (*Commission* v. *Germany*), case 178/84 [1986] *ECR* 1227, paras. 44 and 52, p. 1276. See further Lenaerts and van Nuffel, loc. cit. n. 1, at p. 563, nn. 17 and 18 and accompanying text, and Schermers and Waelbroeck, loc. cit. n. 3, paras. 175-177, pp. 100-101.

46. Compare *Commission* v. *Italy* (the *Radio Tubes* case), case 10/61 [1962] *ECR* 1, at p. 10, in which the Court had simply referred to the principle of international law that 'by assuming a new obligation which is incompatible with rights held under a prior treaty a State *ipso facto* gives up the exercise of these rights to the extent necessary for the performance of its new obligations'. This principle has been codified in Art. 30 of the Vienna Convention on the Law of Treaties (1969). The Court's simple statement of this rule stands in clear contrast to the approach it has taken in the more recent cases considered in this section.

47. *The Queen* v. *Minister of Agriculture, Fisheries and Food, ex parte Anastasiou (Pissouri) Ltd and Others*, case C-432/92 [1994] *ECR* I-3087.

48. Ibid., see pp. 3095-3098 (Opinion of the Advocate-General) for a description of the situation on the island of Cyprus.

49. Art. 5 of the Association Agreement provided that the 'rules governing trade between the Contracting Parties may not give rise to any discrimination between ... nationals or companies of Cyprus'.

the Law of Treaties (1969)[50] as requiring that substantial importance be attached to (i) the object and purpose of a treaty and (ii) to any subsequent practice in its application. With regard to the object and purpose of the treaty, the Court stated that non-discrimination was only one of the aims of the Agreement, which had to be considered in the light of its other objectives, a ruling which accords with well-established general rules of treaty interpretation.[51] The Court found that advantages stemming from the Agreement had on several occasions been made available to the entire population of Cyprus including the northern part, and also that the Community 'must take particular account of its partner to the Agreement when interpreting and applying it.' The Court considered that the Agreement had to be interpreted and applied within the framework of the institutions it established, and not those of a different administration; to do otherwise would be to ignore the objects and purposes of the treaty. With regard to the subsequent practice on the application of the Agreement, the Court stated that:

> 'the practice followed in applying the Agreement after the material events took place does not suffice to establish unequivocally, within the meaning of Article 31 of the Vienna Convention, the existence of an agreement between the parties regarding the relevant provisions of [the agreement].'[52]

The Court proceeded to point out the differing practice of various Member States and the Commission with regard to acceptance of certificates from the northern part of Cyprus, which, in its view, created 'uncertainty of a kind likely to undermine the existence of a common commercial policy and the performance by the Community of its obligations' under the Agreement. Again, while couched in terms of the interest of the Community in maintaining its economic aims, the Court's application of the rule contained in Article 31 of the Vienna Convention is unassailable. That rule, which is well-established in the case-law of international tribunals,[53] provides that subsequent

---

50. Ibid., at paras. 43-54, pp. 3132-3134. The Convention has not been ratified by all the Member States of the Community (see the Opinion of the Advocate-General in *Racke* v. *Hauptzollamt* case (case 162/92 [1998] *ECR* I-3655, at p. 3664, para. 20; accession is open only to States); but the status of Article 31(1) as customary law is well-established; see e.g., Jennings and Watts, loc. cit. n. 10, pp. 1271-1272, para. p632.

51. See e.g., *Competence of the ILO to Regulate Agricultural Labour* case, *PCIJ Rep.* Ser. B, Nos. 2 and 3 (1922) p. 23; *Free Zones of Upper Savoy and Gex* case, *PCIJ Rep.* Ser. A/B, No. 46 (1932) p. 140; *Air Transport Services Agreement* (USA v. France) 38 *ILR* (1963) pp. 182, 228-229; *Italy-United States Air Transport Arbitration* 45 *ILR* (1965) pp. 393, 412-413.

52. Ibid., at para. 50.

53. See e.g., *Competence of the ILO to Regulate Agricultural Labour*, *PCIJ Rep.*, Ser. B, No. 2 (1922) p. 39; *Corfu Channel* case, *ICJ Rep.* (1949) p. 25; *Arbitral Award of the King of Spain* case, *ICJ Rep.* (1960) p. 206; *Young Loan* arbitration, 59 *ILR* p. 495 at pp. 541-543; *Air Transport Services Agreement* arbitration (*USA* v. *France*), loc. cit. n. 50, at pp. 245-248.

practice may be taken into account when it 'clearly establishes the understanding of all parties regarding its interpretation.'[54]

3.2.2 *The principle of good faith*

In *Opel Austria* v. *Council*,[55] the Court of First Instance had to pronounce on the legality of a regulation that withdrew tariff concessions granted to Austria, which was adopted a few days before the Agreement on the European Economic Area came into force. It was argued that that the regulation violated this Agreement. The Court held that the legality of the regulation had to be determined on the basis of the situation at the time the regulation was adopted. It then referred to the principle of good faith, which required that prior to the entry into force of an agreement, the signatories to that agreement were precluded from adopting measures which would defeat its object and purpose. The Court held that the principle was a part of customary international law, one that had been recognized by the International Court of Justice[56] and was *therefore* binding on the Community, and which had also been codified in Article 18 of the Vienna Convention on the Law of Treaties.

Significantly, the Court stated that this principle is the corollary in public international law of the principle of the protection of legitimate expectations. The latter principle was part of the Community legal order.[57] The Court found that, on the basis of the aforementioned principles, the regulation had been adopted in breach of the Agreement. While this case would seem to confirm the view that the Court appears in recent cases to be more open to explicit treatment of international law, it should be noted that the Court did not apply the principle of good faith without reference to the counterpart of that principle that had already been developed in Community law, independently of public international law. This observation is reinforced by the consideration that the Court made no reference to the principle of international law after it had found its corollary in Community law; from that point onwards, the Court applied only the *acquis communautaire*. This consideration should temper any opti-

---

54. This ruling is even more significant when one considers that the Court had uncharacteristically gone further than the Advocate-General, who had not referred to rules of treaty interpretation contained in the Vienna Convention on the Law of Treaties in his Opinion in this case. On the relationship between the role of the Advocates General and the typically exhaustive nature of their opinions compared to the judgments of the Court, see Craig and de Burca, loc. cit. n. 31, at p. 83.
It should also be noted that the Court responded to an argument based on a ruling of the International Court of Justice in the *Namibia* advisory opinion, concerning the consequences of non-recognition. This matter is dealt with at greater length in section 3.4 below.

55. Case T-115/94 [1997] *ECR* II-39, at paras. 37-60, pp. 70-81.

56. *Certain German Interests in Polish Upper Silesia, PCIJ Rep.*, Ser. A, No. 7 (1926) pp. 30 and 39.

57. See also *Danisco Sugar AB* v. *Allmänaa Ombudet*, case 27/96 [1997] *ECR* I-6653, at para. 20, p. 6682, and para. 31, at p. 6686.

mism that may be suggested by the reference to principles and judgments of international law in this case.[58]

3.2.3 *Rebus sic stantibus*

Further occasion for the Court to consider rules of customary international law arose in *Racke* v. *Hauptzollamt Mainz*.[59] The Opinion of the Advocate-General underlines the significance of this case, and is worth quoting:

> 'the Court is largely in uncharted waters ... in *Poulsen* the Court went no further than interpreting a Community regulation in light of the rules of customary international law, and in *Opel Austria* the international law principle of good faith was married to the Community law principle of protection of legitimate expectations ... but the sort of effect which is sought in the present case is much stronger. Racke is seeking to have a Community Regulation declared invalid on the sole basis of an alleged violation of rules of customary international law. It is difficult to envisage any stronger type of effect.'[60]

This places in context the reference by the Court to international law in the earlier cases referred to. This was the first case in which the Court had to consider at length whether customary international law could provide a basis for the invalidity of a Community act.

The question referred to the Court was whether the suspension and denunciation by the Council of the European Communities of the Co-operation Agreement between the Socialist Federal Republic of Yugoslavia and the Community on the basis of an alleged fundamental change of circumstances was valid under customary international law. The Court stated early on in its judgment, regarding the applicable law, that:

> 'By way of preliminary observation, it should be noted that even though the Vienna Convention does not bind either the Community or all its Member States, a series of its provisions, including article 62, reflect the rules of international law which lay down, subject to

58. As will be seen below (in section 3.2.3), an Advocate-General has suggested a limit to the operation of international law as applied in this case. Klabbers, loc. cit. n. 1, at pp. 53-56, notes that the application of Art. 18 of the Vienna Convention on the Law of Treaties in this case is quite unorthodox. However, the Court was not applying Art. 18 or any other international law as such; once it had found the corollary of the applicable principle in Community law, the rest of the judgment was not couched in terms of the law of treaties. This may be considered to result in the unorthodox application of international law by the Court in cases where there are related or similar principles in Community law, so that the obligations undertaken by members of the Community may be more stringent than those undertaken by other parties that are not Member States. This point should not be disquieting from the point of view of international law, which, as illustrated in Art. 27 of the Vienna Convention on the Law of Treaties for example, is concerned with breaches of international law rather than the intricacies of internal (*in casu* Community) law that do not breach international obligations.

59. Case C-162/96 [1998] *ECR* I-3655.

60. Ibid., at para. 76 of the Opinion, p. 3679.

> certain conditions, the principle that a change of circumstances may entail the lapse or suspension of a treaty. Thus the International Court of Justice held that "[t]his principle, and the conditions and exceptions to which it is subject, have been embodied in Article 62 of the Vienna Convention on the Law of Treaties, which may in many respects be considered as a codification of existing customary international law on the subject of the termination of a treaty relationship on account of change of circumstances..."'[61]

The Court later referred to its ruling in the *Poulsen and Diva Corporation* case, and concluded that the Community:

> 'is required to comply with the rules of customary international law when adopting a regulation suspending the trade concessions granted by, or by virtue of, an agreement which it has concluded with a non-member country. Accordingly, the rules of customary international law concerning the termination and the suspension of treaty relations by reason of a fundamental change of circumstances are binding on the Community institutions and form part of the Community legal order'[62]

The Court went on to state that the plea of fundamental change of circumstances was an exception to the *pacta sunt servanda* principle, 'which constitutes a fundamental principle of any legal order and, in particular, the international legal order.' The Court referred first to Article 26 of the Vienna Convention on the Law of Treaties and also to the judgment of the International Court of Justice in the *Gabcíkovo-Nagymaros* case to the effect that 'the stability of treaty relations requires that the plea of fundamental change of circumstances be applied only in exceptional cases.'[63]

The Court then proceeded to apply the plea, but with a qualification that is significant in that it suggests an obstacle in the way of the application of international law within the Community legal order. It stated that:

> 'because of the complexity of the rules in question and the imprecision of some of the concepts to which they refer, judicial review must necessarily, and in particular in the context of a preliminary reference for an assessment of validity, be limited to the question whether, by adopting the suspending regulation, the Council made manifest errors of assessment concerning the conditions for applying those rules.'[64]

Here the Court is introducing a new restriction on the effect of international law, different from those established in its previous jurisprudence in the *International Fruit Company* case.[65] As far as the 'imprecision' of the rules of international law is concerned, the statement is perhaps uncontroversial; if the rules that might adversely af-

---

61. Ibid., at para. 24, p. 3700. The Court was referring to the judgement of the ICJ in the *Fisheries Jurisdiction* case, *ICJ Rep.* (1973), p. 3 at para. 36.
62. Ibid., at para. 45-46, pp. 3704-3705.
63. *ICJ Rep.* (1997) para. 104, at p. 64.
64. Ibid., at para. 52, at p. 3706.
65. Loc. cit. n. 14.

fect the validity of an act are not clear as to what they stipulate, a reluctance to limit the applicability of that act is understandable, particularly if, as has been suggested, there is a presumption of legality of acts of international organizations.[66] However, as far as the 'complexity' of those rules is concerned, it seems unusual that the Court, after identifying and acknowledging the binding nature of those rules, decided that the effect of those rules would be limited because the rules were complex. The complexity of legal rules can hardly be regarded as a reason for restricting their legal effect by a court of law that has decided that is bound to apply those rules. This is true even if the Court considered that the effect of the 'complexity' is to affect the validity of the Community act only if there had been a 'manifest error' on the part of the Council in its appreciation of the rules in question. The complexity of rules surely cannot reduce the obligation of a subject of the law to abide by those rules.

The Advocate-General, in his opinion, had considered the conditions laid down in the *International Fruit Company* case for the review of the validity of Community acts on the basis of international law, and he was of the view that the second condition, namely whether, as he put it, 'the provision of international was capable of conferring rights on citizens', was crucial in this case.[67] In considering whether the rules of customary international law on the plea of fundamental change of circumstances met this condition, he referred to the settled case-law of the Court to the effect that provisions of international agreements could be relied on by individuals[68] when, having regard to the wording and the nature of the agreement itself, the provision contains a clear and precise obligation which is not subject, in its implementation or effects, to the adoption of any subsequent measure. He stated that:

> 'The notion of *rebus sic stantibus* is notoriously difficult and contested ... Its scope has been formulated more clearly in Article 62 of the Vienna Convention, but even that provision contains concepts which easily lend themselves to widely diverging interpretations. What is a "fundamental change" of circumstances? What are the circumstances which "constituted an essential basis of the consent of the parties"? And when does the change in circumstances "radically ... transform the extent of the obligations still to be performed"? It may therefore be doubted whether the conditions for the application of the doctrine of *rebus sic stantibus* are sufficiently clear and precise to confer rights on individuals.'[69]

It would appear that the views of the Advocate-General in this passage were shared by the Court when it referred to 'the complexity of the rules in question and the imprecision of some of the concepts to which they refer.' It appears, however, that the Advocate-General was referring to a particular rule in the Community legal order on

66. See D. Grieg, *International Law*, 2nd edn. (1976) pp. 820-822; E. Lauterpacht, 'The Legal Effect of Illegal Acts in International Organizations', in R. Jennings, ed., *Cambridge Essays in International Law*; E. Osieke, 'The Legal Validity of Ultra Vires Acts of International Organizations', 77 *AJIL* (1983) p. 239. These works all relate to the question of invalidity based on *ultra vires* acts.

67 Ibid., at paras. 82-90.

68. See section 4 below.

69. Ibid., at para. 85, p 3682.

the circumstances under which individuals could contest the validity of a Community act before the Court. The question that is left unanswered both by the Court and the Advocate-General is that the refusal of the Court to review the legality of a Community act for these reasons means that the Community could still be in breach of international law from the point of view of international law if, under international law, the plea of fundamental change of circumstances is not justified for suspension of the Community's treaty obligations.

Of course, on the basis of familiar constitutional principle, judicial restraint in the review of discretionary acts is to be expected. The Advocate-General had referred to the political discretion involved in the making and termination of treaties as a basis for limited review;[70] the Court, in contrast, was basing limited review on the complexity and imprecision of the rules in question. But judicial restraint is one thing, while the refusal of a Court to scrutinize the conduct of a subject of the law on the basis not of this constitutional principle but on the basis of a perceived complexity in the rules that call that conduct into question is quite another.

In addition, and perhaps most fundamentally, the fact remains that the plea of fundamental change of circumstances has been considered and applied in a vast number of cases by international courts and tribunals.[71] There seems to be no basis upon which the Court should attempt to abdicate its responsibility to determine the applicable rules when several other courts and tribunals have not considered themselves to have been faced with this problem identified by the Court. It would seem that the difficulty here related to the task of applying facts to law,[72] a task which is fundamental to legal reasoning; the complexity of either the facts or the law must be an important part of the functions of adjudication. The clarification, elucidation and application of the rules that fall to be considered in a case before a court is surely a fundamental part of the judicial function.

It may be that the Court had chosen to make this statement because, considering that 'in almost all cases in which the doctrine *rebus sic stantibus* has been invoked before an international tribunal, the latter, while not rejecting it in principle, has refused to admit that it could be applicable to the case before it,'[73] the Court, in its deliberations, had decided to uphold the plea in this case. It is doubtful whether this justifies the statement of the Court under consideration, which, on balance, suggests a certain maladroitness on the part of the Court as far as the treatment of international law is concerned. It will be recalled that the basic rule on grounds for judicial review laid down in Article 230 of the Treaty[74] provides that the Court shall have jurisdiction 'on the grounds of lack of competence, infringement of an essential procedural require-

---

70. Ibid., at para. 90.

71. See for example, the wealth of case-law cited in Jennings and Watts, loc. cit. n. 10, at p. 1307, para. 8.

72. See O. Elias and C. Lim, *The Paradox of Consensualism in Interational Law* (The Hague, Kluwer Law International 1998), Chapter 9.

73. Jennings and Watts, loc. cit. n. 10, at p. 1307, para. 651, referring, *inter alia*, to the *Free Zones* case (*PCIJ Rep*. Series A/B, No. 46 (1932) p. 158) and the *Fisheries Jurisdiction* case, loc. cit. n. 51.

74. Formerly Art. 173, on actions for annulment of acts of the institutions.

ment, infringement of a the Treaty or of any rule of law relating to its application, or misuse of powers'. It is doubtful whether this restriction based on the 'complexity' of rules of law upon which the review is based would apply to any of the grounds for review of Community acts other than international law. In other words, it is difficult to imagine that the Court would refer to lack of competence or the breach of procedural rules under Community law or provisions of the EC Treaty as being too 'complex' to be grounds for review.[75]

It is difficult to see why this statement was included in the judgment since the Court nevertheless proceeded to apply, in a rather uncontroversial manner, the customary international law as codified in Article 62 of the Vienna Convention, by referring to the two conditions for the applicability of principle laid down in paragraph 1 thereof.[76] Regarding the first condition, namely that the existence of the fundamental change of circumstances upon which the suspension of the treaty is based must have constituted an essential basis of the consent of the parties to be bound by the treaty, the Court ruled that 'the maintenance of a situation of peace in Yugoslavia, indispensable for neighbourly relations, and the existence of institutions capable of ensuring implementation of the co-operation envisaged by the Agreement throughout the territory of Yugoslavia' was an essential condition, which no longer existed in view of the consequences of the war in Yugoslavia. Regarding the second condition, namely that the changed circumstances must have had the effect of radically transforming the extent of the obligations under the treaty, the Court stated that the consideration that there was no point in continuing to grant preferences with a view to stimulating trade where Yugoslavia was breaking up was sufficient; 'customary international does not require an impossibility to perform obligations.' Accordingly, the conditions laid down were met, and the suspension was held not to conflict with customary international law.

This case is a notable exception to the general trend according to which the plea of fundamental change of circumstances has rarely been applied by international courts and tribunals. The application of the plea in this case does not, however, appear to be unjustifiable. After all, the operation of the plea in this case could be justified in view of the response of the international community to the situation in Yugoslavia on which the Council had based its decision to suspend the application of the Agreement.[77] It may even be suggested that this case contributes to the development of the *rebus sic stantibus* principle, concerning its applicability in situations of illegality or

75. This issue is discussed further, in section 4 below, in the context of a discussion of the 'direct effect' of customary law rules. The discussion above is based on general principle rather than the peculiarities of the Community legal order.

76. At paras. 53-57.

77. The preamble to the decision suspending the application of the Agreement referred expressly to Security Council resolution 713 (1991), in which the Security Council expressed concern that the prolongation of the crisis in Yugoslavia constituted a threat to international peace and security. The Council of the European Communities had made it known, as noted by the Court, that it would terminate the Agreement if the ceasefire agreed by the parties to the conflict was not upheld. For the view that the Court's application of the *rebus sic stantibus* principle was significantly more lenient than is understood to be the case in traditional international law, see Klabbers, loc. cit. n. 1, at pp. 56-59.

where international public policy is involved, such as this case in which international peace and security, as noted in a resolution of the Security Council, are put at risk.

Finally, in response to the argument that the procedural requirements (namely prior notification and a waiting period) laid down in Article 65 of the Vienna Convention had not been complied with, the Court ruled that even if the various statements made by the Community and the Member States were insufficient to meet these requirements, these procedural requirements did not form part of customary international law outside the Vienna Convention, indicating further the Court's explicit handling of the methods and sources of international law.

3.3 State succession

The opportunity arose for the Court to consider, albeit as a secondary matter, the rules on the succession of States in *Belgian State* v. *Banque Indosuez.*[78] The question there was whether anti-dumping duties imposed by Community legislation on imports of products 'originating in Yugoslavia' applied to such products manufactured by a produce/exporter who had been established in the Socialist Federal Republic of Yugoslavia, but as a result of the declaration of independence by the Former Yugoslav Republic of Macedonia (FYROM), was situated in the latter State's territory at the time when the goods were imported into the Community. The Court began by stating, in accordance with its established case-law, that in interpreting a provision of Community law, it was necessary to consider the wording, its context and its aims, and that the purpose of the measures in question was to protect Community industry from products imported from third states at a price below their normal value. Accordingly, since these measures focused on the products and their origin, the geographical criterion, rather than a change in the name or political organization of the geographical area referred to as the country of origin, which has no impact on the economic purpose of the duty imposed, was what mattered.[79] In accepting an argument that suppliers should not be allowed to avoid anti-dumping duties solely because the authorities of the territory declared themselves independent, the Court stated that: '[e]ven if, as a matter of public international law, the supplier came within the jurisdiction of a new State, that does not mean that his practices would cease to injure Community industry.'[80] The Court also ruled that even though Yugoslavia had now split into different states, the term as used in the Community act 'cannot but designate the same geographical area which was once co-extensive with that republic and now corresponds to the territory of those new States collectively', including that of the FYROM.[81] Finally, in response to an argument that based on the international law rules of State succession, the Court held that those rules applied to State debts but not to charges payable by individuals, such as those in the present case.[82]

---

78. Case C-177/96 [1997] *ECR* I-5673.
79. Ibid., at paras. 18-21, pp. 5679-5680.
80. Ibid., at para. 22, p. 5680.
81. Ibid., at para. 23.
82. Ibid., at para. 25, p. 5681.

It is clear that the primary consideration in this case was the nature of anti-dumping duties and the economic interests of the Community in protecting its industry. Thus viewed, it is surely within the Community's powers to set any conditions for the entry into its territory of any goods from a third State, in the absence of any contrary obligations. The rules of State succession were not really in issue, and accordingly, aside from the much noted general lack of uniformity in the international practice on State succession,[83] it is difficult to argue that the rules could apply to the obligations of individuals.

3.4 **Recognition of states**

In the *Anastasiou* case, it has been seen that the Court denied the lawfulness of the acceptance of certificates of origin and physiosanitary health issued by the Turkish Republic of Northern Cyprus, because of the non-recognition policy adopted by the international community,[84] including the European Community, in respect of that entity. The instructive part of the judgment was the Court's treatment of the argument put forward by the Commission and the United Kingdom to the effect that the acceptance of certificates from the Republic of Cyprus but not from the northern part would result in discrimination against individuals based in the latter part. They had argued that the *de facto* acceptance of the certificates in question would not have amounted to recognition of the Turkish Republic of Northern Cyprus, but would rather have ensured that the interests of the whole population of Cyprus were taken into account. They had based this argument on the judgment of the International Court of Justice in the *Namibia* case, to the effect that a policy of non-recognition should not result in depriving individuals of any advantages conferred by treaty. The International Court of Justice had stated in that case that the non-recognition of South Africa's administration of the territory of Namibia pursuant to Security Council resolutions should not result in depriving the people of Namibia of 'any advantages derived from international co-operation', and that the invalidity of acts of the administration 'cannot be extended to those acts, such as, for instance, births deaths and marriages, the effects of which can be ignored only to the detriment of the inhabitants of the Territory'.[85]

The Advocate-General had pointed out that, unlike the situation in the present case, the sanctions imposed on the South African administration were decided specifically in the interest of the Namibian population, as the International Court had stated that 'all States should bear in mind that the injured entity is a people which must

83. See e.g., Jennings and Watts, loc. cit. n. 10, at p. 236.

84. See section 3.2.1 above. Only Turkey has recognized the 'Turkish Republic of Northern Cyprus'. Security Council resolution 541 (1983) states that the declaration of secession of the northern part was 'legally invalid', and called for its withdrawal, while resolution 551 (1984) reiterated 'the call on all States not to recognize the purported state of the 'Turkish Republic of Northern Cyprus' set up by secessionist acts', and called upon States 'not to facilitate or in any way assist the aforesaid secessionist entity.

85. Legal Consequences for States of the Continued Presence of South Africa in Namibia notwithstanding Security Council Resolution 276, *ICJ Rep* (1971) at para. 125.

look to the international community for assistance in its progress towards the goals for which the sacred trust was instituted.'[86] The distinction was thus drawn between the situation of the population in the territory of Namibia and that in the territory of Northern Cyprus, with the Court concluding (correctly, it is submitted) that no analogy could be drawn between them. It is true that the Court appears to have placed more weight on the concern that the objects and purposes of the Agreement between the Community and the Republic of Cyprus should not be frustrated, as it emphasized at greater length that the ends of the co-operation sought by the Agreement depended on strict compliance with the procedures for administrative co-operation, which excludes co-operation with the non-recognized entity. It is however just as true that the Court may be seen to have made a contribution to a difficult area of international law concerning the distinction drawn between those acts of unrecognized entities that will be given legal effect in the interests of the population and those which will not.[87]

Furthermore, the Court also pronounced on the international law principle of non-intervention in the domestic affairs of States when it stated that the requirement of non-discrimination in the application of the Agreement could not confer on the Community the right to interfere in the internal affairs of Cyprus. The Court stated that the 'problems resulting from the *de facto* partition of the island must be resolved exclusively by the Republic of Cyprus, which alone is internationally recognized.'[88] This argument is unassailable if it is considered that the Agreement was concluded with the Republic of Cyprus, and not with an entity that sought to be recognized as being distinct from it, and only the acts of the party to the Agreement would be taken into account.

3.5 Extraterritorial jurisdiction

In *Gencor* v. *Commission*,[89] the Court of First Instance had occasion to consider the validity of a decision of the Commission of the European Communities that declared a concentration involving undertakings based in third States (*in casu* South Africa) to be incompatible with the common market and the functioning of the European Economic Area Agreement because it would have led to the creation of a dominant duopoly position that would have significantly impeded the effective competition. This involved consideration of the principles applied in the *Dyestuffs* and *Wood Pulp* cases

---

86. Ibid., at para. 58, p. 3109.

87. For this reason, it seems that the description of the Court's judgment as 'a retrograde step' (M. Dixon and R. MacCorquodale, *Cases and Materials on International Law* (London, Blackstone Press 1995) p. 189), is somewhat harsh; surely there is a balance to be struck between the requirements of public policy pursuant to Security Council resolutions requiring non-recognition on the one hand, and the interests of the population on the other, a balance that the Court can be seen to have attempted to strike in this case.

88. Ibid., at para. 47, pp. 3133-3134.

89. Case T-102/96 [1999] *ECR* II-753.

discussed above.[90] The Court accepted the Commission's argument to the effect that it was not the location of the undertakings involved that were in issue, but rather the location of the anti-competitive effect of their activities, endorsing the ruling in the earlier cases as to the importance of the implementation, for example through sale, of anti-competitive agreements within the Community.[91] However, in contrast to the judgments in the earlier cases, the Court of First Instance dealt explicitly with the compatibility of the contested Community act with international law. Whereas the Court in *Wood Pulp* had not espoused the Opinion of the Advocate-General in that case to the effect that the only criterion for jurisdiction in the circumstances of that case was the existence of a 'direct, substantial and forseeable effect', the Court here stated that the application of the Community act 'is justified under public international law when it is forseeable that a proposed concentration will have an immediate and substantial effect within the Community.'[92] It then proceeded to examine whether these three criteria had been satisfied in this case, which it found to be the case.

As was the case in *Wood Pulp*,[93] the Court stated that '[t]he applicant's argument that, by virtue of a principle of non-interference, the Commission should have refrained from prohibiting the concentration in order to avoid a conflict of jurisdiction with the South African authorities must be rejected, without it being necessary to consider whether such a rule exists in international law,' since the South African government, in its communications with the Commission, had expressed some concerns but had not called into question the Community's jurisdiction to rule on the concentration at issue; nor had the applicant or the South African government indicated, 'beyond making mere statements of principle, in what way the proposed concentration would affect the vital economic and/or commercial interests of South Africa.'[94] On the one hand, this may perhaps indicate some sensitivity to the objections of principle to assertions of extraterritorial competence, but on the other, the Court's perceived need to examine whether the principle of non-interference does exist in international law is somewhat surprising.[95]

However, the Court did not enter into any detailed discussion of the method it employed in order to arrive at the applicable international law rule, a feature that is char-

90. See text accompanying nn. 23 and 27 above.

91. Ibid., at paras. 76-88.

92. Ibid., at para. 90.

93. Loc. cit. n. 27, at paras. 19-20.

94. Ibid., at paras. 102-108. This may be compared to the recognition of the principle of non-intervention in the *Anastasiou* case, discussed in section 3.2.1 above.

95. 'The exercise of jurisdiction because of the effects of an act within the state may amount to no more than an "objective" application of the territorial principle of jurisdiction, but where the effects relied on are not a constituent part of the offence in question but are mere consequences or repercussions of the acts done, the legitimate bounds of the territorial principle are overstepped, particularly if the effects are only incidental and insubstantial; in this lies the danger of impropriety in resort to the "effects" principle as a basis for jurisdiction and the doubtful consistency of that principle with international law. Concern expressed by many other states has led certain United States courts to have some regard to the legitimate interests of other states, by requiring not only that the foreign conduct of aliens must have actual or intend-

acteristic of its early case-law, particularly in a controversial field of law as that involved in this case. On balance, it is doubtful whether this judgment is significantly different from the Court's earlier judgments on the matter.[96]

3.6 The Court and resolutions of the United Nations

The Charter of the United Nations occupies a privileged position within the Community legal order, for a number of reasons, deriving both from the Charter as well as the EC Treaty. Firstly, according to Article 103 of the Charter of the United Nations, the obligations of States under the Charter take precedence over their obligations under any other international agreement. Secondly, Article 48(2) of the Charter provides that members of the United Nations must carry out decisions for the maintenance of international peace and security directly and through their action in the appropriate international agencies of which they are members. Thirdly, Article 307 of the EC treaty[97] provides that 'the rights and obligations arising from agreements concluded before 1 January 1958 or, for acceding States, before the date of their accession, between one or more Member States on the one hand, and one or more third countries on the other, shall not be affected by the provisions of this Treaty'. Fourthly, Article 297 of the EC Treaty[98] provides that 'Member States shall consult each other with a view to taking together the steps needed to prevent the functioning of the common market being affected by measures which a Member State may be called upon to take in the event of serious internal disturbances affecting the maintenance of law and order, in the event of war, serious international tension constituting a threat of war, or in order to carry out obligations it has accepted for the purpose of maintaining peace and international security.' The combination of the effect of these provisions is to guarantee the effect of resolutions of the Security Council of the United Nations in Community law. While the Community is itself not a party to the Charter of the United Nations,[99] all Member States of the European Community are members of the United Nations. As far as the Community is concerned, it must not hinder the compliance by Member States of their international organizations.[100] These obligations

---

ed effects within the United States, causing sufficient injury there, but also that "the interests of, and links to, the US – including the magnitude of the effects on American foreign commerce – are sufficiently strong, vis-à-vis those on other nations, to justify the assertion of extraterritorial authority'"; Jennings and Watts, loc. cit n. 10, para. 139, pp. 475-476 (quoting from a leading American case on the issue, *Timberlane Lumber Co* v. *Bank of America*).

96. See text accompanying nn. 23-30 above.

97. Formerly Art. 234.

98. Formerly Art. 224.

99. Art. 4 of the Charter of the United Nations provides that membership of the organization is open to States only.

100. See Gilsdorf, 'Les réserves de securité du traité CEE, à la lumière du traité sur l'Union européene', *Revue du Marché Commun et de L'Union Européenne* (1994) p. 17, at p. 21.

have been reflected in a number of judgments, some of which have been considered above.[101]

A group of cases involving the resolutions adopted by the Security Council concerning the situation in the former Yugoslavia illustrates the rule that Community law will be interpreted in a manner that conforms to Charter obligations. In *Ebony Maritime and Loten Navigation* v. *Prefeto della Provinsia di Brindisi*[102], the Court was called upon to determine the scope of a Community regulation adopted pursuant to Security Council resolution 820 (1993), which was designed to reinforce the sanctions against the Federal Republic of Yugoslavia (Serbia and Montenegro) ('Yugoslavia') by resolutions 713 (1991), 757 (1992) and 787 (1992). Resolution 820 prohibited all maritime traffic from entering the territorial sea of Yugoslavia (Serbia and Montenegro) except when authorized, and to detain, pending investigation, all vessels and their cargo found in their territories and suspected of having violated or being in violation of the resolutions mentioned above. In compliance with these obligations, the regulation in question prohibited the entry into Yugoslav territorial waters of all commercial traffic. The question was whether this covered conduct occurring in international waters which gave good reason to believe that the vessel concerned was on course for that territorial sea for the purposes of commercial traffic. The Court ruled that (a) no distinction was drawn on the basis of the vessel's flag or owner, (b) there was no requirement that the breach of the prohibitions had to have occurred on Community territory and (c), rather, the prohibition on entry into the territorial sea of Yugoslavia could only be breached *outside* Community territory.[103] The Court ruled that the regulation covered attempted as well as actual entries into the Yugoslav territorial sea by vessels in international waters, and that any other interpretation would render the prohibition, and the United Nations resolutions it sought to implement, ineffective.[104] Furthermore, in response to the question as to whether a domestic law that prescribed confiscation of the cargo of a vessel found to be in breach of the provisions of the regulation was valid, the Court ruled that, where Community law does not itself prescribe a penalty for breach of its provisions, it was up to the Member States pursuant to Article 5 of the EC Treaty to ensure the effective application of Community law, even to the extent of imposing strict criminal liability. The only requirement was that the national court must determine, in accordance with established principles of the Court's case-law, whether the penalty imposed was 'dissuasive, effective and proportionate'.[105] However, in deciding whether that was the case, the national court 'must take account, in particular, of the fact that the objective pursued by the Regulation, which is to bring to an end the state of war in the region concerned and the massive violations of human rights and humanitarian international law in the

101. See e.g., the *Anastasiou* case, section 3.2.1 above, and the *Racke* case, section 3.2.3 above.
102. Case C-177/95 [1997] *ECR* I-1111.
103. Ibid., at paras. 17-18, pp. 1138-1139.
104. Ibid., at paras. 23-26, pp. 1140-1141.
105. Ibid., at para. 37, p. 1143.

Republic of Bosnia-Herzegovina, is one of fundamental general interest for the international community.'[106]

It would appear that the converse is also true, that an act adopted for the purposes of implementing a resolution could be declared invalid if it does not in fact achieve the results intended by that resolution, or where the terms of the resolution have not been properly applied. In *Bosphorus Hava Yollari ve Ticaret AS* v. *Minister for Transport, Energy and Communications*,[107] the Court upheld the application of a regulation that authorized the impoundment of aircraft in which a 'majority or controlling interest' is held by a person or undertaking in or operating from Yugoslavia, which was adopted pursuant to resolution 820 (1993). The owner of the aircraft was based in or operating from Yugoslavia but at the relevant time had leased it to an undertaking that had no connection with Yugoslavia. The Court held that the idea of 'ownership' was included in the phrase 'majority or controlling interest', so that the impoundment of this aircraft by national authorities was lawful even where the day-to-day operation and control of the aircraft were performed by an undertaking not connected with Yugoslavia. The Court held further, in response to an argument that the impoundment would infringe the fundamental right to peaceful enjoyment of property and freedom to pursue a commercial activity, that:

> 'As compared with an objective of general interest so fundamental for the international community, which consists in putting an end to the state of war in the region and to the massive violations of human rights and humanitarian international law in the Republic of Bosnia-Herzegovina, the impounding of the aircraft ... cannot be regarded as inappropriate or disproportionate.'[108]

In contrast, in *The Queen, ex parte Centro-Com Srl* v. *HM Treasury and Bank of England*,[109] the Court ruled that measures taken by Member States by virtue of their national competence in the field of foreign and security policy, such as the performance of obligations under the Charter, cannot be treated as falling outside the scope of the Community's common commercial policy simply on the ground that such measures have foreign and security objectives. Accordingly, while measures taken by a Member State intended to apply sanctions imposed by a Security Council resolution 'in order to achieve a peaceful solution to the situation in Bosnia-Herzegovina, which forms a threat to international peace and security' can derogate from obligations under the common commercial policy, such measures cease to be justified if there are Community rules that provide for the necessary measures with the same aim.

---

106. Ibid., at para. 38, p. 1143.

107. Case 84/95 [1996] *ECR* 3953.

108. Ibid., at para. 25. See paras. 19-27. See also *Dorsch Consult Ingenieurgesellschaft mbH* v. *Council and Commission*, case T-184/95 [1998] *ECR* II-667, at para. 74, p. 694, for the proposition that loss or damage suffered as a result of the Community acts adopted pursuant to resolutions of the Security Council are not attributable to the Community.

109. Case 124/95 [1997] *ECR* I-81.

On the basis of these cases, it can be seen that the Court is dealing with the obligations imposed by the Security Council resolutions not primarily as such but rather as a matter of Community law. It has been written, concerning the *Bosphorus* case, that the Court utilized its own methods of interpretation of Community law to the interpretation of Security Council resolutions, and that this is far from satisfactory as the Court appeared to be insufficiently sensitive to the 'background and affinities' of those resolutions.[110] The existence of a system or theory of interpretation applied by the Court generally has been the subject of discussion by several commentators (often with negative conclusions),[111] although it is clear that the Court does tend to adopt the teleological approach in its interpretation of Community law. In contrast, there is support for the view that a more literal approach is applied to the interpretation of decisions of the organs of international organizations.[112] But leaving to one side the merits or otherwise of an attempt to state categorically the rules of interpretation to be applied in particular contexts, it is clear that, even if the Court can be criticized in this way, the fact is that the Court, in interpreting the resolutions, appears to have erred in favour of what it perceived to be the requirement of the resolution.[113] The explicit references to the interests of the international community as a basis for interpreting Community law, even if there is always an element of 'transformation' of international rules before they are applied as Community law, is perhaps as much as can be expected from a Court in a specific setting such as the European Communities.[114]

110. I. Canor, '"Can Two Walk Together, Except They Be Agreed?" The Relationship between International Law and European Law: The Incorporation of United Nations Sanctions Against Yugoslavia into European Community Law Through the Perspective of the European Court of Justice', 35 *CMLRev.* (1998) p. 137, at p. 187. '...[e]xamination of the way the Court analysed the text of the resolution reveals that it was strongly influenced by the way it applies these very measures of interpretation domestically. Indeed, the United Nations Resolution was not perceived B and should not have been perceived B by the Court, as being in itself part of "the law of the land" but, was applied since it was incorporated into European law by the Regulation. But that is not sufficient to justify the interpretation of the United Nations Resolution being conceived as a matter of Community act interpretation' (at p. 150).

111. See e.g., H. Rasmussen, 'Between Self-Restraint and Judicial Activism', 13 *ELRev.* (1988) p. 28; J. Weiler, 'The European Court of Justice on Trial', 24 *CMLRev.* (1987) p. 555

112. See e.g., C.F. Amerasinghe, ***Principles of the Institutional Law of International Organizations*** (Cambridge, Cambridge University Press 1996) pp. 59-63.

113. 'Moreover, instead of supporting an activist and influential line of reasoning [the judges] were demonstrating bias to the international activity'; Canor, loc. cit. n. 110, at p. 187. The author also suggest that there may have been other considerations of pragmatism that may have been behind the Court's reasoning.

114. The marked increase in the number of Security Council resolutions adopted since the end of the Cold War will no doubt have played a role. Between 1990 and 2000, the Security Council has adopted more than twice as many resolutions as it adopted between 1946 and 1989. See also Klabbers, loc. cit. n. 1, at pp. 66-68.

4. THE INDIVIDUAL BEFORE THE EUROPEAN COURT OF JUSTICE, 'DIRECT EFFECT' AND THE PRELIMINARY REFERENCE PROCEDURE

It is well-known that while individuals enjoy substantive rights and are the subjects of substantive duties according to traditional international law, the position is different with respect to *procedural* capacity before international tribunals. Generally speaking, this is also the position in the Community legal order. Article 230[115] of the EC Treaty illustrates the position of the individual as a 'non-privileged applicant' for the purposes of instituting proceedings before the Court 'on grounds of lack of competence, infringement of an essential procedural requirement, infringement of this Treaty or of any rule of law relating to its application, or misuse of powers.' In contrast to the position of the Member States, the Council, the Commission, the European Parliament and the European Central Bank, the fourth paragraph of this article provides that '[a]ny natural or legal person may institute proceedings against a decision addressed to that person or against a decision which, although in the form of a regulation or a decision addressed to another person, is of direct and individual concern to the former.' The Court has interpreted this provision restrictively, to limit access to judicial review to Community acts that are essentially particular in aim rather than general, and in which the applicant has a personal interest.[116]

---

115. Formerly Art. 173.

116. See e.g., *Alcan* v. *Commission*, case 69/69 [1970] *ECR* 385; *Bock* v. *Commission*, case 62/70 [1971] *ECR* 897; *Piraiki-Patraiki* v. *Commission*, case 11/82 [1985] *ECR* 207; *Comité central d'enterprise de la Société générale des grandes sources*, case T-96/92 [1995] *ECR* II-1213; *Comité central d'enterprise de la Société anonyme Vittel* v. *Commission*, case T-12/93 [1995] *ECR* II-1247; *Plaumann* v. *Commission*, case 25/62 [1963] *ECR* 95; *Toepfer* v. *Commission*, cases 106-107/63 [1965] *ECR* 405; *Zunis Holdings SA* v. *Commission*, case T-83/92 [1993] *ECR* II-1169; *Stichting Greenpeace Council* v. *Commission*, case T-585/93 [1995] *ECR* II-2205. But see *Parti Ecologiste 'Les Verts'* v. *Parliament*, case 294/83 [1986] *ECR* 1339.

See also Art. 232 (formerly Art. 175), concerning judicial review for failure to act. Access to the Court for individuals is similarly restricted; see e.g., *Bethell* v. *Commission*, case 246/81 [1982] *ECR* 2277; *Lütticke* v. *Commission*, case 48/65 [1966] *ECR* 19; *Star Fruit Co* v. *Commission*, case 247/87 [1989] *ECR* 291. Similarly, Art. 241 (formerly Art. 184), which provides that 'any party may, in proceedings in which a regulation adopted jointly by the European Parliament and the Council, or a regulation of the Council, of the Commission, or of the ECB is at issue, plead the grounds specified in the second paragraph of Article 230 in order to invoke before the Court of Justice the inapplicability of that regulation', is subject to the same restrictions as to standing for individuals.

For critique of the restrictive approach taken by the Court, see e.g., C. Harlow, 'Towards a Theory of Access for the European Court of Justice', 12 *YEL* (1992) p. 213; P. Craig, 'Legality, Standing and Substantive Review in Community Law', 14 *Oxford Journal of Legal Studies* (1994) p. 507; A. Arnull, 'Private Applicants and the Action for Annulment under Article 173 of the Treaty', 32 *CMLRev.* (1995) p. 7.

However, the procedure for references from national courts to the Court under Article 234[117] has provided a means whereby the Court can examine the validity of Community acts, albeit indirectly. This article of the EC Treaty makes provision for the national courts in the Community, before which individuals of course have broad procedural capacity, to obtain from the Court authoritative rulings on the interpretation of European law in cases being considered by those courts.[118] The majority of cases discussed in section 3 above came to the Court through this procedure. Given the increased level of reference to international law in the Court's recent case-law as described thus far, there exists a greater possibility for individuals to obtain indirect challenges to Community acts on the basis of international law than exists under traditional international law.

In *Racke* v. *Hauptzollamt Mainz*, it was argued before the Court that the preliminary reference procedure did not permit the development of arguments based on international law alone without any reference to Community law. The Court however applied its earlier ruling in the *International Fruit Company* case, to the effect that its jurisdiction to give preliminary rulings concerning the validity of acts of the Community institutions could not be limited by the grounds on which the validity of those measures could be contested.[119] With regard to individuals, the *Racke* case involved discussion of the conditions on the reviewability of the compatibility of Community legislation with rules of international law. The second condition laid down in the *International Fruit Company* case[120] was that the rule of international law in question must have direct effect, i.e., be capable of conferring rights on individuals which could be enforced directly in national courts.[121] That case, it will be remembered, involved a treaty rule. In his Opinion in the *Racke* case, the Advocate-General considered the applicability of this condition to rules of customary international law on the plea of fundamental change of circumstances as a basis for the suspension of a treaty.[122] By analogy with the case-law of the Court on the direct effect of international agreements (which was not appropriate because the rules in Vienna Convention on the Law of Treaties were applicable as customary law only), the Advocate-General inferred that there should also be limits to the applicability of customary law. He stat-

117. Formerly Art. 177. For discussion, see e.g., Watson, 'Asser Institute Colloquium on European Law 1985: Experience and Problems in Applying Article 177 EEC', 23 *CMLRev.* (1986) p. 207; A. Arnull, 'References to the European Court', 15 *ELRev.* (1990) p. 375.

118. On the preliminary reference procedure in Community law, see e.g., G. Bebr, 'The Reinforcement of the Constitutional Review of Community Acts under Article 177 EEC', 25 *CMLRev.* (1988) p. 684, and Arnull, loc. cit. n. 117, at p. 375.

119. Loc. cit. n. 59, at paras. 25-27.

120. Loc. cit. n. 14.

121. See the *Van Gend en Loos* case, loc. cit. n. 9; the *International Fruit* case, loc. cit. n. 14. On the doctrine of direct effect generally and its development and treatment by the Court, see Craig and de Burca, loc. cit. n. 31, Ch. 4.

122. 'Are the rules of customary international law such as to create rights in favour of individuals ... such as to permit an individual to challenge a *political* decision by the Community to suspend the operation of an international agreement?'; para. 77 et seq., p. 3679.

ed that the customary law of treaties, including the *rebus suc stantibus* doctrine, was concerned with the regulation of the relations between States and international organizations, rather than individuals. He distinguished between the law of treaties and those rules of international law that intend to confer rights on individuals, such as humanitarian law, and concluded that the nature and purpose of the law of treaties 'was not conducive to direct effect'.[123] He then considered the rule applied in the case-law of the Court concerning the conditions for direct effect, namely that the rules of international law in question must contain clear, precise and unconditional obligations, which he found not to be the case as far as the *rebus sic stantibus* doctrine was concerned.[124] However, considering that the rights of the individual to challenge Community acts were also to be protected, he attempted to strike a balance between the non-reviewability of the political discretion involved in the exercise of the treaty-making powers of the Community institutions on the one hand, and the need to protect the legitimate expectations of individuals based on treaties thus concluded by limiting the scope of judicial review to cases where there had been a 'manifest violation' of customary law of treaties on the other.[125]

For its part, in response to the argument put forward by the Commission that, in order to challenge the validity of a regulation, an individual could not rely on grounds deriving from the relationship between the Community and a third State under international law, the Court ruled that, since customary international law was a part of the Community legal order, an individual relying in legal proceedings on rights derived from a treaty between the Community and a third State 'may not be denied the possibility of challenging the validity of a regulation which ... prevents him from relying on it, and of invoking ... obligations deriving from international law which govern the termination and suspension of treaty relations.'[126]

The only qualification imposed by the Court related to the 'complexity' and 'imprecision' of the rules of customary international law in question, and this has been discussed.[127] It only needs to be noted here that the Court, probably accepting the reasoning of the Advocate-General, did limit the reviewability of the Community act in question on the basis of customary law to cases where there had been a 'manifest error of assessment concerning the conditions for applying those rules.' Setting aside the objections of principle to this statement discussed earlier,[128] it would seem to follow that customary international law, rather than being just a part of Community law, has direct effect. Even the questionable qualification imposed by the Court does not rule out the possibility of review; it merely restricts it. That that qualification is ill-conceived is probably borne out by the consideration that the lack of direct effect of the provisions of the EC or other treaties would exclude the reviewability of Commu-

---

123. Ibid., at paras. 83-85, pp. 3681-3682.
124. See text accompanying nn. 67-69 above.
125. Ibid., at paras. 89-90, p. 3683.
126. Ibid., at paras. 44-51, pp. 3704-3706.
127. See section 3.2.3 above.
128. Ibid.

nity acts on the basis of those treaties entirely, while the lack of direct effect of rules of customary law would not exclude such review, at least not entirely. The paradoxical result is that customary law would in this sense be more compelling than provisions of the EC treaty or international treaties. It is unlikely that the Court intended this result.[129]

The significance of this case lies in the considerations that (i) that this principle of direct effect was extended to customary as distinct from conventional international law, and (ii) the Court did not accept the argument based on the distinction between international law and Community law, since the former was a part of the latter. The preliminary reference procedure as developed by the Court does go a long way in allowing the individual the opportunity of legal redress on the basis of international custom, even if it is for the national court, rather than the individual, to make the reference to the Court.[130]

5. CONCLUSION

On the basis of the cases considered in this survey, it can be argued that the European Court of Justice is becoming a court that applies general international law. Specifically, it has been seen that the Court has been faced with a diverse range of issues as a matter of customary international law, as distinct from treaty law, and given the doctrinal difficulties inherent in the notion of customary law, this must be seen as encouraging from the point of view of the international lawyer, albeit that the most difficult issues of customary international may not have arisen for the Court's consideration. Of course, from the point of view of the traditional international lawyer, there are certain difficulties with the way the Court has handled the international law it applied, ranging from the Court's 'internalization' of the rules of customary law into the Community legal system before applying them (which is not surprising for the Court given its position within the Community legal system[131]) to its apparent unwillingness to broach the difficult task of international law-identification in the *Racke* case (which is more difficult to justify or explain).[132] However, the point is that general interna-

129. Of course, the problem is that the novelty of this pronouncement makes it difficult to know whether the Court was dealing with direct effect or other issues.

130. Klabbers, loc. cit. supra n. 1, especially pp. 53-59, notes, in relation to aspects of the law of treaties, the (realized?) potential of Community law as applied by the Court to ameliorate the position of non-State actors in international law in general, albeit resulting in some unorthodoxy as far as some traditional notions of international law are concerned.

131. Hartley, loc. cit. n. 5, Ch. 7, on the question whether the Community legal system can be described as (i) separate and (ii) independent of the international legal system. See also J.H.H. Weiler and U.R. Haltern, 'The Autonomy of the Community Legal Order B Through the Looking-Glass', 37 *Harvard JIL* (1996) p. 411.

132. See sections 3.2.3 and 4 above.

tional law has been expressly accepted as being a part of the Community legal order, and can be used to examine the validity of acts of and within the Community. It would be interesting to see how the Court's treatment of general international law will develop in coming years.

ENVIRONMENTAL NON-COMPLIANCE PROCEDURES AND INTERNATIONAL LAW*

M. A. Fitzmaurice and C. Redgwell*****

** Professor of Public International Law, Queen Mary University of London.

*** Reader in Public International Law, Oxford University, and Fellow of St. Peter's College.

1. INTRODUCTION

A number of recent environmental treaties provide for a non-compliance procedure (NCP) to address failure by Contracting Parties properly to implement their treaty obligations. Examples include the 1987 Montreal Protocol to the 1985 Vienna Convention on the Protection of the Ozone Layer;[1] the 1991 VOC and 1994 Sulphur Protocols to the 1979 Long-Range Transboundary Air Pollution Treaty;[2] the 1992 Convention for the Protection of the Marine Environment of the North-East Atlantic;[3] and the 1997 Kyoto Protocol to the 1992 Framework Convention on Climate Change,[4] all of which envisage a separate mechanism for compliance being established.[5] This re-

1. 26 *ILM* (1987) p. 1529 (Convention) and p. 1550 (Protocol); see also http://www.unep.ch/ozone Provided for in Art. 8 of the Protocol, the NCP was finalised at the fourth meeting of the parties in 1992: see Decision IV/5.

2. The 1994 Second Sulphur Protocol (33 *ILM* (1994) p. 1542) entered into force on 5 August 1998 and was the first Protocol to LRTAP to require the mandatory application of emission limit values set forth in the Protocol; the 1991 VOC Protocol (31 *ILM* (1992) p. 568) entered into force on 29 September 1997. In 1997 an Implementation Committee was established for review of compliance by the parties with the protocols to LRTAP by Decision 1997/2 of the Executive Body of the Convention. The structure, function and procedures set out in that decision establishing the Implementation Committee have subsequently been adopted for review of compliance in accordance with Art. 3(3) and Art. 7, respectively, of the VOC and Second Sulphur Protocols: Decisions 1997/3 and 1998/6. At the end of 1999 an eighth Protocol was adopted, the Gothenburg Protocol to Abate Acidification, Eutrophication and Ground-Level Ozone, Art. 9 of which provides for regular review of the compliance of each party with the obligations of the Protocol and likewise utilises the Implementation Committee established by Decision 1997/2. By Decision 1998/3, any amendment to Decision 1997/2, and any other decision of the Executive Body pertaining to the Implementation Committee or its procedures, requires the consensus of the parties. See further http://www.unece.org/env/lrtap/conv

3. 32 *ILM* (1993) p. 1069 and http://www.ospar.org/ See Art. 23, which empowers the Commission established pursuant to Art. 10 to assess the compliance of Contracting Parties and to call for steps to bring a non-complying Contracting Party back into compliance. These provisions have not yet been implemented, with the Convention only entering into force on 25 March 1998.

4. 31 *ILM* (1992) p. 1330 (Convention) and 37 ILM (1998) p. 22 (Protocol) and http://www.unfccc.de/ COP-4 established a Joint Working Group on Compliance which produced a draft text for consideration at COP-6 (2000), which was suspended without reaching an agreement on, *inter alia*, this issue. COP-6 *bis* is due to be held in the second half of 2001. See further n. 15.

5. A number of other recent agreements have, or are contemplating the use of non-compliance procedures. Examples of the latter include the 1989 Basel Convention on the Transboundary Movement of Hazardous Wastes and their Disposal and the 1980 Convention on the Conservation of Antarctic Marine Living Resources: see further C. Redgwell, 'Protection of Ecosystems under International Law: Lessons from Antarctica', in A. Boyle and D. Freestone, eds., *International Law and Sustainable Development* (Oxford, Oxford University Press 1999) Ch. 9. Non-compliance procedures are also catered for in the recently concluded regional Aarhus Convention on Public Participation 1998 (Art. 15), the 1998 Rotterdam Convention on the Prior Informed Consent Procedure for Certain Hazardous Chemicals and Pesticides in International Trade (Art. 17) and the 2000 Cartagena Protocol on Biosafey to the 1992 Convention on the Conservation of Biological Diversity (Art. 34). Non-compliance procedures have been established by the International Commission for the Conservation of Atlantic Tuna (ICCAT): see further C. Carr, 'Recent De-

course to non-compliance procedures is evidence of a growing awareness that traditional rules of international law concerned with material breach of treaty obligations and with state responsibility[6] are inappropriate – and, indeed, unable – fully to address problems of environmental treaty compliance. This is a consequence both of the nature of international environmental obligations, in particular their non-reciprocal character, and of the inherent limitations of the present rules relating to treaty breach and state responsibility in addressing harm especially to the global commons. Even the innovative provisions of the current draft articles of the ILC on state responsibility, which address breach of multilateral and *erga omnes* obligations and are discussed further below, do not completely fill the 'responsibility gap'. Nonetheless recent international environmental agreements do not eschew traditional international law mechanisms; indeed, in all of the instances cited above, non-compliance procedures function alongside traditional dispute settlement mechanisms.[7] This duality is possible if one views NCPs as located within a wider category of non-confrontational dispute avoidance procedures[8] which combine classical methods, which have their roots

velopments in Compliance and Enforcement for International Fisheries' 24 *Ecology Law Quarterly* (1997) p. 847, at pp. 847-860.

Churchill and Ulfstein argue that 'subsidiary bodies for operating noncompliance mechanisms could also be established without an explicit provision in the [multilateral environmental agreement] on the basis of "implied powers".' R.R.Churchill and G. Ulfstein, 'Autonomous Institutional Arrangements in Multilateral Environmental Agreements: A Little-Noticed Phenomenon in International Law', 94 *AJIL* (2000) p. 623, at p. 644.

6. As the Third Report of the Special Rapporteur on State Responsibility makes clear, the VCLT and state responsibility operate in separate spheres, a distinction maintained even where suspension of treaty obligations are resorted to as a countermeasure in response to a non-material breach of treaty: cf., Third Report (2000), A/CN.4/507/Add.3, pp. 16-17, paras. 324-325; see also the *Case Concerning the Gabcikovo/Nagymaros Project (Hungary/Slovakia)*, 25 September 1997, *ICJ Rep.* (1997) at pp. 38-39, para. 47 wherein the law of treaties and the law of State responsibility are described as 'two branches of international law [that] obviously have a scope that is distinct. A determination of whether a convention is or is not in force, and whether it has or has not been properly suspended or denounced, is to be made pursuant to the law of treaties. On the other hand, an evaluation of the extent to which the suspension or denunciation of a convention, seen as incompatible with the law of treaties, involves the responsibility of the State which proceeded to it, is to be made under the law of State responsibility.'

7. Indeed, this may be all that is provided for in many agreements, including those recently concluded: see for example, Art. 27 of the 1992 Convention on Biological Diversity which provides for traditional dispute settlement, viz. negotiation, good offices, mediation, arbitration and/or the ICJ or conciliation. The 2000 Biosafety Protocol to the CBD, however, provides in Art. 14 for the negotiation of a non-compliance mechanism. Like the CBD, the 1994 Convention to Combat Desertification contains a dispute settlement provision (Art. 28); however, Art. 27 provides that '[t]he Conference of the Parties shall consider and adopt procedures and institutional mechanisms for the resolution of questions that may arise with regard to the implementation of the Convention,' thus providing the legal foundation for the subsequent development by the parties of compliance procedures and mechanisms.

8. A feature of NCPs which is sometimes overlooked as pointed out by e.g., A.O. Adede, 'Avoidance, Prevention and Settlement of International Disputes', in Sun Lin, Lal Kurukulasuriya and F. Schlingemann eds., *UNEP's New Way Forward: Environmental Law and Sustainable Development* (52 et seq; G. Loibl, 'Comment on the Paper of A. Adede', in W. Lang, ed., *Sustainable Development and International Law* (London, Graham & Trotman 1995) pp. 125 et seq; idem 'Dispute Prevention and

in the dispute settlement mechanisms developed under general international law, with 'innovative procedures for enhancing compliance with, and responding to, non-performance of international obligations.'[9]

It is the purpose of this article more fully to explore the legal relationship between non-compliance procedures (NCP),[10] dispute settlement procedures, material breach of treaty obligations and state responsibility. The fundamental objective is to locate NCPs within a broader international law framework and to suggest that recent procedures, including those under discussion for the 1997 Kyoto Protocol, demonstrate the development of collective responses to breach of treaty and responsibility which focus upon ensuring the credibility and effectiveness of environmental treaty obligations. While the purpose is not exhaustively to describe and analyse existing NCPs, a task which at any rate has been extensively performed in the literature,[11] particular

---

Possible Legal Instruments in the Field of the Environment' in *Österreichische Aussenpolitik Dokumentation Sondernumer, 'UN Green Helmets'* ; Z.O. Gresham, J.M. Schurz, 'Dispute Avoidance and Dispute Resolution in International Environmental Agreements: An Introduction', 9 *Environment and Trade* (1994).

9. C. Chinkin, 'Alternative Dispute Resolution under International Law', in M. Evans, ed., *Remedies in International Law, The Institutional Dilemma* (Oxford, Hart Publishing 1998) p. 128.

10. An interesting issue not considered here is what constitutes compliance. Kingsbury rightly critiques the literature as setting up a (false) dichotomy between compliance and non-compliance, when in practice it is, at best, a continuum: see further B. Kingsbury, 'The Concept of Compliance as a Function of Competing Conceptions of International Law', 19 *Michigan JIL* (1998) p. 345. Nor should compliance be viewed as synonymous with effectiveness: see further n. 34 below. During debate of the Special Rapporteur's Second Report on State Responsibility (1999) the suggestion that 'non-compliance' be employed in the draft articles to refer to a failure to carry out an obligation not involving a breach of international law was rejected: 1999 *ILC Rep.*, para. 115, reproduced at http://www.un.org/law/ilc/reports/1999

11. In addition to the sources cited *infra*, see generally P. Szell, 'The Development of Multilateral Mechanisms for Monitoring Compliance', in Lang, ed., op. cit. n. 8, at Ch. 7; J. Cameron, J. Werksman and P. Roderick, eds., *Improving Compliance with International Environmental Law* (London, Earthscan 1996); G. Handl, 'Compliance Control Mechanism and International Environmental Obligations', 5 *Tulane JIL* (1995) p. 29; D.G. Victor, K. Raustiala and E.B. Skolnikoff, eds., *The Implementation and Effectiveness of International Environmental Commitments: Theory and Practice* (Cambridge MA, MIT Press 1998); E. Brown Weiss and H.K. Jacobson, eds., *Engaging Countries: Strengthening Compliance with International Environmental Accords* (Cambridge MA, MIT Press 1998); R. Wolfrum, 'Means of Ensuring Compliance with and Enforcement of International Environmental Law', 272 *RdC* (1999) pp. 9-154; H.M. Schally, 'The Role and Importance of Monitoring and Non-Compliance procedures in International Environmental Regimes', in The Ozone Treaties and Their Influence in on the Building of International Environmental Regimes, *Special Issue: Österreichische Aussenpolitsche Dokumentation*; Federal Ministry for Foreign Affairs, Vienna, Austria (1996); P. Szell, 'Implementation Control: Non-Compliance Procedure and Dispute Settlement in the Ozone Regime' in ibid.; D.G. Victor, 'The Early Operation and Effectiveness of Montreal Protocol's Non-Compliance Procedure', *IIASA Paper* (May 1996) J. Werksman, 'Designing a Compliance System for the UN Framework Convention on Climate Change', in J. Cameron, J. Werksman and P. Roderick eds., *Improving Compliance with International Environmental Law* (London, Earthscan 1996); A. Chayes and A. Chayes, *The New Sovereignty: Compliance with International Regulatory Agreements* (Cambridge MA, Harvard University Press 1995); A. Chayes and A. Chayes, 'On Compliance', 47 *International Organisation* (1993) pp. 175-205; A. Chayes and A. Chayes, 'Compliance without Enforcement: State Behaviour under Regulatory Treaties', *Negotiations Journal* (1991) pp. 311-330.

reference will be made to the operational NCP under the 1987 Montreal Protocol and to the current negotiation of a non-compliance procedure under the 1997 Kyoto Protocol to the 1992 Framework Convention on Climate Change (FCCC).

2. WHY ESTABLISH A NON-COMPLIANCE PROCEDURE?

The primary objective in establishing any NCP is to provide, within a multilateral context, encouragement to states to comply with their treaty obligations and, in the event of non-compliance, to provide a 'softer' system to address non-compliance than that afforded by traditional dispute settlement procedures under general international law.[12] Accordingly, NCPs are designed to assist the defaulting state in returning to compliance, not necessarily to incriminate for non-compliance.[13] However, as will be illustrated further below, the methods for encouraging compliance range from the facilitative to the coercive; or, as Werksman characterises compliance approaches, from a 'soft managerial approach' relying primarily upon 'cooperative problem solving' to an enforcement approach 'which relies on stronger tactics to deter non-compliance or to coerce non-complying states into complying.'[14] Indeed, these are not mutually exclusive with both approaches manifest in the proposed Kyoto Protocol NCP which envisages a Compliance Committee with both a facilitative branch and an enforcement

12. These objectives are confirmed by the conclusions of the Group of Legal Experts under the Montreal Protocol which state that a NCP 'allows and encourages the parties to assist each other in the implementation of the control measures agreed by them and to a certain degree to prevent them from referring cases of breaches of the Protocol directly to confrontational settlement of disputes procedure.' Ms. C. Bjorklund, the first President of the Montreal Protocol Non-Compliance Implementation Committee, described the Montreal Protocol NCP 'as an assisting rather than dispute solving body which is to act as a new forum of settling disputes outside the traditional judicial framework': cited in I. Rummel-Bulska, 'Implementation Control: Non-Compliance and Dispute Settlement: From Montreal to Basel', in W. Lang, ed., *The Ozone Treaties and Their Influence on the Building of International Legal Regimes; Special Issue: Österreichische aussenpolitische Dokumentation*. See also the Declaration by the Ministers of the Environment of the Region of the UNECE and the Member of the Commission of the EC Responsible for the Environment, 30 April 1993, at p. 8, para. 23.1.

13. G. Handl, 'Controlling Implementation of Compliance with International Environmental Commitments: the Rocky Road from Rio', 5 *Colorado JEL&P* (1994) p. 305, at p. 329. Of course, incrimination for non-compliance may be one mechanism to achieve a return to compliance, analogous to 'name and shame' techniques under international human rights instruments, for example, but going further in providing for specific sanctions, such as trade sanctions. See further discussion in Wolfrum, op. cit. n. 11, at pp. 56 et seq. ('Enforcing Compliance by Confrontational Means').

14. J. Werksman, 'Compliance and the Kyoto Protocol: Building a Backbone into a 'Flexible' Regime', 9 *YIEL* (1998) p. 48, at p. 56 ('Theoretical Approaches to Non-Compliance Responses'). In these admittedly crude characterisations Werksman explicitly relies on the extensive literature on compliance with multilateral environmental agreements, in particular K. Danish, 'Management v. Enforcement: The New Debate on Promoting Treaty Compliance', 37 *Virginia JIL* (1997) p. 789 (enforcement) and Chayes and Chayes, *op. cit. n. 11*, ('managerialist').

branch. This reflects '[t]he objective of the procedures and mechanisms on compliance [which] is to facilitate, promote and enforce compliance with commitments under the Protocol.'[15] This differentiation is a reflection of the various reasons for non-compliance by states with their international obligations. Such reasons may range from the free rider exploiting the economic advantage derived from non-compliance[16] to an inability to meet treaty obligations because of their high cost or a lack of capacity, e.g., lack of relevant technology or expertise.[17] A NCP needs both to reduce or eliminate the economic benefits to be derived from non-compliance[18] and to facilitate compliance where obstacles relating to lack of capacity, particularly for developing States, are identifiable. Practice under the Montreal Protocol reveals a particular reliance on facilitative approaches though the Implementation Committee thereunder is not bifurcated in the manner proposed for the Kyoto Compliance Committee.

A further characteristic feature of NCPs is that a multilateral forum for dispute resolution/avoidance is created for the internal resolution of disputes, without the need for recourse to external adjudication or institutions. Access to the procedure is generally broader than for traditional dispute settlement mechanisms, since NCPs may be invoked by one or more parties regarding another party's implementation or by a party regarding it own implementation; in addition, the role of the secretariat may include reporting upon possible non-compliance revealed through an initial scrutiny of national reports and where administrative and diplomatic efforts to resolve the matter have not proved successful.[19] NCPs are therefore not dependent upon common agreement; that is, unlike traditional dispute settlement mechanisms NCPs need not

---

15. 'Procedures and Mechanisms Relating to Compliance Under the Kyoto Protocol: Text proposed by the Co-Chairmen of the Joint Working Group on Compliance', FCCC/SB/2000/11, 24 October 2000, Section I, para. 1 and Section II, para. 2, respectively.

16. See generally, J. Heister, E. Mohr, F. Stahler, P.T. Stoll and R. Wolfrum, 'Strategies to Enforce Compliance with an International CO2 Treaty', 9 *International Environmental Affairs* (1997) p. 22, at pp. 23-24 ('reasons for non-compliance').

17. Mitchell identifies three principal sources of non-compliance: preference, incapacity and inadvertence. See R.B. Mitchell, 'Compliance Theory: an Overview', in J. Cameron et al., eds., op. cit. n. 11, Ch. 1, at pp. 11-13.

18. As Marauhn observes, 'compliance control is a device for generating confidence of states that the benefits of respecting and implementing the obligations of the treaty outweigh the costs'. T. Marauhn, 'Towards a Procedural Law of Compliance, Control in International Relations', 56 *ZaöRV* (1996) p. 698; see also C. Redgwell, 'Non-Compliance Procedures and the Climate Change Convention', in W. Bradnee Chambers, ed., *Global Climate Governance: Inter-linkages between the Kyoto Protocol and other Multilateral Regimes* (UNU/GEIC/IAS 1998) Ch. 3, p. 14.

19. As is the case, for example, under the Second Sulphur Protocol: see para. 5 of Decision 1997/2. For further discussion of the Montreal Protocol procedure, see below. Wolfrum compares NCPs with the State complaint procedures under the International Covenant on Civil and Political Rights (Art. 41), the Convention on the Elimination of Racial Discrimination (Art. 11), and the Torture Convention (Art. 21): Wolfrum, loc. cit. n. 11, at p. 38 n. 45. The Multilateral Consultative Process envisaged under Article 13 of the 1992 United Nations Framework Convention on Climate Change provides, *inter alia*, that the COP may trigger this process. There is no formal conduit for NGOs to access the compliance procedures under the Montreal Protocol nor under the proposed Kyoto Protocol procedure, though the latter does envisage

be consent-based. Nor is it necessary for there to be 'injured state' in order to invoke NCPs, as is the case under traditional rules of state responsibility. While in its recent deliberations the International Law Commission has broadened the concept of 'injured state', a point returned to below, there remains the question of the status of rules on state responsibility concerning the international community as whole as a matter of general international law, and the point remains a valid one in so far as the existing state of the law is concerned.[20]

NCPs reflect the need to ensure both continuing participation in the treaty and fulfilment of generally non-reciprocal obligations designed to ensure the achievement of common goals.[21] The distinctive character of certain multilateral environmental treaty obligations arises from a number of factors: the pace, magnitude and irreversibility of environmental problems which renders enforcement *inter partes* ineffective; the failure to operationalise traditional rules on state liability and responsibility; the ability accurately to measure compliance against quantifiable targets; and the necessity for national implementation to render international environmental obligations effective. Moreover, in the climate change context the effects of non-compliance may be subtle and cumulative, with the full effects manifest only over a considerable time period. In common with other transfrontier environmental problems, it may also be difficult to attribute particular harm to the actions or omissions of one state or states. This enhances the need for a NCP which places emphasis upon prevention[22] as well as upon cessation of the harmful activity and a return to compliance. The preventive element is reflected in a trend away from relying solely upon dispute settlement pro-

(on the current 2000 draft) the possibility of NGOs providing information relevant to compliance issues: *supra* n. 15, Section III.

20. See further J. Crawford, 'Revising the Draft Articles on State Responsibility', 10 *EJIL* (1999) p. 435, at p. 436. Elsewhere he has observed that earlier formulations of Art. 40 (now 43) in the ILC Draft Articles on State Responsibility conflated two categories of states, namely, 'states whose rights are infringed by the violation of a multilateral obligation and those states with a legal interest in compliance with the obligation.' He notes that in some cases of multilateral obligations there may be no primary obligee, specifically citing the obligation not to emit excess CFCs into the atmosphere under the Ozone Convention and its Montreal Protocol: J. Crawford, 'The Standing of States: A Critique of Article 40 of the ILC's Draft Articles on State Responsibility', in M. Andenas and D. Fairgrieve, eds., *Liber Amicorum in Honour of Lord Slynn of Hadley* (The Hague, Kluwer Law International 2000) Ch. 3, at pp. 41-42; see also the discussion in Bederman, 'Article 40(2)(E) & (F) of the ILC Draft Articles on State Responsibility: Standing of Injured States Under Customary International Law and Multilateral Treaties' State Responsibility in a Multifactor World', *1998 ASIL Proceedings*, p. 293.These categories of States are now addressed as separate (but potentially related) categories in the ILC Draft Articles.

21. As is discussed further below, this feature of NCPs is particularly important given the inadequacies both of the traditional rules on state responsibility and of the law of treaties to address breach of multilateral environmental treaty obligations.

22. Some commentators rightly observe that traditional dispute settlement provisions may also serve a preventive function: see further n. 36 below. Monitoring and information collection can also provide helpful information as to the effectiveness of non-compliance procedures once adopted, thus completing the feedback loop within in an ongoing process of monitoring and information exchange and review.

visions, towards the addition of provisions addressing assessment,[23] monitoring,[24] verification,[25] verification of compliance,[26] and implementation.[27] This is a trend observable not only in the environmental sphere, though of particular import within it.

A broad – and more accurate – conception of NCP views such procedures as comprising a system of national reports and monitoring together with NCP *sensu stricto*, i.e., with an institutional mechanism specifically established to control implementation and compliance by states with their treaty obligations. As evidenced in the ozone and climate change contexts in particular, this broad view of NCPs provides a more accurate picture of the compliance 'continuum', with reporting and data-collecting forming part and parcel of the whole compliance or implementation system. Without them, it would not be possible to verify the degree of compliance by states with their treaty obligations. Indeed, there is little point in adopting a compliance mechanism without the capability to gather information relevant to a determination of whether treaty obligations are being observed. Thus findings based on monitoring and reporting obligations enable the whole NCP to be put into motion.[28] This integrated process may take place in incremental stages, i.e., with monitoring and information gathering preceding the development of non-compliance mechanisms. A good example of this step-by-step process is found under the 1979 Geneva Convention on Long-Range Transboundary Air Pollution (LRTAP),[29] which has seen data collected under the

---

23. Art. 6, 1987 Montreal Protocol to the 1985 Ozone Layer Convention.

24. Art. 9, 1979 Convention on Long-Range Transboundary Air Pollution Treaty ('LRTAP').

25. Art. 19, 1989 Basel Convention on the Control of Transboundary Movements of Hazardous Wastes and their Disposal.

26. This is particularly relevant in arms control treaties, e.g., 1987 US/USSR Treaty on the Elimination of Intermediate Range and Shorter Range Missiles. This is carried out, *inter alia*, through compulsory inspections. See generally, S. Oeter, 'Inspection in International Law: Monitoring Compliance and the Problems of Implementation in International Law', 28 *NYIL* (1997) pp. 101-169. A further example is found in the fisheries context, for example the international observer scheme provided for in Art. 21 of the 1995 Straddling Stocks Agreement. Art. VII of the 1959 Antarctic Treaty and Art. 14 of the 1991 Madrid Protocol provide further examples of compliance linked with inspection. On the latter see further Wolfrum, op. cit. n. 11, at p. 45.

27. Art. 13 FCCC.

28. This appears to be supported by for example Chinkin who includes monitoring and reporting to formalised method for treaty compliance: C. Chinkin, 'International Environmental Law in Evolution', in T. Jewel and J. Steele, eds., *Law in Environmental Decision-Making, National, European, and International Perspectives* (Oxford, Clarendon Press 1998) at p. 247. See also Szell, who observes that '[w]ithout regular, detailed and objective reporting of performance, any meaningful supervision of a state's observance of its commitments [is] impossible': Szell, op. cit. n. 11, at p. 98; see also K. Sachariew, 'Promoting Compliance with International Environmental Legal Standards: Reflections on Monitoring and Reporting Mechanisms', 2 *YIEL* (1991) p. 333.

29. 24 *ILM* (1985) p. 484. See further J. Carlos di Primio, 'Data Quality and Compliance Control in the European Air Pollution Regime', in D.K. Victor, K. Raustiala, and E.B. Skolnikoff, eds., *The Implementation and Effectiveness of International Environmental Commitments: Theory and Practice* (Cambridge, MIT Press 1998) pp. 283–303

EMEP Programme[30] form the basis for an assessment of the first sulphur emissions protocol in 1985[31] which led to agreement on a tightened emission reduction schedule in the second sulphur protocol in 1994 with a non-compliance mechanism.[32] Indeed, the obligation to report is itself a concrete obligation, non-compliance with which may lead to the invocation of a NCP where available.[33] Similar developments may be observed in the climate change context which has proceeded from general commitments without specific timetables and targets to agreement upon such specific commitments with attention turned to implementation thereof and to compliance control.[34] The 1987 Montreal Protocol, the 1994 Second Sulphur Protocol and the 1997 Kyoto Protocol suggest a new cycle of strengthening compliance systems gradually, and in step with the strengthening of commitments.[35]

3. NON-COMPLIANCE PROCEDURES AND DISPUTE SETTLEMENT PROCEDURES

Many recent environmental agreements also incorporate traditional dispute settlement mechanisms,[36] though rarely with provision for compulsory third party dispute

30. 1984 Protocol on Long-Term Financing of the Cooperative Programme for Monitoring and Evaluation of the Long-Range Transmission of Air Pollutants in Europe (EMEP), 24 *ILM* (1985) p. 484.

31. Protocol on the Reduction of Sulphur Emissions or their Transboundary Fluxes by at least 30%, 27 *ILM* (1988) p. 707.

32. See also Art. 3(3) of the 1991 Protocol concerning the Control of Emissions of Volatile Organic Compounds or their Transboundary Fluxes, 31 *ILM* (1992) p. 568.

33. Non-compliance with reporting requirements is explicitly addressed under the Montreal Protocol, for example, which is discussed further below.

34. In this sense, a continuum may be perceived from communication of information and review thereof through to non-compliance and (possibly) culminating in dispute settlement. This is what Szell refers to as 'filling the gap' with an effective mechanism. See Szell, The Development of, loc. cit. n. 11; see also the note on implementation (Art. 13 FCCC) prepared by the interim secretariat, *supra* n. 15, at para. 18 (continuum from communication of information and review - article 12 - to the multilateral consultative process - article 13 - through to dispute settlement - article 14). However, Szell also points out the risk of an inverse relationship between the stringency of NCP and the stringency of the commitments which parties are willing to undertake (*ibid*., at p. 107), at point echoed by Victor, loc. cit. n. 11, at p. 139.

35. Even where concrete obligations have been established, compliance with which has been ensured, the effectiveness of the treaty regime is not thereby ensured. Compliance is not synonymous with effectiveness since the latter depends in part upon the strength of the obligations, their clarity, and their relationship with the overall objectives of the treaty in question. Low standards, and/or ambiguous ones, reduce effectiveness even where 'compliance' has been ensured. On effectiveness, see generally Victor et al., eds., op. cit. n. 29.

36. It is an over-simplification to state that dispute avoidance procedures are preventive in character whereas dispute settlement are only applicable post factum when damage to the environment has been done. Indeed, it has been argued elsewhere that the mere existence of dispute settlement mechanisms has a preventive effect since decision makers generally envisage the possibility that the injured state may have

settlement.[37] Traditionally States have demonstrated reluctance to seek recourse to arbitral or judicial proceedings in environmental disputes, even where bilateral or reciprocal obligations are at stake.[38] Nonetheless the parallel existence of dispute settlement and NCP creates potential legal difficulties. Is there a hierarchy in the application of these systems, or are they mutually exclusive? Is recourse to either of them conditioned by a particular type of breach of a treaty obligation? The difficulties of the interrelationship between the two systems has already been demonstrated in the Working Group entrusted by the Meeting of the Parties of the Montreal Protocol to establish a Non-Compliance Procedure,[39] where no agreement was reached on the priority of these systems. In the event the Montreal Protocol clearly seeks to prioritise traditional dispute settlement mechanisms over NCP, providing in the opening paragraph establishing the NCP under the Protocol that '[t]he following procedure has been formulated pursuant to Article 8 of the Montreal Protocol. It shall apply without prejudice to the operation of the settlement of dispute procedure laid down in Article 11 of the Vienna Convention [on the Protection of the Ozone Layer].'[40] The latter article introduces a hierarchy of application of the methods of dispute settlement: first, parties to a dispute seek a solution through negotiations and if they cannot achieve an agreement, they may seek recourse to good offices or mediation by a third party and finally, upon mutual consent, they may turn to arbitration or to the International Court of Justice. In the absence of mutual acceptance of either of these methods, the dispute shall be submitted to conciliation. Conciliation forms an inter-

---

recourse such mechanisms: G. Hafner, 'Should one fear the proliferation Mechanisms for the Peaceful Settlement of Disputes?', in L. Caflish, ed., *The Settlement of Disputes between States: Universal and European Perspectives* (The Hague, Kluwer Law International 1998) pp. 25, 37.

37. Notable exceptions include the Ozone Layer Convention and Montreal Protocol, and the FCCC and Kyoto Protocol. For further general discussion see M.M.T.A. Brus, *Third Party Dispute Settlement in an Interdependent World* (Dordrecht, Martinus Nijhoff Publishers 1995) p. 37 et seq. ('Dispute Settlement and the Global Environment').

38. Indeed, none of the major environmental catastrophes of recent years such as the 1978 Amoco Cadiz oil spill or 1985 Chernobyl nuclear incident have lead to international judicial proceedings: see e.g., P. Birnie and A. Boyle, *International Law and the Environment* (Oxford, Clarendon Press 1992) p. 137. Only a very few cases brought before the ICJ have involved environmental matters, including: *Case Concerning the Gabcikovo-Nagymaros Project (Hungary/Slovakia)*, 25 September 1997, *ICJ Rep.* (1997); *Case Concerning Certain Phosphate Lands in Nauru, Preliminary Objections*, 26 June 1992, *ICJ Rep.* (1992) pp. 240 et seq; *Case Concerning Delimitation of the Maritime Boundary in the Gulf of Maine Area*, 12 October 1984, *ICJ Rep.* (1984) pp 245 et seq; *Legality of the Use of Nuclear Weapons in Armed Conflict, Advisory Opinion*, 8 July 1996, *ICJ Rep.* (1996) pp. 225 et seq.

39. Szell, 'The Development of', loc. cit. n. 11, at p. 102.

40. The Multilateral Consultative Procedure (MCP) established under Art. 13 FCCC is also expressly stated to be without prejudice to the dispute settlement provisions of Art. 14 FCCC. As with the Montreal Protocol NCP, this begs certain legal questions such as: would invocation of Art. 13 require exhaustion before Art. 14 is pursued? Can a State go directly to Art. 14 before Art. 13 has been invoked? Some States favoured the automatic suspension of Art. 13 when Art. 14 is invoked, but this is not the necessary effect of the terms of reference of the MCP which only stresses that the process is both separate from and without prejudice to the dispute settlement provisions of Art. 14. See further Redgwell, op. cit. n. 18, at pp. 13-26.

mediate step between purely bilateral means of dispute settlement and third party settlement through an international court or arbitration and in general, 'is perceived as a not very effective means of dispute settlement.'[41]

The NCP procedure requires parties involved in the NCP 'to inform...the Meeting of the Parties of the results of proceedings taken under Article 11 of the Convention regarding possible non-compliance, about implementation of those results and about implementation of any decision of the Parties pursuant to paragraph 9' (which refers to recommendation undertaken under the NCP).[42] Paragraph 13 provides that the Meeting of the Parties may, pending completion of dispute settlement proceedings initiated under Article 11 of the Convention, issue an interim call and /or recommendation.

These provisions scarcely serve to clarify the legal relationship between NCP and dispute settlement procedures (DSP) under the Montreal Protocol. Similar difficulties may well arise under the 1992 Climate Change Convention where the NCP provisions of the 1997 Kyoto Protocol co-exist with the dispute settlement provisions (and with the Multilateral Consultative Process) of the Convention.[43] Writing in 1992, the legal relationship between non-compliance and dispute settlement procedures under the Montreal Protocol was a cause of some concern to Koskenniemi particularly in relation to the rights of parties allegedly in breach of their treaty obligations.[44] In consequence of the parallel existence of the NCP and DSP, a defaulting state could find itself subject to both regimes. To further complicate matters, one of the measures available under the Montreal Protocol NCP is the suspension of the rights of a party in default.[45] This facility arguably places certain parts of the NCP within the realm of state responsibility, including countermeasures, as well as giving rise to the potential application of the 1969 Vienna Convention on the Law of Treaties.[46] The relationship of NCP with dispute settlement procedures, with the law of state responsibility and with the law of treaties thus all arise.

The essential issue which arises regarding the first issue, viz., the legal relationship between NCPs and DSPs, is the extent to which recourse to NCPs is conditioned by the availability of, and actual recourse to, DSPs. This relationship is usefully explored in the context of the only treaty both to embody each procedure and to have

41. Brus, op. cit. n. 37, at p. 193.

42. Para. 12 of the Montreal Protocol Non-Compliance Procedure.

43. For recent treatment, see Werksman, op. cit. n. 14. He examines the 'specialized non-compliance systems' under Art. 13 UNFCCC (the Multilateral Consultative Process) and Art. 18 of the Kyoto Protocol (NCP), as well as the systems which will evolve in the implementation of the Kyoto flexibility mechanisms embodied in Arts. 4 (joint implementation), 6 (emissions trading), and 12 (clean development mechanism).

44. M. Koskenniemi, 'Breach of Treaty or Non-Compliance? Reflections on the Enforcement of the Montreal Protocol', 3 *YIEL* (1992) pp. 123-162. The issue of 'due process' for the 'target state' where collective countermeasures are employed is raised in the ILC's Third Report, *supra* n. 6, para. 116.

45. See the indicative list of measures, *infra* n. 50.

46. Though it must be emphasised once again that each has a distinctive field of operation: *supra* n. 6.

experienced considerable practice thereunder, at least in respect to NCPs. This is the 1987 Montreal Protocol[47] to the 1985 Ozone Convention, the first multilateral environmental treaty to go beyond reporting and dispute settlement provisions in providing for a non-compliance procedure.[48] As we have seen, while Article 11 of the Convention provides for traditional dispute settlement, Article 8 of the Protocol envisages a non-compliance procedure, the latter without prejudice to the operation of the former. Article 8 further requires the first MOP to consider and approve procedures and institutional mechanisms for determining non-compliance with the provisions of the Protocol, and for treatment of parties found to be in non-compliance.

The Ad Hoc Working Group of Legal Experts was requested by MOP3 to compile indicative lists of the possible situations of non-compliance with the Protocol and of 'advisory and conciliatory measures to encourage full compliance'.[49] In the event, only an indicative list of response measures is found as Annex V to the Report of MOP4; no designated list of non-complying acts or omissions is provided, thus leaving it in each case as a matter for the Implementation Committee to determine.[50] It sets an escalating response from appropriate assistance, including technical and financial assistance, through to issuing cautions to suspension of rights and privileges under the Protocol. Suspension must be in accordance with the applicable rules of international law concerning the suspension and operation of a treaty, of specific rights and privileges under the Montreal Protocol, whether or not such rights and privileges are subject to time limits, and including those rights and privileges concerned with industrial rationalisation, production, consumption, trade, transfer of technology, financial mechanism, and institutional arrangements.[51] The latter embodies a unique feature of the Montreal Protocol NCP, namely, trade measures, which are linked to Protocol's general ban on trade in regulated substances between parties and non-

47. For recent analysis, see D.G. Victor, 'The Operation and Effectiveness of the Montreal Protocol's Non-Compliance Procedure' in Victor et al., eds., op. cit. n. 11, Ch. 4; O. Yoshida, 'Soft Enforcement of Treaties: the Montreal Protocol's Non-Compliance Procedure and the Functions of Internal International Institutions', 10 *Colorado JIEL* & Poll (1999) pp. 95-141.

48. As Szell observes, it was the first such agreement to 'fill the gap' between reporting and dispute settlement with a 'meaningful procedure': Szell, 'The Development of', loc. cit. n. 11, at p. 99. Thus the accomplishment of the Protocol NCP is two-fold: an internal, possibly self-contained mechanism to address non-compliance combined with 'gap-filling' between monitoring and reporting obligations and dispute settlement procedures. On self-contain regimes, see further below.

49. See Decision III/2(a)(ii), Montreal Protocol MOP3, UNEP/OxL.Pro.3.L.4.

50. UNEP/OxL.Pro4/5/15, 23 November 1992. These are: a. appropriate assistance, including assistance for the collection and reporting of data, technical assistance, technology transfer and financial assistance, information transfer and training; b. issuing cautions; c. suspension, in accordance with the applicable rules of international law concerning suspension of the operation of a treaty, of specific rights and privileges under the Protocol, whether or not subject to time limits, including those concerned with industrial rationalisation, production, consumption, trade, transfer of technology, financial mechanism and institutional arrangements.

51. Report of the Third Meeting of the Parties to the Montreal Protocol, UNEP/OxL.Pro.4/15 (1992).

parties. As Werksman observes, '[t]his feature allows the NCP to treat the ability to trade in regulated substances as a privilege granted by the Montreal Protocol and to incrementally suspend that privilege in order to encourage compliance.'[52] This is also a possible non-compliance response under the Kyoto Protocol, viz., suspension of emissions trading.

The NCP was finalised at the Fourth Meeting of the COP in London in 1992 and updated in 1998 without substantial amendment.[53] As provided for under Articles 8 and 11 of the Protocol, it is for the Meeting of the Parties thereunder to consider and approve the procedures and institutional mechanisms for determining non-compliance with the provisions of the Protocol and for treatment of parties found to be in non-compliance. Under the NCP duly approved, a pivotal role is played by a ten-member Implementation Committee (IC), the composition and functions of which are set forth in paragraphs 5, et seq. of the 1998 NCP. The IC reviews specific cases of non-compliance, debates general issues of implementation and compliance, makes recommendations to other Convention bodies, and issues a publicly available report after each meeting.[54] Though not bifurcated in the manner proposed for the Kyoto Protocol Compliance Committee, the IC performs both facilitative and enforcement functions. However, paragraph 9 NCP underscores the subsidiary character of the IC which has an obligation to report to the MOP, including any recommendations it considers appropriate. It is only after receiving a report by the Committee, with such recommendations, that the MOP may decide upon and call for steps to bring about full compliance with the Protocol; thus, whilst the Committee is obliged to report, the MOP does not have an obligation to act upon such report.

Issues of non-compliance may be referred to the IC by parties concerned with their own, or with other parties', compliance or by the Secretariat.[55] Early issues included data reporting to establish important baselines for assessing compliance with quantitative and temporal obligations (targets and timetables).[56] Non-compliance

52. Werksman, loc. cit. n. 14, at p. 72. A similar approach may prevail under the Kyoto NCP. Amongst other things, Werksman discusses the possible suspension of a party's ability to trade allowances and offsets under the Kyoto Protocol as one possible compliance response.

53. At MOP9 an Ad Hoc Working Group of Legal and Technical Experts on Non-Compliance was established to review the operation of the non-compliance procedure, with suggested modifications adopted virtually verbatim at COP 10: see Decision IX/10. For the report of the Working Group, see UNEP/OzL.Pro/WG.5/1/3/ 18 November 1998.

54. See http://www.unep.ch for the text of the reports (Ozone Secretariat web site). Such reports are required to be available to the parties not later than six weeks before a MOP: Para. 9 NCP (1998); on availability and protection of confidential information, see further paras. 15 and 16 NCP

55. See paras. 1, 3 and 4, NCP Procedure 1998.

56. Art. 7 of the Protocol sets forth detailed data reporting requirements. As Werksman observes, the early work of the Montreal Protocol Implementation Committee focused on concerns raised by the Ozone Secretariat regarding compliance with such requirements: loc. cit. n. 14, at p. 97. One interesting phenomenon has been the Committee's willingness to overlook non-compliance evidenced in data in an effort to ensure participation in and eventual compliance with the Protocol: Kingsbury, loc. cit. n. 10, at p. 366. This emphasis on cooperation over conflict, and a certain flexibility in permitting adherence to treaty obligations over time, suggests a certain progressive character to the obligations.

with reporting requirements is explicitly addressed under the Montreal Protocol, Article 7 of which imposes the duty on each Contracting Party to report data on its production, imports and exports and consumption of controlled and transitional substances within certain time limits. In practice the majority of instances of non-compliance with the Protocol have related to non-reporting of consumption data.[57] Compliance with this obligation has been an acute problem for developing countries and for countries with economies in transition. Lack of capacity, including the technical and financial resources, has been a significant factor in the failure to comply.[58] This has led, *inter alia*, to close cooperation between the Implementation Committee in addressing non-compliance, and the Montreal Protocol Multilateral Fund (administered by UNEP, UNDP and the IBRD) in providing financial support for institution building and strengthening, technical training, and assistance in country programme formulation.[59]

As indicated above, the Montreal Protocol NCP is implemented both by the IC and the MOP, with each body exercising different functions. The role of the IC is generally that of facilitator to the parties in dispute and of advisor to the MOP as to the possible responses to non-compliance. It may 'consider the submissions, information and observations referred to it...with the view of securing an amicable solution of the matter' and 'report to the Meeting of the Parties, including any recommendations it considers appropriate.'[60] However, decision-making power rests with the MOP which is charged with the task of securing full compliance with the Protocol. It is in this sense that, as Koskenniemi rightly observes, the IC is not a judicial but a political organ. From this it logically follows that where the case of non-compliance by one of the parties is pending in the forum of the IC the case 'is not sub judice if discussed, nor res judicata if decided.'[61] The point here is that a matter before the Implementation Committee cannot be *res judicata* since that body is not empowered to take decisions on such matters which are directed to parties; this is a prerogative granted only to the MOP. Support for this approach is derived from the jurisprudence of the ICJ, which has considered the problem of litispendence between legal and political organs in several cases.[62] The Court's practice clearly indicates that when a dispute is being dealt with in a parallel manner by both the legal and the political organs of the United Nations, it does not constitute 'in either organ a bar to its further action, the competence of the Court being limited to the purely legal aspects of the matter.'[63]

A further question arises regarding the legal effect of the MOP's decisions, namely, whether these bind as a matter of treaty law or as a matter of internal law relating

---

57. Response by the Secretariat to the Working Group on Non-Compliance, UNEP/OzL.Pro/WG.4/1/1, para. 8.

58. See for example, the reports by Kenya, Uganda and the Maldives on non-compliance with reporting obligations contained in the Secretariat's Second Report on the Reporting of Data.

59. For further information, see the web site for the secretariat of the Fund at http://www.unmfs.org/

60. Para. 8 and 9 NCP (1998), respectively.

61. Koskenniemi, loc. cit. n. 44, at p. 157

62. In particular see cases: *South- West Africa, Application of the 1971 Montreal Convention, and Application of the Genocide Convention.*

63. S. Rosenne, *The Law and Practice of the International Court 1920-1996, Vol. I The Court and the United Nations* (The Hague, Martinus Nijhof Publishers 1997) p. 155.

to international organisations. Thus far state practice is sparse and inconsistent. For example, Russia's non-compliance decision was adopted on the basis of 'consensus minus one' (Russia abstained) whilst in respect of non-compliance by Poland and Bulgaria, for example, these States joined in the consensus. There is no evidence of a state party's failure to observe non-compliance measures being treated as a breach of treaty obligation or of the internal law of the organisation, though the literature suggests support for the latter.[64]

Resolving any question of conflict between the competence of the IC in respect of the non-compliance and dispute settlement procedures is further complicated by the fact that different dispute settlement procedures are provided for in Article 11, ranging from diplomatic methods such as negotiation and good offices to conciliation and legally binding procedures such as recourse to the ICJ and to international arbitration. The legal relationship between the NCP and DSP will thus depend upon which of the latter methods is being invoked. Negotiations, good offices, mediation and conciliation do not pose a legal impediment to simultaneous proceedings within the IC. Indeed, unless the Protocol were expressly otherwise to provide, such an outcome would be at odds with state practice where negotiations between the parties to a dispute may be ongoing at the time a dispute is submitted for judicial settlement yet, absent express provision to the contrary, this does not constitute a bar to litigation.[65] *A fortiori* simultaneous non-binding diplomatic methods should be accorded similar latitude.[66] Whether as a matter of policy, and with regard to the effective functioning of the Convention, this should be the case is a different matter. On the one hand it could be argued that the invocation of NCP in the face of ongoing diplomatic methods of settlement may imperil the good will upon which such diplomatic means are predicated and thus as a matter of policy should lead to self-restraint.[67] However, diplomatic methods of dispute settlement are very often bilateral in nature and usually conducted outwith the treaty framework, whilst the NCP is a multilateral and collective procedure established within that framework. It may thus be argued that the latter

64. See Koskenniemi, loc. cit. n. 44, at p. 146; and Churchill and Ulfstein, loc. cit. n. 5, at p. 646.

65. In the *Aegean Sea Continental Shelf* case, *ICJ Rep.* (1978) 3, the Court rejected the apparent suggestion from Turkey that judicial proceedings ought not to proceed in the face of active negotiations relying, *inter alia*, upon Art. 33 of the UN Charter (which enumerates negotiation and dispute settlement together). It observed that 'the fact that negotiations are being actively pursued during the present proceedings, is not, legally, any obstacle to the exercise by the Court of its judicial function.' (idem, p. 12). Indeed, as Merrills observes, negotiation is the principal means of handling international disputes: J.G. Merrills, *International Dispute Settlement*, 3rd edn. (Cambridge, Cambridge University Press 1998) p. 2. Koskenniemi considers that ongoing conciliation procedures should not be a bar for a dispute; loc. cit. n. 44, at p. 159. On the relationship between DSPs and countermeasures, see below text following n. 85.

66. There is in any event an overlap between the NCP and diplomatic methods: NCP, Para. 3.

67. Birnie and Boyle, op. cit. n. 38, make the point that pressure upon parties in default is a common method of addressing default under international environmental treaties, even where no treaty-based NCP procedure exists. See, for example, the practice of the COP under the Convention on International Trade in Endangered Species of Wild Fauna and Flora (CITES), 12 *ILM* (1973) p. 1088, which reviews information from the Secretariat on national reports and may identify cases of non-compliance.

is more consistent with the nature of environmental treaty obligations, with the forum of the IC reflecting this collective character and possessing 'an *erga omnes* aspect'.[68]

As for parallel procedures conducted within the IC and before an arbitral panel or the ICJ, Koskenniemi makes an interesting distinction in relation to the function of the IC. In cases when the IC acts as an advisory body to the MOP, putting forward a proposal in respect of a party's non-compliance, it is *de facto* determining that party's future behaviour while the dispute is *sub judice* elsewhere. In such instance, he argues, the proceedings within the IC should be suspended, but not terminated: '[I]t would frustrate the purpose of Article 11 of the Convention if the Implementation Committee were allowed to proceed to make an independent recommendation on the possible countermeasures.' However, apart from the recommendation of measures which amount to countermeasures (e.g., suspension of rights), when the IC is acting as a facilitator in a dispute to bring it to an amicable solution such function is not in a conflict with a dispute sub judice elsewhere and indeed should even be encouraged.[69]

Legal and practical problems may arise regarding not only the possibility of competition, but of actual conflict between the systems, i.e., between the findings of, say, the Conciliation Commission in the absence of another agreed method of third party dispute settlement under the Convention, and the application of NCP measures. In the absence of practice, it is possible only to speculate as to the possible outcome of such conflict, which is reflective of the general problem of the relationship between the parallel yet distinct dispute settlement and non-compliance procedures. In any event, since the Conciliation Commission issues only a recommendatory award, its implementation depends on its consideration by parties in good faith (Art. 11 of the 1985 Ozone Convention). Any disparity between the findings of the Conciliation Commission and the NCP, at least in theory, should not lead to a legal conflict, although for a party concerned, compliance with an award and with the findings under the NCP (if conflicting) may prove to be burdensome. It may be that this is one of the many reasons for absence of recourse to DSP, with parties relying instead on the available NCP. This is not to insulate the matter entirely from the application of DSP since to state that the NCP is 'without prejudice' to dispute settlement is not sufficiently clear to suggest an inevitable priority for, say, the findings of the Conciliation Commission over the NCP. Rather, any party may invoke the DSP at any time, even where the NCP is being invoked simultaneously. In any event, as the experience with Russia demonstrates, conflict is more likely to arise sequentially than simultaneously in the sense that a party (whether the non-complying state or an 'injured state', if such exists) might resort to dispute settlement where dissatisfied with the application of the NCP.

---

68. Koskenniemi, loc. cit. n. 44, at p. 158.

69. Koskenniemi supports his view on the basis of the statement in the Great Belt case wherein the International Court stated that judicial settlement is an alternative to the direct and friendly settlement of disputes between parties and that any negotiations pending the judicial proceedings with a view of achieving a direct and friendly settlement are to be welcomed: *Case Concerning Passage through Great Belt, ICJ Rep.* (1991) p. 61 para. 35 relying upon the *Case of Free Zones of Upper Savoy and District of Gex*, (1930) *PCIJ*, Ser. A . No. 22, 13.

However, there is a possibility that estoppel might operate to prevent such subsequent recourse.

The foregoing serves to underscore the difficulties in defining the relationship between the obligations/procedures to which the NCP and dispute settlement give rise, and the relationship between treaty provisions. Simply to provide that NCP does not prejudice DSP scarcely penetrates the surface. Where NCPs embrace a range of mechanisms from the facilitative to the coercive, there is the real possibility of overlap with DSP such as good offices and negotiation, the crucial difference being the essentially multilateral character of NCP compared with the essentially bilateral character of dispute settlement mechanisms. The Ad Hoc Working Group formed to review the functioning of the NCP in 1998 considered a proposal regarding the need to define the relationship between the NCP and DSP but, '[n]oting the difficulties in determining precedence between different international administrative and judicial proceedings ... decided that no action should be taken on this proposal.'[70] This leaves unamended the text of paragraph 12 of the NCP agreed in 1992 which appears expressly to contemplate the possibility of procedures functioning in parallel at least to a degree. It imposes the requirement on parties where compliance is in issue to report to the MOP the 'results of any proceedings taken under Article 11 in respect of non-compliance, about implementation of those results and about implementation of any decision of the parties pursuant to paragraph 9' of the NCP. This accords with Article 8 of the Protocol, which is reiterated in the opening to the NCP, viz., that the Protocol's Article 8 NCP applies without prejudice to the Convention's Article 11 DSP. Further, paragraph 13 stipulates that the Meeting of the Parties may, pending completion of proceedings initiated under Article 11 of the Convention, issue an interim call and/or recommendation.

The practice of states under the Montreal Protocol does not shed any light on these issues. Thus far states have not initiated parallel proceedings under both Article 11 the Convention and Article 8 of the Protocol. That there may have been a strong temptation to do so is without question given strong pressure on Russia in particular, and the consideration evidently given to remitting the NCP measures taken against it to the GATT/WTO for an assessment of their compatibility.[71] In this case the 'carrot' of financial assistance was offered in conjunction with the 'stick' of financial conditionality and trade restrictions to encourage Russia to fulfil its treaty obligations. This is reflective of subsequent practice under the Protocol, with cases of non-compliance apparently addressed only under the NCP and with the indicative measure most frequently employed being facilitative, viz., assistance.[72] It is also indicative of the IC's

70. Report of the Ad Hoc Working Group of Legal and Technical Experts on Non-Compliance with the Montreal Protocol, UNEP/OzL.Pro/WG.4/1/3/, para. 48.

71. See generally, J.Werksman, 'Compliance and Transition: Russia's Non- Compliance Tests the Ozone Regime', 56 *ZaöRV* (1996) p. 750.

72. This is emphasised in Para. 9 of the NCP, the third sentence of which provides that '[a]fter receiving a report by the Committee the Parties may, taking into consideration the circumstances of the matter, decide upon and call for steps to bring about full compliance with the Protocol, including measures to *assist* the Parties' compliance with the Protocol, and to further the Protocol's objectives' [emphasis added].

preoccupation with compliance by countries with economies in transition, such as Russia and Poland. In such instances, where non-compliance often reflects lack of capacity, facilitative measures are particularly influential. In the case of Russia, Werksman notes that financial assistance was pivotal: released in tranches conditional upon demonstrable progress in coming into compliance, this funding enabled a process for monitoring and enforcement properly to be established.[73]

4. NON-COMPLIANCE PROCEDURES AND STATE RESPONSIBILITY

A further legal issue which arises in the context of NCPs is the extent to which measures taken might be legally classified as countermeasures under the law of state responsibility. [74] For example, might suspension of privileges by the MOP under the Montreal Protocol be viewed as the imposition of collective countermeasures and, if so, with what legal consequences? It is useful briefly to review the current work of the ILC on these issues before returning to this point.

Currently undergoing their second reading in the ILC under the current Special Rapporteur, Professor James Crawford, Draft Articles on State Responsibility were adopted on first reading in 1996 and subsequently commented upon by Governments. The provisions on countermeasures are contained in Part II, Chapter III, Articles 49-54 of the draft articles which were reconsidered at the 53rd session of the ILC in 2001 (Arts. 47-50 on first reading, now Arts. 49-54).[75] The reason for their inclusion in Part II, and 'without any special linkage to dispute settlement', 'is that in general, countermeasures should be seen as performing an instrumental function of ensuring compliance, and not as punitive measures or sanctions.'[76] In particular the role of countermeasures as ensuring compliance with secondary obligations such as cessation and

73. Werksman, loc. cit. n. 14, at p. 71

74. Countermeasures '...are the most difficult and controversial aspect of the whole state responsibility', *Fifth Report on State Responsibility* by G. Arangio-Ruiz, Special Rapporteur, A/CN.4/453, 12 May 1993, para. 27. Special Rapporteur Crawford suggests that one of the reasons for his predecessor's resignation was the intractability of the issue of countermeasures and multilateral obligations: 1998 Report, para. 324.

75. See the ILC's Report of its Fifty-third session, 23 April-1 June and 2 July-10 August 2001, A/CN.4.L/502/Rev.1. The draft articles have been adopted on second reading (18 August 2001). On the draft articles provisionally adopted on second reading at the ILC's Fifty-second session, see J. Crawford, P. Bodeau and J. Peel, 'The ILC's Draft Articles on State Responsibility: Towards Completion of Second Reading', 94 *AJIL* (2000) p. 660. In addition to reproduction on the ILC web site of the three reports to date of the current special rapporteur and of the text of the draft articles adopted on first reading http://www.un.org/law/ilc/index.htm the text of the draft articles with commentary is reprinted in 37 *ILM* 440 (1998). See also http://www.law.cam.ac.uk/RCIL/ILCSR/Statresp.htm For recent debate on the second reading of the controversial issues before the ILC, including the issue of state responsibility and multilateral obligations, see 10 EJIL (1999) passim.

76. A/CN.4/507/Add.3, p. 2, para. 287.

reparation is the clear focus of these draft articles, and is also reflected in the ICJ's consideration of countermeasures in a bilateral context in the *Gabcikovo-Nagymaros* case. There, in addition to generally endorsing the approach of the ILC in the draft Articles in this connection, the Court identified four distinct elements of the law of countermeasures: (1) countermeasures must be taken in response to an unlawful act; (2) such measures must be preceded by a demand for compliance by the injured state; (3) the countermeasure taken must be proportionate (the point on which Slovakia failed); and (4) the purpose of the countermeasure must be 'to induce the wrongdoing state to comply with its obligations under international law, and that the measure must therefore be reversible.'[77] The Court also specifically endorsed the definition of countermeasures contained in then Draft Article 47 (now Art. 49 paragraph 1), viz., 'An injured state may only take counter measures against a state which is responsible for an internationally wrongful act in order to induce that state to comply with its obligations.'

Not specifically addressed by the Court owing to the bilateral nature of the dispute, but raised in the most recent (third) report of the Special Rapporteur, is the question of countermeasures in case of breach of multilateral or *erga omnes* obligations,[78] a question of direct relevance to environmental treaties such as the Ozone Convention. As a whole the draft articles distinguish between (and thus recognise) state responsibility for breaches of multilateral as distinct from bilateral obligations. Indeed, the Special Rapporteur's Third Report sets out three categories of obligations breach of which is addressed in the draft articles: obligations to the international community as a whole (*erga omnes*); obligations owed to all the parties to a particular regime (*erga omnes partes*); and obligations to which some of many States are parties, but in respect of which particular states or groups of states are recognised as legally interested ('multilateral obligations generally').[79] Obligations *erga omnes partes* are of particular relevance in the environmental context, instancing 'the case of the international regime ... the maintenance and implementation of which all states parties have a common interest.'[80] Specific environmental examples cited are biodiversity and global warming,[81] with depletion of the ozone layer clearly also falling within this category of obligation.

77. *Supra* n. 6 at pp. 55-57; see A/CN.4/507/Add.3, p. 2, para. 289. See further R. Lefeber, 'The Gabcikovo-Nagymaros Project and the Law of State Responsibility', 11 *Leiden JIL* (1998) pp. 609-625.

78. See further C. Dominice, 'The International Responsibility of States for Breach of Multilateral Obligations', 10 *EJIL* (1999) p. 353 and K. Zemanek, 'New Trends in the Enforcement of erga omnes Obligations', 4 *Max Planck Year Book of United Nations Law* (2000) p. 1.

79. Third Report, *supra* n. 6, at para. 106, pp. 49-50, with table at p. 50 setting out the three categories and the extent of their application. See also Table 2 'Extent to which differently affected States may invoke the legal consequences of the responsibility of a State', ibid., para. 118, p. 56. It should be noted that these categories of obligation are not mutually exclusive.

80. Ibid., at para. 106 (b), p. 49.

81. Ibid.

Related to the category of obligation is the definition of 'injured state' in Article 42 [40] which recognises the general interest of states in securing compliance with obligations to the international community as a whole.[82] Obligations *erga omnes* in the environmental field are addressed under the heading of '"victimless" breaches of community obligations' where, 'if restitution is materially impossible, then other states may be limited to seeking cessation, satisfaction, and assurances against repetition....[A]ny state party to the relevant collective obligation should be entitled to invoke responsibility in these respects.'[83] Obligations *erga omnes partes* are also catered for in Article 48 which refers to groups of states, including the state invoking responsibility. The obligation not to omit excess CFCs into the atmosphere under the Ozone Convention and Montreal Protocol is a specifically cited example of a multilateral obligation without any particular obligee or beneficiary; '[t]his is a purely solidary obligation and there will never be a demonstrable connection with any particular state party.'[84] Nonetheless under the draft articles countermeasures may be applied for breach of such obligation not only by states acting in concert (collective countermeasures) but also where an individual state, which has not suffered individual injury in consequence of the breach of a multilateral obligation nonetheless asserts a right to react to that breach in the public interest. However, one limitation on the exercise

---

82. In 1998, in response to criticisms of Art. 19 of the Draft Articles adopted on first reading in 1996, the ILC 'decided to resolve the issues raised by Article 19 through the concepts of obligations to the international community as a whole, and peremptory norms': 1998 Report, p. 147, para. 331. These provisions are now located in Draft Articles 42 and 48 which provide as follows:

Article 42 [40] *Notice of claim by an injured state.*

1. An injured state which invokes the responsibility of another state, shall give notice of its claim to that state.

2. The injured state may specify in particular:

(a) The conduct that the responsible state should take in order to leave the wrongful act, if it is continuing:

(b) What forms reparation should take in accordance with the provisions of Part Two.

Article 49 *Invocation of responsibility by States other than the injured State*

1. Any state other than an injured state is entitled to invoke the responsibility if another state in accordance with paragraph 2 if:

(a) The obligation breached is owed to a group of states including that state, and is established for the protection of a collective interest of the group; or

(b) The obligation breached is owed to the international community as a whole.

2. Any state entitled to invoke responsibility under paragraph 1 may claim from the responsible state:

(a) cessation of the internationally wrongful act, and assurances and guarantees of non-repetition in accordance with article 30; and

(b) Performance of the obligation of reparation in accordance with the preceding articles, in the interest of the injured state or beneficiaries of the obligations breached.

3. The requirements for the invocation of responsibility by an injured state under Articles 43, 44 and 45 apply to an invocation by a state entitled to do so under paragraph 1.

83. A/CN.4/507/Add.4, p. 8, para. 379; and see draft article 48, ibid.

84. A/CN.4/507, p. 51, para. 109.

of countermeasures by third states (viz., 'not directly affected' states) where there also exists an injured state is that the latter must request such measures which are then taken on its behalf – a restriction echoing the conditions on the lawful exercise of collective self-defence in the *Nicaragua* case.[85] Outwith consideration under the draft articles are institutional responses in the framework of international organizations.[86] While some doubt may exist as to whether, say, the IC of the Montreal Protocol constitutes such an institutional response, less doubt surely exists as to the potential characterisation of the decisions of the MOP regarding the NCP measures to be applied to a non-complying state in the absence of an injured state (a 'victimless breach') as a collective countermeasure *if* such measures fall within the definition of a countermeasure. Koskenniemi, for one, appears to assume that the Montreal Protocol NCP response measures are synonymous with countermeasures. But such characterisation is not sustained in the theory nor in the practice of NCP under the Protocol since Koskenniemi raised the issue nearly a decade ago (and admittedly raised by him before the NCP had become fully operational). It is clear that of the indicative measures open to the Implementation Committee to recommend and for the MOP to adopt, it is very likely only suspension of rights and privileges under the Protocol which potentially fits within the countermeasures framework, viz., 'counter measures are limited to the non-performance for the time being of international obligations of the state taking measures towards the responsible state.' (ILC draft Art. 49 (2)).

In addition, it will be recalled that the Implementation Committee does not have the power to take any measures against a party in default, including suspension. It's powers are advisory only; it is only the MOP which can take binding decisions. The legal outcome of compliance responses under the Montreal Protocol is thus determined by the powers conferred upon the MOP. This has consequences for the application of the provisions of the ILC draft articles which consider the relationship between countermeasures (which, as indicated above, could conceivably encompass a NCP measure) and dispute settlement. Draft article 53 [48] reflects the compromise achieved within the Commission where, ultimately, proposals to make the resort to the mechanism of peaceful settlement of disputes compulsory, preceding the use of countermeasures, failed.[87] A state resorting to countermeasures is not, however, relieved from fulfilling its obligations under any applicable dispute settlement proce-

85. Art. 54 of the draft articles. As Crawford et al. note, this is a tenable if not a compelling argument: loc. cit. n. 75.

86. Whilst Security Council action, and also the role of the ECJ under Art. 228 EC, clearly fall within this excluded category, less clear is the position of the Montreal Protocol NCP for example. A clear distinction is of course that both the UN and the EC are international organisations possessing international legal personality; the Montreal Protocol MOP, the decision-making body for these purposes, does not. However, to the extent that this provision in the draft articles is intended to exclude e.g., self-contained regimes, this point is returned to below, text following n. 94. On the legal status of 'autonomous institutional arrangements' established by multilateral environmental agreements and the application thereto of international institutional law, see Churchill and Ulfstein, loc. cit. n. 5.

87. Art. 58(2) on first reading; for criticism of this linkage, cf., Second Report, A/CN.4/498/Add.4, pp. 13-15, paras. 384-387.

dure in force between it and the responsible State (draft art. 50[26]). Moreover, draft article 52[48] ('Conditions relating to resort to countermeasures') goes further in imposing important limitations on the taking of countermeasures, viz., that such right is suspended where the dispute is submitted to a court or tribunal with authority to make decisions binding on the parties, if such procedures are implemented in good faith by the responsible state and provided that the internationally wrongful act has ceased. This accords with international practice which appears to indicate that the mere presence of dispute settlement mechanisms does not form an obstacle to the resort to countermeasures. Only when this mechanism has been triggered, and the dispute is *sub judice*, is the use of countermeasures impermissible. This was the stand taken by the ICJ in the *Hostages* case,[88] and is consistent with the relationship between the NCP of the Montreal Protocol and the DSP of the Ozone Convention since the former expressly applies without prejudice to the latter.

An important question is the nature of the dispute settlement mechanism as applied under ILC draft article 52, i.e., whether such mechanism must result in binding and/or enforceable decisions and; whether its powers include the indication of provisional measures. This has clear consequences for the applicability of these provisions to compliance response mechanisms under the Montreal Protocol (and, conceivably, for the NCP adopted under the Kyoto Protocol which may well embody both elements). Under the Montreal Protocol such conflict could only arise under Article 12 thereof if the decision to suspend was taken whilst DSP were also underway which, whilst theoretically possible, is politically highly unlikely under the Protocol.

What then may be concluded regarding the relationship between NCPs and state responsibility? First and foremost, the goal of any NCP, at least in the environmental context, is distinguishable from traditional rules on state responsibility. The primary objective of NCPs is to ensure a return to compliance with treaty obligations rather than to require reparation by the defaulting state for the harm caused to another state or states for breach of international obligation.[89] More specifically in the context of countermeasures, NCP measures are concerned with compliance with primary obligations whilst countermeasures are concerned with compliance with secondary obligations. It will be recalled that the general rule in respect of reparation for a breach of an international obligation requires the state found to be in breach to provide restitution, or if this is not possible, to compensate for the losses.[90] In an environmental

---

88. The Court has said in relation to the US aborted rescue operation that 'an operation undertaken in those circumstances from whatever motive, is of a kind calculated to undermine respect for judicial process in international relations…' *Case Concerning United Sates Diplomatic and Consular Staff in Teheran, ICJ Rep.*(1980) p. 1, para. 93.

89. On environmental harm generally, see P. Wetterstein, ed., *Harm to the Environment: The Right to Compensation and the Assessment of Damages* (Oxford, Clarendon Press 1997) and F. Francioni and T. Scovazzi, eds., *International Responsibility for Environmental Harm* (London, Graham & Trotman 1991); see also J. Peel, 'New State Responsibility Rules and Compliance with Multilateral Environmental Obligations - Some case studies of how the New Rules Might Apply in the International Environmental Context', 10 *RECIEL* (2001) pp. 82-98.

90. *Case Concerning the Factory at Chorzów (Claim for Indemnity; Merits), PCIJ*, Ser. A, No. 17 (1928) p. 47. The relevant passage reads as follows: 'The essential principle […] is that reparation must,

context, the possibility of restoring the *status quo ante* or restitution in kind is not always possible – species extinction or global warming make the point.[91] Indeed, Boyle has observed 'the difficulty of reconciling doctrinal support for state responsibility for environmental damage with the realities of state practice.'[92] There are a number of examples of treaty parties preferring to establish regulatory regimes based on principles such as the precautionary principle, common but differentiated responsibility, and equitable sharing of burdens and benefits, rather than addressing directly compensation for damage.[93] Moreover, the regulatory approach is multilateral in character whilst compensation for damage is generally pursued on a bilateral basis.[94] This is likely to continue to be so notwithstanding the ILC's innovative approach to categories of obligations and to injured parties under the draft articles, not only because in the vast majority of cases regulation is preferable to ex ante remediation but also because increasing recourse to NCPs provides a multilateral forum with wider responses available than under state responsibility.

Finally, to the extent that general principles of state responsibility may apply, certain treaty regimes have actually sought to insulate themselves from the intrusion of general principles of state responsibility through the concept of self-contained regimes. This concept arose in the context of the ILC's earlier work on state responsibility, in particular under Special Rapporteur Riphagen, and has been comprehensive-

as far as possible, wipe out all the consequences of the illegal act and re-establish the situation which would, in all probability, have existed if the act had not been committed. Restitution in kind, or, if this is not possible, payment of a sum corresponding to the value which a restitution in kind would bear.'

91. Matters are further complicated by the distinction drawn in the ILC's deliberations between state responsibility on the one hand, where breach of a primary obligation gives rise to the secondary obligation to make reparation, and reparation for the injurious consequences of an act not prohibited by international law, where the obligation to make reparation arises from the operation of the primary rule itself. In the latter context, restitutio in integrum is not as rigorously observed: see remarks of Barbarosa, Special Rapporteur on Liability for the Injurious Consequences Arising Out of Acts Not Prohibited by International Law, 'The ILC and Environmental Damage', in Wetterstein, ed., op. cit. n. 89, at p. 79.

92. A.E. Boyle, 'Remedying Harm to International Common Spaces and Resources: Compensation and Other Approaches', in Wetterstein, ed., op. cit. n. 89, at p. 89.

93. The Climate Change Convention furnishes one such example. Indeed, where the polluter pays principle is most rigorously applied under international environmental treaties, it is with respect to imposing liability on private actors – ship owners or nuclear operators for example – either exclusively or in conjunction with state responsibility. For example of the former, see the 1992 Protocol to the 1969 Convention on Civil Liability for Oil Pollution Damage; and for the latter, the 1960 Paris Convention on Third Party Liability in the Field of Nuclear Energy and 1963 Brussels Supplementary Convention.

94. As Boyle notes, op. cit. n. 92, the responsibility of Iraq for environmental damage caused during its invasion and occupation of Kuwait, recognised in Security Council Resolution 687, is one of the few examples of exclusively state liability for environmental damage, albeit with claims presented via an international forum, the United Nations Compensation Commission. The *Wimbledon* case, (1923) *PCIJ* Ser. A, No. 1 is an interesting example of both bilateral and multilateral remedies being sought in the context of an obligation erga omnes partes: France sought reparation on its own part in respect of losses suffered, whilst the three other States were concerned to establish the principle in dispute, and thereby achieve cessation of the wrongful act. It is cited in the ILC Third Report, para. 114, n. 206, as an example of the question whether other States 'should be able to seek compensation or take countermeasures on their own account.'

ly analysed in a seminal article by Simma in this *Yearbook*.[95] The issue raised here is not whether the breach of an international environmental obligation may potentially give rise to state responsibility – clearly, as the above discussion supports, it may. Rather, the question is whether specific environmental treaty obligations and the dispute settlement/avoidance procedures linked with them comprise a self-contained regime which, *inter alia*, precludes the use of countermeasures as a matter of general international law and limits state responses to those provided for within the self-contained treaty regime itself.[96] This is a matter partly of treaty interpretation: did the Contracting Parties intend to 'contract out' of the general rules on the consequences of treaty violations, viz., of the general legal consequences of internationally wrongful acts?[97] If the regime permits not the permanent exclusion of such general rules but reserves them as a 'fall-back' position, then Simma's definition of a self-contained regime as 'a certain category of subsystems, namely, those embracing, in principle, a full (exhaustive and definite) set of secondary rules'[98] is not met.[99] The legal relationship between the NCP and DSP under the Montreal Protocol, with the NCP viewed as a 'gap-filler' and without prejudice to the invocation of DSP, supports this view. Nonetheless the theoretical possibility of a self-contained regime is allowed for in Article 56[37] of the current draft articles. It was during discussion of his First Report in 1996 that Special Rapporteur Crawford suggested that the Commission discuss the draft articles on state responsibility on the basis of the assumption that, where other rules of international law, such as specific treaty regimes, provided their own framework for responsibility, that framework would ordinarily prevail.[100] Article 55 accomplishes this goal, though as the Third Report emphasises, where States have made ex-

---

95. For excellent analysis see B. Simma, 'Self-contained regimes', 16 *NYIL* (1985) p. 111; for application see the numerous case studies in the twenty-fifth anniversary volume of the *Yearbook* (1994), in particular M.A. Fitzmaurice, 'International Environmental Law as a Special Field', pp. 181-226. The contributions by de Witte and by Hancher (EC law), Barnhoorn (diplomatic law) and Vierdag (human rights) revisit the three examples explored by Simma in 1985.

96. As Simma observes in the human rights context, one view is that the non-reciprocal character of human rights treaty obligations renders inapposite countermeasures which are built on the edifice of reciprocity. This view is echoed by R. Wolfrum in the environmental context in his Hague lectures, 'Means of Ensuring Compliance With and Enforcement of International Environmental Law', 272 *RdC* (1998) pp. 9-154.

97. See further Simma's conclusion, point (f), loc. cit. n. 95, at p. 136.

98. Ibid., at p. 117.

99. The possibility of viewing the Montreal Protocol as a fully self-contained regime was also considered by Koskenniemi, who observed that: 'this would allow parties its flexible application, but only at the cost of its binding force under general international law. Whether this cost seems worth paying depends on what value one puts on the formalism and the procedural safeguards for sovereignty that form the nucleus of the general law.' loc. cit. n. 44, p. 162.

100. The suggestion was made that then Art. 37 of Part II (which addresses *lex specialis*) be made into a general principle of application to the whole of Part I of the Draft Articles: 1998 *ILC Rep.*, A/53/10. At present Art. 55.

press provision for the legal consequences of breaches of particular rules the extent to which such provision operates in an *exclusive* manner is a question of interpretation.[101]

5. NON-COMPLIANCE PROCEDURES AND THE LAW OF TREATIES

There is further evidence of a link between NCPs and general international law principles in the application of Article 60 of the Vienna Convention on the Law of Treaties (VCLT) regarding material breach. Indeed, NCPs may be viewed as a half-way house between collective suspension of particular *obligations* under a multilateral treaty and collective suspension of the treaty *instrument* as a whole. The former is the purview of countermeasures under state responsibility and the latter is the purview of Article 60 VCLT. NCPs provide for flexible responses outwith both state responsibility/countermeasures and material breach of treaty, though may clearly embody elements of either or both responses. This is a question of construction; while the Montreal Protocol NCP, for example, explicitly links suspension measures under the NCP procedures with the application of Article 60 VCLT, this is not a necessary consequence of such procedures. NCPs may provide for not only suspension of a treaty *obligation* but for the suspension or termination of the *treaty vis-à-vis* the non-complying State, though the latter is unlikely given the purpose for establishing such procedures outlined in Part II above.

Material breach of treaty,[102] is understood as a repudiation of a treaty not sanctioned by Convention or the violation of a provision essential to the accomplishment of the object or purpose of the treaty the commission of which may result in termination or suspension of the operation of a treaty.[103] As indicated the NCP provisions under the Montreal Protocol clearly link suspension as one of the measures in respect of non-compliance to general international law by ruling that it is effected 'in accordance with the applicable rules of international law concerning the suspension of the operation of a treaty.' It may thus be assumed that in case of suspension which is the

101. Ibid., para. 420, p. 27.

102. In general on material breach see: S. Rosenne, *Breach of a Treaty* (Cambridge, Grotius Publications Limited 1985); M.M. Gomma, *Suspension or Termination of Treaties on Grounds of Breach* (The Hague, Martinus Nijhoff Publishers 1996); B. Simma, 'Reflections on Article 60 of the Vienna Convention on the Law of Treaties and its Background in General International Law', 20 *ZaöRV* (1970) pp. 5-83; D. Hutchinson, 'Solidarity and breaches of Multilateral Treaties', 59 *BYIL* (1989) pp. 151-213; L.-A. Sicilianos, 'The Relationship Between Reprisals and Denunciation or a Suspension of a Treaty', 4 *EJIL* (1993) pp. 341-359.

103. Commentary of the ILC see II *YbILC* (1966) p. 255, para. 8. *The Tacna-Arica Arbitration* (*Chile* v *Peru*) 2 *RIAA* (1925) p. 921 established that it is only material breach which justifies termination or suspension, not any breach.

consequence of material breach, Article 60 of the VCLT is applicable.[104] In cases of non-material breach, the link with general international law is effected through countermeasures within the structure of state responsibility, already considered above (and outwith the VCLT regime); the general customary law on countermeasure would permit proportionate retaliation in the event of minor, i.e., non-material, breaches.[105] However, as the Third Report of the Special Rapporteur on State Responsibility makes clear, the law of treaties as reflected in the Vienna Convention and the principles of international law regarding state responsibility operate in separate spheres, even where suspension of treaty obligations are exercised qua countermeasure in response to a non-material breach.[106]

Under multilateral treaties material breach constitutes for a party specifically affected a ground to be invoked to suspend the operation of a treaty; in other words, its effects are dependent upon, in essence, the exercise of a right of election by a specifically affected state to invoke such breach and its consequences, rather than the material breach itself giving rise *ipso facto* to termination or suspension of the treaty. Other parties may seek recourse to the suspension remedy only, where the material breach in question radically changes the position of every party with respect to further performance of their obligations;[107] moreover, a decision to suspend may only be taken unanimously under the VCLT. Material breach has procedural safeguards included in Articles 65-68 of the VCLT. These include the obligation of prior notification of termination (including to the defaulting party) and the stipulation that no measures may be taken during three months after notification; and recourse to compulsory non-binding conciliation machinery for the resolution of any dispute arising from the breach and its consequences.

---

104. An interesting further question is whether this provision incorporates by reference the relevant provisions of the VCLT even for non-parties; however, there is evidence that the Art. 60 regime reflects customary international law (e.g., *South West Africa* Advisory Opinion 1971, para. 91), in which case the only potential residual category of non-applicability is a party to the Montreal Protocol not a party to the VCLT and a persistent objector to any rules of customary international law reflective of Art. 60 VCLT.

105. This is not to suggest that there is an inconsistency between general international law and the provisions of Art. 60 addressing responses to material breach, since the requirement of proportionality would in any event indicate the inappropriateness of termination or suspension in response to a minor breach.

106. See further *supra* n. 6. This also applies to the definition of the injured State in Art. 43(b)(ii) to include State(s) where the breach of the obligation 'is of such a character as to affect the enjoyment of the rights or the performance of the obligations of all the States concerned' and Art. 60(2)(c) VCLT which defines material breach of a treaty 'of such a character that a material breach of its provisions by one party radically changes the position of every party with respect to the further performance of its obligations'. As the Third Report observes, the VCLT formulation is narrower and , '[w]hile applying an a priori test of effect upon other States, it applies to the treaty as a whole and not to the particular obligation breached' (the latter being the approach of the Draft Articles). See A/CN.4/507, p. 42, para. 91.

107. The ILC Commentary to what was to become Art. 60(2)(c) VCLT makes it clear that this response is addressed to treaties 'of a special type' (disarmament treaties are specifically mentioned, for example), 'where a breach by one party tends to undermine the whole regime of the treaty as between all the parties'.

States' behaviour in case of material breach is thus clearly rooted in the general principle of reciprocity. In the case of environmental treaties based largely on non-reciprocally owned rights and duties, difficult questions arise. What is 'a party specially affected by material breach'?[108] Is the relationship between defaulting party and a specially affected party or parties bilateral, or multilateral? A further difficulty – and the reason for recourse to the default rules of the VCLT – is the fact that neither the Montreal Protocol nor the NCP evolved thereunder specify the procedure in cases of suspension (or for that matter in relation to any other measure on the list of indicative measures – an omission unlikely to be repeated in the proposed Kyoto Protocol NCP). If we assume that the provisions of the NCP represent *lex specialis*, then the regime provided for by the Convention in Article 60 is *lex generalis*, which allows derogation by parties to a treaty 'by means of inserting specific treaty provisions applicable in the event of breach'.[109] The purpose of such a derogation may be two-fold: either it renders the response on the part of an injured party more severe, making violations more prohibitive; or it may limit the responses and make them less severe in order to avoid the breakdown of the whole treaty-regime. The *leges specialis* may be of substantive or procedural character. In the latter case recourse may be had to Articles 65-68 of the VCLT. Simma points out, however, that the *leges generalis* re-apply either if the procedural *leges specialis* are affected by the breach from the beginning, or if the state who breached substantive provisions objects to the application of the special procedural rules in the dispute i.e., the provisions of the Vienna Convention are applicable in cases of the break-down of a special regime, viz., the NCP.[110]

If the 'default rules' of the VCLT apply, there remains the key question of the appropriateness of termination or suspension of an international environmental treaty as a response to breach by one party where the treaty in question is normative in character. In his recent Hague lectures, Wolfrum provocatively argues that Article 60 VCLT scarcely touches upon the problem of reaction to treaty provisions owed reciprocally but also serving the interests of the community of states as a whole. He suggests that the normative function of such treaties 'should render the validity and the applicability of international agreements immune against actions in reaction to their breach.'[111] This echoes to a certain extent the thrust of Riphagen's argument in connection with self-contained regimes, wherein he argued that the injured state is not entitled to suspend the performance of its obligations towards the state which has committed an internationally wrongful act. He argued that, where a multilateral treaty imposing the obligations provides a collective decision procedure for the purpose of enforcement of obligations under the treaty, such a decision must be taken prior to suspension.[112] However, the dual character of the NCP and DSP of the Montreal Proto-

108. See also, Koskenniemi, loc. cit. n. 44, at p. 138.

109. Simma, loc. cit. n. 102, at p. 82.

110. Ibid., at p. 82.

111. Wolfrum, loc. cit. n. 96.

112. W. Riphagen, 'Sixth Report on State Responsibility', II *YbILC* (1985) p. 12; for similar views see also, G. Aranguio-Ruiz, 'Third Report on State Responsibility', A/CN.440, 45-46, paras. 84-85.

col and the Ozone Convention arguably fails to satisfy Riphagen's precondition of collective decision at least in so far as such procedure must be exclusive in order for the injured State to be deprived of individual response. Nor does it accord with the more recent work of the ILC on collective response, discussed infra.

6. CONCLUSION

In citing the characteristic features of NCPs under international environmental law, it may be noted that many of these features may be observed in the context of enforcement of domestic environmental law.[113] This lends credence to the view that, regardless of fora, the nature and purpose of environmental laws are such that the quest for new methods of implementation and enforcement is inevitable. That said, it may be questioned whether the claims made for NCP in theory are reflected in the practice, when the accomplishments of NCP are relatively modest. The Montreal Protocol's non-compliance regime is widely regarded as having operated successfully, but has done so within the context of a treaty which has attracted generally high levels of compliance and where instances of non-compliance have been addressed within a pragmatic, managerial approach[114] to compliance. Serious controversies, with the possible exception of the Russian Federation in the mid-1990s, have been avoided.

This is unlikely to be the case under other, potentially far more contentious, instances of non-compliance that may arise under the Kyoto Protocol to the Climate Change Convention, for example.[115] There the Parties have indicated a preference for a more structured and less flexible approach to NCP than is operated under the Montreal Protocol, in anticipation of non-compliance giving rise to a greater potential for conflict.[116] At COP-4 (1998) a Joint Working Group was established to elaborate the NCP of the Protocol,[117] with COP-5 (1999) requesting the work to be completed in

---

113. See for example, S. Bell and D. McGillvray, *Ball & Bell on Environmental Law*, 5th edn., (London, Blackstone Press 2000) Ch. 9 'The enforcement of environment law', whom observe that regulatory enforcement is concerned not only with punishment but also with bringing about compliance (at p. 240). Prevention of harm and the maintenance of a continuing relationship between enforcer and polluter are amongst the reasons cited for the adoption of a cooperative, rather than a confrontational, approach to enforcement (at p. 241).

114. For further discussion of compliance approaches, see *infra* n. 14.

115. On the NCP under the Climate Change see in particular: Redgwell, loc. cit. n. 18; J.E. Butler, 'The Establishment of A Dispute Resolution/Noncompliance Mechanism', *ASIL Proceedings* (1997) pp. 250-256; D. Bodansky, 'The United Nations Framework Convention on Climate Change: A Commentary', 18 *Yale JIL* (1993) pp. 451-558; I. Rowlands, *The Policies Global Atmosphere Change* (Manchester, Manchester University Press 1995); D. Zaelke and J. Cameron, 'Global Warming and Climate Change-An Overview of an International Legal Process', 5 *Am.Univ.JIL & Pol.* (1990) pp. 249-289; J. Werksman, 'Designing a Compliance System for the UN Framework Convention on Climate Change', op. cit. n. 11; and Cameron et. al., op. cit. n. 11, Chapter 4.

116. For recent analysis, see Werksman, loc. cit. n. 14.

117. FCCC/CP/1998/16/Add. 1, Decision 8/CP.4.

order for the compliance system to be adopted at COP-6 (2000) where, it was anticipated, the fleshing out of the flexibility mechanisms[118] of the Protocol would be accomplished. COP-6 failed to reach agreement and, at the time of writing, it seems unlikely that COP-6bis will succeed fully where the Hague meeting failed.[119] As Rajamani relates, the two most controversial aspects of the NCP are the consequences of non-compliance with Article 3(1) of the Protocol, namely, compliance by Annex I parties with the targets and timetables for greenhouse gas emissions,[120] and the composition of the Compliance Committee.[121] Clearly motivating the design of these measures, in particular non-compliance responses, is the perception that facilitative approaches to non-compliance will function less effectively at least in so far as Annex I parties obligations are concerned and that a more enforcement-oriented approach to compliance is necessary. If this is so, then the need to clarify the relationship between NCP and DSP and the residual role for state responsibility and the

118. That is, joint implementation between Annex I parties, the clean development mechanism (Annex I and non-Annex I parties) and emissions trading.

119. For excellent recent analysis of COP-6, see L. Rajamani, 'Re-Negotiating Kyoto: A Review of the Sixth Conference of the Parties to the Framework Convention on Climate Change', *RECIEL* (2001) (forthcoming); see also the 'Summary of the Sixth Conference of the Parties to the Framework Convention on Climate Change: 13-25 November 2000', 12 No. 163 *Earth Negotiations Bulletin* (2000) pp. 1-19. An informal note by President Pronk formed the basis for last-ditch efforts at achieving consensus in the last two days of COP-6, without success: see *Note by the President of COP-6*, 23 November 2000, annexed to Decision 1/CP.6.

120. COP-6 saw consensus emerging regarding the need for legally binding consequences for non-compliance (which, as indicated above, would require amendment of the Protocol - Art. 18) with Art. 3(1) but controversy remains regarding the types of measures which may be taken in response to a finding of non-compliance. In particular whether vireing between commitment periods would be permitted, and the submission of a 'compliance action plan' to the enforcement branch of the Compliance Committee, proved insurmountably contentious. On the first point, the issue is what 'penalty' rate should apply in subtracting excess emissions from one commitment period from the permitted emissions amount for the subsequent commitment period. A compromise figure of 1.5, rising in increments of 0.25 in each subsequent period of non-compliance, was suggested in the President's Note but did not achieve widespread support. Whether approval of the compliance action plan by the enforcement branch of the Compliance Committee would be required was also left unresolved. COP-6 bis adopted a political agreement on the outstanding issues including compliance that needs to be incorporated into the legal document. (Conference of the Parties, sixth session, part two, Bonn 16-27 July 2001, FCC/CP/2001/L.7).

121. The composition of the Compliance Committee, namely, its enforcement and facilitative branches, has defied consensus. The two opposing views are equitable geographic representation versus Annex I/non-Annex I with the former enjoying a numerical majority. Indeed, as regards the enforcement branch the Umbrella Group (a fluid grouping of Annex I countries including Australia, Canada, Japan, New Zealand, Norway and the US) has supported exclusive Annex I membership on the basis that enforcement issues will only arise for such parties. The opposing argument is that non-compliance with commitments affects all countries. President Pronk proposed a compromise formula of representation by the five regional groups but with a 3/4 majority voting rule in combination with a double majority (for Annex I and non-Annex I countries) voting rule for the enforcement branch, with equitable geographic representation on the facilitative branch. See *Note*, supra, n. 119. No consensus emerged on this compromise formula: see further Rajamani, loc. cit. n. 119, at p. 14.

general law of treaties, may become vital given that disputes over the application of the NCP are more likely to arise in this context. Thus whilst non-compliance procedures clearly have a significant role to play in plugging the 'responsibility gap', the effectiveness of such measures will depend on, *inter alia*, their design. The fact that compliance issues under the Kyoto Protocol constituted one of the 'deal-breakers' at COP-6 indicates that the transition from a facilitative to a more enforcement oriented approach to compliance will not be an easy one.

Notwithstanding these difficulties, it is likely that existing and future treaty regimes, particularly in the environmental field, will continue to search for alternatives to state responsibility and material breach. The reasons for this are various. NCPs allow for a return to compliance outwith the shadow of state responsibility. While the ILC draft articles have significantly improved the position in terms of the definition of obligations and of an 'injured state' – indeed, as we have seen, providing for responsibility for 'victimless' breaches of obligations *erga omnes partes* – it is still a requirement that a state is held responsible for breach of an international obligation. To be sure it may be observed that NCPs rely on the identification of a non-complying state, whether by self-incrimination or otherwise; but this distinction between a responsible state and a non-complying state is more than merely semantic. It remains the case that the finding that a state has committed an internationally wrongful act as a matter of international law has significant psychological impact. Indeed, the very remedy of acknowledgement of that fact (*Corfu Channel* case) underscores this point. Yet we have seen that the Montreal Protocol NCP has functioned as an in-house facilitative mechanism in the vast majority of cases, not concerned with a determination of wrongfulness and its consequences but rather to ensure a return to compliance. The ILC draft articles would permit a 'victimless' internationally wrongful act to be addressed in a manner hitherto unlikely under the traditional rules of state responsibility, but do not provide for either the 'softer' approach to non-compliance nor the facilitative remedies of a NCP. This is also the case in respect of material breach: even where coercive in character, i.e., in providing for suspension of treaty rights and privileges, NCPs offer a more nuanced approach than the VCLT which can only address suspension of the treaty where material breach has occurred. A NCP allows a range of responses, including the suspension of treaty rights and privileges, without the need for categorisation of the non-complying act or omission as a material breach, with the serious consequences flowing therefrom.[122]

Ultimately, however, NCPs are subordinate to DSPs in the sense that, at least on the pattern of existing NCPs, such (internal) procedures are expressed to be 'without prejudice to' the invocation of (external) dispute settlement procedures, namely, arbi-

---

122. Churchill and Ulfstein criticise the indicative measures under the Montreal Protocol as unnecessarily restrictive in requiring suspension of rights and privileges thereunder to be in accordance with the applicable treaty law rules, rather than with the (presumably wider) 'appropriate law of international institutions': loc. cit., n. 5, at p. 645. At pp. 643-647 they consider briefly the application of international institutional law to breaches of substantive obligations under multilateral environmental agreements and to the interpretation and application of NCPs (an issue beyond the scope of this article), though conclude that the issue remains rather theoretical in the absence of practice beyond the Montreal Protocol NCP.

tration and judicial settlement. The uncertain legal effect of these qualifying words has been addressed above.[123] At any rate it is clear that DSPs, along with the rules of international law regarding state responsibility and material breach, remain in the wings where an internationally wrongful act is concerned, with the NCP providing a first (and in many cases, last) step along the dispute avoidance/settlement continuum. This is not to suggest that there is no overlap between NCPs and state responsibility: as was elaborated above, NCPs may be applied in such a manner as to constitute de facto the imposition of collective countermeasures under the ILC draft articles. But in the main, especially where functioning in a facilitative manner, NCPs operate in a separate sphere from state responsibility and material breach; indeed, each has a separate though potentially overlapping sphere of operation. What the current ILC draft articles have accomplished is to increase the likelihood that state responsibility will provide a remedy for breach of international environmental obligations of an erga omnes or *erga omnes partes* character even where 'victimless'; that is, the potential field of application of state responsibility will be widened. At the same time it is possible to detect in the proposed design of the Kyoto non-compliance procedure a 'hardening' of the NCP in its enforcement capacity, and as such it could be argued that NCPs are likewise expanding along the continuum towards state responsibility. It could of course be questioned whether the characteristics of NCP are in fact strengths, and argued that failure to comply with international environmental obligations *should* be subject to the full force of the rules on state responsibility and material breach. The point here has not been so much evaluative as factual, in that as the law presently stands the rules regarding responsibility and breach do not and cannot function to address the range of non-complying behaviour by states. Hence the utility of NCPs in plugging the 'responsibility gap'. Even with the progressive development of the law of state responsibility this gap will inevitably narrow but there will remain a sphere of operation for NCPs outwith responsibility and breach.

123. Part 3 *infra*. Note also the potential for estoppel to operate where DSP is invoked subsequent to the conclusion of the NCP.

THE LEGAL STATUS OF THE 1989 AUSTRALIA-INDONESIA TIMOR GAP TREATY FOLLOWING THE END OF INDONESIAN RULE IN EAST TIMOR*

David M. Ong**

** Department of Law, University of Essex, Wivenhoe Park, Colchester, Essex CO4 3SQ, UK. E-mail: daveo@essex.ac.uk. Also principal research fellow on the British Institute of International and Comparative Law's Joint Development Regimes research project.

Netherlands Yearbook of International Law
Volume XXXI - 2000 - pp. 67-129

1. INTRODUCTION

East Timor will soon achieve full independence and statehood. Its initial concerns as a newly independent state are political and economic stability.[1] The current UN presence in East Timor should help ensure that the former concern is addressed so that the transition from a war torn non self-governing territory to a democratically elected government proceeds as smoothly as possible.[2] The latter concern over East Timor's future economic stability is currently tied-up with continuing negotiations over the division of oil and gas revenues derived from a joint development arrangement, namely the Timor Gap Zone of Co-operation Treaty.[3] This bilateral treaty was initially agreed in 1989 between Indonesia, which controlled East Timor from 1975 to 1999, and Australia. Its terms are currently being enforced on a provisional basis as agreed between the United Nations Transitional Administration of East Timor (UNTAET)[4] and Australia while its future is being negotiated.

This essay examines the current legal status of the 1989 Timor Gap treaty with a view to determining whether international law would allow a newly independent East Timor state to repudiate the arrangement, or indeed whether it requires its continued application notwithstanding the change of sovereignty that is taking place in East

---

1. For a recent account of East Timor's rocky road to full independence and statehood, see A. L. Smith, 'East Timor's Difficult Transition to Independence', in Daljit Singh and N.J. Freeman, eds., *Regional Outlook: Southeast Asia 2001-2002* (Singapore, Institute of Southeast Asian Studies 2001).

2. For an analysis of the legal authority of the UN presence in East Timor, see M.J. Matheson, 'United Nations Governance of Post Conflict Societies', 95 *AJIL* (2001) pp. 76-85, at pp. 81-83.

3. Full title: Treaty between the Australia and the Republic of Indonesia on the Zone of Co-operation in an Area between the Indonesian Province of East Timor and Northern Australia, signed (in the air-space) over the Timor Gap on 11 December 1989; entered into force on 9 February 1991. (hereinafter: the Timor Gap treaty) Sources: 29 *ILM* (1990) 469 and V. Prescott, 'Australia-Indonesia (Timor Gap)', Report No. 6-2(5), in J.I. Charney and L.M. Alexander, eds., *International Maritime Boundaries*, Vol. II (The Hague, Martinus Nijhoff 1993) at pp. 1245-1328. Also in H. Fox, ed., *Joint Development of Offshore Oil and Gas*, Vol. II, Part III (London, The British Institute of International and Comparative Law 1990) pp. 235-251. For an early analysis of the background and main features of the Treaty, see V.L. Forbes and F. M. Auburn, 'The Timor Gap Zone of Co-operation', *Boundary Briefing* (1991) No. 9.

4. Full Title: Memorandum of Understanding between the Government of Australia and the United Nations Transitional Administration in East Timor (UNTAET), acting on behalf of East Timor, on Arrangements Relating to the Timor Gap Treaty, 10 February 2000. Adopted in an Exchange of Notes constituting an Agreement between the Government of Australia and the United Nations Transitional Administration in East Timor (UNTAET) concerning the continued operation of the treaty between Australia and the Republic of Indonesia on the Zone of Co-operation between the Indonesian Province of East Timor and Northern Australia of 11 December 1989. Performed at Dili, 10 February 2000. Entry into force: 10 February 2000, but with effect from 25 October 1999. This arrangement was brought into force by an exchange of Diplomatic Notes on 10 February 2000 that retrospectively applied the provisional agreement as from 25 October 1999, i.e., the date when UNTAET took over government functions on behalf of East Timor. See Australian Treaty Series 2000, No. 9, accessed at the following website: http:www.auslii.edu.au/au/other/dfat/treaties/2000/9.html> In April 2000 Australia approved legislation giving effect to the above treaty with UNTAET. See Timor Gap Treaty (Transitional Arrangements) Act 2000.

Timor. The essay begins with a discussion of the background, negotiation and main features of the Timor Gap treaty to highlight its defining characteristics. It will then examine the international law relating to new states, with a view to ascertaining whether a newly-independent East Timor state is obliged to respect the terms of the Timor Gap treaty.[5] Two aspects of this question will be considered: First, whether the Timor Gap treaty can be repudiated by a new East Timor state as invalid on the ground that it was agreed between Indonesia and Australia without consulting the East Timorese people, thereby denying their right of self-determination under international law. Secondly, whether a newly independent East Timor state would succeed to the Timor Gap treaty under international law? This in turn depends on whether the treaty can be described as a territorial boundary treaty, thereby falling within the exception to the general rule of state succession under international law embodying a 'clean slate' approach to treaty obligations. This analysis is essential to determine whether a new East Timor state would succeed to the original 1989 treaty, or whether a new maritime boundary treaty or joint development arrangement is to be negotiated between itself and Australia.

Finally, arguments advocating a joint development arrangement between a new East Timor state and Australia over the disputed continental shelf area and the petroleum resources therein will be examined. Regardless of whether joint development is required by international law, it is argued here that it represents the most effective solution to the immediate problem of exploitation of the shared petroleum resources found in the disputed area. The recent Memorandum of Understanding (MOU) between the Australian government and provisionally continuing the application of the legal regime established by the Timor Gap treaty appears to vindicate this view. However, continuing negotiations between Australia and UNTAET, with the participation of East Timorese representatives,[6] over the future of the present joint development regime in the Timor Gap have encountered problems as to the shape of the new treaty regime.[7]

5. Grant, for example, notes that 'the legal status of East Timor should not be ignored as a factor in the movement of the territory from *de facto* province of Indonesia to independent state *in statu nascendi.*' See T.D. Grant, 'East Timor, the UN System, and Enforcing Non-Recognition in International Law', 33 *Vanderbilt JIL* (2000) pp. 273-310, at p. 275. Moreover, as Crawford notes, '[t]he capacity of entities *in statu nascendi* to acquire rights under other forms of international arrangement is also a matter of some difficulty.' See J. Crawford, *The Creation of States in International Law* (Oxford, Clarendon Press 1979) at p. 394.

6. Namely, the National Council of Timorese Resistance (CNRT), an umbrella group composed of different political hues, presided over by Xanana Gusmao.

7. Triggs reports that the first round of negotiations ended inconclusively and a new round had not yet been convened by the end of 2000, see G. Triggs, 'Legal and Commercial Risks of Investment in the Timor Gap', 1 *Melbourne JIL* (2001) pp. 98-130, at p. 99, citing UNTAET, *First Round of Timor Gap Talks Ends*, Daily Briefing (12 October 2000) Marks reports that further talks in Melbourne also ended without agreement in April 2001. See K. Marks, 'East Timor claims oil and gas rights', *The Independent*. UK newspaper (Friday 20 April 2001) at p. 19.

2. THE BACKGROUND, NEGOTIATION AND MAIN FEATURES OF THE TIMOR GAP TREATY

2.1 Background to the Timor Gap Treaty

The Timor Gap treaty was agreed in 1989 to fill in the gap between the continental shelf boundaries of the respective countries that were delimited by agreements in 1971 and 1972.[8] (see Map 1) The existence of this gap was due to the fact that at the time of the earlier maritime delimitation agreements between Australia and Indonesia, the land territory to which this gap appertained, i.e., East Timor, was controlled by Portugal.[9] However, in late 1975 Indonesia invaded East Timor and formally annexed it on 17 July 1976. Portugal immediately protested against this action in the UN.

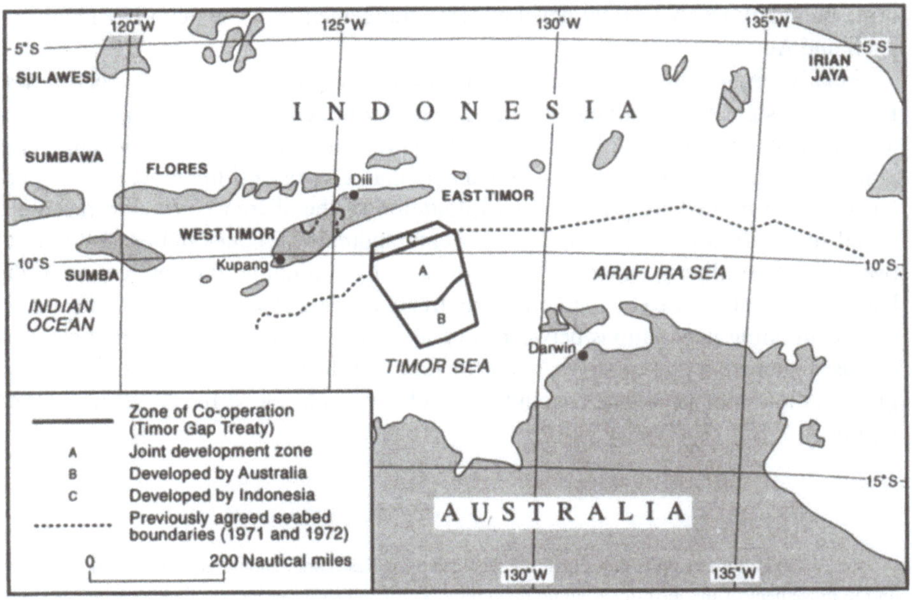

Map 1. Timor Gap Zone of Co-operation

8. Agreement between the Government of the Commonwealth of Australia and the Government of the Republic of Indonesia Establishing Certain Seabed Boundaries, signed at Canberra on 18 May 1971 and the Agreement between the Government of the Republic of Indonesia and the Government of the Commonwealth of Australia Establishing Certain Seabed Boundaries in the Area of the Timor and Arafura Seas, Supplementary to the Agreement of 18 May 1971 signed at Jakarta on 9 October 1972. See V. Prescott, 'Australia-Indonesia (Seabed Boundaries)', Report No. 6-2(1) & 'Australia-Indonesia (Timor and Arafura Seas)', Report No. 6-2(2) in Charney and Alexander, eds., op. cit. n. 3, at pp. 1195-1205, 1207-1218, respectively.

9. Portugal was designated as the 'Administering Power' of East Timor by UNGA Resolution 1542 (XV) of 15 December 1960.

Both the UN General Assembly and Security Council upheld Portugal's condemnation of the Indonesian invasion, although according to Cassese, they did not unequivocally hold that it amounted to an aggressive act.[10] A number of UN Security Council and General Assembly resolutions were passed condemning the Indonesian action principally on the basis of its lack of respect for the self-determination of the East Timorese people.[11] For example, UN Security Council Resolution 389 of 22 April 1976 called upon all states to respect East Timor's territorial integrity and the right to self-determination of its people. UN General Assembly Resolution 31/53 of 1 December 1976 rejected the claim that East Timor had been integrated into Indonesia since its people had not been able to exercise their right to self-determination. The UN General Assembly reaffirmed the inalienable right of the East Timorese people to self-determination and independence in Resolution 33/39 of 13 December 1978.

This illegal Indonesian action stalled negotiations for the Resolution of the Timor Gap because of Australia's initial reluctance to recognise the Indonesian army's enforced incorporation of East Timor into the Indonesian state. After 1982, however, the UN General Assembly no longer discussed the East Timor question. Although several UN bodies continued to consider East Timor issues and adopt Resolutions on its behalf, significantly these did not require an Indonesian withdrawal or East Timor independence.[12] A growing perception of international community indifference[13] and the lack of concerted efforts on the part of the Portugese to resolve the East Timor is-

10. Antonio Cassese, *Self-Determination of Peoples: A Legal Reappraisal* (Cambridge, Cambridge University Press 1995) at p. 224.

11. The question of East Timor has been the subject of two UN Security Council Resolutions and eight General Assembly resolutions. See UNSC Res. 384 (1975) adopted on 22 December 1975, *YUN* (UN Yearbook) (1975) at p. 866; and UNSC Res. 389 (1976) adopted on 22 April 1976, *YUN* (1976); and UNGA Res. 3485 (1975) of 12 December 1975, *YUN* (1975) at p. 865; UNGA Res. 31/53 of 1 December 1976, *YUN* (1976) at p. 754; UNGA Res. 32/34 of 28 November 1977, *YUN* (1977) at p. 890; UNGA Res. 33/39 of 13 December 1978, *YUN* (1978) at p. 869; UNGA Res. 34/40 of 21 November 1979, *YUN* (1979) at p. 1056; UNGA Res. 35/27 of 11 November 1980, *YUN* (1980) at p. 1094; UNGA Res. 36/50 of 24 November 1981, *YUN* (1981) at p. 1185; UNGA Res. 37/30 of 23 November 1982, *YUN* (1982) at p. 1349.

12. See N. Sybesma-Knol, 'The Indispensable Parties Rule in the East Timor Case', in E. Denters and N. Schrijver, eds., *Reflections on International Law from the Low Countries: in Honour of Paul de Waart*, (The Hague, Martinus Nijhoff 1998) pp. 442-457, p. at 445.

13. Calvocoressi, for example, notes that both Portugal and Australia implicitly acquiesced in the Indonesian invasion of East Timor, while '[T]he rest of the world hardly noticed.' See P. Calvocoressi, *World Politics since 1945*, 6th edn. (London, Longman 1991) at p. 472. Cassese postulates that the general apathy displayed by the international community, which amounted to the effective tolerance of the Indonesian occupation of East Timor, can be accounted for by political considerations, in particular the strategic importance of Indonesia for the West. See Cassese, op. cit. n. 10, at p. 227. On the other hand, Symmons observes that the number of recognising states in fact constituted very much a minority of the world community, comprising mainly some Asian and neighbouring states of Indonesia and no European states at all. Moreover, of this small number of states, only Australia expressly recognised the Indonesian take-over *de jure* by the negotiation of the Timor Gap treaty. See C.R. Symmons, 'The International Recognition Position Regarding the Purported Incorporation of East Timor into Indonesia', in P. Pinto Leite, ed., *The East Timor Problem and the Role of Europe* (Lisbon International Platform of Jurists for East Timor (IPJET) 1998) pp. 211-221, at p. 221.

sue[14] led the Australian government to conclude that its national interests were better served by granting *de facto* recognition of Indonesian sovereignty over East Timor. Declining production from Australia's major oilfields in the Bass Strait, coupled with the promisingly large potential for exploitable hydrocarbons in the Kelp structure to the north of the Timor Gap area, further reduced Australian reticence to renewing negotiations with Indonesia over the Timor Gap.

2.2 Negotiations towards the Timor Gap Treaty

Thus, in 1979, Australia resumed the sea-bed boundary negotiations with Indonesia that had initially begun with Portugal. These negotiations culminated in a Joint Statement by the two Foreign Ministers released on 25 October 1988 which, *inter alia,* established a Zone of Co-operation in the Timor Gap in respect of petroleum exploration and exploitation. This Joint statement was followed by the definitive treaty slightly more than a year later, signed on 11 December 1989 by Mr. Gareth Evans, (then) Minister for Foreign Affairs & Trade on behalf of Australia and by Dr. Ali Alatas, Minister for Foreign Affairs on behalf of Indonesia.

Upon signature of the Timor Gap treaty, Portugal delivered a written protest to the Australian government complaining of a flagrant violation of international law and the UN Charter on the basis that the annexation of East Timor by Indonesia was illegal. This protest was followed by legal action filed against Australia at the International Court of Justice (ICJ) on 22 February 1991,[15] claiming that the Timor Gap treaty was illegal and should be declared null and void. On 30 June 1995, the Court delivered its decision, holding by 14 votes to 2 that it lacked jurisdiction to deal with the dispute brought by Portugal against Australia in the absence of Indonesia's participation in the proceedings,[16] which the Court held to be indispensable since the legality of Indonesia's conduct in annexing East Timor was fundamental to the determination of the dispute.[17] The ICJ therefore declined jurisdiction to entertain the Portugese claim on the basis that the relevant legal issues arising from this dispute necessarily

14. See K. Suter, 'Timor Gap Treaty: The continuing controversy', 17 *Marine Policy* (1993) pp. 294-302, at p. 302.

15. The action brought by Portugal against Australia challenged the rights of both Indonesia and Australia to enter into any agreement over the exploitation of hydrocarbons in the continental shelf area pertaining to East Timor. See *Case Concerning East Timor (Portugal* v. *Australia)* Judgment, *ICJ Rep.* (1995) 90 and 34 *ILM* (1995) 1581. See also I. Scobbie, 'The East Timor Case: The Implications of Procedure for Litigation Strategy', 9 *Oil and Gas Law and Taxation Review* (1991) pp. 273-281; and S. Kaye, *Australia's Maritime Boundaries,* Wollongong Papers on Maritime Policy No. 4 (Wollongong, Australia: Centre for Maritime Policy 1995) pp. 75-78.

16. *Case Concerning East Timor, ICJ Rep.* (1995) ibid., at para. 38, p. 106.

17. Ibid., at paras. 33 and 34, pp. 104-105.

involved the actions of a third state, namely Indonesia, which did not accept the compulsory jurisdiction of the Court.[18]

Notwithstanding this Judgment which at least implicitly vindicates the negotiation and adoption of the 1989 Timor Gap treaty,[19] the legal status of the treaty is now cast in shadow following the overwhelming vote for independence cast by the people of East Timor in the UN-organised referendum last August 1999.[20] The UN-sponsored referendum in East Timor saw a resounding vote for independence.[21] While the resulting violence and unrest initially delayed the implementation of this vote,[22] crucially the acceptance of this result by the Indonesian government paves the way for the eventual election of an independent East Timor government.[23] This new government will then be in a position to begin negotiations with the Australian government as to the continued implementation (or otherwise) of the Timor Gap treaty.

18. Ibid., at para. 35, p. 105. Several of the legal issues raised by this case, namely, the Court's jurisdiction, the legal effect of the right of self-determination, and the legality of the Indonesian occupation of East Timor have been discussed in the pages of this *Yearbook*. See C. Antonopoulos, 'Effectiveness v. the Rule of Law Following the East Timor Case', 27 *NYIL* (1996) pp. 75-111. See also G.J. Simpson, 'Judging the East Timor Dispute: Self-Determination at the International Court of Justice', 17 *Hastings I & CLR* (1994) p. 323.

19. It is important to note however, that the Court was careful to state that its conclusion over its lack of jurisdiction in the instant case did not extend to other Australian objections, including the Court's jurisdiction to decide on the validity of the 1989 Timor Gap treaty. See *ICJ Rep.* (1995) *supra* n. 15, at para. 35, p. 105.

20. The UN-sponsored referendum on East Timor's future took place on 30 August, 1999. The vote was organised by UNAMET (UN Mission in East Timor), the predecessor organisation to the present UNTAET (UN Transitional Administration in East Timor). Indonesia agreed to allow the ballot after two days of extensive negotiations in New York between the UN Secretary-General, Kofi Annan and the Indonesian and Portugese foreign ministers during March 1999. The agreement allowed both local East Timorese (pop. 600,000) and the East Timorese diaspora living all over the world (30,000), the majority being in Portugal, Australia and Macau, to participate in a direct ballot to decide whether the territory remained part of Indonesia, or became independent. See J. Aglionby, 'UN pressure gives East Timor vote on independence', *The Guardian*, UK newspaper (Saturday, 13 March 1999) at p. 18.

21. Following a strong voter turn-out (98.6%), UN Secretary General Kofi Annan announced on 4 September 1999, that the result was an overwhelming vote in favour of independence for East Timor. Almost eighty per cent (78.5%) of those registered to vote rejected a proposal for autonomy within Indonesia, thereby supporting East Timor's separation from Indonesia.

22. Cady, for example, observes that in the three weeks following the UN referendum East Timor was almost completely destroyed. 78% of public and private buildings were rendered unusable. Water, electricity, telephone and telecommunications systems, public services, hospitals, the banking system, businesses, infrastructure, the police, national and local institutions, archives – all collapsed. See J.-C. Cady, Deputy Transitional Administrator of East Timor, 'Building the New State of East Timor', Lecture for the Centre of International and Public Law (CIPL) (Canberra, Australia National University on 18 May 2000). Text available from the CIPL and accessible at http://law.anu/edu/au/centres/CIPL/WEB22-0.7.htm (Conferences and Lectures 2000)

23. Indonesia renounced her claims to East Timor on 20 October 1999. In November 1999, the Indonesian People's Consultative Assembly met and officially accepted the result of the East Timor referendum vote.

In the hiatus before a democratically-elected East Timorese government takes over the reins, the United Nations Security Council has established an interim administration, namely the United Nations Transitional Administration in East Timor (UNTAET).[24] It should be noted that this is not the first occasion in which the UN has taken over the administration of a non-self-governing territory. A similar instance also from the Southeast Asian region is the United Nations' Transitional Authority of Cambodia (UNTAC).[25]

A more pertinent example dates back to 1966 when the UN General Assembly terminated South Africa's League of Nations Mandate over South West Africa (later, Namibia) and placed the territory under the direct responsibility of the United Nations. The General Assembly later established a UN Council to administer South West Africa until its independence. As Schrijver notes, the very first Decree enacted by the UN Council was for the Protection of the Natural Resources of Namibia.[26] This in turn directly connected the Namibian people's right of self-determination with their right to exploit the natural resources of their territory.

As previously noted, in the exercise of its mandate, UNTAET has recently entered into a Memorandum of Understanding (MOU) with Australia establishing a provisional arrangement for the continued application of the 1989 Timor Gap treaty. This development raises the question as to whether some variation of the joint development arrangement established by the 1989 Timor Gap treaty will eventually be formally re-adopted between a new East Timor state and Australia.[27] On the other hand, UNTAET has called for a new treaty arrangement to be negotiated,[28] and East Timorese leaders have gone even further in advocating a permanent maritime boundary

---

24. On 25 October 1999, by unanimously adopting UNSC Resolution 1272 (1999), the UN Security Council established UNTAET for an initial period until 31 January 2001. It is responsible for the administration of East Timor and empowered to exercise all legislative and executive authority, including the administration of justice. The Security Council also mandated UNTAET to provide security and maintain law and order throughout East Timor; ensure the co-ordination and delivery of humanitarian, rehabilitation and development assistance; support capacity-building for self-government; and assist in the establishment of conditions for sustainable development. See UNSC res. 1272, 4057th Meeting (am), 25 October 1999, UN Doc. S/RES/1272 (1999) Also see 39 *ILM* (2000) 240. The Security Council established the UNTAET for an initial period until 31 January 2001.

25. See T. Findlay, *Cambodia: The Legacy and Lessons of UNTAC,* SIPRI Research Report No. 9 (Stockholm/Oxford, Stockholm International Peace Research Institute/Oxford University Press 1995) See also Institute of Policy Studies of Singapore and UN Institute for Training and Research (UNITAR), *The UN Transitional Authority in Cambodia (UNTAC): Debriefing and Lessons*, Report of the 1994 Singapore Conference (London, Kluwer Law International 1995).

26. See N. Schrijver, *Sovereignty over Natural Resources: Balancing Rights and Duties* (Cambridge, Cambridge University Press 1997) at p. 147.

27. See W.T. Onorato and M.J. Valencia, 'The New Timor Gap Treaty: Legal and Political Implications', 15 *ICSID Review – Foreign Investment Law Journal* (2000) pp. 59-85.

28. Negotiations are presently continuing in Dili (East Timor) between the UNTAET and Australia on a new arrangement to replace the current Timor Gap treaty regime. See UNTAET, 'First Round of Timor Gap Talks Ends', Daily Briefing (12 October 2000)

agreement based on the median line which favours East Timor in the division of the petroleum resources in the Gap area.[29] A new median line boundary agreement may give East Timor up to 90% of the Timor Gap's petroleum resources. Thus, Australia is now competing with its soon to be independent, new but poor, neighbour for these resources.[30]

However, given that Australian technical expertise and financial aid will be crucial to the East Timor infrastructure and community rebuilding process, the Australian government is at least in public taking a relatively sanguine approach to the dispute. It has stated that Australia will be sensible, reasonable and fair in considering the natural aspirations of the Timorese leadership.[31] For example, the Australian Senate Foreign Affairs, Defence and Trade References Committee's Inquiry into East Timor has recommended that, 'in its negotiations with UNTAET on the future of the Timor Gap Treaty, the Australian Government should take into account current international law in relation to seabed boundaries, the history of (Australia's) relations with the East Timorese people, the need to develop good bilateral relations with East Timor and the need for East Timor to have sources of income that might reduce dependency on foreign aid.'[32]

On the other hand, Australia considers her legal views on continental shelf entitlement as fundamental to her national self-interest. Thus, as Triggs observes, if UNTAET and its East Timor representatives maintain their attempt to negotiate a maritime boundary delimitation agreement with Australia based on the median line principle, there is every chance a further period of unproductive exchanges will ensue.[33]

2.3 Main features of the Timor Gap Treaty

The 1989 Timor Gap treaty is an excellent example of a species of maritime boundary treaty embodying the concept of 'joint development' of shared mineral resources. 'Joint Development' is a generic term given to international agreements between states whose main function is to provide for the co-operative exploitation of hydrocarbon resources that come under the jurisdiction of two states. While the 'joint devel-

29. See J. McBeth, 'Pipe Dreams', *Far Eastern Economic Review* (31 August 2000) at p. 18. See also the comments of Mari Alkatiri of the National Council of Timorese Resistance, as quoted in P. Alford and R. Garran, 'East Timor Wants New Gap Treaty', *The Australian*, Sydney newspaper (15 June 2000) at p. 2; and those of UNTAET's head, S. Vieria de Mello, 'East Timor Receives First Royalty Payment from Oil Exploitation in Timor Gap', in UNTAET, Press Release (24 October 2000).

30. Marks, loc. cit. n. 7, at p. 19.

31. McBeth, loc. cit. n. 29.

32. Available at http://www.aph.gov.au/senate/committee/fadt.ctte.

33. Triggs, loc. cit. n. 7, at p. 125.

opment' concept itself has not been understood or used in a uniform way,[34] joint development arrangements have nevertheless proven to be an effective option for co-operation in the exploration and exploitation of shared offshore mineral resources. There are now numerous examples of bilateral offshore joint development agreements.[35] Significantly, examples can now be found in many different marine regions around

---

34. For example, Sect. IV, para. 1 of the Conclusions and Recommendations of the lawyers' group at the Second Workshop on Geology and Hydrocarbon Potential in the South China Sea and Possibilities of Joint Development, held in Honolulu during August 1983 defined 'joint development' as extending from unitization of shared resources to unilateral development of a shared resource beyond a stipulated boundary, and various gradations in between. See M. Miyoshi, 'The Basic Concept of Joint Development of Hydrocarbon Resources on the Continental Shelf', 3 *International Journal of Estuarine (now Marine) and Coastal Law* (1988) pp. 1-18, at p. 5 and Appendix II, at p. 17.
Gault defines 'joint development' as 'a decision by one or more countries to pool any rights they may have over a given area and, to a greater or lesser degree, undertake some form of joint management for the purposes of exploring and exploiting offshore minerals.' See I. Townsend-Gault, 'Joint Development of Offshore Mineral Resources - Progress and Prospects for the Future', 12 *Natural Resources Forum* (1988) at p. 275.
Lagoni restricted the scope of 'joint development' to co-operation between states with regard to the exploration for and exploitation of certain deposits, fields or accumulations of non-living resources, which either extend across a boundary or lie in an area of overlapping claims. See International Law Association, International Committee on the EEZ, 'Joint Development of Non-Living Resources in the Exclusive Economic Zone' Report of the Sixty-Third Conference, Warsaw (1988). Rapporteur: R. Lagoni (hereinafter, 1988 ILA Warsaw Report) pp. 509-558, at pp. 511-512.
Miyoshi too favours a restrictive version of 'joint development', limited to an inter-governmental agreement, to the exclusion of joint ventures between a government and an oil company, or a consortia of private companies for capital participation. He therefore defines 'joint development' as an inter-governmental arrangement of a provisional nature, designed for functional purposes of joint exploration for and/or exploitation of the hydrocarbon resources of the sea-bed beyond the territorial sea. See M. Miyoshi, 'Basic Legal Issues of Joint Development of Offshore Oil and Gas in relation to Maritime Boundary Delimitation', *Maritime Briefing*, Vol. 2, No. 5 (Durham, International Boundaries Research Unit (IBRU) 1999) at p. 4.
Finally, the British Institute of International and Comparative Law (BIICL) Research Team's definition of 'joint development' is an agreement between two states to develop so as to share jointly in agreed proportions by inter-state co-operation and national measures the offshore oil and gas in a designated zone of the seabed and subsoil of the continental shelf to which both or either of the participating states are entitled in international law. See H. Fox, et al, *Joint Development of Offshore Oil and Gas*, Vol. I (London, British Institute of International and Comparative Law 1988) at p. 45.

35. Other examples of joint development agreements include the following: Agreement concerning the Delimitation of the Continental Shelf in the Persian Gulf between the Shaykhdom of Bahrain and the Kingdom of Saudi Arabia, 22 February 1958, in R. Churchill, M. Nordquist and S. Houston Lay, eds., *New Directions in the Law of the Sea*, Vol. 5 (Dobbs Ferry, NY, Oceana Publications 1973) pp. 207-211, ST/LEG/SER.B/16, 409; Agreement between the state of Kuwait and the Kingdom of Saudi Arabia Relating to the Partition of the Neutral Zone, 7 July 1965, in 4 *ILM* (1965) p. 1134; Agreement on the Settlement of Maritime Boundary Lines and Sovereign Rights over Islands between Qatar and Abu Dhabi, 20 March 1969, ST/LEG/SER.B/16, 403; Memorandum of Understanding between Iran and Sharjah, 18 November 1971, *Middle East Economic Survey*, Vol. 15, No. 28 (1972) Supplement; Convention between the

the world.[36] Both their increasing numbers and geographical diversity preclude any attempt at dismissing their repeated occurrence as merely coincidental state practice. This leads to the preliminary observation that the lack of a binding obligation to co-operate in the joint development of an international common deposit has less to do with the lack of state practice than with the absence of that other imperative in the formation of customary international law, namely the psychological or subjective element of acceptance of the specific obligation as binding in law, *opinio juris sive ne-*

Government of the French Republic and the Government of the Spanish state on the delimitation of the Continental Shelf of the Two states in the Bay of Biscay, 29 January 1974, ST/LEG/SER.B/19, 445, Agreement between Japan and the Republic of (South) Korea concerning Joint Development of the Southern Part of the Continental Shelf adjacent to the Two Countries, 5 February 1974, in Churchill et al., Vol. 4 (1975) pp. 117-133; Agreement between Sudan and Saudi Arabia relating to the Joint Exploitation of the Natural Resources of the Sea-Bed and Sub-soil of the Red Sea in the Common Zone, 16 May 1974, ST/LEG/SER.B/18 452-5; Agreement between the Government of the United Kingdom of Great Britain and Northern Ireland and the Government of the Kingdom of Norway relating to the Exploitation of the Frigg Field Reservoir and the Transmission of Gas therefrom to the United Kingdom, 10 May 1976, entered into force: 22 July 1977, *UKTS* (1977) 113; Memorandum of Understanding between Malaysia and the Kingdom of Thailand on the Establishment of a Joint Authority for the Exploitation of the Resources in the Sea-Bed in a Defined Area of the Continental Shelf of the Two Countries in the Gulf of Thailand, 21 February 1979, entered into force: 24 October 1979, in Appendix I of D. Ong, 'Thailand/Malaysia: The Joint Development Agreement 1990', 6 *International Journal of Estuarine (now Marine) and Coastal Law* (1991) pp. 57-72, at pp. 61-63. Followed by the Agreement between the Government of Malaysia and the Government of the Kingdom of Thailand on the Constitution and Other Matters relating to the Establishment of the Malaysia-Thailand Joint Authority, 30 May 1990, in Appendix II of Ong, pp. 64-72; Agreement on the Continental Shelf between Iceland and Norway, 22 October 1981, 21 *ILM* (1982) pp. 1222-1226; Memorandum of Understanding between Malaysia and Vietnam for the exploration and exploitation of petroleum in the Gulf of Thailand, 5 June 1992, entered into force: 4 June 1993. See T.L. McDorman, 'Malaysia-Vietnam', Report No. 5-19, in Charney and Alexander, Vol.III, op. cit. n. 3, at pp. 2335-2344, text of MOU at pp. 2341-2344; Maritime Delimitation Treaty between Jamaica and the Republic of Colombia, 12 November 1993, entered into force: 14 March 1994, see K.G. Nweihed, 'Colombia-Jamaica', Report 2-18, in Charney and Alexander, Vol. III, op. cit. n. 3, at pp. 2179-2204; Management and Co-operation Agreement between the Government of the Republic of Senegal and the Government of the Republic of Guinea-Bissau, 14 October 1993, and Protocol of Agreement relating to the Organization and Operation of the Agency for Management and Co-operation between Senegal and Gunea-Bissau, 12 June, 1995, both entered into force: 21 December 1995, 31 *LOS Bull.* 40 & 42, respectively (1996). See also J. R. V. Prescott, 'Guinea-Bissau-Senegal', Report 4-4(4) & (5) in Charney and Alexander, Vol. III, op. cit. n. 3, at pp. 2251-2278. Joint Declaration of Argentina and the United Kingdom on Co-operation over Offshore Activities in the South West Atlantic, 27 September 1995, 35 *ILM* (1996) p. 301, 'Current Developments: UK-Argentina', 11 *International Journal of Marine and Coastal Law* (1996) pp. 113-118, see also R.R. Churchill, 'Falkland Islands - Maritime Jurisdiction and Co-operative Arrangements with Argentina', 46 *ICLQ* (1997) pp. 463-477.

36. Specifically, the North Sea, Middle East and East and Southeast Asian regions, and more recently, the Caribbean Sea (Jamaica/Colombia, 1993), eastern (Senegal/Guinea-Bissau, 1993/1995) and southwestern (UK/Argentina, 1995) Atlantic regions. See List of joint development and transboundary unitization agreements, *supra* n. 35.

cessitasis.[37] The lingering uncertainty as to whether a rule of customary international law enjoining co-operation in the form of joint development exists is enhanced by an appreciation of the fact that no particular type or model of joint development agreement would appear to have achieved significant pre-eminence over the rest in numerical terms alone. On the other hand, the Arbitral Tribunal in the *Eritrea-Yemen Arbitration (Phase II-Maritime Delimitation)* case[38] observed that 'in the last thirty years there has grown up a significant body of cooperative state practice in the exploitation of resources that straddle maritime boundaries'.[39] Reisman notes that 'the Tribunal seemed to assume that some of these (state) practices were rapidly acquiring, but have not yet attained, customary international law status.'[40]

The Timor Gap treaty, along with its four annexes,[41] is probably one of the most sophisticated joint development regimes agreed todate.[42] Both the geographical division and institutional design are complex. As Onorato and Valencia note, 'the treaty goes far beyond any previous arrangements for joint development in that it creates, in detail, a comprehensive, interlocking legislative, contractual and fiscal regime to govern joint development in the chosen area ... never before have contracting states purposefully negotiated in advance a complete and area-specific regime, solely for the

---

37. For a fuller discussion of this issue, see David M. Ong, 'Joint Development of Common Offshore Oil and Gas Deposits: 'Mere' State Practice or Customary International Law?', 93 *AJIL* (1999) pp. 771-804.

38. Arbitral Tribunal Award, 17 December 1999. Accessed from: <http:// www.pca-cpa.org>

39. Ibid., at para. 84.

40. W.M. Reisman, 'Eritrea-Yemen Arbitration Award Phase II-Maritime Delimitation', International Decisions, 94 *AJIL* (2000) pp. 721-736, at p. 735.

41. Under Art. 1(o), Annexes A, B, C, and D are included within the meaning of the 'Treaty'. Annex A contains the designation and description including maps and coordinates of the areas A, B and C comprising the Zone of Cooperation and is incorporated into the Treaty by Art. 1. Annex B contains the Petroleum Mining Code for Area A of the Zone of Cooperation. This Code governs operational activities relating to exploration and exploitation of the petroleum resources in Area A subject to the power of the Ministerial Council under Art. 6.1(b) of the Treaty to amend it (Art. 1.1(i)) Annex C to the treaty contains the Model Production Sharing Contract between the Joint Authority and contractors on the basis of which production sharing contracts for Area A are to be concluded subject to modification by the Ministerial Council under Art. 6.1(c) of the treaty (Art. 1.1(g)).

42. For an early analysis of its provisions see A. Bergin, 'The Australian-Indonesian Timor Gap Maritime Boundary Agreement', 5 *International Journal of Estuarine (now Marine) and Coastal Law* (1990) pp. 383-393. It should be noted however that unique as the Timor Gap treaty is, it is but one of three such joint development arrangements in Southeast Asian waters alone. The other two are: The 1979 Memorandum of Understanding between Thailand and Malaysia establishing a Joint Authority for the exploitation of the resources of the sea-bed in a defined area of the continental shelf of the two countries in the Gulf of Thailand, followed by the 1990 Agreement between the same two countries on the Constitution and other matters relating to the establishment of the Malaysia-Thailand Joint Authority, both texts in Ong, loc. cit. n. 35, at pp. 57-72. Also, the 1992 Memorandum of Understanding between Malaysia and the Socialist Republic of Vietnam for the exploration and exploitation of petroleum in a defined area of the continental shelf involving the two countries, in McDorman, Vol. III, op. cit. n. 35, at p. 2341.

purposes of setting the total parameters of their intended joint endeavor.'[43] Consideration of the respective states' legal claims and how these were resolved in the delineation of the Zone of Co-operation will be followed by an examination of the joint development regime that this treaty established for the shared exploitation of the petroleum resources in the overlapping continental shelf claims area.

According to Burmester,[44] the boundaries of the Zone are based on the following criteria: In the east and west, the lines are based on the equidistance principle for adjacent coastlines. The northern and southern limits of the Zone of Co-operation represent the maximum continental shelf limits claimed by the two states and thereby delineate the area of overlapping claims. The line representing the southern limits of Area A is the median line of this overlapping continental shelf claims area. In other words, if Australia and Indonesia had agreed to delimit their continental shelf boundary according to the median line principle, which is equidistant from the opposing coastlines of Australia and East Timor, then the agreed maritime boundary would have been drawn along this line. The northern limits of Area A were drawn along a designated isobath[45] corresponding to the deepest point of the so-called Timor Trough, a sea-bed depression located due south of the East Timor coastline.

The use of different criteria based on distance and geomorphology represent the different legal bases of the respective states during the stalemated delimitation negotiations. Australia based its claim on the principle of natural prolongation that formed the early underpinnings of the continental shelf regime.[46] Australia thus argued that the Timor Trough represented the natural limits of Australia's wide continental shelf and margin and hence the dividing line between the Australian legal continental shelf and the much narrower East Timor shelf.[47] Indonesia, on the other hand, argued that the 'default' limit for a coastal state's legal continental shelf is the 200-nautical mile distance criterion established by the 1982 UN Convention on the Law of the Sea

43. W.T. Onorato and M.J. Valencia, 'International Cooperation for Petroleum Development: the Timor Gap Treaty', Vol. 5, *ICSID Review – Foreign Investment Law Journal* (1990) No. 1, pp. 1-29, at p. 26.

44. H. Burmester, 'The Zone of Co-operation between Australia and Indonesia: A Preliminary Outline with Particular Reference to Applicable Law', in H. Fox, ed., *Joint Development of Offshore Oil and Gas*, Vol. II, (London, The British Institute of International & Comparative Law 1990) pp. 128-140, at pp. 129-130.

45. This is a line drawn on maritime charts that traces every point of a specified ocean water depth.

46. See *North Sea Continental Shelf* cases (1969) *ICJ Rep.* p. 3, at paras. 19 and 43, where the principle of natural prolongation as the legal basis for both the continental shelf regime itself, and the extent of its outer limits, was elaborated. For a recent examination of the relationship between natural prolongation and the delimitation of maritime boundaries, see M. Zahraa, 'Natural Prolongation and Delimitation of Maritime Boundaries', VII *FYBIL* (1996) pp. 378-403.

47. The use of the Timor Trough or Trench as a relevant circumstance to be taken into account in any continental shelf delimitation between East Timor and Australia based on the natural prolongation principle had been noted by Brown. See E.D. Brown, 'The Anglo-French Continental Shelf Case', 16 *San Diego LR* (1979) p. 461, at p. 477, as cited in Zahraa, loc. cit. n. 46, at pp. 381-382, n. 24

(LOSC)[48] and affirmed by more recent international maritime boundary delimitation cases.[49] The northern and southern limits of Area A in the Zone of Co-operation therefore reflect the different legal criteria justifying each of the two states' overlapping continental shelf claims.

The Zone of Co-operation is divided into three areas: A, B, and C, which are subject to three different jurisdictional frameworks.[50] Areas B and C are situated nearest to the Australian and Indonesian coastlines, respectively. These two Areas are subject to the jurisdiction of the Party most proximate to them. Thus, in Area B, Australian jurisdiction and laws prevail, subject to the provision of 10% of gross tax revenues from petroleum resource exploitation in this Area to Indonesia.[51] A similar arrangement occurred in respect of tax revenues from the exploitation of Area C, by the Indonesians to the Australians.[52] Finally Area A, which lies in between the other two Areas, is subject to a truly joint development arrangement, incorporating joint control and revenue sharing.[53] Petroleum resource exploration and exploitation in this area is administered by a Ministerial Council[54] and Joint Development Authority[55] on the basis of production-sharing contracts.[56]

The sophisticated nature of the treaty is evident from the complex institutional framework laid down for the joint development of petroleum resources in Area A. In this sense the Timor Gap treaty is much more than simply a zonal maritime boundary delimitation exercise. The treaty created a hierarchical, two-level arrangement composed of a Ministerial Council and a Joint Authority.[57] The Ministerial Council has the over-

---

48. Art. 76(1) of this Convention provides that 'The continental shelf of a coastal state comprises the sea-bed and subsoil of the submarine areas that extend beyond its territorial sea throughout the natural prolongation of its land territory to the outer edge of the continental margin, or to a distance of 200 nautical miles from the baselines from which the breadth of the territorial sea is measured where the outer edge of the continental margin does not extend up to that distance.'

49. See *Continental Shelf* case (*Libya* v. *Tunisia*) *ICJ Rep.* (1982) p. 18, where the Court held that natural prolongation was not the only important criteria to be considered when establishing the appropriate continental shelf boundary; and *Continental Shelf* case (*Libya* v. *Malta*) *ICJ Rep.* (1985) p. 13, at p. 35, where the Court further marginalised natural prolongation as a relevant criterion in all cases within the 200-nautical mile limit.

50. Art. 2 of the 1989 Timor Gap treaty, op. cit. n. 3.

51. Ibid., Art. 4(1).

52. Ibid., Art. 4(2).

53. Ibid., Art. 2(2)(a) and 3.

54. Ibid., Part III, Arts. 5 and 6.

55. Ibid., Part IV, Arts. 7-11.

56. Ibid. Based on a model production-sharing contract in Annex C.

57. Unlike the Malaysia-Thailand Joint Authority, for example, which ostensibly at least retains control over all aspects of policy and decision-making for the exploration and exploitation of the non-living natural resources in the Joint Development Area. See Art. 3(2) of the 1979 Memorandum of Understanding and Art. 7(1) of the 1990 Agreement on the Constitution of the Joint Authority. For analysis of this issue, see D.M. Ong, 'The 1979 and 1990 Malaysia-Thailand Joint Development Agreements: A Model for International Legal Co-operation in Common Offshore Petroleum Deposits?', 14 *International Journal of Marine and Coastal Law* (1999) pp. 207-246, at p. 233.

all responsibility for petroleum-related activities in Area A of the Zone of Co-operation.[58] It is therefore the principal policy-making body. The Joint Authority is subordinate to the Ministerial Council, and is responsible to the Council for the day-to-day management of the petroleum activities in Area A.[59] Part III established a Ministerial Council (hereinafter MC) for the Zone of Co-operation,[60] consisting of an equal number of Ministers designated by each Party,[61] meeting annually or as often as required,[62] alternately in Indonesia or Australia and chaired alternately by a Minister nominated by each Party.[63] Decisions of the Council shall be taken by consensus and it may establish procedures for taking decisions out of session.[64]

The Ministerial Council (MC) has overall responsibility for all matters relating to the development of the petroleum resources in Area A of the Zone of Co-operation.[65] Its functions include, *inter alia,* giving directions to the Joint Authority (hereinafter JA); amending the Petroleum Mining Code to facilitate petroleum development in Area A; modifying the Model Production Sharing Contract (hereinafter MPSC); approving the agreement, termination, and variation of production sharing contracts between the JA and firms; approving JA petroleum sales; approving the distribution of revenues from production sharing contracts in Area A between Australia and Indonesia; settling disputes in the JA through consultation; approving rules, regulations and procedures for the effective functioning of the JA, including staff regulations; reviewing the treaty operation and making recommendations to the Parties that the Council considers necessary for Treaty amendment; appointing the Executive Directors of the JA; inspecting and auditing the JA's accounts; considering and adopting the annual report of the JA; and finally, reviewing distribution among Indonesia, Australia and third countries, of expenditure on petroleum operations in Area A.[66] The MC shall also ensure optimum commercial utilization of Area A's petroleum resources consistent with good oilfield and sound environmental practice.[67]

Part IV of the treaty established a Joint Authority (JA)[68] that has juridical personality and such legal capacities under the two Parties' laws as necessary to exercise its powers and perform its functions, in particular capacity to contract, acquire and dispose property, to institute and be party to legal proceedings.[69] The JA is responsible to the Ministerial Council (MC).[70] The Joint Authority shall consist of equal numbers

58. Art. 6 of the Timor Gap treaty, op. cit. n. 3.
59. Ibid., Arts. 7(3) and (8).
60. Ibid., Art. 5(1).
61. Ibid., Art. 5(2).
62. Ibid., Art. 5(3).
63. Ibid., Art. 5(4).
64. Ibid., Art. 5(5).
65. Ibid., Art. 6(1).
66. Ibid., Art. 6(1)(a)-(r).
67. Ibid., Art. 6(2).
68. Ibid., Art. 7(1).
69. Ibid., Art. 7(2)
70. Ibid., Art. 7(3).

of Executive Directors appointed by the MC, nominated by each Party;[71] three Directorates, responsible to the executive Directors: a Technical Directorate, a Financial Directorate, and a Legal Directorate,[72] as well as a Corporate Services Directorate.[73] Of the four Directors heading the Directorates, the Executive Directors shall appoint two from each Party.[74] The Executive Directors and the four Directors shall constitute the Executive Board.[75] The Executive Directors and personnel of the JA shall have no financial interest in any activity relating to exploration for and exploitation of petroleum resources in Area A.[76] Decisions of the JA Executive Directors shall be reached by consensus, failing this by reference to the MC.[77] The Joint Authority has its head office in Jakarta and an office in Australia, each of which shall be headed by an Executive Director.[78]

The Joint Authority, subject to directions from the MC, is responsible for the management of petroleum exploration and exploitation activities in area A, in accordance with the treaty, the Petroleum Mining Code and production sharing contracts (PSCs).[79] These management functions include, *inter alia*, dividing area A into contract areas, commissioning environmental investigations before prior to contract areas being advertised and making recommendations to the MC on production-sharing contract applications; entering into production sharing contracts with companies, subject to MC approval, and supervising the contractors pursuant to the requirements of the Petroleum Mining Code; terminating and transferring contractors; collecting and with the approval of the MC distributing the proceeds of the JA's share of the petroleum production from contracts awarded in Area A between the two Parties; preparing annual accounts of the JA for submission to the MC; controlling movements into, within and out of Area A by vessels, aircraft, structures and other petroleum exploration and extraction equipment and, subject to Article 23, authorising the entry of workers.[80] The Joint Authority also establishes safety zones; issues regulations under the Petroleum Mining Code on all matters related to the supervision and control of health and safety, environmental protection and work practices; makes recommendations to MC to amend the PSCs; requests action by the Parties for search and rescue and anti-terrorist operations in Area A; requests assistance with pollution prevention measures from the Parties; prepares annual reports to the MC; with the approval of the MC, varies the terms of the PSCs; with the approval of the MC, markets the petroleum produced; inspects and audits the contractors' accounts; and performs any other functions as may be conferred on it by the MC.[81]

---

71. Ibid., Art. 9(1)(a).
72. Ibid., Art. 9(1)(b)(i)-(iii).
73. Ibid., Art. 9(1)(c).
74. Ibid., Art. 9(2)
75. Ibid., Art. 9(4).
76. Ibid., Art. 9(5).
77. Ibid., Art. 7(4).
78. Ibid., Art. 7(5).
79. Ibid., Art . 8.
80. Ibid., Art. 8(a)-(h).
81. Ibid., Art. 8(i)-(u).

It should be noted that the Australia-Indonesia Joint Authority is only responsible for the development of the *petroleum* resources in Area A under Article 8 of the Timor Gap treaty.[82] This limitation to the regulation of activities pertaining only to petroleum resources has certain implications for the obligations of each Party should other non-hydrocarbon minerals be found within the Zone. It is arguable that the exploitation of such minerals will be outside the jurisdictional and operational ambit of this Treaty. Therefore, should a similar kind of dispute occur with regard to a non-hydrocarbon type mineral deposit situated within the Zone of Co-operation, the respective governments might find themselves needing to negotiate another co-operative agreement to jointly exploit this non-hydrocarbon deposit.

The Joint Authority has juridical personality and more particularly, a contractual capacity for the performance of its functions.[83] The most important contractual function the Joint Authority has performed relates to entering production-sharing contracts (PSCs) with corporations for the extraction of petroleum. In this, however, the Joint Authority is subject to at least two constraints: First, it can only enter such contracts subject to the Ministerial Council's approval.[84] Second, the production-sharing contracts for Area A have been formalised and annexed to the Treaty; any variation of their provisions can again only be made subject to the approval of the Ministerial Council.[85]

In Area A, the Parties shall also co-operate to prevent and minimise pollution of the marine environment arising from the exploration and exploitation of petroleum, in particular by providing assistance to the JA as may be requested pursuant to Article 8(m) and where pollution in Area A spreads beyond it.[86] Pursuant to Article 8(j), the JA shall issue regulations for marine environmental protection in Area A and establish an oil spill contingency plan.[87] Contractors shall be liable for damage or expenses incurred as a result of marine environmental pollution arising out of petroleum operations in Area A in accordance with contractual arrangements with the Joint Authority and the law of the state in which a claim in respect of such damage or expenses is brought.[88]

In the exercise of criminal jurisdiction, a national or permanent resident of a state Party shall be subject to the criminal law of that state for acts or omissions in Area A connected with or arising out of the exploration and exploitation of petroleum resour-

82. Again in contrast with the Malaysia-Thailand Joint Authority which also has control over the other non-living resources aside from merely petroleum. See Arts. 3(2) and 3(4) of the Memorandum of Understanding; and ibid., Art. 7 of the 1990 Agreement on the Constitution of the Joint Authority.

83. Under Art. 7(2) of the Treaty, op. cit. n. 3.

84. Ibid., Art. 8(b).

85. Ibid., Art. 8(o). Annex C to the Treaty contains the Model Production Sharing Contract between the Joint Authority and contractors on the basis of which production sharing contracts for Area A are to be included concluded. Under Art. 1(o), Annexes A, B, C, and D are included within the meaning of the 'Treaty'.

86. Ibid., Art. 18(1)(a) & (b).

87. Ibid., Art. 18(2).

88. Ibid., Art. 19.

ces, provided that a permanent resident of one state Party who is a national of the other Party shall be subject to the criminal law of the latter state.[89] A national of a third state, not being permanent resident of either Party, shall be subject to the criminal law of both state Parties in respect of acts or omissions in Area A, subject to a double-jeopardy clause.[90] In such a case the two Parties shall consult each other as to which criminal law is to be applied, taking into account the nationality of the victim and the interests of the state Party most affected by the alleged offence.[91] All the foregoing provisions are subject to the rule that the criminal law of the flag state shall apply in relation to acts or omissions on board vessels including seismic or drill vessels in, or aircraft in flight over, Area A.[92]

The Parties shall assist and co-operate, through agreements if appropriate, for the purposes of criminal law enforcement, including the obtaining of evidence and information.[93] They also recognise the interest of the other Party where the alleged victim is a national of the other Party and shall keep this Party informed to the extent permitted by the law. The Parties may arrange for officials of one Party to assist in enforcing the criminal law of the other Party. Where such assistance involves detention of a person who under Article 27(1) is subject to the jurisdiction of the other Party, then such detention can only continue until it is practicable to hand the person over to the relevant officials of that other Party.[94]

Claims for damages or restitution of expenses as a result of activities in Area A can be brought in the state Party that has or whose nationals or permanent residents have suffered the damage or incurred the expense. The court in which the action is brought shall apply the law and regulations of that state.[95] The law applicable to production sharing contracts shall be specified in that contract.[96] Other legal areas covered by provisions on the applicable laws include: customs, migration and quarantine laws;[97] employment;[98] health and safety for workers[99]; petroleum industry vessels;[100] and taxation law.[101]

Any dispute arising between the Parties concerning the interpretation or application of this treaty shall be resolved by consultation or negotiation between the Parties.[102] Each production sharing contract entered into by the Joint Authority contains provisions to the effect that any dispute concerning the interpretation or application

89. Ibid., Art. 27(1).
90. Ibid., Art. 27(2)(a).
91. Ibid., Art. 27(2)(b).
92. Ibid., Art. 27(3).
93. Ibid., Art. 27(4)(a).
94. Ibid., Art. 27(5).
95. Ibid., Art. 28.
96. Ibid., Art. 22.
97. Ibid., Art. 23.
98. Ibid., Art. 24.
99. Ibid., Art. 25
100. Ibid., Art. 26.
101. Ibid., Art. 29.
102. Ibid., Art. 30(1).

of such contract shall be submitted to a specified form of binding commercial arbitration. The Parties facilitate the enforcement in their respective courts of arbitral awards made pursuant to such arbitration.[103]

In the event that the treaty ceases to be in force due to the conclusion of a permanent continental shelf boundary and there are in existence immediately prior to this date production sharing contracts with the Joint Authority, these contracts shall continue to apply to each state Party or some other person nominated by the state Party, in place of the JA, in so far as the contract is to be performed in the territorial jurisdiction of each state Party, having regard to the agreed boundary delimitation. In such cases, each Party shall apply to contractors within its territorial jurisdiction a regime no more onerous than that set out in this Treaty and the relevant production sharing contract.[104] The two Parties, namely Australia and Indonesia, made arrangements to give effect to the provisions of Article 34(1) above, at the time of concluding the permanent boundary delimitation. The two state Parties had promulgated the necessary enabling domestic legislation and given the written notifications under Article 32 of the Treaty, 30 days after which the Treaty entered into force on 9 February 1991. This has obvious legal implications should the Timor Gap treaty be repudiated under any of the grounds discussed below. (Section 3) For example, the Australian enabling legislation would also need to be repealed in order to prevent oil and gas companies attempting to exercise their current right to be allowed to operate under a legal regime no more onerous than they are now.

As Onorato and Valencia note, progress in the implementation of the treaty in the ten years or so since its adoption has been good.[105] There are twelve production-sharing contracts (PSCs) currently operating in Area A of the Zone of Co-operation. The first oil discoveries in Area A were made in 1994 and the first gas condensate discoveries in 1995. Subsequent discoveries were made in the 1996-1998 period. There are now seven oil and seven gas condensate discoveries in Area A. Currently under production are the Elang, Kakatua and Kakatua North oil fields. However, the biggest find is the Bayu-Undan field, discovered in 1995 and projected to go on-stream in late 2003/2004.[106]

103. Ibid., Art. 30(2).

104. Ibid., Art. 34(1)(a) and (b).

105. Onorato and Valencia, op. cit. n. 23, at p. 73.

106. The Bayu-Undan project involves two phased developments of the field's natural gas and gas liquids resources. The first phase of development in October 1999, comprising an initial expenditure of approximately US $ 1.4 billion on the liquids stripping/lean gas recycle phase makes it the largest investment proposed to date in the Timor Sea.
The Bayu-Undan field is located in the central Timor Sea about 500 km north west of Darwin Australia and about 250 km south of Suai in East Timor. The field straddles two production sharing contract (PSC) areas (91-12 and 91-13) in Area A of the Timor Gap Zone of Cooperation (ZOCA) just north of the EEZ boundary and median line between Australia and East Timor. The Bayu-Undan field is a single gas/condensate resource with recoverable reserves of approximately 400 million barrels of liquids (condensate and LPG) and 3.4 tcf of gas. The field life is estimated to be 25 years, with first liquids production planned to commence in late 2003.

3. THE LEGAL STATUS OF THE TIMOR GAP TREATY FOLLOWING THE UN REFERENDUM

This Section will consider the different legal bases that would allow a new East Timor state to deny any legal obligations it may have in respect of the treaty.[107] The following discussion will consider at least three alternative modes of analysis that can be utilised to determine whether the Timor Gap treaty has continuing legal effect.[108]

First, it is argued that the Indonesian invasion and consequent annexation of East Timor constituted an illegal act under international law that invalidates any diplomatic acts between Indonesia and third states (apart from Portugal) regarding the East Timorese population and its resources. In particular, the 1989 Timor Gap treaty agreed with Australia was in violation of the principle of self-determination for the East Timorese people and consequently their right of permanent sovereignty over their natural resources. The invalidity of the Timor Gap treaty thus negates any rights and obligations under this treaty in respect of a new East Timor state and Australia.

Second, the international law of state succession may in any case allow a new East Timor state to renounce the treaty, should it so wish. This argument raises complex issues that need to be tackled individually before a definitive answer can be arrived at. These include questions relating to whether maritime boundary treaties generally, and continental shelf boundary treaties in particular, are a species of territorial boundary treaty that may form an exception to the generally applicable 'clean slate' rule for state succession; whether such boundary treaties that are specified to apply only for a prescribed time period also qualify as an exception to the 'clean slate' rule; and whether the joint development treaties can be considered as falling within the category of a territorial boundary treaty for these purposes.

Finally, should it be the case that the treaty is deemed to apply to a new East Timor state, is it nevertheless possible for this new entity to argue that the *rebus sic stantibus* rule applies? According to this rule, a fundamental change of circumstances relating to the application of the treaty would result in its termination.[109]

A second phase downstream development to commercialise the field's valuable gas reserves is also planned and concepts for this are the subject of separate studies and approvals by the co-venture companies and government authorities.

107. For a discussion of the traditional methods by which a treaty may be discharged, see J.L. Brierly, *The Law of Nations: An Introduction to the International Law of Peace*, Sir Humphrey Waldock, ed., 6th edn. (Oxford, Oxford University Press 1963) pp. 327-345.

108. This is notwithstanding Australia's own admission in its submissions before the ICJ in the *East Timor* case, op. cit. n. 15, that the Timor Gap treaty would not bind an independent East Timor. Indeed the Australian government has reportedly given its official approval to the 'clean slate' approach for a succeeding East Timor state in the Attorney-General's submission to the East Timor Senate. Enquiry on 19 April 1999.

109. See A. Vamvoukos, *Termination of Treaties in International Law: The Doctrines of Rebus Sic Stantibus and Desuetude* (Oxford, Clarendon Press 1985) at p. 201.

3.1 Can the Timor Gap Treaty be declared invalid?

We begin this analysis of the legal status of the Timor Gap treaty by asking whether a future East Timor state can claim that the adoption of the Timor Gap treaty was an illegal act, thereby rendering the treaty invalid. Article 69 of the Vienna Convention on the Law of Treaties, 1969 (hereinafter, VCLT, 1969) provides that where the invalidity of the treaty is established, the treaty is void and its provisions have no legal effect. This provision effectively applies the principle that illegal acts cannot result in legally-binding instruments. General support for this view can be derived from the doctrinal literature. McNair, for example, includes the incompatibility or conflict with rules of international law within a list of possible factors that may render a treaty invalid.[110] According to Linehan, international law has always recognised that there are a number of grounds on which a treaty may be held invalid and the Vienna Convention identifies at least eight grounds for such invalidity.[111] Should a claim of invalidity on any of these grounds be upheld in respect of the Timor Gap treaty, the consequences for its continued operation would be dire. As Nahlik notes, the claim of invalidity undermines the very roots of a treaty: 'It compels attention to the moment of the conclusion of the treaty, for at that very moment, something already must have existed which stood in the way of the validity of the treaty.'[112]

The focus here is on the widespread acceptance of the *jus cogens* doctrine as a legitimate reason for rendering a treaty invalid. Article 53 of the VCLT, 1969 provides that a treaty is void if it conflicts with a peremptory norm of general international law *(jus cogens)* at the time of its conclusion. It is arguable that the subsequent doctrinal focus on *jus cogens* has narrowed perspectives to the extent that many publicists now contemplate only breaches of *jus cogens* norms as automatically invalidating treaties, thereby implicitly denying the traditional conception of a possibly wider category of international violations rendering treaties invalid.

On the other hand, present doctrine can be viewed as merely representing a refinement, rather than a limitation, of the possible factors invalidating a treaty. According to McNair, certain customary rules of international law and conventional rules such as the UN Charter stand in a higher category because they are necessary to protect the public interests of international society and are therefore universally applicable.[113] In fact, this is merely an argument for the peremptory nature of such rules, and thereby

110. See A.D. McNair, *The Law of Treaties* (Oxford, Oxford University Press 1961) at pp. 206, and 214-224. He notes that a treaty can be invalidated due to its incompatibility with (a) a rule of customary international law; (b) a rule of general conventional international law; (c) the Charter of the UN; and (d) specific obligations created by other treaties. (at p. 214) This approach has been cited with approval by Sir Ian Sinclair, *The Vienna Convention on the Law of Treaties*, 2nd edn. (Manchester, Manchester University Press 1984) at p. 162.

111. J. Linehan, 'The Law of Treaties', in S. Blay, R. Piotrowicz and B.M. Tsamenyi, eds., *Public International Law: An Australian Perspective* (Melbourne, Oxford University Press 1997) at p. 105.

112. S.E. Nahlik, 'The Grounds for Invalidity and Termination of Treaties', 65 *AJIL* (1971) pp. 736-756, at p. 738.

113. McNair, op. cit. n. 110, at pp. 214-217.

easily subsumed within the relatively new *jus cogens* category that the 1969 Vienna Convention also enshrined in Article 64 as invalidating conflicting treaties. Aust notes that 'there is no agreement on the criteria for identifying which norms of general international law have a peremptory character. Whether a norm of general international law has it depends on the particular nature of the subject matter.'[114] Therefore, should *jus cogens* norms be defined restrictively, then a treaty that conflicts with certain international obligations regarded in the past as invalidating the treaty will not now do so. However, Linehan observes that among the norms that attract clearest support as constituting *jus cogens* are the prohibitions against the use of force and the right to self-determination.[115] In the present context, violations of both these norms have been strongly argued to deny the legality of the Timor Gap treaty.

Sforza, for example, observes that the Timor Gap treaty represents but one instance of repeated violations by Indonesia of the territorial sovereignty of East Timor through its use of armed force and repression of the indigenous East Timor population.[116] Indonesia's actions should thus be considered illegal under international law. This echoes arguments put forward by Portugal in its claim before the International Court of Justice in the *East Timor* case.[117] However, in the *East Timor* case, the Court itself was less convinced by these arguments as it refused to rule on the validity of the Timor Gap treaty in the case before it. The Court noted that 'the argument of Portugal under consideration rests on the premise the United Nations Resolutions and in particular those of the Security Council, can be read as imposing an obligation on states not to recognize any authority on the part of Indonesia over the Territory and, where the latter is concerned, to deal only with Portugal. *The Court is not persuaded, however, that the relevant resolutions went so far.*'[118] (emphasis added) As Simpson correctly points out, 'Portugal's difficulties in the case lay not in showing that there had been repeated breaches of international law but rather in demonstrating that these breaches were Australia's responsibility.'[119] In its Judgment, the Court neither accepted that Indonesia had officially annexed East Timor, nor that Portugal remained the

---

114. A. Aust, *Modern Treaty Law and Practice* (Cambridge, Cambridge University Press 2000) at p. 257.

115. Linehan, op. cit. n. 111, at p. 107.

116. M. Sforza, 'The Timor Gap Dispute: The Validity of the Timor Gap Treaty, Self-Determination, and Decolonization', Note, 22 *Suffolk Transn. LR* (1999) pp. 481-528, at pp. 525-526.

117. Portugal maintained that 'Australia, in negotiating and concluding the 1989 Treaty, in initiating performance of the Treaty, in taking internal legislative measures for its application, and in continuing to negotiate with Indonesia, has acted unlawfully, in that it has infringed the rights of the people of East Timor to self-determination and to permanent sovereignty over its natural resources, infringed the rights of Portugal as the administering Power, and contravened Security Council Resolutions 384 and 389.' See *Case Concerning East Timor (Portugal* v. *Australia) ICJ Rep.* (1995) *supra* n. 15, para. 19. at p. 98.

118. See *East Timor* case, Judgment, op. cit. n. 15, at p. 103, para. 31.

119. See G. Simpson, 'A Stone in Each Shoe: Australian Foreign Policy and East Timor', in Pinto Leite, ed., op. cit. n. 13, at pp. 143-158, at p. 145.

administering Power over the territory.[120] Instead the Court suggested that a novel situation had emerged: East Timor remained a non-self-governing territory with a continuing right of self-determination under Chapter XI of the UN Charter,[121] but it was controlled by a non-traditional administering power, namely Indonesia. The legal implications of this finding are difficult to entangle but they do suggest that the invalidity of the treaty should not be presumed simply because of the alleged illegality of the Indonesian annexation of East Timor. Moreover, the lack of formal protests against the Timor Gap treaty by third states (apart from Portugal) arguably reveals at least a measure of acquiescence on the part of the international community in this exercise.

Balanced against the Court's equivocal view, however, are the persuasive arguments contained in Judge Weeramantry's dissenting opinion.[122] Judge Weeramantry considered the legal force of the relevant UN Security Council and General Assembly Resolutions in line with each of Australia's objections to Portugal's contentions above. First, in respect of Australia's contention that the progressively lessening vote in favour of the General Assembly Resolutions showed that those resolutions were of a diminishing level of authority, he argues that once a General Assembly Resolution has been duly passed, it commands recognition and respect, irrespective of its political history or the voting strength it reflects.[123] Second, as to whether Security Council and General Assembly Resolutions can lapse through desuetude, he observes that once these resolutions are duly passed they do not have to be repeated to retain their validity. It is to be presumed that they would retain their validity until duly revoked or superceded by some later resolution.[124] Third, the notion that these resolutions were nullified by supervening events was also denied by Judge Weeramantry, who suggested that it would be up to the relevant UN bodies, namely the Security Council and General Assembly, to decide whether the situation was altered and act accordingly.[125] Weeramantry thus concludes that Australia's participation in the Timor Gap treaty was incompatible with her obligation to respect and indeed uphold the right of self-determination of the East Timorese people by abstaining from such action.[126] It is important to note however, that this conclusion as to the incompatibility of Australia's actions with international law does not necessarily render the treaty itself void under international law.

This brings us to the final and most important question in this section: whether the Timor Gap treaty constituted a denial of the East Timorese right of self-determination and therefore provides a legitimate justification for its repudiation by a newly independent East Timor. Weeramantry is in no doubt as to the central importance of the

120. As Antonopoulos notes, 'the Court declined to accept as facts certain United Nations General Assembly and Security Council resolutions which affirmed Portugal's status as the administering power of East Timor.' Antonopoulos, op. cit. n. 18, at p. 76.

121. See *East Timor case,* Judgment, op.cit. n. 15, at p. 103, para. 31.

122. See Dissenting Opinion of Judge Weeramantry, ibid., pp. 139-223, at pp. 189-190.

123. Ibid., at pp. 189-190.

124. Ibid., at p. 190.

125. Ibid., at pp. 190-191.

126. Ibid., at pp. 204 and 222.

self-determination principle as a norm of international law and a basic element of the UN Charter.[127] It is interesting to note that the Court also found Portugal's assertion that the right of peoples to self-determination was *erga omnes,* irreproachable.[128] No less a doctrinal authority than Brownlie suggests that this principle is now *jus cogens,*[129] although he does not elaborate upon the legal effects of this appellation.

Unfortunately, the more important question as to whether the treaty is invalidated on the ground that it violates an *jus cogens* obligation, by violating the East Timorese people's right to self-determination and abusing their permanent sovereignty over their natural resources, was not deliberated upon by the Court itself. Even Judge Weeramantry does not explicitly address this question in his dissenting opinion. However, it is this question that is central to the continuing legality (or otherwise) of the treaty when a new East Timor state eventually emerges. In the absence of a definitive Court ruling or any other equivalent legal authority, no conclusion can be reached on this issue beyond asserting that the 1989 treaty was negotiated and agreed in apparent breach of the East Timorese right of self-determination. As this right is now asserted as *jus cogens*, this ostensibly renders the 1989 treaty invalid according to Article 53 of the VCLT, 1969. However, the legal analysis cannot conclude at this point. The difficulty here lies not so much in the legal *status* of the self-determination principle but its legal *effect* in relation to other well-known principles of international law.

In particular, any assertion that the Timor Gap treaty is invalidated pits the principles of self-determination and permanent sovereignty over natural resources against longer standing principles such as the *uti possidetis* rule providing for the sanctity of territorial boundaries at the moment when independence is achieved. In the *Frontier Dispute (Burkina Faso* v. *Mali)* case, an ICJ Chamber held that the *uti possidetis* principle was a general principle of international law that is logically connected with the phenomenon of independence, wherever it occurs.[130] Cassese examines this very issue and concludes that here the self-determination principle is 'trumped' by the overriding legal requirement for the stability of territorial boundaries at the moment of a new state's independence, as provided by the *uti possidetis* rule.[131]

Examining this question in the African context, Klabbers and Lefeber conclude that the conflict between *uti possidetis* and self-determination exemplifies the tension inherent in contemporary international law between the positivist perspective favour-

---

127. Ibid., at p. 194.

128. *East Timor* case, Judgment, ibid, at p. 102, para. 29

129. See I. Brownlie, *Principles of Public International Law,* 5th edn. (Oxford, Oxford University Press 1998) at p. 515, citing the Separate Opinion of Judge Amoun in the *Barcelona Traction* case (Second Phase) *ICJ Rep.* (1970) at p. 304, as authority for the right of self-determination.

130. Case *Concerning the Frontier Dispute* (*Burkina Faso* v. *Republic of Mali*), ICJ Chamber Judgment, *ICJ Rep.* (1986) at para. 20, p. 565.

131. Cassese, op. cit. n. 10, at p. 193.

ing the former principle and the natural law view stressing the latter.[132] As Grant notes, African 'boundaries were in many instances set without regard to the political, ethnic, linguistic, or religious affinities of the indigenous population; yet, in deference to the principle of *uti possidetis juris*, virtually every boundary set by the European colonial powers was preserved as the boundary of an independent state after decolonization.'[133] The ICJ Chamber in the *Frontier Dispute* case justified this African state practice in the following manner: 'The essential requirement of stability in order to survive, to develop and gradually consolidate their independence in all fields, has induced African states judiciously to consent to the respecting of colonial frontiers, and to take account of it in the interpretation of the principle of self-determination of peoples.'[134]

However, unlike in Africa, where the land boundaries are clearly territorial in nature and the problem lies with the uncertain definition of groups of 'peoples' in respect of their respective rights of self-determination, the problem in East Timor at least partly resides in the uncertainty surrounding the territorial nature of maritime boundaries, as we shall see below in Section 3.2. In other words, does the *uti possidetis* principle apply to the unique legal regime established by the Timor Gap treaty for the delimitation and joint development of the petroleum resources in this area?

On the other hand, the possible application of the permanent sovereignty over natural resources principle as a corollary to the exercise of the right of self-determination[135] is somewhat easier to distinguish in the *East Timor* case. Here, it should first be noted that it is now generally accepted under international law that every state in the world exercises permanent sovereignty over its natural resources. This right is embodied in the 1962 UN General Assembly Resolution on Permanent Sovereignty over Natural Resources,[136] and according to Harris, accepted in a number of awards as reflecting customary international law.[137] It was later reaffirmed in Article 2(1) of the Charter of Economic Rights and Duties of States, 1974.[138] These instruments provide generally that the natural resources of a state, both terrestrial and marine, within its international boundaries, belong exclusively to that state, in the sense that such resources can only be exploited by, or for the benefit of, the state concerned.

Chowdhury takes the view that since the permanent sovereignty principle arises from the right of self-determination, which has the status of *jus cogens*, the former

132. J. Klabbers and R. Lefeber, 'Africa: Lost between Self-Determination and *Uti Possidetis*', in C. Brölmann, R. Lefeber and M. Zieck, eds., *Peoples and Minorities in International Law* (Dordrecht, Martinus Nijhoff 1993) pp. 37-76, at p. 76.

133. Grant, loc. cit. n. 5, at p. 281.

134. *Frontier Dispute* case, *ICJ Rep.* (1986) op. cit. n. 15, at para. 25, p. 567.

135. For an account of the evolution of this principle under international law and its relationship with other principles such as self-determination and sustainable development, see Schrijver, op. cit. n. 26, especially at pp. 36-142.

136. UNGA Res. 1803/XVII, adopted by 87 votes to 2, with 12 abstentions.

137. D.J. Harris, *Cases and Material on International Law*, 5th edn. (London, Sweet & Maxwell 1998) at p. 549.

138. UNGA Res. 3281/XXIX (1975) adopted by 120 votes to six, with 10 abstentions.

principle should enjoy the same status under international law.[139] A Declaration of the International Law Association (ILA) confirms the principle of permanent sovereignty over natural resources as a fundamental principle of customary international law, emanating as it does from the *jus cogens* principle of self-determination.[140] However, as Hossain notes, the important question relates to whether the right is inalienable, such that even if the predecessor state entered into a treaty modifying its sovereign rights, this would not affect the permanent nature of this right.[141]

Chowdhury asserts that the right to permanent sovereignty is not defeasible by treaty, but this does not preclude a state from agreeing to specific and temporary limitations of its exercise of the right to permanent sovereignty over its natural resources. This latter conclusion is accepted by the Dutch branch of the ILA in its study of state practice on the issue,[142] and is reflected in Arbitrator Dupuy's award in the *Texaco* v. *Libya* arbitration.[143] In that case, Dupuy held that a state can by agreement accept a partial limitation of the exercise of its sovereignty in respect of certain resources in particular areas for a specific period of time.

It is submitted here that this is exactly what is provided for in the 1989 Timor Gap treaty. Thus, the continuing applicability of this treaty cannot be undermined simply on the basis that it would represent an allegedly undue initial constraint to the right of a newly independent East Timor state to permanent sovereignty over its natural resources in the Gap area. This is because Australia too has a right to assert her permanent sovereignty over natural resources in the continental shelf appertaining to her coastline. As Judge Oda notes in his separate opinion in the *East Timor* case, 'Australia's original title to the continental shelf in the "Timor Gap" cannot be challenged at all by any state or by any people. ... The continental shelves to which both states (i.e., Australia and either one of Portugal/Indonesia/East Timor) are thus entitled to overlap somewhere in the middle of the "Timor Gap".'[144]

The permanent sovereignty principle also implicitly presumes the existence of stable territorial boundaries within which this principle can be applied. However, in a situation like the present one, where the location of the boundary itself is in dispute due to the shared nature of the petroleum resource, the application of this principle as between each state is necessarily also uncertain. Indeed, the principle can equally be invoked by both parties to the dispute, namely a new East Timor state and Australia, as

139. S.R. Chowdhury, 'Permanent sovereignty over natural resources', in K. Hossain and S.R. Chowdhury, eds., *Permanent Sovereignty over Natural Resources: Principles and Practice*, (London, Frances Pinter 1984) pp. 1-41.

140. See 1986 Seoul Declaration of the ILA on the Progressive Development of Principles of International Law relating to a New International Economic Order, in Report of the 62nd Conference (London, ILA 1986) at p. 2. Also published in 33 *NILR* (1986) pp. 328-333.

141. See K. Hossain, 'Introduction', in Hossain and Chowdhury, eds., op. cit. n. 139, at p. xiv, citing Jimenez de Arechaga, *Recueil des cours* (1978) at p. 297.

142. See P. Peters, N.J. Schrijver and P.J.I.M. de Waart, 'Permanent sovereignty, foreign investment and state practice', in Hossain and Chowdhury, eds., op. cit. n. 139, at pp. 88-143.

143. *Texaco* v. *Libya* (1979) 53 *ILR* (1979) 389.

144. See *East Timor* case, *ICJ Rep.* (1995) *supra* n. 15, at pp. 107-118, at para. 4, at p. 110.

each of them can legitimately consider that the principle applies on their behalf in the disputed continental shelf area concerned.

Confirmation that the right of permanent sovereignty is not overriding in favour of any one state but correlative between interested states in the case of shared or trans-boundary natural resources is evidenced by the fact that Article 3 of the 1974 Charter of Economic Rights and Duties of States provides for co-operation and prior consultations to achieve the optimum utilization of such resources. Thus, the application of the permanent sovereignty principle to the present dispute does not bring us closer to its resolution in favour of either party. Instead, it reinforces the procedural requirements leading towards some form of international co-operation in the exploitation of the shared resources in question.[145]

Articles 74(3) (EEZ) and 83(3) (Continental Shelf) of the 1982 UN Convention on the Law of the Sea (CLOS) further provide that, pending EEZ/continental shelf maritime boundary delimitation, the states concerned must make every effort to enter into provisional arrangements of a practical nature. Within this context, as Schrijver notes, '(I)nternational joint development, that is the common exercise of sovereign rights by two or more states, for the purpose of exploration and exploitation of the natural resources in an agreed area, is one such provisional arrangement.'[146]

3.2 Will an independent East Timor state succeed to the Treaty?

Assuming a newly independent East Timor state eventually takes its rightful place on the international stage, the next pertinent question is the extent to which this new state is bound to respect certain obligations under international law. In the context of this essay, the obligations in question relate especially to any treaties entered into by Indonesia,[147] ostensibly on behalf of the East Timor territory she was occupying (albeit illegally) between 1975 and September 1999.[148] Chief among these will certainly be the 1989 Timor Gap treaty. Consideration of these issues necessarily requires an appraisal of the international law of state succession in relation to treaties delimiting territorial boundaries and in particular, maritime boundaries. The extent of any obligations arising from previously agreed bilateral maritime boundary delimitation treaties between the predecessor state and third states should be examined. However, the

145. See Schrijver, op. cit. n. 26, at p. 276.

146. Ibid., at p. 277.

147. Consideration of any maritime boundary treaties entered into by Portugal would also have been pertinent but in this instance is rendered superfluous by their absence.

148. When Indonesia signalled its acceptance of the result of the UN-sponsored referendum in East Timor, thereby allowing UNTAET to fulfil its mandate to administer the territory during its transition period to full independence and sovereignty.

international law on this issue is far from certain.[149] This renders its analysis necessarily speculative.

There are three main schools of thought in respect of state succession, which has been defined as a situation '(w)hen one state takes the place of another and undertakes a permanent exercise of its sovereign territorial rights or powers.'[150] These are the doctrines of universal and partial state succession, and the more recent 'clean slate' approach. The universal state succession theory provides that the complete catalogue of rights and duties involving the predecessor state continues to be applicable to any successor state.[151] The 1978 Vienna Convention on the Succession of States in respect of Treaties,[152] for example, highlights the international responsibilities undertaken by the new state over its territory in its definition of the 'succession of states'.[153] However, by the end of 1998, only fifteen states had ratified this Convention. Thus, the legal authority of the Convention itself as a definitive statement of the legal position of succeeding states under customary international law is uncertain. Mullerson, for example, notes that '[t]he two (1978 and 1983) Conventions on state succession have many clauses which pertain more to the progressive development of existing customary international law than to its codification.'[154]

It is also worth noting here the Dutch state practice in respect of this Convention. Having submitted the Convention for consent by the Dutch parliament in March 1990,[155] by December 1994 the Dutch government withdrew its bill of approval, arguing that the Convention had lost its value as codification of international law, *inter alia*, because State practice was not in accordance with the Convention rules.[156] More recently though, its entry into force has prompted Aust to note that, 'although the

149. O'Connell's view on this subject while dated is still pertinent today: 'The law relating to state succession to treaties has never been completely settled.' See D.P. O'Connell, 'Independence and Succession to Treaties', 38 *BYIL* (1962) pp. 84-180, at p. 84. Brownlie echoes this conclusion more recently when he notes that '(S)tate succession is an area of great uncertainty and controversy.' See Brownlie, op. cit. n. 129, at p. 650.

150. See A.S. Hershey, 'The Succession of States', 5 *AJIL* (1911) pp. 285-297, at p. 285.

151. See S.T. Korman, 'The 1978 Vienna Convention on Succession of States in Respect of Treaties: An Inadequate Response to the Issue of State Succession', Note, 16 *Suffolk Transn. LR* (1992) pp. 174-199, at pp. 178-179, citing Hershey, loc. cit. n. 150, at pp. 285-288. Korman and other writers have noted the failing appeal of the universal theory of state succession. Marek, for example, points out that the existence of universal succession would defeat the sharply defined notion of individual state sovereignty and identity that forms the cornerstone of modern international law. See K. Marek, *Identity and Continuity of State in Public International Law*, 2nd edn. (Geneva, Libraire Droz 1968) at p. 10.

152. Opened for signature: 23 August 1978; in force: 6 November 1996, 30 days after the deposit of its fifteenth instrument of ratification, as required by Art. 49(1) of the 1978 Convention. See *ILM* (1978) at p. 1488.

153. See Art. 2(1)(b) of the 1978 Convention.

154. See R. Müllerson, *International Law, Rights and Politics: Developments in Eastern Europe and the CIS* (London, Routledge 1994) p. 137.

155. Document NL/10 (*Bijl. Hand* II 1989/90 – 21494 (R 1385) No. 1)

156. See Doc. NL/ 48, translation in 27 *NYIL* (1996) at p. 240.

Convention is largely an example of the progressive development of international law, rather than a codification of customary law, and is not therefore a reliable guide to the rules of customary law on treaty succession, its eventual entry into force, recent practice following the end of the Cold War, and decisions of the International Court of Justice, may have now breathed new life into some of its provisions.'[157]

Partial succession on the other hand relies upon a prior determination as to whether the predecessor state's personality has survived the transition to the new state.[158] If the state's personality survived, then the successor state is said to have succeeded to the predecessor state's rights and duties.[159] The universal and partial succession arguments that certain rights and duties of the predecessor pass *ipso jure* to a successor sovereign predate the more recent 'clean slate' notion of state succession. However, they are arguably inapplicable in respect of newly independent states such as a future East Timor state. As Hershey observed nearly ninety years ago, '[t]here is even a greater modification of these principles (of universal or partial succession) in the case of a colony or province which has achieved its independence.'[160]

The question is, does the right of self-determination that justifies the independence of these new states allow them to invoke the 'clean slate' rule in respect of state succession to *all* treaties agreed on their behalf by the former colonial power. The main implication of the right of self-determination for newly independent states is the adoption of a 'clean slate' approach to such treaties. As Koskenniemi notes, '[s]elf-determination is the connecting principle that justifies the application of *tabula rasa* to new states under the 1978 Vienna Convention and, for example, in respect of the Baltic Republics after 1991.'[161]

This approach was accepted by the International Law Commission (hereinafter ILC) in its attempt to codify the international rules on state succession.[162] Indeed, the general rule applicable to newly independent states[163] on questions of state succession

157. See Aust, op. cit. n. 114, at p. 306.

158. Korman, loc. cit. n. 151, at pp. 182-183, citing Hershey, loc. cit. n. 150, at pp. 288-296. Marek too postulates that general international law admits partial succession only, although it is unclear whether she conceives of partial succession in the same way as Hershey, ibid., at p. 11.

159. Korman, loc. cit. n. 151, at pp. 182-183, citing A.R. Cowger, Jr., 'Rights and Obligations of Successor States: An Alternative Theory', Note, 17 *Case Western Reserve JIL* (1985) pp. 285-314, at p. 289.

160. Hershey, loc. cit. n. 150, at p. 289.

161. See M. Koskenniemi, 'The present state of research carried out by the English-speaking section of the Centre for Studies and Research', in Centre for Studies and Research in International Law and International Relations, *State Succession: Codification Tested Against the Facts*, (The Hague, Hague Academy of International Law 1996) at p. 133.

162. See F. Vallat, Special Rapporteur to the ILC, First Report on State Succession in respect of Treaties, Doc.A/CN.4/278. Also in *Yearbook ILC 1974* (New York, United Nations 1975) pp. 1-89, at p. 7. Doc.A/CN/SER.A/1974/Add.1 (Part One)

163. For the purposes of state succession, a 'newly independent state' is defined as a formerly dependent territory for the international relations of which the predecessor state was responsible. See Art. 2(1)(f) of the Vienna Convention on State Succession, 1978, op. cit. n. 152.

to treaty obligations adheres to the 'clean slate' approach.[164] This presumes the inapplicability of treaty obligations entered into by the predecessor state upon the succeeding state. It should be noted here that the 'clean slate' principle does not mean rejecting the continuity of all previous treaties. It merely implies that the newly independent state is entitled to choose which treaties concluded by its predecessor are to be regarded as continuing in force and which are to be considered as terminated. Hence the right of a newly independent state to re-negotiate many of the treaty obligations entered into by the predecessor state.[165] However, even this general rule now enshrined in Article 16 of the 1978 Vienna Convention on State Succession[166] is open to question.[167] As Jenks points out, 'it is not clear why, now that the rules established by multipartite legislative instruments constitute so large a part of the operative law of nations, a new state should be regarded as starting with a clean slate in respect of rules which have a conventional rather than a customary origin.'[168]

In this respect, Beemelmans has noted more recently that 'in spite of a failure to codify state succession matters, a lack of consensus among learned authors, and clear tendencies in older precedents, there seems to be an emerging consensus in recent practice suggesting that state succession should not normally lead to a disruption of legal relationships at all levels.'[169] As Brownlie observes presciently, '[l]eaving questions of state succession on one side, the principle of effectiveness dictates acceptance, for some legal purposes at least, of continuity before and after statehood is firmly established.'[170] In reality, as Craven notes, neither the universal succession thesis,

164. The classic exposition of this rule is by McNair: '[N]ewly established states which do not result from a political dismemberment and cannot fairly be said to involve political continuity with any predecessor, start with a clean slate in the matter of treaty obligations.' See McNair, op. cit. n. 110, at p. 601. Balanced against this approach is the doctrine of universal succession which can be traced all the way back to the writings of Grotius. This doctrine stipulates that a new state succeeds to the *universum jus* of their predecessor states. Their rights and obligations devolving *ipso jure* from the previous state to the new one, without exception or modification. See H. Grotius, *De Jure et Pacis Lib* pp. 315-319 (F. Kelsey transl. 1913)

165. The right to re-negotiate treaties based on the 'clean slate' approach in itself raises further issues. Chief among these is the question whether certain treaties will continue in force during the interim period between independence and the new state declaring which treaties it will succeed to. See J. Mallamud, 'Optional Succession to Treaties by Newly Independent States', Note, 63 *AJIL* (1999) pp. 782-791.

166. Art. 16 provides that: 'A newly independent state is not bound to maintain in force, or to become a party to, any treaty by reason only of the fact that at the date of the succession of states the treaty was in force in respect of the territory to which the succession of states relates.'

167. No less an authority on the subject than Professor O'Connell has argued that state practice belies the application of the 'clean slate' rule and therefore undermines the notion that the Vienna Convention codifies customary international law on this issue, see O'Connell, Reflections on the State Succession Convention', 39 *ZaöRV* (1979) pp. 725-739.

168. See C.W. Jenks, 'State Succession in respect of Law-Making Treaties', 29 *BYIL* (1952) pp. 105-144, at p. 107.

169. See H. Beemelmans, 'State Succession in International Law: Remarks on Recent Theory and State Praxis', 15 *Boston Univ. ILJ* (1997) pp. 71-123, at p. 75.

170. Brownlie, op. cit. n. 129, at p. 78, footnotes in text deleted.

nor the 'clean slate' approach to state succession is generally applicable, nor do they resolve the majority of problems thrown up by state succession.[171] Finally, as O'Connell points out succinctly, '[W]hat is striking about the state practice in respect of succession to treaties in recent years (prior to 1979) is that it is the territorially-connected treaties alone which have given rise to controversy.'[172]

Moreover, the 'clean slate' rule itself is acknowledged to contain a number of exceptions.[173] It is therefore the extent to which any of the acknowledged exceptions to this rule may be applicable in the present situation that concerns us here. Legal doctrine has evolved a distinction between 'personal' and 'real' or dispositive treaties.[174] The latter category is regarded as providing legal obligations that succeed from the predecessor state to the new state. In this respect, territorial boundary treaties are regarded as examples *par excellence* of dispositive treaties whose obligations succeed to the new state.[175] State practice on this issue is heavily in favour of the principle that boundary treaties remain unaffected by the succession of states. The *opinio juris* of states may be discerned from their oral and written comments to the ILC draft articles on state succession. This is also broadly in favour of the inclusion of boundary regimes as an exception to the general 'clean slate' rule in respect of succession to treaties.[176]

Publicists too generally accept that boundary treaties devolve upon successor states despite the change of sovereignty. As Shaw notes, 'The basic reason for the rule is accepted as that of necessity to maintain the stability and continuity of boundaries as an essential condition of international life as emphasised in the recognised principle of respect for the territorial integrity of states.'[177] Koskenniemi observes that '(c)ommunal stability and the need to prevent what the Chamber of the ICJ called 'fratricidal struggles' speak for the need of continued opposability of territorial and boundary regimes on new states.'[178]

171. M.C.R. Craven, 'The Problem of State Succession and the Identity of States under International Law', 9 *EJIL* (1998) pp. 142-162, at pp. 147-149.

172. O'Connell, loc. cit. n. 165, at p. 736.

173. As Jenks notes, 'The only clear and widely accepted exception (to the clean slate rule) being treaties creating local obligations which can be regarded as having the character of executed conveyances.' See Jenks, loc. cit. n. 168.

174. O'Connell attributes the initial distinction drawn between these two categories of treaties to Vattel. See D.P. O'Connell, *The Law of State Succession* (Cambridge, Cambridge University Press 1956) at p. 49, citing Vattel, *Le Droit des gens*, bk. II, c.xiii, para. 203, English trans. Classics of International Law Series of the Carnegie Institute, Vol. III (1916).

175. See International Law Association, Committee on State Succession to Treaties and Other Governmental Obligations, *The Effect of Independence on Treaties*, Rapporteur: D.P. O'Connell (London, Stevens & Sons 1965) at p. 361.

176. See Vallat, *ILC Yearbook 1974*, op. cit. n. 162, at pp. 73-87.

177. M. Shaw, *Title to Territory in Africa: International Legal Issues* (Oxford, Clarendon Press 1986) at pp. 233-234.

178. Koskenniemi, loc. cit. n. 161, at p. 133.

This exception to the 'clean slate' rule was therefore accepted as part of customary international law even before the 1978 Vienna Convention on State Succession was negotiated. As the ICJ Chamber observes in the *Frontier Dispute (Burkina Faso v. Mali)* case, '(t)here is no doubt that the obligation to respect pre-existing international frontiers in the event of a state succession derives from a general rule of international law, whether or not the rule is expressed in the formula *uti possidetis.*'[179] Thus, Articles 11 and 12 of the 1978 Vienna Convention providing that boundary and other forms of local treaties are not considered to be put into question when new states succeed to them merely codifies this exception to the 'clean slate' rule that was already accepted under customary international law.[180] On the other hand, at least two states voiced concerns in their comments to the ILC draft articles on state succession that might also be taken up by a newly independent East Timor state in respect of the Timor Gap treaty. First, Afghanistan in its oral comments to the exception raised its fears that the phrasing of the exception for territorial boundary treaties should not preclude the invalidity of an unequal boundary treaty agreed to by the predecessor state or the non-application of a boundary treaty due to a fundamental change of circumstances. Second, despite approving the application of the clean slate principle and its exception relating to territorial boundaries, Tanzania expressed the view that the Administering Authority of a Trust Territory could not conclude a treaty that binds the soon to be independent state in perpetuity.[181] This is apparently without exception as to the type of treaty entered into by the Administering Authority concerned. The stance adopted by these two formerly colonial countries has obvious legal implications for East Timor in respect of the current re-negotiation of the 1989 Timor Gap treaty between UNTAET and Australia. According to this view, a new East Timor state will have complete discretion to disregard any re-negotiated treaty agreed in the current re-negotiation process between UNTAET and Australia.

The generally well-accepted exception to the 'clean slate' rule is also denied by some writers. Makonen, for example, provides useful counter arguments against the usual reasons why boundaries are held to succeed changes in the statehood of a defined territory.[182] O'Connell too cautioned against any presumption of succession based on treaty categorisation alone, preferring to examine the nature of each treaty on a case by case basis. He adhered to the notion that 'the question of state succession to treaties is more a question of treaty interpretation than of the existence or otherwise of general rules of law concerning the fate of treaties upon change of sover-

---

179. See *ICJ Rep.* (1986) op. cit. n. 130, at para. 24, p. 566.

180. See A. Zimmermann, State Succession in respect of Treaties', in J. Klabbers, M. Koskenniemi, O. Ribbelink and A. Zimmermann, eds., *State Practice regarding State Succession and Issues of Recognition* (The Hague, Kluwer Law International 1999) at p. 82.

181. Vallat, *ILC Yearbook 1974*, op. cit. n. 162, at p. 75.

182. See Y. Makonnen, *International Law and the New States of Africa: A Study of the International Legal Problems of State Succession in the Newly Independent States of Eastern Africa* (Medford MA, Tufts University 1973) at pp. 441-453.

eignty.'[183] He would therefore assess the compatibility of the treaty with the changed situation caused by a new state succeeding a previous state.[184] He points out that ultimately, 'the difference between the ways in which treaties are disposed of following change in sovereignty and other changes of circumstances (under the *rebus sic stantibus* principle) is a matter of degree.'[185]

Several further questions therefore arise regarding boundary treaties: First, do succeeding territorial boundary treaties include maritime, as well as land boundaries? The answer to this question is not as axiomatic as one might suppose. It is noteworthy that most, if not all, adduced examples of succeeding territorial treaties relate to land, rather than maritime, boundaries. Land boundaries are therefore examples *par excellence* of the permanent demarcation of territorial sovereignty. This does not necessarily imply that state succession to maritime boundary treaties has been treated differently from land boundary treaties. Given the relatively recent vintage of the extension of coastal state maritime jurisdiction to incorporate the continental shelf and exclusive economic zone (EEZ) regimes, there are understandably fewer examples of bilateral continental shelf or EEZ boundary delimitation treaties that have been subject to questions of state succession.

However, it should be realised that the delimitation of maritime jurisdictions, especially regarding maritime zones beyond territorial waters, is arguably less connected *per se* with notions of territorial sovereignty than land boundaries. While such maritime jurisdictions as the continental shelf and the EEZ of course derive from territorial sovereignty, they are by their very nature less all-encompassing than their land-based counterparts. Bin Cheng, for example, notes that '(t)he position regarding the continental shelf and the EEZ is more ambiguous, neither of which is, strictly speaking, part of a State's national territory.'[186]

Maritime boundaries do not delimit the complete bundle of jurisdictions normally available to a sovereign state within its land territory. As Marston notes, 'the maritime area is not jurisdictionally homogeneous and contains areas under coastal state sovereignty (internal waters and territorial sea) and areas under a less intensive regime (contiguous zone, exclusive economic or fisheries zone, continental shelf).'[187] Continental shelf and/or EEZ boundary delimitation agreements between states only

183. D.P. O'Connell, 'State Succession and Problems of Treaty Interpretation', 58 *AJIL* (1964) pp. 41-61, at p. 41.

184. O'Connell, op. cit. n. 165, at p. 735.

185. Ibid., at p. 738.

186. See B. Cheng, 'Legal and Commercial Aspects of Data Gathering by Remote Sensing', in Bin Cheng, ed., *Studies in International Space Law* (Oxford, Clarendon Press 1997) pp. 572-597, at p. 575, n. 9, citing President Reagan's Proclamation of 10 March 1983 of the United States' EEZ: '... the EEZ remains an area *beyond* the territory and territorial sea of the United States ...' (emphasis added), see 22 *ILM* (1983) at p. 465.

187. G. Marston, 'The Stability of Land and Sea Boundary Delimitations in International Law', in G.H. Blake, ed., *World Boundaries, Vol. 5: Maritime Boundaries* (London, Routledge 1994) pp. 144-167, at p. 152.

represent a spatial divide of the sovereign rights and specified maritime jurisdictions available to the delimiting states under international law,[188] no more and no less. As Marston points out, '[t]he question is whether these and other distinctions give to maritime delimitations a quality of stability different from that of land delimitations.'[189] Since these maritime jurisdictions do not encompass the full sovereignty of a state, unlike that of territorial jurisdiction on land, maritime delimitation treaties may not be automatically subject to the same rule upon state succession as their land-bound brethren.

Thus, the underlying reasons why boundary treaties *per se* succeed to newly independent states, and others do not, must first be examined. Here, one may conclude that the 'real' nature of boundary treaties, in that they show an intrinsic connection with the territory, provides the legal basis for their permanency, notwithstanding state succession. After all, as Udokang notes, a new state succeeds not to the treaty itself but in fact to the territorial boundaries established by this treaty.[190] Mullerson confirms this view, observing that '(w)ith respect succession and boundaries, it is not exactly a treaty which is succeeded to, but rather the boundary itself as an objective reality having its own *de facto* and *de jure* existence regardless of whether the treaty itself is in force.'[191] Brownlie affirms that international law doctrine has long accepted that a change of sovereignty does not as such affect international boundaries.[192] He notes that the International Court of Justice has applied this principle in the *Frontier Dispute*[193] and *Temple*[194] cases.

Moreover, Article 11(a) of the Vienna Convention on State Succession to Treaties, 1978 provides that any boundaries established by treaties, without exception, are not as such affected by state succession. Quite apart from the 1978 Convention, the relevant principle is well-established in custom. Numerous examples of state practice confirming the general permanency of territorial boundaries can be adduced in support of this principle. Therefore, in the absence of any state practice distinguishing be-

---

188. As provided in Arts. 56(1) (EEZ) and 77 (continental shelf), respectively, of the 1982 UN Convention on the Law of the Sea (UNCLOS, 1982).

189. Marston, op. cit. n. 187, at pp. 152-153.

190. O. Udokang, *Succession of New States to International Treaties* (Dobbs Ferry, NY, Oceana 1972) at p. 380, fn. 124 citing Jenks, 29 *BYIL* (1952) at p. 107; O'Connell, *The Law of State Succession* (Cambridge, Cambridge University Press 1956) at p. 49; and A. Lester, 'State Succession to Treaties in the Commonwealth', 12 *ICLQ* (1963) at p. 492.

191. R. Müllerson, 'Law and Politics in Succession of States: International Law on Succession of States', in B. Stern, ed., *Dissolution, Continuation and Succession in Eastern Europe* (The Hague, Martinus Nijhoff 1998) pp. 5-32, at p. 19.

192. I. Brownlie, *The Rule of Law in International Affairs: International Law at the Fiftieth Anniversary of the United Nations* (The Hague, Martinus Nijhoff 1998) p. 55. See also I. Brownlie, *Boundary Problems and New States,* Josephine Onoh Memorial Lecture, 27 February 1996 (Hull, University of Hull Press 1996) at p. 5.

193. Case *Concerning the Frontier Dispute* (*Burkina Faso* v. *Republic of Mali*) *ICJ Rep.* (1986) p. 554, at p. 566, para. 24.

194. Case *Concerning the Temple of Preah Vihear* (*Cambodia* v. *Thailand*), Merits, *ICJ Rep.* (1962) p. 6.

tween land and maritime boundary treaties, both types of boundary treaties being dispositive by nature succeed sovereignty changes. As Marston concludes in his study, there does not appear to be any difference in legal principle between the internal and external stability of maritime boundary delimitations and their land counterparts.[195] This view appears to be confirmed by the definition of 'territory' adopted in the ILC's commentary to the draft articles on state succession.[196] Moreover the commentary explained that the Commission considered this definition of the word to be its natural meaning in the context of state succession and thus did not find it necessary to specify it in the draft article concerned.[197]

The parallel development of the legal principle of *uti possidetis juris* provides further support for the notion that territorial boundaries transcend state succession.[198] As Udokang notes, 'The legal significance of stability and definitiveness in boundary delimitation has been recognised in international arbitral and judicial decisions relating to boundary disputes.'[199] The *uti possidetis* principle is now accepted as a rule of general customary international law and provides that 'after the achievement of independence, existing delimitations acquire the protection of international law, and any subsequent changes must be achieved without the use or threat of force and through peaceful means.'[200]

However, the question arises, as in the foregoing discussion on state succession, whether the *uti possidetis* rule is applicable to maritime as well as land boundaries. The 1989 *Guinea-Bissau* v. *Senegal Arbitration*,[201] adjudicated upon just this issue. This case concerned the legal effect of a maritime boundary agreement concluded between former colonial powers upon their successor states. A majority of the Tribunal held that previous International Court of Justice cases and Asian state practice in the decolonization period following the Second World War supported the notion that state succession and the *uti possidetis* rule also applied to maritime boundaries.[202] The Tribunal also dismissed an argument put forward by Guinea-Bissau that maritime boundaries which delimited only certain activities, like the exploitation of natural resources, cannot succeed to a new state.[203] Thus, the Tribunal decided by a majority decision (two votes to one) that the maritime boundary agreement concluded between their former colonial powers continues to have the force of law in relations between

195. Marston, op. cit. n. 187, at p. 159.

196. See *Yearbook of the ILC* (1974) op. cit. n. 162, para. 460, at p. 87.

197. Ibid., at para. 461.

198. As Mullerson notes in the context of treaty succession issues following the break-up of the USSR and Yugoslavia, the rule of state succession in the context of boundaries merely confirms the continuing viability of the *uti possidetis* rule. See Rein Müllerson, 'New Developments in the Former USSR and Yugoslavia', 33 *Virginia JIL* (1993) pp. 299-322, at pp. 313-314.

199. Udokang, op. cit. n. 190, at p. 378.

200. Mullerson, op. cit. n. 191, at p. 20.

201. Case *Concerning the Arbitral Award* of 31 July 1989 (*Guinea-Bissau* v. *Senegal*) 83 *International Law Report* (1990) pp. 1-120.

202. Ibid., at pp. 36-37, paras. 63-64.

203. Ibid., at p. 37, para. 65.

Guinea-Bissau and Senegal, but solely with regard to the maritime jurisdictions established by the agreement, namely the territorial sea, contiguous zone, and continental shelf (i.e., not including the EEZ, as this maritime zone was not delimited by the disputes agrrement).[204]

On the other hand, the Dissenting Opinion of Bedjaoui should be noted here. He considered that the *uti possidetis* principle was inapplicable in this case because it pertains only to land boundaries delimiting sovereign territories, and not to maritime boundaries delimiting areas of less exclusive jurisdictions.[205] According to Bedjaoui, the *uti possidetis* principle constitutes an exception to the otherwise sacrosanct norm of state sovereignty and must be applied and interpreted restrictively. Maritime boundaries therefore cannot be automatically included within the application of this principle because unlike land boundaries they do not, strictly speaking, delimit sovereign territory.[206] After examining the case precedents and state practice relied upon by the Tribunal to arrive at its decision, Bedjaoui refines his objection to the application of the *uti possidetis* rule to boundaries delimiting maritime zones beyond the territorial sea.[207] In other words, according to him, this rule only applies to land and territorial sea boundaries and *not* to continental shelf or EEZ boundaries. Even more interesting is the Declaration appended to the Award by the President of the Tribunal, Julio Barberis, whereby he notes that, in his view, the disputed boundary agreement applied to the territorial sea, the contiguous zone, and the continental shelf between Senegal and Guinea-Bissau, but *not* the EEZ waters.[208] He thus makes explicit the otherwise implicit restriction by the Tribunal of the application of the *uti possidetis* rule only to the specific maritime boundaries agreed in the initial treaty.

State practice on this issue since the fall of the Iron Curtain in 1989/1990 corresponds with the majority arbitral decision in this case. A good example is the 1978 Turkey-Soviet Union continental shelf agreement,[209] and the 1986/1987 exchange of notes between the same two countries on the delimitation of their respective exclusive economic zones in the Black Sea.[210] On 27 January 1992 the permanent representative of the Russian Federation to the United Nations sent a note to the UN Secretary-General stating, *inter alia*, that the Russian Federation continues to exercise its rights and honour its commitments in the international treaties concluded by the

204. Ibid., at p. 47, para. 88

205. Ibid., at p. 64, para. 34.

206. Ibid., at p. 67, para. 40.

207. Ibid., at pp. 71-73, paras. 48-52.

208. Ibid., at p. 48.

209. Full title: Agreement between the Government of the Republic of Turkey and the Government of the Union of Soviet Socialist Republics on the Delimitation of the Continental Shelf in the Black Sea. Signed 23 June 1978; entered into force: 15 May 1981. See T. Scovazzi, 'Turkey-Soviet Union (Continental Shelf)', Report No. 8-10(2) in Charney and Alexander, eds., Vol. II, op. cit. n. 3, pp. 1693-1700, text of agreement at pp. 1698-1700.

210. Made on 23 December 1986 and 6 February 1987. See T. Scovazzi, 'Turkey-Soviet Union (Exclusive Economic Zone)', Report No. 8-10(3) in Charney and Alexander, eds., op. cit. n. 3, pp. 1701-1707, text at pp. 1706-1707.

former Soviet Union, and requesting that the Russian Federation be considered a party to all international agreements in force, instead of the Soviet Union. In the instant case between Turkey and the former Soviet Union in the Black Sea, the Russian Federation sent a note to Turkey on 17 September 1992 confirming that it is the successor to the Soviet Union for both the 1978 continental shelf agreement and the 1986/1987 exchange of notes on the EEZ.[211]

Another example deriving from the break-up of the former Yugoslavian Federation relates to the Croatian Republic's succession to the 1968 Yugoslavia-Italy continental shelf agreement,[212] by provision in its domestic legislation. Article 43, paragraph 2, of the Croatian Maritime Code of 27 January 1994 states that 'the boundary line of the continental shelf between the Republic of Croatia and the Republic of Italy has been established by the agreement between Italy and the former Socialist Republic of Yugoslavia in 1968.'[213]

On the other hand, the fact that *uti possidetis* is an obligatory norm of international law does not legitimatise territorial changes imposed during the illegal occupation and annexation of a state. As Müllerson notes in this context, '[o]n the one hand, *uti possidetis* requires leaving the borders as they were at the moment of restoration of independence; on the other hand, the necessity to remedy the results of illegal occupation and annexation means that frontiers existing before the loss of independence should be restored.'[214] The ensuing dilemma between these two conflicting principles will resonate with decision-makers on the East Timor issue, whether they be the states involved, empowered third parties, international institutions or an adjudicatory body. As Müllerson concludes, the decision will be an outcome of two different legal maxims originating from Roman law: *ex injuria non jus oritur* (illegal acts do not create law) and *ex factis jus oritur* (facts have a tendency to become law).[215]

The break-up of the former Soviet Union raised this issue in respect of existing maritime boundary treaties with the Baltic states of Estonia, Lithuania and Latvia that have newly regained their independence.[216] All three states have made declarations denying their successor state status vis-à-vis the Soviet Union.[217] According to

211. See T. Scovazzi, 'Black Sea Update: The Former Republics of the Soviet Union and Turkey', Report No. 8-10(4), in Charney and Alexander, eds., Vol. III, op. cit. n. 3, pp. 2443-2445.

212. Full title Agreement between Italy and Yugoslavia Concerning the Delimitation of the Continental Shelf between the Two Countries, signed 8 January 1968, entered into force 21 January 1970. See T. Scovazzi and G. Francalanci, 'Italy-Yugoslavia (Continental Shelf)', Report No. 8-7(1), in Charney and Alexander, eds., Vol. II, op cit. n. 3, pp. 1627-1637, text at pp. 1634-1637.

213. See T. Scovazzi, 'Adriatic Sea Update: Croatia-Italy-Slovenia', in Charney and Alexander, eds., Vol. III, op, cit. n. 3, pp. 2437-2442, at p. 2437, citing *Narodne Novine* of 7 March 1994

214. Müllerson, op. cit. n. 191, at p. 21.

215. Ibid., at p. 21.

216. See E. Franckx, 'Baltic Sea Update' Report No. 10-14 in Charney and Alexander, eds., op. cit. n. 3, pp. 2557-2573, at p. 2559.

217. Cf., The relevant Declarations in *Multilateral treaties deposited with the Secretary-General* (Status as of 31 December 1994) at p. 9, and *Multilateral treaties deposited with the Secretary-General* (Status as of 31 December, 1995) also at p. 9.

Franckx, the alleged illegality of their annexation by the Soviet Union *ab initio* acts to deny the validity of any boundary treaty agreed between the Soviet Union and third states on the behalf of the Baltic states during the 1949 and 1990 period.[218] Koskenniemi notes that Norway, for example, has recognised the illegality of the Soviet occupation of Latvia and Lithuania[219] and consequently the non-succession by the two states to Soviet treaties, as well as the continued validity of bilateral treaties entered into between Norway and the respective states between 1920 and 1940.[220] France too considered that bilateral treaties concluded with one or more of the Baltic states between 1919 and 1940 were still in force.[221]

These legal developments involving the Baltic states are clearly analogous to the present East Timor situation. A newly independent East Timor state could attempt to rely on the precedent set by the Baltic states to argue that any treaties agreed between Indonesia and third states during its allegedly illegal occupation of East Timor between 1975 and 1999 would be invalid in respect their succession to the new East Timor state. This would obviously include the 1989 Timor Gap treaty that is the subject of discussion here.

The 'clean slate' stance of the three Baltic states even in respect of territorial boundary treaties is affirmed by the fact that they have not automatically accepted the maritime boundary agreements concluded by the former USSR with third states in the Baltic Sea.[222] In practice, however, as Zimmerman observes, '[*d*]*e facto,* a certain number of bilateral treaties concluded between third states and the Soviet Union between 1949 and 1990 continue to be applied with regard to the territory of one or more of the Baltic states.'[223] Moreover, with respect to maritime boundary delimitation, treaties concluded by the Soviet Union and third states were taken as a basis for the delimitation of these same maritime zones by one or more of the Baltic states. This is especially the case in relation to the delimitation agreement between Sweden and the Soviet Union which now remains in force between Sweden and the Baltic states,[224] as well as the maritime boundary delimitation agreements between Finland and the Soviet Union.[225] which were initially provisionally continued between Finland and Estonia,[226] and are now similarly provided under a new treaty.[227]

---

218. Franckx, in Charney and Alexander, eds., op. cit. n. 3, at p. 2562.

219. By an exchange of diplomatic notes between Norway and Lithuania on 20 April 1994.

220. Koskenniemi, op. cit. n. 161, at p. 111, n. 71.

221. See *Liste des Traites et Accords de la France* (Status as of October, 1992) Vol. II, at p. 681, 741 and 744, as cited in Zimmermann, in Klabbers et al., eds., op. cit. n. 180, at p. 96, n. 218.

222. Franckx, op. cit. n. 216, at p. 2563.

223. Zimmermann, in Klabbers et al., eds., op. cit. n. 180, at p. 96.

224. Ibid.

225. Franckx provides details of these agreements in Franckx, op. cit. n. 216, at p. 2564, footnotes 49, 50, 51, and 52

226. See Agreement on the Provisional Application of Some Treaties between Finland and the Soviet Union in the Relations between Finland and Estonia, signed: 20 March 1992 initially covering the period until 9 January 1995 but later extended for two more years. As Koskenniemi notes, however, this agree-

A second, perhaps more serious question that may be raised in respect of the Timor Gap treaty relates to its temporary nature. Article 2(3) of this treaty assumes as much when it provides, *inter alia*, that nothing contained in the treaty shall be interpreted as prejudicing the position of either Contracting state on a *permanent* continental shelf delimitation in the Zone of Co-operation. [emphasis added] Indeed, according to Onorato and Valencia, the main purpose of the treaty was to allow the development of the Zone's petroleum resources to proceed without delay, while negotiations towards a permanent continental shelf boundary continued.[228] Article 33 envisages the treaty being applicable for an initial period of forty (40) years,[229] before continuing for successive terms of twenty (20) years, unless by the end of each term, including the initial term, the two states have concluded an agreement on a permanent continental shelf delimitation in the Zone of Co-operation area.[230] Moreover, Article 34 explicitly provides that the conclusion of a permanent continental shelf boundary will have the consequent legal effect of voiding the present treaty,[231] with certain exceptions in relation to contractors' rights under previously awarded concessions.[232]

These provisions raise the question whether the Timor Gap treaty is only a temporary maritime boundary treaty and therefore cannot be regarded as succeeding to a new East Timor state under the terms of Article 11(a) of the Vienna Convention on State Succession, 1978. Kaye, for example, is of the view that the joint development arrangements established by Malaysia and Thailand in the Gulf of Thailand, as well as between Australia and Indonesia in the Timor Gap, are temporary.[233] Prescott on the other hand, suggests that what is provisional today may in time acquire permanency.[234]

Any argument on this issue depends on the definition of a 'boundary' in the context of state succession being limited to permanent rather than merely temporary boundaries. This assumption of the permanency of boundaries could well be read into the meaning of 'boundary' given the need to retain its connection with the 'real' nature of the territory concerned in order to succeed to a new state claiming sovereignty over this territory. On the other hand, it can be maintained, using O'Connell's analytical insight, that whether a boundary is permanent or temporary does not de-

ment was made on the clear understanding that the treaties themselves were not applied as such, only their provisions. See Koskenniemi, op. cit. n. 161, at p. 111.

227. Full title 'Agreement between the Republic of Finland and the Republic of Estonia on the Boundary of the Maritime Zones in the Gulf of Finland and the Northern Baltic Sea, 1996', text in 12 *International Journal of Marine and Coastal Law* (1997) at p. 375.

228. Onorato & Valencia, loc. cit. n. 27, at p. 60.

229. Art. 33(1) of the Timor Gap treaty, *supra* n. 3.

230. Ibid., Art. 33(2).

231. Ibid., Art. 34(1)(a).

232. Ibid., Art. 33(1)(b).

233. S.B. Kaye, 'The Use of Multiple Boundaries in Maritime Boundary Delimitation: Law and Practice', 19 *Australian YBIL* (1998) pp. 49-72, at p. 63.

234. J.R.V. Prescott, 'The Gulf of Thailand: Maritime Limits to Conflicts and Co-operation', *Maritime Briefings* (Durham, International Boundaries Research Unit 1998) at pp. 32-33

tract from its intrinsically 'real' nature in the sense that both permanent and temporary boundaries are territorial in character and thus fall within the category of treaties that are exempt from the 'clean slate' rule. However, it is clear that the temporary nature of the Timor Gap treaty in this respect has contributed to efforts by East Timorese representatives to rescind its future application to an independent East Timor and somewhat undermined Australia's negotiating position.

Finally in this context it must also be questioned whether offshore joint development agreements such as the Timor Gap treaty are to be regarded as maritime boundary treaties for the purpose of state succession? This view suggests that the joint development regime established by this treaty does not fall within the traditional conception of a 'boundary'. Should this view be substantiated, it will be a strong argument for the discontinuance of the treaty by a new East Timor state. After all, the treaty provides for an area (Area A of the Zone of Co-operation) that is subject to the joint control and jurisdiction of the two contracting states. This arguably represents the very antithesis of territorial delimitation providing for the permanent separation of sovereignty and jurisdiction that we have come to expect from boundaries.

On the other hand, the Timor Gap treaty can be put forward as an example of a new breed of maritime boundary treaty that establishes a legal regime for the management of various sea-use activities within a designated area. Such management-type boundary regimes represent a progressive attempt to move away from the strictures imposed by conventional boundary-making practice, in favour of a functional approach designed to resolve the real issues arising from such boundary disputes.[235] These usually involve disputed ownership of natural resources and/or conflicting sea-use activities. Again it is possible to refer to the Vienna Convention for support for the proposition that such boundary treaty regimes, as opposed to mere boundary delimitation treaties are covered by the general rule providing for their continued effect notwithstanding state succession. Article 11(b) provides that the obligations and rights established by a treaty and relating to the *regime* of a boundary are also not affected by state succession. [emphasis added]. Moreover, Article 12(1) extends this continuity to cover treaty rights and obligations relating to the use or benefit of any territory, or to restrictions upon its use, for the benefit of any territory of a foreign state and considered as attaching to the territories in question.

The issue therefore turns on the question whether the joint development framework and institutions established by the present Timor Gap treaty relate to the boundary regime. And what if certain provisions are deemed to be boundary-related but others are not? As Sharma notes, '[e]very now and then boundary treaties will contain additional provisions in the text or annexure for the exercise of reciprocal rights and duties that are only notionally connected with the territory. ... The question then arises whether the treaty devolves *in toto* or does not devolve, or whether it is possible to sever provisions which are transmissible to the successor from those not so transmis-

---

235. See D.M. Johnston, *The Theory and History of Ocean Boundary-Making* (Kingston and Montreal, McGill-Queen's University Press 1988) at pp. 227-229, citing O.R. Young, *Resource Regimes: Natural Resources and Social Institutions* (Berkeley CA, University of California Press 1982).

sible.'[236] This type of dilemma was highlighted by O'Connell to substantiate his argument against the pre-emptive categorisation of individual treaties into either 'personal' or 'real' treaties.[237] According to Sharma, several approaches have been utilised to determine which parts of a boundary treaty are severable from the rest of the treaty and thus transmissible to the succeeding state.[238] State practice suggests that rights relating to, *inter alia,* commercial navigation, fisheries and cattle grazing have in the past been regarded as severable from the straightforward boundary line stipulations in a succeeding treaty.[239]

While there is little doubt about the 'real' or dispositive character of certain provisions of the Timor Gap treaty,[240] not all of these provisions can readily be described as such, especially when they regulate the commercial transactions involving the sale and supply of the extracted petroleum resource. On the other hand, these provisions are intimately linked to the joint development regime established by the treaty. It would be difficult in these circumstances to distinguish between the so-called 'personal' aspects of the treaty from its 'real' or dispositive aspects for the purpose of succession.

Yet another argument denying a new East Timor state's succession to the Timor Gap treaty can be made on the basis that it is an unequal treaty.[241] This view suggests that the so-called automatic succession formula for new states in the case of boundary treaties should be suspended where it can be shown that these treaties are not consistent with the interests of the people of that new state.[242] This is especially pertinent in respect of territorial treaties that are the products of colonialism and thereby contrary to self-determination.

In the present context, it would be interesting to speculate whether Indonesia's annexation of East Timor after the Portugese withdrawal amounted to the re- or neo-colonisation of this territory. Thus, any boundary treaty entered into between the effective colonial power and third states should not succeed to the new state as it would not have represented the consent of the colonised population. Chen recommends that 'the successor or other concerned states suffering from unequal boundary treaties should have the right to demand negotiation for a new boundary treaty based on the principles of equality, independence, reciprocity and freedom of consent, provided that pending the conclusion of a new boundary treaty the territorial *status quo* be respected as *fait accompli*.'[243]

236. S.P. Sharma, *International Boundary Disputes and International Law: A Policy-Oriented Study* (Bombay, N.M. Tripathi 1976) at p. 239.

237. O'Connell, loc. cit. n. 165, pp. 735-736.

238. Sharma, op. cit. n. 236, at pp. 239-240.

239. Ibid., pp. 241-242.

240. Namely, Annex A containing the designation and description, including maps and co-ordinates of Areas A, B, and C of the Zone of Co-operation incorporated into the treaty by Art. 1(1)(p).

241. See Lung-Fong Chen, *State Succession Relating to Unequal Treaties* (Connecticut, Archon 1974) esp. from p. 175.

242. Ibid., at p. 177.

243. Ibid., at p. 214.

However, it is doubtful whether general international law accords with this view. Few examples of state practice can be adduced in support of it.[244] Moreover, in at least one instance where a treaty was abrogated due to its allegedly unequal nature, the actions of the abrogating state were condemned by the other party as a flagrant violation of the treaty rights 'and the most elementary standards of international usage and conduct.'[245] Merely to argue that disputes concerning the succession of boundary treaties arise primarily due to their unequal nature does not in itself provide an adequate legal pretext for changing the present legal position supporting their continuation. To presume otherwise would surely result in calls for the re-negotiation of many international boundary treaties across the globe, thereby undermining their fundamental purpose of providing stability and continuity in international relations between states.

3.3 Has there been a fundamental change of circumstances allowing termination of the Treaty?

According to Shaw, '[t]his rule states that a party to a treaty may unilaterally invoke as a ground for terminating or suspending the operation of the treaty the fact that there has been a fundamental change of circumstances from those which existed at the time of the conclusion of the treaty.'[246] Lissitzyn observes that 'a treaty should not be applied in circumstances which are so different from those for which the parties sought to provide that its application would be contrary to the parties' shared expectations and would defeat their apparent objectives.'[247]

The *rebus sic stantibus* rule, as it is also known, is now provided included in Article 62 of the 1969 Vienna Convention on the Law of Treaties. However, as Fitzmaurice notes, its formulation is particularly cautious.[248] In particular, the threshold whereby the change of alleged circumstances is so fundamental as to allow for the unilateral termination of a treaty is undefined.[249] As David observes, the doctrine of fundamental change of circumstances as a reason for terminating treaties pits the two

244. Kontou, for example, cites the abrogation by the newly-installed communist government in China of a US treaty-acquired right to use land it occupied in Peking on the basis that this right had been obtained under an unequal treaty. See N. Kontou, *The Termination and Revision of Treaties in the Light of New Customary International Law* (Oxford, Clarendon Press 1994) at p. 96.

245. Ibid., at p. 97.

246. Shaw, op. cit. n. 177, at p. 230.

247. O.J. Lissitzyn, 'Stability and Change: Unilateral Denunciation or Suspension of Treaties by Reason of Changed Circumstances', *Proceedings of the American Society of International Law,* 61st Meeting, April 25-29 1967, pp. 186-193, at p. 187.

248. M. Fitzmaurice, 'The Gabcikovo-Nagymaros Case: The Law of Treaties', 11 *Leiden JIL* (1998) pp. 321-344, at p. 332.

249. As Vamvoukos notes, 'the lack of any precise definition of the notion of changed circumstances may be due to the fact that the provisions do not, as a rule, accord the parties a right of unilateral action in the first instance. The party invoking the provision has to initiate negotiations with the other party and, only if such negotiations fail, has it a right to unilateral denunciation of or withdrawal from the treaty.' See Vamvoukos op. cit. n. 109, at p. 150.

main tenets of international relations, namely stability and flexibility, against each other: 'Concern with stability militates against the frequent termination of former arrangements, while flexibility, as the term was understood in the nineteenth century, favours frequent termination of former agreements in pursuance of short-term interests.'[250]

It is possible to argue that the status of a newly-independent state of East Timor alone constitutes a fundamental change of circumstance that has the legal effect of terminating the Timor Gap treaty. However, this is not reflected in state practice. Mere change in the legal status of a state does not of itself constitute a fundamental change of circumstance resulting in termination of the treaties agreed by the previous state.[251] If this were the case then the rules relating to state succession of treaties would be rendered almost superfluous. In the *Gabcikovo-Nagymaros* case, for example, Hungary requested the Court to adjudge, *inter alia,* that the bilateral Treaty of 16 November 1977 agreeing to invest in and build a series of dams and tidal barrages along the course of the Danube river had never been in force between Hungary and Slovakia, thereby implying that Slovakia did not succeed to the rights and obligations that were formerly provided to Czechoslovakia under this 1977 treaty.[252] The ICJ, however, disregarded this alleged distinction between the former Czechoslovakia and the present Slovakia for the purpose of state succession to treaty obligations. It apparently assumed that state succession naturally followed the consensual division of one state into two (or more) new states. As Klabbers notes, the Court 'simply re-iterated that it did not need to express itself on the legal nature of the alleged automatic succession rule.'[253] The Court also accepted that the political and economic situation, as well as the state of environmental knowledge, had changed considerably in the intervening years since the treaty was first signed in 1977. Nonetheless it held that these changes had not transformed the 1977 treaty obligations in such a radical manner so as to provide a justification for the termination of the treaty by either party.

This presumption against finding that a fundamental change of circumstances has occurred appears to extend to changes in substantive legal concepts and rules too.

250. A.E. David, *The Strategy of Treaty Termination: Lawful Breaches and Retaliations* (New Haven, Yale University Press 1975) at pp. 13-14.

251. See Art. 62 of the Vienna Convention on the Law of Treaties, 1969. As the International Court of Justice re-affirmed in the *Gabcikovo-Nagymaros* case, 'The negative and conditional wording of Article 62 of the Vienna Convention on the Law of Treaties is a clear indication moreover that the stability of treaty relations requires that the plea of fundamental change of circumstances be applied only in exceptional cases.' See *Case Concerning the Gabcikovo-Nagymaros Project* (Hungary/ Slovakia) Judgment of 25 September 1997, *ICJ Rep.* (1997) p. 7, at p. 65, para. 104.

252. Ibid., at p. 15, para. 11.

253. J. Klabbers, 'Cat on a Hot Tin Roof: The World Court, State Succession and the *Gabcikovo-Nagymaros* Case', 11 *Leiden JIL* (1998) pp. 345-355, at p. 349.

This is especially true in the case of boundary treaties,[254] as with the case of state succession considered above. As Vagts notes, '[t]reaties fixing boundaries or other territorial rights are usually treated as fixed and thus survive the vicissitudes that might cause other agreements to be terminated by *rebus sic stantibus*.'[255] In other words, it is not open for a new East Timor state to argue that the change in the legal basis for continental shelf boundary delimitation from geomorphological criteria to the more explicit 200-nm distance criterion in itself constitutes a fundamental change of circumstances meriting the termination of the treaty.

An analogous situation to this occurred in the *Fisheries Jurisdiction* case,[256] where Iceland invoked both legal and factual changes in the waters around Iceland as reasons to terminate an agreement with the UK providing for the right to refer any dispute concerning Iceland's extended fisheries jurisdiction to the ICJ. In respect of the former, legal changes, Iceland contended that the evolving legal opinion on fisheries jurisdiction, as embodied in the Icelandic declaration of a 50-nm exclusive fishing zone, constituted grounds for invoking the *rebus sic stantibus* rule.[257] The Court held that 'while changes in the law may under certain conditions constitute valid grounds for invoking a change of circumstances affecting the duration of the treaty, the Icelandic contention is not relevant to the present case.'[258]

However, as Vamvoukos notes, this was mainly because the present case only concerned the validity of the compromissory clause providing for referral to the ICJ and jurisdictional issues arising therefrom.[259] On the other hand, in rejecting Iceland's arguments, the Court held that any change of circumstance must be fundamental,[260] and result in a radical transformation of the obligations still to be performed.[261] The cautious attitude of the Court in its interpretation of the *rebus sic stantibus* rule in this

---

254. Art. 62(2)(a) of the 1969 Vienna Convention provides: 'A fundamental change of circumstances may not be invoked: (a) as a ground for terminating or withdrawing from a treaty establishing a boundary ...' While the overall purpose of Art. 62 represents a leaning towards closely circumscribing the operation of the *rebus sic stantibus* doctrine, according to Lissitzyn, this provision (Art. 62(2)(a)) is especially forthright, not because provisions in such boundary treaties should be regarded as already 'executed', but because such treaties were intended to create a stable situation between the relevant states and thus needed to be excluded from the operation of the doctrine. See O.J. Lissitzyn, 'Treaties and Changed Circumstances (*Rebus Sic Stantibus*)', 61 *AJIL* (1967) pp. 895-922, at p. 915 and p. 917, citing Sir Humphrey Waldock, Special Rapporteur to the ILC on the Law of Treaties, in the Second Report on the Law of Treaties, in the *1963 ILC Yearbook* (II).

255. D.F. Vagts, 'State Succession: The Codifiers' View', 33 *Virginia JIL* (1993) pp. 275-297, at p. 289, citing the following case-law authorities that treated boundary lines as surviving decolonization, namely, the Award of the Arbitration Tribunal in the *Guinea-Guinea-Bissau Maritime Delimitation* case 77 *ILR* (1989) p. 635, at p. 667; *Frontier Dispute* case (*Burkina Faso* v. *Mali*) (1986) *ICJ Rep.* p. 554, at p. 656; *Continental Shelf* (*Tunisia* v. *Libya*) *ICJ Rep.* (1982) pp. 18, 65-66.

256. *Fisheries Jurisdiction* case (Jurisdiction) (*United Kingdom* v. *Iceland*), *ICJ Rep.* (1974) p. 3.

257. See Vamvoukos, op. cit. n. 109, at p. 169.

258. *Fisheries Jurisdiction* case (Jurisdiction) (1974) op. cit. n. 256, at p. 17.

259. Vamvoukos, op. cit. n. 109, at p. 169.

260. *Fisheries Jurisdiction* case (Jurisdiction) (1974) op. cit. n. 256, at p. 18, paras. 37 and 38.

261. Ibid., at para. 43.

case, and its general reluctance to allow this rule to overturn the more fundamental principle of the stability of treaties has been noted by Fitzmaurice.[262]

The effect of substantive new legal developments was also adjudicated on in the *Gabcikovo-Nagymaros* case. In this case, Hungary argued that the advent of international law for environmental protection in the intervening years between the adoption of a bilateral treaty between itself and Czechoslovakia (now Slovakia) constituted a fundamental change of circumstances[263] and precluded performance of the treaty,[264] thus entitling it to terminate the treaty. While agreeing that recently evolved norms of environmental law are relevant to the implementation of the treaty and should be inserted into the relevant treaty provisions concerning the project,[265] the International Court of Justice refused to accept that the need to consider the inclusion of these principles constituted a fundamental change of circumstances such that the *rebus sic stantibus* rule should be applied.[266]

On the other hand, it should be emphasised that the legal situation between Slovakia and Hungary in the *Gabcikovo* case was quite different from the present one between East Timor and Australia in respect of the Timor Gap treaty. To begin with, there was little doubt that Slovakia was fully entitled under international law to act as a successor state to the former Czechoslovakia, whereas this is precisely one of the crucial questions that needs to be resolved in respect of the succession or otherwise of a newly-independent East Timor to the Timor Gap treaty agreed between Indonesia and Australia. Secondly, the substantive issues regulated by each of these treaties are not comparable for the purpose of determining whether the 'change of circumstances' rule would apply equally in the latter case involving East Timor and Australia, even if it has been held to be applicable in the former case of Slovakia and Hungary.

4. IS JOINT DEVELOPMENT OF THE TIMOR GAP REQUIRED BY INTERNATIONAL LAW?

The foregoing section has considered some of the difficult issues relating to the possible invalidity, lack of succession and fundamental change of circumstances that may combine, jointly or severally, to deny the application of the present Timor Gap treaty between Australia and a new East Timor state in the near future. The final section of this essay will be devoted to an exploration of the legal and practical arguments that can be utilised to propose a similar type of joint development arrangement to replace the current Timor Gap treaty regime should it be deemed to be discontinued under in-

262. Fitzmaurice, loc. cit. n. 248, at pp. 333 and 343.
263. *Gabcikovo-Nagymaros* case, op. cit. n. 251, at p. 64, para. 104.
264. Ibid., at p. 67, para. 111.
265. Ibid., at p. 67, para. 112.
266. Ibid., at pp. 64-65, para. 104.

ternational law. The conceptual bases for these arguments are developed elsewhere[267] and will not be re-trodden here. Rather the problem will be considered anew.

This problem essentially consists of two states with opposing coastlines, namely Australia and a newly-independent East Timor. Both states are legally entitled to claim at least 200-nm of continental shelf,[268] thereby creating an overlapping claims area in the Timor Gap area, where oil and gas deposits are known to exist. As Shihata and Onorato have observed, the development of petroleum resources in these circumstances is even more problematic than usual.[269]

Assuming the Timor Gap treaty is discontinued due to the legal difficulties considered above, the usual question facing the parties at this juncture would be the negotiation of a permanent continental shelf boundary delimitation.[270] The UN Transitional Authority for East Timor (UNTAET) and the East Timor Transitional Administration (ETTA)'s formal opening position in these negotiations is that the application of current international law would result in *all* the Zone of Co-operation resources accruing to a newly-independent East Timor. However, UNTAET/ETTA acknowledges that the presence of overlapping claims in the area requires solution by negotiations and thus demands some flexibility on their part.[271] Onorato and Valencia note that as East Timor moves closer to independence, its leaders have begun openly to call on Australia to renegotiate the (Timor Gap) treaty on the principle of equidistance,[272] rather than the *status quo* applicable under the normal state succession rule discussed above (in Section 3.2). The fledgling East Timor leadership thus argues that the boundary should be drawn exactly midway between the opposing Australian and East Timor coastlines. This would enable East Timor to receive almost twice the benefit (i.e., up to 90% of the estimated Timor Gap resources) it would otherwise receive under the current joint development arrangement. Onorato and Valencia also favour the application of the equidistance principle, concluding that if the continental shelf boundary were to be renegotiated today, equidistance would probably prevail.[273]

---

267. See Ong, loc. cit. n. 37. The relative merits of the Malaysia-Thailand joint development agreements in comparison with the Timor Gap treaty and the Malaysia-Vietnam transboundary unitization agreement are considered in Ong, loc. cit. n. 57.

268. See Art. 76 of the 1982 LOSC, *supra* n. 48.

269. I.F.I. Shihata and W.T. Onorato, 'The Joint Development of International Petroleum Resources in Undefined and Disputed Areas', *ICSID Review – Foreign Investment Law Journal*, 11 (1996) pp. 299-317, at p. 299.

270. In this respect, both formal and informal talks between on the one hand, the UNTAET and the East Timor Transitional Administration (ETTA) and on the other hand, Australia have taken place through April and May 2001. Formal talks took place in Melbourne from 4-6 April 2001 and again in Dili on 28 May 2001.

271. UNTAET, Daily Press Briefing, Dili, 12 April 2001, accessed at: http:// www.un.org/peace/etimor.

272. See Onorato and Valencia, op. cit. n. 27, at p. 80.

273. Ibid.

Failing such negotiations,[274] recourse may be had to any number of international dispute settlement procedures, including the judicial modes of determining the applicable international law to this situation. Triggs, for example, has already explored the possibility of an application to the International Court of Justice to resolve this issue.[275]

The international legal framework governing such continental shelf boundary disputes has at its heart the application of equitable principles,[276] with a view to achieving an equitable solution by agreement.[277] The precise nature of these equitable principles has been the subject of some legal obfuscation by the Court that has subsequently provoked much doctrinal debate.[278] While the use of the equidistance or median line to delimit the maritime boundary may be agreed between the two states, it is by no means legally required,[279] unless it can be shown to be the only possible delimitation technique for achieving the often elusive equitable solution. Thus, advocates of a median line solution delimiting a continental shelf and/or Exclusive Economic Zone (EEZ) boundary,[280] in line with the recently agreed 1997 Australia-Indonesia EEZ 'water column' maritime boundary in the same area,[281] must provide authoritative legal authority to substantiate their arguments to this effect. Neither is it

274. The second official round of talks in Melbourne between the UNTAET/ETTA and Australia were described by the ETTA Cabinet Member for Economic Affairs, Mari Alkatiri, as a 'setback'.

275. Triggs, loc. cit. n. 7, at pp. 114-125.

276. As developed by the International Court of Justice in successive maritime boundary dispute cases beginning with the *North Sea Continental Shelf* cases (1969) *supra* n. 46.

277. As required by Art. 74(1) of the 1982 LOSC for EEZ delimitation and Art. 83(1) for continental shelf delimitation.

278. The literature on this issue is extensive and cannot be fully referred to here. Examples include: M.D. Blecher, 'Equitable Delimitation of Continental Shelf', 73 *AJIL* (1979) pp. 60-88; B. Kwiatkowska, 'Equitable Maritime Boundary Delimitation - A Legal Perspective', 3 *International Journal of Estuarine (now Marine) and Coastal Law* (1988) pp. 287-304; P. Weil, *The Law of Maritime Delimitation - Reflections* (Cambridge, Grotius Publications 1989); and S.P. Sharma, *Delimitation of Land and Sea Boundaries Between Neighbouring Countries* (New Delhi, Lancers Books 1989).

279. Art. 6(1) of the 1958 Continental Shelf Convention requiring the application of the median line in such situations in the absence of an agreement has been superceded in this respect by Arts. 74(1) and 83(1) of the 1982 LOSC, both in international conventional law and arguably also in customary international law.

280. See G.A. McKee, 'The New Timor Gap: Will Australia now break with the past?', No. 62 *Inside Indonesia* (April-June 2000) citing J.J. Smith who argues that a new East Timor state will benefit from recent international law developments which 'strongly suggest that a median line will ultimately form the EEZ boundary between East Timor and Australia.' See also R. Tanter, M. Selden and S.R. Shalom, 'East Timor Faces the Future', Vol. 32, Nos. 1 & 2 *Bulletin of Concerned Asian Scholars* (January-June 2000) pp. 113-124, especially at pp. 118-120.

281. Full title: Treaty between the Government of Australia and the Government of the Republic of Indonesia establishing an Exclusive Economic Zone Boundary and Certain Seabed Boundaries, signed in Perth, Western Australia on 14 March 1997. Not yet in force. See http://www.austlii.edu.au/au/other/dfat/treaties/2000/index.html for text. The legal status of this agreement is presumably also being reappraised following the UN-sponsored referendum result and consequent relinquishment of Indonesian sovereignty over East Timor.

necessarily the case that the continental shelf boundary delimiting the sea-bed between the two countries must be the same line as the EEZ boundary delimiting the superjacent water column.[282] There is no provision in the 1982 LOSC, nor customary international rule prescribing such a course of action.[283] State practice expressing a preference for a common continental shelf and EEZ boundary based on the median line,[284] amounts to a persuasive, but not prescriptive, legal argument in favour of this proposal. Nor does state practice alone,[285] without a perceived legal imperative to this effect, fulfil the requirement for the formation of a customary rule.[286] As Churchill and Lowe correctly observe, '[A]lthough state practice exhibits an overwhelming trend towards EEZ and continental shelf boundaries coinciding, the practice is not such as to *require* a single boundary.'[287] Thus, despite the problems that might face the two countries should any new continental shelf boundary settlement differ from the present median line EEZ 'water column' boundary,[288] there is no legal compulsion upon them to arrive at a common boundary solution.

---

282. For an analysis of the possible legal problems raised by the overlapping nature of the Indonesian EEZ jurisdiction in the water column superjacent to the Australian continental shelf jurisdiction in some areas delimited by the 1997 Treaty, see M. Herriman and M. Tsamenyi, 'The 1997 Australia-Indonesia Maritime Boundary Treaty: A Secure Legal Regime for Offshore Resource Development?', 29 *Ocean Development & International Law* (1998) pp. 361-396.

283. As Churchill and Lowe note, 'Although the provisions of the Convention governing continental shelf and EEZ boundaries are the same, their wording is sufficiently imprecise for the continental shelf and EEZ boundaries to differ - a situation fraught with potential conflict...' See R.R. Churchill and A.V. Lowe, *The Law of the Sea,* 3rd edn. (Manchester, Manchester University Press 1999) at p. 196.

284. For example, para. 7 of Malaysia's Declaration following her ratification of the 1982 LOSC on 14 October 1996, in accordance with Art. 310 of this Convention, states that: 'The Malaysian Government interprets article 74 and article 83 to the effect that in the absence of agreement on the delimitation of the exclusive economic zone or continental shelf or other maritime zones, for an equitable solution to be achieved, the boundary shall be the median line, namely a line every point of which is equidistant from the nearest points of the baselines from which the breadth of the territorial sea of Malaysia and of such other states is measured. Malaysia is also of the view that in accordance with the provisions of the Convention, namely article 56 and article 76, if the maritime area is less [than] or to a distance of 200 nautical miles from the baselines, the boundary for the continental shelf and the exclusive economic zone shall be on the same line (identical).' It should be noted that Art. 310 of the LOSC provides that the declarations or statements made by states when signing, ratifying or acceding to this Convention 'do not purport to exclude or modify the legal effect of the provisions of this Convention in their application to that state.'

285. Churchill and Lowe note that 'Since the late 1970s the trend, particularly outside Europe, has been to conclude agreements establishing a single maritime boundary for all zones ... Of the single maritime boundaries that have so far been agreed, many, particularly in the case of opposite coasts, are based on the equidistance (or median) principle ...', op. cit. n. 284, at p. 197.

286. Using the threshold of proof applied by the Court in the *North Sea Continental Shelf* cases, for example. See *ICJ Rep.* (1969) at pp. 43-44, paras. 75-77.

287. Churchill and Lowe, op. cit. n. 283, at p. 196 [emphasis added].

288. See S.B. Kaye, 'Multiple Boundaries in Maritime Boundary Delimitation: The Problems of Common Jurisdiction', in Australia and New Zealand Societies of International Law (ANZSIL) *Proceedings of the 6th Annual Conference, 1998* (Canberra, Centre for International and Public Law (CIPL), Australian National University 1999) pp. 185-193.

Moreover, there is a further, extremely significant, but so far neglected legal issue that militates against the use of the median line to delimit a common boundary. This relates to the use of a proportionality test by the ICJ to ascertain the equity of maritime boundary solutions presented in their judgements.[289] The most relevant case for our purposes here is the *Libya v. Malta Continental Shelf* case, where the Court shifted the recommended boundary from the initial median line drawn between Libya and Malta in the Mediterranean Sea closer to Malta in recognition of Libya's longer coastline and consequently greater land mass facing Malta.[290]

In the *Libya* v. *Malta* case, the Court noted that the principle of proportionality between the extent of the continental shelf areas appertaining to the coastal state and the length of its coast was first enunciated in the *North Sea Continental Shelf* cases.[291] The proportionality test is employed to verify the equity of delimitation between opposite coasts, as well as between adjacent coasts. The Court elaborated the criteria that need to be taken into account for the application of the proportionality test to determine whether an equitable delimitation would ensue. This involved first, the identification of 'relevant coasts' and 'relevant areas' of continental shelf, second, the calculation of the mathematical ratios and lengths of the coasts and the areas of shelf attributed, and finally the comparison of such ratios.[292] However, the Court was very much aware of the possible practical difficulties involved in the identification the 'relevant coasts' and 'relevant areas' for the application of the proportionality test. Thus, the Court limited the application of this test to the continental shelf areas immediately adjacent to the modified median delimitation line already established.

The Court found it necessary to adjust the initial median delimitation line northwards by exactly 18' (eighteen minutes) of latitude so that it lay closer to the Maltese coastline to achieve an equitable solution between the continental shelf areas appertaining to the two Parties, namely Libya and Malta.[293] (See Map 2, page 116) Brown cautions against the conclusion that this adjustment of the initial median line was an application of the proportionality test. He argues that the Court simply took into consideration the marked disparity in the comparative coastal lengths as a relevant circumstance.[294] Brown admits however, that it would have been very surprising to later find the Court had held the net effect of this modification did not satisfy the pro-

289. Churchill and Lowe note at least three cases where the proportionality principle was utilised, namely the *Greenland* v. *Jan Mayen* case, and the *Libya* v. *Malta* and *Libya* v. *Tunisia* cases. See Churchill and Lowe, op. cit. n. 283, at p. 189.

290. See *Case Concerning the Continental Shelf (Libya* v. *Malta)*, Judgment, *ICJ Rep.* (1985) p. 13, at pp. 43-46 and 49-50.

291. Ibid., at p. 44, para. 74, citing *ICJ Rep.* (1969) at p. 54, para. 101.

292. Ibid., at p. 44, para. 74.

293. Ibid., at pp. 42-43, paras. 71-73.

294. See E.D. Brown, 'The Libya-Malta Continental Shelf Case (1985)', in B. Cheng and E.D. Brown, eds., *Contemporary Problems of International Law: Essays in honour of Georg Schwarzenberger on his eightieth birthday* (London, Stevens & Sons 1988) pp. 3-18, at pp. 14-15, citing the *Libya* v. *Malta* Judgment at p. 49, para. 66.

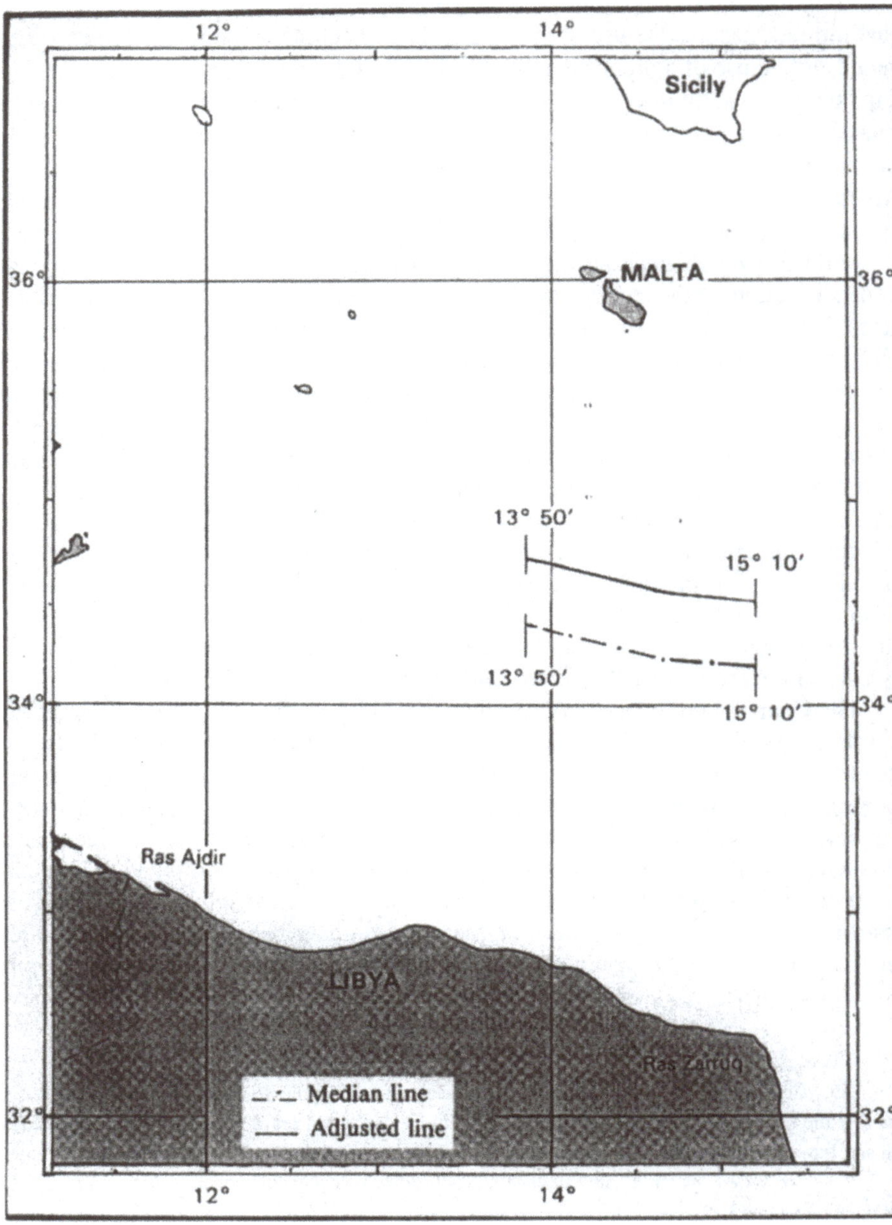

Map 2. Adjusted Median line proposed by the ICJ in the Case Concerning the Continental Shelf, (Libya/Malta) Judgment, ICJ Reports (1985) 13, at 54.

portionality test as one of the criteria for an equitable result.[295] This leads to the conclusion that although the proportionality principle is conceived by the Court as an *ex post facto* test to determine the equity of a proposed delimitation line; in reality it is applied by the Court throughout its deliberations to ascertain that the eventual result it arrives at will necessarily be an equitable one.

Given the large disparity in coastal lengths and land masses facing each other across the Timor Gap between Australia and a newly-independent East Timor state, a similar readjustment to the proposed median line continental shelf boundary is eminently possible by any tribunal tasked with adjudicating the matter. A putative median line boundary between a new East Timor state and Australia would thereby also be moved northwards like in the *Libya* v. *Malta* case to compensate for the disparity between the opposing coastal lengths of East Timor and Australia. The Australian negotiating position *vis-à-vis* a new East Timor state on this issue would also be based upon this premise.

Thus, the expectation that a median line continental shelf boundary would follow the 1997 Australia-Indonesia EEZ boundary line along the southern limits of Area A of the current Zone of Co-operation and thereby surrender most, if not all, of the current joint development area to a new East Timor state may be premature.[296] Instead, we may find that a suitably modified median line continental shelf boundary will in fact cut across the oil and gas fields currently being primed for exploitation, especially the Bayu-Undan gas project in what is currently within Area A. (see Map 3, page 118)

It is precisely at this juncture that a further co-operative arrangement is needed to deal with any straddling deposits. Indeed, it may be argued that the applicable international law is embodied in Articles 74(3) and 83(3) of the 1982 UN Convention on the Law of the Sea (CLOS). This requires just such a provisional arrangement for the joint development of the petroleum resources in the area as previously obtained under the 1989 Timor Gap treaty.[297] As Triggs notes, 'If Australia and East Timor do not agree upon a sea-bed boundary, either during the transitional period of UNCLOS or upon the independence of East Timor, cooperative arrangements for joint development are a sensible means of unlocking resources to the benefit of all stakeholders.'[298] The Arbitral Tribunal in the *Eritrea-Yemen, Phase II-Maritime Delimitation Award*, for example, held that the two Parties are bound to inform and consult one another on

295. Brown, ibid., at p. 17.

296. See G.A. McKee, 'The New Timor Gap: Will Australia now break with the past?', No. 62 *Inside Indonesia* (2000). McKee is of the opinion that 'a median line settlement under UNCLOS [sic] will enable East Timor to receive almost twice the benefit offered by a (Timor Gap) treaty Indonesia and Australia concluded in darker times.' See also Tanter, Selden and Shalom who quote McKee as arguing that 'the median line principle, which was given weight by Australia in the 1997 treaty with Indonesia, is significant for the new nation of East Timor since all the significant petroleum discoveries have been in the area north of the line. Thus East Timor may be entitled to the entire tax revenues.' loc. cit. n. 280, at p. 119, citing a letter to the authors by McKee, dated 5 November 1999.

297. See Triggs, loc. cit. n. 7, at p. 125.

298. Ibid.

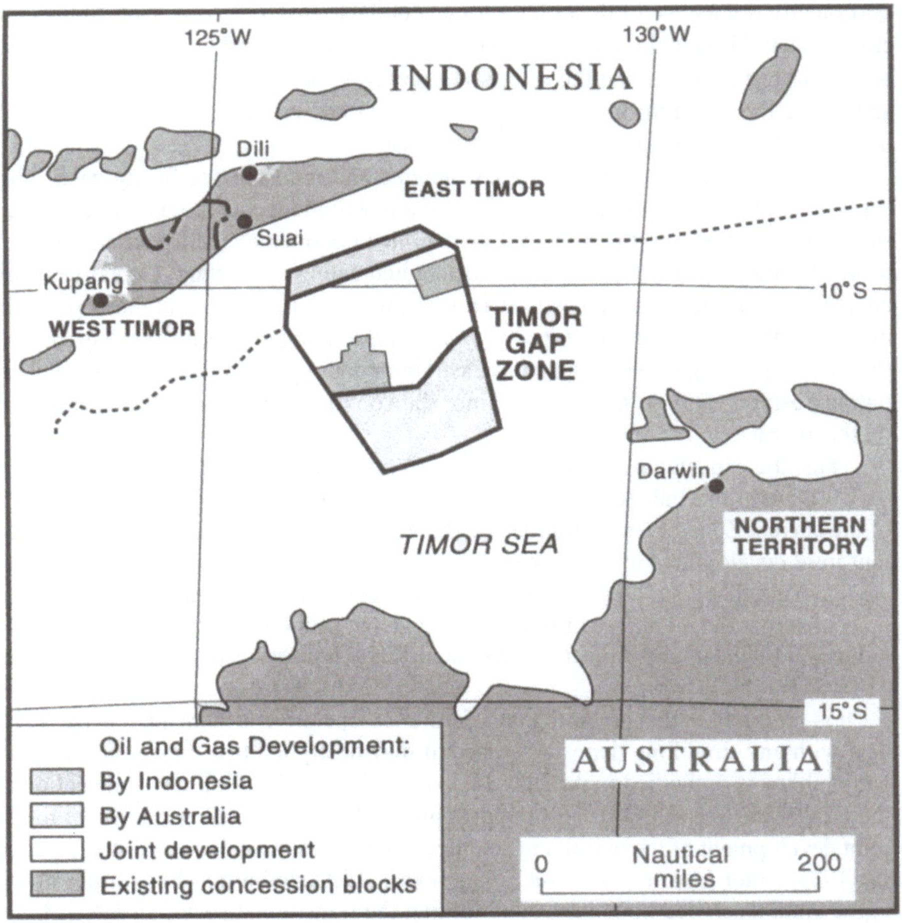

Map 3. Oil and Gas Development in the Timor Gap Zone of Co-operation.

any oil and gas deposit that may be discovered to straddle the recommended single maritime boundary between them or lie in its immediate vicinity.[299] The Tribunal inferred that, *inter alia,* state practice dictates that Eritrea and Yemen should give every consideration to the shared or joint or unitised exploitation of any straddling deposits.[300]

Moreover, the 1997 maritime boundary treaty delimiting the respective Australian and Indonesian EEZs would have provided a legal basis for the unitisation of such de-

299. *Eritrea-Yemen* (1999) *supra* n. 38, at para. 86.

300. Ibid., at para. 86.

posits.[301] Significantly, it echoes Article 20 of the Timor Gap treaty itself, which also provides for the unitisation of any hydrocarbon deposit found to extend across any boundary lines of Area A of the Zone of Co-operation. International transboundary unitization agreements based on similar straddle deposit clauses are especially prevalent in the North Sea.[302] These unitization agreements are arguably merely applying an alternative version of the joint development concept currently provided for in the 1989 Timor Gap treaty.[303] They too require an element of co-operation and further negotiation regarding the different legal issues arising from the implementation of the joint regime, even if this regime is nowhere near as complex as the current Timor Gap treaty regime. Thus these transboundary unitization agreements will not necessarily result in the financial windfall and consequent autonomy for the newly-independent East Timor state as envisaged by the proponents of a new median line continental shelf boundary replacing the Timor Gap treaty.

Indeed, worse may follow. Unlike the joint development model implemented by the Timor Gap treaty that envisages a straightforward 50:50 split of all government revenues between the two parties from petroleum development anywhere within Area A of the Zone of Co-operation,[304] many transboundary unitization agreements dealing with situations where a boundary is already drawn tend to arrive at very specific breakdowns of the revenue split between the two governments. These revenue splits are usually directly proportionate to how much (or little) of the deposit lying across the boundary is estimated to be located within the continental shelf of each state. For example, the Frigg Gas field lying across the UK-Norway continental shelf boundary was calculated as being 60.82% in the Norwegian sector and 39.18% in the UK sector.[305]

301. Art. 9 of the 1997 treaty provides that '[I]f any single accumulation of liquid hydrocarbons or natural gas, or if any other mineral deposit beneath the seabed, extends across the lines described in Arts. 1 and 3 of this Treaty, and the part of such accumulation or deposit that is situated on one side of the line is recoverable in fluid form wholly or in part from the other side of the line, the two Parties will seek to reach agreement on the manner in which the accumulation or deposit shall be most effectively exploited and on the equitable sharing of the benefits arising from such exploitation.

302. See UK-Norway Agreement Relating to the Exploitation of the Frigg Field Reservoir and the Transmission of Gas Therefrom to the United Kingdom, 10 May 1976, at 1977 *UK TS* No. 113 (Cmnd. 7043), 1098 *UNTS* 3. See J.C. Woodliffe, 'International Unitization of an Offshore Gas Field', 26 *ICLQ* (1977) at p. 338. Similar agreements relating to the Murchison and Statfjord Fields were also concluded between the United Kingdom and Norway on 16 October 1979, 1981 *UK TS* No. 39 (Cmnd. 8270) & No. 44 (Cmnd. 8282). The Anglo-Dutch Agreement Relating to the Exploitation of the Markham Field Reservoirs and the Offtake of Petroleum Therefrom, 26 May 1992, is a similar type of international transboundary unitization agreement. See 1993 *UK TS* No. 38 (Cmnd. 2254).

303. See Ong, loc. cit. n. 57, pp. 788-792, where a typology of three different categories of joint development models is described.

304. Art. 2(2)(a) of the 1989 treaty, op. cit. n. 3.

305. Det Norske Veritas, Draft Technical Report of Frigg Field Cessation Environmental Impact Assessment, prepared for TotalFinaElf, Report No. 99-4030, at p. 4.

Therefore, should a permanent continental shelf boundary applying a modified median line cut across the Bayu-Undan field, or indeed any other field in such a way that most of the deposit lies on the Australian side of the line, then in fact the percentage split of the government revenues derived from the exploitation of the resulting transboundary deposit may reflect very badly upon the new East Timor state, whereas presently it is entitled to 50% of these revenues from a petroleum deposit found anywhere in Area A of the Zone of Co-operation.

An appreciation of the foregoing legal and practical difficulties arising from the proposed replacement of the Timor Gap joint development regime with a median line continental shelf boundary appears to underlie the pragmatic stance adopted by the UNTAET in its negotiating relationship with Australia on the subject of the continuing implementation of the Timor Gap treaty.

This is regardless of the possible adoption by a succeeding new East Timor state of the 'clean slate' rule in its approach to the treaty and Australian acquiescence with the legality of this approach. Thus, it is perhaps unsurprising that the 2000 Memorandum of Understanding agreed between UNTAET and Australia provides for the continued applicability of the terms of the Timor Gap treaty including, *inter alia,* all actions taken by either the Ministerial Council for the Zone of Co-operation or the Joint Authority for Area A of the Zone, as well as all existing Production Sharing Contracts. (paras. 2(b) and (c), respectively) The joint development principle embodied in the Timor Gap treaty therefore continues to apply under the terms of the 2000 MOU. It is submitted here that regardless of the political stance taken up by a new East Timor state with regard to the Timor Gap treaty itself, joint development will continue to be a cornerstone of the diplomatic relations between this new state and Australia over the Timor Gap area, albeit with some fine tuning as to the exact boundaries of the Zone of Co-operation and the proportions of the petroleum revenues shared between the contracting parties.

In this respect, the present continuation of the joint development approach to the hydrocarbon resources of the Timor Gap, accords with Koskenniemi's observation that '[t]he absence of clear-cut rules (in the international law of state succession) on continuation and disruption of treaty relations or detailed lists of fundamental rights of states, for instance, makes it possible to combine continuation at the level of abstract status with important changes at the level of specific rights and duties.'[306]

5. CONCLUSIONS

In the not too distant future, East Timor will take up its rightful place as a new sovereign state. Traub suggests that the UNTAET and the National Council of Timorese Resistance (CNRT) have agreed on the road to independence.[307] The process will be-

306. Koskenniemi, op. cit. n. 161, at p. 93.

307. J. Traub, 'Inventing East Timor', Vol. 79, No. 4, *Foreign Affairs* (2000) pp. 74-89, at p. 88.

gin with a mass convocation of East Timorese to debate constitutional principles, followed by the drafting of a constitution and the election of a Constituent Assembly. Latest reports suggest that this election will take place on 30 August 2001. The Assembly elections will lead to the drafting of a new Constitution within ninety (90) days, following which the Assembly will transform itself into Parliament. Then, in what is expected to be late 2001 or early 2002, the elected Assembly/Parliament will sign the constitution and the country will declare its independence.[308]

This new legal status raises several questions in respect of the continuing application of Timor Gap treaty. These questions have been enumerated in this essay as follows: Are new states bound to accept maritime boundary treaties agreed by predecessor states? Is the Timor Gap treaty to be regarded as a maritime boundary treaty for this purpose? Will a new East Timor state succeed to the Timor Gap treaty initially agreed between Indonesia and Australia? Finally, even if the Timor Gap treaty is found to be inapplicable in this context, is there nevertheless a legal requirement to jointly develop the hydrocarbon deposits found in the overlapping continental shelf claims area that will result from the treaty being rendered invalid, or otherwise inapplicable?

At least three major aspects of the many legal issues discussed above suggest that the Timor Gap treaty instrument in itself will *not* succeed to a newly independent East Timor state. These outstanding legal issues are firstly, the general uncertainty as to whether the Timor Gap treaty falls within the category of continental shelf boundary treaties that can in turn be considered to be territorial boundary treaties, thereby constituting an exception to the 'clean slate' rule embodied in the 1978 Vienna Convention, such that it continues to bind the successor state, namely the newly independent East Timor state. Secondly, the specific uncertainty surrounding the question whether the Timor Gap treaty providing for joint development in the continental shelf can be included within the category of continental shelf boundary treaties. Finally, the fact that the Timor Gap treaty was established as a provisional, and therefore temporary, joint development arrangement for shared hydrocarbon resources in the continental shelf and not a permanent continental shelf boundary delimitation means that it is unlikely to fall within the exception to the 'clean slate' rule. The overall uncertainty over the categorisation of the Timor Gap treaty leads to an initial conclusion that it would *not* apply to a newly independent East Timor state, especially when the presumption of a 'clean slate' embodied in the 1978 Vienna Convention is taken into account.

On the other hand, it is submitted here that the very nature of the legal problem that now confronts the two parties with the Timor Gap treaty's discontinuation will almost inevitably lead them to contemplate a similar type of joint development arrangement to resolve the outstanding legal issues raised by the shared hydrocarbon resour-

308. The gradual process towards laying the foundations for democratically elected government in East Timor is continuing and was recently boosted by the news that one of East Timor's biggest and best known political groups, *Freitilin*, which spearheaded the bloody 24-year struggle for independence from Indonesia has begun the process of transforming itself from a revolutionary front to a mainstream political party. See M. Dodd, *Sydney Morning Herald*, Australia newspaper (May 2000).

ces in their overlapping continental shelf claims. This is evidenced by the interim agreement between UNTAET and Australia to continue the current joint development regime while negotiating a new treaty as noted above. In other words, a newly independent East Timor state will need to negotiate an alternative joint development regime with Australia to exploit the shared hydrocarbons coveted by both parties. The legal arguments developed in the course of this essay conspire to suggest that the joint development principle currently embodied in the present Timor Gap arrangement is sufficiently robust to stand the test of time. The precise application of the joint development principle, whether in its present form, or through a system of compulsory transboundary unitizations of straddling hydrocarbon deposits across a modified median line continental shelf boundary, is reliant upon the political will of the future parties. International law does not currently prescribe a specific solution for this problem of hydrocarbon deposits situated in a disputed area of overlapping continental shelf claims. It merely provides for several different models of co-operation in the joint development of these deposits, any model of which can be utilized by agreement between the parties concerned.[309]

Therefore, it is clear that the intense co-operative effort by both Australia and Indonesia, engendered and maintained by the negotiation, agreement and implementation of the 1989 Timor Gap treaty throughout the 1990s, will need to continue at a high diplomatic level in the new bilateral relationship between Australia and an independent East Timor state. Continued high level co-operation is imperative to prevent possible disruption of the oil and especially natural gas supplies from Area A of the current Zone of Co-operation. Thus, modifying the present joint development arrangements in the Timor Gap, rather than beginning negotiations anew for a permanent maritime boundary settlement under the 'clean slate' approach represents the politically astute, economically viable and arguably also legally correct, if not legally imperative, solution to the Timor Gap dilemma.

---

309. See Ong, op. cit. n. 57, at pp. 788-792, for a basic typology of the main joint development models adopted by states in their bilateral practice on this issue.

POSTSCRIPT

The 2001 Memorandum of Understanding between Australia and the UNTAET providing for the Timor Sea Arrangement to be adopted between Australia and East Timor upon East Timor's independence

1. INTRODUCTION

Very soon after this article was accepted for publication by the *Netherlands Yearbook of International Law*, news arrived that the UN Transitional Administration for East Timor (UNTAET), negotiating on behalf of a future independent East Timor state, had signed a new joint development agreement with Australia.[1] This agreement, called the Timor Sea Arrangement, is to be adopted by the two states upon East Timor's full independence. This is indeed a significant achievement in the prospects for future joint development of the petroleum resources in the Timor Gap area. The *Netherlands Yearbook* has kindly allowed me to add a postscript to this article dealing with the implications of this latest development in the Timor Gap saga. Space and time constraints however do not permit me to do more than highlight the particular aspects of the new agreement that are especially pertinent to arguments I put forward in the article.

Accordingly, I shall structure the postscript in the following manner: First, I shall briefly examine the legal status of the 2001 Memorandum of Understanding (MOU), especially as it pertains to a newly-independent East Timor state. Secondly, I shall compare the joint development regime to be established by the new Timor Sea Arrangement with the regime that prevailed under the 1989 Timor Gap treaty and continued by the 2000 MOU. Finally, I shall assess how far the new Arrangement embodies the joint development solution I advocated over the straightforward continental shelf boundary delimitation for the overlapping continental shelf claims dispute in the presence of common offshore oil and gas deposits. My conclusions to this postscript reaffirm the view that this new joint development agreement provides the most pragmatic alternative to an otherwise intractable legal dispute that cannot be resolved merely by submission to an international tribunal.

1. Memorandum of Understanding (MOU) between Australia and the UNTAET, 2001 incorporating the Timor Sea Arrangement as Attachment 'A'. Adopted on 5 July 2001. The MOU also includes Annexes A to F. Under Art. 1(a), the 'Arrangement' also means these Annexes and any others subsequently agreed between East Timor and Australia. The Arrangement will enter into force 30 days after both parties have notified each other in writing that their respective requirements for its entry into force have been fulfilled (Art. 25).

2. THE UNCERTAIN LEGAL STATUS OF THE NEW TIMOR SEA ARRANGEMENT

At the outset of this analysis, it is important to note the uncertain legal status of this arrangement under international law in respect of a future, newly-independent East Timor state. The present 2001 MOU, like the 1989 Timor Gap treaty and the 2000 MOU before it (both discussed in the article above), will not necessarily be legally enforceable against the new East Timor state that will soon rise to take its place in the international community of states. This is because none of these treaties have directly involved the fledgling East Timor state itself. The 1989 Timor Gap treaty was agreed between Australia and Indonesia, and the two later agreements in 2000 and 2001 were between Australia and the UN Transitional Administration in East Timor (UNTAET). Although the new Timor Sea Arrangement purports to apply to an East Timor state, this is belied by the MOU itself. It merely provides that the Arrangement forming Attachment 'A' to the MOU 'is *suitable* for adoption as an agreement between Australia and East Timor upon East Timor's independence.'[2] Moreover, the final recital of the Preamble to the Arrangement itself only notes 'the *desirability* of Australia and East Timor entering into a Treaty providing for the continued development of the petroleum resources in an area of seabed between Australia and East Timor' [emphasis added]. The clear legal implication here is that both the 2001 MOU and the new Arrangement it embodies cannot of themselves be binding upon a newly-independent East Timor state without its future, formal consent.

The East Timor Transitional Cabinet reaffirms this view in its press release on the eve of the adoption of the 2001 MOU. It pointed out that before entering into force, the new Arrangement must be approved by the elected government of East Timor in accordance with its constitutional processes.[3] In other words, 'it will be up to the newly elected East Timor government to decide whether it wants the treaty or not.'[4] This view is also confirmed in the Australian government's own joint media release. This provides that 'the terms of the (new) Arrangement are to be incorporated into a new treaty upon East Timor's independence, replacing the existing agreement.'[5]

Therefore, as a newly-independent state, East Timor will be fully entitled to argue for the application of the 'clean slate' rule of state succession to deny the future application of the Timor Sea Arrangement and indeed even the 2000 and 2001 MOUs between Australia and the UNTAET. Balanced against this view are the arguments I have made in Section 3.2 above concerning the possible succession of a new East Timor state to the joint development regime established by the 1989 Timor Gap treaty. These arguments may also be utilised for the succession of a new East Timor state

---

2. MOU, 2001, ibid. [emphasis added].

3. Press Release, *Timor Sea Arrangement approved by East Timor Cabinet* (Dili, 3 July 2001).

4. Statement by P. Galbraith, 'East Timor Transitional Cabinet Member for Political Affairs and Timor Sea', in Press Release, ibid.

5. Joint Media Release by the (Australian) Minister for Foreign Affairs, the Minister for Industry, Science and Resources and the Attorney-General, *Australia, East Timor and UN agree on new resources deal for the Timor Sea.*

to both the 2000 and 2001 agreements between the UNTAET and Australia. They relate mainly to the arguably territorial nature of the arrangements, which constitute an almost uniformly accepted exception to the 'clean slate' rule for state succession among newly-independent states.

However, these arguments are increasingly difficult to sustain in legal, policy and plain factual terms. It is clear that neither the UNTAET, nor the East Timorese representatives, nor even the Australians themselves regard these agreements as continuing to be applicable upon a future East Timor state under the state succession doctrine. The apparent consensus on all sides as to their lack of succession means that none of these agreements will in themselves be regarded as legally binding upon a newly-independent East Timor state should it choose to reject them upon full independence.

Thus, in the absence of an explicit undertaking by the new East Timor government to accept them unconditionally once full independence from the UN transitional administration has transpired, neither the present nor proposed joint development regime will be applicable. The new East Timor state will therefore retain full discretion to reject the 2000 and 2001 MOUs between Australia and the UNTAET. This is despite the endorsement of this new arrangement by the East Timor Transitional Cabinet.[6] Even explicit undertakings by a provisional East Timor government to the outgoing UNTAET administration in the immediate period prior to full independence will not necessarily bind the new East Timor state.

A further legal uncertainty arising from adoption of the 2001 MOU embodying the Timor Sea Arrangement concerns the timing of its initiation. The Australian joint media release suggests that the revenues from the petroleum development in the designated Area will only flow from 2004,[7] although East Timor itself is widely expected to achieve independence within the next year or so (2001/2002).[8] Therefore, in the interim period before the 2001 Arrangement is formally adopted by the new East Timor state, it should be presumed that the 2000 MOU providing for the *status quo* is to be applied, namely the 1989 Timor Gap treaty regime with equal division of the upstream petroleum revenues.

3. A COMPARATIVE ANALYSIS OF THE PRINCIPLES APPLIED IN BOTH JOINT DEVELOPMENT REGIMES

Moving on from the legal uncertainty surrounding the enforceability of the 2001 Arrangement in respect of a newly-independent East Timor state, we can now compare the joint development regime it purports to establish with the previous 1989 treaty regime, which was in turn continued by the 2000 agreement. First, we focus on the new-

6. Press Release (Dili, 3 July 2001) *supra* n. 3.

7. Australian Joint Media Release, *supra* n. 5.

8. The first post-independence East Timor elections for a Constituent Assembly will take place on 30 August 2001. For latest news on East Timor's progress towards full independence and statehood, see: http://www.un.org/peace/etimor/news.

ly designated Joint Petroleum Development Area (JPDA) and the radically different division of upstream revenues established by the 2001 Arrangement. Next, the main features of the proposed new joint development regime will be examined.

3.1 The designated joint development area

The latitude and longitude co-ordinates of the designated Joint Petroleum Development Area (JPDA) established by Article 3 of the new Timor Sea Arrangement are provided in Annex A to the 2001 MOU. The JPDA covers precisely the same area as Area A of the 1989 Zone of Co-operation treaty, which was subject to a 50:50 split in the government revenues derived from the upstream petroleum development activities undertaken there. The 2000 MOU continues the terms of the previous treaty until the 2001 Arrangement enters into force.

The new Arrangement however incorporates a major distributional realignment in the division of upstream revenues whereby the future East Timor state will receive 90% of the proceeds with Australia's share reduced to only 10%. (Art. 4(a)) East Timor's share of the revenues is estimated to be more than A$7 billion (US$ 4 – US$ 5 billion) over the next 20 years from 2004. Australia stands to gain about A$ 1billion in direct revenue over that period. On the other hand, the downstream benefits that will accrue to Australia are potentially highly lucrative, as virtually all the oil and gas found is to be refined or otherwise industrially processed in Darwin, Australia.[9] Australia is likely to make more than four or five times the amount of its direct revenues from refining Timor Sea oil and gas as the new East Timor state is not expected to build the facilities to do so in the near future.[10]

3.2 The non-prejudice clause

This is a standard clause incorporated in most joint development agreements of this kind, involving an as yet undelimited area of overlapping continental shelf claims. Its main purpose here under Article 2(b) is to ensure that neither the provisions of the new Arrangement, nor any acts undertaken during the time it is in force, can be interpreted as prejudicing or affecting either parties' legal positions and rights to the seabed concerned.

3.3 The joint development principle

It is imperative to note the extent to which the joint development principle underlies overall regime despite the uneven 90:10 division of revenues in favour of East Timor. This principle manifests itself most vividly in the joint development of common deposits found in the designated JPDA. For example, Article 3(b) provides for the joint

9. Australian Joint Media Release, *supra* n. 5.

10. See J. Aglionby, 'East Timor signs lucrative oil deal', *The Guardian*, UK newspaper (6 July 2001) at p. 14.

control, management, exploration, development and exploitation of the petroleum resources in the designated JPDA. Moreover, Article 4(a) first provides that East Timor and Australia shall have title to all petroleum produced in the JPDA, before the 90:10 division is introduced. Thus, the joint development principle itself is clearly applied by the 2001 Arrangement, albeit ultimately unequally.

The joint development principle also applies to the provision for the unitisation of deposits found to straddle the designated joint development area, in the sense that any petroleum deposit extending across the JPDA boundary is treated as a single entity for management and development purposes, under Article 9(a). Article 9(b) further provides that the two parties shall reach an agreement on the effective exploitation and equitable sharing of the benefits from such unitisations. Pursuant to this provision, Annex E of the Arrangement contains a unitisation agreement for the 'Greater Sunrise' deposits such that 20% of production is attributed to the JPDA and the remaining 80% to Australia. The joint development principle is also evident in the requirement that both parties shall make every possible effort to agree on joint fiscal arrangements for petroleum activities in the JPDA (Art. 5(a)(i)).

3.4 **Jurisdiction**

Another aspect of the proposed joint development regime to be instituted once the newly-independent East Timor state adopts the new Arrangement relates to the criminal jurisdiction powers exercised by both parties to the 2001 Arrangement. Essentially these powers are similar to those provided under the corresponding provisions of the 1989 Timor Gap treaty. Article 14(a) of the 2001 Arrangement initially provides for the application of the nationality principle of jurisdiction in relation to crimes perpetrated in the JPDA by nationals and permanent residents of either of the two countries. In other words, a crime committed by an Australian will be subject to Australian criminal law and *vice versa*.

However, Article 14(b) applies both East Timor and Australian criminal laws to any offence committed in the JPDA by a third state's national, thus reaffirming the joint exercise of criminal jurisdiction powers held by both parties. This rule is of course subject to the usual protection against double jeopardy, thus preventing a person from being tried and discharged or acquitted, or convicted for the same offence twice. A further exception is provided in Article 14(d) for crimes committed aboard vessels in JPDA waters or flights over the area. These are subject to the flag state jurisdiction as per the international norm.

3.5 **Institutional framework**

Finally we examine the extent to which the joint development principle underlies the institutional framework to be introduced for overseeing the petroleum activity in the JPDA. Article 6(a) of the Arrangement establishes a three-tiered joint administrative structure comprising of a Designated Authority (DA), Joint Commission (JC) and Ministerial Council (MC). This appears to be different from the two-tier system established under the 1989 treaty and continued by the 2000 MOU, incorporating a

Ministerial Council and Joint Authority. In practice, however, the different institutional design of the 2001 Arrangement does not necessarily depart from the essential principle of joint decision-making at the highest institutional level.

For example, the Ministerial Council (MC) shall consist of an equal number of ministers from East Timor and Australia (Art. 6(d)(i)). It is mandated to consider any matter relating to the operation of this Arrangement that is referred to it by either East Timor, Australia, (Art. 6(d)(i)) or their Joint Commission (JC) members (Art. 6(c)(iii)). However, in the event that the MC is unable to resolve a matter, either party may invoke the dispute resolution procedures set out in Annex B to the Arrangement (Art. 6(d)(ii)). The only exception to the decision-making authority of the MC relates to the issue of the construction of pipelines from the JPDA to the territory of either state party (Art. 8(c)). This is the sole preserve of the JC.

The Commissioners are also appointed by East Timor and Australia, the only difference with the equally balanced MC membership here being that East Timor shall appoint one more commissioner than Australia. The JC shall establish policies and regulations relating to petroleum activities in the JPDA and oversee the work of the Designated Authority (DA) (Art. 6(c)(i)). A more detailed but non-exhaustive list of the powers and functions of the JC is set out in Annex D (Art. 6(c)(ii)). The JC shall meet annually or as required and shall be chaired by a Commissioner nominated by the parties on an alternate basis (Art. 6(c)(iv)).

Finally, the Designated Authority (DA) will play the same role as the Joint Authority under the 1989 treaty. It is responsible to the JC and carries out the day-to-day regulation and management of petroleum activities (Art. 6(b)(iv)). A non-exclusive listing of more detailed powers and functions of the DA is set out in Annex C (Art. 6(b)(v). Significantly, bearing in mind the one-sided (90:10) breakdown of upstream revenues, the DA is designated by the JC,[11] but after the first three years of the Arrangement coming into force, the DA shall revert to the East Timor Government Ministry responsible for petroleum activities, or an East Timor statutory authority (Art. 6(b)(ii)). During these three years, the DA will have juridical personality and such legal capacities under the laws of both East Timor and Australia as necessary for the exercise of its powers and performance of its functions (Art. 6(b)(iii)).

4. CONCLUSIONS

Notwithstanding the uncertain legal status of the proposed Timor Sea Arrangement, 2001 *vis-à-vis* a newly-independent East Timor state, it is important to highlight the joint development principle that this new agreement embodies. As I noted in section 4 of the article above, there are several legal arguments suggesting that joint development is the most practical legal solution for the resolution of the overlapping claims dispute in the Timor Sea. Even leaving aside the question as to whether the parties

---

11. Unlike for the JC and MC, there is no provision in either Art. 6 or Annex C for the membership of the DA beyond the requirement that it must be designated by the JC.

concerned should succeed to the joint development regime first introduced by the 1989 Timor Gap treaty, it is possible to note more compelling legal arguments for such international co-operation over shared natural resources generally.[12]

In particular, Article 83 of the 1982 UN Law of the Sea Convention is specifically invoked by Article 2(a) of the 2001 Arrangement as requiring states to make every effort to enter into provisional arrangements of a practical nature pending a final continental shelf delimitation agreement between them. In line with this provision, international tribunals are increasingly proposing joint development agreements as a means of resolving overlapping continental shelf claims in the presence of hydrocarbon deposits. The latest example comes from the Permanent Court of Arbitration in the *Eritrea-Yemen Arbitration (Phase II-Maritime Delimitation).*[13] According to the Tribunal, cooperative state practice in the exploitation of resources that straddle maritime boundaries had particular relevance in the instant case between Yemen and Eritrea as they face each other across a relatively narrow body of water,[14] very much like the present situation between Australia and East Timor. The Tribunal concluded that 'Eritrea and Yemen should give *every consideration* to the shared or joint or unitised exploitation of any such (straddling) resources'[15] [emphasis added].

Finally, it should always be borne in mind that the submission of this continental shelf dispute to an international tribunal will not necessarily result in the award of the entire disputed area to a new East Timor state. Quite apart from the delay this adjudication process would entail for the parties concerned, there is a real possibility that the continental shelf boundary line proposed by a tribunal will cut across already discovered hydrocarbon deposits, inevitably requiring renewed bilateral negotiations as to how these deposits will be divided. Thus, despite continuing media speculation as to whether a new East Timor state might be able to secure an even better legal result by bringing the dispute to an international adjudication procedure, I would conclude unequivocally that the proposed joint development regime in the 2001 Timor Sea Arrangement represents the fairest and most pragmatic legal solution that could be arrived at given the circumstances of this case.

12. See D.M. Ong, 'Joint Development of Common Offshore Oil and Gas Deposits: 'Mere' State Practice or Customary International Law?', 93 *AJIL* (1999) pp. 771-804.

13. See Arbitral Tribunal Award, 17 December 1999. Accessed at Permanent Court of Arbitration website: <http://www.pca-cpa.org>

14. Ibid., at paras. 84 and 85.

15. Ibid., at para. 86.

DOCUMENTATION

The material in the Documentation Section is, for the most part, based on the surveys carried out in the T.M.C. Asser Instituut and edited by members of the Institute's staff.

The systematic classification scheme used for the surveys, and for the Documentation Section, is set out on the following pages. It is based on the 'Model Plan for the Classification of Documents concerning State Practice in the field of Public International Law', as adopted by the Committee of Ministers of the Council of Europe in Resolution 68 (17) of 28 June 1968. The 'Model Plan' has been considerably enlarged and elaborated in order to meet the specific needs of the Institute's projects; the classification numbers appearing in the original 'Model Plan' are preceded by an asterisk.

CLASSIFICATION SCHEME

Part One	International Law in General
Part Two	Sources of International Law
Part Three	Subjects of International Law
Part Four	The Position of the Individual in International Law
Part Five	Organs of the State
Part Six	The Law of Treaties
Part Seven	Personal Jurisdiction of the State
Part Eight	State Territory and Territorial Jurisdiction
Part Nine	Seas, Waterways
Part Ten	The Air Space, Outer Space
Part Eleven	Responsibility
Part Twelve	Pacific Settlement of Disputes
Part Thirteen	Coercion and Use of Force Short of War
Part Fourteen	Armed Conflicts (War)
Part Fifteen	Neutrality, Non-Belligerency
Part Sixteen	Legal Aspects of International Relations in Various Matters

The classification numbers preceded by an asterisk appear in the 'Model Plan for the Classification of Documents concerning State Practice in the field of Public International Law', as adopted by the Committee of Ministers of the Council of Europe in 1968.

*	1.	**Part One:**	**INTERNATIONAL LAW IN GENERAL**
	1.0	0	HISTORY
*	1.1	I	NATURE, BASIS, PURPOSE
	1.10		A. In general
	1.11		B. Theoretical and philosophical aspects of international law
	1.12		C. Impact of ideologies and religions on international law (see also 1.17)
	1.13		D. The nature of international rights and duties
	1.131		1. *Jus cogens* in international law (see also 6.426)
	1.132		2. Effectiveness
	1.133		3. Abuse of rights
	1.134		4. Estoppel
	1.135		5. Prescription
	1.136		6. General principles of international law (see 2.2)
	1.14		E. Relation between public international law and other fields of law relating to transnational relationships
	1.15		F. Political, economic and other non-legal aspects of international relations and their impact on international law
	1.16		G. Role of law in international relations (see also 12.12)
	1.17		H. Attitude of various groups of States towards international law (see also 1.12)
	1.171		1. Western States
	1.172		2. American States
	1.173		3. Newly independent States
	1.174		4. Communist States
	1.175		5. Other groups of States
	1.176		6. Dutch practice
	1.18		I. Regional international law (see also 3.222)
	1.19		J. General – particular international law
*	1.2	II	RELATIONSHIP BETWEEN INTERNATIONAL LAW AND MUNICIPAL LAW
*	1.20		A. In general
	1.201		1. Monist and dualist theories
	1.202		2. Enforcement of international law in municipal law
	1.203		3. Conflict between international law and municipal law
	1.204		4. Self-executing provisions of treaties or decisions of international organizations
*	1.21		B. International law in municipal courts
*	1.22		C. Municipal remedies for violation of international law
	1.23		D. Supranational law and municipal law
	1.3	III	PEACE RESEARCH

*	**2.**	**Part Two:**	**SOURCES OF INTERNATIONAL LAW**
	2.0	0	In general
	2.01		A. Conflicts between sources (see also 6.223 and 6.224)
*	2.1	I	TREATIES (see also 6.)
*	2.2	II	CUSTOM
	2.21		A. Usage
*	2.3	III	GENERAL PRINCIPLES OF LAW
*	2.4	IV	JUDICIAL DECISIONS (see also 12.26 et seq.)
*	2.5	V	OPINIONS OF WRITERS
*	2.6	VI	EQUITY
*	2.7	VII	UNILATERAL ACTS
	2.71		A. Unilateral acts of States (see also 13.1)
*	2.72		B. Acts and decisions of international organizations (see 3.213)
*	2.73		C. Acts and decisions of international conferences (see also 6.)
*	2.8	VIII	CODIFICATION AND PROGRESSIVE DEVELOPMENT
*	2.9	IX	COMITY (for diplomatic custom: see 5.271)
	2.10	X	CODES OF CONDUCT
*	**3.**	**Part Three:**	**SUBJECTS OF INTERNATIONAL LAW**
	3.0	0	In general
*	3.1	I	STATES
*	3.11		A. International status; fundamental rights and duties
	3.110		0. In general
*	3.111		1. Sovereignty and independence (see also 8.21)
*	3.112		2. Non-intervention (see also 13.14 and 13.222)
*	3.113		3. Domestic jurisdiction
*	3.114		4. Equality of States
	3.1141		a. Immunity of foreign States and of their organs and property
	3.1142		b. Recognition and enforcement of acts of foreign States (see 8.24)
	3.115		5. Economic rights and duties of States
	3.116		6. Other fundamental rights and duties of States (see also 11.215 and 14.1124)

*	3.12		B. Recognition (see also 2.71, for recognition of insurgency and belligerency: see 3.31, 3.32)
	3.120		0. In general
*	3.121		1. Recognition of States
*	3.122		2. Recognition of governments
*	3.123		3. Forms of recognition
*	3.1231		a. *De facto* and *de jure* recognition
*	3.1232		b. Conditional recognition
*	3.1233		c. Implied recognition
*	3.1234		d. Collective recognition
*	3.124		4. Retroactive effect of recognition
*	3.125		5. Non-recognition
*	3.13		C. Types of States
*	3.131		1. Unitary States, federal States and confederations
*	3.132		2. Personal unions, real unions (also the Commonwealth and the Kingdom of the Netherlands)
*	3.133		3. Permanently neutral States (see also 15.2 and 15.3)
*	3.134		4. Dependent States (see also 3.34)
*	3.1341		a. Protectorates
*	3.1342		b. Vassal States
	3.1343		c. 'Satellite' States
	3.135		5. Divided States
*	3.14		D. Formation, continuity and succession of States (for succession of international organizations: see 3.216)
*	3.141		1. Formation
	3.1411		a. Self-determination
	3.1412		b. Decolonization
*	3.142		2. Identity, continuity
*	3.143		3. The effect of territorial change
*	3.144		4. The effect of extinction of States
*	3.2	II	INTERNATIONAL ORGANIZATIONS (see also 12.28)
*	3.21		A. In general
*	3.211		1. Legal status
	3.2111		a. Personality, recognition
*	3.2112		b. Powers, including treaty-making power (see also 6.61)
	3.21121		(i) Competence of various organs
	3.21122		(ii) Procedure of decision-making
*	3.2113		c. Privileges and immunities
	3.2114		d. Financial arrangements
*	3.212		2. Participation of States in the activities of international organizations
*	3.2121		a. Admission
*	3.2122		b. Suspension, withdrawal, expulsion
*	3.2123		c. Obligations (and rights) of membership
*	3.2124		d. Representation of States

*	3.213		3. Legal effect of acts of international organizations
*	3.214		4. International officials
	3.2141		a. Legal status
	3.2142		b. Administrative jurisdiction
*	3.215		5. Responsibility of international organizations (see Part Eleven)
	3.216		6. Succession of international organizations
	3.217		7. Co-operation and co-ordination between international organizations
*	3.22		B. Particular aspects
*	3.221		1. Universal organizations (in alphabetical order)
*	3.222		2. Regional organizations (in alphabetical order; see also 1.18)
*	3.223		3. Organizations constituting integrated (economic, etc.) communities (in alphabetical order)
*	3.224		4. Other types of organizations (in alphabetical order; including non-governmental organizations)
*	3.3	III	OTHER SUBJECTS OF INTERNATIONAL LAW
*	3.31		A. Insurgents; national liberation movements
*	3.32		B. Belligerents
*	3.33		C. The Holy See
	3.34		D. Non-autonomous territories (see also 3.134)
*	3.341		1. Mandated territories
*	3.342		2. Trust territories
*	3.343		3. Condominiums
*	3.344		4. Special regimes (e.g., Cracow, Danzig, territories under UN administration, etc.)
	3.345		5. Colonies and similar regimes
	3.35		E. Natural persons (see also 3.214; for international responsibility: see 11.241)
	3.36		F. Corporations (for international responsibility: see 11.243)
	3.361		1. National corporations
	3.362		2. International corporations
	3.363		3. Transnational corporations
*	3.37		G. Miscellaneous (tribes, chartered companies, etc.)
*	**4.**	**Part Four:**	**THE POSITION OF THE INDIVIDUAL (INCLUDING THE CORPORATION IN INTERNATIONAL LAW** (see also 3.35 and 3.36)
*	4.1	I	NATIONALITY
	4.10		A. In general; function; nationality and citizenship; 'protected persons'
	4.11		B. Rights and duties attached to nationality
	4.12		C. Acquisition
	4.13		D. Loss
	4.14		E. Option
	4.15		F. Multiple nationality
	4.16		G. Married women

	4.17		H. Right of expatriation and repatriation
	4.18		I. Corporations
*	4.2	II	DIPLOMATIC PROTECTION (see part Eleven)
*	4.3	III	ALIENS OR NON-NATIONALS (for enemy persons and property: see 14.1223)
	4.31		A. Admittance (for expulsion: see 4.65)
	4.311		1. Freedom of establishment
	4.32		B. Passports and visas
	4.33		C. Status of aliens; general standard of treatment
	4.34		D. National jurisdiction over aliens (see also 8.233 and 11.3)
	4.340		0. In general
	4.341		1. Exhaustion of local remedies (see 11.21712)
	4.342		2. Denial of justice
	4.343		3. Calvo clause
	4.35		E. Extraterritorial jurisdiction (see 7.2 et seq.)
	4.36		F. Rights and duties of aliens (see also 4.311)
	4.361		1. Duties
	4.362		2. Property rights (see also 16.141)
	4.3621		a. Nationalization, expropriation
	4.3622		b. Reparation (see 11.216)
	4.363		3. Other rights
*	4.4	IV	MINORITIES (see also 4.7 et seq.)
	4.41		A. Genocide (see also Part Eleven)
*	4.5	V	STATELESSNESS, REFUGEES, SLAVERY
	4.51		A. Statelessness (including factual statelessness)
	4.52		B. Refugees
	4.53		C. Slavery (see 16.52)
*	4.6	VI	IMMIGRATION, EMIGRATION, EXTRADITION, EXPULSION, ASYLUM
	4.61		A. Immigration
	4.62		B. Emigration
	4.63		C. Extradition
	4.64		D. Other assistance in criminal matters (for judicial assistance in other fields: see 16.7241)
	4.65		E. Expulsion
	4.66		F. Asylum (for diplomatic asylum: see 5.28)

*	4.7	VII	PROTECTION OF HUMAN RIGHTS AND FUNDAMENTAL FREEDOMS (the various rights successively)
	4.71		A. Individual right of petition
	4.72		B. Universal Declaration, 1948
	4.73		C. European Convention, 1950
	4.74		D. UN Covenants
	4.741		1. Civil and Political Rights
	4.742		2. Economic and Social Rights
	4.75		E. European Social Charter
*	4.8	VIII	RESPONSIBILITY OF THE INDIVIDUAL (see Part Eleven)
*	**5.**	**Part Five:**	**ORGANS OF THE STATE**
	5.0	0	In general: representation of States (for representation in international organizations: see 3.2124)
	5.01		A. Diplomacy
*	5.1	I	THE HEAD OF STATE, THE FOREIGN MINISTER, THE GOVERNMENT, Etc.
	5.10		A. In general
	5.11		B. Head of State
	5.12		C. The Government
	5.13		D. The Ministers
	5.14		E. Other central State organs
*	5.2	II	DIPLOMATIC MISSIONS
	5.21		A. Diplomatic relations: right of legation
	5.210		0. In general
	5.211		1. Establishment
	5.22		B. Internal structure of the foreign service and of the diplomatic mission
	5.23		C. Ranks, level, and precedence
	5.231		1. [Heads of] missions
	5.232		2. Staff members and other personnel
	5.233		3. Diplomatic corps; precedence
	5.24		D. Appointment
	5.241		1. Head of the mission
	5.242		2. Staff members
	5.243		3. Other personnel
	5.25		E. Commencement and termination of the mission
	5.251		1. Commencement
	5.252		2. Termination, declaration of *persona non grata*, severance of diplomatic relations (see also 13.18 and 14.1221)
	5.26		F. Functions (for diplomatic protection: see 11.2171)

	5.27		G. Status of the diplomat in the host State
	5.271		1. Diplomatic custom (see also 2.9)
	5.272		2. Duties
	5.273		3. Inviolability of person, premises and archives, freedom of movement and communication
	5.274		4. Immunities
	5.275		5. Privileges
	5.276		6. Waiver of immunities and privileges
	5.28		H. Diplomatic asylum (for territorial asylum: see 4.66)
	5.29		I. Diplomatic representation in common
	5.291		1. Temporary representation of another State
	5.292		2. Joint representation
*	5.3	III	CONSULS AND CONSULATES
	5.31		A. Consular relations: general, historical development
	5.32		B. Internal structure of the consular service and of the consular mission
	5.33		C. Establishment of consular relations: consular treaties
	5.34		D. Ranks and appointment
	5.341		1. Ranks
	5.342		2. Appointment
	5.35		E. Commencement and termination of the mission
	5.36		F. Functions
	5.360		0. In general
	5.361		1. Trade
	5.362		2. Shipping
	5.363		3. Protection of citizens (see also 11.2171)
	5.364		4. Passports and visas
	5.365		5. Public functions in the field of private law
	5.366		6. Consular jurisdiction (see 7.232)
	5.367		7. Diplomatic functions
	5.37		G. Status of the consul in the host State
	5.370		0. In general
	5.371		1. Inviolability of person, premises, archives, etc.
	5.372		2. Immunities
	5.373		3. Privileges
	5.374		4. Waiver of immunities and privileges
*	5.4	IV	SPECIAL MISSIONS (Ad hoc diplomacy)
*	5.5	V	TRADE DELEGATIONS, INFORMATION CENTRES, Etc.
*	5.6	VI	ARMED FORCES (see also 7.25)
	5.7	VII	MISSIONS OF STATES TO INTERNATIONAL ORGANIZATIONS
	5.8	VIII	EXPERTS, TECHNICIANS, Etc.
*	**6.**	**Part Six:**	**THE LAW OF TREATIES**

	6.0	0	In general (for peace treaties: see 14.1292)
	6.01		A. Reciprocity
	6.02-6.03		*reserved*
	6.04		D. International contracts: 'quasi-international law'
	6.05		E. Concordats
*	6.1	I	CONCLUSION AND ENTRY INTO FORCE
*	6.11		A. Conclusion
	6.111		1. Adoption and authentication of the text
	6.112		2. Signature
	6.113		3. Ratification, acceptance, approval
	6.114		4. Accession
	6.115		5. Exchange or deposit of instruments of ratification, acceptance, approval or accession
*	6.12		B. Reservations to multilateral treaties
*	6.13		C. Entry into force
*	6.2	II	OBSERVANCE, APPLICATION AND INTERPRETATION OF TREATIES
*	6.21		A. The observance of treaties
	6.211		1. *Pacta sunt servanda*
*	6.22		B. The application of treaties
	6.221		1. [Non-]retroactivity
	6.222		2. Application to territory (for State succession: see 3.143)
	6.223		3. Application of successive treaties (see also 2.01)
	6.224		4. Conflicts between treaties (see also 2.01)
	6.225		5. Application of provisions contained in treaties not yet in force
*	6.23		C. The interpretation of treaties
*	6.24		D. Treaties and third States or their nationals
	6.240		0. In general
	6.241		1. Treaties providing for obligations for third States
	6.242		2. Treaties providing for rights for third States
*	6.3	III	AMENDMENT AND MODIFICATION OF TREATIES
*	6.4	IV	INVALIDITY, TERMINATION AND SUSPENSION OF OPERATION
*	6.41		A. General rules
*	6.42		B. Invalidity
	6.421		1. Municipal provisions
	6.422		2. Error
	6.423		3. Fraud
	6.424		4. Corruption of the representative of the State

	6.425		5. Coercion (for peace treaties: see 14.1292 et seq.)
	6.4251		a. 'Unequal treaties'
	6.426		6. Treaties conflicting with a peremptory norm of general international law (*jus cogens*) (see also 1.131)
*	6.43		C. Termination and suspension of operation
	6.431		1. By consent of the parties
	6.432		2. As a consequence of breach
	6.433		3. As a consequence of war (see 14.1222)
	6.434		4. Unilateral denunciation
	6.4341		a. Fundamental change of circumstances
*	6.44		D. Procedure
*	6.45		E. Consequences
*	6.5	V	DEPOSITARIES, NOTIFICATIONS, CORRECTIONS AND REGISTRATION
	6.6	VI	PARTICULAR KINDS OF TREATIES (for peace treaties: see 14.129 et seq.)
	6.61		A. Treaties concluded by international organizations (see also 3.2112)
*	**7.**	**Part Seven:**	**PERSONAL JURISDICTION OF THE STATE**
*	7.1	I	GENERAL CONCEPTION
*	7.2	II	EXERCISE
	7.21		A. Extraterritorial scope of legislative acts
	7.211		1. Personality principle
	7.212		2. Protection principle
	7.213		3. Universality principle
	7.22		B. Extraterritorial effects of acts of State (see 8.24)
	7.23		C. Extraterritorial regimes
*	7.231		1. Capitulations (see also 6.4251)
*	7.232		2. Consular jurisdiction
*	7.233		3. Mixed courts (see also 12.273)
	7.24		D. Governments in exile (see also 14.1262)
*	7.25		E. Military jurisdiction (see also 5.6)
*	7.26		F. On the high seas including artificial islands and foreign ships (see 9.6 et seq.)
*	7.27		G. In polar regions
*	7.28		H. On *terra nullius*
	7.29		I. In aircraft (see also 10.23)

*	**8.**	**Part Eight:**	**STATE TERRITORY AND TERRITORIAL JURISDICTION**
*	8.1	I	PARTS OF TERRITORY, DELIMITATION
*	8.11		A. Frontiers
*	8.12		B. Relations of '*voisinage*'
*	8.13		C. The subsoil
*	8.14		D. The territorial sea (see 9.1 et seq.)
*	8.15		E. Lakes, inland and land-locked seas (see 9.8)
*	8.16		F. The air space (see 10.1 et seq.)
*	8.2	II	TERRITORIAL JURISDICTION
*	8.21		A. Territorial sovereignty (see also 3.111)
*	8.22		B. Limitations upon territorial jurisdiction
	8.221		1. Servitudes
	8.222		2. Leases
	8.223		3. Right of transit (see also 9.121, 9.618 an 16.411)
*	8.23		C. Concurrent territorial jurisdiction and extra-territoriality
	8.231		1. Immunity of foreign States and of their organs and property (see 3.1141, 5.274 and 5.372)
	8.232		2. Immunity of international organizations (see 3.2113)
	8.233		3. Concurrent jurisdiction of the flag State and another State
	8.24		D. Recognition and enforcement of acts of foreign States
	8.241		1. 'Act of State' doctrine (see also 7.2)
*	8.3	III	ACQUISITION AND TRANSFER OF TERRITORY
*	8.31		A. Acquisition (various modes of)
*	8.32		B. Transfer (various modes of)

*	**9.**	**Part Nine:**	**SEAS, WATERWAYS**
	9.0	0	In general
*	9.1	I	THE TERRITORIAL SEA
*	9.11		A. Admeasurement
	9.111		1. Archipelagos
	9.112		2. Historic waters
	9.113		3. Ports and roadsteads
*	9.12		B. Legal status
*	9.121		1. The right of innocent passage
*	9.122		2. The regime of merchant vessels
*	9.123		3. The regime of public ships other than warships
*	9.124		4. Warships
	9.125		5. Fishery

*	9.2	II	THE CONTIGUOUS ZONE
*	9.3	III	BAYS AND GULFS
*	9.4	IV	STRAITS
*	9.5	V	CANALS
*	9.6	VI	THE HIGH SEAS
*	9.61		A. Freedom of the seas
*	9.611		1. Navigation (see also 16.44)
*	9.612		2. Fishery
	9.6121		a. Fishery zones
*	9.613		3. Submarine cables and pipelines
*	9.614		4. The right of overflight
*	9.615		5. Scientific research and hydrography
*	9.616		6. Exploration and exploitation of the seabed and the subsoil
	9.6161		a. Artificial islands (see also 9.634)
	9.617		7. Radio and television transmissions (see also in general: 10.4 and 16.47)
	9.618		8. Land-locked States
	9.619		9. Exclusive economic zone
*	9.62		B. The status of ships (nationality of vessels, the flag, and other questions) (see also 16.44)
	9.63		C. Jurisdiction of a State on the high seas
*	9.631		1. Hot pursuit (for hot pursuit in general: see 8.21; in the air: see 10.13)
*	9.632		2. Visit and search
*	9.633		3. Piracy
	9.634		4. Artificial islands
*	9.64		D. Conservation of living resources
*	9.65		E. Pollution (see also 16.55)
	9.66		F. Collisions, assistance, salvage (see 16.441)
*	9.7	VII	THE CONTINENTAL SHELF
*	9.8	VIII	INLAND AND LAND-LOCKED SEAS
	9.81		A. Inland seas and lakes
	9.82		B. [International] land-locked seas
	9.83		C. Internal waters
*	9.9	IX	RIVERS
	9.91		A. National rivers
	9.92		B. International rivers
	9.921		1. Status
	9.922		2. Shipping
	9.923		3. Other uses
	9.924		4. Pollution (see also 16.55)
	9.925		5. Salinization

*	**10.**	**Part Ten:**	**THE AIR SPACE, OUTER SPACE**
*	10.1	I	SOVEREIGNTY OVER AIR SPACE
*	10.11		A. Extent
*	10.12		B. Limitations, international air space
	10.13		C. Hot pursuit (see also 8.21 and 9.631)
*	10.2	II	AIR NAVIGATION
*	10.21		A. Civil aviation (for traffic and transport matters: see also 16.45)
*	10.211		1. Legal status of aircraft
*	10.212		2. Treaty regime
*	10.22		B. Military aviation
	10.23		C. Unlawful seizure of aircraft and interference with aviation (see also 7.29)
*	10.3	III	OUTER SPACE
*	10.4	IV	TELECOMMUNICATIONS (see also 9.617 and 16.47)
	10.5	V	AIR POLLUTION AND POLLUTION FROM NOISE (see also 16.55)
	10.6	VI	METEOROLOGY
*	**11.**	**Part Eleven:**	**RESPONSIBILITY**
*	11.1	I	GENERAL CONCEPTION
	11.12	A.	International tort and delict
*	11.2	II	RESPONSIBLE ENTITIES
*	11.21		A. States
*	11.211		1. The elements of responsibility (unlawfulness of the act, imputability to the State)
	11.2111		a. Acts of private persons
	11.2112		b. Acts of organs (see 11.212-11.214)
*	11.212		2. Executive acts
*	11.213		3. Legislative acts
*	11.214		4. Judicial acts
*	11.215		5. Factors excluding responsibility (self-defence, necessity, reprisals) (see also 3.116 and 13.1)
*	11.216		6. Reparation (restitution *in integrum*, damages, satisfaction, guarantees)
*	11.217		7. Procedure
*	11.2171		a. Diplomatic protection
*	11.21711		(i) Nationality of claims
*	11.21712		(ii) Exhaustion of local remedies
*	11.2172		b. Peaceful settlement (see Part Twelve)
*	11.22		B. International organizations
*	11.23		C. Other subjects of international law

*	11.24		D. Individuals and groups of individuals, including corporations (see also 11.3)
	11.241		1. Individuals
	11.242		2. Groups of individuals
	11.243		3. Corporations
	11.3	III	'INTERNATIONAL CRIMES', WAR CRIMES, CRIMES AGAINST PEACE, CRIMES AGAINST HUMANITY (for genocide: see also 4.41; for piracy: see 9.633; for unlawful seizure of aircraft and interference with aviation: see 10.23)
	11.31		A. Terrorism
*	**12.**	**Part Twelve:**	**PACIFIC SETTLEMENT OF DISPUTES**
*	12.1	I	THE CONCEPT OF AN INTERNATIONAL DISPUTE
	12.11		A. Distinction between legal and political disputes
	12.12		B. The role of law in the pacific settlement of disputes (see also 1.16)
*	12.2	II	MODES OF SETTLEMENT
	12.20		In general
	12.21		A. Negotiation and consultation
*	12.211		1. Negotiation, diplomacy
*	12.212		2. Consultation
*	12.22		B. Enquiry and finding of facts
*	12.23		C. Good offices
*	12.24		D. Mediation
*	12.25		E. Conciliation
*	12.26		F. Arbitration
	12.260		0. General questions
	12.2601		a. Composition of the tribunal
	12.2602		b. Competence of the tribunal; admissibility; *non liquet*
	12.2603		c. Arbitration *ex aequo et bono*
	12.2604		d. Rules of procedure
	12.2605		e. Execution and other consequences of the decision
	12.261		1. Arbitration other than between States
	12.2611		a. Between a State and an international organization
	12.2612		b. Between a State and an individual
	12.2613		c. Other cases of arbitration
*	12.262		2. The Permanent Court of Arbitration
*	12.263		3. Other arbitral tribunals and commissions
*	12.27		G. Judicial settlement by international courts
	12.270		0. General questions
	12.2701		a. Competence of the court; admissibility; *non liquet*
	12.2702		b. Rules of procedure
	12.2703		c. Advisory opinions
	12.2704		d. Execution and other consequences of the judgment
	12.271		1. Adjudication other than between States
	12.2711		a. Individuals in criminal matters

	12.2712 et seq.		b. Other cases (e.g., European Convention on Human Rights) (for administrative jurisdiction over international civil servants: see 3.2142; for individual right of petition: see 4.71; for national jurisdiction over aliens: see 4.34)
*	12.272		2. The Permanent Court of International Justice and the International Court of Justice
*	12.273		3. Other judicial tribunals (see also 3.223, 4.74, 7.233)
	12.274		4. European Commission of Human Rights
*	12.28		H. Settlement within international organizations
	12.281		1. The role of international organizations in the maintenance of peace (see also 3.22 et seq., 13.2)
*	12.29		I. Other means of settlement
*	**13.**	**Part Thirteen:**	**COERCION AND USE OF FORCE SHORT OF WAR**
*	13.1	I	UNILATERAL ACTS
*	13.11		A. Retortion
*	13.12		B. Reprisals
*	13.13		C. Pacific blockade
*	13.14		D. Intervention (see also 3.112)
	13.15		E. Quarantine
	13.16		F. Embargo
	13.17		G. Boycott
	13.18		H. Severance of diplomatic relations (see also 5.252)
*	13.19		I. Other unilateral acts
*	13.2	II	COLLECTIVE MEASURES ('Collective security') (see also 12.281)
*	13.21		A. Regime of the League of Nations
*	13.22		B. Regime of the United Nations
	13.221		1. Peace-keeping operations
	13.222		2. Intervention (see also 3.112)
	13.223		3. Embargo, boycott, blockade
	13.224		4. UN Forces; international police-force
	13.225		5. Other military sanctions
	13.23		C. Regime of other international organizations
*	13.24		D. Other collective measures
*	**14.**	**Part Fourteen:**	**ARMED CONFLICTS (WAR)**
	14.0	0	In general
*	14.1	I	INTERNATIONAL WAR
*	14.11		A. Resort to war
*	14.111		1. Definition of war
	14.1111		a. War as means of self-help
	14.1112		b. 'Cold war'
	14.1113		c. 'Limited war'
	14.1114		d. 'War of liberation'

	14.1115	e. 'Total war'
*	14.112	2. Limitation and abolition of the right of war
	14.1121	a. *Jus ad bellum*, just war
	14.1122	b. Aggression
	14.1123	c. Limitation and abolition by international organizations
	14.1124	d. Self-defence (see also 3.116 and 11.215)
*	14.113	3. Limitation and reduction of armaments, disarmament (see also 16.8)
	14.1130	a. In general
	14.1131	b. Conventional weapons
	14.1132	c. Nuclear weapons
	14.1133	d. Chemical and biological weapons
*	14.12	B. The laws of war (for war crimes: see 11.3)
*	14.121	1. Sources and sanctions
*	14.122	2. The commencement of war and its effects
*	14.1221	a. Diplomatic and consular relations
*	14.1222	b. Treaties
*	14.1223	c. Enemy persons and property
*	14.12231	(i) Nationality
*	14.12232	(ii) *Persona standi in judicio*
	14.12233	(iii) Internment
	14.12234	(iv) Requisition, sequestration, war booty (see also 14.1261)
	14.12235	(v) Effect of war on private legal relationship
*	14.12236	(vi) Trading with the enemy
	14.123	3. Land, sea and air warfare
*	14.1231	a. Land warfare
*	14.1232	b. Sea warfare
	14.12321	(i) Blockade, contraband
	14.12322	(ii) Prize law
*	14.1233	c. Air warfare
*	14.124	4. The distinction between combatants and non-combatants
	14.1241	a. Guerrilla fighters, *levées en masse* and other irregular resistance movements
	14.1242	b. Hostages

*	14.125		5. Humanitarian law (*'droit humanitaire'*)
	14.1251		a. Red Cross [Conventions]
	14.1252		b. Prisoners of war
	14.1253		c. Mercenaries
*	14.126		6. Belligerent occupation
	14.1261		a. Competence of occupant (see also 11.3 and 14.12234)
	14.1262		b. Competence of the Government in exile (in general: see 7.24)
	14.1263		c. Effect of occupation regime on private legal relationships
	14.127		7. Weapons
*	14.1271		a. Conventional
*	14.1272		b. Nuclear
*	14.1273		c. Bacteriological
*	14.1274		d. Chemical
*	14.128		8. Treaty relations between combatants (cartels, armistices, etc.)
*	14.1281		a. Cartels
*	14.1282		b. Armistices
	14.1283		c. Capitulation
*	14.129		9. Termination of war, treaties of peace
	14.1291		a. Modes of termination
	14.1292		b. Peace treaties
	14.1293		c. Other arrangements
	14.1294		d. War reparations
*	14.2	II	CIVIL WAR
*	14.21		A. Rights and duties of States (see also 14.125)
*	14.22		B. Recognition of insurgency or belligerency (see 3.31 and 3.32)
*	14.3	III	OTHER ARMED CONFLICTS
*	**15.**	**Part Fifteen:**	**NEUTRALITY, NON-BELLIGERENCY**
*	15.1	I	THE LEGAL NATURE OF NEUTRALITY (traditional doctrine)
*	15.11		A. Land warfare
*	15.12		B. Sea warfare
*	15.13		C. Air warfare
	15.14		D. Neutralized, demilitarized territories
*	15.2	II	NEUTRALITY IN THE LIGHT OF THE CHARTER OF THE UNITED NATIONS
*	15.3	III	NEUTRALITY AS THE POLICY OF A STATE (see also 3.133)
*	15.4	IV	NON-BELLIGERENCY
	16.	**Part Sixteen:**	**LEGAL ASPECTS OF INTERNATIONAL RELATIONS IN VARIOUS MATTERS**

16.1	I	GENERAL ECONOMIC AND FINANCIAL MATTERS (for international organizations: see 3.22)
16.11		A. Trade
16.110		0. In general
16.111		1. Trade agreements
16.1111		a. Most-favoured-nation clause
16.112		2. Measures resulting in promotion or restriction of trade and other traffic of goods
16.113		3. Free trade areas
16.114		4. Customs and economic unions (see also 3.223)
16.115		5. Other forms of economic integration
16.116		6. State trading
16.117		7. Commodity agreements
16.12		B. Anti-trust measures
16.13		C. Loans
16.131		1. Loan agreements (for 'soft' loans: see also 16.2)
16.132		2. Drago doctrine
16.14		D. Investments
16.141		1. Protection of foreign investments (see also 4.362 and 16.2)
16.142		2. Other capital movements
16.143		3. Control of foreign investments
16.15		E. Taxes
16.151		1. Tax agreements
16.152		2. Double taxation
16.16		F. Natural resources (see also 8.21)
16.160		0. In general
16.161		1. Agriculture
16.162		2. Marine resources (for fisheries: see 9.612; for conservation of living resources of the sea: see 9.64)
16.163		3. Mineral resources
16.164		4. Protection of plants and animals
16.165		5. Water resources
16.166		6. Energy
16.17		G. Weights and measures
16.18		H. Technology
16.181		1. Peaceful use of nuclear energy
16.2	II	INTERNATIONAL LEGAL ASPECTS OF ECONOMIC DEVELOPMENT AND DEVELOPMENT CO-OPERATION (for international organizations: see 3.22)
16.3	III	MONETARY MATTERS (for international organizations: see 3.5)
16.31		A. General problems
16.32		B. Foreign exchange control
16.4	IV	TRANSPORT, TRAFFIC, COMMUNICATION (for international organisations: see 3.22)
16.41		A. Transport in general (for river traffic and transport: see 9.922)
16.411		1. Right of transit

16.42		B. Road traffic and transport
16.43		C. Rail traffic and transport
16.44		D. Sea traffic and transport (see also 9.611 and 9.62)
16.441		1. Sea traffic (including collisions, assistance, salvage)
16.442		2. Maritime transport
16.4421		a. Conferences (see also 16.12)
16.45		E. Air traffic and transport (see also 10.21)
16.46		F. Postal communications
16.47		G. Telecommunications (see also 10.4)
16.5	V	SOCIAL AND HEALTH MATTERS (for international organizations: see 3.22)
16.51		A. Labour and related matters
16.52		B. Slavery
16.521		1. Traffic in women and children
16.522		2. Forced labour
16.53		C. Narcotics
16.54		D. Health matters
16.55		E. Environmental questions (see also 9.65, 9.924 and 10.5)
16.56		F. Accidents and disasters
16.6	VI	CULTURAL MATTERS (for international organizations: see 3.22)
16.61		A. Cultural agreements
16.62		B. Education
16.63		C. Monuments
16.64		D. Science
16.65		E. Exhibitions
16.66		F. Sports
16.7	VII	LEGAL MATTERS (for international organizations: see 3.22)
16.71		A. Unification and harmonization (see also 16.72 et seq.)
16.72		B. International regulation (see also 1.14)
16.721		1. Private law
16.7211		a. Multual assistance in private law matters
16.722		2. Commercial law
16.723		3. Intellectual property
16.724		4. Law of civil procedure
16.7241		a. Mutual assistance in judicial matters
16.725		5. Private international law
16.726		6. Criminal law

16.727		7. Law of criminal procedure
16.7271		a. Mutual assistance in judicial matters (see 4.63 and 4.64)
16.728		8. Administrative law
16.8	VIII	MILITARY AND SECURITY MATTERS (for international organizations: see 3.22, see also 14.113)
16.81		A. Military alliances, guarantees
16.82		B. Non-aggression pacts
16.83		C. Military assistance and arms trade
16.84		D. Espionage
16.9	IX	INTERNATIONAL EVENTS AND DEVELOPMENTS WITH LEGAL IMPLICATIONS (in alphabetical arragement of key words)

NETHERLANDS STATE PRACTICE FOR THE PARLIAMENTARY YEAR 1998-1999

P.C. Tange[1]

Although this sets out to be an annual survey, it may also include material which dates from a different parliamentary year from that given in the heading. This has proved to be inevitable in those cases when texts do not become available to the editor until long after their original date of drafting; written submissions to international organizations made by the Netherlands representatives frequently fall into this category.

Where a text has been issued in English, the issued version has been printed without alteration, the others having been translated by Mr D. Stephens.

1.2 RELATIONSHIP BETWEEN INTERNATIONAL LAW AND MUNICIPAL LAW

See also: 1.176, 6.113, 8.22

Applicability of Article 91(3) of the Constitution as concerns the transfer of judicial powers[2]

On 6 November 1998 the Ministers of Justice and Foreign Affairs sent a Note to Parliament on the above-mentioned subject related to the establishment of a Scottish Court sitting in the Netherlands.[3] It reads, *inter alia*, as follows:

'Before discussing the meaning and application of Article 91(3) of the Constitution regarding the evaluation of the question whether a treaty conflicts with the Constitution, we note that in our constitutional system there is no constitutionally established norm of absolute national sovereignty that cannot be surrendered at all, or only after the revision of the Constitution. This was confirmed in the constitutional revisions of 1953 and 1956 and is expressed in the Constitution (current Articles 91 and 92 thank their existence to these revisions). In its 1983 opinion on the Agreement regulating the stationing of cruise missiles, the Council of State

1. Associate Research Officer.
2. See also this Yearbook under Municipal Legislation, 8.22.
3. 30 NYIL (1999) pp. 272-273.

Netherlands Yearbook of International Law
Volume XXXI - 2000 - pp. 153-214

therefore rightly concluded that "a treaty does not conflict with the Constitution on the sole grounds that it is accompanied by a loss of sovereignty" (Hand. II, 1983/84, 17 980, No. 7, p. 3).

The text of Article 92 of the Constitution establishes that the transfer of powers as such does not encounter any constitutional objections. The Article establishes that 'legislative, executive, and judicial powers may be conferred on international institutions by or pursuant to a treaty.' In its opinion, the Council rightly concluded that this provision may not be interpreted in such a way as to prohibit the conferral of powers on individual States by or pursuant to a treaty. It is clear, therefore, that in the case at hand Article 92 presents no obstacle to the conferral of powers on the United Kingdom in this agreement. This is all the more true because the agreement links up with and forms part of the cooperation on this issue within the framework of the United Nations, which has adopted a resolution on the matter.

It appears from the opinion of the Council of State that Article 92 contains no other restrictions regarding the transfer of powers than those already mentioned in the Article. Besides the prescribed procedural requirement 'by or pursuant to a treaty', the provision refers to Article 91(3) which should be observed, if need be, when powers are conferred. It has already been explained that the procedure outlined in Article 91(3) should not be observed on the sole grounds that there is a question of a transfer of powers by or pursuant to a treaty. Article 91(3) implies that a treaty containing provisions that conflict with the Constitution, or which lead to conflicts with it, may only be ratified by Parliament if at least two-thirds of the votes cast are in favour. In its 1983 opinion, the Council of State declared that the 1953 revision of the Constitution established that there can only be a question of a conflict with the Constitution within the meaning of Article 91(3) 'when treaty provisions are not in accordance with specific constitutional provisions' (Hand. II, 1983/84, 17 980, No. 7, p. 3.) Therefore, the identification of the specific provisions of the Constitution with which the treaty in question conflicts forms an essential condition for the application of Article 91(3). From a constitutional viewpoint, mere doubts in this regard do not provide adequate cause for the prescribed application of the procedure of Article 91(3), nor do they furnish the constitutionally required identification of the provision(s) of the Constitution with which the treaty supposedly conflicts.

The Government was and remains of the opinion that Article 91(3) of the Constitution does not apply in the case at hand. Nevertheless, in its detailed report, the Government explicitly tested the treaty against a number of specific provisions in the Constitution on a hypothetical basis, in order to determine whether there is a conflict with the Constitution within the meaning of Article 91(3). In the process, the treaty was tested against Articles 15 and 17 of the Constitution. These provisions contain guarantees for persons who arrive in the Netherlands and are transferred to the Scottish Court following a request for their extradition. After their arrival in the Netherlands, these persons will have unlimited access to the Dutch Court examining the legality of their detention and the extradition request. Following the transfer of these persons to the Scottish Court, the latter has full competence. Article 17 of the Constitution, the provision mentioned by the Members of Parliament in the report, does not contain a condition to the effect that the Court must be a Dutch Court. From an historical viewpoint, it is possible that the time-honoured principle of *ius de non evocando* was taken to mean a national or local Court. The Constitution does provide, however, that access to a Court should exist. The legislature will not diminish this fact by ratifying the agreement. Furthermore, it is not new for foreign courts to exercise criminal jurisdiction in this country with the approval of the Netherlands and pursuant to a treaty. The Act ratifying the NATO Convention previously made this possible.

The Members of Parliament have sought to clarify the interpretation of Article 91(3) with realistic examples. The procedure outlined in Article 91(3) has previously been applied on two occasions. The first time was in the framework of the ratification of the Treaty establishing the European Defence Community in 1953, which was concluded on 27 May 1952. At the time of the submission of a Memorandum of Amendment, the Government referred to two provisions in the Constitution with which, in its opinion, the Treaty could come into conflict. The second case concerns the ratification in 1962 of the Agreement between the Republic of Indonesia and the Kingdom of the Netherlands concerning West New Guinea, which was concluded on 15 August 1962. During the deliberations concerning the submission of an amendment to the bill, it became clear that the Second Chamber was of the opinion that the Agreement conflicted with a specific provision in the Constitution concerning the constitutional system of Netherlands New Guinea. As a result of the aforementioned opinion of the Council of State of 1983 on the Agreement regulating the stationing of cruise missiles (which contains an extensive and enlightening analysis and refers to both the examples mentioned above), the Government and both Chambers concluded that the application of the procedure outlined in Article 91(3) of the Constitution was not required in that case.'[4]

3.221 UN COMMITTEE AGAINST TORTURE
See also: 4.65, 4.7

Request of the Committee Against Torture to suspend the expulsion of a complaint pending investigation by the Committee

On 16 April 1999 the State Secretary of Justice answered questions on the expulsion of an asylum seeker who lodged a complaint against the State of the Netherlands. He stated, *inter alia*, as follows:

'Requests from the Committee against Torture, on the basis of Rule 108(9) of the Rules of Procedure of the Committee, to suspend the expulsion of complainants during the consideration of their cases are being seriously and carefully considered. In doing so, the Government's starting point is that, in principle, such requests are granted. It follows from this premise that the rejection of an asylum request in itself is not a strong enough reason not to comply with a request by the Committee, unless a situation occurs in which an exception to this premise is justified.

On 26 March 1999, the President of the Court of First Instance in The Hague, which also sits in Haarlem, did not consider the policy that I have pursued to be manifestly unreasonable.

4. Bijl. Hand. I 1998/99 – 26211 No. 36b, pp. 1-3.

In addition, the President decided that the person in question was not entitled to a suspension of his expulsion on the basis of this policy and that there did not appear to be special circumstances that suggested that the expulsion should be suspended.

Taking into account the information provided by the person in question during the asylum procedure, and in the light of the general situation in Sri Lanka and the position of the Tamils in particular, I am of the opinion that there is no reason to suppose that there are sound reasons to believe that this person would be in danger of being subjected to torture if he were to return to Sri Lanka.

2. From information obtained from the Secretariat of the Committee against Torture, it emerges that the Committee does not maintain general guidelines to decide whether a request will be made to suspend the expulsion of the complainant pending investigation by the Committee.

This decision will take into account the human rights situation in the country of origin of the alien and the personal situation of the alien that emerges from the case, as well as any supplementary information provided by the alien. As a matter of fact, I would like to point out that Rule 108(9) of the Rules of Procedure expressly states that 'such a request addressed to the State party does not imply that any decision has been reached on the question of the admissibility of the communication.' In addition, in a letter dated 15 December 1998 in which the Committee made its request with regard to the case in question on the basis of Rule 108(9) of the Rules of Procedure, the Committee states categorically that 'this request does not imply that any decision has been reached on the admissibility of the communication, not does it prejudge the Committee's final views on the merits of the communication.' From the information provided by the Secretariat of the Committee it also emerges that approximately 110 Article 3 cases have so far been considered, and that 49 of these are still under consideration. The Committee does not maintain records of the number of cases in which a request was made on the basis of Rule 108(9) of the Rules of Procedure. The Secretary estimates that this number may be around 70 per cent of the cases. In approximately thirteen cases, the Committee was of the opinion that the expulsion of the alien would contravene the Convention against Torture and Other Cruel, Inhuman or Degrading Treatment or Punishment.

The large difference between the number of cases handled and the number of cases in which the Committee is of the opinion that the expulsion of the complainant contravenes the Convention is partly explained, according to the Secretariat of the Committee, by the fact that many cases are declared nonsuits after submission because, for example, not all national legal remedies have been exhausted, and by the fact that many cases are not continued by the complainants because, for example, they have received a residence permit. It appears from the above-mentioned figures that although a request on the basis of Rule 108(9) of the Rules of Procedure is not made in all cases, it does occur in a sizeable proportion of those cases. It is impossible here to provide a well-grounded evaluation of the manner in which the Committee generally exercises its competence under Rule 108(9) of the Rules of Procedure, because I do not possess the necessary insight into the files concerning complaints against other countries. The fact that the Committee has so far submitted only four cases to the Dutch Government, including the case in question, also plays a role in this.

[...]
4. The Netherlands actively supported the conclusion of the United Nations Convention against Torture and aims to promote compliance with the Convention with the same sense of dynamism.

By not adopting the substance of Rule 108(9) of the Rules of Procedure in its present form as a binding provision in the Convention, the framers of the Convention have chosen to grant the Contracting Parties a certain amount of freedom on this point. The fact that, in the case in question, the Government is making use of this freedom for the first time does nothing to diminish its commitment to the protection and promotion of human rights in general, and the objectives of the Convention against Torture in particular.'[5]

3.221 UNITED NATIONS SECURITY COUNCIL

See also: 1.176, 3.212

Membership Security Council

On 20 November 1998 the Ministers of Foreign Affairs and for Development Cooperation sent a Letter to Parliament on the above-mentioned subject. The Letter reads in full:

'On 8 October 1998, after a successful campaign, the Netherlands was elected by the United Nations General Assembly, with 122 of 175 votes, as a non-permanent member of the Security Council for the period of 1999-2001. This success is the result of the efforts of many, not least those of the overseas parts of the Kingdom. Membership of the Security Council provides the Kingdom, which has always had an international outlook and has incorporated promotion of the international legal order into its Constitution, with a welcome opportunity to contribute to the realization and maintenance of international peace and security.

The Member States of the United Nations have charged the Security Council with the primary responsibility for the maintenance of peace and security. The Security Council has the authority to settle disputes peacefully, but also to use force when a serious threat to peace and stability exists. The measures (resolutions) adopted by the Council can be of a political, economic (sanctions) or military nature.

The emphasis in the activities of the Security Council is on the management of conflicts. The actual Agenda of the Council is determined by current political developments and by the discussion of matters such as the review of sanctions régimes, the formulation and extension of the mandates of peacekeeping operations and reports by the Secretary General, which are prepared at the behest of the Security Council. In practice, the Council's Agenda was dominated in recent years by conflicts in Africa, the Gulf, the former Yugoslavia and the Caucasus and by the Cyprus question. Naturally, the first task of the Kingdom is to make a reasoned and substantial contribution to discussions and decision-making concerning important current issues of this kind.

---

5. Bijl. Hand. II 1998/99 No. 1207, pp. 2375-2376.

The Dutch government does not wish to limit its membership of the Security Council to matters merely concerning the daily Agenda of the Security Council, but has opted for an integrated approach involving other, broader aspects of security and conflict management that fall within the competency of other branches of the United Nations family. Conflicts cannot, after all, be considered in isolation. Therefore, the Netherlands aims to pay special attention to the pre-conflict stage, by means of preventive diplomacy and early warning, as well as to peace-building during conflicts and the reconstruction that follows them. The humanitarian aspects of conflicts also deserve greater emphasis. Peace-building and humanitarian needs have already received more attention from the Security Council in recent years; the Netherlands wishes to reinforce this trend.

Pre-conflict and post-conflict

In the Security Council, the Netherlands will therefore make the best possible use of the various methods of dispute settlement offered by Chapter VI of the United Nations Charter. The Secretary General and his Special Representatives play an important role in preventive diplomacy, but the Council itself could, where possible, demonstrate a more direct involvement through missions of the presidency, for example. These have been conducted in the past, but they were predominantly for the purpose of fact-finding. In our opinion, a more operational approach should be sought for such missions. The Council could also pay more attention to the possibility of achieving agreement between parties with the aid of the peaceful methods mentioned in Chapter VI: negotiation, inquiry, conciliation, arbitration and so forth. Another problem that frequently presents itself is that once a conflict breaks out, too much time passes before the Council reaches a decision. Swifter decision-making by the Council is a Dutch priority.

As a result of the definition of the role of the Security Council, problems that occur in post-conflict situations may also not receive the attention they deserve. The Netherlands will attempt to introduce coherence into the transition from conflict situations to so-called post-conflict peace-building. Considering the role of non-governmental organizations and the United Nations funds and programmes, there is every reason to increase the contacts between these institutions and to secure better coordination between them. The coherence between these activities and those of the United Nations peacekeeping forces should also be reinforced. Although the Security Council itself has only limited room for manoeuvre in the area of post-conflict peace-building, the Netherlands will at least be able, through an integrated approach, to encourage the design of mechanisms for follow-up and systematic review following conflict situations. This requires a coordinated Dutch approach on the so-called Executive Boards of the various United Nations programmes and funds and of the World Bank.

Humanitarian aspects

Besides the (military) aspects of peace and security, which are dealt with mainly in the Security Council itself, the related socio-economic and humanitarian aspects that fall within the competency of other United Nations organs also deserve emphasis. As a member of the Security Council, the Kingdom will request that more attention be paid to these aspects and it will make use of special knowledge in these fields to do so. The contacts between the Council and humanitarian organizations must be reinforced, for example, at the stage of informal consultations. Organizations operating in the humanitarian field have a clear need for increased contact with the Security Council, as recently indicated by the United Nations High Commissioner for Refugees, Ms. Ogota.

As a result, *inter alia*, of the continuing erosion of humanitarian law, humanitarian workers are increasingly becoming victims of violence. In 1997, the Netherlands, in its capacity as holder of the presidency of the European Union, appealed to the Security Council to devote more attention to the protection of humanitarian workers. The Netherlands intends to continue this line of policy during the next two years. In view of the importance of restoring civil authority in the early stages of peacekeeping operations, thereby reducing the risks to refugees, United Nations personnel and humanitarian workers, the Netherlands will in certain cases push for a greater role for civilian police in peacekeeping operations.

Sanctions

In the judgement of the Dutch Government, sanctions régimes should be tailored more to specific situations. When the Council considers action unavoidable, but cannot or does not wish to resort to military action, there is a tendency to impose (economic) sanctions. This often occurs under considerable time pressure, a fact which does not contribute to the effectiveness of the sanctions régime and which may also have unintended negative effects on a humanitarian level. The Netherlands will strive to ensure that new sanctions régimes are better tailored to their intended objectives, that their effectiveness will be tested on a regular basis and that special attention will be paid to their humanitarian aspects.

(Sub-)regional organizations

In a different sense, the Government has also chosen to adopt an integrated approach to its membership of the Security Council. Although the Security Council bears primary responsibility for the maintenance of international peace and security, this task has proven to be too great for the Security Council alone and even for the United Nations as a whole. According to Chapter VIII of the United Nations Charter, regional and sub-regional organizations bear a special responsibility of their own for conflict management in their own regions. They can and must play an important complementary role, mandated by the Security Council if necessary and/or possible. It emerges from the report of the United Nations Secretary General on Africa of April of this year, that regional organizations (such as the Organization of African Unity) have an important role to play in the resolution of conflicts in Africa. The Security Council should therefore encourage such organizations to assume greater responsibility for developments in their region. In doing so, the United Nations should recognize its own responsibility by making such initiatives possible and by supporting them.

Africa

In this context, Africa deserves special attention. Since 1970, the continent has been struck by more than thirty wars. In addition to the indescribable human suffering that has been and continues to be caused by these conflicts, they have also had deeply negative consequences for the development and stability of large parts of the continent. During the next two years, the Netherlands will devote special attention to Africa in the Security Council, as well as in other United Nations organs and in the World Bank, on the basis of the broad approach that it has adopted. In doing so, both the undersigned will opt for an approach in which their efforts in the fields of foreign policy and development cooperation will mutually reinforce each other as much as possible.

Non-proliferation
Another special point of interest concerns the promotion of concrete steps to prevent the proliferation of weapons of mass destruction in regions where such proliferation is threatened. The authority of the Council to act in a more general sense in the field of proliferation is disputed, but this is not the case where a real threat of proliferation of weapons of mass destruction is concerned. In this area, the Kingdom will press for a vigilant approach on the part of the Security Council.

Information and transparency
The conduct of the Netherlands in the Security Council will also be determined by its membership of the European Union and NATO. The Treaty of Amsterdam indicates that Member States that are also members of the United Nations Security Council will consult amongst themselves and keep the other Member States fully informed (Art. J.9). The Netherlands intends to honour this commitment. Transparency is also an important aspect of the activities of the Council. Since the Security Council summit of 1992, under the presidency of the then Prime Minister of the United Kingdom, Mr. Major, decided to take action on this specific issue, there has been much improvement, in particular in the area of consultations with troop-supplying countries. Nevertheless, many Member States of the United Nations that are not members of the Security Council feel excluded and much opposition exists to the informal consultations of the Council. The Netherlands will strive to disseminate more information without losing sight of confidentiality. Relations with the General Assembly are also in need of improvement, for example, by increasing the frequency of consultations with the President of the General Assembly.

The Dutch Parliament will be provided with as much information as possible during our membership of the Security Council. The monthly Agenda, which is drawn up by the monthly rotating Presidency, will be placed at the disposal of the Permanent Committee for Foreign Affairs as soon as possible. This also applies to the work programme, which is prepared for the Presidency by the Secretariat.

In addition, a review of issues that have arisen in the Security Council will be prepared on a regular basis. Information regarding current events will naturally be provided on an *ad hoc* basis as necessary. The Dutch representation to the United Nations in New York has set up an internet site on which relevant information will be made available.

For a meaningful implementation of Security Council membership, the words of the governmental declaration are most applicable: 'We are idealistic with regard to our principles and aims, pragmatic with regard to the protection of the Netherlands' position and values and realistic with regard to what can be attained and to taking concrete measures.' In this spirit, our country will occupy its seat in the Security Council from 1 January 1999.[6]

3.222 NATO
See: 13.23

---

6. Bijl. Hand. II 1998/99 – 26301 No. 1.

4.3 ALIENS OR NON-NATIONALS
See also: 4.52, 4.65, 4.66

Revision Aliens Act

The Explanatory Memorandum to the Bill for parliamentary approval of the total revision of the Aliens Act[7] reads, *inter alia*, as follows:

'A large number of proposals in the field of asylum policy have been included in the coalition agreement (Hand. II, 1997/98, 26 024, No. 9). One of the proposals concerns the amendment of the Aliens Act. In the field of immigration and asylum policy, the existing international commitments that the Netherlands has entered into are and remain of overriding importance. Within this international legal framework, there is a certain (limited) amount of room to influence the flow of aliens to the Netherlands as a result of migratory pressures in other parts of the world. The policy is aimed at regulating migration to the Netherlands, insofar as this is possible, and at controlling the consequences of this migration for Dutch society as much as possible. Recent policy measures are aimed at regulating the influx and exit of asylum seekers within the existing legal framework. The proposed new Aliens Act cannot be uncoupled from these policy measures, which were described in a letter to the Chairman of the Second Chamber of Parliament, dated 9 October 1999 (Hand. II, 1998/99, 19 637, No. 367), nor from measures that are to be concluded at the international level, in view of the forthcoming harmonization (both procedural and substantive) of European asylum and immigration policy.
[...]

Simplification of the System of Residence Permits

The coalition agreement mentions the possibility of a system of two parallel forms of asylum status: temporary and permanent. Persons qualifying for permanent status in such a system would include the current holders of A-status, as well as those persons that qualify for a residence permit on humanitarian grounds *(vtv-hum)* on the basis of Article 3 of the European Convention on Human Rights (ECHR, *Trb.* 1951, 154), or on the grounds of severe traumatic experiences. Persons qualifying for temporary status would include the current holders of a provisional residence permit *(vvtv)*. In addition to the presentation of the above-mentioned dual status system, the coalition agreement also states that the possibility of further simplification will be examined. This simplification is based on a system of residence permits which allows one to apply, in succession, for a permit for a limited period and, after a period of three years, for a permit for an unlimited period.

The current bill has been chosen to introduce this simplified system of successive residence permits. In a system with two consecutive residence permits, it is not necessary to explain, when granting an application for a residence permit for a limited period, whether the protection is required because of circumstances relating to the alien in question, or because of the general situation in the country of origin of the alien. This has been included in the bill (Article 40(2)). During the preparation of an order on an application for a residence

7. See also this NYIL under Municipal Legislation, 4.3.

permit, time no longer needs to be devoted to setting out why the alien may qualify for one status, but not for the other. This is not the case when the intention is to withdraw the residence permit or not to extend it.

A residence permit may be withdrawn regardless of whether it was issued for a limited period or an unlimited period. In the case of a permit for a limited period, this may be done, *inter alia*, if the person in question presents a threat to public order or if the grounds on which the permit was issued have since disappeared (see Article 16(1) under (e) and (f), in conjunction with Article 17, for regular cases, and Article 30, under (b) and (c), for asylum cases). The grounds for the withdrawal of a residence permit are the same as the grounds for not extending a permit, with the exception of Article 16(1) under (b) (required possession of a valid international travel document).

If circumstances remain unchanged, a residence permit for an unlimited period may be issued after three years (asylum cases) or after five years (regular cases) (Articles 19 and 32). A residence permit for an unlimited period cannot be withdrawn if the grounds on which the permit was issued have disappeared. However, it can still be withdrawn as a result of a violation of public order or if the alien has established his main residence outside the Netherlands.

At the time of the withdrawal of a residence permit, as described in Article 26 and 31, or if there is an intention not to extend a residence permit for a limited period, it is important whether or not a prohibition on *refoulement* applies on the basis of international commitments. If an alien is a refugee within the meaning of the Convention, his residence permit may only be withdrawn if one of the so-called cessation clauses of Article 1C of the Refugees Convention applies, or otherwise if the alien (in short) has provided incorrect information, or presents a threat to public order. This is of significance when a permit is withdrawn on the grounds of public order, because it has to be established whether the alien in question can actually be expelled following the withdrawal of the permit. With a view to the possible withdrawal or non-extension of a residence permit, the file that was prepared at the time of the decision on the application should contain all the information that is necessary for a determination to be made, at the time of the planned withdrawal, whether the alien is a refugee within the meaning of the Convention, or whether he requires protection on the grounds of Article 3 of the European Convention on Human Rights or Article 3 of the Convention against Torture.

Information relating to the asylum request can still be important at such a time. It is therefore essential that files contain as much personal information as possible concerning the alien's nationality, identity, account of his flight from his country of origin and asylum request. On the basis of this information, as well as fresh information concerning the situation in the country of origin of the alien, a decision will be made whether the residence permit can be withdrawn.

The public order criterion can be found in various places in the Act. An application for a residence permit for a limited period on regular grounds (Article 14(1) under (d)) and on asylum grounds (Article 29(2) under (j)) may be turned down if an alien presents a threat to public order or national security. The same applies to the withdrawal and extension of a permit for a limited period. Once a permit for an unlimited period has been issued, the (continued) residence of an alien can be terminated only if the alien has been convicted by final judgment for a crime that carries a prison sentence of three years or more, or if the measure described in Article 37(a) of the Penal Code (detention at the pleasure of the State) has been imposed on him. These norms are elaborated in the so-called sliding scale, which is currently set down in the Aliens Policy Brief. The starting point of the sliding scale is that the longer the alien resides in the Netherlands, the heavier the imposed sentence or measure must be in order to terminate his residence.

Incidentally, public order is understood to include the public peace; the latter term therefore no longer appears in the new Act. Threats to public order, finally, are understood to include, *inter alia*, threats to public morality, international relations and public health.

All information relating to nationality, identity, flight from country of origin and asylum request are to be collected and recorded in a file during the so-called first instance stage. As a result of the cancellation of the appeal stage in asylum cases, the quality of the orders of the Immigration and Naturalization Service *(IND)* must be improved. Guarantees concerning the quality of the orders of the *IND* on applications for residence permits on asylum grounds are set down partly in the Act and partly in subordinate regulations. As in the current Aliens Act, the new Act provides that, with regard to the application, the alien should be given the opportunity to express himself in a language that he may reasonably be assumed to be familiar with (Article 36). The Act also includes a so-called informational procedure. This procedure provides that the draft order on the application, consisting of either a rejection (Article 37) or a withdrawal (Article 39(2)), is submitted to the alien. The alien can then submit his opinions in writing. The measures relating to the order on applications for asylum are meant to guarantee that the appellate court receives a file containing sufficient information, on the basis of which it can decide whether or not to reverse the earlier decision. In this manner, facts that previously came to light only at the appeal stage can also be considered at first instance.

In addition to contributing to the simplification of procedures and, as a result, the possible shortening of the period needed by the Immigration and Naturalization Service to determine whether an application can be granted, a system of successive permits also prevents so-called 'continuing applications'. Because only one type of residence permit is available initially, it will no longer be possible to initiate a procedure to receive a different residence permit. Under the current Act, holders of a provisional residence permit often apply for the stronger A-status or a residence permit on humanitarian grounds. Under the new Aliens Act, this will no longer be possible.

Another, not insignificant cause of continuing applications is that different welfare packages are attached to the various types of status that currently exist. In order to prevent continuing applications for reasons of this kind, it is not enough to limit the number of residence permits. If different welfare provisions and rights were attached to different grounds for admittance, it would no longer be possible to apply for a different permit, but it would still be possible to apply for a different welfare package. The prevention of continuing applications therefore presupposes that, regardless of the grounds on which the permit is issued, the same rights and welfare provisions are attached to a residence permit in every case. The level of these rights and welfare provisions is determined, on the one hand, by binding international law agreements on the matter and, on the other hand, by the policies of the Dutch Government within the framework of these international agreements. In order to prevent that aliens with residence permits have an interest in continuing applications because the welfare package attached to one ground is better than the one attached to another, all aliens that are in possession of a residence permit for a limited time will, on the grounds of treaty commitments to which the Kingdom is bound, have to be offered a welfare package at the level of those received by aliens who are defined as refugees in accordance with the Convention.

If all welfare packages are made uniform, the alien has no particular interest in the grounds on which his residence permit was issued being expressly stated: the welfare package is always the same, regardless of the grounds on which it was issued. It is impossible to acquire a different residence permit with a different welfare package. Therefore, the alien has no legally relevant interest to familiarize himself with the grounds on which the permit was actually issued. For this reason, Article 40(2) provides that any reference to the reasoning behind the order granting the application may be omitted. It goes without saying that the fact that the reasoning is not given with the order does not mean that the order is arbitrary. As with all other orders, the facts and circumstances have been established and a decision is reached on the basis thereof. A reasoning exists, but the actual grounds on which the permit is issued are not referred to in the order.

The non-reference to the grounds on which the residence permit is issued does not conflict with the Refugees Convention or any other agreement.

The rationale of the current bill is that those that require protection actually receive it. The interests of Dutch society and the interests of the alien have been weighed against each other on that basis. In that context, the costs associated with continuing applications in order to discover on what grounds one has been admitted were contrasted with the interest of the alien in continuing applications.

Legal certainty only requires that the alien has insight into the grounds on which the residence permit was originally issued to him at the time that the permit is being withdrawn or is not extended. Only then does the alien have a legally relevant interest to be able to establish whether the grounds on which the permit was issued have indeed disappeared. However, the announcement of the grounds at the time that the permit is issued does not provide the alien with legally relevant certainty: whether and, if so, when those grounds have disappeared and the residence permit can be withdrawn, or not extended, remain uncertain. Moreover, it also uncertain whether the authorities will actually proceed with the withdrawal or non-extension.'[8]

4.31 ADMITTANCE

See also: 4.52, 11.3

Residence in the Netherlands of asylm seekers who are suspected of war crimes

On 1 December 1998 the State Secretary of Justice answered questions on the above-mentioned subject. He stated, *inter alia*, as follows:

---

8. Bijl. Hand. II 1998/99 – 26732 No. 3, p. 1, 3-6.

'3. and 7. The Aliens Act, in Article 8, presents the possibility of refusing entry at the external borders of the Netherlands to persons presenting a danger to public peace, public order or national security. Such a situation may arise when it is known that the alien in question is a war criminal. In practice, however, it may only become evident that the person in question is a war criminal after he has submitted an application for admission as a refugee and has been heard on it, or even later when, for example, he is recognized by victims. In light of the above, there are no conceivable measures that could prevent the aforementioned category of persons from entering the Netherlands. However, every effort is being made within the confines of national and treaty law to discourage this category of aliens from remaining in the Netherlands. You are familiar with the measures mentioned in the policy memorandum concerning Article 1F of the Refugees Convention, which my predecessor sent to your Chamber on 28 November 1997 (Hand. II 1997-98, 19 637, No. 295).[9]

4. During the last two years, Article 1F of the Refugees Convention has been employed against approximately sixty asylum seekers. In at least ten cases, the procedure was terminated and the decision prevailed, either as the result of a court decision, or as a result of the fact that the alien in question did not file an objection or an appeal against the decision. In the remaining cases, a decision has yet to be made regarding an objection or an appeal.

5. Since mid-1997, when reports first began to filed in cases such as these, the Immigration and Naturalization Service *(IND)* has filed reports with the Public Prosecutor in approximately forty cases. In the cases of aliens to whom Article 1F(a) of the Refugees Convention has been applied – sub-paragraph (a) of Article 1F deals with war crimes and crimes against humanity – the Public Prosecutor examines whether there are sufficient leads for an investigation. The information in the possession of the *IND* is tested against the criteria mentioned in the action plan concerning the investigation in the Netherlands of war crimes and crimes against humanity.

6. In just one specific case, in my opinion, the application of Article 1F of the Refugees Convention does not provide an adequate reason for refusing to provide protection here in the Netherlands: if the denial of refugee status takes place on the basis of Article 1F of the Refugees Convention, but return to the country of origin carries a real risk of the violation of Article 3 of the European Convention on Human Rights. In such a case, the person in question is neither expelled nor granted residence. This policy was accepted by the relevant judicial body, the *Rechtseenheidskamer (REK)* in its judgment of 11 September 1997. In practice, this implies that the person in question remains in the Netherlands without a residence permit, but that he is excluded from government-financed reception facilities and other government-financed services. In such cases, it is unavoidable that the alien may receive hospitality and shelter from, for example, family members or fellow-countrymen, residing in the Netherlands, who sympathize with him.'[10]

---

9. See 30 NYIL (1999) pp. 178-189.
10. Bijl. Hand. II 1998/99 No. 416, pp. 847-848.

4.52 REFUGEES

See also: 3.221 UNHCR, 4.1, 4.3

Reaction of the United Nations High Commissioner for Refugees proposal to amend the Aliens Act

On 19 January 1999 the State Secretary of Justice stated the following:

'The next issue concerns the UNHCR. I believe that I have some explaining to do regarding this issue, if only to clarify how it came about that the Government assumed that the first reaction of the UNHCR was a reaction to the original bill, which refers to "demonstrating" and not to "making credible". I cannot say otherwise than that we assumed in absolute good faith that the reaction of the UNHCR could only have been based on the amended bill. The Chamber will no doubt be willing to take my word for this. Reading the reaction of the UNHCR, we were under the impression that it could only be referring to "demonstrating" and not to "making credible". I was therefore astonished by the reaction following the consideration of the bill in the Second Chamber, not so much by the exact wording of the bill, but by the tone of the debate and by the explanation of the bill in the Memorandum of Reply and the discussion. I say now roughly what I said then in slightly greater detail. To my surprise, the UNHCR stated again, as reported in the *Trouw* newspaper, that the bill was exceptionally harsh.

If I was to be asked precisely on what the difference of opinion with the UNHCR is based, I could not answer otherwise than by saying that I do not know. The essence of the position of the UNHCR may be found in the sentence that was just read out by Ms. Le Poole. Allow me to read it out again to be on the safe side. This is a sentence with which I am entirely in agreement from start to finish: "the UNHCR believes that when an applicant's account appears plausible and credible, the asylum seeker should be given the benefit of the doubt and granted access to the regular asylum procedure."

That is precisely what should happen. The only thing that I can imagine is that this problem may have been related to language. The UNHCR may have focused very closely on the wording of the bill, without considering it in the light of the Refugees Convention. Because I was convinced then, as I am convinced today, that we were dealing with an unfortunate misunderstanding, we indirectly contacted the UNHCR again through the Ministry for Foreign Affairs when its reaction became clear at the beginning of December.

[...]

I have just explained that all texts in the field of aliens law can only be understood in relation to the Refugees Convention. Once again, I do not, ultimately, understand the problem. Furthermore, the UNHCR need not have read the whole pack, because how the bill should be understood is explained repeatedly in the Memorandum of Reply to the Second Chamber and the Memorandum of Reply to the First Chamber, which are almost identical. This is neither the first time, nor the last, that the wording of a bill requires some explanation. To prevent this kind of misunderstanding, I have no objection to wording the new bill in such a way that its purpose is immediately apparent from its text. I do not regard this as essential, however, because the bill cannot be understood in any way other than the one I have just explained. This is the simple truth, because any court would overturn a ruling of the Immigration and Naturalization Service *(IND)* that was not composed in this manner. And it would be justified in doing so! Hence, the bill cannot be understood in any other way. I therefore do not understand how things went the way they did.

Mr. Holdijk has asked how the Government deals with UNHCR documents and in what manner the UNHCR is taken into account in the formulation of new legislation. Existing UNHCR documents are particularly important to the Dutch Government. The UNHCR is an international organization that sets an example that we are keen to follow for all manner of reasons. As an organization that is formed by all its member countries, the UNHCR sets policy guidelines with regard to the refugee issue all over the world. All approaches to this issue come together here as well. Still, this does not mean that we always blindly agree with the UNHCR. However, texts from the UNHCR are particularly important to the Dutch Government. When it wishes to deviate from such texts, the Dutch Government constantly asks itself what arguments can be supplied in support of this. The Government also feels that very strong arguments should be provided for doing so.

Consequently, the next question is whether it is not a pity in this case – and possibly in future cases – that communication with the UNHCR did not take place sooner, because misunderstandings could then perhaps have been prevented. I offer no opinion on the subject at this time. However, we have resolved – in fact, we have already taken practical steps – to involve the UNHCR in the review of the Aliens Act. Naturally, we will only involve the UNHCR insofar as it is within our power to do so, because the independent status of the UNHCR, which does not want to be too closely associated with the Dutch policy, does not always make things very easy.

Mr. Chairman! I would just like to add a few words about the "benefit of the doubt". The position the Government has taken on this matter should be clear from what has been said so far. An asylum seeker who registers himself in the Netherlands has a right to receive the benefit of the doubt. In the Memorandum of Reply, however, we have determined that doubt should be deemed to exist when an asylum seeker fails to provide a sufficiently plausible explanation as to why he has no documents. When such doubt arises, it can no longer be said at that point that the asylum seeker should receive the benefit of the doubt. This does not mean – not even in the aforementioned case – that the final decision cannot be that, given the rest of his account, the asylum seeker should receive the benefit of the doubt. It is definitely not the case that the Government is trying to reverse matters on this issue. That would indeed constitute a reversal of the burden of proof. I have already said that this is absolutely not our intention.' [11]

Application of Article 1C Refugees Treaty

On 6 May 1999 the State Secretary of Justice sent a Letter to Parliament on the above-mentioned subject. It reads, *inter alia*, as follows:

11. Hand. I 1998/99 No. 16, pp. 493-494.

'1. Article 1C of the Convention Relating to the Status of Refugees (Refugees Convention)

1.1 Definition

Article 1A of the Refugees Convention (Trb. 1954 No. 88) states that for the purposes of the Convention, the term refugee shall apply to any person who owing to a well-founded fear of being persecuted for reasons of race, religion, nationality, membership of a particular social group or political opinion, is outside the country of his nationality and is unable or, owing to such fear, unwilling to avail himself of the protection of that country; or who, not having a nationality and being outside the country of his former habitual residence, is unable or, owing to such fear, is unwilling to return to it.

Article 1C of the Refugees Convention establishes the circumstances under which recognition as a refugee ceases to exist. The Article states that the Convention shall cease to apply to any person falling under the terms of Article 1A of the Convention if:

(1) He has voluntarily re-availed himself of the protection of the country of his nationality; or

(2) Having lost his nationality, he has voluntarily reacquired it; or

(3) He has acquired a new nationality, and enjoys the protection of the country of his new nationality; or

(4) He has voluntarily re-established himself in the country which he left or outside which he remained owing to fear of persecution; or

(5) He can no longer, because the circumstances in connection with which he has been recognized as a refugee have ceased to exist, continue to refuse to avail himself of the protection of the country of his nationality;

(6) Being a person who has no nationality he is, because the circumstances in connection with which he has been recognized as a refugee have ceased to exist, able to return to the country of his former habitual residence.

These six grounds for termination of recognition as a refugee are known as the cessation clauses.

Clauses 5 and 6 of Article 1C of the Convention do not apply to a refugee falling under Article 1A of the Convention who is able to invoke compelling reasons, arising from previous persecution, for refusing to avail himself of the protection of the country of his nationality (Clause 5), or for refusing to return to the country of his former habitual residence (Clause 6).

With the application of a cessation clause, recognition as a refugee ceases to exist. This can be a reason to withdraw the right to admission to the Netherlands as a refugee. A decision to withdraw admission on the basis of Article 1C of the Convention should be distinguished from a decision to refuse admission to the Netherlands as a refugee on the basis of Article 2(2) of the Aliens Act, which establishes that the admission (to the Netherlands) of a person who is a refugee within the meaning of the Convention can only be refused for compelling reasons of national interest. In such cases, in which recognition as a refugee does not cease to exist, admission to the Netherlands as a refugee is nevertheless not granted on the grounds of compelling reasons of national interest, despite the fact that the Netherlands recognizes the refugee status of the person in question, in connection with the prohibition on *refoulement*. Such reasons present themselves when situations as described in Article 33(2) of the Refugees Convention arise. Article 33(2) of the Convention establishes that the benefits of the prohibition on *refoulement* in the Convention may not be claimed by a refugee whom there are reasonable grounds for regarding as a danger to the security of the country in which he is, or who, having been convicted by final judgment of a particularly serious crime, constitutes a danger to the community of that country.

1.2 Rationale of Article 1C of the Convention

The rationale for the existence of Article 1C of the Convention is the primacy of national protection in refugee law. This implies that international protection – recognition as a refugee – is justified only when national protection for a person is regarded as being non-existent.

It inevitably follows from the above that, if it can reasonably be assumed that national protection exists (again), recognition as a refugee ceases to exist. This starting point was articulated clearly during the conference of plenipotentiaries – the conference charged with drafting the Refugees Convention in 1951 – by the first United Nations High Commissioner for Refugees, Mr. G. J. van Heuven Goedhart. He argued that refugee status should not be granted for one day longer than absolutely necessary, and that this status ceases to exist when the person in question has acquired the *(de facto)* citizenship of a particular State, in accordance with the general aims of the Convention.

1.3 Elaboration of the four 'personal' clauses of Article 1C

In each individual case, the application of one of the six mutually exclusive cessation clauses should take place on the basis of an independent evaluation of the facts and circumstances. Nevertheless, on the basis of the Handbook of Procedure and Criteria for Determining Refugee Status (1979) of the UNHCR, the following can be stated, at least, with regard to the general scope of the clauses.

The cessation clauses may be divided into two categories. The first category consists of the first four clauses, which reflect a change in the personal circumstances of the refugee as a result of his own actions. These are therefore strictly personal clauses. A further distinction can be made between, on the one hand, a refugee re-availing himself of the national protection of his country of origin (Clauses 1, 2 and 4) and, on the other hand, a refugee availing himself of the national protection of another country (Clause 3). The second category consists of the last two clauses (5 and 6), which reflect a change in the objective circumstances that were involved in the recognition of refugee status. These are general, objective reasons which may provide a basis for terminating the recognition of the status of several refugees. The four "personal" clauses will be briefly considered below. The two "general" clauses will be considered in Section 1.4.

Paragraph 119 of the Handbook establishes three requirements for the withdrawal of refugee status on the basis of Clause 1 of Article 1C of the Convention: (a) the refugee must act voluntarily; (b) the refugee must intend by his action to re-avail himself of the protection of the country of his nationality; (c) the refugee must actually obtain such protection. The term "voluntarily" means without pressure from the authorities of the country of origin. Circumstances beyond the control of the refugee are not regarded as being voluntary. The Handbook mentions divorce as an example. If a refugee can only apply for a divorce in his country of origin, such an application cannot be regarded as a voluntary re-availment of the national protection of the authorities of his country of origin. Incidental contacts with the diplomatic mission of the country of origin in the country of refuge equally cannot be regarded as such. However, if the refugee applies to the authorities of his country of origin for a passport, such an act is regarded, in principle, as falling under Clause 1 of Article 1C of the Convention. Likewise, if the refugee has returned to his country of origin on a travel document other than the passport of that country, for example, such an act is regarded, in principle, as falling under Clause 1 of Article 1C of the Convention. The Handbook indicates that the nature of the visit can have an effect on such an evaluation:

"Cases of this kind should, however, be judged on their individual merits. Visiting an old or sick parent will have a different bearing on the refugee's relation to his former home country than regular visits to that country spent on holidays or for the purpose of establishing business relations."

I regard the return of a refugee to his country of origin as evidence that the person in question is no longer a refugee within the meaning of the Convention. This implies that if there are clear indications that the person in question has, in fact, returned to his country of origin, I will withdraw his admission as a refugee, unless the person in question can demonstrate that he is nevertheless still a refugee within the meaning of the Convention. In my opinion, by returning to his country of origin, the person in question has himself expressed that he no longer requires the protection afforded by the Convention. Consequently, the burden will be on him to present new and credible information to confirm that he is still a refugee within the meaning of the Convention. Incidentally, in cases in which a refugee returns to his country of origin, it will also be possible to apply the grounds for withdrawal of refugee status provided in Article 14(1) of the Aliens Act, under (a) (the provision of incorrect information leading to admission as a refugee).

Clause 2 of Article 1C of the Convention applies to cases in which a refugee voluntarily re-acquires his nationality. According to Paragraph 128 of the Handbook, this involves the explicit acceptance by the refugee of an offer to re-acquire the nationality of his country of origin.

Clause 4 of Article 1C of the Convention applies to cases in which a refugee has voluntarily returned to his country of origin. Paragraph 134 of the Handbook indicates that a temporary visit by a refugee to his country of origin on the basis of a travel document issued by his country of residence, rather than a passport, cannot necessarily be regarded as voluntary return within the meaning of this clause.

Clause 3 of Article 1C of the Convention applies when a refugee has acquired a new nationality, either of the country of residence or of another country. This clause therefore forms the legal basis on which admission to the Netherlands as a refugee is terminated if the person in question has acquired Dutch nationality. Likewise, the acquisition of the nationality of another country can also lead to the withdrawal of admission to the Netherlands as a refugee. Paragraph 130 of the Handbook sets the requirement that the acquisition of the new nationality also carries the effective protection of the country concerned.

1.4 Change of circumstances

Conclusion 69 (XLIII) 1991 off the Executive Committee of the UNHCR is devoted to the application of Clauses 5 and 6 of Article 1C of the Convention (supplement 2 to this letter). The Conclusion sets out a number of starting points for decision making with regard to these cessation clauses. Firstly, Conclusion 69 emphasizes the role that the UNHCR can play in the decision-making process. In the framework of its role of supervising the application of the provisions of Refugees Convention, the UNHCR issues declarations concerning the application of Clauses 5 and 6 of Article 1C of the Convention. These declarations can be of use to States that are party to the Convention in the determination of their own positions. In this context, the most recent declaration of the UNHCR, concerning the category of refugees that left Bulgaria and Romania before 1990, dates from October 1997. In the period preceding this declaration, the UNHCR issued declarations concerning approximately fifteen other countries of origin. These declarations are based on fundamental changes that were related to the introduction of democracy in those countries. In addition to Bulgaria and Romania, recent examples include: Chile (28 March 1994), as a result of elections and democratic developments, Namibia (18 April 1995), as a result of independence and elections, South Africa (18 April 1995), as a result of the dismantling of apartheid and the transition to a democratic régime, Malawi (31 December 1996), as a result of the transition to a multiparty system, elections, the new Constitution and the successful integration of repatriates and, finally, Mozambique (31 December 1996), as a result of the peace agreement, the transition to a multiparty system, the transition to a democratic régime and successful large-scale repatriation.

In addition, Conclusion 69 emphasizes the importance of a thorough examination of the nature of the change of circumstances in the country of origin. States considering the application of Article 1C of the Convention should therefore carefully assess whether the changes in the country of origin are of a fundamental character. In the case of the Netherlands, this implies that (1) a report containing an overview of the changes in the country of origin is requested from the Minister for Foreign Affairs, (2) the opinion of the UNHCR is sought, and (3) an examination takes place to establish whether any of the neighbouring countries have already applied the Article, or whether they intend to do so, before the Government comes to a similar decision. In my opinion, it will be possible, by employing these three sources, to determine in a sufficiently objective and verifiable manner whether the Government can take the position that the changes in the country of origin justify the application of the cessation clause.

Conclusion 69 emphasizes that fundamental changes can relate to the observance of human rights in general, as well to the specific circumstances that formed the basis for the fear of persecution. It must be established that the situation that justified recognition as a refugee has ceased to exist as a result of the stable and durable character of the fundamental changes. It appears from the Handbook that basic assurances are required in this regard. Refugees should not be confronted with unnecessary re-evaluations of their status in the light of temporary or non-fundamental changes in the situation prevailing in their country of origin.

2. Withdrawal of admission on the Grounds of the Aliens Act

2.1 The legal grounds for withdrawal of admission

Article 15(3) of the Aliens Act provides the option of withdrawing admission as a refugee. The right to admission as a refugee may be withdrawn on the grounds listed in Article 14(1) of the Aliens Act, as well as in cases in which, as a result of a change of circum- stances, the alien has the opportunity to establish himself outside the Netherlands without danger of persecution, unless he has compelling reasons, resulting from earlier persecution, not to make use of this opportunity.

Article 14(1) of the Aliens Act lists four grounds for the withdrawal of admission:
(a) the person in question provided incorrect information leading to his admission;

(b) he has repeatedly committed an act that is punishable by law;
(c) he has been convicted by final judgment of deliberately committing crime carrying a prison sentence of three or more years;
(d) he constitutes a serious danger to national security.

The grounds for withdrawal in Article 14(1) of the Aliens Act should be distinguished from the cessation clauses. The fact is that these grounds are related to circumstances in the country of residence as established after the admission of the refugee. All cases relate to new facts that become known to the Dutch authorities only after the admission of the refugee. If the alien had not yet been admitted, these facts would have led either to a rejection of the application, or to a refusal of admission as a refugee on the grounds of compelling reasons of national interest. However, none of these facts are related to the importance that is attached to the primacy of national protection, which, as previously stated, forms the rationale for the existence of Article 1C of the Convention.

The main points of current decision-making practice and jurisprudence in the Netherlands with regard to the international grounds for withdrawal are elaborated below. The policy regarding the international grounds for withdrawal is set down in the Aliens Policy Brief and does not, in my opinion, require further explanation in this context. It should further be established in advance that a combination of national and international grounds of withdrawal is not impossible. On a few occasions in the recent past, the withdrawal of admission as a refugee has been based both on reasons of public order and on the absence of fear of prosecution.

2.2 Policy and jurisprudence in the Netherlands

The first starting point is that the term 'change of circumstance' in Article 15(3) of the Aliens Act refers to all situations as described in the cessation clauses of Article 1C of the Convention. The Administrative Law Division of the Council of State confirmed this in its decision of 21 November 1996 (*RO*2.93 4639).

The second starting point is that, in view of the wording and general aims of Article 1C of the Convention, it is legally established that a person no longer falls under the Convention if one of the cessation clauses can be applied to him. Recognition of refugee status is declaratory; *ipso facto* the termination of that recognition is also declaratory.

However, in the aforementioned decision, the Administrative Law Division of the Council of State did consider that the fact that recognition as a refugee legally ceases to exist does not imply that admission to the Netherlands as a refugee is also legally withdrawn. The Division considered that because Article 15(3) of the Aliens Act provides the Minister with discretionary competence on this point, an explicit decision in favour of withdrawal of admission as a refugee is required in each case. This implies that admission as a refugee can only be withdrawn on the grounds of Article 15(3) of the Aliens Act after it has been established that the person in question is not (or no longer) a refugee in accordance with the definition of the Convention and the Aliens Act.

The third starting point is that, in principle, there must be fundamental changes in the country of origin before a general decision can be made to apply Article 1C(5) or (6) of the Convention. This follows from the state practice as set down, *inter alia*, in the Handbook and Conclusion 69. It also follows from sparing references in the jurisprudence of the Division of the early 1990s, concerning the changes in Chile, from which the criterion of 'restoration of the legal order' may, with some good will, be inferred. In my opinion, fundamental changes may be deemed to have taken place during a dramatic change in the country of origin in which the political system undergoes considerable improvement. This point of view is in accordance with declarations of the UNHCR in practice (see Section 1.4), as well as with the essence of the reasoning of the plenipotentiary representing France – the country that proposed the cessation clause in 1950. The plenipotentiary put forward the argument that protection should no longer be granted to refugees from countries where democracy has been restored, and that France, at least, would no longer consider itself bound to grant such protection. In my opinion, indications that such a dramatic change has taken place include, *inter alia*, the success of constitutional reforms, the holding of democratic elections, the establishment of a democratic régime or a multiparty system, successful large-scale repatriation, the introduction and implementation of amnesty regulations, a general improvement in the human rights situation, and the completion of other social developments marking the end of systematic repressive government action. Examples of such social developments include the termination of an emergency situation, the withdrawal of measures relating to censorship, the establishment of a criminal tribunal, a national commission on reconciliation, an ombudsman or a human rights committee, and the disbandment of security services or militias. The final judgment does not depend so much on one or more of these indications, but on the general picture of the situation that eventually emerges from the country of origin. Experience has taught us that, in many cases, when changes are evaluated over a period of three years following the initial reforms (peace agreements or dramatic changes), a balanced assessment of the general situation in the country of origin can be rendered. Incidentally, I consider it important to emphasize once again that the fundamental changes described in Article 1C(5) and (6) of the Convention are of a different order than the circumstances that may lead to a change in policy with regard to provisional residence permits *(vvtv)*, as described in the supplement to the letter on indicators regarding provisional residence permits (Bijl. Hand. II 1997/98, 19 637, No. 308).

The fourth starting point is that the asylum request of the person in question must be reviewed in the light of the situation in his country of origin, in order to establish whether he no longer has reason to fear persecution. Thus, an individual evaluation takes place with regard to the withdrawal of admission as a refugee on the grounds of Article 1C(5) or (6) of the Convention. In my opinion, this evaluation should take place on the basis of those objective facts and circumstances regarding the situation in the country of origin that are relevant in the light of the specific asylum request of the person in question. The result of this may be that the aforementioned conditions regarding fundamental changes in the situation in the country of origin have been met, but that, in one or two individual cases, the conditions for the application of Article 1C(5) of the Convention have not been met. Viewed from the opposite angle, the result may also be that although the aforementioned conditions regarding fundamental changes in the situation in the country of origin may not have been met in their entirety, the conditions regarding the application of Article 1C(5) of the Convention have been met.

By way of illustration, the reader is referred to a decision of the President of the Court of First Instance of The Hague, which also sits in Zwolle, of 2 February 1995 (*RV* 1995, no. 39), which considered that the evaluation of whether the person in question had reason to fear persecution if he returned to his country of origin should be made on the basis of his declaration, and that his asylum request should be evaluated in the light of the 'current' situation in his country of origin. The Court considered that it was of particular significance whether, generally speaking, the group to which the alien belonged had problems with the Government or with other local population groups. The asylum request of the person in question was based on his professed membership of the Pentecostal community. The Court considered that the situation in his country of origin, namely Romania, had changed to such an extent that membership of such a community was no longer considered a prohibited activity and that it could not be assumed, therefore, that the person in question still had reason to fear persecution within the meaning of refugee law. According to the Court, therefore, the refugee status of the person in question had rightly been withdrawn.

This decision dates from 2 February 1995. The UNHCR only issued a declaration concerning the applicability of Article 1C(5) of the Convention to Romanian refugees on 1 October 1997. It follows, therefore, that the application of this cessation clause is not solely dependent on declarations issued by the UNHCR.

The final starting point is that, during the consideration whether to withdraw admission to the Netherlands as a refugee on the grounds of a change of circumstances, it should also be considered whether the person in question has compelling reasons, arising from previous persecution, not to make use of the opportunity to return to his country of origin. Conclusion 69 orders States Parties to the Refugees Convention to grant a different status in such cases to maintain previously established rights.

The academic literature refers to the intention of the drafters of the Refugees Convention to take into account, by way of this exception, the psychological problems of persons who are returned to the very countries that were responsible for their mistreatment. Reference is also made to their intention to protect victims of such abuse against further mistreatment by fellow citizens who have not (yet) embraced the basic principles of the dramatic changes in their country of origin. Family circumstances and disability are not considered to represent compelling reasons, nor are economic motives.

In my opinion, the current system of residence law contains a sufficient number of guarantees to do justice to this starting point. In the Netherlands, a residence permit may, in certain cases, be granted on the grounds of prolonged residence or compelling reasons of a humanitarian nature.'[12]

4.64 OTHER ASSISTANCE IN CRIMINAL MATTERS

See also: 4.31, 4.52, 4.63, 11.3, 12.273 ICC and ICTY

Investigation of war crimes and crimes against humanity

On 22 December 1998, the Minister of Justice stated, *inter alia*, as follows:

'The Minister noted that, first and foremost, the Netherlands wished to honour its commitments on the basis of agreements that it has concluded. This also applies to the judicial aspects of these commitments. Globally speaking, the national war crimes investigation team (*NOVO* team) is almost unique. Most cases concern the entry into the Netherlands of persons to whom aliens law would normally be applicable, but who may have committed serious crimes, so that criminal law should be applied to them instead. It should be recalled that significant differences exist between aliens law and criminal law. If persons are not refused

12. Bijl. Hand. II 1998/99 – 19637 No. 438, pp. 2-8.

admittance directly upon entry and they apply for asylum, they enter into the asylum process. Even if they do not acquire any formal status, they cannot be deported, on the grounds of Article 3 of the European Convention on Human Rights, if they fear inhuman or cruel treatment in their own country. However, criminal law employs different criteria from aliens law. It is therefore not a foregone conclusion that they will be automatically prosecuted and tried.

[...]

The transfer of cases to individual countries by the International Criminal Tribunal for the Former Yugoslavia (ICTY) is controlled by Article 11 *bis* of the Rules of Procedure and Evidence, which establishes that the Tribunal can transfer a case to a country if 'it appears to the Trial Chamber that the authorities of the State in which the accused was arrested are prepared to prosecute the accused in their own courts; and it is appropriate in the circumstances for the courts of that State to exercise jurisdiction over the accused...' As far as we know, the ICTY has yet to transfer a case to the Netherlands or to any other country.

At present, the *de facto NOVO* team consists of four persons: a team leader, a tactical coordinator, a tactical investigator and two intelligence coordinators. In addition, two interpreters are employed on a freelance basis. The two coordinators are also liaison officers with the ICTY. Once a month, consultations take place between the Public Prosecutor and the ICTY. From 1 March 1999, the team will be expanded by five tactical investigators and an information processor. In the meantime, the selection and appointment process for this expansion has largely been completed. It is expected that, after this, a further two tactical investigators and a scientist will be engaged. At the present time, the *NOVO* team possesses 87 files, half of which concern cases relating to the former Yugoslavia. The remaining files relate to cases in other countries, including Afghanistan. In the case of a few files, active investigations are currently taking place. For reasons of an operational nature it is not possible to elaborate on this matter.

A strong case did not exist against Pinochet in 1994, nor does it exist today. In addition, no complaints have been received from interested parties in the Netherlands and, consequently, the Public Prosecutor is not able to launch a criminal investigation against Pinochet. When asked, the Minister noted that it is possible that persons suspected internationally of committing serious crimes might leave after a stay in the Netherlands before sufficient material is collected to proceed with an arrest, because it is an impossible task for the Public Prosecutor to collect sufficient material and information beforehand, in order to proceed with a prosecution. If the Internal Security Services are aware of the arrival of such a person, this information will be forwarded to the collegiate body of Public Prosecutors so that the appropriate Public Prosecutor can collect relevant information. In response to a question regarding the establishment of a database with a Europol connection, the Minister pointed to developments that are already underway. It is no coincidence that an International Criminal Court is being established in the Netherlands and international data collection forms a part of this. The expansion of Europol's mandate is currently being examined, but this will be a difficult task. Even to this day, unfortunately, all attempts to render Europol operational have failed. It remains to be seen whether this will be different as of next January.

[...]

No normal legal assistance régime exists as yet with the States that currently occupy the territory of the former Yugoslavia. No legal assistance treaties exist as yet. However, since 1994, the Netherlands has amply assisted the ICTY prosecutor with so-called on-site investigations within these jurisdictions into mass executions and on-site legal investigations.

The results of these on-site legal investigations are primarily intended for the ICTY, but at the request of the Dutch Minister of Justice the documents are made available by the Public Prosecutor for prosecutions on the basis of the Criminal Law in Wartime Act.

The mandate of the *NOVO* team runs until 2004. An evaluation can take place halfway through the period in 2001. A memorandum concerning the legislation is anticipated prior to the implementation process required by the advent of the International Criminal Court. In February, an official committee with the task of drafting an annex defining the elements of responsibility for war crimes will meet again in New York. This annex will form part of the Statute. Once this Statute has been completed, it is the intention that a memorandum on the legislative policy that should be followed in these matters will be presented to the Chamber. This will occur in March, provided that the committee has reached agreement. It is intended that the memorandum will appear at such a time as to permit its inclusion in the discussion of the bill approving the establishment of the International Criminal Court. If it proves impossible to confirm this arrangement by January, the Chamber will be informed of this. The cases for which the witnesses are already in the Netherlands will be handled first. In the cases that have been heard so far, witnesses have frequently been located outside the Netherlands. In practice, a great deal of effort has been required to locate these witnesses. For witnesses that are in danger the same arrangements apply as in the Netherlands.

The plan of action was sent to the Second Chamber on 11 June. After that, written questions were submitted on 6 October and answered on 23 October.

In response to a question regarding the 100 day period of administrative detention, the Minister noted that the existing provision in the Penal Code offers sufficient scope through the so-called *pro forma* warrant and trial under Article 282(4) together with Article 66, Part II of the Penal Code. In other words, it is always possible to hold persons in administrative detention for longer than 100 days. Article 68(3) of the Penal Code, which relates to the principle of *ne bis in idem*, will require amendment in view of the implementation in the Netherlands of commitments under the Statute of the International Criminal Court (ICC Statute). The Statute includes a separate provision in Article 20(3) concerning the principle of *ne bis in idem*. The International Criminal Court will have the authority to disregard the principle of *ne bis in idem* if a prior prosecution for war crimes, for example, was purely for the purpose of shielding the accused from criminal responsibility. In such cases, there is a question of a sham procedure, an abuse of national trial law. This relativization of the principle of *ne bis in idem* also applies to the Contracting Parties. They must ensure that such a procedure cannot form a barrier to prosecution in their national systems. This also applies to the Netherlands, which will have to amend Article 68 of the Penal Code to this effect. Article 20 of the Statute concerns only gross violations of human rights and war crimes. The jurisdiction of the International Criminal Court covers only violations of this kind. Nevertheless, this Article of the Statute establishes a clear norm regarding the meaning, reach and limitation of the international principle of *ne bis in idem*. In this respect, Article 20 recodifies international criminal law. States Parties can introduce this into national law on the basis of their implementation commitments.

In response to the question how to verify whether the country of origin of the accused is merely attempting to shield him from criminal responsibility, the Minister noted that for this purpose a general norm should be established in the law. On the basis of facts and circumstances, a test must be conducted by a court against the background of what is possible on the basis of Article 20 of the Statute. It was asked what would happen if a Dutch Court determined that a criminal trial in another country had been a sham, so that the prosecution in the Netherlands could be continued. If the country of origin was to disagree with such a finding, two courts in two different countries would be up against one another. The Minister noted that in the case of Bouterse, the latter would presumably not end up in prison in the case of a conviction in the Netherlands and an acquittal in Suriname. Once the person in question enters the Netherlands, it is obviously an entirely different matter. Such a situation would form the basis of an extradition request if he were to appear in a third country. The Minister pointed to the fact that the international law principle of good faith applies with regard to the principle of *ne bis in idem*. One should assume that the third country has made use of its trial law in an appropriate manner. Only a very serious suspicion to the contrary justifies a renewed prosecution in the Netherlands. A proposal to amend Article 68 of the Penal Code will come up for discussion prior to, or concurrently with the introduction of the bill to ratify the treaty on the International Criminal Court.

Persons suspected of war crimes cannot be barred from the asylum process. International law establishes that everyone has a right to request asylum. That is the basis of Articles 1 and 33 of the Refugees Convention. In practice, an exception to this rule can only be made if a person previously sojourned in a safe third country and if that country can be regarded as willing to readmit the person in question to its asylum process. The Universal Declaration of Human Rights also takes the line that everyone may seek asylum. The Declaration provides just one exception to this rule in Article 14(2) which establishes that no appeal may be made to this right in cases of criminal prosecutions for crimes of a non-political nature or actions contrary to the aims and principles of the United Nations. This points to the fact that the international community is of the opinion that an asylum application can be rejected only after a penal procedure has been initiated.

The Aliens Act provides the possibility to withdraw the status granted to an alien if it was awarded on the basis of incorrect data. The condition for such a withdrawal is that the person in question provided incorrect data to the Immigration and Naturalization Service *(IND)* and that the decision to admit the person as a refugee was made on the basis of this data. It will not be possible in all cases to withdraw refugee status on this ground. For a long time, the courts and the *IND* presupposed a very high burden of proof with regard to Article 1F, the Article that makes it possible to withhold refugee status on account of war crimes. Only after further study in 1997, did a new understanding of the implications of this Article arise. This resulted in the Memorandum that was sent to the Chamber in November 1997 by the previous State Secretary.

Measures are being taken to enhance cell capacity, even though current needs are amply met, and to counter security threats. Entry can be refused at the border only if an alien is known to be a war criminal. A reevaluation of penalties for crimes against humanity and war crimes will take place in the framework of the implementation of the Rome Statute, which contains a recodification of substantive international criminal law on these points. The ICTY has yet to refer any cases to third countries, but it is trying to hand over four convicted persons to other countries, including Norway and Denmark, for execution of their sentences. These countries, however, are little inclined to execute these sentences, in part because of all the risks and prison unrest that this would involve. Until now, there has been no question of the transfer of prosecutions. With a view to the establishment of the International Criminal Court in the Netherlands, this means that other countries will have to be approached. All countries must share the burden of the absorption of persons convicted by the International Criminal Court.

At this time, cases are being heard against nationals of the former Yugoslavia. When the *NOVO* team is up to strength at the beginning of next year, cases against persons from other countries will also be heard. The plan of action states that, for every two investigators, four cases will be heard per year. There will also be cases that are less time-consuming. Depending on the weight of the cases, more than sixteen cases could be heard during 1999. Should this number prove to be too low, a revision will take place.

During the last two years, there were roughly sixty Article 1F rulings. These rulings consist of rulings of the *IND* in first instance and on appeal. Consequently, they do not necessarily involve sixty different persons. The Minister is not aware of the exact number.

The ICTY focuses on leaders and larger cases. This restriction of competency stems from the way in which the tasks of the ICTY were defined in the Security Council's resolution. This is an important consideration in the distribution of cases, in which capacity is also an issue. Thus far, there has been no evidence of a need to establish criteria. Decisions of this kind are made on a case by case basis. The plan of action states that, in each case, consultations will be held in advance with the ICTY regarding the question of who will hear the case. The constant coordination between the Netherlands and third countries with regard to the prosecution of war criminals is aided by a legal assistance régime based on classic legal assistance and extradition treaties. The Netherlands also has a specific treaty relationship with the ICTY as a result of the Agreement regulating the sitting of the Tribunal. However, these treaties do not provide for financial compensation. Legal assistance continues to be at the expense of the party providing it, which cannot request compensation for providing legal assistance, not even from the United Nations.

The transfer of information from the criminal investigation to the petitioners appears to present serious problems with regard to privacy legislation. The cases are heard in open court.

The Netherlands has offered itself as the host country for an International Criminal Court with a permanent jurisdiction to try cases of war crimes and crimes against humanity. However, the Netherlands is fundamentally unwilling to serve as the host country for the trial of crimes if that would lead to excessive disorder in the countries that possess original jurisdiction. The idea that Öcalan should stand trial before a European criminal court arose only because certain countries are involved in a process that may end in his extradition to Turkey, which would entail numerous complications of an international nature. The International Criminal Court that was established in Rome would not have jurisdiction to try Öcalan, because the acts of which he stands accused do not fall within the jurisdiction of the Court. In any case, the Netherlands has no arrangements with the United Nations regarding the establishment of a court that could exercise such jurisdiction. The Netherlands certainly does not welcome such a form of *ad hoc* jurisdiction. In the case of Lockerbie, it was the United Nations that approached the Netherlands. This was an unusual situation in which the parties concerned could not reach agreement and the Netherlands provided a solution.

In cases in which a policy of delayed departure to the country of origin applies, a delay is not granted, because Article 1F counts as a counter indication in the same way as a criminal record. A deportation order is then issued, unless a situation as described in Article 3 of the European Convention of Human Rights exists. If this is the case, the person in question is neither admitted nor sent back.'[13]

---

13. Bijl. Hand. II 1998/99 – 26262 No. 3, pp. 7-12.

Dutch detainees in foreign prisons and foreigners in Dutch prisons [14]

On 11 May 1999 the Minister of Justice sent a Letter to Parliament on the above-mentioned subject. It reads, *inter alia*, as follows:

'The reasons behind the treaty requirement in the Act concerning the transfer of responsibility for the execution of criminal sentences

Article 2 of the Act concerning the transfer of responsibility for the execution of criminal sentences contains, as its first condition for the adoption of responsibility for the execution of a criminal sentence of a foreign court, a treaty requirement. It establishes that the execution of foreign judgments in the Netherlands can only take place pursuant to a treaty. Art. 2 conforms to the traditional approach of Dutch constitutional law, which requires a treaty base for the provision of far-reaching forms of legal assistance to foreign countries by the Dutch justice system (compare Art. 2(3) of the Constitution, Arts. 2 and 51 of the Extradition Act and Art. 552(m) and (o) of the Penal Code). For a better understanding of Article 2 of the Act concerning the transfer of responsibility for the execution of criminal sentences, I believe that it would be helpful to take another look, on the basis of the legislative history, at the reasons behind the extension of the traditional approach to this form of international cooperation in criminal cases.

In the Explanatory Memorandum (Hand. II, 1983/84, 18 129, No. 3), the following is stated concerning the choice in favour of the treaty requirement for the execution of foreign criminal sentences in the Netherlands. As in the case of extradition law, the motive for this choice lies in the judgment that such a system of international cooperation can only function properly if the States that are involved in it have sufficient confidence in the quality of each other's administration of criminal justice. The starting point is that foreign criminal judgments are recognized and accepted, and that they can not be subjected to review, as far as the establishment of the facts is concerned.

Not only the determination of the criminality of the facts, but also the manner in which the facts were established in the convicting State, are exempt from evaluation by the authorities of the State that adopts responsibility for the execution of an imposed sanction. Therefore, the adopting State should be able to trust that the decision of the foreign court was reached in accordance with the basic principles of what constitutes proper criminal procedure. Ultimately, these considerations must carry more weight than considerations of a humanitarian nature, which argue for the creation of the option for Dutch nationals to be transferred to the Netherlands to complete their sentences when have been convicted and detained in countries with which the conclusion of treaties raises too many objections, because of insufficient trust in their criminal procedures.

Because the transfer of responsibility for the execution of criminal sentences implies that several States can exercise authority in the same area, a treaty-based arrangement offers the additional advantage that guarantees can be provided for the convicted person against the risk of being subjected to sentence for the same acts on several occasions, as well as against

---

14. See also 30 NYIL (1999) pp. 192-193.

other potential consequences of the transfer that could have a negative impact on his position with respect to detention.

The treaty requirement implies that Dutch nationals who are detained in a country with which the Netherlands does not have a treaty providing for their transfer will not qualify for transfer to the Netherlands. This implication was heavily debated during the parliamentary consideration of the bill concerning the transfer of responsibility for the execution of sentences.

As a solution to the problem, it was proposed, *inter alia*, that an exception be made to the treaty requirement in cases where the convicted person consents to his transfer to the Netherlands. The Government rejected this proposal in the Memorandum of Reply (Hand. II, 1984/85, 18 129, No. 6, p. 5) because: "it would be wrong to assume that the consent of the person in question would relieve the Dutch authorities (including the justice system) of the responsibility to concern themselves with the quality of the legal régime of a foreign country." It appeared to the Government, "that the Dutch authorities cannot hide behind the consent of a convicted person and use it as a justification to close their eyes to the quality of the administration of criminal justice in third countries. If the Netherlands adopts responsibility for the execution of a foreign criminal decision, this implies recognition of that decision, and it appears that the Netherlands could be challenged on this recognition, also on the international level."

The option of simply dropping the treaty requirement in its entirety was also considered. At the time, the Government judged that, all things considered, the arguments in favour of maintaining the treaty requirement were more compelling than the arguments that called for abandoning it. In the note that was issued in connection with the final report (Hand. II 1985/86, 18 129, No. 9, pp. 1-2), it was explained, *inter alia*, as follows. 'The core of those arguments is that we regard it as being our duty to prevent, insofar as possible, that the court is placed in a position in which it may become a participant in an international dispute resulting from fundamental differences of opinion, between the Netherlands and other countries, with regard to ideas concerning the quality of the administration of criminal justice and the minimum standards to be observed therein. Moreover, the knowledge that such disputes may easily develop with countries that have legal traditions that are fundamentally different from our own, and that the management of such disputes is the responsibility of the Government, could put considerable pressure on the independence and impartiality of the courts in their judgments. The legislature should avoid placing the courts in such a position."

It should not be concluded from the above that we are not concerned about the humanitarian aspect of the fate of Dutch nationals who are detained in certain countries. On the contrary, it is very important to us to try to alleviate their suffering and we will do everything in our power to achieve this. However, it is our contention that the instruments of international criminal law, that is to say, the laws regulating international cooperation in criminal cases, are not designed for this, and that it would be better to try using other means and modalities that have already been applied with some success in the past.' [15]

15. Bijl. Hand. II 1998/99 – 25203 No. 12, pp. 1-3.

4.7 PROTECTION OF HUMAN RIGHTS AND FUNDAMENTAL FREEDOMS

Dutch view on the 'Memorandum of Understanding' between the UN and Afghanistan

On 16 October 1998 the Ministers of Foreign Affairs and of Development Cooperation answered questions on the above-mentioned subject. They stated, *inter alia*, as follows:

'1. We did not agree in any way with the document that was drafted last May. In this context, we would like to draw attention to the fact that, as a result of the subsequent change in the situation in Afghanistan, no further elaboration or implementation of the Memorandum of Understanding will take place. At the end of July, most non-governmental organizations had evacuated their employees from Kabul, while the United Nations had minimized its staff and was carrying out only so-called life saving activities. Recently, there has been talk of significant military victories by the Taliban and accompanying territorial expansion.

2. In view of the many obstacles that the Taliban had placed in the path of the United Nations during the performance of its humanitarian tasks, it had become necessary to reach an agreement with the Taliban concerning the continuation of humanitarian assistance. The present Memorandum of Understanding is the result of talks that were held between the United Nations and the Taliban on this matter. The Memorandum of Understanding in no way constitutes an endorsement of the policy pursued by the Taliban or a recognition of the Taliban as the legitimate government of Afghanistan. We saw no immediate reason to intervene with criticisms in the work of United Nations, although we have reservations concerning a number of specific elements in the Agreement.

3. It goes without saying, in our opinion, that it may be expected of United Nations personnel that they show respect for the values and traditions of the population of the country in which they are employed.
[...]

5. Article 12 clearly expresses the basic right of men *and* women to education and health care. Article 13, however, states that the access of women to health care and education and their participation in them will need to be gradual. Although some may see in this Article a legitimization of the reprehensible policies of the Taliban, the provision may actually offer the prospect of the gradual achievement of the ultimate objective, namely, unrestricted, equal access to and participation in health care and education for women, an objective to which the Taliban have also committed themselves in writing. Unfortunately, current Taliban policy flatly contradicts such a gradual approach. In mid-June, the closure of all informal schools for girls in Kabul, which had been tolerated until then, was ordered. In addition, it was decreed at the end of June that all women seeking medical treatment must be accompanied by a close male relative, an act which further limits the access of women to health care. As

a result, the already extremely poor state of health of women in Afghanistan will deteriorate even further.
6. Naturally, human rights and human rights agreements are, and will remain applicable to men and to women. The Memorandum of Understanding can do nothing to diminish this and confirms as much in Article 12 of the Memorandum of Understanding, in relation to the right to education and access to health care.' [16]

8.22 LIMITATIONS UPON TERRITORIAL JURISDICTION

See also: 1.2, 4.64, 7.21, 8.24, 12.2711, 12.273, 16.726

Establishment of a Scottish Court sitting in the Netherlands

The Explanatory Memorandum to the provisions for the Establishment of a Scottish Court sitting in the Netherlands to try the persons referred to as 'the two accused' in the Resolution 1192 (1998) of the Security Council of the United Nations, which was adopted during its 3920th meeting on 27 August 1998, in respect of the criminal offences referred to in the Preamble of the treaty between the United Kingdom of Great Britain and Northern Ireland and the Kingdom of the Netherlands of 18 September 1998 for the establishment of a Scottish court sitting in the Netherlands reads, *in full*, as follows:

'In a letter dated 24 August 1998 (Bijl. Hand. II, 1997/98, 26 127 Nos. 1-2), we brought to your attention the initiative of the United Kingdom and the United States regarding the possible criminal prosecution of the two Libyan suspects of the 1988 bombing of PanAm flight 103 over Lockerbie (Scotland). According to this initiative, the prosecution would take place before a Scottish Court, sitting on Dutch territory. Naturally, such a Court would apply Scottish criminal and trial law. In the aforementioned letter, the second signatory of this Memorandum presented a few additional documents, including the proposed British-Dutch Agreement regulating the sitting of the Court and the British bill for an Act establishing a Scottish Court in the Netherlands.

On 27 August, the United Nations Security Council adopted Resolution 1192 (1998), wholly in line with the above-mentioned initiative. This Resolution has also been brought to your attention. The Resolution welcomes the initiative undertaken by the United States and the United Kingdom and the willingness demonstrated by the Kingdom of the Netherlands to assist in the realization of this initiative by permitting the exercise of Scottish jurisdiction on Dutch territory. The Council calls on the three cooperating States to undertake the necessary steps to realize the proposed jurisdiction, which is to be entrusted to a Scottish Court in accordance with a letter from the United Kingdom of Great Britain and Northern Ireland and the United States to the United Nations Secretary General (S/1998/759), which was presented to your Chamber as an annex to our aforementioned letter. In order to

16. Bijl. Hand. II 1998/99 No. 181, pp. 367-368.

implement this initiative, as mentioned by the Security Council, two judicial steps are indispensable at this stage as far as the Netherlands is concerned, in its capacity as the proposed host country. The first is the conclusion of an Agreement regulating the sitting of the Court between the United Kingdom and the Netherlands. The second is a procedural implementation law, in which the legal consequences of the acceptance of this foreign jurisdiction in the Dutch legal system are regulated. The Agreement regulating the sitting of the Court will, first and foremost, carefully determine the boundaries of the jurisdiction that is to be exercised by the Scottish Court. The purpose of this jurisdiction is the criminal prosecution of the persons described by the Security Council as 'the two accused', also described in the Resolution as 'the two persons charged with the bombing of PanAm flight 103'. The jurisdiction to be exercised by the Scottish Court is thus of a personal and temporary nature: it can only be exercised for the purpose of prosecuting the two suspects. This temporal jurisdiction will be brought into force on Dutch territory. In a manner of speaking, a spatial immunity will be created within the territorial jurisdiction of the Netherlands and, within this immunity, a foreign, Scottish Court will be permitted to exercise criminal jurisdiction on an *ad hoc* and *ad personam* basis, as described in the Agreement regulating the sitting of the Court. To a certain extent, therefore, the Netherlands will be waiving internal sovereignty on the basis of an agreement. Stated differently, the spatially bound immunity described in the Agreement regulating the sitting of the Court – criminal exterritoriality in classic terms – limits Dutch jurisdiction based on the principle of territoriality, as formulated in Article 2 of the Penal Code. The applicability of this principle is directly limited by Article 8 of the Penal Code, which establishes that such an international law exception to the principle carries over immediately into the Dutch legal system. Naturally, the Netherlands' jurisdictional position is only temporary, for the duration of the criminal prosecution, as established in the Resolution and the Agreement regulating the sitting of the Court. In fact, Dutch law will remain in force within the spatial immunity. However, for the duration of the Agreement regulating the sitting of the Court it cannot be enforced via normal channels, including the possible use of force, without the permission of the Scottish Court, which has been granted immunity. If, according to Dutch law, a criminal act is committed within the spatial immunity, the Dutch authorities can act insofar as the Scottish Court permits them to do so. Naturally, in the case of criminal offences that are intended to disrupt the criminal procedure, such as breaches of the peace or the intimidation of witnesses or officials, the Scottish Court can request the assistance of the authorities of the host State. Under such circumstances, this request would constitute a waiver of immunity.

Precedents exist for the exercise in the Netherlands of such a temporary, non-national criminal jurisdiction: the jurisdiction exercised by the so-called International Criminal Tribunal for the Former Yugoslavia (ICTY) and that exercised by the Appeals Chamber of the Rwanda Tribunal, which also sits in The Hague. The most important current legal phenomenon – to wit, the limitation of Dutch territorial jurisdiction and its entrustment to a Scottish Court on an *ad hoc* basis – displays many similarities to the relationship between ICTY jurisdiction and Dutch jurisdiction. As in the case of ICTY jurisdiction, it will be established that Dutch law is not applicable to measures relating to the deprivation of liberty and the limitation of freedom of movement of persons by order of the Scottish Court in premises that have been placed at the disposal of the Court by the Netherlands in accordance with the Agreement regulating the sitting of the Court. This will be achieved through the current bill, the first article of which follows the wording of Article 17 of the law establishing the jurisdiction of the ICTY. In essence, the bill concerns the following. The Scottish Court will want to take steps to ensure the appearance of both suspects in Court. This desire will arise immediately after the completion of the Dutch extradition process, which begins the moment that both requested Libyan suspects set foot on Dutch territory. At such a time, there must be an arrest warrant based on the Dutch Extradition Act. In principle, it would be sufficient at this time for the requesting party, the United Kingdom, to have made a request for provisional arrest to the Netherlands in accordance with Article 16(1) of the European Extradition Convention of 13 December 1957 (*Trb.* 1965 No. 9). The Public Prosecutor can then act in accordance with Article 13(1) of the Extradition Act of 1967, depending on the point of arrival in this country. However, if possible, we would prefer to receive a fully developed extradition request from the United Kingdom, in which it requests the Netherlands to arrest the requested persons and then to deliver them to the Scottish Court exercising jurisdiction within a defined space in the Netherlands. This space, or area, is defined in the Agreement regulating the sitting of the Court, in which the Netherlands has committed itself to the Court to provide premises (Art. 3(1) of the Agreement). In accordance with Article 5 of the Agreement, these premises will enjoy immunity for the duration of the trial. Within this area of immunity, a temporary enclave inside Dutch jurisdiction, only Scottish law is applicable and enforceable and, as such, the transfer by the Netherlands of the requested persons to this Scottish Court corresponds with extradition as defined in the Article 1 of the relevant treaty, namely, the European Extradition Convention. The Netherlands is physically providing both suspects in accordance with the request of the United Kingdom (as, for the sake of brevity, we identify the requesting party in this context), so that they may undergo criminal prosecution within the jurisdiction of this party for acts that are criminal both according to the law of the requesting party and according to the law of the Netherlands. The admissibility and approval of this extradition request will, of course, be evaluated in accordance with the procedures provided in the Extradition Act of 1967.

This implies, therefore, that a Dutch Court will examine – on the basis of the legal procedures embodied in the Dutch Extradition Act – whether the detention and preventive measures, which are to be taken with a view to the transfer of the requested persons to the Scottish Court, are in accordance with the Convention, legislation and law. In this regard, the requested persons will be entitled to the same legal protection that all persons in special categories are entitled to on Dutch territory. This legal status is guaranteed from the moment that the requested persons arrive in the Netherlands until the moment of their transfer to the Scottish Court. The transfer itself also takes place by virtue of a judicial decision: the decision that the extradition of the requested persons to the Scottish Court is admissible in accordance with law and treaty. After transfer, the requested persons remain under the exclusive competence of the Scottish Court. With regard to the Scottish Court, the Dutch extraditing Court will be bound by the restrictions that stem from the international law principle of good faith: it will have to assume that, with regard to the requested persons, the Court will act in accordance with the basic legal principles and guarantees on which the European Convention for the Protection of Human Rights and Fundamental Freedoms is based and which it partly articulates. This assumption is also justified by the fact that the United Kingdom is party to this Human Rights Convention. We refer the reader to the decision of the Supreme Court of 1 July 1985)[17]. Once they are in the custody of the Scottish Court, the requested persons will immediately enjoy the legal protection that arises from the principle of *habeus corpus*, on which Article 5 of the European Convention on Human Rights is based.

The current bill concerns the fact that the measures relating to deprivation of liberty and the limitation of freedom of movement that are to be taken by the Scottish Court under Scottish law should be viewed as separate from the examination conducted by the Dutch Court and the compatibility of Dutch law. Formally speaking, the law must ensure that the Scottish Court, not the Dutch Court, possesses exclusive authority. In this context, one may think especially of a measure such as administrative detention, to which both suspects will be subjected immediately upon transfer to the Scottish premises. The possibility that, on the basis of Article 15 of the Dutch Constitution, the suspects could turn to a Dutch Court for an injunction by way of a *habeas corpus* procedure must be ruled out. Otherwise, this could lead to an irresolvable conflict of jurisdiction. In this context, we wish, also for the sake of brevity, to refer the reader to the point made by the then Minister of Justice during the debate concerning the Act implementing the ICTY in the Second Chamber. According to the Minister, it would "create the wrong impression" if the Dutch legislature was to determine that the ICTY could detain or hold persons whose arrests as suspects it had ordered. In this case, the Minister stated, it is not the Dutch legal order that applies, but that of the United Nations. We refer the reader to the debate of 3 March 1994 (Hand. II 1993/94 No. 57, pp, 4223-4258; 4308). and the Memorandum of Amendment introducing the aforementioned Article 17 of the Act implementing the ICTY.[18] The Dutch legal order must be suspended to a certain extent; this is the inevitable consequence of admitting a "foreign criminal jurisdiction" to the Netherlands. This case is no different. Article 1 is meant to prevent the above-mentioned "wrong impression" by providing the Dutch Court with a formal legal basis to dismiss claimants who apply for *habeas corpus* with respect to the detention measures of the Scottish Court. Unlike in the case of the Act implementing the jurisdiction of the Rwanda Tribunal (Act of 18 December 1997, *Stb.* 754), we have refrained from simply declaring that Article 17 of the Act implementing the ICTY applies equally to the Scottish jurisdiction. The reason for this is that the Netherlands had to adhere to specific definitions contained in the Act implementing the ICTY, such as "tribunal", "statute", "surrender" and "transfer", which correspond to standard United Nations terminology, as included in Security Council Resolution 955 of 8 November 1994. In the United Nations context, "surrender" is a new legal concept in which a requested person is transferred to a supranational jurisdiction that is hierarchically superior to national jurisdictions, including the national judicial authorities. In this context, in which the Netherlands is contributing through traditional channels to the maintenance of Scottish criminal law, which is obviously not hierarchically superior to Dutch law, the legal concept of "surrender" clearly does not apply. The Netherlands is employing regular legal assistance relations, as established and defined by treaty and by law, for the purpose of the physical presentation of the suspects to the

17. *NJ* (1986) No. 162.
18. Bijl. Hand. II, 1993/94, 23 542, No. 10.

Scottish jurisdiction. It appears to us, therefore, that it would suffice to include in the text of the Act that the suspension of Dutch law relates to measures relating to deprivation of liberty and the limitation of freedom of movement initiated by the Scottish Court, as agreed by the United Kingdom and the Netherlands in the Agreement regulating the sitting of the Court. Articles 2 to 16 of the Act implementing the ICTY are not needed to ensure the exercise of the above-mentioned Scottish jurisdiction, because the national enforcement measures and preventive competences granted to the Dutch authorities by the Extradition Act are being employed with regard to the Scottish jurisdiction. We have already pointed out that the Extradition Act provides the authority for administrative detention, after which a shift can be made to detention under Article 14 *(inverzekeringstelling)*. After that, the Public Prosecutor can demand further detention *(inbewaringstelling)* and, after a fully developed asylum request has been received in compliance with Article 18 of the Act, he can proceed in accordance with Section B of Chapter III of the Extradition Act. Aside from "extradition", no other forms of legal assistance are provided, but should a requesting party require such legal assistance, it can apply for this under existing legal assistance agreements. Of course, there is absolutely no question at all of the Netherlands carrying out the Scottish judgment, as is the case with regard to ICTY judgements as regulated in Articles 11, 12, 13 and 14 of the Act implementing the ICTY.

In this context, it is worth mentioning that, in accordance with Article 3(3) of the Agreement regulating the sitting of the Court, the Court is also authorized, pending the procedures, to take other measures restricting freedom of movement aside from administrative detention in order to ensure the continuity of the integrity of justice. The Court will be authorized to act with regard to offences directed against the integrity of the Court, so-called contempt of court offences, as well as offences directed against officials and functionaries of the Court. Furthermore, the Court will be allowed to detain witnesses who have been transferred to the Court by other States. This measure may be taken at the expense of the witnesses to ensure the presentation of testimony at trial. This authority ends the moment that the jurisdiction granted to the Scottish Court for the trial of both suspects, to which the extradition relates, expires. In this context, it is also true that pending judgment, the ICTY possesses similar powers on the basis of its own procedural rules to act against persons who threaten the progress of the case, for example, by committing perjury.

With regard to the remaining provisions of the Agreement regulating the sitting of the Court, it may be noted that they contain the privileges and immunities that are required for the proper functioning of the Court. In addition, some practical provisions have been included in the Agreement with regard to the presence in the Netherlands of suspects and witnesses. These provisions are comparable to those of the Agreement with the United Nations regulating the ICTY (*Trb.* 1994 No. 189). The Chairman of the Second Chamber was informed of these matters in letters dated 24 August and 25 August 1998 (Bijl. Hand. II, 1997/98, 26 127, No. 1).' [19]

---

19. Bijl. Hand. II 1998/99 – 26211 No. 3.

9.616 EXPLORATION AND EXPLOITATION OF THE SEABED AND THE SUBSOIL

See: 9.619

9.619 EXCLUSIVE ECONOMIC ZONE[20]

See also: 9.616, 9.63, 9.7

Exclusive Economic Zone

In a Note referring to the Report concerning the Kingdom Act concerning the establishment of the Exclusive Economic Zone of 17 December 1998, the Ministers of Foreign Affairs and of Transport, Public Works and Water Management stated, *inter alia*, as follows:

'The Netherlands already enjoys sovereign rights for the purpose of the exploration and exploitation of the natural resources of the continental shelf. The establishment of an Exclusive Economic Zone does not affect these rights.

The Members of Parliament for the *VVD* (liberals) have also asked about the possible implications of the establishment of an Exclusive Economic Zone for the maintenance of the external border in the context of the Schengen agreement, as well as the possibility of combatting illegal drug traffic by ships. In accordance with Article 56 of the United Nations Convention on the Law of the Sea, the coastal State has rights and duties in the Exclusive Economic Zone in the areas of natural resources, economic exploration and exploitation, artificial islands and installations, marine scientific research and the marine environment. The aim of the establishment of an Exclusive Economic Zone is not territorial expansion, but the extension of rights and duties over an area bordering the territory of the State. For this reason, the boundary of the Exclusive Economic Zone cannot be regarded as an external border in the sense intended by the Members. Furthermore, we would like to point out that the scope of the Schengen agreement is limited to the territory of the Netherlands.

The Government would like to point out that, with regard to the combatting of drug trafficking at sea, cooperation agreements exist both at the European level and in the framework of the United Nations Convention against Illicit Traffic in Narcotic Drugs and Psychotropic Substances (*Trb.* 1989 No. 97), which was concluded in Vienna on 20 December 1988.

Furthermore, we are cooperating with the United States in particular on a bilateral agreement concerning maritime law enforcement in the Caribbean, aimed at preventing illegal drug trafficking on the high seas. This will be accompanied by an implementation agreement concerning a new ship riders programme that will allow the investigating officers of both parties to sail on board each other's vessels when they are involved in an investigation and to intercept suspect ships from these vessels on the basis of their own warrants. In addition, there are, of course, classic legal assistance treaties in which States mutually guarantee to

20. See 30 NYIL (1999) pp. 197-198.

provide reciprocal legal assistance with regard to crimes committed on the high seas on board vessels that fly their flags or that are of their registry.

The law of the sea itself does not grant specific powers in the Exclusive Economic Zone with regard to the prevention of illegal drug trafficking. In this regard, the same rights and duties apply in the Exclusive Economic Zone as on the high seas.
[...]

The Members of Parliament for the *SGP* have asked what the national and international legal ramifications of the establishment of an Exclusive Economic Zone will be for the Kingdom's existing sovereign rights regarding the use of the continental shelf. The answer to this question is as follows. Currently, the Dutch continental shelf exists on the basis of the Convention on the Continental Shelf (*Trb.* 1959, 126), which was concluded in Geneva on 29 April 1958. On the basis of the Convention, the coastal State possesses sovereign rights with regard to the exploration and exploitation of the natural resources of the area in question. In the Netherlands, the manner in which sovereign rights over minerals in the continental shelf may be exercised is laid down in the Act regulating the mining of the continental shelf.

In the recent provisions of the United Nations Convention on the Law of the Sea, a distinction is made between the Exclusive Economic Zone, a zone with a breadth no greater than 200 miles, and the continental shelf, which, depending on the geographical situation, can extend seawards beyond the Exclusive Economic Zone. In the Exclusive Economic Zone, the coastal State possesses rights and duties in a number of defined areas, as well as sovereign rights with regard to the exploration and exploitation of natural resources. On the continental shelf, beyond the 200 miles, the coastal State possesses only sovereign rights with regard to the exploration and exploitation of natural resources. Because the Kingdom's Exclusive Economic Zone will not reach a breadth of 200 miles at any point, the Kingdom will not be able to claim a portion of the continental shelf beyond the 200 mile limit in accordance with Article 76 of the United Nations Convention on the Law of the Sea. The establishment of the Exclusive Economic Zone will therefore have no consequences for sovereign rights regarding the utilization of the continental shelf within the meaning of the United Nations Convention on the Law of the Sea.'[21]

On 4 March 1999 the Parliament held a debate on the Kingdom Act concerning the establishment of an EEZ.[22] In that debate, the State Secretary of Internal Affairs stated, *inter alia*, as follows:

'The current bill makes use of the opportunity provided to coastal States by the Convention on the Law of the Sea to establish an Exclusive Economic Zone. The Convention, which was concluded in 1982, but only came into force in 1994, offers a comprehensive codification of the law of the sea. The Netherlands ratified the Convention three years ago.

The Exclusive Economic Zone is important to the Kingdom in the first place because of the additional scope it offers for the maintenance of international regulations concerning the discharge and dumping of waste at sea that apply to shipping. Recent developments, however,

21. Bijl. Hand. II 1998/99 – 25446 (R1594) No. 5, p. 6-7.
22. For the Kingdom Act see this Yearbook under Municipal Legislation, 9.619.

such as the planned erection of transmitters at sea and the discussion concerning the construction of an airport at sea, demonstrate that the Exclusive Economic Zone can also be of importance in connection with other issues.

What rights does the coastal State have in the Exclusive Economic Zone? These are sovereign rights for the purpose of exploring and exploiting, conserving and managing the natural resources, whether living or non-living, fish, oil, gas, sand and gravel, of the sea, the seabed and its subsoil. In addition, there are sovereign rights with regard to other activities for the economic exploitation and exploration of the Exclusive Economic Zone, such as the production of energy from the water, currents and winds. In this context, I can think not only of windmills, but also of the tidal turbines that Mr. Herrema spoke about in his contribution. Finally, there is jurisdiction with regard to the establishment and use of artificial islands, installations and structures and with regard to marine scientific research and the protection and preservation of the marine environment. This makes it possible for more factors to be included in the evaluation.

The Exclusive Economic Zone forms a basis for further regulation regarding transmitters. This bill does not achieve enough, however, to make it possible to declare that Dutch legislation can be immediately applied.

[...]

Mr. Chairman! What may we expect from the Exclusive Economic Zone? By establishing this zone, the Kingdom will make optimal use of the possibility offered by the United Nations Convention on the Law of the Sea to exercise jurisdiction with regard to a number of uses of the sea. The current bill presents the best legal framework for achieving this. Expectations should not be too great, particularly because the possibilities are, after all, only limited. One of the original motives was to use the bill to deal with ships that have made illegal discharges when they are actually at sea. The United Nations Convention on the Law of the Sea, however, sets a number of fairly high thresholds in this regard. There must, *inter alia*, be question of an intentional discharge causing a significant pollution of the marine environment or major damage or threat of damage to the coastline or related interests. In fact, this does not happen all that frequently. In cases in which a ship does need to be seized, the Exclusive Economic Zone provides the required legal framework. It may be expected that sporadic action will also have a strong preventive effect. At present, it is not possible to seize a ship flying the flag of another country in the Exclusive Economic Zone. In any case, one should not think that a ship may be seized immediately if it is suspected of engaging in certain activities. Other regulations set fairly high thresholds in this regard.'[23]

9.63 JURISDICTION OF A STATE ON THE HIGH SEAS

See: 9.619

9.7 THE CONTINENTAL SHELF

See: 9.619

---

23. Hand. II 1998/99 No. 53, p. 3436.

13. COERCION AND USE OF FORCE SHORT OF WAR

See: 14.1132

13.22 REGIME OF THE UNITED NATIONS

See: 13.23, 14.113 UN Collective Measures

13.221 PEACE-KEEPING OPERATIONS

See: 13.23

13.23 COLLECTIVE SECURITY REGIME OF THE NORTH ATLANTIC TREATY ORGANIZATION

Military aerial actions against the FRY

On 8 October 1998 the Ministers of Foreign Affairs and Defence sent a Letter to Parliament concerning the situation in former Yugoslavia. On the above-mentioned subject it reads, *inter alia*, as follows:

'Military action is only in order when all political and diplomatic means have been exhausted. If military means are employed they are aimed, as part of a broader process of international efforts, at the achievement of a primary political-strategic objective. Potentially necessary military action is therefore aimed at enforcing immediate compliance with Resolution 1199. This is not a punitive expedition.

This is in accordance with the framework of evaluation, which refers to the Van Traa motion of 27 June 1999 (21 991, no. 26). The framework of evaluation mentions that "a gross violation of human rights, such as genocide, can also be the reason for military intervention by the international community." The Van Traa motion proclaimed that military action in an international context is possible "in order to avert large-scale and massive violation of basic human rights in the framework of a humanitarian emergency operation."

As you are aware, the Netherlands has made available sixteen F-16 aircraft, eight of which are already in Villafranca. A number of these F-16s have been modernized in the framework of the so-called "Midlife Update". Depending on the duration and intensity of the aerial actions, NATO can call upon these aircraft. The F-16s are deployed by NATO's air traffic control centre (Combined Air Operations Center) in Vicenza, which is part of the integrated command structure of NATO. This guarantees both a clear command structure and coordination with SFOR: both operations are under the command of the same NATO commander. The deployment of F-16s does not threaten the execution of (NATO) tasks in Bosnia-Herzegovina. In addition, the Netherlands has made tanker capacity available in the form of two KDC-10s. The pilots have received explicit Rules of Engagement.

The carrying out of any operation, in which a majority of NATO countries participates, will be authorized by the NATO Council. The intensity and duration of the aerial attacks depend on Milosević's response. In the planning, a number of stages are anticipated, in which various military targets can be attacked. Each subsequent stage will only be implemented after permission has been granted by the NATO Council.

The Government is fully aware of the risks involved in military action against the Federal Republic of Yugoslavia (FRY). Counter-actions cannot be ruled out in advance. As a result, the level of alertness of all SFOR units in Bosnia-Herzegovina has been increased. A negative travel advisory has also been issued for the FRY. Dutch nationals in the FRY have been advised to leave the country. A number of embassy employees and family members of embassy employees have left the FRY. Attention is also being given to the safety of the Dutch observers in KDOM and ECMM. Everything is aimed at achieving a cessation of hostilities in Kosovo through the implementation – with or without the use of military force – of Resolution 1199, as a result of which displaced persons will gain sufficient confidence to return to their homes and a favourable climate for negotiations between the parties will develop. Such confidence will only develop when a verifiable ceasefire has been established. At a certain point, compliance with such a ceasefire will need to be supervised. International humanitarian assistance will also need to be supported.

It is likely that this will require an international presence on the ground. A decision concerning the participation of the Netherlands in the deployment of ground forces will only be in order, as far as the Netherlands is concerned, when there is clarity concerning the circumstances prevailing at such a time. In any case, military involvement is inconceivable unless authorized by a new Security Council resolution. Participation of United States infantry units is a further prerequisite. During the any deployment, maximum attention will naturally be given to the safety of the Dutch units. Subsequently, all other aspects of the framework of evaluation must also be considered. According to the framework of evaluation, the Chamber will be involved in this process.

Concerning any Dutch participation in aerial actions, the Dutch Government has decided that such participation is justified if, in addition to the principles of the framework of evaluation mentioned in this letter, the following conditions are also satisfied. It must be clear that a decision in favour of the activation order (ACTORD) is supported by the whole of NATO and also that the largest possible majority of the allies will participate actively in the operations. This implies that there must be agreement within NATO with regard to the legitimacy of military action. During all subsequent stages, maximum use must be made of all conceivable diplomatic – by the OSCE among others – and political means in order to obtain a peaceful implementation of Resolution 1199. In addition, during the entire process, constant political control over each individual stage of any military action must be guaranteed and, during each stage, the consequences and implications for decision-making during the next stage(s) will have to be considered. The decision of the Dutch Government in the NATO Council to agree to the authorization of the ACTORD and the ensuing Dutch participation in aerial actions is thus tied to the above-mentioned conditions.'[24]

---

24. Bijl. Hand. II 1998/99 –22181 No. 213, pp. 2-4.

In a debate on 24 March 1999 on the above-mentioned subject, the Minister of Foreign Affairs stated, *inter alia*, as follows:

'All the speakers have devoted attention to Resolutions 1199 and 1203. I believe that Resolution 1199 dates from 8 October 1998, while Resolution 1203 was passed after an agreement had been concluded between Milosević and NATO. Both Resolutions provide the basis for the aerial actions that are currently taking place. The demands that were presented in the Resolution of the Security Council are also based on Chapter VII of the United Nations Charter. This means that, because of its consequences for regional peace and security, the situation in Kosovo can no longer be regarded by the international community as an internal matter of the Federal Republic of Yugoslavia. This is the position that the Dutch Government has taken consistently during the past months, a position that, fortunately, has been shared by this Chamber.

Mr. Chairman! In a general sense, but also as a matter of principle, the Government is of the opinion – and I also mentioned this yesterday in the debate on the budget of the Ministry for Foreign Affairs – that for operations of this kind there must be an authorization in the form of a Security Council resolution, which should be linked to the United Nations Charter. However, I also consider it important to mention – although it is not relevant in this case – that circumstances are conceivable, in particular with regard to humanitarian crises, in which the possibility to act without a resolution of this kind should also exist. This applies to exceptional cases, but in this case, at least, it is not relevant.
[...]

Mr. Chairman! It goes without saying that I have discussed the situation in the Former Yugoslav Republic of Macedonia (FYROM) in detail with the Chief of Defence Staff. A large number of questions have been asked about the situation, especially regarding the position of the extraction force, and rightly so. This complex situation was discussed in detail in the Cabinet on Friday. In a certain sense, it may be argued that the mission of the extraction force was concluded with the withdrawal of the observers. Because the Dutch Cabinet – the Dutch Chamber – issued a mandate exclusively for activities of Dutch soldiers on behalf of the extraction force, the rationale for activities of Dutch soldiers has disappeared. At the same time, the Chamber is aware that a number of other countries have stationed additional units in FYROM in the framework of the transformation of the extraction force into an enabling force, in case an agreement can be concluded after all. If an agreement is concluded, NATO units must be able to move into Kosovo as swiftly as possible to stabilize the situation in preparation for KFOR.

Although, on the one hand, logic states that Dutch units be withdrawn once their mandate and activities are concluded, Dutch involvement in KFOR, on the other hand, may be expected in light of the discussion of the matter in the Chamber. In this context, it would be very strange if these units were withdrawn at this stage. I would like to emphasize that Dutch units will not operate other than within the mandate provided by the Chamber. Activities of Dutch units in the extraction force are also limited to defensive measures. This fact was emphasized by the placing of a radar mortar detection unit at the disposal of the extraction force.'[25]

In a debate on 11 June 1999, on the above-mentioned subject, the Minister of Foreign Affairs stated, *inter alia*, as follows:

'NATO forces confirmed yesterday afternoon that the withdrawal of Serbian units had started. This allowed the Secretary General of NATO to make the decision to suspend the aerial actions. This was reported to the Secretary General of the United Nations. The Chamber has received the relevant letter. With this suspension, the last obstacle to the acceptance by the Security Council of Resolution 1244, authorizing the deployment of an international force in Kosovo, was also removed. Unfortunately, the People's Republic of China abstained from the vote. Fortunately, however, the fears and suspicions that the People's Republic of China would ultimately make use of its right of veto were not realized. The fact that the Russian Federation cooperated fully both in the establishment of the Military Technical Agreement and with regard to the deployment of Russian troops in Kosovo is very significant. It says something about the level of involvement of the Russian Federation. It is important that the Russian Federation played such a constructive role in the passage of this Resolution.

In essence, this Resolution translates a political mandate into a military assignment. The execution of this assignment is framed in the plan of operation of KFOR, which has been approved by the NATO Council and is related to the Military Technical Agreement. Chapter 7 of the Charter of the United Nations unambiguously points out the international law and legal bases for the legitimacy of the deployment of KFOR, without leaving any room for discussion whatsoever. Naturally, this is one of the important elements. The Military Technical Agreement reflects the political consent of the Federal Republic of Yugoslavia to the deployment of KFOR. Thus the structure is provided: a firm political and legal basis for the deployment of KFOR.

This legal basis was also a crucial factor in the consideration by the Dutch Government whether to allow Dutch troops to participate in KFOR. On the one hand, the Government regards as beyond question that the presence of an international military force is required to achieve a situation in which hundreds of thousands of refugees and displaced persons consider it safe to return to their homes. On the other hand, the Government considers it to be of vital importance to have an undisputed political and legal basis for Dutch participation in such a military force. That is also the reason why, in our opinion, it seemed most sensible to hold the debate today, now that the legal basis is 100 per cent certain, following the passage of the Resolution in the Security Council.'[26]

The strategic concept of the NATO

In answer to questions on, *inter alia*, the above-mentioned subject, the Minister of Foreign Affairs on 1 December 1998 stated the following:

---

25. Hand. II 1998/99 No. 61, pp. 3793, p. 3975.
26. Hand. II 1998/99 No. 87, p. 5081.

'Mr. Pitstra and Mr. Van Eekelen have submitted questions regarding NATO's Strategic Concept. The intention is that it will be one of the main topics at the Washington summit, alongside the issue of the "open door" policy. The Strategic Concept forms the guideline for NATO's military activities in particular. In addition, the Strategic Concept guides national defence efforts and is therefore also a matter of national concern. On Dutch initiative, it was decided to review this Concept, which dates from as long ago as 1991, and in doing so to give expression to new relationships and new developments in the area of security and the role of NATO therein.

What are the Netherlands' objectives with regard to the Strategic Concept? An important point for us is that a new NATO task is adopted in the area of crisis management and peacekeeping operations. NATO is not familiar with this task at the present time; its role in the fourth pillar is still clearly aimed at the situation that existed during the Cold War. However, we no longer need to define that role. On the contrary, we require that a clear task is laid down in the Strategic Concept within the whole range of activities from peacekeeping to peace-enforcing. In part, this is a natural reflection of the peacekeeping operations to which NATO is contributing in the former Yugoslavia, but it also represents an ambition to play a more active role in the future.

The discussion is certainly far from being concluded. We wish to conduct this discussion in all openness. It also forms one of the points of contention in the discussion accompanying the review of the Strategic Concept. A number of our allies fear that with the adoption of a central task of this kind on behalf of NATO, the importance of the common defence of NATO territory (the Article 5 task of the NATO treaty) will be more or less pushed to the background, or will even be at risk. For the time being, this opinion is held in the Federal Republic of Germany in particular. In the judgment of the Dutch Government, however, these two tasks, the classic task (self-defence, as expressed in Article 5 of the NATO treaty), on the one hand, and peacekeeping operations, on the other hand, can mutually strengthen each other. In our opinion, one task need not be at the expense of the other. As mentioned, this discussion will continue to be conducted in full for the foreseeable future in the build-up to the Washington summit in April next year.

Furthermore, it is important to the Dutch Government that a greater emphasis is placed in the Concept on the means that are employed for the defence of the Alliance, as well as for the new tasks. Thought should be given to issues of mobility, flexibility and technological adaptability and to issues relating to the readiness and the deployability of the Alliance's armed forces. It is also important that multinationalism and international cooperation between the army, navy and air force, which the Netherlands seeks to prioritize, receive a place in the Strategic Concept.

Mr. Van Eekelen and Mr. Pitstra also sought information regarding the possibility of NATO action, if necessary without the authorization of the Security Council of the United Nations. Naturally, the approaches of both men differed. It is a known fact that the Dutch Government has a preference for actions that have the authorization of the United Nations, and that of the Security Council in particular. I remind you that, in the opinion of the Dutch Government, the decision made by the NATO Council in the context of the crisis in Kosovo (the authorization of the activation order) was a direct consequence of Security Council Resolution 1199. A thread runs from that resolution to the decision made by the NATO

Council in mid-October. The Dutch Government has a clear preference for such a course of events, as expressed in the written documents.'[27]

Role and tasks of the NATO

On 25 January 1999 the Ministers of Defence and Foreign Affairs, together with the State Secretary of Defence, sent a Letter to Parliament titled 'Strategic Concept 2000'. On the above-mentioned subject it stated, *inter alia*, as follows:

'NATO remains the undiminished cornerstone of Dutch security policy. Other international organizations, such as the United Nations, the OSCE, the European Union and the WEU, also play an essential role. The Netherlands recognizes the fundamental importance of the political and diplomatic efforts of the United Nations and United Nations peacekeeping operations for the promotion of international peace and security. As far as peacekeeping operations are concerned, this applies in particular to preventive deployment, "classic" tasks falling under Chapter VI of the United Nations Charter and post-conflict peace-building. In this context, the Government supports the reinforcement of the United Nations's rapid reaction capability, *inter alia* through the United Nations Stand-by Arrangements System (UNSAS). The Netherlands has therefore played an active role in the establishment of the Stand-by Forces High Readiness Brigade (SHIRBRIG). The participating States have united their UNSAS contributions in this stand-by Brigade so that collectively they are able to deploy a brigade in support of peacekeeping operations within fifteen to thirty days of a political decision. The Brigade should be operational before the end of the year. To this end, we intend to make a brigade headquarters, a company of engineers, a mechanized or infantry battalion and a detachment of helicopters available to the Brigade's pool of resources. For the swift transfer of (part of) the Brigade to the theatre of operations an appeal can also be made to the Dutch strategic transport capability.

1.3 NATO

Amidst the great changes that have taken place in the international security situation, NATO has proven to be a source of continuity and stability and has played a leading role in the design of the new international order. During the Washington summit in April 1999, the Czech Republic, Hungary and Poland will be welcomed as NATO allies. With regard to further expansion, the Netherlands supports the Membership Action Plan, which prepares candidate countries for potential membership in a better manner than has so far been the case. The Dutch position is that all countries that are candidates for NATO membership should be eligible to participate in such a programme, with the exception of Albania, owing to the specific circumstances in which this country finds itself. This means that, as far as the Netherlands is concerned, Slovenia, Romania, Bulgaria, the Former Yugoslav Republic of Macedonia, Slovakia and the Baltic States will be able to participate in the intensive preparatory programme.

---

27. Hand. I 1998/99 No. 10, pp. 232-233.

Although an acute military threat no longer exists, the principle of collective self-defence expressed in Article 5 of the NATO treaty remains the best expression of allied solidarity and the interconnectedness of European and American security interests. In addition, NATO has adopted wide-ranging new tasks. These involve, in particular, consultation and cooperation with the Russian Federation and the countries of Central and Eastern Europe. The concrete cooperation programmes in the framework of the Partnership for Peace are the pre-eminent expression of this. Moreover, attention is not directed exclusively towards the countries of Central and Eastern Europe; a dialogue has also been established between NATO and the countries around the Mediterranean Sea.

In addition to its commitments under Article 5, NATO can carry out crisis management and peacekeeping operations to promote or maintain international peace and security when there are sufficient grounds to do so under international law (preferably a United Nations or an OSCE mandate). In this manner, NATO can make a valuable contribution to the maintenance of stability on the periphery of the Alliance's territory. In fact, crisis management operations on the periphery of NATO's territory generally require the same resources as operations carried out in the framework of collective self-defence. This important development will be addressed later in this Memorandum. Excessive expectations with regard to NATO's contribution to the maintenance of international peace and security should nevertheless be avoided. As the distance between trouble spots and the Alliance's territory increases, NATO intervention becomes less of a foregone conclusion.

1.3.1 NATO's New Strategic Concept

The Netherlands is actively participating in the discussions regarding the new Strategic Concept, which will be defined at the NATO summit in Washington DC. The starting-points formulated in this Memorandum form the Dutch contribution to the Alliance's deliberations on this matter. The Government emphasizes the undiminished importance of NATO for peace and security in Europe. NATO is also essential as a transatlantic forum for allied consultations and for deterrence and defence against threats to the territory of the Member States. In this context, NATO would also benefit from closer defence cooperation between the European allies.

The Strategic Concept will have to address important new tasks that NATO has been performing since 1991, such as military action outside Alliance territory and cooperation with the countries of Central and Eastern Europe. We urge that these new tasks be given full-fledged expression in the Strategic Concept. In the view of the Netherlands, this can be best achieved by formulating a new central NATO task: making available allied resources for crisis management and peacekeeping operations.

In the new Strategic Concept, attention should also be given to the compatibility of the various tasks. In general, more emphasis should be placed on resources that can be employed both for collective defence and for crisis management and peacekeeping operations. In the current security situation, threats to the Alliance's territory will surely be of a local nature, probably as the result of tensions in countries along NATO's external border. It would not be appropriate to respond to a threat of this kind with a massive deployment of troops or by calling up large stand-by units. The resources required for such instances of regional collective defence will often barely differ from the resources required for conflict management or internationally mandated peacekeeping operations. Units that are kept on alert are of crucial importance for both collective defence and crisis management. The requirements of operations based on Article 5 and crisis management operations flow over into one another. The timely deployment of directly deployable resources can prevent the need for total mobilization.

Military contributions to multinational frameworks may be regarded as modules that should fit well into a larger whole. Therefore, much thought must be given to flexibility, mobility, technological suitability and preparedness – in other words, the deployability – of units and to the capacity to maintain operations for extended periods. It is important that the new Strategic Concept emphasizes these characteristics of modern military units. NATO planning should also be geared to such a qualitative approach. After all, military intervention is no longer primarily about the ability to raise large numbers of troops, but the ability to make the necessary resources available in a timely manner.

Multinationalism deserves an important place in the Strategic Concept. This is expressed in the strengthening of operational cooperation, both within NATO and with the countries participating in the Partnership for Peace. States will have to adapt their land, sea and air forces for simultaneous action by different branches of the armed forces (joint action) of two or more countries (combined action).

The Netherlands urges that special attention be given in the Strategic Concept and during the NATO summit in Washington DC to the security risks that flow from the spread of nuclear, biological and chemical (NBC) weapons and their means of delivery. The development of resources for coping effectively with these risks ought to be expedited. This may be achieved, *inter alia*, by prioritizing the interception of ballistic and cruise missiles which may be equipped with weapons of mass destruction, the so-called theatre missile defence. In this context, it is of crucial importance that NATO possesses accurate information that is also made available to the allies in a timely manner. To supplement existing facilities, the establishment of an Alliance database containing information on the programmes of States and non-State, terrorist groups for the development and delivery of NBC weapons should therefore be considered. On the basis of a clear and common need and an allocation of tasks, the Member States of NATO should make the necessary efforts to acquire the means to defend themselves against weapons of mass destruction. This applies to the protection of troops (in the field) and the civilian population, as well as to active defence, including extended air defence. The Netherlands wishes to make a substantial contribution in this area.

The Netherlands supports the revision of the nuclear clause in the Strategic Concept. The changes that have taken place in the field of security since the formulation of the current Strategic Concept in 1991 make this a necessity. The allied nuclear arsenal has meanwhile been reduced by 80 per cent. In addition, it may be emphasized how far we are removed from circumstances under which the use of nuclear weapons might be an option. It may also be recalled that the state of readiness of nuclear weapons has been lowered. The review of the nuclear clause also provides an opportunity to consider how the nuclear states' unilateral negative security guarantees regarding the use of nuclear weapons relate to NATO's current nuclear policy. Nevertheless, the Netherlands sees no reason for a drastic revision of the nuclear clauses of the Concept. Nuclear weapons still play a crucial deterrent role against the manifold threats of today; potential aggressors should be left in maximum uncertainty regarding the circumstances under which NATO would consider using these weapons.'[28]

Justification of NATO intervention

On 23 March 1999 the Minister of Foreign Affairs stated, *inter alia*, the following:

'This brings me to a number of questions regarding the justification of NATO intervention. Ms. Gelderblom and Ms. Zwerver have discussed the matter. Mr. Van Gennip has posed some penetrating questions on the subject. Last week, during the debate on the NATO budget, I promised Mr. Hirsch Ballin an answer to a question concerning Article 52 of the United Nations Charter.

My answer to this question is as follows. I already stated last week that there has to be, in a general sense and in principle, a resolution from the Security Council of the United Nations authorizing military action. With regard to Kosovo, the Security Council pronounced its opinion last year. I went into this in greater detail last week, in connection with Security Council Resolutions 1199 and 1203. The questions go further, however, addressing situations in which the Security Council has not provided, or has not clearly provided, authorization. Circumstances may arise that necessitate a deviation from the general rule that Security Council authorization is required. One may think of a grave humanitarian disaster with regard to which the Security Council cannot reach agreement on a resolution as a result, for example, of the opposition of a permanent member of the Security Council. According to Mr. Hirsch Ballin, consideration should perhaps also be given to the amendment of Article 52 of the United Nations Charter with respect to regional security organizations in cases of this kind. Having had the opportunity to think this over for a few days, I would say that it is questionable whether we should take this approach. It immediately raises the problem of amending the Charter and, in reality, this cannot be achieved within the foreseeable future. Nevertheless, it would also be unacceptable if the failure of explicit support to emerge in the Security Council were to bind all countries to a form of non-action or inactivity. Law would then lead to injustice, in my opinion. The Dutch Government is therefore of the opinion that in extreme circumstances sufficient grounds can be found in recent international law for humanitarian operations, if necessary outside NATO territory as well. This should still be regarded as an exception to the rule and, in the opinion of the Dutch Government, this rule should not be broken lightly.'[29]

---

28. Bijl. Hand. II 1998/99 – 26382 No. 1, pp. 13-15.
29. Hand. I 1998/99 No. 24, p. 1067.

14.113 LIMITATION AND REDUCTION OF ARMAMENTS, DISARMAMENT

UNSCOM

On 3 February 1999 the Minister of Foreign Affairs answered questions relating to the cooperation between UNSCOM and the Secret Services of Israel and the United States. He stated, *in full*, as follows:

'1., 2. and 4. In Security Council Resolution 699, the Security Council of the United Nations encouraged all Member States to provide maximum assistance, in cash and in kind, in support of the work of UNSCOM. This may also be understood to include the provision of information by national intelligence services, since the United Nations clearly does not possess its own capacity in this area. In addition, precisely as a result of the obstruction of its inspections by Iraq, UNSCOM is heavily dependent on the material collected by intelligence services. It should not be the case, however, that intelligence services use UNSCOM for the collection of material intended for national purposes. It therefore speaks for itself that the greatest possible discretion is required of the Member States during the provision of such assistance, precisely because of the importance of maintaining the integrity of the activities of UNSCOM. This discretion applies both for the Member States and for the Special Commission itself. The Government is not acquainted with the details of the cooperation with the intelligence services of the United States and Israel. Furthermore, the Government regrets that the involvement of national intelligence services has led to a media controversy that plays into the hands of the opponents of UNSCOM, in particular Saddam Hussein.

3. The Government has not changed its views regarding the proportionality and legitimacy of the aerial actions carried out against Iraq since it outlined these views in a letter to the Second Chamber dated 17 December. The British and American authorities have indicated that the aerial actions served their purpose of damaging Iraq's military potential to a significant extent. However, both countries, in common with the Netherlands, are also of the opinion that, in the longer term, an effective inspection régime requires the presence of arms inspectors on the ground.

5. and 7. The debate in the Security Council concerning the interrelated aspects of the inspection régime, the sanctions régime and the improvement of the living conditions of the Iraqi population is only now getting underway. I described the Dutch contribution to this debate in my aforementioned letter dated 19 January. Of course, this contribution is also aimed at repairing the consensus in the Security Council. I have resolved to inform the Chamber at regular intervals of any progress achieved in this regard. Regarding cooperation with intelligence services, I refer you to my answer to questions 1, 2 and 4.

6. Recent reports concerning UNSCOM, as well as the aerial actions last December, have unquestionably contributed to the fact that the status of the Special Commission has become the subject of discussion.

However, the current discussion in the Security Council is foundering on the form and substance of the future disarmament of Iraq, in particular with regard to the conditions under which it would be possible to change over to a régime of ongoing monitoring and verification (OMV). Countries such as Russia and China wish to change over to such a régime at the present time. The Netherlands is of the opinion, together with the United States and the United Kingdom, that the conditions for such a changeover have not been fulfilled, at least not as far as biological and chemical weapons are concerned. France is also of the opinion that the shift to ongoing monitoring and verification can be made, but is not opposed to an evaluation of the current state of affairs in the area of disarmament, as a precursor to ongoing monitoring and verification.

The continued absence of UNSCOM naturally carries the risk that Iraq may once again begin to devote itself to the development of weapons of mass destruction. The Dutch Government therefore takes the position that the weapons inspections in Iraq must be resumed as soon as possible. For more details, I refer to my letter dated 19 January.

8. The Government refers to the European Union Action Plan, adopted on 26 January 1998, which is aimed at stemming the flow of immigrants from Iraq and the neighbouring region. This Action Plan unites a broad range of activities, including combatting illegal immigration, tackling elements of organized crime that are involved in illegal immigration and a joint analysis of the political, economic and humanitarian situation in the region. The High Level Working Group (HLWG), which was established on Dutch initiative, has prepared a list of countries of origin (including Iraq) for which an integrated approach in the area of asylum and migration is proposed. This list and the mandate of the High Level Working Group were drawn up by the General Affairs Council on 25 January. The way things are looking now, Northern Iraq will soon also be on this list. Furthermore, preparations are being made for an official Dutch mission (with participants from the Ministry of Justice and the Ministry for Foreign Affairs) that aims to map out the possibilities, in cooperation with the relevant parties in the region, for the return of migrants to Northern Iraq. To improve the humanitarian situation of the population of Northern Iraq, the starting point of Dutch humanitarian assistance is that such assistance should be complementary to activities in the framework of the Oil for Food programme. In 1999, as previously, only activities that can be charged under the heading of emergency assistance will be financed. Under this budgetary heading, it will also be possible to finance initial moves towards rehabilitation. Where possible, the Netherlands will continue to support projects and programmes that aim to improve the economic situation of the population in Northern Iraq.

9. Assuming that the term "containment strategy" refers to the totality of measures that have been instituted by the Security Council against Iraq's potential for weapons of mass destruction since the Gulf War, the answer to the question is that these measures are still justified and that compliance with them should be stringently enforced. It will be a long time before Iraq receives a clean bill of health. In addition, the human rights situation in Iraq itself is still particularly alarming. For example, the minorities living in Northern and Southern Iraq (Kurds and Shi'ites) still require a measure of protection from the régime in Baghdad in the form of no-fly zones.

Finally, sounds have recently been emanating from Baghdad indicating that the discussion of the borders, if not of the very right of existence of Kuwait, has started up again. We therefore need to guard against recidivism on the part of Saddam Hussein in this regard.'[30]

14.1131 LIMITATION AND REDUCTION OF CONVENTIONAL WEAPONS
See also: 14.125, 14.1271

Mines, booby traps and blinding laser weapons

On 12 November 1998, the Parliament debated on the Bill concerning the approval of the Protocol on prohibition or restrictions on the use of mines, booby traps and other devices,[31] and of the additional protocol concerning blinding laser weapons.[32] The Minister of Foreign Affairs answered several questions and stated, *inter alia*, as follows:

'As the Chamber has observed, an important step has been taken today towards the ratification of Protocol II as amended and a new Protocol IV to the Convention on Conventional Weapons. These are important instruments for the humanitarian law of war. Protocol II as amended forms the first response of the international community to the growing land mine problem, which manifested itself at the beginning of the 1990s. The amendment has been a long time in the making: the preparations were started in 1993 and, fortunately, agreement was reached in 1996. I will convey the gratitude of the Chamber to those who worked on the amendment directly, in particular the members of the civil service who were involved in this effort in a broad manner. Naturally, I also wish to thank my predecessor.

However, as has been previously indicated to the Chamber, the Government was not entirely satisfied with the results. For this reason, the Netherlands has played a very active role in the process that ultimately led to the Convention on the prohibition of the use, stockpiling, production and transfer of anti-personnel mines and on their destruction, the Ottawa Convention, which at the present time has been submitted to the Chamber for consideration. The current state of affairs is that a memorandum must be submitted in connection with the report. The Chamber will receive this memorandum as soon as possible, as it has now been completed. If it is up to me, the Chamber will receive the memorandum at the beginning of next week.

Even as concluded, the Protocols now under discussion contain enough of the elements of the Ottawa Convention to make them worthwhile. The Government hopes that these rules will be sharpened in the future. In addition, the Protocol binds a number of countries that are not yet willing to sign the Ottawa Convention. Ms. Van Ardenne has already pointed out

---

30. Bijl. Hand. II 1998/99 No. 722, pp. 147-1474.

31. Protocol II as amended on 3 May 1996, *Trb.* 1996 No. 260.

32. Protocol IV of 13 October 1995 related to the Convention on prohibitions or restrictions on the use of certain conventional weapons, which may be deemed to be excessively injurous or to have indiscriminate effects. *Trb.* 1999 No. 122.

this fact. The Protocol thus constitutes a good methodology: Protocol II as amended remains the only form of regulation of the use and transfer of mines for these countries. As the Chamber will be aware, this point was incorporated in the Protocol as a result of pressure exerted by the Netherlands.

In my opinion, it is clear that the ratification of the amended Protocol contributes to the strengthening of norms governing the use of land mines that are binding on countries. Protocol IV is entirely new and forms a response to the threat of modern weapons technology. I am referring in particular to the prohibition on the use of laser weapons specifically designed to cause permanent blindness. The Protocol prohibits the use and transfer of a category of weapons that, as far as we know, are not employed by any army.

It is the fervent hope of the Dutch Government that the development of these weapons can be permanently halted as a result of this Protocol. It was pointed out in the written submissions that the Netherlands had wanted to go further on this point by restricting permanent blinding as a form of warfare. I will come back to this point later. However, no agreement existed on the issue.

I now come to the restriction on the transfer of mines that was incorporated in both Protocols. As I have already stated, this is an issue that was actively advocated by the Netherlands during the negotiation process. This restriction hinders the unrestricted transfer of mines, also with regard to countries that have not signed the Convention.

What else will the Netherlands do? During the next few years, the Netherlands will dedicate itself, both individually and together with other countries, in particular our partners in the European Union, to increasing the universality of both Protocols, as well as the Ottawa Convention. Naturally, the Netherlands will take part very actively in the conferences of the Contracting Parties, as provided for in Protocol II. As we have done in the past, we will continue to advocate far-reaching restrictions on the use and transfer of anti-tank mines. There is more work to be done.

The Netherlands supports the extension of the rules of the humanitarian law of war to include all types of weapons. Mr. Hoekema has mentioned sea mines, but there are also many kinds of low calibre weapons that must be dealt with in this context. This subject matter is not undisputed at the international level, but together with like-minded countries the Netherlands is considering ways in which to raise these issues. At the time of the United Nations General Assembly, a meeting was held by a number of countries under the chairmanship of Canada and Norway to examine how the discussion may be advanced and in what manner further results may be achieved. The Dutch Government is full of ambition with regard to the humanitarian law of war.

Mr. Apostolou has asked about the initiatives of the European Union. As a result of differences of opinion within the European Union with regard to the nature and content of these initiatives, none were undertaken. However, with the exception of Finland, all European Union countries support the resolutions calling for accession to the Protocols and the Ottawa Convention.

[...]

A number of Members of Parliament have asked what is being said on this issue in the framework of NATO and what is being done with regard to the United States and Turkey. Matters of this kind must be addressed constantly in the NATO context, also with regard to the countries that were mentioned. The implementation of the Ottawa Convention in particular is the subject of deliberations within the NATO framework. Turkey has been pressed to ratify the Convention as soon as possible. The United States has announced – I believe that one of the Members just mentioned this as well – that it will accede to the Ottawa Convention, albeit not immediately. During the consideration of the Ottawa Convention, which will take place soon, I hope, as a result of the Memorandum that we have submitted on the matter, we will be able to exchange views with one another on this issue in more detail. We are thus not wasting time in NATO.

Mr. Apostolou has asked about the financial support that the Netherlands is providing to UNMAS. The Netherlands supports the activities of the United Nations in various countries that are affected by mines. The Netherlands favours an improvement in the coordination of these activities by UNMAS.

In addition, Mr. Apostolou has spoken about anti-tank mines. As far as this issue is concerned, the Netherlands has acted as one of the pioneers in recent years. During the negotiation of Protocol II as amended, we argued in vain for a total ban on non-detectable anti-tank mines, a ban on the transfer of this type of mine, especially to non-Contracting Parties, and a total ban on remotely delivered mines without mechanisms for self-neutralization and self-detection. I believe that Ms. Van Ardenne has also spoken about this. Almost all countries, including most of our partners in the European Union, opposed these proposals. Only the United States and Ireland supported far-reaching restrictions on the use of these mines. These proposals therefore belong on the list of issues that the Dutch Government, in line with its actions in recent years, will continue to advocate vigorously wherever this is deemed expedient and in whatever forum.

Mr. Apostolou has inquired about the ban on the production of laser weapons. Naturally, the Netherlands supports such a ban and will raise this issue, *inter alia*, during the review conference that is mentioned in the Protocol.

I have already discussed the state of affairs with regard to the Ottawa Convention. Mr. Hoekema has also made a general request, in light of the slow genesis of the two Protocols, to attempt greater speed in this context. In addition, with regard to the other Convention, I have already stated – and I have discussed this within the Ministry – that we should make faster progress towards the ratification of these Conventions. Indeed, it would not look good if the Netherlands, which has a good reputation on these issues, would allow the ratification process to advance so slowly, albeit that – there is an explanation for everything and this case is no different – the process lasted somewhat longer this time as the result of a discussion on the question of how to deal with the overseas parts of the Kingdom with regard to the implementing legislation. This caused a certain delay. It is also a factor in other areas, but that is the explanation. This is not to say that, in such a process, conclusions cannot be reached a little more quickly.

I have already responded to Mr. Hoekema's remarks concerning our ambitions with regard to raising the issue of anti-tank mines. Mr. Van den Doel has asked about the state of affairs regarding Protocol II as amended and Protocol IV. On 1 November 1998, Protocol II as amended was adopted by 26 States. It will come into force on 1 December 1998. On 1 November 1998, Protocol IV was adopted by 31 States. It came into force on 30 July.

Mr. Van den Doel has also asked about the political position of the Netherlands with regard to countries that continue to use anti-personnel mines. As I have already indicated, the Netherlands, both individually and together with like-minded countries, is urging other countries to halt the use of anti-personnel mines and will continue to do so. In addition, it is being examined during mine clearance operations whether the countries receiving assistance are themselves contributing to the solution of the problem. A country that continues to lay and make use of mines does not qualify for support, also not in the wider framework of development cooperation, except of course in humanitarian emergencies. The Memorandum from the Minister for Development Cooperation provides the initial incentive for a discussion of the relevant criteria in the Chamber. It would make sense to raise this issue during such a discussion. The Memorandum is not so detailed and does not cover all possible cases. The aim of the Memorandum is to provoke a discussion in the Chamber on criteria, including in particular the criterion of good governance and the related issue of human rights.

Mr. Van den Doel has recalled that there is a ban on the production of mines. He has asked whether this ban also applies to the production of components for mines and whether these may nevertheless be exported. It appears from a letter by the State Secretary for Economic Affairs from some time ago that components and relevant technology fall under the Implementation Memorandum. Mr. Van den Doel has also asked about the results of an inquiry into the production of components for anti-personnel mines that was to be initiated by the Minister of Justice. The Minister of Justice agreed to examine whether an explicit ban on production could be drawn up. I believe that she agreed to do so in response to the motion introduced by Mr. Houda in April 1996. A ban on the production of anti-personnel mines will be included in the framework Act for the implementation of treaties on arms control, arms limitation and arms reduction, which I discussed with the Chamber in the context of the Comprehensive Nuclear Test Ban Treaty.

Mr. Van den Doel has also asked about mine clearance operations by the European Union. In international terms, the European Union is the largest donor where mine clearance operations are concerned. During the 1992-1998 period, the European Union provided 181 million ecu for this purpose. This aid has been and continues to be used for mine clearance in Angola, Bosnia, Cambodia, Croatia, Ethiopia and Mozambique. The European Union also supports the development of new and improved techniques for humanitarian mine clearance. In addition, the European Union has seen community action with regard to land mines since 1995. Support of mine clearance has formed a part of this. In this context, the European Union expends approximately 700 to 800 million ecu annually on such support. Support has been provided, for example, to the United Nations, the Red Cross and a number of countries, including Angola, Mozambique, Bosnia and Croatia.

Mr. Van den Doel has asked whether there is a list of countries that have stockpiles of mines. Institutes such as the Stockholm International Peace Research Institute (SIPRI) can only provide rough estimates. Clear insight into these matters does therefore not yet exist. If the system is successful, countries will have to provide information of this kind to the United Nations under the terms of the Ottawa Convention.

Mr. Van den Doel and Mr. Apostolou have inquired about blinding laser weapons. I have already indicated that no weapons with the purpose of causing permanent blindness are being produced at the moment. As far as we know, no army has this type of weapon at its disposal. It appears to me to be beyond doubt that it is sensible to argue in favour of a ban on the production of blinding laser weapons. In fact, we should do so at the review conference. Mr. Van den Doel announced that he might ask the Chamber for a statement on this matter. However, his line of thought enjoys the Government's full support.

Mr. Van den Doel has asked whether it would not be possible to organize a conference on the development of new mine clearance technologies with a number of other countries, in order to share knowledge and learn from one another, instead of each country working in isolation. I find Mr. Van den Doel's idea very attractive and interesting. I will consult with the Minister of Defence on this matter, as well as with the Minister for Development

Cooperation. I will be supporting this idea during my discussion with them. On behalf of the Government, I can say that, at the very least, there is support for this idea. Moreover, I believe that the European Commission has organized a seminar on this issue, but it could certainly be discussed in a wider forum than the European Union.

Ms. Van Ardenne has asked what pressure is being exerted on countries that have not yet signed the Ottawa Convention. I have already indicated that we are exerting pressure on the United States and Turkey, in particular. Ms. Van Ardenne has further asked what the Protocol contributes in the area of anti-personnel mines. Viewed on its own, Protocol II contributes nothing, but it is of great significance with regard to countries that have not signed the Ottawa Convention, because it ensures that they are also bound.

Ms. Van Ardenne has further asked if, when it ratifies Protocol IV, the Netherlands will declare that it will refrain from using blinding laser weapons under all circumstances. On the basis of the statements that I have just made to Mr. Hoekema and Mr. Apostolou, it should be obvious that the Netherlands intends to do so. I believe that we have already incorporated this idea in the written papers. In answer to the question whether this topic will remain on the agenda, I can respond with a straightforward "yes".

Ms. Chairman! Ms. Van Ardenne has asked me an exceedingly complex question about the range of 500 metres that serves as one of the criteria of what constitutes a remotely-delivered mine. She has asked whether this concerns a large number of devices that are similar to anti-personnel mines. In fact, the Netherlands wanted to lower this criterion, we even wished to prevent its application altogether. Unfortunately, this could not be achieved during the negotiations.

Mr. Hoekema has inquired about the nine-year transition period. The Netherlands delegation tried to reduce this period, but countries such as China, India and Russia refused to accept a shorter period. That is the explanation for the transition period. I share the sentiments of the Chamber regarding the length of the period.'[33]

14.1132 LIMITATION AND REDUCTION OF NUCLEAR WEAPONS

Nuclear Test Ban Treaty

On 3 November 1998, the First Chamber debated on the Bill of Approval of the Comprehensive Nuclear Test Ban Treaty (10 September 1996, New York; *Trb.* 1997 No. 62). The Minister of Foreign Affairs stated, *inter alia*, as follows:

'During the consideration of the Comprehensive Nuclear Test Ban Treaty in the Second Chamber, I immediately pointed out the great importance of the Treaty. I also pointed out that, with regard to the issue of nuclear disarmament as a whole, we should not only do our work with a liberal measure of idealism, but that we also require realism in this context. It was not an instance of hallucination when I spoke in the Second Chamber of the importance of reducing the role of these weapons and, ultimately, eliminating them from the face of the earth. It is part and parcel of the idealism with which the Government wishes to proceed –

33. Hand. II 1998/99 No. 24, pp. 1572-1574.

in fact, the Government would be maintaining continuity by doing so – if only for the fact that Article 6 of the Comprehensive Nuclear Test Ban Treaty presents a clear assignment for the Dutch Government, namely, to do everything in its power to conduct negotiations that lead to measures which, in turn, lead to the termination of the arms race and, ultimately, to nuclear disarmament. The Dutch Government is bound to this. In the coming years, the Cabinet will continue its work in this spirit.

This does not imply in any way that I do not share the analysis of Mr. Van Eekelen. He is absolutely right when he says that everything that has been achieved in recent years is and continues to be, for the most part, the result of the deterrent effect of nuclear weapons. Idealism is necessary, but so is realism. I would like to say to Mr. Pitstra that this Cabinet needs to act and work at the point where idealism and realism intersect, and it will.

Mr. Chairman! Mr. Hirsch Ballin has asked a few questions which I believe I can link to a question from Mr. Pitstra, as the latter was wondering whether the Minister himself believes what he has been saying. At least, I believe – paraphrasing slightly – that this was the gist of the comment that Mr. Pitstra made. What are we doing? Mr. Hirsch Ballin and Mr. Pitstra have mentioned the Court. To my knowledge, however, we are not dealing with a judgment of the Court, but rather with an opinion. We must demonstrate that we plan to be very active on this issue. I have already indicated that what is written in the Treaty on the Non-Proliferation ofNuclear Weapons should be taken very seriously. The Government will actively pursue the realization of this objective. This must be done in a balanced manner, in which countries that possess nuclear weapons should take the initiative. Individually and in the European Union framework, the Netherlands is encouraging the nuclear powers to speed up this process. Later, I will discuss the motion introduced by Mr. Hoekema, which was unanimously adopted by the Second Chamber of Parliament. This motion calls for the same type of action, and the Dutch Government will therefore act accordingly. On the multilateral level, the Netherlands will contribute to the negotiations for the next agreement – the so-called cut-off agreement – which forbids the production of fissionable material for weapons use. The negotiations that will lead to this agreement are expected to start in January 1999. Incidentally, the agreement is completely unrelated to the coming into force of the Comprehensive Nuclear Test Ban Treaty. This is the action that we will be taking on this issue in the short term. The Netherlands will do everything in its power to lay the groundwork for achieving progress on this issue. I would like to thank Mr. Hirsch Ballin and Mr. Pitstra for the well-deserved praise that they addressed to those who were involved in the negotiation of the Treaty. I believe that the Netherlands should continue working on the implementation of the Treaty in the same manner in the coming years.

Another important issue is the contribution that the Netherlands can provide in the context of the technical and financial challenges surrounding nuclear disarmament. This is particularly relevant in the case of the Russian Federation, where there is plenty to be done by the Netherlands.

Mr. Hirsch Ballin and Mr. Van Eekelen have asked whether the Explanatory Memorandum was not rather a long time in the making. I speak of a period during which I was in a position to observe, but did not bear any direct responsibility. I believe that this delay is related to the fitful progress of the negotiations and the fact that, during this process, the civil servants were fully committed to the negotiations. The preparation of the Explanatory Memorandum was only started later, at the end of 1996. This is merely an explanation. Mr. Hirsch Ballin undoubtedly knows from his own experience of the legislative process how these things are, especially when five Departments are involved in the preparation of an explanatory

memorandum. In addition, time was also spent on the drafting of the implementing legislation for the Treaty. All in all, I would conclude that all those involved worked on the Treaty to the best of their ability. However, I cannot hide the fact that, to a certain extent, I can understand the murmuring of criticism emerging from the Chamber, as expressed in the words of Mr. Hirsch Ballin and Mr. Van Eekelen. This is especially true when one considers the fact that the Netherlands has a certain reputation to maintain, since it played such an important role in the negotiation of the Treaty. The Chamber can rest assured that the comments made in connection with the Treaty have not fallen on deaf ears.
[...]

Mr. Hirsch Ballin has also inquired about the activities that the Netherlands is developing to prevent the illegal trade in military materials and equipment, and their use by terrorists. The Netherlands is party to the Convention on the Physical Protection of Nuclear Material of 1980. This Convention obliges the Contracting Parties to take precautionary measures with regard to the transport, storage and use of nuclear material to ensure that it does not end up in the wrong hands. The Convention also provides an international registry in the shape of the International Atomic Energy Agency in Vienna. In addition, the Agency offers a system of safeguards and important guarantees against the withdrawal of material from the nuclear fuel cycle, in order to prevent this material subsequently ending up in the wrong hands. In this context, the Netherlands is cooperating with the Nuclear Suppliers Group.

The illegal trade in nuclear material enjoys the full attention of the investigation and security services. To my knowledge, the Central Criminal Investigation Department *(CRI)* is not directly involved in the activities of the services, but it does form the point of contact for Europol. Suspicious information, including information concerning nuclear transactions, enters the system through the *CRI*, which is in contact with the Economic Control Department *(ECD)*. The latter is the body that registers suspicious transactions of nuclear material.

Within the framework of the European Union, the Netherlands is participating in meetings of experts on this issue. In addition, the Dutch investigation and security services inform their sister services abroad in cases of suspicious incidents. There is also a Europol mandate, but Europol has yet to commence actual operational activities on the basis of it. At any rate, Europol has a mandate.
[...]

A number of aspects of this Resolution, and of the opinions that were expressed in the Group of Eight, definitely appeal to us, but this is not the case with regard to some of the other points, albeit that I have still not received the final texts concerning these points, nor had I received them last week, when I discussed them in the Second Chamber. There were a number of aspects in the initiative of this group of eight countries that encountered the opposition of the Dutch Government, for example, the implication that the nuclear powers would not comply with their obligations under the Treaty on the Non-Proliferation of Nuclear Weapons to strive for nuclear disarmament. In view of what is happening, for example, in France and the United Kingdom, I now believe that this assumption is incorrect. I refer to the Strategic Defence Review that appeared recently. Another issue is the problematic nature of the concept of 'no first use'. This was already pointed out by Mr. Pitstra. There is thus continuity with regard to this issue. In March of this year, an interesting debate developed between Mr. Pitstra and my predecessor. I fully share the opinions expressed by Mr. Van Mierlo in this Chamber on that occasion. If we annul this declaration and state that we no longer have a need for it, the 'weapon of last resort' will lose its deterrent effect and may then become a destabilizing factor.

Furthermore, and this is another aspect of the Resolution, or at least of the opinions and ideas of the Group of Eight, it is surprising that the Draft Resolution completely disregards the nuclear tests in India and Pakistan, as well as, for example, the position of countries such as Iraq and North Korea. Precisely because there are countries such as the latter two in the world, I believe that it is good that the NATO alliance has the strategy that it does, which means that it therefore has nuclear weapons and arrangements at its disposal, as pointed out by Mr. Pitstra in his argument.'[34]

Developments after the nuclear tests conducted by India and Pakistan[35]

On 23 November 1998 the Minister of Foreign Affairs sent a Letter to Parliament on the above-mentioned subject. It reads, *in full*, as follows:

'In response to the nuclear tests in India and Pakistan in May 1998, the previous Cabinet decided on certain bilateral measures to give expression to the concern and indignation of the Netherlands. The Second Chamber was informed of these measures in a letter dated 19 June (Bijl. Hand. II 1997/98, 26 085, No.1), which was discussed with the Permanent Committee for Foreign Affairs on 24 June. At that time, it was duly noted that neither the international community nor the European Union had managed to present a common front towards India and Pakistan on the issue of sanctions. The Chamber was told that the Netherlands would strive for closer coordination of policy with other countries providing development assistance. This has not, however, produced any results. Therefore, the Dutch position with regard to multilateral credit provision will be eased and bilateral aid for economic development, employment and regional development and the business programme will be resumed. In addition, our arms export policy will be brought closer into line with that of our partners in the European Union.

An overview of developments since June follows below. In addition, the approach outlined above will be further explained.

Developments in India and Pakistan

In the months since the nuclear tests, the situation in India and Pakistan has developed in a promising direction in certain respects. The condemnatory response of the international community and the pressure of international sanctions, in particular the freezing of multilateral credit, have led to a number of guarantees from India and Pakistan. Following the tests, both countries declared a moratorium on further nuclear explosions and both declared during the General Assembly of the United Nations that they were prepared to sign the Comprehensive Nuclear Test Ban Treaty, albeit not unconditionally and without mentioning a specific target date for signature. India and Pakistan also lifted their objections to negotiations on a ban on the production of fissionable material for weapons use at the Conference on Disarmament in Geneva. In addition, they have declared their intention to

---

34. Hand. I 1998/99 No. 5, pp. 84-85, 86, 87.
35. See also 30 *NYIL* (1999) pp. 211-216.

exercise strict controls on the export of sensitive technology. Finally, India and Pakistan have resumed their bilateral dialogue, which includes the issue of security (including Kashmir). The first round of talks in mid-October did not produce any tangible results.

It would not be realistic to expect that India and Pakistan will be willing to agree with the international community on all the issues in question. The complete termination of their nuclear weapons and missile programmes is unlikely in current circumstances. For that, the regional security situation is too complicated, considerations of national prestige are too much at stake and, in relation to the latter, it seems that too much national support exists for the programmes. Meanwhile, India has announced a basic nuclear doctrine that is based on the maintenance of a minimum level of nuclear deterrence, a guarantee not to initiate the deployment of nuclear weapons and another guarantee not to deploy nuclear weapons against countries that do not possess nuclear weapons (or are not protected by them).

It is therefore improbable that India and Pakistan will become parties to the Non-Proliferation Treaty in the short term. Such a move is more likely to represent the last stage of an extended process.

International dialogue and confidence-building measures

It does not seem likely that, with the means currently being employed, including the sanctions, further changes in conduct can be exacted from India and Pakistan as long as there is no improvement in their negative perception of the regional security situation. In light of this, a constructive international dialogue is of particular importance. Such a dialogue will require initiatives that are more concrete than those that were developed so far. The designated initiators include the Geneva Conference on Disarmament, the G8+ Task Force and the five nuclear powers. Renewed interest in non-proliferation places a heavy responsibility on the shoulders of the five nuclear powers (P5) to clarify their positions on nuclear disarmament. Initially, as part of such a clarification, further steps are required from the two countries with by far the largest nuclear arsenals – Russia and the United States. In this context, the early ratification of START II, followed by negotiations on START III, is a priority. It is also important that, through the provision of foreign assistance, the Russian Federation is granted the capacity to dismantle larger numbers of nuclear weapons in a safe manner. A number of countries, including the United States and Norway, are already active in this area. The Netherlands is currently in talks with the Russian Federation with regard to a cooperation programme. In addition, it is significant that the next realizable step towards nuclear arms control is now being implemented, namely, the negotiation of a treaty to ban the production of fissionable material for weapons use. The Netherlands will dedicate itself to the success of these negotiations.

The question whether the time is now ripe, more so than in the past, for a more active involvement of the international community in the Kashmir dispute cannot be answered unequivocally. Until now, Kashmir has been regarded as a bilateral issue that was to be resolved by India and Pakistan on the basis of the so-called Simla Accord. At present, it may be argued that as a result of the open nuclearization of both countries the dispute has transcended its bilateral context and has acquired considerable international significance. As yet, however, India strongly rejects this point of view. The Netherlands will canvass its partners in the European Union and other countries to determine the level of willingness to devote more attention to this question in the United Nations.

Bilateral sanctions
The Netherlands forms part of a group of countries that have decided to announce bilateral and multilateral measures against India and Pakistan. In future decision-making, it is important that the Dutch position reflects solidarity with the consensus within the group. This consensus is characterized by a positive assessment of the steps taken by India and Pakistan, but also by caution regarding the durability of their declarations of intent.

It makes no sense for the Netherlands to go further than other countries in its sanctions policy. On the bilateral level, the previous Cabinet decided no longer to issue any licences for military exports to India and Pakistan and to provide no new assistance of a macroeconomic nature to these countries. Repeated consultations with our partners in the European Union have not led to greater policy unity. The countries that described the sanctions as undesirable held on to their positions. Therefore, the measures adopted differ from country to country. It should be noted in this regard that the Netherlands has set a high standard. We intend to bring the bilateral measures closer into line with those of other (European) countries.

I. Development cooperation
In practice, bilateral aid for economic development, employment and regional development and the business programme will be resumed (categories 1(a) and 1(d) in the Appendices), as well as the co-financing of loans from multilateral banks aimed at poverty elimination. However, for the time being, the freeze on bilateral financial support at the macroeconomic level and debt reduction will be maintained. This does not alter the fact that the Netherlands will have to cooperate in a multilateral arrangement in the framework of the Paris Club, stemming from an approved IMF programme, which will have financial consequences for the Netherlands. In addition, the extent to which the nuclear tests will affect the future distribution of project aid is being considered. It is being examined whether more aid can be provided through non-governmental organizations and decentralized authorities.

II. Multilateral credit
After the nuclear tests, the Netherlands came out strongly in favour of the suspension of multilateral credit to India and Pakistan. The Dutch position, as presented to the Chamber, corresponded to the first European Union declarations on the matter. At the end of June, however, the Netherlands threatened to become isolated in the Executive Council of the World Bank when it became apparent that the other shareholders concurred with the "basic human needs" exception recommended by the G7. We are of the opinion that the Netherlands should not take a more radical position than the rest of the international community, the more so because we wish to be cautious regarding the introduction of considerations into the decision-making of the Bretton Woods institutions that fall outside the mandate of these institutions. This applies both to humanitarian loans and to the evaluation of other projects and programmes. In light of the grave, possibly destabilizing economic situation in Pakistan, the Netherlands would welcome an agreement between that country and the IMF and would judge it on its economic merits, aware that such an agreement through the Paris Club could result in a request to delay bilateral debt repayments (see above). As a matter of fact, the main reason for the suspension of IMF assistance to Pakistan was disagreement concerning economic policy.

III. Military exports
In view of the fact that the Netherlands has adopted relatively far-reaching measures in the field of military exports, as well as the desirability of a more unified position on the part of the Member States of the European Union, exceptions will be made for shipments based on commitments entered into before the tests took place. As usual, the licence applications in question will be tested very carefully against the eight criteria of the arms export policy and the European Union Code of Conduct. We are also considering the possibility of handling other licence applications according to the strict guidelines of our arms export policy, the Code of Conduct and possible future European initiatives in this area.'[36]

14.125 HUMANITARIAN LAW
See: 14.1131

14.127 WEAPONS
See: 16.112

14.1271 CONVENTIONAL WEAPONS
See: 14.1131

16.112 MEASURES RESULTING IN PROMOTION OR RESTRICTION OF TRADE AND OTHER TRAFFIC OF GOODS

Arms export policy related to United Nations Weapons Registry

On 4 December 1998, the Ministers of Foreign Affairs and Development Cooperation together with the State Secretary of Economic Affairs, sent a Letter to Parliament on Arms Export Policy. It reads, *inter alia*, as follows:

'The coalition agreement states that efforts will be made to introduce a new criterion into arms export policy, preferably together with the largest possible number of relevant Member States of the European Union, namely, not to grant export licences to countries that do not agree to join the United Nations Weapons Registry. The Government attaches great value to the United Nations Weapons Registry. This should be clear from the fact that every year the Netherlands submits a resolution during the General Assembly of the United Nations calling on United Nations Member States to provide information to the Registry. Participation in the Registry is intentionally on a voluntary basis in order to do justice to its character as a confidence-building measure. Countries can find out about the flow of arms in their region

36. Bijl. Hand. II 1998/99 – 26085 No. 4.

with relative ease by consulting the Registry. As expected, this has a moderating effect on regional arms purchases.

Meanwhile, the experience of the Registry has confirmed that countries can have various reasons for not making information available to the Registry. These reasons may relate to administrative incapacity, as well as to countries' perceptions of the devel- opment of the security situation in their region. For instance, the Registry scarcely offers information concerning the flow of arms in the Middle East and the Gulf region, because the situation there is that, if one country does not report, the neighbouring country will not want to do so either. In addition, there are countries that for some reason or other make information available one year, but fail to do so the following year. Furthermore, some countries regard the Registry as a form of Western tutelage. The reasons that move countries not, or not always, to report information to the Registry are thus quite diverse.

The Netherlands is seeking to involve as many countries as possible in the United Nations Weapons Registry. If non-participation in the Registry is linked to consequences regarding the granting of export licences, this could lead to more countries joining the Registry. It goes without saying that this effect will emerge above all if as many arms-exporting countries as possible are willing to link such consequences to non-participation in the Registry. Therefore, the Government will seek to win over as many like-minded countries as possible to participate in this endeavour. In view of the European dimension of arms export policy, it would make sense to begin by seeking the support of our partners in the European Union. The support of at least the United Kingdom, France, Germany, Italy and Sweden, those being the most important European arms exporters, would appear to be essential for realizing this objective within the European Union framework and making sure that it is effective. This support should preferably be expressed in an amendment along the above-mentioned lines to the European Union Code of Conduct on Arms Exports. The Government will also search outside the European Union for supporters that wish to maintain the Registry as a yardstick for arms export policy.

At the same time, it will be necessary to guard against the possibility that this effort will lead arms-importing countries to transfer their procurement to countries that do not maintain the requirement of participation in the Registry. As a result of this, on balance, control over the export of arms and willingness to participate in the Registry could both diminish.

It is conceivable that support for the Dutch initiative will not emerge. In that case, the Government will take into account whether the country of final destination is participating in the Registry in the implementation of Dutch arms export policy. The Government will consider the reasons for which the country in question may not be participating. It will evaluate the issue in light of the sixth criterion of the arms export policy. This criterion focuses, *inter alia*, on the behaviour of the country of final destination towards the international community. In anticipation of such a conclusion, it was established on a Dutch initiative at the beginning of November in the framework of the Wassenaar Arrangement that participation in the United Nations Weapons Registry can be one of the factors in the evaluation of the conduct of countries of final destination.'[37]

---

37. Aanh. Hand. II 1998/99 – 22054 No. 40, pp. 5-6.

16.55 ENVIRONMENTAL QUESTIONS

Prevention of transboundary environmental damage

On 9 March 1999 the State Secretary of Foreign Affairs answered questions on the safety of nuclear installations in Eastern Europe and GOS. One of the questions read:

'4. In the light of international law, what are the rights and duties of the relevant international organizations and the governments of countries in the region with regard to effective preventive action concerning transboundary environmental damage?

The State Secretary answered as follows:

4. In general, it may be argued that on the basis of international law there is a duty on all countries to take all the precautionary measures within their power to prevent serious transboundary environmental damage. In this context, it is possible to refer to generally accepted principles, such as Principle 21 of the Declaration of the United Nations Conference on the Human Environment, which was adopted in Stockholm in 1972, and Principles 2, 18 and 19 of the Rio Declaration on Environment and Development, adopted during the United Nations Conference on Environment and Development in Rio de Janeiro in 1992. In addition, more specific obligations may be found in the Convention on Nuclear Safety of 1994 (*Trb.* 1995, 105), which was concluded under the auspices of the International Atomic Energy Agency in Vienna. The objectives of this Convention are to achieve and maintain a high level of nuclear safety through the enhancement of national measures and international cooperation, to establish and maintain effective defences in nuclear installations against potential radiological hazards in order to protect individuals, society and the environment from the harmful effects of ionizing radiation from such installations, as well as to prevent accidents with radiological consequences and to mitigate such consequences should they occur. Bulgaria, Hungary, Lithuania, Ukraine, Poland, Romania, the Russian Federation, Slovakia and the Czech Republic are party to the aforementioned Convention.'[38]

Inspection and repair of unsafe foreign nuclear installations

On 2 April 1999 the State Secretary of Foreign Affairs answered questions on the above-mentioned subject. He stated, *inter alia*, as follows:

'1. According to current international law, except with the approval of the countries concerned, there is no way for international organizations (and third countries) to take preventive action in the form of inspection or repair of nuclear installations located in those

38. Aanh. Hand. II 1998/99 No. 912 pp. 1867-1868.

countries, not even in the light of a threat of serious transboundary environmental pollution or other damage, in the case of an accident.

2. The Convention on Nuclear Safety is aimed at achieving and maintaining a high level of nuclear safety by means of international cooperation. The cooperation foreseen in this Convention does not consist of the provision of assistance in specific cases, but the mutual review and discussion of the national reports of the Contracting Parties. This will occur for the first time at the Review Conference, which will take place in Vienna from 12-23 April. As such, the Convention does not provide any basis for the provision of international assistance to the countries of Eastern Europe. However, the Review Conference will discuss the functioning of the national regulatory agencies, which bear responsibility for making nuclear installations Y2K compatible.

3. The Convention on Nuclear Safety is aimed exclusively at the safety of (civilian) nuclear installations. The Convention on Early Notification of a Nuclear Accident also covers accidents in nuclear fuel cycle facilities and accidents involving nuclear weapons. The Convention on Assistance in the Case of a Nuclear Accident or Radiological Emergency concerns nuclear accidents in general and therefore possesses the widest scope of all three of the Conventions mentioned. However, the last two Conventions cover cooperation after an accident has taken place. This does not diminish the fact that international cooperation did evolve between the United States and Russia, as well as between NATO and Russia, in the framework of efforts to make defence-related computer systems Y2K compatible (see also my response of 10 February 1999 to questions from Members of Parliament Hoekema, Van 't Riet and Augusteijn-Esser, reference 2989907390). The Netherlands continues to be actively involved in these efforts and will strive for their further intensification.

4. As I have explained in my previous answers, the aforementioned Conventions present no possibility for international organizations or third countries to take preventive action in the form of inspection or repair of unsafe nuclear installations, and they bear no relation to efforts to make nuclear weapons and related facilities Y2K compatible. Therefore, I see no reason to raise these points of international law in the organizations mentioned in the question.'[39]

16.56 ACCIDENTS AND DISASTERS

See: 16.55

39. Bijl. Hand.II 1998/99 No. 1107, pp. 2269-2270.

TREATIES AND OTHER INTERNATIONAL AGREEMENTS TO WHICH THE KINGDOM OF THE NETHERLANDS IS A PARTY
Conclusions and Developments 1999

D. Vleugels*

This survey covers the treaties, international agreements, and other international instruments mentioned in the '*Tractatenblad van het Koninkrijk der Nederlanden*' – Treaty Series of the Kingdom of the Netherlands (abbr.: Trb.). Its purpose is to record the legal consequences of such agreements and instruments for the Netherlands, and Netherlands State acts in respect of them, such as signature, parliamentary approval, ratification, entry into force, provisional application, extension or limitation of territorial application, termination and abrogation. Signature by the Netherlands, however, is mentioned separately only if, in the case of multilateral treaties, such signature has taken place on a date different from the official date of conclusion of the treaty.

The issue-number of the *Tractatenblad* mentioned as the source of each entry refers to the issue recording the relevant legal consequence or State act. The text of the treaty or agreement itself may thus be included in a different (earlier) issue of the *Tractatenblad.* By use of the consecutive annual surveys published in the Yearbook a systematically arranged view of the developments with regard to the treaty or agreement in question may be obtained. In relevant cases references will be made to additional sources of the treaty texts, such as the European Treaty Series (ETS) and the Official Journal of the European Communities (OJ).

Treaties will only be concluded by the Kingdom of the Netherlands as a whole. The Kingdom consists of three countries: the Netherlands (the part in Europe), the Netherlands Antilles and Aruba (both in Latin America). If an instrument or act affects only one or two of the parts of the Kingdom this will be expressly mentioned.

For an explanation of the formal aspect of Dutch treaty law see H.H.M. Sondaal, 'Some features of Dutch Treaty Practice', 19 NYIL (1988) pp. 179-257. The new Act on the Approval and Promulgation of Treaties of 1994 is dealt with in 26 NYIL (1995) pp. 316-320.

* Research Assistant, T.M.C. Asser Instituut.

Netherlands Yearbook of International Law
Volume XXXI - 2000 - pp. 215-244

3.1141 IMMUNITY OF FOREIGN STATES AND OF THEIR ORGANS AND PROPERTY
See: 4.64 (Trb. 1999 Nos. 1 and 208)

3.211 LEGAL STATUS
See also: 3.223 Association of Caribbean States (ACS) (Trb. 1999 Nos. 28 and 111)

— Agreement with the Permanent Court of Arbitration concerning the Headquarters of the Permanent Court of Arbitration, The Hague, 30 March 1999.
Parliamentary approval: not required, Art. 7(a) Approval Act of 1994.
(Trb. 1999 No. 68)

— Amendment, The Hague, 8/25 June 1999, to the Agreement with the International Service for National Agricultural Research (ISNAR) concerning the headquarters of ISNAR, The Hague, 2 June 1980.
Entry into force: 25 June 1999 (for the Netherlands).
(Trb. 1999 No. 145)

3.2113 PRIVILEGES AND IMMUNITIES
See also: 4.6 (Trb. 1999 Nos. 186 and 187)

— Exchange of Notes with Denmark regarding an Agreement concerning privileges and immunities for liaison officers who are employed at Europol, The Hague, on behalf of the Danish government, Copenhagen, 10/17 December 1998.
Parliamentary approval: not required, Art. 7(b) Approval Act of 1994.
Entry into force: 1 May 1999 (for the Netherlands).
(Trb. 1999 Nos. 25 and 81)

— Exchange of Notes with Finland regarding an Agreement concerning privileges and immunities for liaison officers who are employed at Europol, The Hague, on behalf of the Finnish government, Helsinki, 9/21 December 1998.
Parliamentary approval: not required, Art. 7(b) Approval Act of 1994.
Entry into force: 1 February 1999 (for the Netherlands).
(Trb. 1999 No. 26)

— Exchange of Notes with Spain regarding an Agreement concerning privileges and immunities for liaison officers who are employed at Europol, The Hague, on behalf of the Spanish government, Madrid, 27 January 1999.
Parliamentary approval: not required, Art. 7(b) Approval Act of 1994.
Provisional application: 11 February 1999 (for the Netherlands).
(Trb. 1999 No. 32)

— Exchange of Notes with Sweden regarding an Agreement concerning privileges and immunities for liaison officers who are employed at Europol, The Hague, on behalf of the Swedish government, Stockholm, 21 December 1998/3 February 1999.
Parliamentary approval: not required, Art. 7(b) Approval Act of 1994.
Entry into force: 1 January 1999 (for the Netherlands).
(Trb. 1999 No. 40)

— Agreement with the European Space Agency concerning the European Space Research Technology Centre, Noordwijk, 10 February 1999.
Parliamentary approval: not required, Art. 7(a) Approval Act of 1994.
Entry into force: 1 April 1999 (for the Netherlands).
(Trb. 1999 No. 41)

— Exchange of Notes with Ireland regarding an Agreement concerning privileges and immunities for liaison officers who are employed at Europol, The Hague, on behalf of the Irish government, Dublin, 8/11 February 1999.
Parliamentary approval: not required, Art. 7(b) Approval Act of 1994.
Entry into force: 1 May 1999 (for the Netherlands).
(Trb. 1999 Nos. 42 and 88)

— Exchange of Notes with Belgium regarding an Agreement concerning privileges and immunities for liaison officers who are employed at Europol, The Hague, on behalf of the Belgium government, Brussels, 23 December 1998/19 February 1999.
Parliamentary approval: not required, Art. 7(b) Approval Act of 1994.
Provisional application: 11 March 1999 (for the Netherlands).
(Trb. 1999 No. 49)

— Exchange of Letters with the International Atomic Energy Agency concerning an Agreement and meeting regarding the 'Preparation of an Atlas on quality control and troubleshooting in nuclear medicine images', Amsterdam 19/23 April 1999; Vienna, 8/26 February 1999.
Parliamentary approval: not required, Art. 7(c) Approval Act of 1994.
Entry into force: 1 March 1999 (for the Netherlands).
(Trb. 1999 No. 55)

— Exchange of Notes with Germany regarding an Agreement concerning privileges and immunities for liaison officers who are employed at Europol, The Hague, on behalf of the German government, Bonn, 2/10 March 1999.
Parliamentary approval: not required, Art. 7(b) Approval Act of 1994.
Entry into force: 10 March 1999 (for the Netherlands).
(Trb. 1999 No. 57)

— Exchange of Letters with the International Atomic Energy Agency concerning an Agreement on a 'Technical Committee Meeting on PSA Applications', in the Netherlands, 21/25 June 1999; Vienna, 17 December 1998/15 February 1999.
Parliamentary approval: not required, Art. 7(c) Approval Act of 1994.
Entry into force: 17 February 1999 (for the Netherlands).
(Trb. 1999 No. 60)

— Exchange of Notes with France regarding an Agreement concerning privileges and immunities for liaison officers who are employed at Europol, The Hague, on behalf of the French government, Paris, 10 December 1998/16 February 1999.
Parliamentary approval: not required, Art. 7(b) Approval Act of 1994.
Entry into force: 1 June 1999 (for the Netherlands).
(Trb. 1999 Nos. 63 and 114)

— Exchange of Notes with Greece regarding an Agreement concerning privileges and immunities for liaison officers who are employed at Europol, The Hague, on behalf of the Greek government,

Athens, 26 January/5 March 1999.
Parliamentary approval: not required, Art. 7(b) Approval Act of 1994.
Entry into force: 1 July 1999 (for the Netherlands).
(Trb. 1999 Nos. 64 and 135)

— Exchange of Notes with Great Britain and Northern Ireland regarding an Agreement concerning privileges and immunities for liaison officers who are employed at Europol, The Hague, on behalf of the government of Great Britain and Northern Ireland, London, 9 December 1998/9 March 1999.
Parliamentary approval: not required, Art. 7(b) Approval Act of 1994.
Entry into force: 1 May 1999 (for the Netherlands).
(Trb. 1999 Nos. 65 and 89)

— Exchange of Letters with Italy regarding an Agreement concerning privileges and immunities for liaison officers who are employed at Europol, The Hague, on behalf of the Italian government, Rome, 22 March 1999.
Parliamentary approval: not required, Art. 7(b) Approval Act of 1994.
Entry into force: 1 July 1999 (for the Netherlands).
(Trb. 1999 Nos. 67 and 137)

— Exchange of Letters with the United Nations Population Fund (UNFPA) concerning a 'Forum associated with the five-year review of Implementation of the Programme of Action of the International Conference on Population and Development (ICPD)', New York, 4 February 1999.
Parliamentary approval: not required, Art. 7(c) Approval Act of 1994.
Entry into force: 4 February 1999 (for the Netherlands).
(Trb. 1999 No. 71)

— Exchange of Notes with Austria regarding an Agreement concerning privileges and immunities for liaison officers who are employed at Europol, The Hague, on behalf of the Austrian government, Vienna, 9 February/18 March 1999.
Parliamentary approval: not required, Art. 7(b) Approval Act of 1994.
Entry into force: 1 July 1999 (for the Netherlands).
(Trb. 1999 Nos. 73 and 136)

— Exchange of Notes with Luxembourg regarding an Agreement concerning privileges and immunities for liaison officers who are employed at Europol, The Hague, on behalf of the Luxembourg government, Luxembourg, 18 December 1998/16 March 1999.
Parliamentary approval: not required, Art. 7(b) Approval Act of 1994.
Entry into force: 1 June 1999 (for the Netherlands).
(Trb. 1999 Nos. 82 and 97)

— Exchange of Letters with Portugal regarding an Agreement concerning privileges and immunities for liaison officers who are employed at Europol, The Hague, on behalf of the Portuguese government, Lisbon, 24 March/22 April 1999.
Parliamentary approval: not required, Art. 7(b) Approval Act of 1994.
Entry into force: 1 July 1999 (for the Netherlands).
(Trb. 1999 Nos. 96 and 138)

— Protocol drawn up, on the basis of Article K.3 of the Treaty on European Union and Article 41(3) of the Europol Convention, on the privileges and immunities of Europol, the members off its organs, the deputy directors and employees of Europol, Brussels, 19 June 1997.

Parliamentary approval: not required, Art. 7(a) Approval Act of 1994
Ratification: 3 July 1998 (for the Netherlands).
Entry into force: 1 July 1999 (for the Netherlands).
(Trb. 1999 No. 134)

— Exchange of Letters, The Hague, 1/8 May 2000, with the Food and Agriculture Organization of the United Nations concerning an Agreement regarding the 32nd Session of the Codex Committee on Pesticide Residues, Rome, 24 September 1999 and 20 October 1999.
Parliamentary approval: not required, Art. 7(c) Approval Act of 1994.
Entry into force: 20 October 1999 (for the Netherlands).
(Trb. 1999 No. 195)

3.221 UNIVERSAL ORGANIZATIONS

Food and Agricultural Organization (FAO)
See: 3.2113 (Trb. 1999 No. 195)

International Atomic Energy Agency (IAEA)
See: 3.2113 (Trb. 1999 Nos. 55 and 60); 14.1132 (Trb. 1999 No. 147)

International Labor Organization (ILO)
See: 16.51 (Trb. 1999 No. 182); 16.522 (Trb. 1999 No. 177)

International Mobile Satellite Organization (Inmarsat)
See: 10.3 (Trb. 1999 No. 79)

International Organization for Migration
See: 4.6 (Trb. 1999 Nos. 186 and 187)

International Service for National Agricultural (ISNAR)
See: 3.211 (Trb. 1999 No. 145)

United Nations Population Fund (UNFPA)
See: 3.2113 (Trb. 1999 No. 71)

3.222 REGIONAL ORGANIZATIONS

European Space Agency (ESA)
See: 3.2113 (Trb. 1999 No. 41)

North Atlantic Treaty Organisation (NATO)
See: 16.8 (Trb. 1999 No. 54)

Organisation For Joint Armament Cooperation

— Convention between Great Britain and Northern Ireland, France, Germany, and Italy, on the establishment of the Organisation for Joint Armament Cooperation, with Annexes, Farnborough, 9 September 1998.

Parliamentary approval: pending.
Note: This Convention shall, in accordance with Article 52, enter into force, 30 days after deposit of the fourth instrument of ratification or acceptance.
(Trb. 1999 No. 174)

3.223 ORGANIZATIONS CONSTITUTING INTEGRATED COMMUNITIES

Association of Caribbean States (ACS)

— Agreement with the Association of Caribbean States defining the modalities of participation of the Netherlands Antilles as an Associate Member, Bridgetown, Barbados, 10 December 1998.
Parliamentary approval: pending.
Authentic languages: English, French, Spanish
(Trb. 1999 No. 28)

— Agreement with the Association of Caribbean States defining the modalities of participation of Aruba as an Associate Member, Santo Domingo, 26 March 1999.
Parliamentary approval: pending.
(Trb. 1999 No. 111)

Benelux

— Protocol, Brussels, 16 February 1990, concerning amendment to Article 81 of the Treaty to establishment of the Benelux economic union, The Hague, 3 February 1958.
Parliamentary approval: by Act of 3 July 1991.
Ratification: 22 October 1991 (for the Netherlands).
Entry into force: 1 September 1999 (for the Netherlands).
(Trb. 1999 No. 181)

Euratom
See: 14.1132 (Trb. 1999 No. 147)

European Communities (EC)

— Partnership and Cooperation Agreement between the European Communities and its member states, on the one hand, and Kazakhstan, on the other, with Annexes and Protocol, Brussels, 23 January 1995.
Parliamentary approval: by Act of 11 September 1997.
Ratification: 30 October 1997 (for the Netherlands).
Entry into force: 1 July 1999 (for the Netherlands).
(Trb. 1999 No. 128)

— Partnership and Cooperation Agreement between the European Communities and its member states, on the one hand, and Kirghizistan, on the other, with Annexes and Protocol, Brussels, 9 February 1995.
Parliamentary approval: by Act of 11 September 1997.
Ratification: 30 October 1997 (for the Netherlands).
Entry into force: 1 July 1999 (for the Netherlands).
(Trb. 1999 No. 129)

— Partnership and Cooperation Agreement between the European Communities and its member states, on the one hand, and Armenia, on the other, with Annexes and Protocol, Luxembourg, 22 April 1996.
Parliamentary approval: 9 July 1998, tacit.
Ratification: 17 July 1998 (for the Netherlands).
Entry into force: 1 July 1999 (for the Netherlands).
(Trb. 1999 No. 130)

— Partnership and Cooperation Agreement between the European Communities and its member states, on the one hand, and Azerbaijan, on the other, with Annexes and Protocol, Luxembourg, 22 April 1996.
Parliamentary approval: 9 July 1998, tacit.
Ratification: 17 July 1998 (for the Netherlands).
Entry into force: 1 July 1999 (for the Netherlands).
(Trb. 1999 No. 131)

— Partnership and Cooperation Agreement between the European Communities and its member states, on the one hand, and Georgia, on the other, with Annexes and Protocol, Luxembourg, 22 April 1996.
Parliamentary approval: 9 July 1998, tacit.
Ratification: 17 July 1998 (for the Netherlands).
Entry into force: 1 July 1999 (for the Netherlands).
(Trb. 1999 No. 132)

— Partnership and Cooperation Agreement between the European Communities and its member states, on the one hand, and Uzbekistan, on the other, with Annexes and Protocol, Florence, 21 June 1996.
Parliamentary approval: 9 July 1998, tacit.
Ratification: 17 July 1998 (for the Netherlands).
Entry into force: 1 July 1999 (for the Netherlands).
(Trb. 1999 No. 133)

— Protocol, Brussels, 25 June 1999, to adaption of the institutional aspects of the Europe-Agreement establishing an association between the European Communities and its member states, on the one hand, and Poland, on the other, taking into account the accession of Austria, Finland and Sweden to the European Union, with Annexes, Brussels, 16 December 1991.
Parliamentary approval: not required, Art. 7(a) Approval Act of 1994.
Note: This Protocol shall, in accordance with Article 4, enter into force on the first day of the second month following the date whereupon the contracting parties give notice to each other of the completion of the procedures to entry into force of the Agreement.
(Trb. 1999 No. 156)

— Protocol, Brussels, 25 June 1999, to adaption of the institutional aspects of the Europe-Agreement establishing an association between the European Communities and its member states, on the one hand, and Slovakia, on the other, taking into account the accession of Austria, Finland and Sweden to the European Union, with Annexes, Brussels, 16 December 1991.
Parliamentary approval: not required, Art. 7(a) Approval Act of 1994.
Note: This Protocol shall, in accordance with Article 4, enter into force on the first day of the second month following the date whereupon the concluding parties give each other notice of their completion of the procedures to entry into force of the Agreement.
(Trb. 1999 No. 157)

— Protocol, Brussels, 25 June 1999, to adaption of the institutional aspects of the Europe-Agreement establishing an association between the European Communities and its member states, on the one hand,

and Hungary, on the other, taking into account the accession of Austria, Finland and Sweden to the European Union, with Annexes, Brussels, 16 December 1991.
Parliamentary approval: not required, Art. 7(a) Approval Act of 1994.
Note: This Protocol shall, in accordance with Article 4, enter into force on the first day of the second month following the date whereupon the concluding parties give each other notice of their completion of the procedures to entry into force of the Agreement.
(Trb. 1999 No. 158)

— Protocol, Brussels, 25 June 1999, to adaption of the institutional aspects of the Europe-Agreement establishing an association between the European Communities and its member states, on the one hand, and Romania, on the other, taking into account the accession of Austria, Finland and Sweden to the European Union, with Annexes, Brussels, 16 December 1991.
Parliamentary approval: not required, Art. 7(a) Approval Act of 1994.
Note: This Protocol shall, in accordance with Article 4, enter into force on the first day of the second month following the date whereupon the concluding parties give each other notice of their completion of the procedures to entry into force of the Agreement.
(Trb. 1999 No. 159)

— Protocol, Brussels, 25 June 1999, to adaption of the institutional aspects of the Europe-Agreement establishing an association between the European Communities and its member states, on the one hand, and Bulgaria, on the other, taking into account the accession of Austria, Finland and Sweden to the European Union, with Annexes, Brussels, 16 December 1991.
Parliamentary approval: not required, Art. 7(a) Approval Act of 1994.
Note: This Protocol shall, in accordance with Article 4, enter into force on the first day of the second month following the date whereupon the concluding parties give each other notice of their completion of the procedures to entry into force of the Agreement.
(Trb. 1999 No. 160)

European Community (EC)

— Framework Agreement regarding cooperation in preparation for an association of a political and economic nature between the European Community and its member states, on the one hand, and Chile on the other, with Annexes, Florence, 21 June 1996.
Parliamentary approval: 9 July 1998, tacit.
Ratification: 17 July 1998 (for the Netherlands).
Entry into force: 1 February 1999 (for the Netherlands).
(Trb. 1999 No. 56)

— Interregional Framework Agreement for cooperation between the European Community and its member states, on the one hand, and the Mercado Comun del Sur and its participating states, on the other, with declaration, process-verbal of signature, and letters, Madrid, 15 December 1995.
Parliamentary approval: 17 April 1998, tacit.
Ratification: 5 May 1998.
Entry into force: 1 July 1999 (for the Netherlands).
(Trb. 1999 No. 166)

European Union
See: 4.64 (Trb. 1999 No. 16); 12.273 ECJ (Trb. 1999 No. 15); 16.725 (Trb. 1999 No. 14)

Europol

See: 3.2113 (Trb. 1999 Nos. 25, 26, 32, 40, 42, 49, 57, 63, 64, 65, 67, 73, 81, 82, 88, 89, 96, 97, 114, 134, 135, 136, 137 and 138)

Mercosur

See: 3.223 EC (Trb. 1999 No. 166)

4.31 ADMITTANCE

— Agreement between the Benelux countries and Estonia regarding the taking over of irregular resident persons, with executive protocol, Brussels, 3 February 1999.
Parliamentary approval: pending.
Provisional application: 1 July 1999 (for the Netherlands).
Entry into force: This Agreement shall, in accordance with Article 17, paragraph 1, enter into force on the first day of the second month that follows the date of receipt of the note whereby the last of the conforming parties gives notice to the Depository of Belgium of the completion of the entry into force required internal formality.
(Trb. 1999 Nos. 78 and 115)

— Agreement between the Benelux and Letland regarding the taking over of persons who are staying irregularly (Taking over Agreement), with Annex, Brussels, 9 June 1999.
Parliamentary approval: pending.
Provisional application: 1 July 1999 (for the Netherlands).
Note: The Agreement and Annex shall, in accordance with article 17, paragraph 1, of the Agreement, enter into force on the first day of the second month that follows the date on receiving the note whereby the latest of the agreed parties gives notice to the Belgium government for the required entry into force internal judicial formality.
(Trb. 1999 No. 117)

— Agreement between the Benelux and Lithuania regarding the taking over of persons who are staying irregularly (Taking over Agreement), Brussels, 9 June 1999.
Parliamentary approval: pending.
Provisional application: 1 July 1999 (for the Netherlands).
Note: The Agreement shall, in accordance with Article 17, paragraph 1, enter into force on the first day of the second month that follows the date on receiving the note whereby the latest of the agreed parties gives notice to the Belgium government for the required entry into force internal judicial formality.
(Trb. 1999 No. 119)

— Agreement between the Benelux and Croatia regarding the taking over of persons who have entered or are staying irregularly, with Appendices, Zagreb, 11 June 1999.
Parliamentary approval: pending.
Provisional application: 15 November 1999 (for the Netherlands).
Note: This Agreement shall, in accordance with Article 10, paragraph 1, enter into force on the first day of the second month that follows the date of receipt of the note whereby the latest of the four concluding parties give notice to the Belgium government of the entry into force internal judicial formality.
(Trb. 1999 Nos. 140 and 192)

4.32 PASSPORTS AND VISAS

— Agreement between the Benelux countries and Malawi on the abolition of visas, London, 3 December 1969.
Termination: 1 February 1999.
(Trb. 1999 No. 37)

— Agreement between the Benelux countries and Jamaica on the abolition of visas, Kingston, 7 October 1970.
Termination: 1 February 1999.
(Trb. 1999 No. 38)

— Exchange of Letters between the Benelux and Estonia concerning an Agreement on the abolition of visa requirements, Brussels, 9 June 1999.
Parliamentary approval: pending.
Provisional application: 1 July 1999 (for the Netherlands).
Note: The Agreement shall, in accordance with point 9 of the letters, enter into force on the first day of the second month that follows the date on receiving the note whereby the latest of the agreed parties gives notice to the Belgium government for the required entry into force internal judicial formality.
(Trb. 1999 No. 116)

— Exchange of Letters between the Benelux and Latvia concerning an Agreement on the abolition of visa requirements, Brussels, 9 June 1999.
Parliamentary approval: pending.
Provisional application: 1 July 1999 (for the Netherlands).
Note: The Agreement shall, in accordance with point 9 of the letters, enter into force on the first day of the second month that follows the date on receiving the note whereby the latest of the agreed parties gives notice to the Belgium government for the required entry into force internal judicial formality.
(Trb. 1999 No. 118)

— Exchange of Letters between the Benelux and Lithuania concerning an Agreement on the abolition of visa requirements, Brussels, 9 June 1999.
Parliamentary approval: pending.
Provisional application: 1 July 1999 (for the Netherlands).
Note: The Agreement shall, in accordance with point 9 of the letters, enter into force on the first day of the second month that follows the date on receiving the note whereby the latest of the agreed parties gives notice to the Belgium government for the required entry into force internal judicial formality.
(Trb. 1999 No. 120)

— Exchange of Letters between the Benelux and Croatia concerning an Agreement on the abolition of visa requirements, Zagreb, 11 June 1999.
Parliamentary approval: pending.
Provisional application: 15 November 1999 (for the Netherlands).
Note: This Agreement shall, in accordance with point 9 of the letters, enter into force on the first day of the second month that follows the date of receipt of the note whereby the latest of the concluding states informs the government of Belgium of the entry into force required internal judicial formality.
(Trb. 1999 Nos. 141 and 193)

— Exchange of Letters between the Benelux and Bulgaria concerning an Agreement regarding abolition of visa requirements, Sofia, 10/11 June 1999.

Parliamentary approval: not required, Art. 7(c) Approval Act of 1994.
Note: This Agreement shall, in accordance with pt. 8 of the letters, enter into force on the first day of the second month that follows the date of receipt of the note whereby the latest of the concluding states informs the government of Belgium of the entry into force required internal judicial formality.
(Trb. 1999 No. 178)

4.6 IMMIGRATION, EMIGRATION, EXTRADITION, EXPULSION, ASYLUM

— Agreement with the International Organization for Migration on the Organization's operational activities in the Netherlands, The Hague, 1 May 1990.
Termination: 20 October 1999.
(Trb. 1999 No. 186)

— Cooperation Agreement with the International Organization for Migration, Geneva, 24 July 1997.
Parliamentary approval: 8 October 1999, tacit.
Entry into force: 20 October 1999 (for the Netherlands).
(Trb. 1999 No. 187)

4.62 EMIGRATION

— Agreement with Brazil concerning emigration and colonization, with Final Protocol, Rio de Janeiro, 15 December 1950.
Termination: 22 December 1998.
(Trb. 1999 No. 194)

4.64 OTHER ASSISTANCE IN CRIMINAL MATTERS

— Agreement with Great Britain and Northern Ireland concerning a Scottish trial in the Netherlands, with Annexes, The Hague, 18 September 1998.
Parliamentary approval: by Act of 11 November 1998.
Entry into force: 8 January 1999 (for the Netherlands).
Note: Exchange of notes, The Hague, 18 September 1998, with Great Britain and Northern Ireland concerning the interpretation of contempt of court.
(Trb. 1999 No. 1)

— Convention, drawn upon the basis of Article K.3 of the Treaty on European Union on driving disqualifications, with Annexes, Brussels, 17 June 1998.
Parliamentary approval: pending.
Note: This Convention shall, in accordance with Article 15, paragraph 3, enter into force ninety days after the notification referred to in paragraph 2 by the member state which, being a member of the European Union on the date of the adoption by the Council of the act drawing up this Convention (17 June 1998), is the last to fulfil this formality.
(Trb. 1999 No. 16)

— Agreement with Lithuania on mutual administrative assistance for the proper application of customs law and for the prevention, investigation and combating of customs offences, with Annexes, Vilnius, 8 December 1998.

Provisional application: pending.
Authentic languages: Lithuanian, Dutch, English (English prevails)
(Trb. 1999 No. 18)

— Agreement with Latvia on mutual administrative assistance for the proper application of customs law and for the prevention, investigation and combating of customs offences, with Annex on data protection, The Hague, 8 October 1999.
Parliamentary approval: 15 February 1999, tacit.
Entry into force: 1 May 1999 (for the Netherlands).
(Trb. 1999 No. 59)

— Protocol, Brussels, 12 March 1999, drawn up on the basis of Article K.3 of the Treaty of the European Union, on the scope of the laundering of proceeds in the Convention on the use of information technology for customs purposes and the inclusion of the registration number of the means of transport in the Convention, with declarations, Brussels, 26 July 1995.
Parliamentary approval: pending.
Note: This Protocol shall, in accordance with Article 3, paragraph 3, enter into force ninety days after the notification, referred to in paragraph 2, by the member state which, being a member of the European Union on the date of adoption by the Council of the Act drawing up this Protocol, is the last to fulfil that formality. However, it shall at the earliest enter into force at the same time as the Convention.
(Trb. 1999 No. 163)

— Agreement on cooperation in proceedings for road traffic offences and the enforcement of financial penalties imposed in respect thereof, with Annexes, Luxembourg, 28 April 1999.
Parliamentary approval: pending.
Entry into force: This agreement shall, in accordance with Article 20, paragraph 2, enter into force on the first day of the second month following the date of deposit of the last instrument of ratification, acceptance or approval by the States for which the 19 June 1990 Convention has been brought into force as pursuant to paragraph 1, indent 2, of the Final Act of the above mentioned Convention.
(Trb. 1999 No. 191)

— Convention with Morocco regarding the transfer of sentenced persons, Rabat, 30 November 1999.
Parliamentary approval: pending.
Provisional application: 30 December 1999 (for the Netherlands).
Authentic languages: Dutch, Arabic, French
(Trb. 1999 No. 198)

— Exchange of Notes, The Hague, 16 December 1999, to extend the Agreement concerning a Scottish trial in the Netherlands, The Hague, 18 September 1998.
Entry into force: 16 December 1999.
(Trb. 1999 No. 208)

4.73 EUROPEAN CONVENTION ON HUMAN RIGHTS, 1950
See: 12.273 ECHR (Trb. 1999 No. 21)

6.1 CONCLUSION AND ENTRY INTO FORCE OF TREATIES
See: 10.21 (Trb. 1999 No. 48)

6.4 INVALIDITY, TERMINATION AND SUSPENSION OF OPERATION

See: 4.6 (Trb. 1999 No. 186); 4.32 (Trb. 1999 Nos. 37 and 38); 4.62 (Trb. 1999 No. 194); 10.21 (Trb. 1999 No. 50); 16.141 (Trb. 1999 No. 91); 16.152 (Trb. 1999 Nos. 76 and 143); 16.42 (Trb. 1999 No. 200); 16.51 (Trb. 1999 Nos. 203, 204, 205 and 206)

7.25 MILITARY JURISDICTION

— Exchange of Letters with Denmark regarding an Agreement concerning the status of the brigade staff of the United Nations Stand by Forces High Readiness Brigade (Shirbrig) in Denmark, with Annexes, Copenhagen, 5 March/11 May 1998.
Parliamentary approval: 17 December 1998, tacit.
Entry into force: 1 March 1999 (for the Netherlands).
(Trb. 1999 No. 31)

— Exchange of Letters concerning the establishment of support for American armed forces on the Netherlands Antilles in connection with drugs combating activities, The Hague, 9/13 April 1999.
Parliamentary approval: not required, Art. 7(c) Approval Act of 1994.
Entry into force: 13 April 1999 (for the Netherlands Antilles and Aruba).
(Trb. 1999 No. 98)

8.11 FRONTIERS

— Agreement with Belgium regarding amendment of the border in the channel of Terneuzen to Gent, with Annex, Brussels, 6 January 1993.
Parliamentary approval: 7 January 1994, tacit.
Entry into force: 23 June 1999.
(Trb. 1999 No. 125)

8.12 RELATIONS OF 'VOISINAGE'

— Protocol No. 2, Strasbourg, 5 May 1998, to the European Outline Convention on transfrontier cooperation between territorial communities or authorities concerning interterritorial co-operation, Madrid, 21 May 1980.
Parliamentary approval: pending.
Note: This Protocol shall, in accordance with Article 9, paragraph 1, enter into force three months after the date on which four member states of the Council of Europe have expressed their consent to be bound by this Protocol in accordance with Article 8.
(Trb. 1999 No. 43)

9.5 CANALS

See: 8.11 (Trb. 1999 No. 125)

9.64 CONSERVATION OF LIVING RESOURCES

See: 16.164 (Trb. 1999 No. 45)

9.65 POLLUTION

— Resolution MEPC.75(40), adopted on 25 September 1997, amending the Annex of the Protocol of 1978 relating to the International Convention for the prevention of pollution from ships, 1973 (Amendments to regulation 10 and new regulation 25A of Annex I of MARPOL 73/78).
Acceptance: 1 August 1998.
Entry into force: 1 February 1999.
(Trb. 1999 No. 167)

— Resolution MEPC 77(41), adopted on 2 April 1998, establishing the date on which the amendments to regulation 10 of Annex I of MARPOL 73/78 in respect of the North West European Waters special area shall take effect.
Acceptance: 1 August 1998.
Entry into force: 1 August 1999.
(Trb. 1999 No. 167)

— Protocol, with Annex, London, 26 September 1997, to amend the International Convention for the prevention of pollution from ships, 1973, as modified by the Protocol of 1978 relating thereto.
Parliamentary approval: pending.
Entry into force: This Protocol shall, in accordance with Article 6, paragraph 1, enter into force 12 months after the date on which not less than fifteen States, the combined merchant fleets of which constitute not less than 50 per cent of the gross tonnage of the world's merchant shipping, have become Parties to it in accordance with Article 5 of the present Protocol.
(Trb. 1999 No. 169)

9.92 INTERNATIONAL RIVERS

— European Agreement on main inland waterways of international importance (AGN), with Annexes, Geneva, 19 January 1996.
Parliamentary approval: 2 March 1998, tacit.
Ratification: 21 April 1998 (for the Netherlands).
Entry into force: 26 July 1999 (for the Netherlands).
(Trb. 1999 No. 106)

— Additional Protocol No. 5, with declaration, Strasbourg, 28 April 1999, to the revised navigation act of the Rhine, Mannheim, 17 October 1868.
Parliamentary approval: pending.
Provisional application: 1 January 2000 (for the Netherlands).
(Trb. 1999 No. 171)

9.924 POLLUTION

— Convention concerning the protection of the Rhine, with Annexes and Protocol, Bern, 12 April 1999.
Parliamentary approval: pending.

Note: This Convention shall, in accordance with Article 17, enter into force on the first day of the second month that follows the receipt to the Swiss state of the latest announcement of the contracting parties to this Convention that the national requirements for the entry into force of this Convention are fulfilled.
(Trb. 1999 No. 139)

10.21 CIVIL AVIATION

— Protocol, Montreal, 10 May 1984, to insert Article 3 bis in the Treaty on civil aviation, Chicago, 7 December 1944.
Entry into force: 1 October 1998.
(Trb. 1999 No. 6)

— Agreement with the Dominican Republic for air services between and beyond their respective territories, Santo Domingo, 15 December 1998.
Parliamentary approval: pending.
(Trb. 1999 No. 11)

— Protocol, Montreal, 1 October 1998, relating to an amendment to the Convention on international civil aviation, Chicago, 7 December 1944.
Parliamentary approval: not required, Art. 7(b) Approval Act of 1994.
(Trb. 1999 No. 47)

— Protocol, Montreal, 1 October 1998, on the authentic six-language text of the Convention on international civil aviation, Chicago, 7 December 1944.
Parliamentary approval: not required, Art. 7(b) Approval Act of 1994.
Note: This Protocol shall, in accordance with Article IV, paragraph 1, enter into force on the thirtieth day after twelve States shall, in accordance with the provisions of Article III, have signed this Protocol without reservation as to acceptance or accepted it and after entry into force of the amendment of the final clause of the Convention adopted on 1 October 1998, which provides that the text of the Convention in the Chinese language is of equal authenticity.
(Trb. 1999 No. 48)

— Air transport agreement with the United States, with Annexes, Washington, 3 April 1957.
Termination: 16 February 1999.
(Trb. 1999 No. 50)

— Air transport agreement with the United States relating to air transport between the Netherlands Antilles and the United States, with Annexes, Washington, 14 July 1998.
Parliamentary approval: 14 December 1998, tacit.
Ratification: 16 February 1999 (for the Netherlands Antilles)
(Trb. 1999 No. 51)

— Agreement with Zimbabwe for air services between and beyond their respective territories, Harare, 30 January 1984.
Parliamentary approval: 13 April 1984, tacit.
Ratification: 18 February 1999 (for the Netherlands).
(Trb. 1999 No. 52)

— Agreement with Costa Rica for air services, with Annex, San Jose, 21 December 1994.
Parliamentary approval: 20 May 1995, tacit.
Entry into force: 11 March 1999 (for the Netherlands).
(Trb. 1999 No. 66)

— Exchange of Notes, 6 November 1998, with Kuwait to insert Article 13 bis in the Agreement with Bahrain concerning air services between and beyond their respective territories, with Annex, Manama, 11 July 1990.
Parliamentary approval: 13 December 1998
Entry into force: 26 December 1998 (for the Netherlands).
(Trb. 1999 No. 80)

— Annexes to the Convention on international civil aviation of 1944.
Promulgation: 26 June 1999.
(Trb. 1999 No. 108)

— Amendments I-IV, Beijing, 11/13 June 1999, to the Agreement with China concerning civil aviation, with Annex, Beijing, 2 May 1996.
Parliamentary approval: Nos. I and II: pending. Nos. III and IV: not required, Art. 7(f) Approval Act of 1994.
Entry into force: Nos. III and IV: 20 July 1999 (for the Netherlands)
(Trb. 1999 No. 183)

10.3 OUTER SPACE

See also: 16.4 (Trb. 1999 No. 142)

— Amendments, during the 12th sitting of the Assembly of Inmarsat, 24 April 1998, to the Convention on the International Mobile Satellite Organization (Inmarsat), with Annexes, and to the Operating Agreement, with Annex, London, 3 September 1976.
Parliamentary approval: pending.
Note: The Amendment shall, in accordance with Article 34 of the Convention, enter into force one hundred and twenty days after the Depository has received notices of acceptance from two-thirds of those States which, at the time of adoption by the Assembly (28 April 1998), were Parties.
The Agreement shall, in accordance with Article XVIII of the Agreement, enter into force one hundred and twenty days after the Depository has received notice of its approval by two-thirds of those Signatories which at the time of confirmation by the Assembly (28 April 1998) were Signatories and then held at least two-thirds of the total investment shares.
(Trb. 1999 No. 79)

11.3 'INTERNATIONAL CRIMES', WAR CRIMES, CRIMES AGAINST PEACE, CRIMES AGAINST HUMANITY

See: 12.273 International Criminal Court (ICC) (Trb. 1999 No. 13)

12.262 PERMANENT COURT OF ARBITRATION

See: 3.211 (Trb. 1999 No. 68)

12.273 OTHER JUDICIAL TRIBUNALS

European Court of Human rights (ECHR)

— European Agreement relating to persons participating in proceedings of the European Court of Human Rights, Strasbourg, 5 March 1996.
Parliamentary approval: 14 October 1996, tacit.
Ratification: 21 January 1997.
Entry into force: 1 January 1999.
(Trb. 1999 No. 21)

Court of Justice of the European Communities (ECJ)
See also: 16.724 (Trb. 1999 No. 104)

— Protocol, drawn up on the basis of Article K.3 of the Treaty on European Union, on the interpretation by the Court of Justice of the European Communities of the Convention on jurisdiction and the recognition and enforcement of judgements in matrimonial matters, Brussels, 28 May 1998.
Parliamentary approval: pending.
Note: This Protocol shall, in accordance with Article 9, paragraph 3, enter into force ninety days after the notification referred to in paragraph 2 by the third State which, being a member of the European Union at the time the Council adopts the act drawing up this Protocol (28 May 1998), completes that formality. However, it shall at earliest enter into force at the same time as the Convention.
(Trb. 1999 No. 15)

International Criminal Court (ICC)

— Rome Statute of the International Criminal Court, Rome, 17 July 1998.
Parliamentary approval: pending.
Note: This Statute shall enter into force on the first day of the month after the 60th instrument of ratification, acceptance or accession with the Secretary-General of the United Nations.
(Trb. 1999 No. 13)

14.113 LIMITATION AND REDUCTION OF ARMAMENTS, DISARMAMENT

— Treaty with Russia concerning Dutch assistance with the destruction of stockpiles of chemical weapons in Russia, The Hague, 22 December 1998.
Parliamentary approval: 10 July 1999, tacit.
Entry into force: 1 November 1999 (for the Netherlands).
Provisional application: 1 February 1999 (for the Netherlands).
(Trb. 1999 Nos. 19 and 179)

14.1131 CONVENTIONAL WEAPONS

— Additional Protocol to the Convention on prohibitions or restrictions on the use of certain conventional weapons which may be deemed to be excessively injurious or to have indiscriminate effects, Vienna, 13 October 1995.
Parliamentary approval: by Kingdom Act of 4 February 1999.
Ratification: 25 March 1999 (for the Netherlands).

Entry into force: 25 September 1999 (for the Netherlands).
(Trb. 1999 No. 122)

— Protocol on prohibitions or restrictions on the use of mines, booby-traps and other devices as amended on 3 May 1996 (Protocol II as amended 3 May 1996) annexed to the Convention on prohibitions or restrictions on the use of certain conventional weapons which may be deemed excessively injurious to or have indiscriminate effects, Geneva, 3 May 1996.
Parliamentary approval: by Kingdom Act of 4 February 1999.
Ratification: 25 March 1999 (for the Netherlands).
Entry into force: 25 September 1999 (for the Netherlands).
(Trb. 1999 No. 123)

14.1132 NUCLEAR WEAPONS

— Additional Protocol, with Annexes, Vienna, 22 September 1998, to the Agreement between Austria, Belgium, Denmark, Finland, Germany, the Hellenic Republic, Ireland, Italy, Luxembourg, the Netherlands, Portugal, Spain, Sweden, the European Atomic Energy Community and the International Atomic Energy Agency on implementation of Article III, paragraphs 1 and 4, of the Treaty on the Non-Proliferation of Nuclear Weapons (with Protocol), Brussels, 5 April 1973.
Parliamentary approval: pending.
Signature: 28 September 1998 (for the Netherlands).
Note: This Protocol, with Annexes, shall, in accordance with Article 17, enter into force on the date on which the Agency receives from the Community and the States written notification that their respective requirements for entry into force have been met.
(Trb. 1999 No. 147)

14.125 HUMANITARIAN LAW ('DROIT HUMANITAIRE')

— Second Protocol to the Hague Convention of 1954 for the protection of cultural property in the event of armed conflict, The Hague, 26 March 1999.
Parliamentary approval: pending.
Note: This Protocol shall, in accordance with Article 43, enter into force three months after twenty instruments of ratification, acceptance, approval or accession have been deposited.
(Trb. 1999 No. 107)

14.127 WEAPONS

See: 3.222 Organisation for Joint Armament Cooperation (Trb. 1999 No. 174)

16.112 MEASURES RESULTING IN PROMOTION OR RESTRICTION OF TRADE AND OTHER TRAFFIC OF GOODS

See also: 16.55 (Trb. 1999 No. 30)

— Convention on the control and marketing of articles of precious metals, with Annexes, Vienna, 15 November 1972, as amended until March 1992.
Parliamentary approval: 21 November 1996, tacit.
Accession: 16 April 1999 (for the Netherlands).

Entry into force: 16 July 1999 (for the Netherlands).
(Trb. 1999 No. 168)

16.114 CUSTOMS AND ECONOMIC UNIONS

— Amendment of 30 November 1998 to the Customs Convention on the temporary importation of private road vehicles, with Annexes, New York, 4 June 1954.
Parliamentary approval: pending.
Acceptance: 5 August 1999.
Entry into force: 5 November 1999.
(Trb. 1999 No. 176)

16.117 COMMODITY AGREEMENTS

— Resolution number 384, 21 July 1999, Extension of the International Coffee Agreement, London, 30 March 1994.
Parliamentary approval: not required, Art. 7(e) Approval Act of 1994.
Provisional application: 1 October 1999 (for the Netherlands).
(Trb. 1999 No. 199)

16.141 PROTECTION OF FOREIGN INVESTMENTS

— Agreement with Chile on the encouragement and reciprocal protection of investments, with Protocol, Santiago, 30 November 1998.
Parliamentary approval: pending.
Authentic languages: Spanish, Dutch, English (English prevails).
(Trb. 1999 No. 7)

— Agreement on the encouragement and reciprocal protection of investments with South Africa, Cape Town, 9 May 1995.
Parliamentary approval: 14 December 1998, tacit.
Entry into force: 1 May 1999.
Authentic languages: English, Dutch (English prevails)
(Trb. 1999 No. 39)

— Agreement with Georgia on the encouragement and reciprocal protection of investments, Tbilisi, 3 February 1998.
Parliamentary approval: 26 December 1998, tacit.
Entry into force: 1 April 1999.
(Trb. 1999 No. 70)

— Agreement with the Socialist Federal Republic of Yugoslavia concerning the protection of investments, Belgrade, 16 February 1976.
Termination: 1 June 1999 (for Croatia by Agreement of 28 April 1998).
1 June 1999 (for Macedonia by Agreement of 7 July 1998).
(Trb. 1999 No. 91)

— Agreement with Croatia on the encouragement and reciprocal protection of investments, Zagreb, 28 April 1998.
Parliamentary approval: 8 March 1999, tacit.
Entry into force: 1 June 1999.
(Trb. 1999 No. 92)

— Agreement with Macedonia on the encouragement and reciprocal protection of investments, Skopje, 7 July 1998.
Parliamentary approval: 20 March 1999, tacit.
Entry into force: 1 June 1999.
(Trb. 1999 No. 93)

— Agreement with Costa Rica on the encouragement and reciprocal protection of investments, The Hague, 21 May 1999.
Parliamentary approval: pending.
Authentic languages: Dutch, Spanish, English (English prevails)
(Trb. 1999 No. 112)

— Agreement with Ecuador on the encouragement and reciprocal protection of investment, Rio de Janeiro, 27 June 1999.
Parliamentary approval: pending.
(Trb. 1999 No. 127)

— Agreement with Tunisia on the encouragement and reciprocal protection of investments, with Protocol, The Hague, 11 May 1998.
Parliamentary approval: 22 March 1999, tacit.
Entry into force: 1 August 1999.
(Trb. 1999 No. 165)

— Agreement with Mexico on promotion, encouragement and reciprocal protection of investments, Mexico City, 13 May 1998.
Parliamentary approval: 11 January 1999, tacit.
Entry into force: 1 October 1999.
(Trb. 1999 No. 175)

— Agreement with El Salvador on the encouragement and reciprocal protection of investments, The Hague, 12 October 1999.
Parliamentary approval: pending.
Authentic languages: Dutch, Spanish, English (English prevails)
(Trb. 1999 No. 197)

— Agreement with Cuba on the encouragement and reciprocal protection of investments, Havanna, 2 November 1999.
Parliamentary approval: pending.
Authentic languages: Dutch, Spanish, English (English prevails)
(Trb. 1999 No. 211)

16.142 OTHER CAPITAL MOVEMENTS

— Convention with Tunisia concerning the promotion from capital investments and the protection from ownership, with letters, Tunis, 23 May 1963.
Termination: 1 August 1999.
(Trb. 1999 No. 173)

16.15 TAXES
See: 16.728 (Trb. 1999 No. 113)

16.152 DOUBLE TAXATION

— Protocol, The Hague, 25 August 1997, amending the Convention with Canada for the avoidance of double taxation and the prevention of fiscal evasion with respect to taxes on income, with Protocol, signed at The Hague on 27 May 1986, as amended by the Protocol signed at The Hague on 4 March 1993.
Parliamentary approval: 17 June 1998, tacit.
Entry into force: 15 January 1999 (for the Netherlands).
(Trb. 1999 No. 5)

— Protocol, Pretoria, 15 December 1998, amending the Convention with South Africa for the avoidance of double taxation and the prevention of fiscal evasion with respect to taxes on income, with Protocol, Cape Town, 15 March 1971.
Parliamentary approval: pending.
(Trb. 1999 No. 27)

— Protocol, The Hague, 4 December 1996, amending the Agreement with Malaysia for the avoidance of double taxation and the prevention of fiscal evasion with respect to taxes on income, with Protocol, and Exchange of Letters concerning the Agreement, The Hague, 7 March 1988.
Parliamentary approval: by Act of 18 December 1997.
Entry into force: 5 February 1999 (for the Netherlands).
(Trb. 1999 No. 35)

— Protocol, The Hague, 18 July 1995, amending the Agreement with Malta for the avoidance of double taxation and the prevention of fiscal evasion with respect to taxes on income andon capital with Protocol, signed at The Hague on 18 May 1977, with Letters.
Parliamentary approval: by Act of 17 December 1998.
Entry into force: 28 March 1999 (for the Netherlands).
(Trb. 1999 No. 44)

— Convention, Brussels, 21 December 1995, concerning the accession of Austria, Finland and Sweden to the Convention on the elimination of double taxation in connection with the adjustment of profits of associated enterprises, Brussels, 23 July 1990.
Ratification: 30 May 1996 (for the Netherlands).
Entry into force: 1 May 1999 (for the Netherlands).
(Trb. 1999 No. 69)

— Protocol, 6 November 1999, The Hague, amending the Agreement with Korea for the avoidance of double taxation and the prevention of fiscal evasion with respect to taxes on income, with Protocol, Seoul, 25 October 1978.
Parliamentary approval: 8 March 1999, tacit.
Entry into force: 2 April 1999 (for the Netherlands).
(Trb. 1999 No. 75)

— Agreement with the Socialist Federal Republic Yugoslavia for the avoidance of double taxation with respect to taxes on income and on capital, with Protocol, Belgrade, 22 February 1982
Continuation: 21 April 1999 (for Bosnia Herzegovina, Croatia and Slovenia).
Termination: 21 April 1999 (for Macedonia).
(Trb. 1999 No. 76)

— Convention with Macedonia for the avoidance of double taxation with respect to taxes on income and on capital, with Protocol, Skopje, 11 September 1998.
Parliamentary approval: 6 March 1999, tacit.
Entry into force: 21 April 1999 (for the Netherlands).
(Trb. 1999 No. 77)

— Agreement with Romania for the avoidance of double taxation and the prevention of fiscal evasion with respect to taxes on income and capital, with Protocol, Bucharest, 27 March 1979.
Termination: 29 July 1999.
(Trb. 1999 No. 143)

— Convention with Romania for the avoidance of double taxation and the prevention of fiscal evasion with respect to taxes on income and capital, The Hague, 5 March 1998.
Parliamentary approval: 29 October 1998.
Entry into force: 29 July 1999 (for the Netherlands).
(Trb. 1999 No. 144)

— Protocol, Brussels, 25 May 1999, to amend the Convention on the elimination of double taxation in connection with the adjustment of profits of associated enterprises, Brussels, 23 July 1990, and Final Act of the Conference of Representatives of the Governments of the Parties, meeting within the Council.
Signature of the Final Act: 25 May 1999.
Parliamentary approval: not required, Art. 7(e) Approval Act of 1994.
Note: The Protocol shall, in accordance with Article 3, enter into force on the first day of the third month following the deposit of the instrument of ratification, acceptance or approval by the last Signatory State to take this step.
(Trb. 1999 No. 148)

— Convention with Lithuania for the avoidance of double taxation and the prevention of fiscal evasion with respect to taxes on income and on capital, with Protocol, Vilnius, 16 June 1999.
Parliamentary approval: pending.
Authentic languages: Dutch, Lithuanian, English (English prevails)
(Trb. 1999 No. 149)

— Convention with Portugal for the avoidance of double taxation and the prevention of fiscal evasion with respect to taxes on income and on capital, with Protocol, Oporto, 20 September 1999.

Parliamentary approval: pending.
(Trb. 1999 No. 180)

— Agreement with Egypt for the avoidance of double taxation and the prevention of fiscal evasion with respect to taxes on income, with Protocol, Cairo, 21 April 1999.
Parliamentary approval: pending.
Authentic languages: Dutch, Arabic, English (English prevails)
(Trb. 1999 No. 188)

16.164 PROTECTION OF PLANTS AND ANIMALS

— Inter-American Convention for the protection and conservation of sea turtles, with Annexes, Caracas, 1 December 1996.
Parliamentary approval: pending.
Note: This Convention shall, in accordance with Article XXII, paragraph 1, enter into force ninety days after the date of deposit of the eighth instrument of ratification.
(Trb. 1999 No. 45)

16.181 PEACEFUL USE OF NUCLEAR ENERGY

— Exchange of Notes between the Netherlands, Germany and Great Britain and Northern Ireland, on the one hand, and the United States, on the other, concerning the application from non-proliferation assurances to Taiwan produced low enriched uranium, with Annex, Washington, 21 July 1999.
Parliamentary approval: pending.
Note: This Exchange of Notes shall, in accordance with Note No. II, enter into force on the first day of the second month following the date on which the last of the following named states, the Netherlands, Germany and Great Britain and Northern Ireland, has informed the Department of State of the United States that the national requirements for the entry into force of the Agreement have been fulfilled.
(Trb. 1999 No. 170)

16.2 INTERNATIONAL LEGAL ASPECTS OF ECONOMIC DEVELOPMENT AND DEVELOPMENT CO-OPERATION

— Administrative Arrangements with Egypt under the Agreement on technical cooperation, Cairo, 30 October 1976, concerning:
1) 'Strengthening the Integrated Pest Management Knowledge System in Fayoum', Cairo, 18 November 1998;
2) 'the Fayoum Horticultural Development Project- Phase IV', Cairo, 18 November 1998.
Parliamentary approval: not required, art. 7(b) Approval Act of 1994.
Entry into force: 1) 18 November 1998, with retroactive effect to 1 September 1997.
2) 18 November 1998.
(Trb. 1999 No. 8)

— Administrative Agreement with Ethiopia concerning technical assistance to strengthen: 1) the Mekelle University College for Dry Land Agriculture and Natural Resources, Addis Ababa, 4

November 1998; 2) to strengthen Alemaya University of Agriculture and specifically the Departments of Extension and Animal Science of the Faculty of Agriculture, Addis Ababa, 4 November 1998.
Entry into force: 1) & 2) 4 November 1998.
Provisional application: 1) & 2) from 1 January 1997.
(Trb. 1999 No. 9)

— Agreement on development cooperation with Uganda, Kampala, 20 January 1998.
Parliamentary approval: 12 October 1998, tacit.
Entry into force: 1 January 1999 (for the Netherlands).
(Trb. 1999 No. 36)

— Agreement with Kyrgyzstan regarding the agricultural development project in the Naukat rayon, Osh Oblast, Bishkek, 17 February 1999.
Parliamentary approval: pending.
Provisional application: 17 February 1999 (for the Netherlands).
(Trb. 1999 No. 61)

— Treaty with Bulgaria concerning technical and financial cooperation, The Hague, 30 September 1998.
Parliamentary approval: 2 April 1999, tacit.
Entry into force: 14 April 1999 (for the Netherlands).
(Trb. 1999 No. 83)

— Agreement with China on scientific and technological cooperation, Beijing, 12 April 1999.
Parliamentary approval: pending.
Authentic languages: Chinese, Dutch, English (English prevails)
(Trb. 1999 No. 84)

— Agreement with the Ukraine concerning technical and financial cooperation, Kiev, 11 May 1998.
Parliamentary approval: 12 October 1998, tacit.
Entry into force: 20 April 1999 (for the Netherlands).
(Trb. 1999 No. 90)

— Agreement with Georgia on technical and financial cooperation, The Hague, 23 June 1999.
Parliamentary approval: pending.
Authentic languages: Dutch, Georgian, English (English prevails)
(Trb. 1999 No. 124)

— Agreement with the Dominican Republic concerning economic and technical cooperation between the Dominican Republic, the Netherlands Antilles and Aruba, Santo Domingo, 24 June 1992.
Parliamentary approval: 26 December 1992, tacit.
Entry into force: 1 July 1998 (for the Netherlands Antilles and Aruba)
(Trb. 1999 No. 126)

— Administrative Arrangements with Egypt under the Agreement of technical cooperation, Cairo, 30 October 1976, concerning:
1) 'Training Programme for the Development of Managers and Supervisors for the National Cadastre at the Egyptian Survey Authority', Cairo, 28 February 1999;
2) 'Water Boards Project', Cairo, 19 May 1999.
Parliamentary approval: not required, Art. 7(b) Approval Act of 1994.

Entry into force: 1) 28 February 1999.
2) 19 May 1999.
(Trb. 1999 No. 150)

— Administrative Arrangement with Bangladesh under the Agreement on technical cooperation, Dhaka, 19 May 1977, concerning 'Meghna Estuary study, phase II', Dhaka, 3 February 1999.
Parliamentary approval: not required, Art. 7(b) Approval Act of 1994.
Entry into force: 3 February 1999, with retroactive effect to 1 October 1998.
(Trb. 1999 No. 151)

— Administrative Arrangement with Yemen under the Agreement on technical cooperation, The Hague, 3 October 1978, concerning 'Hodeidah Primary Health Systems Support Project', Sana'a, 2 February 1999.
Parliamentary approval: not required, Art. 7(b) Approval Act of 1994.
Entry into force: 2 February 1999.
(Trb. 1999 No. 152)

— Administrative Arrangement with Kenya under the Agreement on technical cooperation, Nairobi, 29 April 1980, concerning 'Environmental and Urban Development Training Project II (EUDTP II)', Nairobi, 5 March 1999.
Parliamentary approval: not required, Art. 7(b) Approval Act of 1994.
Entry into force: 5 March 1998, with retroactive effect to 15 July 1996.
(Trb. 1999 No. 153)

— Administrative Arrangement with Mozambique under the Agreement on technical cooperation, Maputo, 12 July 1984, concerning 'Sistemas de Aguas Sustentaveis (SAS)', Maputo, 6 April 1999.
Parliamentary approval: not required, Art. 7(b) Approval Act of 1994.
Entry into force: 6 April 1999, with retroactive effect to 1 October 1999.
(Trb. 1999 No. 154)

— Administrative Accord with Nicaragua under the Agreement on technical cooperation, Managua, 26 August 1992, concerning 'Fortalecimiento del Sistema de Atencion Primaria 1996-1998/FORSAP III', Managua, 28 April 1999.
Parliamentary approval: not required, Art. 7(b) Approval Act of 1994.
Entry into force: 28 April 1999, with retroactive effect to 1 September 1996.
(Trb. 1999 No. 155)

16.4 TRANSPORT, TRAFFIC, COMMUNICATION

— International Agreement concerning the establishment and operation of the civil LORAN C navigation system in North West Europe and the North Atlantic, with Annexes, Oslo, 6 August 1992.
Parliamentary approval: 14 February 1994, tacit.
Ratification: 3 March 1994 (for the Netherlands).
Entry into force: 2 April 1994 (for the Netherlands).
(Trb. 1999 No. 142)

16.42 ROAD TRAFFIC AND TRANSPORT

— Agreement with Czechoslovakia on international road transport, Prague, 15 November 1967.
Termination: 1 December 1999.
(Trb. 1999 No. 200)

— Agreement with Slovakia on international road transport, Bratislava, 16 March 1999.
Parliamentary approval: 8 October 1999, tacit.
Entry into force: 1 December 1999 (for the Netherlands).
Authentic languages: Slovakian, Dutch, English (English prevails)
(Trb. 1999 Nos. 72 and 201)

16.43 RAIL TRAFFIC AND TRANSPORT

— Amendment of Article 5, Lausanne, 4 June 1999, to the Convention with regard to the establishment of the 'Eurofima' (European company to financing of railway material), with Annexes, Bern, 20 October 1955.
Entry into force: 4 June 1999.
(Trb. 1999 No. 162)

16.47 TELECOMMUNICATIONS

— Final Act of the World Administrative Radio Conference and Revised radio regulations with Annexes, Geneva, 17 November 1995.
Parliamentary approval: 10 February 1999 (Final Act).
Entry into force: 10 February 1999 (Revised radio regulations).
(Trb. 1999 No. 46)

16.51 LABOUR AND RELATED MATTERS

— Agreement with Austria on social security, Vienna, 9 December 1998.
Parliamentary approval: pending.
(Trb. 1999 No. 10)

— ILO Convention No. 181 concerning private employment agencies, Geneva, 19 June 1997.
Parliamentary approval: 12 July 1999, tacit.
Ratification: 15 September 1999 (for the Netherlands).
Entry into force: 15 September 2000 (for the Netherlands).
(Trb. 1999 No. 182)

— Agreement with Austria on social security, with final protocol, The Hague, 7 March 1974.
Termination: 1 February 2000.
(Trb. 1999 No. 203)

— Accord to give effect to the Agreement with Austria concerning social security, with Annex, The Hague, 7 March 1974.

Termination: 1 February 2000.
(Trb. 1999 No. 204)

— Additional Agreement to the Agreement with Austria of 7 March 1974 on social security, The Hague, 5 November 1980.
Termination: 1 February 2000.
(Trb. 1999 No. 205)

— Administrative Agreement with Austria, Vienna, 1 October 1982, supplementary to the Administrative Agreement with Austria concerning the manner of application of the Agreement with Austria on social security, signed at The Hague on 7 March 1974.
Termination: 1 February 2000.
(Trb. 1999 No. 206)

— Agreement with Austria concerning social security, Vienna, 9 December 1998.
Parliamentary approval: 9 October 1999, tacit.
Entry into force: 1 February 2000 (for the Netherlands).
(Trb. 1999 No. 207)

16.522 FORCED LABOUR

— ILO Convention No. 182 concerning the prohibition and immediate action for the elimination of the worst forms of child labour, Geneva, 17 June 1999.
Parliamentary approval: pending.
Note: This Convention shall, in accordance with Article 10, paragraph 2, enter into force 12 months after the date on which the ratifications of two members have been registered with the Director-General of the International Labour Office.
(Trb. 1999 No. 177)

16.53 NARCOTICS

See also: 7.25 (Trb. 1999 No. 98)

— Convention on psychotropic substances, with Annexes, Vienna, 21 February 1971.
Entry into force: 10 March 1999 (for the Netherlands Antilles and Aruba).
(Trb. 1999 No. 189)

— United Nations Convention against illicit traffic in narcotic drugs and psychotropic substances, with Annexes, Vienna, 20 December 1988.
Entry into force: 10 March 1999 (for the Netherlands Antilles and Aruba).
(Trb. 1999 No. 190)

16.55 ENVIRONMENTAL QUESTIONS

— Rotterdam Convention on the prior informed consent procedure for certain hazardous chemicals and pesticides in international trade, with Annexes, Rotterdam, 10 September 1998.
Parliamentary approval: pending.

Note: This Convention shall, in accordance with Article 26, paragraph 1, enter into force on the ninetieth day after the date of deposit of the fiftieth instrument of ratification, acceptance, approval or accession.
(Trb. 1999 No. 30)

— Amendments, 1/11 December 1997, to Annex I of the United Nations Framework Convention on climate change, with Annexes, New York, 9 May 1992.
Entry into force: 13 August 1998.
(Trb. 1999 No. 53)

— Modifying Annex I, and amending Annex VIII and IX, Basel, 27 February 1998, to the Basel Convention on the control of transboundary movements of hazardous wastes and their disposal, Basel, 22 March 1989.
Entry into force: 6 November 1998 (for the Netherlands).
(Trb. 1999 No. 105)

— Amendment, 4 December 1998, to Annex II of the Convention on the conservation of European wildlife and natural habitats, with Annexes, Bern, 19 September 1979.
Parliamentary approval: not required, Art. 7(f) Approval Act of 1994.
Entry into force: 4 March 1999 (for the Netherlands).
(Trb. 1999 No. 109)

— Convention on international trade in endangered species of wild fauna and flora, with Annexes, Washington, 3 March 1973.
Ratification: 7 April 1999 (for the Netherlands Antilles).
Entry into force: 6 July 1999 (for the Netherlands Antilles).
(Trb. 1999 No. 146)

— Joint Convention on the safety of spent fuel management and on the safety of radioactive waste management, Vienna, 5 September 1997.
Parliamentary approval: pending.
Note: This Convention shall, in accordance with Article 40, paragraph 1, enter into force on the ninetieth day after the date of deposit with the Depository of the twenty-fifth instrument of ratification, acceptance or approval, including the instruments of fifteen states each having an operational nuclear power plant.
(Trb. 1999 No. 164)

16.63 MONUMENTS

See: 14.125 (Trb. 1999 No. 107)

16.66 SPORTS

See: 16.728 (Trb. 1999 No. 87)

16.723 INTELLECTUAL PROPERTY

— Protocol, Brussels, 13 April 1999, amending the Regulations of implementation of the Uniform Benelux Act concerning drawings and models, Brussels, 31 May 1989.

Parliamentary approval: not required, Art. 7(b) Approval Act of 1994.
Entry into force: 1 January 1999 (for the Netherlands)
(Trb. 1999 No. 85)

— Protocol, Brussels, 13 April 1999, amending the Regulations of implementation of the Uniform Benelux Act on trademarks, Brussels, 20 November 1995.
Parliamentary approval: not required, Art. 7(b) Approval Act of 1994.
Entry into force: 1 January 1999 (for the Netherlands).
(Trb. 1999 No. 86)

— Protocol, Brussels, 28 March 1995, amending the Uniform Benelux Act concerning drawings and models, Brussels, 25 October 1966.
Parliamentary approval: by Act of 29 May 1997 (for the Netherlands).
Ratification: 12 February 1999 (for the Netherlands).
Entry into force: 1 May 1999 (for the Netherlands).
(Trb. 1999 No. 95)

16.725 PRIVATE INTERNATIONAL LAW
See also: 12.273 ECJ (Trb. 1999 No. 15)

— Convention, drawn up on the basis of Article K.3 of the Treaty on European Union, on jurisdiction and the recognition and enforcement of judgements in matrimonial matters, Brussels, 28 May 1998.
Parliamentary approval: pending.
Note: This Convention shall, in accordance with Article 47, paragraph 3, enter into force ninety days after the notification referred to in paragraph 2 by the State which, being a member of the European Union at the time the Council adopts the Act drawing up this Convention (28 May 1998), is the last to complete that formality.
(Trb. 1999 No. 14)

— Convention on the accession of Austria, Finland and Sweden to the Convention on jurisdiction and the enforcement of judgements in civil and commercial matters and to the Protocol on its interpretation by the Court of Justice, with the adjustments made to them by the Convention on the accession of Denmark, Ireland and Great Britain and Northern Ireland, by the Convention on the accession of the Hellenic Republic and by the Convention on the accession of Spain and Portugal, Brussels, 29 November, 1996.
Ratification: 4 July 1997 (for the Netherlands and Aruba).
Entry into force: 1 December 1998 (for the Netherlands and Aruba).
(Trb. 1999 No. 104)

16.728 ADMINISTRATIVE LAW
See also: 8.12 (Trb. 1999 No. 43)

— Treaty with Belgium concerning cross-border police-action to maintain public order and security during the European Championship football for national teams in the year 2000, Bergen op Zoom, 26 April 1999.
Parliamentary approval: not required, Art. 7(c) Approval Act of 1994.
Entry into force: 20 May 2000 (for the Netherlands).
(Trb. 1999 No. 87)

— Agreement with Germany concerning mutual administrative assistance by the introduction of tax arrears and the distribution of documents, The Hague, 21 May 1999.
Parliamentary approval: pending.
(Trb. 1999 No. 113)

16.8 MILITARY AND SECURITY MATTERS

— Agreement between the parties of the North Atlantic Treaty for the security of information, with Annexes, Brussels, 6 March 1997.
Parliamentary approval: 3 January 1999, tacit.
Ratification: 24 February 1999 (for the Netherlands).
Entry into force: 26 March 1999 (for the Netherlands).
(Trb. 1999 No. 54)

NETHERLANDS MUNICIPAL LEGISLATION INVOLVING QUESTIONS OF PUBLIC INTERNATIONAL LAW, 1999*

P.C. Tange**

This survey covers municipal regulations relevant to international law that could not be dealt with adequately in the State Practice section. Translations of all or part of the text are usually given, together with descriptive or analytical notes where appropriate.

4.31 ADMITTANCE OF ALIENS OR NON-NATIONALS

Act of 21 January 1999 amending the Aliens Act (undocumented applications) (Stb. 1999 No. 29)

The present Act amends the Aliens Act in order to limit the difficulties that arise when investigating whether an application for admission as a refugee as referred to in Article 15a of the Aliens Act is eligible to be granted. The great majority of asylum-seekers state that they do not possess any travel document. In the Netherlands there is a requirement that an application for a decision or permit should be accompanied by certain documents. In the absence of such documents the application may in some cases not be processed and may in other cases, even where it is processed, not be granted.

Article 15b of the Aliens Act lists the grounds that can result in a decision on an application for admission as a refugee being refused because it is not admissible. Under Article15b(f) an application may be held to be inadmissible in a case where an alien does not have a cross-border travel document required for the Netherlands, unless he immediately reports to a competent official.[1] In a judgment of 29 December 1994[2] the Aliens Law Uniform Application Chamber held that as in this case the declaration of inadmissibility was accompanied by an expulsion order a clear and reasoned view should have been given on

*. Associate Research Officer.

**. Translated by P. Kell.

1. "A request for admission as a refugee will be refused on the ground that it is inadmissible if: [...] f. the alien did not possess the requisite document for crossing the national border into the Netherlands, unless he/she immediately reported to a State official charged with border surveillance or the supervision of aliens, stating the place where or through which he entered the Netherlands, and he made the application because he had reason to fear persecution as set out in Art. 15. [...]"

2. *AB* 1995 227, with note by T.P. Spijkerboer, *RV* 1994 No. 23, with note by B.P. Vermeulen.

the question of whether there was a risk of refoulement as referred to in Article 33 of the Convention relating to the Status of Refugees.[3] This means that in such a case there must be a substantive test to ascertain whether expulsion to the country of origin is possible.

The present Act therefore adds a new provision to Article 15c of the Aliens Act in relation to the submission of applications for asylum, which require in so far as necessary a substantive investigation but which must be dismissed as manifestly unfounded even on a *prima facie* assessment. This therefore guarantees a substantive assessment of an application for admission in so far as this is necessary under the various conventions.[4] Article 15c (f) now therefore reads as follows:

> 'A request for admission as a refugee will not be granted because it is manifestly unfounded if:
> [...]
> (f) the alien is unable to submit in support of his application travel or identity papers, documents or papers that are necessary for assessment of his application for admission, unless the alien can make a plausible case that the lack of these documents is not attributable to him [...]'

The present Act also adds a new Article 17b, under which officials charged with border surveillance and supervision of aliens are given the power to search asylum seekers in order to obtain such information as is necessary for an assessment of the application for admission as a refugee.
This Act took effect on 1 February 1999.[5]

4.32 PASSPORTS AND VISAS
See: 4.31

4.36 RIGHTS AND DUTIES OF ALIENS
See: 4.6

3. Convention of 28 July 1951 189 *UNTS* p. 137; *Trb.* 1975 No. 131, amended by Protocol of 31 January 1967, 606 *UNTS* p. 267; *Trb.* 1967 No. 76.

4. It is, incidentally, assumed in the present Act that if the documents necessary for assessment of the application for admission are missing it is up to the alien to make a plausible case as to why this cannot be attributed to him.

5. *Stb.* 1999 No. 32.

4.6 REMIGRATION

Act of 22 April 1999 containing rules on the making of provisions for remigration (Remigration Act)(Stb. 1999 No. 232)

The present Act makes provision for remigration. The principles on which remigration policy is based are: 1. that there must be a voluntary, personal and well-considered choice by the person concerned; 2. that after arrival in the country of destination the person concerned must have a reasonable certainty of adequate means of subsistence, and 3. that there must be good opportunities for people who consider remigration to obtain objective information.[6]
'The aim (of the Remigration Act) is to create facilities for remigration for people who are unable to fulfil their wish independently to be repatriated to their country of origin and come from the target groups of integration policy.'[7] Those eligible for these facilities are:

> '[...] (a) an alien of full age as referred to in Article 1(e) of the Kingdom Act on Netherlands Nationality, who belongs to a minority group, and (b) a Dutch national of full age who does not also have another nationality, belongs to a minority group and declares that he is prepared to do everything reasonably possible to obtain the nationality of the destination country with all due speed [...].'[8]

The facilities have been broadened for refugees and asylum-seekers who have been admitted to the Netherlands on the basis of an asylum application in the Netherlands for urgent reasons of a humanitarian nature, in that the present Act applies to them not only in cases where they emigrate back to their country of origin but also where they emigrate to a third country.[9]

Articles 3-7 list the facilities which the repatriated person can invoke. Under Article 8 persons who have been repatriated on the basis of the present Act can return to the Netherlands no later than one year after the date on which they have settled outside the Netherlands.

Pursuant to Article 7, paragraph 1, of the Present Act the Remigration Act Facilities Decree[10] lays down further rules on the facilities for remigration.

Both the Act and the Decree took effect on 1 April 2000.[11]

9.615 SCIENTIFIC RESEARCH AND HYDROGRAPHY

See: 9.619

---

6. Lower House 1997/98 – 25 741 p. 4
7. Lower House 1997/98 – 25 741 No. 3 p. 3
8. Art. 2 para. 1
9. Art. 1 para. 2
10. Decree of 14 October 1999 to impose further rules on facilities for remigration (*Stb.* 1999 No. 446)
11. Decree of 15 March 2000 (*Stb.* 2000 No. 129)

9.616 EXPLORATION AND EXPLOITATION OF THE SEABED AND THE SUBSOIL
See: 9.619

9.6161 ARTIFICIAL ISLANDS
See also: 9.619

Decree of 20 September 1999 declaring some regulations of the Public Works Management Act to be applicable to platforms at sea (Marine Installations Licensing Obligation Interim Decree) (Stb. 1999 No. 412)

The present Interim Decree[12] is the first step towards a statutory system of instruments that provides for the possibility that the authorities carry out a binding assessment (having a wider scope than the telecommunication legislation already applicable) of a private installation in the North Sea, in the Dutch part of the continental shelf.

The basic premise of the Interim Decree is 'that short-term or other plans to maintain installations at sea should be subject to a binding assessment by the authorities as part of a licensing system in order to protect relevant public interests both in connection with man's use of the sea and in connection with nature and the environment. The aim is to prevent the possibility that the statutory rules for the Dutch exclusive economic zone that are yet to be formulated could be undermined in advance.'[13] The establishment of an exclusive economic zone will offer the Dutch authorities an explicit basis on which to take regulatory action in relation to installations in this zone.

The present Decree took effect on 6 October 1999.

9.619 EXCLUSIVE ECONOMIC ZONE
See also: 9.6161

Kingdom Act of 27 May 1999 establishing an exclusive economic zone of the Kingdom of the Netherlands (Exclusive Economic Zone Establishment Act) (Stb. 1999 No. 281)

The present Act establishes an exclusive economic zone of the Kingdom of the Netherlands, the Netherlands Antilles and Aruba. The establishment of an exclusive economic zone is desirable in order to make the best possible use of the possibilities offered by the United Nations Convention on the Law of the Sea, with annexes, which was concluded at Montego Bay on 10 December 1982 (UNCLOS).[14] The Convention was approved for the Kingdom by the Kingdom Act of 26 June 1996[15] together with the Agreement relating to the implementation of part IX of the Convention, New York , 29 July 1994. The Convention and the Agreement were ratified for the European part of the Kingdom on 28 June 1996.

The main articles of the present Act read as follows:

---

12. This Interim Decree is of a provisional nature and must be followed by formal legislation.
13. Explanatory Memorandum, *Stb.* 1999 p. 3
14. *Trb.* 1983 No. 83
15. *Stb.* 1996 No. 357

'Article 1
There is an exclusive economic zone of the Kingdom.
The exclusive economic zone of the Kingdom is the area beyond and adjacent to the territorial sea of the Kingdom which does not extend more than two hundred nautical miles from the baselines from which the breadth of the territorial sea is measured.
[...]

Article 3
The Kingdom has, subject to the limits imposed by international law, in the exclusive economic zone: :
sovereign rights for the purpose of exploring and exploiting, conserving and managing the natural resources, whether living or non-living, of the waters superjacent to the sea-bed and of the sea-bed and its subsoil, and with regard to other activities for the economic exploitation and exploration of the zone, such as the production of energy from the water, currents and winds;
jurisdiction with regard to the establishment and use of artificial islands, installations and structures, marine scientific research and the protection and preservation of the marine environment.
[...]'[16]

The present Act will take effect on a date to be determined by Royal Decree, which may differ for each of the countries of the Kingdom. The Act took effect for the Netherlands on 28 April 2000.[17]

9.7 THE CONTINENTAL SHELF

See: 9.6161

13. COERCION AND USE OF FORCE SHORT OF WAR

Decree of 18 March 1999 confirming the regime of sanctions on Yugoslavia (Yugoslavia Sanctions Decree 1999) (Stb. 1999 No. 153)

Under Article 8 of the Sanctions Act 1977 the Yugoslavia Sanctions Regulation 1998[18] adopted on 2 November 1998 will cease to have effect no later than 10 months after its entry into effect. The Regulation took effect on 5 August 1998 and will therefore cease to have effect on 5 June 1999. The present Decree confirms the measures that were adopted when the Regulation took effect.

---

16. For the complete text of the Explanatory Memorandum, see 29 *NYIL* (1998) pp. 167-180
17. Decree of 13 March 2000, *Stb.* 2000 No. 167.
18. *Stc.* 1998 No. 210, see 30 *NYIL* (1999) p. 274.

Yugoslavia Aviation Sanctions Regulation 1999-2 (Stc. 1999 No. 241, p. 8)

The Yugoslavia Aviation Sanctions Regulation 1999-2 of 10 December 1999 tightens up the existing rules by repealing Article 6 of the Yugoslavia Sanctions Decree[19] and providing that infringement of the prohibition on flights between the territory of the Federal Republic of Yugoslavia and that of the European Community is a criminal offence. An exception is made for flights between the territory of the EC and that of the Republic of Montenegro or the region of Kosovo. This Sanctions Regulation replaces a previous Sanctions Regulation of 2 July 1999.[20]

Yugoslavia Financial Sanctions Regulation 15 July 1999 (Stc. 1999 No. 135, p. 7)

The Yugoslavia Financial Sanctions Regulation 1999 also repeals Articles 2-5 of the above-mentioned Yugoslavia Sanctions Decree, as a result of the repeal of Council Regulations (EC) Nos. 1295/98 and 1607/98.[21] The Sanctions Regulation prohibits acts in contravention of Articles 3, 4 and 5 of Council Regulation (EC) No. 1294/1999.[22]

Decree of 3 March 1999 amending the Angola Sanctions Decree 1998 in connection with the establishment of Council Regulation (EC) No. 1705/98 of 28 July 1998 (Stb. 1999 No. 162)

The present Decree confirms the measures adopted in the Angola Sanctions Regulation of 2 October 1998 and resulting from EC Regulation 1705/98 concerning the interruption of certain economic relations with Angola[23] in order to induce the União Nacional para a Independência Total de Angola (Unita) to fulfil its obligations in the peace process, and repealing Council Regulation (EC) No. 2229/97.[24]

---

19. Under Art. 6 it was prohibited to act in breach of Regulation 1901/98, which included a prohibition on flights of Yugoslav airlines between the Federal Republic of Yugoslavia and the EC. When repealing Council Regulation (EC) No. 1901/98, Council Regulation (EC) No. 1064/1999 adopted a prohibition on flights between the Federal Republic of Yugoslavia and the territory of the EC.

20. Yugoslavia Aviation Sanctions Regulation 1999, Stc. 1999 No. 126, p. 13.

21. The Regulations in question were repealed by Art. 13 of Council Regulation (EC) No. 1294/1999 of 15 June 1999 concerning a freeze of funds and a ban on investment in relation to the Federal Republic of Yugoslavia.

22. Other sanction schemes adopted as a result of prohibitions introduced by the Council of the European Communities against the Federal Republic of Yugoslavia concern oil and oil products. (Yugoslavia Oil and Oil Products Sanctions Regulation 1999, *Stc.* 1999 No. 106, p. 7 and No. 208, p. 7).

23. *OJ* 1998 L 215, p. 1.

24. *OJ* 1997 L 309, p. 1.

Act of 2 December 1999 renewing the operation of rules laid down pursuant to the Import and Export Act with regard to the import and export of goods (Stb. 1999 No. 539)

Pursuant to Article 2c(6) of the Import and Export Act, an import or export decree ceases to have effect three years after it takes effect, unless provided otherwise by law. The Act of 4 September 1996[25] extended the term of operation of certain decrees until 1 January 2000. The present Act extends the operation of the Industrial Goods Import and Export Decree 1963, the Strategic Goods Export Decree 1963, the Agricultural Goods Import and Export Decree 1980, the Countries Import Decree 1981 and the Tobacco Import and Export Decree 1982 until 1 January 2003.

Repeal of Libya Sanctions Decree 1993, 12 May 1999 (Stc. 1999 No. 92, p. 9)

The cooperation by Libya in the trial of two persons suspected of the bomb attack on PanAm flight 103 above Lockerbie[26] in 1988 resulted in suspension of the sanctions against that country. As a result of Resolution 1192 (1998) of the Security Council[27] and suspension of Council Regulation (EC) No. 3274/93,[28] the Dutch legislation on this subject must be amended.

Pursuant to Article 7 of the Sanctions Act 1977 the Libya Payments Transactions and Financial Services Dealings Sanctions Decree 1994[29] and (under the present Regulation) the Libya Sanctions Decree 1993 have been repealed.

Indonesia Sanctions Regulation 1999, 8 December 1999 (Stc. 1999 No. 238, p. 7)

The present Regulation has been adopted to implement the Common Position of the Council of the European Union of 16 September 1999[30] concerning limiting measures against the Republic of Indonesia and Council Regulation (EU) No. 2158/99 of 11 October 1999[31] concerning a prohibition on the supply to Indonesia of equipment that might be used for internal repression or terrorism. Under Article 1, it is prohibited to supply or transfer to Indonesia, arms, weapons of destruction, ammunition, military equipment, goods or parts, or military technology as designated in the annex to the Strategic Goods Implementation Decree 1963. Article 2 provides that infringement of Article 1, paragraph 1, of the Regulation is a criminal offence.

---

25. See 28 *NYIL* (1997) p. 318
26. See 31 *NYIL* (2000) p. 182.
27. On 5 April 1999 effectuated by the Secretary General of the United Nations.
28. 29 November 1993, *OJ* 1993 L 295, p. 1.
29. 26 *NYIL* (1995) p. 322. Repealed by Regulation of 19 April 1999, Stc. 1999 No. 75.
30. 1999/624/GBVB, *OJ* 1999 245, p. 53.
31. *OJ* 1999 L 265.

NETHERLANDS JUDICIAL DECISIONS INVOLVING QUESTIONS OF PUBLIC INTERNATIONAL LAW, 1998-1999*

L.A.N.M. Barnhoorn**

The decisions in this survey are taken from the documentation system of the Public International Law Department of the T.M.C. Asser Instituut, which now contains abstracts from approximately 5000 decisions dating from 1839 to the present day. Most of the texts are taken from various Reports and Journals, but the Institute also receives the texts of decisions involving questions of public international law directly from the Courts concerned by special agreement between the Institute, the Ministry of Justice, and the Courts. If the decision has not (yet) been published elsewhere, the source of the text is given as 'Institute's Collection' followed by the administrative sequence number.

Not all the decisions in the documentation system of the Institute are included in this survey. Some are left out because they contain very minor points of (international) law. Those decisions which are included are given either in an extensive form, with verbatim extracts from the judgment, or in a summarized form, depending on their relevance to international law.

A two-year period is covered by the survey, one year of which overlaps the period covered by the survey in last year's volume of the NYIL. This is made necessary by the fact that the text of the decisions is sometimes available only after a considerable time. This is also why, by way of exception, decisions are occasionally included although given at a time prior to the period covered by the survey.

---

* This section has been translated by P. Kell.

** Senior Research Officer, Department of Public International Law, T.M.C. Asser Instituut.

Netherlands Yearbook of International Law
Volume XXXI - 2000 - pp. 253-315

1.202 ENFORCEMENT OF INTERNATIONAL LAW IN MUNICIPAL LAW
See: 1.204 (pp. 254-257); 13.223, 16.164

1.203 CONFLICT BETWEEN INTERNATIONAL LAW AND MUNICIPAL LAW
See: 1.204; 3.1141 (pp. 265-267); 3.143; 8.23; 13.223

1.204 SELF-EXECUTING PROVISIONS OF TREATIES OR DECISIONS OF INTERNATIONAL ORGANISATIONS
See also: 4.52 (pp. 278-282); 8.23; 13.223

H., the heirs of A.R., and A., v. the Country of Aruba, Supreme Court, 9 January 1998, RvdW (1998) No. 10, NJ (1998) No. 724,[1] AB (1999) No. 149.[2]

— In view of the principle of legality, where means of coercion such as searches of premises, seizure of documents and the transfer of such documents to the judicial authorities of the United States involving infringements of fundamental rights are to be applied in the context of international mutual assistance in criminal matters it is essential that they have a statutory or treaty basis.
— Such a basis cannot be derived from the Treaty between the Kingdom of the Netherlands and the United States of America on mutual assistance in criminal matters, which was concluded in 1981. It must be inferred from the wording of Articles 1 and 6 that they are intended merely to create obligations for the Contracting States themselves.[3]
— Although implementation of the Treaty in the Code of Criminal Procedure of the Netherlands Antilles and Aruba occurred in 1997, this is not applicable here since the request for assistance pre-dates the implementation.
— Nor can other national legislation of Aruba in force at that time provide such a basis.

The Facts: The Director of the Office of International Affairs of the US Department of Justice addressed a request for assistance relating to H. to the Country of Aruba under the Treaty on mutual assistance in criminal matters, which was concluded between the Kingdom of the Netherlands and the United States of America in 1981. He made this request in the course of a criminal investigation in the United States against H., who was suspected of illegally importing narcotics into that country and of laundering the proceeds of such trafficking. By decision of 6 May 1992 the examining magistrate responsible for dealing with criminal cases in the Court of First Instance of Aruba ordered a search at a number of premises and a number of banks for the purpose of seizure. This resulted in the seizure of a large number of documents. H. then applied to the Court of First Instance for an interim injunction ordering that such documents be

1. Note by T.M. Schalken.
2. Note by T.G. Drupsteen.
3. 1359 *UNTS* p. 209; *ILM* (1982) p. 48. *Trb.* 1981 No. 188. For the text of the relevant parts of Arts. 1 and 6, see under Held.

handed over to third parties. This application was dismissed by the President of the Court by judgment of 9 May 1992. Some of the documents were then transferred to the United States and others were returned to H. Together with A.R. and A.,[4] H. then appealed to the Court of First Instance against the decision of the examining magistrate. They applied for a declaration that the seizure and transfer of the documents be declared unlawful on the grounds that there was no adequate legal basis for this action. The Court of First Instance dismissed the claim (judgment of 26 April 1995), as did the Joint Court of Appeal of the Netherlands Antilles and Aruba on appeal (judgment of 20 August 1996). H., the heirs of A.R. (who had died in the meantime) and A. then appealed in cassation to the Supreme Court of the Netherlands.

Held: '... 3.3. In assessing the question raised in this ground of appeal, it should be stated at the outset that in view of the principle of legality, where means of coercion such as searches of premises, seizure of documents and the transfer of such documents to the judicial authorities of the United States "which involve infringements of fundamental rights" are to be applied in the context of international mutual assistance in criminal matters it is essential that they have a statutory or treaty basis.

3.4. Since 1 October 1997 international mutual assistance in criminal matters has been statutorily regulated in Aruba in Articles 555-565 of the Code of Criminal Procedure of the Netherlands and Aruba, which took effect on that date. Previously no provision was made in the legislation of Aruba governing international mutual assistance in criminal matters.[5]

The arrangement that took effect on the said date, which 'in so far as relevant here' corresponds to the arrangement contained in Title X, Part 1 (Arts. 552h-552q) of the Dutch Code of Criminal Procedure, provides a statutory basis for the application of means of coercion such as the present ones in the course of international mutual assistance in criminal matters.

It concerns in particular Article 562, which corresponds to Article 552o of the Dutch Code of Criminal Procedure, and provides, in brief, that an application which is made by the public prosecutor to the examining magistrate with a view to acceding to a request for international assistance in legal matters that is capable of being granted and is based on a treaty and which contains a description of the acts required of the examining magistrate, has the same legal consequences as an application for the institution of a preliminary judicial investigation.

The question that needs to be answered is whether a sufficient basis was available for the application of the means of coercion disputed by H. et al., taking into account that such application occurred at a time when no statutory arrangement concerning international mutual assistance in criminal matters was in force in Aruba.

3.5. Such a basis cannot be derived from the Treaty itself. In Article 1(1) the Contracting Parties undertake to afford each other, upon request and in accordance with

---

4. The interest of the other two parties – A.R. and A. – lay in the fact that they too were the subject of a criminal investigation in the United States as a result of the seized documents.

5. The Joint Court of Appeal of the Netherlands Antilles and Aruba had previously anticipated the entry into effect of this legislation by applying it in its judgment of 20 October 1992 in the case of Aruba v. O.A.L. and three others (*Tijdschrift voor Antilliaans Recht-Justitia* (1992) p. 238, with note by J.M. Reijntjes). However, the Supreme Court rejected this advance application of the legislation in its judgment of 4 March 1994 (*NJ* (1994) No. 575, with note by T.W. van Veen).

the provisions of this Treaty, mutual assistance in criminal investigations and proceedings. Under paragraph 2, opening words and (f), of Article 1, assistance is deemed to include "but not be limited to" executing requests for search and seizure.

Article 6(1) obliges the Requested State to execute requests for search and seizure Ain accordance with its laws and practices, if the subject offence is punishable under the laws of both Contracting Parties by deprivation of liberty for a period exceeding one year, or, if less, is specified in the Annex of the Treaty.

It must be inferred from the wording of these provisions that they are intended merely to create obligations for the Contracting States themselves. As the Treaty does not contain an arrangement for search and seizure which is direct applicable, it must be interpreted in such a way that it is not in this respect binding on any person in that it provides a basis in treaty law for the infringements of fundamental rights of the citizens concerned as a result of the search and seizure.[6]

Nor does the national legislation of Aruba applicable at that time provide the requisite basis. This applied in particular to the arrangement concerning search, contained in Article 99 et seq. of the Code of Criminal Procedure, which applied in Aruba in 1992. This arrangement related exclusively to the application of this measure of coercion in the context of a preliminary judicial investigation, and not therefore in the course of executing a request for assistance in criminal matters made by the authorities of a foreign State.

This leaves open the question of whether the requisite basis can be found in the provisions of Article 35, paragraph 1, of the 1985 Uniform Act of the Netherlands Antilles and Aruba on the Judicial Organisation, under which provision the Joint Court of Appeal of the Netherlands Antilles and Aruba, the courts of first instance and the Public Prosecution Service are obliged to execute requests for assistance in criminal matters from foreign courts or officials.

This question too should, however, be answered in the negative. Taking into account the connection with paragraph 1 of the Article, which relates to assistance in criminal matters within the Kingdom of the Netherlands, a reasonable interpretation of paragraph 2 of this Article is that it is not intended to create a power independently to infringe fundamental rights in the course of international mutual assistance in criminal matters, and is instead intended merely to determine in cases where such power exists on other grounds which authorities should exercise this power.

3.6. It follows from the above that a sufficient basis in law did not exist for the disputed searches. The ground of appeal is therefore well founded and need not be dealt with further. The disputed judgment cannot be upheld …'

The Supreme Court then referred the case back to the Joint Court of Appeal for further consideration and decision.[7]

---

6. It is evident from the judgment of the Court of First Instance of 5 June 1992 that the requirement of double criminality contained in Art. 6 should, however, be applied by the court (*Tijdschrift voor Antilliaans Recht-Justitia* (1992) p. 11 of 3, with note by J.M. Reijntjes).

7. In the subsequent assessment of the request for the extradition of H., which dated from 1997, the Joint Court of Appeal initially took the view that the request was based on evidence unlawfully obtained and that supplementary evidence was necessary (interim judgment of 31 January 1998). However, the United States refused to comply with this request, after which the Joint Court of Appeal

A. v. the State Secretary for Justice, District Court of The Hague (sitting in Zwolle), 21 October 1998, RV (1998) No. 16.[8]

— Articles 4-10 of the 1990 Convention of Dublin[9] *regulate the responsibility of the various Member States among themselves. The provisions do not therefore have direct effect. This means that an alien cannot derive rights directly from these provisions. This does not alter the fact that before submitting a claim to another Member State the State Secretary for Justice should carefully assess whether another Member State is obliged to accept responsibility in accordance with these Articles for examining the application for asylum. There is no evidence that the State Secretary observed this duty of care.*
— Article 3(4) of the Convention[10] *confers on the State Secretary the right to accept responsibility for examining an application for asylum notwithstanding the provisions of Articles 4-8. This right gives the State Secretary a discretionary freedom, and any review by the courts of the manner in which this right is exercised must therefore be restricted to determining whether the exercise was reasonable.*
— The account of the flight need not be reviewed upon application of the provisions of Article 15b(1)(a) of the Aliens Act.[11] *The only exception is where the alien can successfully invoke the 'unless clause'.*
— Invocation of Article 3 of the European Convention on Human Rights does not preclude transfer to Germany.[12] *Germany is, after all, a party to the Convention and it is*

---

recommended in its opinion to the Governor of Aruba of 15 April 1998 that H. be extradited on the basis of the documents that had by that time come to the attention of the Joint Court of Appeal ex officio. The Governor subsequently decided on 17 April to grant the extradition (cf., the commentary of J.M. Socrona in 'Extradition on Aruba: Supreme Court and defence offside'), *NJB* (1998) pp. 865-866). H. appealed in cassation to the Supreme Court against the opinion of the Joint Court of Appeal. The Supreme Court held that the appeal was not admissible. The cassation arrangement for the Netherlands Antilles and Aruba did not, after all, provide for the possibility of appealing in cassation against opinions of the Joint Court of Appeal in extradition cases. This was not altered by the fact that fundamental principles of law were alleged to have been infringed. Furthermore, the courts should observe restraint in matters relating to the Kingdom, particularly if the problem was already under consideration by the Kingdom legislator (judgment of 6 July 1999, *NJ* (1999) No. 107).

8. Note by B.P. Vermeulen.

9. *OJ* 1997 No. 254 p. 1; *Trb.* 1991 No. 129. The full title reads: Convention determining the State responsible for examining applications for asylum lodged in one of the Member States of the European Communities.

10. Art. 3(4) reads: '1. Each Member State shall have the right to examine an application for asylum submitted to it by an alien, even if such examination is not its responsibility under the criteria defined in this Convention, provided that the applicant for asylum agrees thereto. The Member State responsible under the above criteria is then relieved of its obligations, which are transferred to the Member State which expressed the wish to examine the application. The latter State shall inform the Member State responsible under the said criteria if the application has been referred to it.'

11. Art. 15b(1)(a) reads: 'An application for admission as a refugee shall not be granted if it is not advisable because: (a) another country, party to the Geneva Convention relating to the Status of Refugees in accordance with a treaty or a decision of an international organisation binding this country and the Netherlands, is responsible for processing the application, unless such an application is founded on relevant facts which could not have played any role in the decision by the authorities of that country.'

12. 213 *UNTS* p. 221; *ETS* No. 5; *Trb.* 1964 No. 69. Art. 3 reads: 'No one shall be subjected to torture or two inhuman or degrading treatment or punishment.'

therefore up to Germany as the responsible State to determine whether possible expulsion would be contrary to Article 3.

The Facts: A., who came from the Federal Republic of Yugoslavia, requested entry as a refugee on 10 February 1998 and the issue of a residence permit for compelling humanitarian reasons. The application for admission as a refugee was refused by decision of 24 July 1988 under Article 15b(1)(a) of the Aliens Act, because Germany was responsible under the Convention of Dublin for examining the asylum application and Germany had also indicated that it was willing to accept responsibility for examining the application. The application for a residence permit was also refused and A. was given notice to leave the Netherlands immediately. In addition, he was not permitted to remain in the Netherlands pending the processing of his notice of objection. A. appealed against this decision to District Court of The Hague. He also requested the President to stay the implementation of the decision.

Held: '... 2.1. Pursuant to Article 8:81 of the General Administrative Law Act the President of the District Court who is or may become competent in the main action, if objection has been lodged against an order, may on request make a provisional remedy if speed is of the essence in view of the interests involved.

2.2. The President shall, in so far as the expulsion decision is connected with the refusal of the application for entry as a refugee, check whether no doubt can reasonably be said to exist that there is no danger of persecution within the meaning of asylum law as a result of the transfer of the applicant to Germany and, in so far as the expulsion decision is connected with the refusal of the application for entry as a refugee, check whether the objection has a reasonable chance of success.

2.3. The applicant has alleged that the defendant failed to mention in the transfer request to Germany that the applicant left Germany and travelled to Kosovo. It follows that Germany very probably accepted the claim on the basis of incomplete information. The applicant's interests are therefore prejudiced, particularly since he is not able to show that he had exhausted all his legal remedies in Germany. The defendant will be aware of the fact that Germany always accepts the claims in principle, regardless of whether it is actually responsible. There is no apparent reason why a claim was not made to the Italian authorities. The defendant should have carried out further investigation into the journey to and residence in Kosovo.

2.4. In the disputed order, the defendant took the position – in brief – that under the Convention of Dublin the German authorities were responsible for dealing with the application for asylum and that it should be assumed that Germany would observe its obligations under the Refugee Convention and the (European) Convention for the Protection of Human Rights and Fundamental Freedoms. The applicant has failed to demonstrate plausibly that he has exhausted his legal remedies. Nor has he demonstrated that he actually left the territory of the Member States.

In the statement of defence the defendant has submitted that the applicant cannot invoke the provisions of Articles 4-8 of the Convention of Dublin because these provisions do not have direct effect. The defendant observes for the record that the applicant has not plausibly shown by means of documents that he left the Dublin Area.

2.5. The question that needs to be answered at the outset is which country – Germany or the Netherlands – is responsible for examining the application for asylum.

The applicant submits that he stayed outside the Dublin Area. The Member States have recorded in the Convention of Dublin the criteria according to which it must be determined which Member State is responsible for examining an application for asylum submitted to one of these States. Essentially, the Convention of Dublin provides that an alien can and may submit an application for asylum to only one Member State. This results among other things from the aim which the Member States set themselves in the Treaty establishing the European Community, namely the creation of an area without internal borders.

Articles 4-10 of the Convention of Dublin which provide how it is to be decided which State is responsible for examining applications for asylum regulate the responsibility between the different Member States. The provisions do not therefore have direct effect. This means that an alien cannot derive rights directly from these provisions. This does not alter the fact that before submitting a claim to another Member State the defendant should carefully assess whether another Member State is obliged to accept responsibility in accordance with these Articles for examining the application for asylum. There is no evidence that the defendant observed this duty of care. The defendant did not have to accord decisive significance to the submission of the applicant that he had left the Dublin Area, since the applicant had not produced objectively verifiable documents to support this submission. It should also, incidentally, be noted that the statement of the applicant concerning the travel route was included in point 24 of the standard form (enclosed with the transfer request) for determining which Member State is responsible for examining an application for asylum. The German authorities were therefore informed of the applicant's submission that he had left the Dublin Area.

Since Germany has accepted responsibility for the asylum application pursuant to Article 5(4) of the Convention of Dublin, the responsibility of Germany has now been established.[13]

2.6. Article 3(4) of the Convention of Dublin confers on the State Secretary the right to accept responsibility for examining an application for asylum notwithstanding the provisions of Articles 4-8. This right gives the State Secretary a discretionary freedom, and any review by the courts of the manner in which this right is exercised must therefore be restricted to determining whether the exercise was reasonable.[14] There is no evidence of special reasons which could mean that the defendant should exercise the right referred to in Article 3(4) of the Convention of Dublin.[15]

---

13. In the same sense see District Court of The Hague (sitting in Zwolle), 9 September 1998, *JV* (1998) No. 201 with note by R. Fernhout. But see also District Court of The Hague (sitting in Zwolle), 8 May 1998, *JV* (1998) No. 123 with note by R. Fernhout. In this judgment, however, the matter is reviewed directly by reference to Art. 10. District Court of The Hague also held in its judgment of 15 March 1999 that Art. 10(3) of the Convention of Dublin and Art. 8 of Order 1/97 of the Implementing Committee written to supplement and clarify that article (Aliens Circular No. C42) had been written partly in the interests of citizens. The District Court then reviewed the policy of the State Secretary by reference to Art. 8 (*NAV* (1999) No. 70 and *JV* (1999) No. S158).

14. The Dutch term used is *marginale toetsing*, which can be literaly translated in marginal review.

15. In the judgment of District Court of The Hague (sitting in Zwolle) of 7 June 1999, the guideline applied by the State Secretary – namely that the application for asylum under Art. 3(4) need not be processed if six months have not yet elapsed between the claim agreement and the disputed decision – was held not to be unreasonable. Since it is stated in the preamble to the Convention of Dublin that asylum-seekers should not be left in doubt for too long as regards the likely outcome of

2.7. Under the established case law the account of the flight need not, in principle, be reviewed upon application of the provisions of Article 15b paragraph 1, opening words and (a), of the Aliens Act. The only exception is where the alien requesting asylum can successfully invoke the 'unless clause' provided for in Article 15b, paragraph 1, opening words and (a) of the Alien's Act. It is necessary for this purpose that he should plausibly demonstrate "in brief" that he has exhausted his legal remedies in the country having first responsibility.

In addition, it should be plausibly demonstrated that the asylum application in the Netherlands is based on relevant facts which could not play a role in the decision in the country having first responsibility. For this purpose, the person concerned will in principle have to lodge the decisions of the relevant administrative body and the administrative court from the country having first responsibility. The assessment made in the context of the 'unless clause' is not intended as a disguised form of appeal.

2.8. In the view of the president, the defendant had good grounds for taking the position that the applicant had not plausibly demonstrated that he had exhausted his remedies in Germany. The applicant has, after all, failed to lodge the relevant decisions taken against him, and this was something that could be expected of him and not of the defendant. Nor is this altered by the mere unsupported submission of the applicant that he cannot demonstrate that he has exhausted his legal remedies.

2.9. In view of the above there cannot reasonably be said to exist any doubt that there is no danger of persecution within the meaning of asylum law as a result of the transfer of the applicant to Germany.

2.10. Pursuant to Article 11, paragraph 5, of the Aliens Act the issue of a residence permit, including a provisional residence permit, may be refused on the grounds that this is not in the public interest.

2.11. In so far as Article 3 of the (European) Convention for the Protection of Human Rights and Fundamental Freedoms is invoked in the application of the applicant, this would not prevent the transfer of the applicant to Germany. Germany is also a party to the European Convention. It is up to Germany as the responsible State to determine

---

their applications, the State Secretary should nevertheless make use of Art. 3(4) when the occasion arises. This is the case for example where five months and four days have elapsed between the application for asylum and the claim request (the maximum period is stated in Art. 11(1) to be six months). When this is added to the period of three months and eleven days for the above-mentioned period between the claim agreement and decision, the total period is too long (*NAV* (1999) No. 114 with note by H. Tiemersma). Idem District Court of The Hague (sitting in Zwolle), 24 June 1999, *JV* (1999) No. 208 with note by R. Fernhout and *RV* (1999) No. 14 with note by B.P. Vermeulen. But see District Court of The Hague (sitting in Haarlem), 24 September 1999, *JV* (1999) No. 228 and District Court of The Hague, 29 October 1999, *RV* (1999) No. 17 with note by B.P. Vermeulen. District Court of The Hague (sitting in Zwolle) had previously held that where the period specified in Art. 11(5) – i.e., a month – was exceeded by nine months it was necessary to apply Art. 3(4) (judgment of 13 January 1999 (*NAV* (1999) No. 28 with note by H. den Haan). On 19 January 1999 the same District Court held that the total period between the asylum request and the transfer could not exceed six months (excluding the time taken by the requested State for consideration), (*JV* 1999) No. 79, *GV* No. 18b-24, see also article by H. Tiemersma 'Overeenkomst van Dublin, een onderonsje tussen staten?' [Convention of Dublin: a deal between States?], *NAV* (1999) pp. 257-264). The District Court changed its opinion towards this again in its above-mentioned judgment of 7 June 1999: the total period may exceed six months.

whether expulsion to the country of origin would be contrary to Article 3 of the European Convention.

2.12. There is also no evidence of grounds that would support a claim to the issue of a residence permit.

2.13. It follows from the above considerations that the requested remedy should be refused.

2.14. Since the president concluded after the examination in court that the principal case is clear and that further examination could not reasonably be expected to be of assistance in the assessment, a decision should be taken at the same time, pursuant to Article 33b of the Aliens Act, on the dismissal of the applications for admission.

2.15. The president has not seen any evidence of circumstances on the basis of which either party should be ordered to pay the other party's costs.'

III. Decision

The President:

— dismisses the application for provisional remedy;

— declares the objection to be unfounded ...'

2.01 CONFLICT BETWEEN SOURCES

See: 3.1141

2.2 CUSTOMARY LAW

See: 3.1141

2.3 GENERAL PRINCIPLES OF LAW

See: 4.52 (pp. 278-282); 8.23; 16.164

2.4 JUDICIAL DECISION AS SOURCE OF INTERNATIONAL LAW

See: 4.52 (pp. 278-282); 12.2704

2.5 OPINION OF WRITERS AS SOURCE OF INTERNATIONAL LAW

See: 3.1141; 4.52

2.72 ACTS AND DECISIONS OF INTERNATIONAL ORGANIZATIONS AS SOURCE OF INTERNATIONAL LAW

See: 4.52; 13.223; 16.164

3.11 FUNDAMENTAL RIGHTS AND DUTIES OF STATES

See: 5.26; 8.23

3.1141 IMMUNITY OF FOREIGN STATES
See also: 3.132; 16.164

A.I. Arias v. The Republic of Venezuela, District Court of The Hague, 4 February 1998, JAR (1998), No. 67, NIPR (1998) No. 238.

— Venezuela enjoys immunity from jurisdiction in respect of a labour dispute with a secretary employed at the Embassy in The Hague. The secretary had Argentinian nationality at the time she took up her employment in 1980, but also acquired Dutch nationality in 1987.
— This state immunity is not regulated in the Vienna Convention on Diplomatic Relations of 1961.[16] *However, the preamble to the Convention does indicate that the rules of customary international law should continue to govern questions not expressly regulated by the Convention.*
— It can be inferred from international provisions and draft provisions, including the European Convention on State Immunity of 1972[17]*, the International Law Commission* draft of 1986[18] *and the International Law Association draft of Montreal (1982)*[19] *that a foreign state cannot claim immunity in respect of the present kind of disputes, unless the employee concerned is neither a national of the host country at the time when the employment contract is entered into nor permanently resident in the receiving country. This situation arises in the present case.*
— This is not altered by the fact that for practical and financial reasons the person concerned cannot submit the dispute to the courts in Venezuela. Moreover, her access to the Venezuelan courts is assured in view of statements by Venezuela.

The Facts: A. was employed as a secretary in the Embassy of Venezuela in The Hague from 15 April 1980 onwards, where she was a member of the clerical staff. She was born in Argentina and obtained dual nationality in 1987 when she became a naturalised Dutch national. She was dismissed on 1 September 1995. She then issued a writ of summons against Venezuela before Sub-District Court of The Hague and claimed payment of a substantial sum of money on account of irregular and manifestly unreasonable dismissal, as well as an adequate pension provision. The judge of the Sub-District Court held that he lacked the jurisdiction to take cognizance of the application owing to the immunity from jurisdiction to which Venezuela was entitled (judgment of 28 November 1996).[20] A. appealed against this judgment to the District Court of The Hague.

Held: '... 4.2. In answering the present question it is necessary to state at the outset that, pursuant to Article 13a of the General Provisions of Legislation Act, the jurisdiction of the Dutch courts is limited by exceptions recognised in international law. The court would refer in this connection to the provisions of the Vienna Convention on Diplomatic

---

16. 500 *UNTS* p. 95; *Trb.* 1962 No. 101.
17. *ETS* No. 74; *Trb.* 1973 No. 43.
18. *ILM* (1987) p. 625; *ETS* No. 74. For the final draft of 1991 see 30 *ILM* (1991) p. 1565.
19. *ILA Report of the Sixtieth Conference,* Montreal, 1982, p. 325 et seq. For the amended draft of 1994 see *ILR Report of the Sixty-Sixth Conference*, Buenos Aires, 1994, p. 488.
20. Reported for the most part in *NIPR* (1998) No. 238.

Relations of 18 April 1961, to which both Venezuela and the Netherlands are a party. Venezuela ratified the Convention on 16 March 1965. The Netherlands approved the Convention by Act of 11 April 1984 (Stb. 147). It must, moreover, be assumed that the content of the Convention reflects the present state of international customary law. The fact that the Convention came into force for the Netherlands after the date on which A. entered the employ of the Embassy of Venezuela does not therefore detract in the present case from the validity of the rules contained in the Convention.

4.3. It has to be granted to A. that application of the rules included in this Convention does not of itself warrant the conclusion that Venezuela is entitled to claim immunity from jurisdiction. The Convention itself makes no provision about this. However, the preamble to the Convention does indicate that the rules of customary international law should continue to govern questions not expressly regulated by the provisions of the Convention.

4.4. As regards the substance of the generally held views on public international law and of the rules of international customary law, the court would refer first of all to the European Convention on State Immunity of 16 May 1972 (which is not directly applicable in the present case), to the draft arrangement concerning Jurisdictional Immunities of States and their Property of July 1986 (26 ILM (1987) 625), drawn up in the context of the United Nations, and also to the Draft Articles for a Convention on State Immunity of the International Law Association Report of the Sixtieth Conference of Montreal. The court assumes that the current views are recorded in these treaty texts and draft treaty texts. In all of these international treaty texts and draft treaty texts a foreign State may not claim immunity in respect of disputes that result from relations entered into under labour law by the foreign state in the host country, save in cases where the employee concerned is neither a national of the host country nor permanently resident in the receiving country at the time when the employment contract is concluded.

4.5. It follows from the above that what is of primary importance in answering the question whether Venezuela can claim immunity from jurisdiction in the present case is whether A. was a Dutch national or already permanently resident in the Netherlands at the time when the employment contract was concluded, i.e., on 15 April 1980. The court assumes in this connection, as did the Sub-District Court, that permanent residence in the above-mentioned sense must be taken to mean residence with a legal status.

4.6. It is not disputed that A. had Argentinian and not Dutch nationality on the said date. Venezuela has also expressly contended that A. was not permanently resident in the Netherlands at that time, and has referred in this connection to the said letter of 14 July 1980 mentioned in finding of law 4.1 and the note made on this, showing that the Embassy notified the [Dutch] Ministry of Foreign Affairs that A. had arrived in the Netherlands on 15 May 1980. As against this, A. has merely submitted that she had been in the Netherlands for a few months before taking up her employment, without submitting that this residence was of a permanent nature in the above-mentioned sense and also without explaining and properly substantiating her position on this point, although this would have been an obvious course of action for her in view of the considerations of the Sub-District Court judge on this point. Nor is it possible to find any evidence in the statements of D. Smittenaar-Aponte and A.I. Fiege-van Merrebach (exhibits 12 and 13 with the statement of defence in the interim counterclaim) to support the view that there was permanent residence in the Netherlands prior to the entry into employment. Moreover, the entry in the Population Register of The Hague on 20

November 1995 does not support her submission. Clearly, she was not entered in the register previously, for example in 1980. Under these circumstances the Court will disregard this submission and need not formulate an instruction to adduce proof.

4.7. The Court considers in this connection that it is also of importance that, according to the documents in the action, on the basis of the above particulars known at the time when she took up her employment, A. enjoyed the privileges of diplomatic status: at the request of the Embassy she was supplied in 1980 and again in 1992 by the Dutch Ministry of Foreign Affairs with an identity card for people in foreign diplomatic service and did not pay any tax or social security contributions until the time of her dismissal. Under Article 37 of the Vienna Convention, members of the administrative staff of a mission enjoy such privileges only if they are not nationals of or permanently resident in the receiving State. The Court would also observe in this connection that even after A. acquired Dutch nationality in 1987 she continued to enjoy the privileges of diplomatic status.

4.8. In view of the above, the Court is also of the opinion that Venezuela is entitled to claim immunity from jurisdiction. Contrary to what A. contends in the notes on her third ground of appeal, it follows, in the view of the Court, that it is no longer important whether Venezuela acted as a government body (*acta iure imperii*) or as a private person (*acta iure gestionis*) in dismissing A., since the granting of immunity is not dependent on this in the present situation.

4.9. The submission by A. in her fourth ground of appeal that she is unable for practical and financial reasons to submit the dispute to the courts in Venezuela must be disregarded by the Court "quite apart from whether the submission is correct" since it cannot result in a situation in which Venezuela can no longer claim immunity from jurisdiction. As regards her submission that there is no forum for her claim in Venezuela, the Court considers that, in view of the statements made in this respect by the Republic of Venezuela, it must be assumed that A.'s access to the Venezuelan courts is assured on the basis of the legislation mentioned by the Sub-District Court judge in his judgment.

4.10. Since the grounds of appeal of A. cannot succeed, the Court will uphold the judgment of the Sub-District Court judge. A. will be ordered to bear the costs of these proceedings as the party held to be in the wrong ...'[21]

State of the Netherlands v. Azeta BV, District Court of Rotterdam, 14 May 1998, KG (1998) No. 251, NIPR (1999) No. 88.

— Establishing, maintaining and running embassies is an essential part of the function of government and hence of the public service. Moneys intended for the performance of this function must therefore be treated as property intended for the public service.

— The statements of the deputy Chilean Foreign Minister and the Chilean Embassy in The Hague to the effect that the credit balances attached in the possession of ABN-AMRO Bank are used for the functioning of the Embassy are sufficient evidence that the moneys are intended for Chile's public service.

---

21. A. appealed in cassation against this judgment to the Supreme Court. Venezuela did not thereafter respond to calls for procedural action. The parties finally decided to settle the matter out of court, after which the appeal was struck out on 15 October 1999.

— *As Azeta has failed to show that this is not the case, Chile is entitled to immunity from execution. Chile cannot be required to provide further information about the nature and purpose of the credit balances. This would amount to an unacceptable interference in the internal affairs of the Embassy.*
— *Since greater importance should be attributed to the rules of international law than to the rules of Dutch law and Dutch procedure, the interests of the uninterrupted functioning of a diplomatic mission should in this case prevail over the interests of executing a judgment given in the Netherlands.*
— *The State of the Netherlands is entitled to act since it has its own interest in preventing infringements of the immunity of diplomatic missions established in its territory.*

The Facts: On 24 April 1998 Azeta arranged for the credit balances of the Chilean Embassy in an account at ABN-AMRO Bank in Amsterdam to be attached by way of execution of a judgment against Chile. The attachment involved the execution of a judgment given by the District Court of Rotterdam on 5 December 1984 under which Chile was ordered to pay an amount of NLG 15,000,000.[22] After the Bank had informed the Chilean ambassador of the attachment, he lodged a protest with the Dutch Ministry of Foreign Affairs. The ambassador demanded that the Minister take steps to arrange for termination of the attachment on the ground of the Netherlands' obligation under international law to maintain the immunity of the diplomatic mission of Chile from attachment. As the Ministry did not respond immediately, Chile applied to the District Court on 6 May for an interim injunction ordering termination of the attachment. Only after the Netherlands had indicated on 11 May that it would apply for an interim injunction to secure termination of the attachment did Chile withdraw its own application for an interim injunction.[23]

Held: '... 2.2. The plaintiff is now applying for termination of the above-mentioned attachment by way of execution and an order that the defendant be ordered to pay the costs of the action.

The plaintiff has submitted in this connection that the attachment infringes the immunity from attachment which the Republic of Chile enjoys in respect of property such as the funds in the present case, which are intended for the public service. This would amount to a situation which is contrary to the international obligations to which the State (the plaintiff) is subject under international law, as recorded, *inter alia*, in the Vienna Convention on Diplomatic Relations ... The plaintiff submits that it therefore has an urgent interest in claiming termination of this attachment under Article 438 of the Code of Civil Procedure.

2.3. In disputing the submissions of the plaintiff, the defendant has submitted reasoned arguments, including the contention that the attachment is not contrary to the obligations to which the plaintiff is subject under international law since it is not clear

22. 17 *NYIL* (1986) pp. 256-257.

23. It was not until 30 July 1998 that Chile issued a writ of summons against Azeta in the proceedings for an objection to the 1984 default judgment. These proceedings were still under way when this case was being dealt with (5 July 2000).

whether the attached moneys are intended for the public service. The defendant has also alleged that the immunity of a foreign State may not be at the expense of the protection which Dutch companies receive from their government or at the expense of the immunity of the Dutch administration of justice.

3. The assessment

3.1. As the parties are agreed that the plaintiff is entitled to act in this matter since it has its own interest in preventing infringements of the immunity from attachment of diplomatic missions established in its territory, this will be taken as the basis of the assessment.

3.2. The starting point in this dispute is that – pursuant to (unwritten) international law – a foreign State is entitled to immunity from execution when execution measures are employed against the State concerned involving the attachment of property intended for the public service of that State. Establishing, maintaining and running embassies is an essential part of the function of government and hence of the public service. Moneys intended for the performance of this function must therefore be treated as property intended for the public service.

In the present case the defendant denies that (all) bank balances which it has caused to be attached are intended for the functioning of the Chilean Embassy. The plaintiff has lodged in this connection a letter of 8 May 1998 from the deputy Foreign Minister of the Republic of Chile and a "note verbale" from the Chilean Embassy in The Hague of 11 May 1998, in which it is stated that the credit balances in the attached bank account are intended for the running of the Chilean Embassy.

Contrary to what the defendant has alleged in this connection, the President considers that these statements are sufficient in this case to support the assumption that the present moneys are intended for the public service of the Republic of Chile.

It was up to the defendant to adduce evidence of facts and/or circumstances to support its submission that this was not the case. As the defendant has failed to do so, and as such facts and/or circumstances have not become known in any other way either, the Republic of Chile is – in view of the above – in principle entitled to claim immunity from execution.[24] The defendant wrongly demands that the Chilean Embassy should provide more detailed information about the nature and scope of the bank balances held by it, since this would entail an unacceptable interference under international law in the internal affairs of this mission. The defendant's submission that the State of the

---

24. The District Court of Amsterdam applied comparable reasoning in the case of *E.A. Sodipo* v. *ABN-AMRO Bank* in which Sodipo's application to attach the credit balances of the bank accounts of the Embassy of Nigeria by way of execution of judgment was refused. The District Court based its decision on a declaration of the Embassy, lodged by the Bank, in which it was stated that the funds were intended 'for the day-to-day running of the Embassy' (judgment of 24 February 1999, *NJ* (1999) No. 622, *NIPR* (1999) Bo. 42). The application for attachment was made in execution of a judgment of The Hague Sub-District Court of 24 April 1997, in which Nigeria was ordered by default to pay NLG 70,204 on account of the unlawful dismissal of Sodipo on account of arrears of salary and compensation. Sodipo, who had Dutch nationality, worked at the Embassy of Nigeria (Institute's Collection No. 4743). As Nigeria, which had been served with the writ of summons at the address of Republic of Nigeria in Lagos, did not enter an appearance, the District Court gave leave by interim judgment of 20 February 1997 for Nigeria to be served with the writ anew by accelerated procedure at the address of the Nigerian Embassy in The Hague. However, Nigeria did not enter an appearance at the hearing and a default judgment was therefore given against it.

Netherlands should also defend the interests of its national companies does not detract from the above.

3.3. The defence put forward by the defendant that recognition of the immunity from execution would jeopardise the immunity of Dutch administration of justice is rejected. Quite apart from whether such a general principle exists in [the Dutch] legal system, a higher importance should in principle be attached to the rules of international law than to the rules of Dutch law (in particular Dutch procedural law), with the result that the interests of the uninterrupted functioning of a diplomatic mission should in this case prevail over the interests of executing (by expeditious means) a judgment given in the Netherlands.

3.4. In view of the above, the requested relief will be granted and the defendant will be ordered to bear the costs of the action as the party held to be in the wrong.'

3.132 KINGDOM OF THE NETHERLANDS
See also: 1.204

L.M. v. the State of the Netherlands, the Minister for the Netherlands Antilles Affairs and Aruban Affairs, J.J.C. Voorhoeve and A. Koerten, Joint Court of Appeal of the Netherlands Antilles and Aruba, 20 January 1998, NIPR (1998) No. 250, KG (1998) No. 100.

— The State of the Netherlands is not entitled to rely on the rules of State immunity in proceedings before the Aruban courts. These rules, as contained for example in the European Convention on State Immunity of 1972, do not relate to the powers of the courts in respect of legal claims against countries within the same state constitution such as the Kingdom of the Netherlands.
— An immunity of this kind cannot be derived from the provisions of the Charter of the Kingdom of the Netherlands.

The Facts: Koerten, who lived in the Netherlands and was interim head of the Aruban Security Service, had drawn up a report on the instructions of the Minister for General Affairs of Aruba and the Minister for Netherlands Antilles Affairs and Aruban Affairs, Mr J.J.C. Voorhoeve, on the security and integrity of Aruba. This secret but nonetheless leaked report contained passages stating that L.M., who was resident in Aruba, had engaged in money laundering. L.M. then instituted legal proceedings against the State of the Netherlands, the Minister for Netherlands Antilles Affairs and Aruban Affairs and Koerten before the Court of First Instance of Aruba, demanding the issue of a statement that they had no evidence that he had been involved in money laundering. The State of the Netherlands claimed, *inter alia*, immunity from jurisdiction. The Court of First Instance granted this claim and held that it lacked the jurisdiction to take cognizance of the claim against the State. It went on to hold that the claim against the Minister was not admissible since he had not acted as an organ of the State. The Court dismissed the claim against K., holding that he had not acted without due care (judgment of 16 July 1997).[25] L.M. appealed against this judgment to the Joint Court of Appeal of the Netherlands

25. Partly reproduced in *NIPR* (1998) No. 250.

Antilles and Aruba. The Joint Court of Appeal held that it had jurisdiction to hear the appeal against the State of the Netherlands, but went on to dismiss the application. In other respects, it upheld the judgment of the Court of First Instance.

Held: '... 4. Assessment

4.1. The third ground of appeal relates to the legal considerations in the appealed judgment which are based on the European Convention on State Immunity of 16 May 1972 (Trb. 1973, 43) and which led the Court of First Instance of Aruba to hold that it lacked jurisdiction to take cognizance of the claim against the State of the Netherlands.

4.2. This Convention is not in force in Aruba. In fact, it contains only rules of international jurisdiction law designed to give effect to the attempt to limit the cases in which a State in the international law sense can claim immunity before a foreign court. These rules do not relate to the powers of courts in respect of applications against countries within the same state constitution such as the Kingdom of the Netherlands. Nor are they suitable for application as principles of interregional jurisdiction law.

4.3. Article 41, para. 1, of the Charter of the Kingdom of the Netherlands provides that the Netherlands, the Netherlands Antilles and Aruba can regulate their internal affairs independently. The autonomy of the countries in representing their own interests in such matters does not, however, mean that a country is entitled to immunity in a civil dispute in which it becomes involved in one of the other countries. The Kingdom Act governing matters of private law of an interregional nature referred to in Article 38, paragraph 3, of the Charter, under which such immunity could be arranged, has not been concluded. Article 40 of the Charter provides that judgments given by a court in one of the countries may be enforced throughout the Kingdom. A judgment against a country other than the one where it has been given is not excepted from this, with the result that the possibility of enforcement or otherwise does not constitute a ground for assuming that an order cannot be made against a country in such a dispute by a court in another country ...'[26]

3.143 THE EFFECT OF STATE SUCCESSION

Lam Sau Hing v. B. et al., Court of Appeal of Arnhem, 3 March 1998, NJ (1998) No. 992, NIPR (1999) No. 79.

---

26. In the interim injunction proceedings brought by Aruba against the State of the Netherlands concerning the validity of the amendment of the 6th OCT Decision the Netherlands once again claimed that the court lacked jurisdiction to hear the case, referring in this instance to the fact that the Charter did not contain a provision for the resolution of disputes between the countries of the Kingdom. By judgment of 3 April 1998 the District Court of The Hague held that it lacked jurisdiction. AIt should be stated at the outset that this concerns what can best be described as an inter-State dispute, namely between Aruba and the State. Neither of these countries has accepted the jurisdiction of the national courts for the resolution of their disputes. If the national courts were to assume this power, it would be contrary to the principle of international law of immunity from jurisdiction in inter-State disputes. The Dutch courts therefore lack the international jurisdiction to take cognizance of this dispute and the claims of Aruba therefore founder on this ground alone.

— Until the transfer of sovereignty over Hong Kong by the United Kingdom to China on 1 July 1997, Article III of the Supplementary Convention between the Kingdom of the Netherlands and the Kingdom of Great Britain and Northern Ireland regarding Legal Proceedings[27] *prevented the granting of an application for the provision of security under Article 152 of the Dutch Code of Civil Procedure*[28] *against inhabitants of Hong Kong.*
— As China has not acceded to that Convention since that date or announced that it considers itself bound by it in relation to inhabitants of Hong Kong. the provisions of Article III of the Convention can no longer be invoked by them.

The Facts: In proceedings instituted by Lam Sau Hing, resident in Hong Kong, against B. et al., the latter claimed in an interim application that Lam Sau Hing should provide security under Article 152 of the Code of Civil Procedure.

Held: '… 3.1. In the absence of any rebuttal, it has been established between the parties that Lam, resident in Hong Kong in the People's Republic of China, is an alien within the meaning of Article 152 of the Code of Civil Procedure and that the plaintiffs have an interest in the application which they have made.

Until 1 July 1997 the Supplementary Convention between the Kingdom of the Netherlands and the Kingdom of Great Britain and Northern Ireland regarding Legal Proceedings, which took effect for the former British Crown Colony of Hong Kong on 22 April 1971, prevented the granting of such an application. It follows from Article III of that Convention, which applied, *inter alia*, to Hong Kong, that no security for costs or court fees could be required.

As a result of the transfer of sovereignty over Hong Kong by the United Kingdom on 1 July 1997, however, the situation is now different. As the People's Republic of China has not acceded to the Convention since that date or announced that it considers itself bound by it in relation to inhabitants of the former British Crown Colony of Hong Kong, the provisions of the Convention do not (at present) apply to Hong Kong.

What has been claimed by the plaintiffs in the interim application can therefore be granted as having not been disputed …'

3.2113 IMMUNITIES OF INTERNATIONAL ORGANISATIONS

Bausch Datacom B.V. v. the Benelux Trade Marks Office and Bausch Connect Services, District Court of The Hague, 12 May 1999, KG (1999) No. 150.

— Legal proceedings against the Benelux Trade Marks Office.

---

27. *Trb.* 1967 No. 196. Art. III reads: 'The nationals of one High Contracting Party shall not be obliged in the territories of the other High Contracting Party to give security for costs or court fees in any case where a national of the latter High Contracting Party would not be so obliged in similar circumstances.'

28. Art. 152 reads: 'All aliens, whether plaintiffs or third parties, must, at the request of the opposing party, give security for costs, damages and interest which might be awarded against them, before the opposing party is bound to answer the complaint.'

— Contrary to the provisions of Article 11C of the Uniform Benelux Act on Trade Marks of 1962[29] *in conjunction with Article 8 of the Implementing Regulation of 1995*[30]*, the Benelux Trade Marks Office failed to take adequate steps to ascertain the existence of an instrument regulating the transfer of the trade mark.*
— Order to the Benelux Trade Marks Office to cancel the registration. A periodic penalty [astreinte] need not be imposed since it may be assumed that the Trade Marks Office will automatically comply with the order.

The Facts: At the request of Bausch Connect Services (BCS) the Benelux Trade Marks Office registered the transfer of a number of trade marks to BCS by A.J. Bausch in the Benelux Register on 26 June 1998. Bausch had transferred these trade marks to BCS by agreement of 7 February 1997. After the Sub-District Court in Roermond had quashed on 24 July 1998 a decision given earlier that year granting the request of BCS for cancellation of the removal from the register of A.J. Bausch as executive director of Bausch Datacom, Bausch Datacom requested the Benelux Trade Marks Office to cancel the change in the name in which the marks were registered. In reply, the Trade Marks Office indicated that it would do this only on the basis of a court order addressed to it. Bausch Datacom thereupon issued a writ of summons against the Trade Marks Office and BCS before the District Court of The Hague requiring that the change of name be cancelled on pain of a periodic penalty [astreinte].

Held: '... *Assessment of the dispute.*

5. Pursuant to the provisions of Article 11C of the Uniform Benelux Act on Trade Marks in conjunction with Article 8 of the Implementing Regulation, the Benelux Trade Marks Office is required to ascertain the existence of an instrument regulating the alleged transfer of a trademark. Whether the instrument of transfer (or an extract from it) lodged for this purpose with the Trade Marks Office or a declaration relating to it had been signed by persons competent to represent the parties was not a matter to be decided by the Trade Marks Office, as was indeed acknowledged at the hearing by Bausch Datacom.

6. It has been established that Bausch Datacom was originally registered as the proprietor of the trade marks referred to in this legal action. As justification for its claims to these trade marks BCS relied in its correspondence with the Benelux Trade Marks Office on two separate transfers, namely a transfer dated 24 March 1994 from Bausch Datacom to A.J. Bausch and a transfer dated 7 February 1997 from A.J. Bausch to BCS. It has not been alleged or shown that a deed of transfer dated 24 March 1994 (or an extract from it) was at any time produced to the Benelux Trade Marks Office. The letter of 13 July 1998 cannot be regarded as such an instrument, nor as a declaration within the meaning of Article 11C of the Uniform Benelux Act on Trade Marks, since the letter was not signed on behalf of Bausch Datacom (and A.J. Bausch would no longer have been competent to do so at that time). Moreover, the declaration contained in that letter does not refer to a transfer in 1994 from Bausch Datacom to A.J. Bausch since, as the letter states, the words used were evidently Aremain vested in me in my personal capacity, which would be incompatible with such a transfer.

29. 704 *UNTS* p. 301; *Trb.* 1962 No. 58.
30. *Trb.* 1995 No. 294.

7. It must therefore be assumed for the time being that the Trade Marks Office did not correctly discharge its duty as contained in Article 11C of the Uniform Benelux Act on Trade Marks in conjunction with Article 8 of the Implementing Regulation by effectuating the change requested by BCS in the name in which the litigious trademarks were registered in the Benelux Register. The primary claim made against the Trade Marks Office at 1 above will therefore be granted, with the exception of the part relating to the penalty payment, since it may be assumed that the Office will automatically comply with the order ...'

3.213 LEGAL EFFECTS OF ACTS OF INTERNATIONAL ORGANISATIONS
See: 3.2113; 4.52; 13.223; 16.164

3.221 UNITED NATIONS
See: 4.52 (pp. 272-277); 13.223

3.221 UNITED NATIONS COMMITTEE AGAINST TORTURE
See: 12.28

3.221 UNITED NATIONS HIGH COMMISSIONER FOR REFUGEES
See: 4.52

3.222 BENELUX TRADE MARKS OFFICE
See: 3.2113

3.223 EUROPEAN UNION
See: 4.52 (pp. 278-282)

3.34 NON-AUTONOMOUS TERRITORIES
See: 3.143

4.1 NATIONALITY
See: 3.1141

4.31 ADMITTANCE OF ALIENS
See: 1.204 (pp. 257-261); 4.52; 5.26 (n. 59); 6.224; 8.2

4.32 PASSPORTS AND VISAS
See: 1.204 (pp. 254-257)

4.36 RIGHTS AND DUTIES OF ALIENS
See: 3.143; 8.2

4.52 REFUGEES
See also: 1.204 (pp. 257-261); 6.224; 12.28

A. v. State Secretary for Justice, District Court of The Hague, 2 July 1998, JV (1998) No. 135,[31] RV (1998) No. 10.[32]

— In its judgment of 12 April 1995 the District Court of The Hague identified three situations in which refusal of military service or desertion could result in refugee status, namely (a) disproportionate punishment, (b) conscientious objections based on deeply held beliefs, and (c) the wish not to become involved in military action that has been condemned by the international community or which is contrary to the fundamental standards that apply during an armed conflict or in which an alien is likely to be deployed against his own people or family.[33]
— Since the punishment of people of Kurdish origin who refuse military service in the Turkish armed forces does not differ from that of others who refuse that service the situation at (a) does not occur.
— Nor does the first situation described at (c) occur since there is no evidence that there has actually been condemnation by the international community of the military action in South-East Turkey on the ground that it is contrary to fundamental principles of humane behaviour or in breach of the fundamental standards that apply during an armed conflict. Such condemnation by the Security Council or the General Assembly of the UN has not been alleged or shown. Reliance on a resolution of a sub-committee of the UN, a resolution of the European Parliament and a statement of the Secretary-General of the UN must fail since they cannot be regarded as expressing the opinion of the international world community.
— The plaintiff did not wish to be deployed against his own people or family. This should be treated as a possible conscientious objection under (b). It is, after all, an example of a situation that could qualify under the Avalid reasons of conscience referred to in paragraph 170 of the UNHCR Handbook.
— However, not every deployment against one's own people or family would be sufficient for the granting of refugee status. Consideration must be given to all relevant factors, as

---

31. Note by T. Spijkerboer.

32. Note by R. Fernhout, summarised and discussed by B.P. Vermeulen in *NAV* (1998) p. 645. See also F. Lankers, 'Diepgewortelde band met eigen volk' [Strong bond with own people], *NAV* (1999) pp. 91-97.

33. *AB* (1995) No. 592 with note by T. Spijkerboer, *RV* (1995) No. 7, with note by B.P. Vermeulen, *NAV* (1995) p. 367, discussed on p. 302, *GV* No. 18d-7. The District Court based its decision on previous judgments of the Judicial Division of the Council of State and on paras. 168-172 of the UNHCR Handbook.

raised by the person concerned, the ultimate determinant being whether the bond with his own people and family is strong enough to allow his reasons of conscience to be a ground for refugee status.

The Facts: A., who was of Turkish nationality, applied on 16 September 1993 for admission as a refugee and for the granting of a residence permit on the grounds of compelling humanitarian reasons. The application was rejected on 14 October 1993. An application for reconsideration of the decision was also dismissed. A. then applied to the District Court of The Hague for a review of the decision and also for a provisional measure. He subsequently retracted the latter application when the State Secretary for Justice granted him a residence permit on 8 November 1996 on account of delay. In the proceedings before the District Court A. submitted that he feared problems on account of his Kurdish origin. In addition, he stated that he did not wish to obey the call-up for military service since he feared that he would be deployed against his own people, the Kurds, in South-East Turkey.

Held: '... 5. The Court finds as follows. Pursuant to Article 1 (A) of the Convention of Geneva relating to the status of refugees of 1951 (Trb. 1954, 88), as amended by the Protocol of New York of 1967 (Trb. 1967, 76)[34] and Article 15, paragraph 1, of the Aliens Act,[35] the term refugee is applicable if the person concerned comes from a country in which he has a well-founded fear of being persecuted on account of his religious or political beliefs or his nationality or for belonging to a particular race or to a particular social group.

6. It should be said at the outset that the general situation in Turkey is not such that people from this country and belonging to the Kurdish population group can automatically be treated as refugees. The plaintiff must therefore make out a plausible case that the facts and circumstances of his personal situation are such that he has a well-founded fear of persecution within the meaning of refugee law.

7. In the view of the Court, the plaintiff has not succeeded in making out a plausible case that he has reason to fear persecution on account of the political activities alleged by him.

[...]

8. As regards the plaintiff's submissions concerning his refusal to do military service in Turkey, the Court finds as follows.

8.1. First of all, it is necessary to determine whether the plaintiff has made out a plausible case that he was called up for military service in Turkey and is listed there as having evaded conscription.

[...]

9. Since a plausible case has been made that plaintiff is treated in Turkey as a person who has evaded conscription or as a deserter, the case should be assessed by reference to the criteria formulated by the Aliens Law Uniform Application Chamber in the judgment concerning C. of 12 April 1995 (no. 94/12 134, *NAV* April 1995, no. 4). In that judgment it was held that a person who evades conscription or a deserter is a refugee if (a) he has a

---

34. 189 *UNTS* p. 137; *Trb.* 1951 No. 131, amended by Protocol of 31 January 1967, 606 *UNTS* p. 267; *Trb.* 1967 No. 76. For the text of Art. 1(a) see *infra* n. 45.

35. For the text of Art. 15(1) see *infra* n. 46.

well-founded fear, on account of his race, religion, nationality, membership of a particular social group or political persuasion, of disproportionate or discriminatory punishment or implementation of the punishment for his refusal to do military service or if he has a well-founded fear, on account of one or more of the reasons referred to at the start of this category, of other discriminatory treatment or of excessive punishment or implementation of a punishment; (b) his refusal is based on serious and insuperable conscientious objections based on his religion or other deeply held convictions that compel him to refuse military service, and there is no possibility in his country of origin of performing non-military service as a replacement for military service; (c) he has evaded conscription or has deserted because he does not wish to become involved in a military action (of any kind) which has been condemned by the international community as being contrary to the fundamental principles of human behaviour or which is in breach of the fundamental standards that apply during an armed conflict. This also applies if he has decided to desert or refuse military service because he has a well-founded fear of being deployed against his own people or family.

[...]

10. The Court finds as follows.

10.1. Even in cases in which a person invokes the consequences of evading conscription but does not apply for admission as a refugee (this is the situation in a number of the joined cases) the matter should, in the view of the Court – as held in the judgment dated 21 March 1997[36] – be assessed by reference to the criteria formulated by the Aliens Law Uniform Application Chamber in the judgment concerning C. This is subject to the proviso that where these criteria are fulfilled in these cases, a residence permit will, in principle, be granted (without limitations).

10.2. As regards the category referred to at (a) in the judgment of the Aliens Law Uniform Application Chamber concerning C., the Court finds "as in the judgment dated 21 March 1997" that it cannot be inferred either from the official communications of the Ministry of Foreign Affairs or from the documents lodged on behalf of the plaintiff that punishment of people of Kurdish origin who refuse military service in the Turkish armed forces differs from that of others who refuse such service. This alone means, therefore, that the plaintiff cannot be brought within this category.

10.3. As regards the category referred to at (c) in the judgment of the Aliens Law Uniform Application Chamber concerning C., the District Court finds as follows. The Court has not seen any evidence in the present case that the military action in South-East Turkey has actually been condemned by the international community for being contrary to the fundamental principles of humane behaviour or in breach of the fundamental standards that apply during an armed conflict.[37] The Court does not agree with the position taken by the defendant that condemnation by the international community can be said to exist only in the case of condemnation by the Security Council of the UN. A recommendation by the General Assembly of the UN too could be treated as condemnation of this kind. It has not been alleged or shown that the actions of the Turkish army in South-East Turkey have been condemned by the Security Council or the General Assembly of the UN. The plaintiff's reliance on a resolution of a sub-committee

36. *GV* No. 18e-28, discussed by N. Hoogenberk in *NAV* (1997) p. 339.

37. In the cited judgment of 12 April 1995 the same view was taken in respect of Armenia in the context of the conflict in Nagorno Karabach.

of the UN, a resolution of the European Parliament[38] and a declaration of the Secretary-General of the UN[39] must fail because the Court cannot regard these expressions as reflecting the opinion of the international community in the above-mentioned sense. To this extent too, the plaintiff's application fails. Since, as indicated below under 10.4, the Court will assess the criterion of 'deployment against one's own people' as a form of conscientious objection, it sees this as a reason for classifying it under ground (b) of the judgment of the Aliens Law Uniform Application Chamber concerning C.

10.4. As regards the category referred to at (b) in the judgment of the Aliens Law Uniform Application Chamber concerning C., the Court finds that it has not been shown plausibly that plaintiff refused his military service because he has serious and insuperable conscientious objections on the basis of his religious convictions. The plaintiff has indicated that he refused military service only because he did not wish to fight against his own population group. Refusal of military service on account of a well-founded fear of being deployed against one's own people or family can, in the view of the Court, constitute a ground for refugee status. The criterion of 'deployment against one's own people' can be regarded as constituting a 'valid reason of conscience' as referred to in paragraph 170 of the UNHCR Handbook. In its letter of 27 March 1998 on the subject the UNHCR states as follows:

"UNHCR takes the view that valid reasons of conscience to refuse to participate in an armed conflict include not only those relating to the persons political, religious or moral convictions, but may also included those stemming from person's inner and profound feelings of attachment to a group. Membership in an ethnic group is, therefore, the relevant factor to be considered. Mere membership is not, however, sufficient to establish that the person has valid reasons of conscience to refuse to participate in a military action. Each claim must be examined in the light of all relevant factors. Careful consideration of the person's background and experiences is essential to determine whether the bond that exists between the person and the group is strong enough to provide credibility to the person's claimed conscientious objection."[40]

In view of the position of the UNHCR, the Court takes as the criterion that deployment against one's own people or family is not of itself sufficient for recognition as a refugee, but that account must also be taken of all relevant factors concerning the alien, as submitted by him, the ultimate determinant being whether the bond of the alien with his own people or family is strong enough to allow his reasons of conscience to be treated as a ground for refugee status. The Court notes that the defendant has not assessed the question whether the plaintiff's bond with the Kurdish people is so strong that the plaintiff can therefore be regarded as a conscientious objector (and hence as a refugee). The Court rejects the submission of the defendant that "profound feelings of attachment to a group" can never cover solidarity with the Kurdistan Workers' Party (PKK). It is, after all, common knowledge that the supporters of the PKK in South-East Turkey are only people of Kurdish origin. The PKK supporters are fighting for Kurdish interests as they see them. In these circumstances, solidarity with the PKK and its political objectives can certainly play a role in the question whether there is a strong bond with the Kurdish population group. Nor does the Court agree with the defendant's

38. Dated 17 July 1997.
39. Dated 14 May 1997.
40. Letter to P.J. van Krieken attached as a file document to the judgment.

submission that the activities of the Turkish army against the PKK can never constitute deployment against one's own people, because the struggle between the Turkish army and the PKK has major repercussions for the civilian population in South-East Turkey. For example, the Turkish army has evacuated and burned down a large number of villages in the Kurdish region (for reasons of military strategy), thereby depriving the local population of their means of existence. In other villages in the Kurdish region young men are forced to act as village watches, which involves using them to inform on PKK activities and on people who assist the PKK. In general, the armed struggle between the Turkish army and the PKK over a period of many years has resulted in an atmosphere of intimidation and violence, from which the Kurdish civilian population too has suffered to a serious extent. As a result, Kurds who are called up for military service may be deployed as soldiers against civilians in the Kurdish region. In the view of the Court, there can in these circumstances be said to be deployment against one's own people.

10.5. For an assessment of whether the alien concerned has a well-founded fear of being deployed against his own people or family, it is also important to determine what likelihood there is of a Kurdish conscript from South-East Turkey having to perform his military service in that part of Turkey and being deployed there in the armed struggle. The District Court holds as follows in this respect.

Since the judgment of the three-judge section of the District Court of The Hague of 21 March 1997 (AWB 95/7581 VRWET), in which it was held that, in view of the official report of the Minister for Foreign Affairs of 2 July 1996, there was little likelihood of the plaintiff being deployed against his own people, counsel for the plaintiff in that case produced information showing that the likelihood could no longer be said to be small. As a result of this information, it has been held in the majority of judgments since that date that in view of the information that has become available it is the duty of the defendant to make inquiries in this respect and to take a reasoned position (see for example the judgment of the District Court of The Hague, sitting in Zwolle, of 29 August 1997, AWB 96/7745 VRWET and 96/11 799 VRWET).

[...]

In the opinion of the Court, it is still not possible to say with certainty how great is the chance that a Kurdish conscript from South-East Turkey would have to perform his military service in that part of Turkey. The conclusion of the Minister for Foreign Affairs in his official report of 27 March 1998 on this point is that "in view of the above, there seems to be a growing likelihood that young Kurdish men will be deployed as members of the Turkish Armed Forces in South-East Turkey." In view of the information generally known to the Court about the armed conflict in South-East Turkey, it has become plausible that if a conscript is posted to South-East Turkey there is a real likelihood that he will also be deployed in the armed conflict. The defendant has indicated at the hearing that the extent of this likelihood is still being investigated. The Court believes that the defendant's assertion that the conscript must show that he will actually be posted in South-East Turkey and deployed in the armed conflict is too far-reaching. It is evident from the above description of the actual induction into military service that it becomes clear only at the last moment where a conscript will be posted. The Court also holds, *ex abundantia*, that if the inquiries still being made by the defendant do not yield any substantial information rebutting the positions taken by the plaintiff in this respect, the Court does not consider in advance that these positions are insufficient to support the contention that there is a real likelihood that Kurdish conscripts may be posted to South-east Turkey and deployed there in the armed conflict.

11. On the basis of the above, the Court is of the opinion that in preparing the disputed decision the defendant failed to gather the necessary information about the relevant facts and the interests to be weighed, as referred to in Article 3:2 of the General Administrative Law Act. Nor is the disputed decision based in all respects on proper reasoning as referred to in Article 7:12 of the General Administrative Law Act. The Court will therefore declare the application for review to be well-founded and quash the disputed decision ...'

A. v. State Secretary for Justice, District Court of The Hague (Aliens Law Uniform Application Chamber) 27 August 1998 No. 157,[41] NAV (1998) p. 806,[42] AB (1998) No. 398,[43] GV No. 18d-29.[44]

— *The texts of Article 1A(2) of the Convention of Geneva relating to the Status of Refugees*[45] *and Article 15(1) of the Aliens Act*[46] *do not warrant the conclusion that there cannot be persecution within the meaning of refugee law if the persecution is by third parties and no protection can be afforded against it because there is a complete lack of actual government authority in the relevant area. Nor can such a conclusion be inferred from the history of the Refugee Convention.*

— *In view of the object and scope of the Refugee Convention of 1951 – i.e., the provision of protection to people who will have a well-founded fear of persecution in their country of origin on account of one or more of the grounds of persecution referred to in Article 1A (2) and who are unable to obtain protection or sufficient protection in that country – there is no reason to refuse such protection in this situation.*

— *In view of the preamble to Article 35 of the Convention*[47]*, one of the functions of the*

41. Note by B.P. Vermeulen.

42. Note by H. Tiemersma.

43. Note by I. Sewandono.

44. Also reported in GV No. 18d-30.

45. Art. 1(A), at 2, of the Convention relating to the Status of Refugees reads: 'The term refugee shall apply to any person who [...] (2) as a result of events occurring before 1 January 1951 and owing to a well-founded fear of being persecuted for reasons of race, religion, nationality, membership of a particular social group or political opinion, is outside the country of his nationality and is unable or, owing to such fear, is unwilling to avail himself of the protection of that country; or who, not having a nationality and being outside the country of his former habitual residence as a result of such events, is unable or, owing to such fear, unwilling to return to it.'

46. Art. 15, para. 1, of the Aliens Act reads: 'Aliens originating from a country where they have a well-founded fear of persecution because of their religious or political opinion or their nationality, or because they belong to a certain race or to a certain social group, may request Our Minister to grant them admission as a refugee.'

47. The relevant passage of the preamble reads: 'Noting that the United Nations High Commissioner for Refugees is charged with the task of supervising international conventions providing for the protection of refugees, and recognising that the effective coordination of measures taken to deal with this problem will depend on the cooperation of States with the High Commissioner.' Art. 31 reads: '1. The Contracting States undertake to cooperate with the Office of the United Nations High Commissioner for Refugees, or any other agency of the United Nations which may succeed it, in the exercise of its functions, and shall in particular facilitate its duty of supervising the application of the

UNHCR is to ensure the correct application of the provisions of the Refugee Convention. It is therefore important, among other things, that UNHCR sees no reason to make the answer to the question whether persecution should be dependent on the presence of some form of government authority (the UNHCR applies in this connection the general principles of interpretation as codified in Article 31 of the Vienna Convention on Treaties of 1969).[48]

— A different view cannot be defended by citing the practice in some Member States of the European Union, the Joint Position of the EU of 4 March 1996[49] *or objections of a practical nature.*

— It follows that the question whether and, if so, from what date and in what regions forms of government authority once again exist in Somalia can be disregarded.

—The text of Article 1A (2) does not preclude the fact that where no government authority exists, protection may be afforded by parties other than the State, provided that such protection can be described as effective and lasting in relation to the feared persecution. Whether this is so must be decided individually from case to case.

The Facts: A., who was of Somalian nationality, applied for admission as a refugee on 29 April 1993. This request was refused. However, he was granted a residence permit valid for one year. A. then requested reconsideration of the decision refusing him admission as a refugee. The State Secretary for Justice dismissed this request on 31 March 1994. A.'s application for review to the District Court of The Hague (sitting in Haarlem) was held to be well-founded, and the State Secretary was directed to decide on the case anew (judgment of 2 June 1995). On 25 November 1997 the State Secretary once again dismissed the application for reconsideration (following the recommendation of the Advisory Committee on Aliens Affairs). A. then applied a second time to the District Court of The Hague (sitting in Haarlem) for review of the decision. The District Court referred the case to its own Aliens Law Uniform Application Chamber. This was done because of the judgment of the Administrative Law Division of the Council of State of 6 November 1995, in which it was held that if there was no government authority in the country of origin, there could be no persecution within the meaning of Article 1A(2) of the Refugee Act and Article 15(1) of the Aliens Act.[50] This decision was later narrowed in a judgment of 19 March 1997 to a situation in which any form of

---

provisions of this Convention.'

48. 8 *ILM* (1969) p. 679, *Trb.* 1972 No. 51. Art. 31 reads: '1. A treaty shall be interpreted in good faith in accordance with the ordinary meaning to be given to the terms of the treaty in their context and in the light of its object and purpose. 2. The context for the purpose of the interpretation of a treaty shall comprise, in addition to the text, including its preamble and annexes: (a) any agreement relating to the treaty which was made between all the parties in connection with the conclusion of the treaty; (b) any instrument which was made by one or more parties in connection with the conclusion of the treaty and accepted by the other parties as an instrument related to the treaty. 3. There shall be taken into account, together with the context: (a) any subsequent agreement between the parties regarding the interpretation of the treaty or the application of its provisions; (b) any subsequent practice in the application of the treaty which establishes the agreement of the parties regarding its interpretation; (c) any relevant rules of international law applicable in the relations between the parties. 4. A special meaning shall be given to a term if it is established that the parties so intended.'

49. *OJ* (1996) No. L63/2.

50. 28 *NYIL* (1997) pp. 353-354.

government authority was absent in the region concerned.[51] The State Secretary had conformed to this view in his policy.

Held: '... 9. The first question which arises is, in the opinion of the Court, whether there cannot be persecution within the meaning of the Refugee Convention if the persecution is by third parties and no protection can be afforded against it because there is a complete lack of actual government authority in the relevant area.

10. The Court is of the opinion that neither the text of Article 1A, opening words, and 2 of the Refugee Convention nor the text of Article 15, paragraph 1, of the Aliens Act warrants the conclusion that there cannot be persecution in the above-mentioned sense if the persecution is by third parties and no protection can be afforded against it because there is a complete lack of actual government authority in the relevant area.

Nor can such a conclusion be inferred from the history of the Refugee Convention.

In view of the object and scope of the Refugee Convention, i.e., the provision of protection to people who have a well-founded fear of persecution in their country of origin on account of one or more of the specified grounds of persecution and are unable to obtain protection or sufficient protection in that country, there is no reason to refuse such protection because of a lack of actual government authority in the country.

11. In view of the preamble and Article 35, paragraph 1, of the Refugee Convention, one of the functions of the UNHCR is to ensure the correct application of the provisions of the Refugee Convention. For this reason the Court considers it important, among other things, that UNHCR sees no reason for the answer to the question whether persecution exists to be dependent on the presence of some form of actual government authority.

The Court refers in particular to the following passages in the UNHCR Position Paper with regard to Persecution by Non-State Agents, of 30 January 1996: "2. There is nothing in the wording of Article 1A of the 1951 Convention to indicate that persons who fear persecution otherwise than by state authorities should be excluded from refugee status (...) 3. The general principles of interpretation, as codified in Article 31 of the Vienna Convention on the Law of Treaties, require a treaty to be interpreted in accordance with the ordinary meaning to be given to its terms in their context and in the light of the treaty's object and purpose. The ordinary meaning of the term 'persecution', as explained above, is that it embraces all persecutory acts irrespective of whether or not the complicity of the State is involved. Moreover, the object and purpose of the 1951 Convention is to ensure that individuals who have a well-founded fear of persecution on the grounds enumerated in the Convention be granted international protection as a substitute for the, lacking, national protection. Having regard to these considerations, a restricted interpretation, according to which individuals fleeing from the threat of persecution by non-State agents would be excluded from refugee status, would be clearly contrary to the object and purpose of the 1951 Convention. (...) In the opinion of the UNHCR, the preambular text of the European Union Joint Position on the harmonised application of the definition of the term "refugee" allows the Member States to differ in the practice of refugee law and does not necessarily oblige them to follow the application of Article 1A of Germany or France to its full extent. In the opinion of the UNHCR, the interpretation of the Administrative Law Division of the Council of State undermines one of the basic principles of refugee law and may result in the denial of refugee status to

51. 29 *NYIL* (1998) pp. 259-262.

those who, according to the objective and spirit of the 1951 Refugee Convention, are in need of international protection."

The representative in London of the UNHCR repeated this position at the hearing.

12. The Court would observe that the case-law of the Administrative Law Division of the Council of State was entirely in accordance with the stated position of the UNHCR until the judgment of 6 November 1995. In the view of the Court, there is no convincing reason for holding that this position of the UNHCR, which – as held above – is not in breach of the text, object and scope of the Refugee Convention, is incorrect. Such a reason cannot, in the view of the Court, be that administrative law bodies and/or the executive in some Member States of the European Union exclude refugee status if State authority is lacking in the country of origin. After all, in other Member States of the European Union no specific requirements are made in respect of the existence of forms of actual government authority when determining whether there can be refugee status in the above-mentioned sense. The Court refers in this connection to the report entitled 'Persecution by Third Parties' by B. Vermeulen, T. Spijkerboer, K. Zwaan and R. Fernhout, Catholic University of Nijmegen, May 1998, which has been lodged by both parties.

Nor can the Joint Position on harmonised application of the definition of the term "refugee" in Article 1 of the Refugee Convention (OJ L 63/2) as adopted by the Council of the European Union on 4 March 1996 be treated as such a reason. It is important in the first place in this connection that the Joint Position literally states that this has been adopted within the limits of the constitutional powers of the Government of the Member States; it does not bind the legislative bodies and does not affect the decisions of the judicial bodies of the Member States.

Furthermore, the Court would point out that some 130 States are now parties to the Refugee Convention, and it is not likely that the Joint Position in the broadest sense is endorsed by the States that are not members of the European Union. It is, incidentally, evident from the current rulings of the defendant that although the defendant has in fact acquiesced in the present view of the Administrative Law Division of the Council of State, he still assesses the substantive merits of each application for admission as a refugee.

Finally, any practical objections to the acceptance of the position of the UNHCR also provide insufficient reason for abandoning this position, which was also the position taken by the defendant until 6 November 1995.

On the contrary, the Court considers that there are practical objections to the application of the position taken by the defendant since 6 November 1995, in keeping with the judgment of the Administrative Law Division. The Court holds as follows in this connection. The question whether or not actual government authority (or any form of such authority) exists is a question of fact. Where the situation in a country is sharply fluctuating and unstable the answer to this question may vary over a short space of time depending on whether the instability increases or decreases. If it were to be assumed that refugee status could exist only where actual government authority (or any form of such authority) exists, this would mean that in the course of a asylum procedure persecution within the meaning of the Refugee Convention could exist at certain times and not at other times.

13. As a consequence of findings of law Nos. 10, 11 and 12 the question whether

and, if so, from what date and in what regions forms of government authority once again exist in Somalia can be disregarded.

14. If the persecution is by third parties and no protection is afforded by State authorities because they do not exist, the question should still be answered whether refugee status would nonetheless exist if protection were to be afforded by parties other than the government authorities.

15. The Court is of the opinion that the text of Article 1A, opening words and 2, of the Refugee Convention does not exclude the possibility that, whether there are no government authorities, protection may be afforded by parties other than such authorities. The article refers to protection by the country of the alien's nationality, which is broader than protection by the state authorities. In addition, the notion of protection in the Refugee Convention means that protection by persons other than the State authorities may be sufficient provided that such protection can be considered to be effective and lasting in relation to the feared persecution. Whether this is so must be decided individually from case to case. As regards the view of the defendant that rejected asylum-seekers from Somalia are, in general (with the exception of the categories of Somali nationals referred to in the official communication of 9 January 1997), no longer eligible for a provisional residence permit because their safety in their clan area is sufficiently guaranteed, the Court would observe that this does not necessarily mean that a Somali asylum-seeker who has made out a plausible case that he fears persecution by a hostile clan always receives in his own clan area or sub-clan area the effective and lasting protection to which he is entitled under the Refugee Convention

Individual assessment

16. The Court is of the opinion that the general and human rights situation in Somalia gives cause for concern, but not to such an extent that asylum-seekers from Somalia are automatically entitled to refugee status. Nor is the mere fact that an asylum-seeker comes from Somalia or belongs to the Darod clan in Somalia a circumstance that in itself creates a presumption that a legal ground for admission as a refugee exists.

In order to claim refugee status successfully, plaintiff must therefore make out a plausible case that the facts and circumstances of his personal situation are such that he has a justified fear of persecution within the meaning of refugee law ...

The Uniform Law Application Chamber did not consider these facts and circumstances to have been proved. It therefore held A.'s application for review to be unfounded.

4.63 EXTRADITION

See: 1.204; 6.224

4.64 OTHER ASSISTANCE IN CRIMINAL MATTERS

See: 1.204 (pp. 257-261)

4.65 EXPULSION

See: 1.204 (pp. 257-261); 6.224; 8.2; 12.28

4.66 ASYLUM
See: 1.204 (pp. 257-261); 4.52; 6.224; 12.28

4.7 PROTECTION OF HUMAN RIGHTS AND FUNDAMENTAL FREEDOMS
See: 6.224; 12.28

4.73 EUROPEAN CONVENTION ON HUMAN RIGHTS
See: 1.204 (pp. 254-257); 4.52 (pp. 272-277); 5.26 (n. 59); 6.224; 12.2704; 12.28

5.13 ORGANS OF THE STATE: THE MINISTERS
See: 5.26

5.22 INTERNAL STRUCTURE OF THE FOREIGN SERVICE AND OF THE DIPLOMATIC MISSION
See: 3.1141

5.26 FUNCTIONS OF THE DIPLOMAT

C.D. v. the Minister for Foreign Affairs, Administrative Law Division of the Council of State, 18 February 1999, AB (1999) No. 143,[52] JB (1999) No. 52,[53] JV (1999) No. 76,[54] RV (1999) No. 40.[55]

— *Legalisation of foreign documents used in Dutch legal transactions entails the declaration by a competent Dutch authority that a document is authentic. The decision is effected by the placing of a declaration (stamp) on the document.*
— *This involves a decision taken by or on behalf of the Minister for Foreign Affairs. The decision is of a public law nature.*
— *Although it is true that there is no specific statutory basis (under public law), legalisation takes place in international legal transactions by a sovereign State, in which connection there is a legal ground under international law as expressed in the 1961 Convention abolishing the requirement of legalisation for public documents.[56] No one other than the State authorities may legalise documents.*

52. Note by M. Schreuder-Vlasblom.
53. Note by R.J.N. Schlossels.
54. Note by R. Fernhout.
55. Note by P. Boeles. Summarised in *NJB* (1999) p. 608, No. 14. Discussed by P.A. Nollkaemper, 'Volkenrechtelijke aspecten van legalisatie en verificatie van documenten [*International Law aspects of legalisation and verification of comments*], *HR* (2000) pp. 123-127 and by B.K. Olivier, 'Twee onafhankelijke gebieden in de wereld van het recht' [*Two independent means in the world of law*], *MR* (2000) pp. 160-164.
56. 527 *UNTS* p. 189; *Trb.* 1963 No. 28.

— Moreover, the Dutch government is required under Article 90 of the Constitution to promote the development of the international legal order and it is the function of the Minister to be responsible for foreign relations. The legal ground under international law can therefore be said to take effect in internal law.
— Although the intended legal consequence of legalisation – the provision of proof – first becomes visible or concrete in a different procedure, this does not alter the fact that it constitutes a juristic act and hence an order as referred to in Article 1:3 of the General Administrative Law Act, against which an application for review may be lodged.[57]

The Facts: By letter of 13 February 1997 the Dutch Ambassador to Ghana refused to legalise a birth certificate submitted by D. D.'s objection to this decision was dismissed as unfounded by the Minister for Foreign Affairs. Although D.'s application for a review of this order was held by the District Court of Amsterdam in its judgment of 8 June 1998 to be well-founded and the decision of the Minister was quashed, the original objection was still held to be inadmissible.[58] D. as well as the Minister then appealed to the Administrative Law Division of the Council of State.

Held: '... 2. Findings

2.1.1. The dispute concerns the question of whether legalisation or the refusal of legalisation (whether or not after verification) of foreign documents for use in Dutch legal transactions can be treated as an order within the meaning of Article 1:3, paragraph 1, of the General Administrative Law Act, namely a written decision of an administrative authority constituting a juristic act under public law.

2.1.2. Legalisation of foreign documents should be taken to mean the declaration by a competent Dutch authority that a document is authentic, in order that the document can be admitted for use in the Dutch legal order. The decision is effected by the placing of a declaration (stamp) on the relevant document.

A decision to legalise a document is often based on an examination of the signature and/or stamps of the authority of the country concerned on the relevant document. It concerns the authenticity of the (external) form of the document. In a number of cases the content of the document is also verified. Verification of this kind has been prescribed by the Minister for documents emanating from Ghana, Nigeria, India, Pakistan and the Dominican Republic.[59]

---

57. Act of 1992. Art. 1:3 reads: 'Order means a written ruling of an administrative authority constituting a juristic act under public law.'

58. *JV* (1998) No. 112, with note by B.K. Olivier.

59. The verification of documents from these countries has taken place since 1 April 1996; see Circular of the State Secretary for Justice to the registrars of births, death and marriages of 8 May 1986, reference 555949/96/6, Aliens Circular, C4 Appendix 1, discussed by A. van der Weij in '*Legalisatie en verificatie van buitenlandse documenten: helderheid gewenst*' [Legalisation and verification of foreign documents: clarity desired], *MR* (1997 pp. 99-103 and K. Wouters and M. Meijers, '*Voortgaande verificatie perikelen*' [Ongoing developments concerning verification], MR (1998) pp. 222-223, J.A. Kroes and M.A.G. Reurs, '*Nederland als probleemland-Voortdurende perikelen rond legalisatie en verificatie in de probleemlanden*' [Netherlands as problem country: ongoing developments concerning legalisation and verification in the problem countries], *MR* (1998) pp. 287-292 and (1999) pp. 3-8.

2.2. In the appealed judgment – which has been published in JV 1998/112 – the District Court held that the refusal of the Minister to legalise a document can have far-reaching consequences for the person concerned, although these consequences are not intended as such by the Minister. Policy rules of other authorities ultimately determine what consequences are attached to the possession or non-possession of legalised documents. The question whether refusal of legalisation can and should, from the point of view of the legal protection to be afforded, be treated as an order against which objection and review lie under the General Administrative Law Act was answered by the District Court in the negative.[60] It took into account in this connection first of all the fact that since a document whose legalisation has been requested can be used for numerous purposes, the fact of legalisation or refusal of legalisation cannot as a rule be treated as a necessary link leading to a specific order, and second that the question whether legalisation of a document has been refused on good grounds may be submitted to the courts in the context of the underlying dispute.[61]

2.3. The appellants have disputed the decision of the District Court by means of reasoned arguments. The Minister has contained in this connection, *inter alia*, that he does indeed intend legalisation to have a legal consequence, namely the determination of the legal status of the relevant document, as a result of which it becomes legally suitable for use in the Dutch legal order.

2.4. The Division finds in this respect that in the case of legalisation (or refusal of legalisation) of documents emanating from foreign government authorities, the decision is taken by an administrative authority, namely the Minister or, on his behalf, the Ambassador to the relevant country. This decision is of a public law nature. Although it is true that there is no specific statutory basis (under public law), legalisation takes place in international legal transactions by a sovereign State, in which connection there is a

---

In the case of *J.O.* v. *the Minister for Foreign Affairs*, a request for legalisation was submitted before the relevant date. In consequence, the District Court of Dordrecht held that the new guidelines were not yet in force and that the Minister had therefore acted wrongly by himself immediately arranging for the documents to be verified in Lagos, thereby circumventing the Nigerian Ministry of Foreign Affairs. Nonetheless, there would be no legalisation since the documents had been shown to be false. This was not altered by the fact that they had been previously legalised by the Ministry of Foreign Affairs in Lagos (judgment of 21 August 1998, *JB* (1999) No. 227 with note by H.J. Simon). The District Court of Haarlem held that the distinction between the five problem countries and the other countries was not contrary to Art. 14 of the European Convention on Human Rights (judgment of 10 August 1998, *AB* (1999) No. 380, with note by I. Sewandono).

60. But for a different decision see District Court of Haarlem, 10 August 1998, and District Court of Dordrecht, 21 August 1998, see note 59 above and Nationale Ombudsman, 1 May 1998, *AB* (1998) No. 291. In the latter case the Ombudsman held that the Dutch Embassy in Ghana had taken a decision on legalisation at a very late stage.

61. The District Court referred in this connection to the judgment previously given by the District Court of The Hague to the effect that the Minister of Justice was required to give his own opinion on the procedural and substantive correctness of individual official communications of the Minister of Foreign Affairs in aliens matters (judgment of 16 April 1998, *JV* (1998) No. 74). Olivier considered this referral to be rather unfortunate since an official communication of this kind entails a recommendation to the Minister of Justice. By contrast, legalisation is of an independent nature (see *supra* n. 7). As regards the status of official communications and the relationship between the Minister for Foreign Affairs and the Minister of Justice, see also the Public Report of the National Ombudsman of 19 August 1998 (*JB* (1998) No. 195).

legal ground under international law. This legal ground is also reflected in the Convention abolishing the requirement of legalisation for public documents, concluded in the Hague on 5 October 1961 (Trb. 1963 No. 28: the "Apostille Convention"). No one other than the State authorities may legalise documents. Nor may it be overlooked that the government is required under Article 90 of the Constitution to promote the development of the international legal order and that it is the function of the Minister to be responsible for foreign relations. The legal ground under international law can therefore be said to take effect in internal law. A decision concerning legalisation is therefore taken in the discharge of a public duty.[62]

Legalisation has consequences under the law of evidence: a legalised document has evidential value and can be used as proof in appropriate cases, and the facts included in it are deemed to be correct. This legal consequence is also intended. Contrary to what the District Court held, this is not altered by the fact that this (abstract) legal consequence first becomes visible or concrete in a different procedure (e.g. with regard to the obtainment of a residence permit, the celebration of a marriage, an application for child benefit allowance or an entry in the municipal personal records database) because it is only at this juncture that the relevant legalised document is first used in legal transactions. There is therefore a juristic act.

2.5. It follows from the finding at 2.4 above that the question raised under 2.1.1 should, contrary to what the District Court decided, be answered in the affirmative. The decision of the District Court to hold that the application for review by the appellant at 1. was well-founded and to quash the disputed order of 10 September 1997 because the objection should have been declared inadmissible is therefore incorrect. The District Court wrongly held the objection to be inadmissible. The appeals are well-founded. Since the District Court did not arrive at a substantive assessment of the case, the Division will quash the appealed judgment in its entirety and refer the case back to the District Court pursuant to Article 44, paragraph 1, opening words, and (b) of the Council of State Act ...'

5.273 DIPLOMATIC INVIOLABILITY OF PREMISES AND ARCHIVES

See: 3.1141 (pp. 265-267)

5.365 CONSULAR PUBLIC FUNCTIONS IN THE FIELD OF PRIVATE LAW

See: 5.26

6.1 CONCLUSION AND ENTRY INTO FORCE OF TREATIES

See: 3.132

---

62. The District Court of Haarlem (see *supra* n. 59) held that the Apostille Convention merely specified that the power of a State to determine whether a foreign document should be accorded significance in that State is assumed by virtue of international transactions. The basis for this power is, however, not the Convention, but the sovereign authority of a State over its own territory.

6.114 ACCESSION TO TREATIES
See: 3.143

6.21 OBSERVANCE OF TREATIES
See: 1.204 (pp. 257-261); 6.224

6.224 CONFLICT BETWEEN TREATIES

H.B. v. the State of the Netherlands, District Court of The Hague (application for interim injunction), 28 October 1997, RV (1997) No. 99[63] and H.B. v. State Secretary for Justice, District Court of The Hague, 28 October 1997 (provisional remedy pursuant to the General Administrative Law Act), JV (1998) No. 20, RV (1997) No. 17.[64]

— Pursuant to the recommendation made by the Supreme Court, it is assumed that B. has in the past been exposed to treatment by Turkish police officers that cannot be reconciled with Article 3 of the European Convention on Human Rights[65] and Article 3 of the Anti-Torture Convention[66], and that this must, in principle, be taken into account in connection with extradition.
— Although the Turkish government has admittedly given assurances, on request, that B. will not be subjected to a violation of his fundamental rights, the question is whether these assurances are sufficiently far-reaching to provide certainty that this will still be the case if the proceedings are continued and the custody resumed.
— Extradition of B. to Turkey is therefore in breach of Article 3 of the European Convention and accordingly prohibited.
— Nor is it possible to determine with sufficient certainty that B.'s expulsion will not constitute a violation of Article 3. This too is therefore prohibited.

The Facts: Turkey requested the extradition of B., who was of Turkish nationality, in order to prosecute him for his involvement in the purchase of a large quantity of heroin in Pakistan and its transport to Turkey in the period from the summer of 1991 to 15 December 1992. The District Court in Breda declared on 13 March 1996 that extradition was admissible, but advised the Minister of Justice not to grant the request. B. appealed in cassation against this judgment to the Supreme Court. The Supreme Court quashed the judgment of the District Court of 15 October 1996. Giving judgment anew the Supreme Court declared on 17 December 1996 that the extradition was admissible. However, the

63. Note by A.H.J. Swart.
64. Note by B.P. Vermeulen.
65. For the text of Art. 3, see *supra* n. 12.
66. 1465 *UNTS* p. 85; *ILM* (1984) p. 1027; *Trb* 1985 No. 69. The text of Art. 3 reads: '1. No State Party shall expel, return ("refouler") or extradite a person to another State where there are substantial grounds for believing that he would be in danger of being subjected to torture.
2. For the purpose of determining whether there are such grounds, the competent authorities shall take into account all relevant considerations including, where applicable, the existence in the State concerned of a consistent pattern of gross, flagrant or mass violations of human rights.'

Supreme Court too advised the Minister of Justice not to grant the request for extradition.[67] The District Court then stayed B.'s detention for the purpose of extradition on condition that he would not leave the Netherlands. The Minister of Justice then requested the Turkish authorities for assurances that after B.'s extradition he would not be subjected to treatment contrary to Articles 2 and 3 of the European Convention.[68] These assurances were given in a letter of 14 February 1997 from the Public Prosecutor at the Court of State Security in Istanbul and were confirmed, on request, by the Turkish ambassador to The Hague by letter of 20 June 1997. The Minister then decided on 29 July 1997 to permit the extradition. B. applied to the District Court of The Hague for an interim injunction restraining the State of the Netherlands from extraditing him until the European Commission of Human Rights had decided on the merits of the complaint submitted by him. The President of the District Court granted the injunction on 28 October 1997.

On the same day the President also granted the provisional remedy that B. should not be expelled to Turkey. This was a consequence of the fact that B. had previously submitted an application on 1 March 1996 for admission as a refugee and for the issue of a residence permit. On 29 June 1997 these requests were rejected by the State Secretary for Justice. B. then lodged an objection on 10 September 1997. He was informed on 29 August that this objection would not have the effect of staying the expulsion. B. then applied to the President of the District Court in The Hague under Article 8:81 of the General Administrative Law Act for a provisional remedy directing that the objection would have the effect of staying the expulsion pending the hearing of the objection.

Held (with regard to the application for an interim injunction):

'... 3. Assessment of the dispute

3.1. The question is whether the Minister acted reasonably in arriving at the view that there was insufficient reason to assume that that in the event of extradition to Turkey the plaintiff would be subjected to treatment contrary to Article 3 of the European Convention on Human Rights.

3.2. The plaintiff has alleged that if extradited to Turkey he will run the great risk of being tortured again and that the assurances given will not prevent this. As against this, the defendant has argued that there is no imminent risk of a violation of Article 3 of the European Convention and that in view of the assurances given there are no longer any obstacles to the extradition of the plaintiff.

3.3. Pursuant to the recommendation made by the Supreme Court, it is assumed that B. has in the past been exposed to treatment by Turkish police officers that cannot be reconciled with Article 3 of the Anti-Torture Convention and Article 3 of the European Convention on Human Rights and that this same risk must, in principle, be taken into account in connection with extradition.

3.4. In view of the assurances given and in the expectation that the Turkish government attaches importance to honouring these assurances, it may be assumed that during his interrogation by the Public Prosecution Service in Istanbul the plaintiff will

---

67. 29 *NYIL* (1998) pp. 272-278.

68. Art. 2(1) reads: 'Everyone's right to life shall be protected by law. No one shall be deprived of his life intentionally save in the execution of the sentence of a court following his conviction of a crime for which this penalty is provided by law.'

not be the victim of a violation of his fundamental rights. The question is, however, whether these assurances are sufficiently far-reaching to provide certainty that this will still be the case if the proceedings are continued and the custody resumed. This question is answered in the negative since it has not been plausibly shown that the Turkish authorities will be able to continue providing the protection promised by the Public Prosecutor at the Court of State Security in Istanbul, for example in the case of transport to and subsequent residence in a penal institution. The start made by the Turkish government in implementing a programme to improve the human rights situation is a positive development. However, this does not alter the fact that the situation with regard to the plaintiff remains uncertain. The Minister did not therefore act reasonably in arriving at the conclusion that there was sufficient certainty that the plaintiff would not be subjected to treatment contrary to Article 3 of the European Convention.

3.5. In view of the above, it must be concluded that the application should be granted in the manner referred to below ...'

Held (with regard to the application for a provisional remedy):

'... 3. In so far as the decision to expel the alien results from the refusal to admit him as a refugee, it must be decided whether his expulsion should not proceed owing to Article 32, paragraph 1, opening words and (a), of the Aliens Act. This article provides that an alien should not be expelled if he has applied for admission as a refugee, unless there can be no reasonable doubt that there is no risk of persecution on account of religious, political or other belief or on account of nationality or belonging to a particular race or social group.

4. The question that arises in connection with the request by the applicant for the issue of a residence permit is whether there are grounds for assuming that the objection against the refusal of the request has a reasonable chance of success. Pursuant to Article 32, paragraph 1, opening words and (b), of the Aliens Act, expulsion should not take place in that case. Such a situation arises, *inter alia*, if there are urgent reasons of a humanitarian nature on the basis of which residence should be permitted in the Netherlands.

[...]

'... 14. As regards the substantive aspects of the applicant's request for admission as a refugee, the President is of the opinion that the defendant could not automatically conclude, pursuant to Article 15c, paragraph 1, opening words and (a), of the Aliens Act, that the application for admission as a refugee was manifestly ill-founded because it was based on circumstances which, either in themselves or in conjunction with other facts, could not reasonably give rise to even the merest suspicion that there was a legal ground for admission.

15. In view of the President, it must be concluded in the present proceedings that the fact that the alien is not a refugee within the meaning of the Refugee Convention and the Refugee Act is not beyond doubt. The President finds in this connection that it has in any event been established that the applicant was exposed to torture in Turkey by the Turkish police in 1989. This torture took place during an interrogation concerning (alleged) involvement in a drug offence. The applicant has stated that he was acquitted by a Turkish Court in respect of this charge in 1991. This statement by the applicant is confirmed by the letter of the Turkish Public Prosecutor of 14 February 1997 in which he stated that the applicant was acquitted of drug trafficking by a Turkish court in 1991.

In addition, the applicant has contended that he was involved in Kurdish opposition groups, which would also seem to be plausible to a certain extent of the plausible in view of the documents lodged. The President would observe in this connection that it is a matter of common knowledge that the Turkish authorities pursue a policy of hard repression against Kurdish opposition movements.

Viewing these factors together, it must be concluded for the time being that doubt can reasonably be said to exist as to whether the applicant is not a refugee within the meaning of the Refugee Convention and the Aliens Act. The possibility can therefore not be excluded in advance that, if the applicant fulfils the conditions of the Refugee Convention, his expulsion to Turkey would be contrary to the prohibition of *refoulement* contained in Article 33, paragraph 1, of the Refugee Convention. This is not altered by the fact that the applicant's extradition is requested merely for an offence under ordinary criminal law. It follows from the above that the criterion referred to above under 3 for staying the extradition under Article 32, paragraph 1, opening words and (a), of the Aliens Act has been fulfilled.

The request for the provisional remedy can therefore be granted for this reason alone.

16. The President notes that it is the established case-law of both the European Court of Human Rights and the Dutch administrative courts that expulsion to a country where there is a real risk of treatment contrary to Article 3 of the European Convention constitutes a violation of that article. In view of the assessment that takes place in the request for the provisional remedy, the criterion for review to be applied in the present proceedings is whether it can be assumed with a sufficient degree of certainty that the alien concerned will not, in the event of his compulsory return to his country of origin, be exposed to a real risk of violation of Article 3 of the European Convention.

17. Unlike the defendant, the President provisionally takes the view that it cannot be assumed with a sufficient degree of certainty that the applicant will not, in the event of expulsion to Turkey, run a real risk of being subjected to a violation of Article 3 of the European Convention. The President would refer in this connection first of all to the recommendation made by the Supreme Court on 17 December 1996 that the request for extradition should not be granted owing to the possibility of a violation of, *inter alia*, Article 3 of the European Convention on Human Rights. Although the President does not doubt the sincere intention of the Turkish Public Prosecution Service and the Turkish government to honour unconditionally the assurances given for the personal safety of the applicant, the fact cannot be overlooked that, despite the efforts made by the Turkish government, violations of human rights frequently occur in Turkey.

The President would refer in this connection to recent reports of the US Department of State and of human rights organisations such as Amnesty International and Human Rights Watch. The President also refers to the official communication of the Minister for Foreign Affairs of 3 September 1997 concerning the general situation in Turkey (reference DPC/AM, No. 67688), in which it was stated among other things that despite the fact that Turkey is a party to a large number of human rights conventions, including the European Convention on Human Rights, the Anti-Torture Convention and the Refugee Convention, it still clearly fails to observe human rights; for example, ill-treatment and torture frequently occur in Turkey, in particular during pre-trial detention. According to the official circular, the main targets are people who have openly worked for the Kurdish cause. It is also stated in the official communication that the European

Committee for the Prevention of Torture and Inhuman or Degrading Treatment or Punishment found convincing proof of torture and ill-treatment by the Turkish police during visits to Turkey in 1994 and 1996. Moreover, the President would refer, with regard to the personal situation of the applicant, to the experts' statements that have been lodged and which suggest that it is very plausible that on his return to Turkey the applicant will run a real risk of being subjected to treatment contrary to Article 3 of the European Convention on Human Rights.

In view of this background, the President is not, for the time being, convinced that the assurances given by the Turkish Public Prosecution Service and the Turkish government provide, in view of their scope, sufficient protection for the applicant against treatment contrary to Article 3 of the European Convention.

18. In these circumstances the provisional remedy should be granted ...'

6.225 APPLICATION OF PROVISIONS CONTAINED IN TREATIES NOT YET IN FORCE

See: 8.23

6.23 INTERPRETATION OF TREATIES

See: 1.204; 4.52; 6.224; 8.23; 12.28; 16.164

7.21 EXTRA-TERRITORIAL SCOPE OF LEGISLATIVE ACTS

See: 8.2; 8.23

8.12 RELATIONS OF 'VOISINAGE'

See: 8.23

8.2 TERRITORIAL JURISDICTION

See also: 5.26; 8.23

A. v. the State Secretary for Justice, District Court of The Hague (sitting in Zwolle), 9 December 1998, JV (1999) No. 28.

— As Article 19(1) of the Aliens Act cannot be applied outside Dutch territory, an alien may be stopped and questioned about his identity as referred to in this article only after he has crossed the Dutch border.[69] *This is not altered by the fact that the actual transfer*

69. Art. 19(1) reads: 'The controllers are authorised, either on the grounds of concrete indications about illegal residence or to combat illegal residence, to stop persons as quickly as possible after they cross the border in order to establish their identity, nationality and status for residence purposes. A person who alleges that he is a Dutch national but is unable to prove this may be subjected to the means of coercion referred to in paragraphs 2 and 4. The documents which an alien must possess for the establishment of his identity, nationality and status for residence purposes shall be designated by order

of the alien took place previously, namely in the working areas of the 'Schengen Information Point' (SIP), which was situated in German territory.
— The question whether apprehension in the SIP was lawful can be assessed only by the German authorities. The Dutch courts can assess the lawfulness of a deprivation of liberty only in so far as it has taken place in Dutch territory.

The Facts: A., who was not entitled to residence in Germany, was transferred to the Royal Netherlands Military Constabulary "in the working areas of the Schengen Information Point", which was situated in German territory, at 4.30 p.m. on 16 October 1998 under the terms of the Schengen Implementation Agreement of 1990 between the Netherlands and Germany. He was then handed over to the Aliens Department for the North-East Gelderland Region, and subsequently stopped for questioning about his identity at 8.30 p.m. This clearly took place in Dutch territory. Subsequently he was detained for questioning at 9.45 p.m. pursuant to Article 19(2) of the Aliens Act.[70] Thereafter he was detained at 11 p.m. A. applied to the District Court for termination of the detention.

Held: '... The District Court agrees with the defendant that, since the actual transfer of the alien occurred in German territory in the present case, the alien could not be stopped for questioning about his identity in the working areas of the SIP since Article 19 of the Aliens Act cannot be applied outside Dutch territory. This is not altered by the fact that the alien had in fact been under the control of the Dutch authorities since 4.30 p.m. It was therefore correct that the alien was stopped for questioning by the Aliens Service only after he had crossed the Dutch border, at around 8.30 p.m.. After he had been stopped for questioning the alien was taken as quickly as possible to a place for interview. It cannot be therefore said that the procedure preceding and leading to the detention of the alien was not lawful. It should, however, be noted that the duration of apprehension in the working areas of the SIP was longer than appears strictly necessary. The District Court considers that the apprehension was not, however, of such a length that the detention must be deemed to be unlawful on the grounds that the Dutch authorities failed to deal with the matter with sufficient urgency. The Court takes into account in this connection that the period that elapsed between the moment when the alien was transferred by the German authorities in the SIP to the Royal Netherlands Military Constabulary and the time when the alien was detained was 6.5 hours and was thus within acceptable limits. The submission that the apprehension in the working areas of the SIP lacked any legal basis and was therefore unlawful cannot be accepted in the context of the present assessment. Since the alien was, after all, in German territory at that time, determination of the lawfulness of this apprehension is a matter for the German authorities. The lawfulness of a deprivation of liberty may be reviewed by the Dutch courts only in so far as the deprivation of liberty occurred in Dutch territory. As already

---

in council.'

70. Art. 19(2) reads: 'If the identity of the person stopped for questioning cannot be established immediately or it is not immediately apparent that he is allowed to reside in the Netherlands, he may be taken to a place of interview. He shall not be detained there for more than six hours, subject to the proviso that the time between midnight and 9 a.m. is disregarded.'

held above, the Court has not seen any evidence of irregularities in the procedure preceding and leading to the detention.

The Court is of the opinion that, in view of the personal circumstances of the alien as revealed in the case documents and during the hearing, there is sufficient evidence that the grounds for detention still exist. In the opinion of the Court, it is reasonable for the defendant to take the position that since the alien does not possess documents proving his identity and makes use of various aliases, he will seek to evade the existing expulsion order if set at liberty.

This means that the application or implementation of the detention of the alien is not in breach of the Aliens Act and cannot reasonably be judged to be unjust in the light of all the interests involved in this case.

The application for review is therefore declared to be unfounded. The detention will not be terminated ...'

8.23 CONCURRENT TERRITORIAL JURISDICTION

Dutch Society for the Preservation of the Waddenzee v. Minister of Agriculture, Nature Management and Fisheries, Administrative Law Division of the Council of State, 29 September 1998, JB (1998) No. 255.[71]

— The licence granted by the Minister of Agriculture, Nature Management and Fisheries for the dumping of dredging spoil from the entrance to the Zeehaven Canal in the Mouth of the Dollard and/or in the Bight of Watum (Bocht van Watum) related to dumping sites in the so-called Disputed Area in the Ems-Dollard Estuary, over which both Germany and the Netherlands claim territorial sovereignty.
— It can be inferred, inter alia, from the Ems-Dollard Environmental Protocol of 1996[72] *that the Ems-Dollard Treaty of 1960*[73] *relates to this activity.*
— It follows from Article 21 of that Treaty, which provides that in carrying out 'river-management functions'[74] *each Contracting Party should apply its own laws and regulations, that a licence as referred to in Article 12 of the Nature Conservancy Act*[75] *is required for the activity in question. This also follows from the history of the Ems-Dollard Cooperation Treaty of 1984.*[76]
— Articles 21 and 22 of the 1960 Treaty contain only rights and duties for the Contracting Parties.[77] *Private individuals cannot derive any rights from these provisions and cannot therefore invoke them in the event of a conflict with other regulations applicable in the Disputed Area.*

---

71. Note by A.R. Neerhof; summarised in *AB Kort* (1998) No. 657.
72. *Trb.* 1996 No. 258.
73. 509 *UNTS* p. 64, *Trb.* 1960 No. 69.
74. In the unofficial English version of the Treaty included in the United Nations Treaty Series, the term 'river police functions' is used.
75. Art. 12 (1) reads: 'It is forbidden, without a licence from Our Minister or in contravention of conditions contained in such a licence, to perform acts, to cause acts to be performed or to tolerate acts which are harmful to an area of natural beauty or to the scientific significance of a protected nature conservation area or which mar such a nature conservation area.'
76. *Trb.* 1984 No.118.
77. For the text of Arts. 21 and 22 see under *Held.*

— The licences and exemptions policy of the Nature Conservancy Act is linked to the policy pursued in the context of the entirely revised Waddenzee Key Planning Decision, which also applies to the Ems-Dollard Estuary.
— Pursuant to this Key Planning Decision the principles of 'the best possible information', 'translocation' and 'precaution' should be applied when taking decisions.
— This also follows from Articles 1 and 4 of the Ems-Dollard Environmental Protocol.[78] *Although this Protocol had not yet been approved at that time, the Netherlands was required under Article 18 of the Vienna Convention on the Law of Treaties to refrain from acts that would defeat the object and purpose of the Protocol.*[79]
— On the basis of the best information available at the time of the granting of the licence, the Minister had not been wrong to conclude – after weighing the interests – that clear doubt did not exist as to the absence of potentially serious adverse effects of the dumping on the ecosystem. The precautionary principle had not therefore prevented the granting of the licence. The same applies to the translocation principle.

The Facts: By order of 24 November 1994 the Minister of Agriculture, Nature Management and Fisheries granted the Northern Department of the Directorate General for Public Works and Water Management (Rijkswaterstaat) in Leeuwarden a licence as referred to in Article 12 (1) of the Nature Conservancy Act (referred to below as the Act) for the annual dumping of a maximum of 100,000 cubic metres of dredging spoil in the Mouth of the Dollard, close to the Dollard nature conservation area and the Dollard and Waddenzee II state nature conservation areas and/or in the Bight of Watum, close to the Waddenzee II state nature conservation area, subject to the conditions specified in the order, the licence being valid until 1 January 2000.[80] By letter of 5 January 1995 the Dutch Society for the Preservation of the Waddenzee objected to this order. On 19 May 1995 the Minister ruled that the objection was unfounded. The Society then appealed to the Administrative Law Division of the Council of State. On 7 August 1997 the holder of the licence was granted a new licence under which dredging spoil could also be dumped outside the normal period (October to February), albeit only in the Watum Bight.

Held: The Division held first of all that it was competent to take cognizance of the appeal. In doing so it considered that the appeal was also directed against the order of 7 August 1997. As the previous order of 1994 had been repealed by this order, the Division held that the appeal by the Society against the previous order was no longer admissible.

"... As regards the other matters raised in the case, doubt has been raised on behalf of the licence holder as to whether a licence as referred to in Article 12 of the Act may be required for the dumping of dredging spoil at the relevant locations. It has pointed out in this connection that the spoiling grounds are situated in the so-called Disputed Area, over

78. For the text of Arts. 1(2) and 4, see under Held.

79. *Trb.* 1972 No. 51. Art. 18 reads: 'A State is obliged to refrain from acts which would defeat the object and purpose of a Treaty when: (a) it has signed the treaty or has exchanged instrument constituting the treaty is subject to ratification, acceptance or approval, until it shall have made its intention clear not to become a party to the treaty; or (b) it has expressed its consent to be bound by the treaty, pending the entry into force of the treaty and provided that such entry into force is not unduly delayed'.

80. The license, and consequently the decision too, wrongly referral to the 'Mouth of the Ems-Dollard Estuary' instead of the 'Mouth of the Dollard'. The place where the spoil had to be dredged was further specified in the licence as Paap Sand Süd. See map on p. 295.

which both the Federal Republic of Germany and the Kingdom of the Netherlands claim territorial sovereignty.

Before being able to assess the objections of the appellant to the licence that has been granted, it is therefore necessary to examine whether the acts in question required the granting of a licence, given the fact that the spoiling grounds are situated in the so-called Disputed Area.

The General Treaty between the Kingdom of the Netherlands and the Federal Republic of Germany for the settlement of frontier questions and other problems outstanding between the two countries (General Treaty), Trb. 1960, 67, was concluded on 8 April 1960. This General Treaty was approved by Kingdom Act of 9 May 1963 (Stb. 1963, 198). Under Article 1 of the General Treaty[81] it was provided, in so far as relevant here, that the Ems-Dollard Treaty was thereby concluded with a view to regulalating arrangements for cooperation in the Ems Estuary. The Ems-Dollard Treaty (Trb. 1960, 69) was also approved by Kingdom Act of 9 May 1963 (Stb. 1963, 198) and entered into force on 1 August 1963.

Under Article 1 of the Ems-Dollard Treaty the Contracting Parties are required, bearing in mind their common interests and having due regard to the special interests of the other Contracting Party, to cooperate in the Ems Estuary in a spirit of good neighbourliness, in accordance with the following articles, for the purpose of ensuring that their ports have such access to the sea as they may at any time require. This objective is to be attained - subject to the maintenance by both Parties of their legal positions with respect to the course of the international frontier – through the medium of practical arrangements with respect to questions affecting both States. Under Article 2 of the Ems-Dollard Treaty the Contracting Parties took as their point of departure the existing main fairway, the Emden fairway, and the south passage from the main fairway to the Bight of Watum, and undertook - in accordance with the terms of chapter 2 – to take all necessary measures to keep open and, if necessary, improve these fairways, and to give their support to measures of the same kind taken by the other Contracting Party. They also undertook to refrain from any measures detrimental to the aforementioned purpose. A Contracting Party would be deemed to have complied with this undertaking if, for example, in carrying out works it made arrangements which prevent any harmful effects on the fairways leading to the ports of the other Contracting Party.

Under Article 4, paragraph 1, first sentence, of the Ems-Dollard Treaty it is provided that in the event that the now existing south passage from the main fairway to the Bight of Watum can no longer be kept open or, if necessary, improved in accordance with the interests of the Port of Delfzijl at a cost considered by the Government of the Kingdom of the Netherlands to be economically justified, the Kingdom of the Netherlands shall be entitled to create a new channel.

Under Article 19, paragraph 1, of the Ems-Dollard Treaty it is provided, in essence, that the Kingdom of the Netherlands is responsible for 'river-management functions' relating to, among other things, the Bight of Watum and the north and south passages from the main fairway to the Bight of Watum.

Under Article 20, paragraph 1, of the Ems-Dollard Treaty, the river-management functions are deemed to include the supervision and protection of hydrological conditions, the state

81. 508 *UNTS* p. 20.

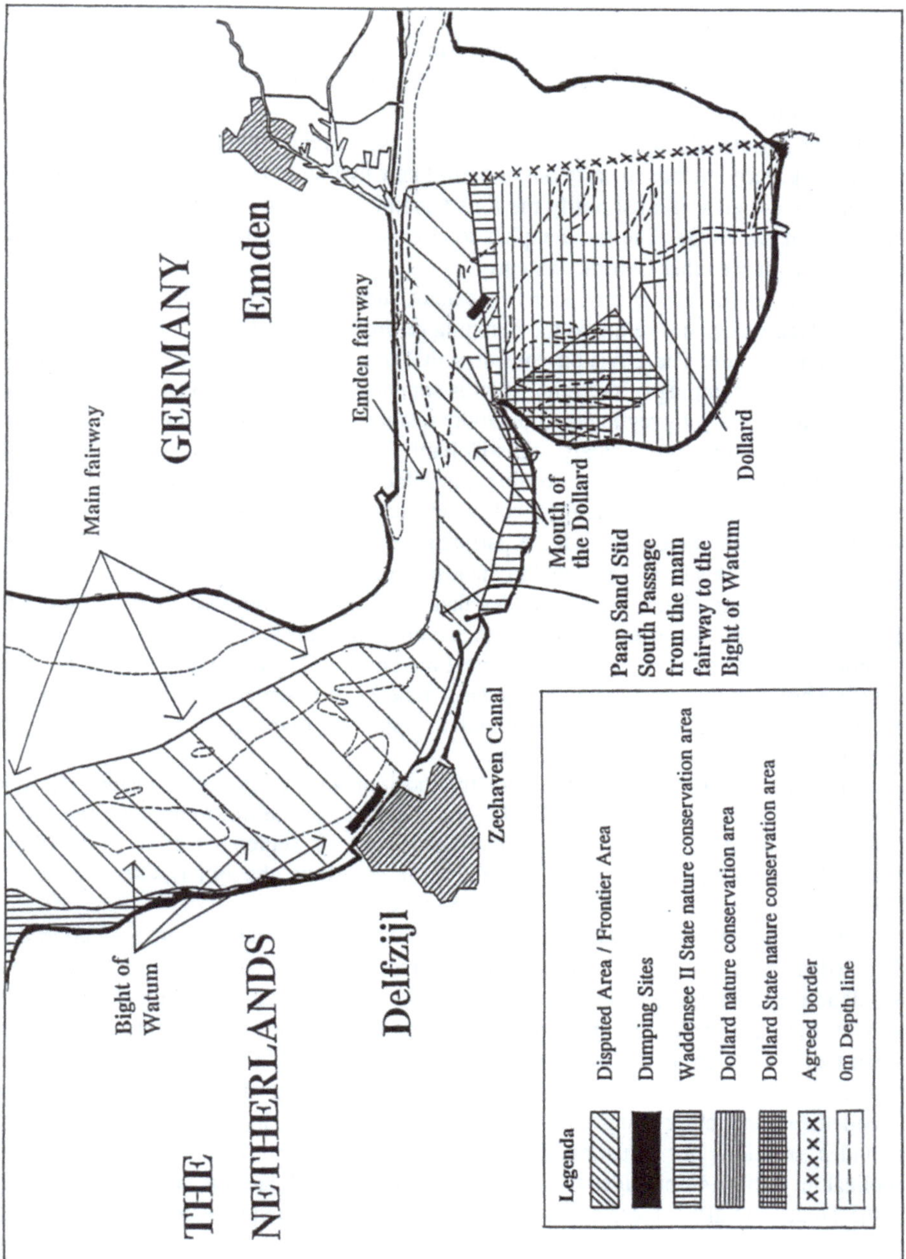

The Ems-Dollard Estuary

of the fairways, and works and installations in the Ems Estuary, and supervision of the use of the Ems Estuary by third parties.

Under Article 21 of the Ems-Dollard Treaty, each Contracting Party is obliged to apply its own laws and regulations. These laws and regulations must be brought to the attention of the Ems Commission.

Under Article 22, paragraph 1, of the Ems-Dollard Treaty, it is provided that if either Contracting Party intends to carry out or permit new hydraulic works or works connected with new sea-marks, it must notify the Ems Commission as soon as possible before the initiation of the works. The same applies to river-management measures that may affect the interests of the other Contracting Party.

In view of the above provisions, it cannot successfully be argued that the Ems-Dollard Treaty does not relate to the dumping of dredging spoil, which is the subject of the present dispute. The Division considers that the view that the Ems-Dollard Treaty also covers the dumping of dredging spoil is supported in the Additional Protocol to the Ems-Dollard Treaty to regulate cooperation relating to water management and nature management in the Ems Estuary (Ems-Dollard Environmental Protocol of 22 August 1996). In particular, the Division would refer to the provisions of Article 5, paragraph 4, opening words and (m), of this Protocol, which states that the cooperation in relation to water management should include, in particular, evaluation of the dumping of dredging spoil in so far as this is not regulated in the Ems-Dollard Treaty.

The argument of the licence holder that no licence as referred to in Article 12, paragraph 1, of the Act is required since the spoiling grounds are situated in the so-called Disputed Area to which – inter alia - the Ems-Dollard Treaty relates, also fails. The Division holds in this connection that under Article 21, first sentence, of the Ems-Dollard Treaty each Contracting Party is required to apply its own laws and regulations in carrying out river-management functions.

The Division also finds support for this position in the legislative history (Lower House of Parliament, 1985-1986,19 343, nos. 1 and 2) of the bill to approve the Ems-Dollard Cooperation Treaty concluded in Emden on 10 September 1984 (Trb. 1984, 118). The memorandum in respect of the final report on the bill (Lower House of Parliament, 1985-1986, 19 343, no. 9, page 8) states as follows:

"As regards the question [...] of the extent to which the Dutch acts are applied in the disputed area, it may be said that the basic premise in this connection is that Dutch legislation applies throughout the territory of the Netherlands, including the disputed area. In the case of the disputed area in the Ems Estuary, however, Treaty obligations mean that the Dutch legislation is not automatically applicable there. For example, the application is limited by the Ems-Dollard Treaty of 8 April 1960. This Treaty is intended, among other things, to make joint arrangements in a number of fields. It provides solutions for situations in which both Dutch and German law might be applicable. Article 48 provides that as regards matters which are not expressly regulated in the Treaty and affect these common interests the parties should cooperate in a spirit of good neighbourliness.

The dredging of the Zeehaven Canal close to Delfzijl and the dumping of the dredging spoil obtained as a result at the disputed locations come within the scope of the river-management functions referred to in the Ems-Dollard Treaty. This means that in view of Article 21, first sentence, of this Treaty Dutch laws and regulations are in principle applicable to these activities. This also means that the requisite licences should be issued for these activities by the competent Dutch authorities. There is no ground whatever for the view that an exception should be made to this as regards a licence as referred to in Article 12, paragraph 1, of the Act if such a licence is in itself required for the relevant acts (as in this case). It cannot be inferred from the fact that Article 21, first sentence, of the Ems-Dollard Treaty relates to river-management functions that the laws and regulations referred to in this sentence are intended to mean only those laws and regulations that explicitly relate to river-management functions.

It has not been alleged or shown that the issuing of the present licence is otherwise contrary to the regulations in force in respect of the Disputed Area. Moreover, it should be pointed out in particular in this connection that Articles 21 and 22 of the Ems-Treaty were drafted in the interests of the Contracting Parties and create rights and duties only for the Contracting Parties. Private individuals cannot invoke these provisions.

[...]

Nor is it in dispute that the dumping of dredging spoil at the locations disputed by the appellant requires a licence under the Act owing to the fact that parts of the Dutch section of the Dollard have been designated as protected areas or, as the case may be, as a state nature conservation area known as the Dollard and a significant part of the Dutch Waddenzee area has been designated as a protected conservation area as well as a state nature conservation area (Waddenzee II). This area adjoins the state nature conservation area known as Waddenzee designated by decision of 18 May 1991 (referred to as Waddenzee I in the decision of 17 November 1993), which already includes large parts of this sea area (approx. 125,000 hectares). The Waddenzee II area also includes parts of the Dollard Estuary. According to the explanatory notes accompanying the decision designating Waddenzee II – which form an integral part of and also replace the explanatory notes on Waddenzee I – the licence and exemption policy under the Act is linked to the policy pursued in the context of the entirely revised Waddenzee Key Planning Decision (Lower House, 1992-1993, 22 605, no. 34).

The key planning decision also relates to the Dutch part of the Ems-Dollard Estuary. The area covered by the key planning decision includes a large part of the above-mentioned Disputed Area, in which the disputed spoiling grounds are also located. The explanatory notes to the designation decision mention the dumping of dredging spoil as an activity that requires a licence under the Act.

According to the decision designating Waddenzee II and pursuant to the key planning decision, any licence to be granted under the Act should be tested against the principal objective of the key planning decision, namely the sustained protection and development of the Waddenzee as a nature conservation area. The aim of the policy is to achieve sustained protection and the most natural possible development of water movements and the accompanying geomorphologic and sedimentation processes, of the quality of the water, soil and air, and of the (seabed) flora and fauna. Subject to these constraints, human activities of an economic and/or recreational nature are possible.

In the context of the orders for the granting of licences, section 2.3 of the key planning decision provides that when the various interests are weighed use should be made of the best information available on the expected impact of an activity on, in particular, the natural environment of the Waddenzee. In addition, the public interest in the activity to be licensed should be demonstrated in this connection, one factor of importance being the extent to which the activity is tied to the particular location. Activities that can be carried out elsewhere - or could indeed be better carried out other than in the Waddenzee - are avoided (translocation principle). Where the importance of the public interest increases, there will be more reason to permit the impact that this is bound to have on the natural environment, subject to constraints.

The precautionary principle is also important when interests are weighed. This principle means that if, when the interests are weighed on the basis of the best available information, there is a clear doubt as to the absence of potentially serious effects on the ecosystem, the benefit of the doubt should be given to the conservation of the Waddenzee, which means that the principal objective is decisive.

In section 3.4.3 of the key planning decision it is also stated that only dredging spoil from the Waddenzee and ports with open links to it should be eligible for dumping in the Waddenzee. A solution outside this area should be found for contaminated dredging spoil that cannot, according to the assessment system still in preparation, be dumped in the Waddenzee. Besides the degree of contamination, another factor of importance is the quantity of dredging spoil to be dumped.

This assessment system is laid down in the 1992-1996 Management Plan for State Waters of May 1993 (Lower House, 1992-1993, 23 230, no. 1). This system, under which decisions on whether the spreading of dredging spoil is permissible are taken on the basis of the so-called content test of the degree of contamination of the spoil, is also included in section 5.3.6 'Methods for removing dredging spoil', subsection 2 'Distribution of dredging spoil in salt water', of the Water Evaluation Policy Document (Lower House, 1993-1994, 21 250, nos. 27-28).

The Division would also observe that pursuant to Article 1, paragraph 2, of the Ems-Dollard Environment of Protocol of 22 August 1996, Germany and the Netherlands are guided, in their cooperation in the Ems Estuary in respect of water and nature management, by the following principles: good neighbourliness, precaution, prevention, 'the polluter pays', the standstill principle, the need for sustainable development, the application of the best existing technology and of the best environmental practice within the context of the law of the European Union then obtaining, and of the principle that environmental loading should not be shifted to other environmental compartments.

Under Article 4 of the Ems-Dollard Environmental Protocol, the Contracting Parties will in this context endeavour, among other things, to preserve and improve the water quality and natural environment in the Ems Estuary and to improve the quality of the sediments in such a way that the ecosystem does not suffer any damage.

Under Article 18 of the Vienna Convention on the Law of Treaties, the Netherlands was obliged at the time when the defendant made the order of 7 August 1997 to refrain from acts which would have defeated the object and purpose of the Ems-Dollard Environmental Protocol, even though this Protocol had not yet been approved by law at that time. The Division considers that the policy described above is not incorrect or manifestly unreasonable.

According to the disputed orders and the explanation given of them, two types of contamination in particular played a role for the defendant in granting the licence under the Act, namely mercury and hexachlorobenzene (referred to below as HCB). Under a transnational arrangement in place for both substances in the port of Delfzijl, the concentrations of both these substances present in the dredging spoil from this port may be higher than the uniform test contents specified in the Water Evaluation Policy Document. Different conditions are also specified for mercury.

[...]

In view of the policy pursued by the defendant, of which the elements described above form part, the Division considers that, as the defendant has indeed acknowledged, there was not yet complete clarity – on the basis of the research data available at the time when the disputed order was made – about the answer to the question whether the dumping of the licensed quantities of dredging spoil at the desired locations would have a major adverse impact on the seabed flora and fauna both at the spoiling grounds and their immediate surroundings and at more distant locations. The fact that there was insufficient clarity was connected among other things with the limited number of chemical parameters used in determining the quality of dredging spoil and with the limited usability and reliability of the toxicity tests.

As the defendant has already indicated, no reliable eco-toxicological risk analyses were possible at the time when the disputed order was made, despite the fact that they were desirable. Such tests work being developed at that time, but the studies (which were still partly experimental) had not yet produced clear results.

It is evident from the disputed order that a factor in the decision was that the sediment to be dredged and removed from the Zeehaven Canal was considerably less toxic than the sediment from other dredging areas, which might have been expected to be less contaminated. In addition, the degree of contamination of the sediment to be dredged from the Zeehaven Canal scarcely differed from that of the sediment at and near the spoiling grounds, and it was also believed that the contamination would decline further in the future.

It is also important to note that the dredging of the Zeehaven Canal is of great economic importance to the port of Delfzijl and that, as became apparent at the hearing, the dumping of the dredging spoil at more distant spoiling grounds would involve substantial extra costs. Alternatives to the processing of dredging spoil, such as storage on land or the use of the spoil for land reclamation in coastal areas, had to treated as financially unfeasible at the time the disputed order was made.

In view of the above, the Division concludes that on the basis of the best information available at the time when the disputed order was made, the Minister was not wrong to conclude – after weighing all the interests concerned – that clear doubt did not exist as to the absence of potentially serious adverse effects of the dumping on the ecosystem. The precautionary principle applicable to the licensing of dumping activities did not, in the opinion of the Division, therefore prevent the granting of the requisite licence for this activity as referred to in Article 12 of the Act.

This also applies to the translocation principle, taking into account what is stated in section 3.4.3 of the key planning decision concerning the public interest.

Although the research results that have become available since the date of the disputed order may warrant the conclusion that the precautionary principle or the translocation principle or any other principle or national and/or international rule or treaty rule should possibly prevent the granting or renewal of licences under the Act, this does not alter the above finding since the question of whether a license as referred to in Article 12 of the Act can be granted should be assessed by reference to the position and on the basis of the best available information at the time when the order was made on the application for such a licence. This order should be completely reviewed in any objection procedure, at which point any newly acquired information and knowledge can also play a role.

Since there is nothing in the appellant's submissions to show that the disputed order of 7 August 1997 should be quashed, the appeal will be held to be unfounded . . .'[82]

9.83 INTERNAL WATERS
See: 8.23

9.924 POLLUTION OF INTERNATIONAL RIVERS
See: 8.23

11.211 THE ELEMENTS OF STATE RESPONSIBILITY
See: 1.204 (pp. 257-261); 3.1141 (pp. 265-267); 4.52 (pp. 278-282); 6.224; 8.2; 12.2704; 12.28; 16.164

11.216 REPARATION
See: 3.2113; 12.2704; 12.28; 16.164

11.22 RESPONSIBILITY OF INTERNATIONAL ORGANISATIONS
See: 3.2113

12.2704 EXECUTION AND OTHER EFFECTS OF THE JUDGMENT

Application by H. van M. for revision, Supreme Court, 6 July 1999, NJ (1999) No. 800,[83] NJCM-Bulletin (1999) p. 912.

---

82. On the same day the Division gave a virtually identical judgment in respect of these legal issues in an appeal brought by the Dutch Society for the Preservation of the Waddenzee against the licences granted on 30 December 1993 (900,000 cubic metres until 1 January 1996), 9 August 1995 (an extra 300.000 cubic metres until 1 January 1996) and 28 September 1995 (extension of both licences until 1 January 1998), *JM* (1999) No. 13, with note by Van der Meijden.

83. Note by J. de Hullu.

— The judgment of the European Court of Human Rights (ECHR) of 23 April 1997[84]*, in which the European Court held that a complaint of Van M. was well-founded on account of a violation of Article 6(1) and (3)(d) of the European Convention on Human Rights*[85]*, cannot in itself be deemed to be a circumstance as referred to in Article 457(1)(2) of the Code of Criminal Procedure.*[86] *It follows that the application by Van M. for revision of his conviction would not be admissible unless the Supreme Court were to break with its present case-law on revisions in order to fill the existing gap as regards the consequences to be attached to a judgment of the European Court holding that the Convention has been violated in criminal proceedings in the Netherlands.*
— However, in view of the current position and given the fundamental nature of any such procedure (which could involve overturning a final and binding decision that has the force of res judicata*) and the fact that there are various ways in which reparation can be provided, it is up to the legislator to make provision for such a procedure.*

The Facts: Van M. was sentenced on 4 February 1991 by the Court of Appeal in 's-Hertogenbosch to 14 years' imprisonment as a co-perpetrator in attempted murder and

---

84. *NJ* (1997) No. 635, with note by G. Knigge. Summarised and discussed by P. Baauw in NJCM-Bulletin (1997), pp. 1052-1065. Discussed by B.E.P. Myjer in 'Getuigen, dienders en Straatburgse rechtsbescherming' [Witnesses, coppers and Strasbourg legal protection], *NJB* (1997) pp. 883-889; by T. Spronken in 'De hoge Amsterdamse diender en de presumptie van onschuld' [The tall Amsterdam copper and the presumption of innocence], *NJB* (1997) pp. 1128-1130 with postscript by B.E.P. Myjer, pp. 1130-1131; by T. Schalken and K. Rozemond in 'Nieuwe Europese verassingen in Hollandse strafzaken' [New European surprises in Dutch criminal cases], *NJB* (1997) p. 894; by A. van Hoorn and H. Nijboer in 'Nog steeds onder de maat. Van Mechelen c.s. en de inquisitoire stijl van procederen' [Still not up to scratch. Van Mechelen et al. and the inquisitorial style of procedure]. *NJB* (1997) pp. 892-893; by C. Gare and T. Spronken in 'Wet bedreigde getuigen niet 'Straatsburg-proof: De zaak "van Mechelen e.a. tegen Nederland' [Threatened Witnesses Act still not Strasbourg-proof: The case of Van Mechelen et al. v. the Netherlands], *Advocatenblad* (1997) pp. 545-550; by E. Myjer in 'Nu toch maar in revisie?' [Ready for an overhaul after all?], *NJCM-Bulletin* (1998) pp. 4-13; by P.H.P.H.M.C. van Kempen in 'Rechtsvinding als oplossing voor verwerking van EHRM-beslissingen in strafzaken' [Judge-made law as a solution to the implementation of ECHR decisions in criminal cases], *Trema* (1998) pp. 104-108; by E. Myjer in 'To be revised? Revision of res judicata sentences in Dutch criminal cases' in T. Barkhuysen, M.L. van Emmerik and P.H. van Kempen, eds., *The Execution of Strasbourg and Geneva Human Rights Decisions in the National Legal Order*, (The Hague, Martinus Nijhoff 1999) pp. 243-253, and by P.H.P.H.M.C. van Kempen in 'Judicial interpretation and amendment of the law: review of criminal law decisions on account of Strasbourg judgments' in ibid., at pp. 323-339.

85. Art. 6(1) reads: 'In the determination of ... any criminal charge against him, everyone is entitled to a fair and public hearing ... Judgment shall be pronounced publicly, but the press and public may be excluded from all or part of the trial in the interests of morals, public order or national security in a democratic society, where the interests of juveniles or the protection of the private life of the parties so require, or to the extent strictly necessary in the opinion of the court in special circumstances where publicity would prejudice the interests of justice ...'
Art. 6(3) reads: 'Everyone charged with a criminal offence has the following minimum rights: ... (d) to examine or have examined witnesses against him and to obtain the attendance and examination of witnesses on his behalf under the same conditions as witnesses against him.'

86. For the text of Art. 457(1)(2), see under Held.

robbery.[87] The appeal in cassation was dismissed by the Supreme Court on 9 June 1992.[88] Van M. then lodged a complaint with the European Court of Human Rights. The European Court held the complaint to be well-founded on account of a violation of Article 6(1) and (3)(d) of the European Convention on Human Rights (judgment of 23 April 1997). The judgment prompted the Minister of Justice to direct that the sentence of Van M., who was still in prison at that time, should be interrupted for three months. In that period he was informed that as reparation the remainder of the prison sentence would not have to be served. In its decision of 30 October 1997 the European Court of Human Rights awarded Van M. damages of NLG 50,000[89] pursuant to Article 50 of the European Convention.[90] Finally, Van M. applied to the Supreme Court for revision of the criminal judgment of 1991, pursuant to Article 457 (1)(2) of the Code of Criminal Procedure. He argued that if the judgment of the European Court of Human Rights had been known to the Court of Appeal in 's-Hertogenbosch at that time, this would have led to his acquittal.

Held: '... 5. Assessment of the application

5.1. The applicant has always denied that he was guilty of the offences with which he was charged and of which he was convicted. The Court of Appeal in 's-Hertogenbosch used as evidence in this case statements by police officers who were questioned anonymously as witnesses by the examining magistrate at the request of the Court of Appeal. In its judgment of 23 April 1997 the European Court of Human Rights held that the evidence accepted by the Court of Appeal was contrary to the provisions of the Article 6 of the European Convention on Human Rights since the evidence was based to a decisive extent on the anonymous testimony of the police officers referred to above.

5.2 The Dutch legislation does not make provision for a procedure intended as a follow-up to a judgment of the European Court of Human Rights in which it is held that one or more provisions of the European Convention on Human Rights have been violated in criminal proceedings in the Netherlands.

---

87. The Court of Appeal quashed the judgment of the District Court of 's-Hertogenbosch of 12 May 1989, in which Van M. had been sentenced to 10 years' imprisonment for the same offences.

88. *NJ* (1992) No. 772, with note by G. Knigge.

89. As damages for pain and suffering caused by the wrongful imprisonment, see C.C. Engering and N.A. Liborang in 'Judgments of the ECHR against the Netherlands' in T. Barkhuysen, M.L. van Emmerik and P.H. van Kempen, eds., *The Execution of Strasbourg and Geneva Human Rights Decisions in the National Legal Order* (The Hague, Martinus Nijhoff 1999) p. 51. In the earlier judgment of 23 April 1997. Van M. had already been awarded an amount for the procedural costs incurred before the European Commission of Human Rights and the European Court of Human Rights. In the case of *Dombo Beheer B.V.* v. *the State of the Netherlands* the Court of Appeal of The Hague held that the costs of proceedings in the Netherlands were also eligible for compensation under Art. 50 of the Convention (judgment of 17 July 1997, *NJ Kort* (1997) No. 75). The European Court of Human Rights had previously granted an amount for the costs of proceedings before the European Commission and the European Court (judgment of 27 October 1993, *NJ* (1994) No. 534).

90. Art. 50 reads: 'If the Court finds that a decision or a measure taken by a legal authority or any other authority of a High Contracting Party is completely or partially in conflict with the obligations arising from the present Convention, and if the internal law of the said Party allows only partial reparation to be made for the consequences of this decision or measure, the decision of the Court shall, if necessary, afford just satisfaction to the injured party.'

On the basis of Article 457 of the Code of Criminal Procedure, revision of a final conviction which has the force of *res judicata* is possible only (in so far as relevant here): "On the basis of any circumstance which was not revealed during the examination at the trial in court and which is, either of itself or in conjunction with evidence previously supplied, incompatible with the judgment in the sense that there is a serious presumption that if it had been known the examination of the case would have resulted either in acquittal of the convicted person or in acquittal on a point of law on the ground that the act in the question was not punishable or in a finding that the case brought by the Public Prosecution Service was not admissible, or in a declaration that a less serious criminal provision is applicable."

5.3. The question whether a judicial decision creates a circumstance in a given case as referred to in the provision under 5.2 cannot be answered in general terms, and is instead dependent on the extent to which the opinion given in that decision is bound up with findings of fact.

5.4. The judgment of the European Court of Human Rights of 23 April 1997 contains an opinion on the extent to which the statements made by the police officers in this case can be used in evidence, having regard to the procedure followed in their examination as anonymous witnesses and having regard to all the circumstances in which that examination took place. This is not in itself a circumstance as referred to above under 5.2, which gives rise to the serious presumption referred to therein.

First of all, there is no new fact in the sense that this was something hitherto unknown on the basis of which the deliberation of the court would have resulted in a different opinion on the question – in so far as relevant in this case – of whether the applicant committed the acts with which he is charged. The possibility can also not be excluded that if the Court of Appeal had known beforehand of the opinion of the European Court of Human Rights, it would have been very likely to decide that a further examination of the police officers in question should take place in accordance with that opinion and that this would not have resulted in an acquittal of the applicant.

5.5. It follows from the above that the argument that has been submitted as a basis for the application cannot of itself be deemed to be a circumstance as referred to in Article 457, paragraph 1, opening words and (2), of the Code of Criminal Procedure. It follows that in connection with the provisions of Articles 459 and 460 of the Code of Criminal Procedure the application would not be admissible unless the Supreme Court were to break with its present case-law on revisions in order to fill the existing gap as regards the consequences to be attached to a judgment of the European Court holding that the Convention has been violated in criminal proceedings in the Netherlands.

5.6. It should, however, be noted as follows in this connection. The Dutch legislation, unlike that of the other Member States of the Council of Europe (as explained in the statements of the Public Prosecution Service), does not make provision for a special judicial procedure in which effect can be given to a judgment of the European Court of Human Rights holding that a violation of the European Convention on Human Rights has occurred in criminal proceedings in the Netherlands. The need for such a procedure allowing reparation is evident. After all, the possibility of granting compensation and deciding not to execute a sentence or terminating its execution – as has in any event occurred in the present case – is not sufficient to in all circumstances to provide reparation. It leaves intact the final judgment in which the conviction is pronounced. Moreover, it provides no solution to cases in which the ascertained violation of the European Convention is not of such a nature as to be incompatible with a conviction. As held above in 5.4, the latter situation could occur here too. As matters stand at present, no solution can therefore be provided in a revision procedure.

5.7. Various ways of providing for such a procedure are conceivable. The choices that must be made in this connection are of a political nature. For example, it will be necessary to decide whether reopening of the original procedure is appropriate and, if so, which court would be eligible for this purpose, who should make application to the court, according to what criteria this court should accept such a procedure, what decisions the court may take and whether and to what extent the original judgment remains in force and whether legal remedies also exist against a judgment given after a new trial.

5.8. In the light of the above it is not up to the courts to fill this legal gap, and certainly not by analogy with the revision arrangements. First of all, the Supreme Court would have to interpret more broadly than it has done hitherto the revision ground included in Article 457, paragraph 1, opening words and (2), of the Code of Criminal Procedure, namely in a manner that would not be compatible with its real meaning. A broad interpretation of this kind would stretch the meaning of revision beyond its true sense, as a result of which the consequences too could not be defined with sufficient certainty. Second, the courts should, in the given constitutional structure, be cautious about intervening in this way. Moreover, the legislator has this issue under consideration, as is stated in the further pleading of the Public Prosecution Service at points 4 and 15.

The Supreme Court is of the opinion that in this position and given the fundamental nature of a procedure of the kind referred to here, which might involve overturning a final and binding decision that has the force of *res judicata* and the fact that there are various ways in which reparation can be provided, it is up to the legislator to make provision for such a procedure.

5.9. In view of the above it must be decided as follows.

6. Decision

The Supreme Court declares that the application is not admissible ...'

12.273 EUROPEAN COURT OF HUMAN RIGHTS

See: 12.2704

12.28 CONSEQUENCES OF REQUESTS BY THE COMMITTEE ON TORTURE

A. v. State Secretary for Justice, District Court of The Hague (sitting in Haarlem), 26 March 1999, JV (1999) No. 116,[91] NAV (1999) No. 54,[92] GV No. 23-8.[93]

---

91. Note by R. Fernhout. See also E. Rieter, Th. Van Boven and C. Flinterman in 'Nederland wil asielzoeker uitzetten in strijd met een interim maatregel van het VN-Comité tegen Folteringen' [Netherlands will expulse an asylum seeker in conflict with an interim ruling of the UN Committee against Torture], *NJB* (1999) pp. 908-909.

92. With note.

93. Also mentioned under *GV* No. 24-74.

— There is no obligation in law for a State that is a party to the United Nations Convention for the Prevention of Torture (the Anti-Torture Convention) of 1984 to comply with a request of the Committee against Torture (CAT) to suspend expulsion of an alien pending the consideration by the Committee of a communication. Neither in the Convention nor in Article 108(9) of the Committee's Rules of Procedure can a basis for such an obligation be found.[94]

— The fact that such a request is made also provides no indication that the Committee will indeed conclude that there has been a violation of the Convention.

— The Dutch government evidently has a policy that such requests should, in principle, be granted, although situations may occur in which an exception to this principle is justified. This is, for example, the case where (1) the application for admission as a refugee is deemed by the Dutch courts to be manifestly unfounded and (2) where the alien has been refused admission to the Netherlands in the course of controls at the external border of the Schengen area.

— This is not unreasonable since the criteria for determining refugee status and for determining whether there has been a violation of Article 3 of the European Convention on Human Rights[95] *and Article 3 of the Anti-Torture Convention*[96] *are for the most part the same in terms of the estimate of the risk.*

— The Committee has indicated that its estimate of the situation in Sri Lanka is not such that belonging to a risk group as referred to in the official reports of the Dutch Ministry of Foreign Affairs is in itself sufficient to warrant the conclusion that Article 3 of the Anti-Torture Convention has been violated.

The Facts: A., of Sri Lankan nationality, arrived at Schiphol on 24 November 1998 and filed an application that same day for admission as a refugee. Two days later the application was rejected on the grounds that it was manifestly unfounded and the decision was handed to A. in the reporting office. On the same day A. applied to the District Court in The Hague (sitting in Haarlem) for review of this decision. At the same time he requested by way of provisional remedy that the decision of the State Secretary not to defer expulsion pending the hearing of the application for review be stayed. The District Court dismissed both applications on 7 December.[97] A. then filed a communication with the Committee Against Torture under Article 22 of the Anti-Torture Convention on 8 December in which he complained of the action taken by the State of the Netherlands. The Committee subsequently requested the Netherlands on 15 December under Article 108(9) of the Committee's Rules of Procedure not to expel A. pending the consideration of the communication. On 5 February 1999 the Netherlands informed the Committee that it would not comply with this request. A. then filed an objection against this decision with the State Secretary on 10 February and sent a copy to the District Court of The Hague (sitting in Haarlem), in which he requested that this

94. For the text of Art. 108(9) see under Held.

95. For the text of Art. 3 see *supra* n. 12.

96. For the text of Art. 3 see *supra* n. 66.

97. *NAV* (1998) No. 52. The District Court also declared that A.'s application for review of the custodial measure was unfounded. The District Court repeated this in its judgment of 12 February 1999, which concerned A.'s application for review of the order continuing the measure (*NAV* (1999) No. 53).

notice of objection be treated as a notice of appeal. On the same day A. requested the District Court to grant provisional remedy by staying the decision of the State Secretary not to defer expulsion until a decision had been taken on the communication to the Committee or the application to the District Court for review. A. then filed a new application for admission as a refugee on 15 February 1999, which was rejected on 17 February. Finally, on 18 February, A. supplied the District Court with more detailed reasons for the notice of appeal.

Held: '... 2.4. In view of the above, the first matter to be determined in the present proceedings is whether there are grounds for staying the expulsion until the Committee Against Torture has assessed the communication filed with it. Second, it has to be determined to whether the expulsion of the plaintiff should be stayed pending disposal of the notice of application for review.

2.5. The plaintiff has contended as follows.

(1) The refusal to comply with a request of the Committee Against Torture to stay the expulsion pending the proceedings before the Committee is, *de facto*, a violation of the Anti-Torture Convention. As long as it is not clear that the communication is unfounded, it may, after all, be well-founded. It follows that by taking this position (and acting accordingly) the State of the Netherlands runs the risk of violating the prohibition on refoulement. Owing to the absolute character of this article and the irreversible consequences that expulsion may have, the expulsion should be stayed in all cases in which it is not manifestly clear that the communication is unfounded. Such a case exists where the Committee requests the State concerned to defer expulsion. Confirmation that this is also the view of the Committee is evident from paragraph 8 of an opinion of the Committee numbered 110/1998 of 10 November 1998 (CAT/C/21/D/110/1998).

(2) In addition, the Dutch government has complied with two previous requests of the Committee for a stay of expulsion. The Committee's opinion of 13 November 1998, (CAT/C/91/1997) published in the 1999 NAV, 26, shows how desirable this was in one of the two cases: the Committee concluded in that case that a violation of Article 3 of the Anti-Torture Convention had taken place. Against this background, the defendant has not indicated in this case why the request of the Committee has not been complied with.

(3) The second application for admission as a refugee is based on the fact that a communication has been filed with the Committee. The possibility cannot be excluded in advance that these proceedings will result in the communication being held to be well-founded, with the result that the application for review has a reasonable chance of success. In addition, the defendant has not reacted in the disputed decision to the argument based on Article 3 of the Anti-Torture Convention. The defendant is obliged to hear the plaintiff on his objection. Furthermore, the plaintiff has once again put forward reasoned arguments, supported by the lodging of a number of documents, for disputing the correctness of the conclusions concerning the general situation in Sri Lanka as contained in the judgments of this Court of 9 October 1998 numbered AWB 98/652 and 98/125 VRWET H.

2.6. The defendant has put forward a reasoned defence as shown in the statement of 8 March 1999 and the notes of counsel's closing speech, which are among the case documents.

The president holds as follows:

2.7. The first point at issue is whether the defendant is obliged to comply with the request of the Committee to stay the expulsion. The basis of such a request is the provision in Article 108(9) of the Committee's Rules of Procedure, which deals with the procedure upon receipt of a communication such as the present one. The provision reads as follows: "In the course of the consideration of the question of the admissibility of a communication, the Committee or the Working Group or a special rapporteur designated under rule 106, paragraph 3, may request the State Party to take steps to avoid a possible irreparable damage to the person or persons who claimed to be victim(s) of the alleged violations. Such a request addressed to the State Party does not imply that any decision has been reached on the question of the admissibility of a communication."

2.8. The court has to agree with the defendant that there is no obligation in law on a State that it is a party to the Anti-Torture Convention to comply with a request as referred to here. No basis for such obligation can be found in the Anti-Torture Convention, nor can any such obligation be inferred from the wording of the cited Article 108(9) of the Rules of Procedure, quite apart from the issue of the effect of these rules. Nor is there any ground for assuming that the circumstance that the request has been made constitutes an indication that there is a likelihood that the Committee will conclude there has been a violation of the Convention. Reference should be made to the second sentence of the cited provision, in which connection it should also be noted that the criteria on the basis of which the Committee decides on such a request are not known. It cannot be inferred from the opinion lodged by the plaintiff that the Committee would not share the view expressed above, quite apart from the fact that an opinion of the Committee concerning this problem is not binding on the States that are parties to the Anti-Torture Convention.

2.9. This therefore brings the court to the second argument advanced by the plaintiff. According to the statement of 26 February 1999 submitted by the State of the Netherlands in answer to the questions raised by a member of the Lower House of Parliament (Halsema of the Green Party) dated 29 January 1999 (Lower House, 1998-1999, Annex to Proceedings, No. 897), the Dutch government evidently has a policy that such requests should, in principle, be granted, although situations may occur in which an exception to this principle is justified. Such an exception occurs, *inter alia*, where two circumstances occur together: where (1) the application for admission as a refugee is rightly deemed by the Dutch courts to be manifestly unfounded and (2) the alien has been refused admission to the Netherlands in the course of controls at the external border of the Schengen area.

2.10. The president considers for the time being that this policy is not manifestly unreasonable. This is because the criteria for determining refugee status and for determining whether there has been a violation of Article 3 of the European Convention on Human Rights and Article 3 of the Anti-Torture Convention are for the most part the same in terms of the estimate of the risk, save for certain exceptions (in particular the cases in which refugee status is claimed, but no evidence of a ground for persecution can be demonstrated). After all, a decision based on an estimate of risk to the effect that there cannot reasonably be any doubt – save where the said exceptions occur – that the person concerned is not a refugee is, after all, not compatible with the possibility that there are concrete grounds for assuming that he would run a real risk (Art. 3 of the European Convention on Human Rights) or danger (Art. 3 of the Anti-Torture Convention) of being subjected to treatment that is prohibited under the provisions of the Conventions. If the defendant therefore arrives at the conclusion on the basis of such a determination that the asylum request is manifestly unfounded and if the court agrees with this, the defendant need not take account of the possibility that the Committee will find that there has been a violation of the Anti-Torture Convention.[98]

2.11. In the present case it has been determined in law, on the basis of an estimate of the risk, that the application for admission as a refugee is manifestly unfounded, in other words that it is beyond doubt that there is no danger of persecution. Moreover, this is a case in which the person concerned was refused admission to the Netherlands as a result of controls at the external border of the Schengen area. This means that the plaintiff cannot derive any entitlement to a stay of expulsion from with the said policy, which also explains the difference in treatment from the other cases, always assuming that the policy existed at that time too.

2.12. There is no evidence of special circumstances which would require the defendant, contrary to the policy, to stay the expulsion, for example subsequent information about facts that the court that has already heard the case could not take into account. The following point should also be made in this connection.

2.13. In its statement of 26 February 1999 sent to the Committee in support of its position, the Dutch government referred to an opinion of the Committee, number 94/1997, adopted on 19 May 1998 in respect of a communication by a Sri Lankan asylum-seeker who had been refused entry to Switzerland. In the opinion of the president, the Committee indicated in the opinion that its estimate of the situation in Sri Lanka was not such that belonging to a risk group as referred to in the official reports of the Minister for Foreign Affairs of 24 March 1998 and 6 November 1998 was in itself sufficient to warrant the conclusion that Article 3 of the Anti-Torture Convention had been violated. The situation in Sri Lanka has not changed since then in a way that would justify the assumption that the Committee will deviate from this approach in the present case. The documents lodged by the plaintiff in these proceedings were for the most part already known and do not shed such new light on the situation that the previous conclusions of this court in the judgments of 9 October 1998, numbers AWB 98/652 and 98/125 VRWET H, are no longer tenable.

---

98. The District Court of The Hague held in its judgment of 30 March 1998 in the case of *D.M.* v. *State Secretary for Justice* (*JV* (1998) No. 77, with note by T. Spijkerboer, summarised and discussed by K. Pastoors in *NAV* (1998) p. 317), that it could be inferred from the case-law of the European Court of Human Rights and the rulings of the Committee Against Torture that the same criterion applied in determining the extent of the risk for the acceptance of refugee status under Art. 15(1) of the Aliens Act in conjunction with Art. 1(A)(2) of the Refugee Convention and violation of Art. 3 of the European Convention on Human Rights and Art. 3 of the Anti-Torture Convention of 1984. According to the District Court, the three instruments did not provide international protection against the purely arbitrary risk that someone might run in the event of a (compulsory) return. In order to invoke these instruments successfully, it is necessary to make out a plausible case that the person concerned personally runs the risk expressed by the words 'well-founded fear' or 'real risk'. The designation of risk categories of Tamils in the official reports of the Minister for Foreign Affairs should therefore be interpreted as meaning that with regard to these categories of persons a fear of persecution or a real risk of violation of Art. 3 of the European Convention on Human Rights or of torture within the meaning of the Anti-Torture Convention should be readily assumed if it is plausibly demonstrated not only that the person concerned belongs to one or more of the risk categories but also that there are special circumstances giving rise to a suspicion that the 'negative attention' of the Sri Lankan authorities is focused on the person concerned.

2.14. In the context of his second application for admission as a refugee the plaintiff has also not adduced evidence of any new facts or circumstances that would shed new light on his story. Even if the letters of a bishop from Jaffna could be regarded as new evidence, they cannot play a role if only because they have not been lodged.

2.15. It follows from the above that there is no ground for staying the expulsion of the plaintiff and that the request to this effect will therefore be dismissed.

2.16. On the grounds of the above the president considers that there is every likelihood that the notice of appeal that has been lodged will not result in a different outcome than in the procedure for provisional remedy. As it has not been shown that further consideration of the notice of appeal could reasonably contribute to an assessment of the case, there is reason in this case to exercise the power contained in Article 8:86 of the General Administrative Law Act. The president will hold that the notice of appeal against the decision not to grant the application for admission as a refugee is unfounded ...'[99]

12.29 OTHER MEANS OF SETTLEMENT
See: 16.164

13.223 UN EMBARGO, BOYCOTT, BLOCKADE

P.J.F. de Kerf v. Minister of Finance, Trade and Industry Appeal Tribunal, 19 August 1999.[100]

— Acts as referred to in Article 1 of the Sanctions Decree on International Payments and Financial Services against Iraq of 1991[101] *of a legal entity established in the Netherlands*

---

99. On 12 May 1999 the Committee held in an interim ruling that A.'s communication was admissible (*NAV* (1999) No. 86, *JAV* (1999) No. 160). It requested the Netherlands to make clear what measures had been taken to have A. examined by a doctor in connection with the torture that he had suffered. Finally, the Committee noted as follows: 'Furthermore, the Committee notes the State party's statement that it saw no reason to honour the Committee's request under rule 108, paragraph 9, of its rules of procedure not to expel the author while his communication is under consideration. The Committee considers that the State party, in ratifying the Convention and voluntarily accepting the Committee's competence under Art. 22, undertook to co-operate with it in good faith in applying the procedure. Compliance with the provisional measures called for by the Committee in cases it considers reasonable is essential in order to protect the person in question from irreparable harm, which could, moreover, nullify the end result of the proceedings before the Committee.

Under rule 110, paragraph 3, of the rules of procedure the Committee reiterates its view that it would be desirable not to return the author to Sri Lanka while his communication is under consideration by the Committee. However, such expression of its views does not prejudge the Committee's final decision on the merits of the communication.'

100. Note by J.H. van der Veen. Summarised in *AB Kort* (1999) No. 485 and *NJB* (1999) p. 1702 (No. 12).

101. For the text of Art. 1 see under Held. As regards the previous Decision on Sanctions on International Payments and Financial Services against Iraq, see 22 *NYIL* (1991) p. 370. For the new Iraq Sanction Decree of 2 August 1997, see 19 *NYIL* (1998) p. 234.

and in liquidation can, since the only person connected with the legal entity has Iraqi nationaltiy, be equated substantively with acts in respect of moneys or assets that belong to a person living or resident in Iraq.
— The Sanctions Decree must be regarded as the implementation by the Dutch legislator of Resolutions 660, 661, 687 and 778 of the Security Council of the United Nations.[102] *It follows that the resolutions do not therefore contain provisions that can be binding on any person and do not therefore prevent the possibility of dispensation referred to in Article 1 of the Decree from being applicable.*
— Where this possibility is invoked, it will be necessary to indicate, having regard, inter alia, to the provisions of Article 9 of the Sanctions Act,[103] *what special interests would, on balance, necessitate refusal in the case of the applicant. Refusal by means of a simple reference to the resolutions is not sufficient.*

The Facts: Mass Holland International B.V., a private company, was incorporated in 1992 on behalf of A.I. Saleh, who possessed Iraqi nationality and was the owner of a chicken fattening business in Iraq. According to an extract from the Commercial Register, Saleh was the sole shareholder and managing director. The Minister of Justice issued a certificate of no objection to the incorporation of the company. At some point the assets of the company were frozen. By decision of 10 June 1996 of the Chamber of Commerce of North-East Brabant, the company was wound up and P.J.F. de Kerf was appointed as liquidator. De Kerf then wrote to the Dutch Central Bank on 4 October 1996 requesting that he be granted a dispensation from the Sanctions Decree on International Payments and Financial Services against Iraq of 1991. The Bank forwarded the request to the Minister of Finance for consideration. The latter, acting also on behalf of the Minister for Foreign Affairs, refused the request on 27 March 1997. De Kerf appealed to the Trade and Industry Appeal Tribunal against this refusal.

Held: '... 2. The basis of the dispute.

2.1. Pursuant to Article 2 in conjunction with Article 3, paragraph 1, of the Act of 15 February 1980, Bulletin of Acts and Orders 1980, 93, for the taking of sanctions against certain States or areas (referred to below as the Sanctions Act 1977), rules may be laid down concerning the movement of goods, services and payments, shipping, civil aviation, road transport, post and telecommunications in respect of the States or areas designated in the Sanctions Decree, in order to comply with resolutions or recommendations of bodies of international organisations or with international agreements relating to the maintenance or restoration of international peace and security or the promotion of the international legal order.

Pursuant to Article 9, paragraph 1, of the Sanctions Act 1977, the government ministers designated in the Sanctions Decree or the Sanctions Order may grant exemption from rules and regulations as described in Article 3 and, on request, dispensation. Pursuant to paragraph 2, an exemption or dispensation may be granted subject to conditions or obligations.

---

102. For the relevant text and dates of the resolutions see under Held.

103. For the text of Art. 9 see under Held. As regards the Act in general see also 12 *NYIL* (1981) p. 292, and P.J. Kuyper, 'The Netherlands in International Law of Export Control', *Jurisdictional Issues* (1992) pp. 117-145.

Article 1 of the Royal Decree of 2 April 1991, Bulletin of Acts and Orders 1991, 167, which contains financial sanctions against Iraq (the Sanctions Decree on International Payments and Financial Services against Iraq of 1991), reads as follows: "Everyone is forbidden, without dispensation granted by or on behalf of Our Minister for Foreign Affairs and Our Minister of Finance, to perform any act of management or disposal with regard to moneys or assets that are kept at banks or other financial institutions established in the Netherlands and that belong directly or indirectly, wholly or to a great extent, to the Republic of Iraq, persons resident or staying there, public bodies established there, legal entities established there and branches or sub-offices in that country of legal entities that are established elsewhere."

Pursuant to Article 1 of the Act of 31 May 1994, Bulletin of Acts and Orders 382, which extends the term of operation of the Sanctions Decree on International Payments and Financial Services against Iraq, the term of operation of the Sanctions Decree has been extended for an indefinite period.

The Sanctions Decree is intended to comply with international agreements concerning Iraq, and in particular Resolutions 660 and 661 of the Security Council of the United Nations. The following paragraph of Resolutions 661 is important to the present case:

"4. Decides that States shall not make available to the government of Iraq, or to any commercial, industrial or public utility undertaking in Iraq or Kuwait, any funds or any other financial or economic resources and shall prevent their nationals and any persons within their territories from removing from their territories or otherwise making available to that Government or to any such undertaking any such funds or resources and from remitting any other funds to persons or bodies within Iraq or Kuwait, except payments exclusively for a strictly medical or humanitarian purposes and, in humanitarian circumstances, foodstuffs."

This is elaborated in Resolutions 687 of 3 April 1991 and Resolution 778 of 2 October 1992. Paragraph 20 of Resolution 687 reads:

"Decides, effective immediately, that the prohibitions against the sale or supply to Iraq of commodities or products other than medicine and health supplies and prohibitions against financial transactions related thereto contained in resolution 661 (1990), shall not apply to foodstuffs notified to the Security Council Committee established by resolution 661 (1990) concerning the situation between Iraq and Kuwait or, with the approval of that Committee, under the simplified and accelerated Ano-objection procedure, to materials and supplies for essential civilian needs has identified in the report to the Secretary-General dated 20 March 1991, and in any further findings of humanitarian need by the Committee."

Finally, paragraph 11 of resolution 778 reads as follows:

"11. Decides that no further Iraqi assets shall be released for purposes set forth in paragraph 20 of resolution 687 (1991) except to the sub-account of the escrow account, established pursuant to paragraph 8 of resolution 712 (1991), or directly to the United Nations for humanitarian activities in Iraq;"[104]

[...]

---

104. Resolution 660 of 2 August 1990 and Resolution 661 of 6 August 1990.

3. The disputed decision and the position of the respondent
In essence, the disputed decision is as follows. Saleh is the sole shareholder of Mass Holland International B.V. and, according to the available information, is resident in Iraq. It follows that Article 1 of the Sanctions Decree is applicable.

The condition on which dispensation can be granted is described in Resolution 778 of the United Nations. Under this resolution, blocked accounts can be released only for the purpose of transmission to the escrow account of the United Nations. As the Netherlands is subject to the obligation to implement sanctions measures against Iraq in accordance with the resolutions of the Security Council, there is no reason in this case to grant the requested dispensation. The position taken by the appellant, namely that it is being made impossible for him to discharge his statutory duties as liquidator owing to the lack of moneys to pay his accounts cannot mean that other statutory provisions, including the provisions of the Sanctions Act 1977, the implementing decrees based on the Sanctions Act 1977 and the policy in this regard, should not be applied.

In the statement of defence and at the hearing, it was once again emphasised on behalf of the respondent that the various interests had not been weighed against one another. In particular, paragraph 11 of Resolution 778 should be interpreted so strictly as to contain a prohibition on allowing any acts of management or disposal other than payments to the escrow account. This prohibition is absolute and does not allow the respondent any scope for deviation from it.

4. The position of the appellant

In support of the appeal the appellant has, in brief, submitted the following arguments against the disputed decision.

The appellant's primary submission is that Article 1 of the Sanctions Decree does not apply since this case does not involve a Dutch company. The fact that the shareholder is resident or staying in Iraq does not make any difference. It has, incidentally, not been established in any way that Saleh, who is of Kurdish origin, is still present in Iraq.

It has been argued alternatively that Article 9 of the Sanctions Act 1977 provides for the possibility of granting a dispensation as requested. The granting of an exemption or dispensation may be necessary for reasons of fairness, as is also evident from the explanatory memorandum to the Act. This is the case here. As liquidator the appellant has the duty of liquidating the assets of the legal entity that has been wound up. It is evident for the time being from the accounts of Mass Holland International B.V. that there are substantial claims that must be examined in more detail. In order to carry out this examination the appellant must have access to the assets on the bank account.

The fact that requests such as this one have always been refused need not mean that this should occur in the present case. The case of the appellant differs substantially from the previous cases disposed of by the respondent, which always involved requests by creditors of a legal entity. The respondent has wrongly failed to consider the possibility of granting dispensation subject to the condition that no payments are made to Saleh, except where permitted by law.

5. Assessment of the dispute

As regards the primary ground of appeal of the appellant, the Tribunal holds that the respondent had good grounds for taking the position that Article 1 of the Sanctions Decree also covers act of management or disposition that relate to moneys or assets belonging to Mass Holland International B.V. in liquidation. It is held in this respect that Saleh, who, in view of the entry in the Commercial Register, must be deemed to be living or resident in Iraq and to possess Iraqi nationality, is the sole person connected with this legal entity. Acts as referred to in the above-mentioned Article 1 relating to moneys or assets of the legal entity in liquidation should therefore be substantively equated, for the purposes of the Sanctions Decree, with acts relating to moneys or assets belonging to a person living or resident in Iraq. The primary ground of appeal of the appellant therefore fails.

As regards the alternative ground of appeal, the Appeal Tribunal holds as follows. The respondent has taken the position that he is bound by the resolutions of the Security Council cited above to such an extent that a dispensation of the kind requested by the appellant can never be granted.

The Appeal Tribunal holds in this regard in the first place that the said resolutions of the Security Council do not contain provisions that can be binding on any person and do not therefore prevent the applicability of the possibility of dispensation referred to in Article 1 of the Decree. The legislator implemented the agreements contained in the resolutions in the Dutch legislation by including them in the Sanctions Decree. The possibility of dispensation contained in the Sanctions Decree, in conjunction with Article 9 of the Sanctions Act 1977, is part of this implementation. If this is invoked, it will have to be shown in respect of each request what special interests necessitate refusal of the request by the applicant. A mere reference to the resolutions is not sufficient for this purpose since the possibility of dispensation is, as mentioned above, part and parcel of the implementation.

This is all the more relevant here since there is a special situation, in the sense that a request has been submitted by the Dutch liquidator of a legal entity that is in liquidation under Dutch law. The respondent has not indicated any reasons that would prevent a dispensation subject to safeguards that no payments are made in the direction of Iraq other than to the escrow account, for example by the attachment of a condition as suggested by the appellant.

In view of the above, the Appeal Tribunal holds that the disputed decision is contrary to Article 7:12, paragraph 1, of the General Administrative Law Act, which requires that a decision on an objection be based on sound reasons. The appeal is well-founded and the disputed decision must therefore be quashed. It will therefore be directed that the respondent make a fresh decision taking into account the reasoning in this judgment ...'

14.125 HUMANITARIAN LAW

See: 4.52 (pp. 272-277)

16.164 PROTECTION OF ANIMALS

Republic of Madagascar v. State of the Netherlands, District Court of The Hague, 16 March 1999, KG (1999) No. 125.

— Legal proceedings by the Republic of Madagascar against the State of the Netherlands in Dutch courts.
— Granting of a claim that the Netherlands should cooperate in the return to Madagascar of 35 tortoises seized in the Netherlands. The wish of the Netherlands to exclude all risk is an insufficient justification for refusing cooperation in the short term.

The Facts: Thirty-five tortoises of the species *Geochelone Yniphora* were seized (under the criminal law) in Vlissingen on 15 November 1996. This species is included in Schedule I to the 1973 Convention on International Trade in Endangered Species of Wild Fauna and Flora.[105] It was not until 22 June 1998 that the CITES Authority[106] in the Netherlands notified Madagascar of this seizure. Evidently it was only at this juncture that it became certain that the tortoises were part of a consignment of 75 tortoises that had been stolen from a breeding station in Madagascar in May 1996. The CITES Authority also stated that the animals would not be sent back to Madagascar owing to the health risks (bacterial infection), and would instead be sent to the Wildlife Preservation Trust in Jersey (UK). Madagascar then gave notice that it wished the animals to be returned immediately. However, on 15 December the CITES Authority sent all but two of the animals to the Wildlife Conservation Society in the United States. Madagascar then applied to the President of the District Court of The Hague for an interim injunction ordering the State of the Netherlands to cooperate in securing the immediate return of the 35 tortoises to Madagascar. Madagascar claimed that the Netherlands had acted unlawfully by wishing to dispose of the animals as though it had the absolute say over them. The protection provisions in the Convention and in EC Regulation No. 338/97[107] did not give it the right to determine what happened to the animals.

Held: '... Applicable law

4.2. The plaintiff contends that the defendant acted unlawfully in the Netherlands. The plaintiff's claim is therefore governed by Dutch law as *lex loci delicti.*

Tort?

4.3. The dispute between the parties concerns the question of whether the duty of care of the defendant goes so far that it can retain possession of the tortoises against the will of the plaintiff, who is their lawful owner.

4.4. Article VII, paragraph 4, of the CITES Convention provides that: "When live animals are confiscated by government authorities, these authorities have a responsibility to dispose of them appropriately."[108] In view of this provision, it may be concluded that it

---

105. 993 *UNTS* p. 243; 12 *ILM* (1973) p. 1085; *Trb.* 1975 No. 23 (the species is mentioned on page 53).

106. This is the national 'Management Authority' referred to in Art. XI of the Convention. In the Netherlands, this authority is part of Laser, which is itself part of the Ministry of Agriculture, Nature Management and Fisheries.

107. Council Regulation on the protection of species of wild fauna and flora by regulating trade therein, 9 December 1996, *OJ* (1997) p. L 61/1.

108. This is not the text of Art. VII(4). Presumably this should be a reference to Art. VIII(4). The complete text of this provision reads as follows: 'Where a living specimen is confiscated as a result of measures referred to in paragraph 1 of this Article: (a) the specimen shall be entrusted to a Management Authority of the State of confiscation; (b) the Management Authority shall, after and consultation with the State of export, and returned the specimen to that State at the expense of that

was reasonable for the defendant to wish to make due arrangements for the care of the tortoises and for their safe disposal and destination.

4.5. There is no evidence that the tortoises are sick. However, it is possible that their intestinal flora contain bacteria that do not occur in tortoises of the same species in Madagascar. It is impossible to say at present whether this constitutes a danger to other tortoises of the same species or to other reptiles in Madagascar. The defendant clearly takes the position that all risk must be excluded and that until such time as all the tests have been completed the tortoises should certainly not be returned.

4.6. It should be observed that the tortoises have already been outside Madagascar for 22 years without any apparent damage to their health. The desire of the defendant to exclude all risk is an insufficient justification for refusing to cooperate in the handing over the tortoises in the short term. The defendant has not demonstrated sufficiently to the satisfaction of the court that on the basis of the present test results the animals cannot be returned to Madagascar and examined there for possible sicknesses, if necessary being held in quarantine.

4.7. It follows from the above that the claim will be granted as follows. The 33 tortoises should be returned to Madagascar after the completion of the second test stage referred to in Dr Behler's[109] letter of 18 February 1999, and in any event by 1 May 1999 at the latest. The two tortoises currently in the rescue centre in Vlissingen should also be returned to the plaintiff by 1 May 1999 at the latest.

There is no occasion to impose a periodic penalty [astreinte] for the eventuality of failure to comply with this order since the State always complies with court judgments without the need for a sanction of this kind ...'

16.55 ENVIRONMENTAL QUESTIONS

See: 8.23; 16.164

16.723 INTERNATIONAL REGULATION OF INTELLECTUAL PROPERTY

See: 3.2113

State, or to a rescue centre or such other place as the Management Authority deems appropriate and consistent with the purposes of the present Convention; and (c) the Management Authority may obtain the advice of a Scientific Authority, or may, wherever it considers it desirable, consulted the Secretariat in order to facilitate the decision under subparagraph (b) of this paragraph, including the choice of a rescue centre or other place.'

109. Director of the Wildlife Conservation Society.

DUTCH LITERATURE IN THE FIELD OF PUBLIC INTERNATIONAL LAW AND RELATED MATTERS, 1999

M. Filet*

This survey is intended to provide information for international lawyers and law students, both in the Netherlands and abroad, on materials concerning international law published in and outside the Netherlands by Dutch authors. A few articles not meeting these criteria are also included. Furthermore, 'international law' has been interpreted widely, so as to include related matters, if the work in question deals with international law considerations. Fiscal law, polemology and specific regulations under European law are generally not included. The survey lists books, articles, inaugural lectures, dissertations and reports.

1. INTERNATIONAL LAW IN GENERAL

See also: 1.11, Kooijmans, P.H.

— *Adviesraad Internationale Vraagstukken* 'Jaarverslag 1999' [Annual Report 1999 of the Advisory Council on international affairs] (The Hague, Adviesraad Internationale Vraagstukken 1999) 32 pp.

— *Commissie van Advies inzake Volkenrechtelijke Vraagstukken* – 'Jaarverslag 1999' [Annual Report 1999 of the Advisory Committee on issues of public international law] (The Hague, Commissie van Advies inzake Volkenrechtelijke Vraagstukken 2000) 13 pp. and 5 Annexes.

— *Realism and Moralism in International Relations: Essays in Honor of Frans A.M. Alting von Geusau*, W.J.M. van Genugten, E.M.H. Hirsch Ballin, E.J. Janse de Jonge, P.H. Kooijmans, eds. (The Hague, Kluwer Law International 1998) 298 pp.

Dekker, I.G.; Schrijver, N.J. — 'Volkenrecht' [Public international law], 48 *Ars Aequi* (1999) Katern No. 70, pp. 3476-3481; No. 72, pp. 3616-3621.

— *International Law and The Hague's 750th Anniversary*, W.P. Heere, ed. (The Hague, T.M.C. Asser Press 1999) 466 pp.

Kooijmans, P.H. — 'International law: placebo or medication?', in W.J.M. van Genugten, E.M.H. Hirsch Ballin, E.J. Janse de Jonge, P.H. Kooijmans, eds., *Realism and Moralism in*

1. Research associate in Public International Law, T.M.C. Asser Institute.

International Relations; Essays in Honor of Frans A.M. Alting von Geusau (The Hague, Kluwer Law International 1999) pp. 87-92.

Kooijmans, P.H. — 'Kroniek van het internationaal publiekrecht' [Chronicle of international public law], 74 *Nederlands Juristenblad* (1999) pp. 482-485.

1.0 HISTORY

See also: 12.273 ICC, Hebel, H.A.M. von
14.1252, Roodt, E. de

Kalshoven, F. — 'De Eerste Haagse Vredesconferentie van 1899' [The First Hague Peace Conference of 1899], 92 *Militair Rechtelijk Tijdschrift* (1999) pp. 257-266.

Myjer, E.P.J. — 'Honderd jaar Haagse vredesconferentie; heeft Den Haag eindelijk een profiel?' [One century of Hague Peace Conferences; does The Hague finally have a profile?], 74 *Nederlands Juristenblad* (1999) pp. 852-859.

1.11 THEORETICAL AND PHILOSOPHICAL ASPECTS OF INTERNATIONAL LAW

See also: 1.203, Simon, H.J
3.223 EMU, Amtenbrink, F.

Cliteur, P.B. — *De filosofie van mensenrechten* [The philosophy of human rights] (Nijmegen, Ars Aequi 1999) 166 pp.

Kooijmans, P.H. — 'Fin de millénaire' [Fin de millénaire], 74 *Nederlands Juristenblad* (1999) pp. 2117-2119.

1.13 THE NATURE OF INTERNATIONAL RIGHTS AND DUTIES

See: 14.1121, Aalbers, C.T.

1.15 POLITICAL, ECONOMIC AND OTHER NON-LEGAL ASPECTS OF INTERNATIONAL LAW

— *Internationale Organisatie; Samenwerking en regimevorming in de internationale betrekkingen* [International organisation; cooperation and regime development in international relations] A.G. van Harry, J. van der Harst, P.M.E. Volten, eds. (Assen, Van Gorcum 1999) 294 pp.

1.17 ATTITUDE OF VARIOUS GROUPS OF STATES TOWARDS INTERNATIONAL LAW

See: 4.7, Grondrechten, etc.

1.2 RELATIONSHIP BETWEEN INTERNATIONAL LAW AND MUNICIPAL LAW

See also: 4.7, Akkermans, P.C.W.; Bax, C.J.; Verhey, L.F.M.
4.73, Rozemond, K.
6., Brouwers, J.G.

— *Flexibility in Constitutions*, A.A.M. Schrauwen, ed. (Amsterdam, Hogendorp Centre for European Constitutional Studies 1999) 140 pp.

Burg, F.H. van der — *Europees gemeenschapsrecht in de Nederlandse rechtsorde* [European community law in the Dutch legal system] (Deventer, Tjeenk Willink 1998) 153 pp.

Jessurun D'Oliveira, H.U. — 'Rechters die afstemmen en afhouden; Vragen over de verenigbaarheid van coördinatiestrategieën met Artikel 17 Grondwet en Artikel 6 EVRM' [Judges who tune in and withhold: questions on the compatibility of coordination-strategies to Article 17 Constitution and Article 6 ECHR], 74 *Nederlands Juristenblad* (1999) pp. 377-384.

Kambel, E.R. — 'Mijn land of ons land?' [My land or our land?], *Nemesis* (1999) No. 5, pp. 144-151.

Kortmann, C.A.J.M. — 'Secundair gemeenschapsrecht en de nationale constituties' [Secundairy community law and the national constitutions], 47 *Sociaal-Economische Wetgeving* (1999) pp. 82-88.

Kummeling, H.R.B.M.; Kortmann, C.A.J.M. — 'Naar een nieuwe Gondwet?/Een beetje wel, maar verder niet' [Towards a new constitution?/ just a bit, but not too much], 48 *Ars Aequi* (1999) pp. 233-238.

Stroink, F.A.M. — 'De betekenis van de Straatsburgse jurisprudentie inzake de onafhankelijkheid en de onpartijdigheid voor het Nederlandse recht' [The meaning of Strassburg jurisprudence concerning the independence and impartiality of Dutch law], 24 *NJCM Bulletin* (1999) pp. 5-32.

Vlemminx, F.M.C — 'Een ieder verbindend verdragsrecht en de bevoegdheden van de (bestuurs)rechter' [Binding treaty law and the competence of the (administrative) judge], 74 *Nederlands Juristenblad* (1999) pp. 949-955.

Vlies, I.C. van der; Widdershoven, R.J.G.M. — *De betekenissen van de Nederlandse grondwet binnen de Europese rechtsorde* [The meaning of the Dutch Constitution within the European legal order] (Deventer, Tjeenk Willink 1998) 72 pp.

1.201 MONIST AND DUALIST THEORIES
See: 1.2, Vlemminx, F.M.C

1.202 ENFORCEMENT OF INTERNATIONAL LAW IN MUNICIPAL LAW
See also: 12.2704,

Boer, M. den — 'Booming business in Brussel: JBZ-instrumenten rollen in hoog tempo van de lopende band' [Booming business in Brussels, justice and internal affairs 'instruments' come at high speed from the assembly line], *Trema* (1999) No. 2, pp. 38-41.

— *Compliance and Enforcement of European Community Law,* J.A.E. Vervaele, ed. (The Hague, Kluwer Law International 1999) 426 pp. European Monographs 20.

1.203 CONFLICT BETWEEN INTERNATIONAL LAW AND MUNICIPAL LAW
See also: 4.73, Boone, M.; Franken, A.A; Klip, A.; Meer van der, I.; T. Prakken

Brouwer, J.G.; Schilder, A.E. — 'Het wetsvoorstel bestuurlijke ophouding; Een verkenning van de rechtsstatelijke grenzen' [The bill on administrative detainement; a reconnaissance of the state judicial boundaries], 74 *Nederlands Juristenblad* (1999) pp. 1640-1648.

Franken, A.A.; Jurgens, M. — 'Geen bewijs, toch betalen of zitten' [No proof, still pay or do your time], 79 *Advocatenblad* (1999) pp. 922-925.

Graaff de, B.J.G.; Janse de Jonge, E.J. — 'De wet op de inlichtingen- en veiligheidsdiensten' [The Act on Intelligence- and Security Services], 74 *Nederlands Juristenblad* (1999) pp. 1925-1931.

Kortmann, C.A.J.M. — 'De Eerste Kamer uit de bocht' [The Senate is at it again], 74 *Nederlands Juristenblad* (1999) 255 pp. (Comment on this article by E. Jurgens, in 74 *Nederlands Juristenblad* (1999) pp. 396-397; further comment by A. Postma, in 74 *Nederlands Juristenblad* (1999) pp. 694-650).

Kraus, S. — 'Alleen kostwinners voldoende geintegreerd in Nederland?' [Are only breadwinners sufficiently integrated in the Netherlands?], *Nemesis* (1999) No. 3, pp. 99-100.

Pennings, F.J.L. — 'Invloed van het internationale recht in de Koppelingswet jurisprudentie; Sociale zekerheid en verdrag' [The influence of international law in the linking law; social security and treaty], *Migrantenrecht* (1999) pp. 95-103.

Simon, H.J — 'Bestuursrecht en mensenrechten; Top down of bottom up?' [Administrative law and human rights; top down or bottom up?], 74 *Nederlands Juristenblad* (1999) pp. 1187-1197.

1.204 SELF-EXECUTING PROVISIONS OF TREATIES OR DECISIONS OF INTERNATIONAL ORGANIZATIONS

See: 4.66, Fleuren, J.; Zwaan, K.

1.21 INTERNATIONAL LAW IN MUNICIPAL COURTS

See also: 1.202, Vervaele, J.A.E., ed.

Brans, E.H.P.; Veen, G.A. van der — 'Publiek domein en aansprakelijkheid voor milieuschade veroorzaakt door olieverontreiniging: de Patmos en de Haven' [Public domain and liability for environmental damage caused by oil pollution: Patmos and Haven], *Tijdschrift voor Milieuaansprakelijkheid* (1999) pp. 109-118.

2.4 JUDICIAL DECISIONS AS SOURCE OF INTERNATIONAL LAW

See: 1.2, Stroink, F.A.M.
6.12, Velde, J. van der

3.111 SOVEREIGNTY AND INDEPENDENCE

See: 9.1, Hoeven, R. van der
13.222, Haandrikman, Y.

3.1141 IMMUNITY OF FOREIGN STATES AND OF THEIR ORGANS AND PROPERTY

— *Advies inzake: Immuniteit van staten en hun eigendom; De ontwerp-artikelen van de International Law Commission* [Advisory Committee on issues of public international law; advisory report on: immunity of states and their property; draft articles of the International Law Commission], Commissie van Advies inzake Volkenrechtelijke Vraagstukken Jaarverslag 1999 (The Hague 2000) Annex 4, pp. 1-19.

3.132 PERSONAL UNIONS, REAL UNIONS (ALSO THE COMMONWEALTH AND THE KINGDOM OF THE NETHERLANDS)

See also:	4.63,	Wisse, C.
	4.64,	Kruit, P.J.J. van der
	4.7,	Kelk, C.
	4.73,	Hartog, A. den

Meel, P. — *Tussen autonomie en onafhankelijkheid; Nederlands-Surinaamse betrekkingen 1954-1961* [Between autonomy and independence; Dutch-Surinam relations 1954-1961] (Leiden, Koninklijk Instituut voor Taal-, Land-, en Volkenkunde Uitgeverij 1999) 450 pp.

Korthals Altes, T.E. — *Koninkrijk aan zee; De lange vlucht van liefde in het Caribisch-Nederlands bestuur* [Kingdom at sea; the long flight of love in the Caribian-Dutch government] (Zutphen, Walburg Press 1999) 208 pp.

3.12 RECOGNITION

See:	3.14,	Klabbers, J.; Koskenniemi, M.; Ribbelink, O.; Zimmermann, A. eds.

3.14 FORMATION, CONTINUITY AND SUCCESSION OF STATES

See also:	3.132,	Meel, P.
	3.344,	Genugten, W.J.M. van

Klabbers, J., Koskenniemi, M., Ribbelink, O., Zimmermann, A. — *State Practice Regarding State Succession and Issues of Recognition: the Pilot Project of the Council of Europe* [The pilot project of the Council of Europe regarding state succession and issues of recognition] (The Hague, Kluwer Law International 1999) 521 pp.

Couwenberg, S.W. — 'Supra-nationale staatsvormen of terug naar de Middeleeuwen?' [Supra-national state structures or return to the Middle Ages?], 53 *Internationale Spectator* (1999) pp. 436-442.

Dijkstra, G.S.A. — 'Bosnie en Hercegovina; tussen onafhankelijke staat en internationaal protectoraat' [Bosnia-Hercegovina; between an independent state and an international protectorate], 53 *Internationale Spectator* (1999) pp. 402-408.

3.2 INTERNATIONAL ORGANIZATIONS

See:	1.,	Realism and Moralism, etc.
	1.15,	Internationale Organisatie, etc.
	4.7,	Human Rights and Ethnic, etc.

3.211 LEGAL STATUS

Zwaan, J. de — 'The Legal Personality of the European Communities and the European Union', 30 *Netherlands Yearbook of International Law* (1999) pp. 75-113.

3.2112 POWERS, INCLUDING TREATY-MAKING POWER

See also:	1.,	Realism and Moralism, etc.
	3.221 WTO,	Bronckers, M.E.C.J.
	3.223 EMU,	Amtenbrink, F.
	3.223 EU,	Barents, R.; Brinkhorst, L.J.; Eijsbouts, W.T.
	13.23,	Daalder, I.H.; Leurdijk, D. A.
	16.723,	Bonofacio, M.

Kummeling, H.R.B.M. — 'Verdere democratisering van de Europese Unie?' [More democratising of the European Union?], *Iust* (1999) pp. 52-59.

Ooik, R.H. — *De keuze der rechtsgrondslag voor besluiten van de Europese Unie* [The choice for the legal basis for decisions of the European Union] (Deventer, Kluwer 1999) 483 pp. Europese Monografieën 63.

Pijpers, A. — *De mythe van het democratisch tekort. Een discussiebijdrage over de Europese politiek* [The myth of the democratic deficiency. A discussion on European politics] (The Hague, Clingendael Occasional Papers 1999) 41 pp.

3.21121 COMPETENCE OF VARIOUS ORGANS

See:	3.223 EU,	Rood, J.Q.T
	12.273 ECJ,	Curtin, D.M.; Ooik, R.H. van; Werner, W.G.

3.21122 PROCEDURE OF DECISION-MAKING

See also: 3.222 NATO, Zandee, D.

Blokker, N. — 'Decisions of International Organizations: The Case of the European Union', 30 *Netherlands Yearbook of International Law* (1999) pp. 3-45.

3.2114 FINANCIAL ARRANGEMENTS

See also: 3.222 NATO, Zwan, D.M. van der

— *Transnationale handhaving van de financiële bepalingen van de Europese Unie* [Transnational preservation of the financial provisions of the European Union], J.A.E. Vervaele, ed. (Antwerpen, Intersentia 1999) 252 pp.

3.212 PARTICIPATION OF STATES IN THE ACTIVITIES OF INTERNATIONAL ORGANIZATIONS

See: 3.223 EU, Hoetjes, B.J.S.
12.273 ICC, Henquet, T.

3.217 CO-OPERATION AND CO-ORDINATION BETWEEN INTERNATIONAL ORGANIZATIONS

Cobelens, P.W.C.M. — 'De Navo Vergelijkenderwijs' [Comparing NATO], 109 *Marineblad* (1999) pp. 153-158.

Haar, B. ter — 'An Alliance for Human Rights and Democracy', 10 *Helsinki Monitor* (1999) No. 4, pp. 49-56.

3.2121 ADMISSION

See: 3.223 EMU, Inclusion of, etc.
4.6, Meulen, J.W. van der

3.213 LEGAL EFFECTS OF ACTS OF INTERNATIONAL ORGANIZATIONS

See: 3.21122, Blokker, N.
3.223 EU, Hoetjes, B.J.S.

3.217 CO-OPERATION AND CO-ORDINATION BETWEEN INTERNATIONAL ORGANIZATIONS

See: 3.222 WEU, Teunissen, P.

3.221 UNIVERSAL ORGANIZATIONS

International Labour Organization

Heijden, P.F. van der — 'Handhaving van ILO-(minimum)normen' [Maintain the ILO-(minimum)norms] Mededelingen [Proceedings] of the Dutch Branch of the International Law Association, (1999) No. 119, pp. 3-49.

Sybesma-Knol, R.G. — 'Rechtsontwikkeling binnen de Internationale Arbeids Organisatie' [Legal development in the ILO], Mededelingen [Proceedings], of the Dutch Branch of the International Law Association, (1999) No. 119, pp. 51-142

Organization for the Prohibition of Chemical Weapons

See:	1.0,	Myjer, E.P.J.

United Nations

See:	12.272 ICJ,	Werner, W.G.
	13.2,	Cras, M.F.A.; Wecke, L.

United Nations Commission on Human Rights

Adviesraad Internationale Vraagstukken — 'Het functioneren van de VN-commissie voor de rechten van de mens' [The functioning of the UN-Commission of Human Rights] (The Hague, Advisory Council of International Affairs, Advisory 1999) Report No. 11, 30 pp. [English translation available, 26 pp.].

United Nations Committee Against Torture

See:	4.66,	Boven, T. van; Flinterman, C.; Rieter, E.
	4.7,	Ingelse, H.C.

United Nations Human Rights Committee

Boerefijn, I. — The Reporting Procedure under the Convenant on Civil and Political Rights: Practice and Procedures of the Human Rights Committee (Antwerpen, Intersentia 1999) 417 pp. Hart, School of Human Rights Research Series, Vol. 2. Dissertation at the University of Utrecht.

World Trade Organization

See also:	16.55,	Wiers, J.

Bronckers, M.E.C.J. — 'Betere regels voor een nieuw millenium; Een waarschuwing tegen ondemocratische ontwikkelingen in de WTO' [Beter rules for a new millenium; a warning against undemocratical developments in the WTO], 47 *Sociaal-Economische Wetgeving* (1999) pp. 414-423.

Kuilwijk, K.J. — 'Kroniek van het WTO-recht' [Chronicle of the law of the WTO], 74 *Nederlands Juristenblad* (1999) pp. 1540-1545.

Kuilwijk, K.J. — 'Stik in bananen en verdwijn!' [Take your bananas and go!], 74 *Nederlands Juristenblad* (1999) pp. 1200-1202.

3.222 REGIONAL ORGANIZATIONS

Association of South East Asian Nations

See also:	13.2,	Cras, M.F.A.; Wecke, L.

Pelkmans, J. — 'Southeast Asian Puzzles in international organization', in *Realism and moralism in international relations; essays in honor of Frans, A.M. Alting von Geusau*, W.J.M. van Genugten, E.M.H. Hirsch Ballin, E.J. Janse de Jonge, P.H. Kooijmans, eds. (The Hague, Kluwer Law International 1999) pp. 107-128.

Commonwealth of Independent Nations

Feldbrugge, F. — 'The commonwealth of independent states: the legal and political re-integration of eastern Europe', in W.J.M. van Genugten, E.M.H. Hirsch Ballin, E.J. Janse de Jonge, P.H. Kooijmans, eds., *Realism and moralism in international relations; essays in honor of Frans, A.M. Alting von Geusau* (The Hague, Kluwer Law International 1999) pp. 21-34.

Council of Europe

See:	3.217,	Haar, B. ter

European Centre for Space Law

Dunk, F.G. van der — 'International Organisations and Space Law - Their Role and Contribution, 3rd ECSL Colloquium, 6-7 May 1999, Perugia' (Report of Conference), 24 *Air and Space Law* (1999) pp. 164-168.

European Committee for the Prevention of Torture and Inhumane or Degrading Treatment or Punishment

See:	4.7,	Berkhout-Van Poelgeest, A.M.; Kelk, C.; Munneke, H.F.

North Atlantic Treaty Organization

See also:	3.217,	Cobelens, P.W.C.M.
	13.2,	Cras, M.F.A.; Wecke, L.
	13.222,	Dekker, G.R. den; Wessel, R.A.
	13.23,	Daalder, I.H.; Leurdijk, D.A.

Duursma, J. — 'Justifying NATO's Use of Force in Kosovo?', 12 *Leiden Journal of International Law* (1999) pp. 287-295.

Hirsch Ballin, E.M.H. — 'Nato and international law: the vocation of a military alliance in an interdependent world', in W.J.M. van Genugten, E.M.H. Hirsch Ballin, E.J. Janse de Jonge, P.H. Kooijmans, eds., *Realism and moralism in international relations; essays in honor of Frans, A.M. Alting von Geusau* (The Hague, Kluwer Law International 1999) pp. 93-105.

Rusman, P.; Colijn, J. — 'Good old NATO, wat nu?' [Good old NATO, now what?], 109 *Marineblad* (1999) pp. 136-140.

Wijk, R. de — 'De Navo: nieuwe taken, nieuwe problemen?' [NATO: new tasks, new problems?], *Jaarboek Vrede en Veiligheid* (1999) pp. 61-81.

Wijk, R. de — 'What is NATO?', 23 *Atlantisch Perspectief* (1999) No. 6/7, pp. 4-8; 24 *Jason Magazine* (1999) No. 3/4, pp. 3-6.

Zandee, D. — 'Crisisbesluitvorming in de NAVO' [Crisisdecision-making at NATO], 109 *Marineblad* (1999) pp. 185-188.

Zwan, D.M. van der — 'NATO Common Fund Resources', 168 *Militaire Spectator* (1999) pp. 437-444.

Organization for Security and Co-operation in Europe

See also:	3.217,	Cobelens, P.W.C.M.; Haar, B. ter
	4.4,	Zaagman, R.
	13.2,	Cras, M.F.A.; Wecke, L.

Cohen, J. — 'Conflict Prevention in the OSCE. An Assessment of Capacities' (Den Haag, Clingendael Notitie Reeks 1999) 150 pp. Notitie 9.

Kwaasteniet, M. de — 'Sub-regionalism and the OSCE: An Artificial Relationship?', 10 *Helsinki Monitor* (1999) No. 2, pp. 39-48.

Organization of African Unity

See:	13.2,	Cras, M.F.A.; Wecke, L.

Western European Union

See also:	3.217,	Cobelens, P.W.C.M.
	16.8,	Vierhout, R.

Teunissen, P. — 'Europese defensiepolitiek: plannen en realiteiten' [European defence politics: plans and realities], 53 *Internationale Spectator* (1999) pp. 493-499.

Teunissen, P. — 'Het smalle pad naar Europese defensie samenwerking; Institutionele opzet en politieke doelstellingen' [The narrow trail to European defence cooperation; institutional structure and political goals], 53 *Internationale Spectator* (1999) pp. 91-97.

3.223 ORGANIZATIONS CONSTITUTING INTEGRATED (ECONOMIC, ETC.) COMMUNITIES

European Community

See:	1.2,	Kortmann, C.A.J.M.; Kummeling, H.R.B.M.
	1.202,	Vervaele, J.A.E., ed.

3.21122,	Blokker, N.
3.211,	Zwaan, J. de
3.2112,	Ooik, R.H.
4.66,	Steenbergen, J.D.M.
4.73,	Heringa, A.W.
11.22,	Lawson, R.A.
16.6,	Albers, H.S.J.
16.723,	Bonofacio, M.

European Monetary Union

— *Inclusion of Central European Countries in the European Monetary Union*, P. de Grauwe, V. Lavrac, eds. (Dordrecht, Kluwer Academic Publishers 1999) 223 pp.

Amtenbrink, F. — 'The European Central Bank-democratically accountable or unrestrained', 74 *Nederlands Juristenblad* (1999) pp. 72-78.

European Union

See also:	1.,	Realism and Moralism, etc.
	1.15,	Internationale Organisatie, etc.
	1.202,	Vervaele, J.A.E., ed.
	3.211,	Zwaan, J. de
	3.2112,	Kummeling, H.R.B.M.; Ooik, R.H.; Pijpers, A.
	3.21122,	Blokker, N.
	3.2114,	Transnationale handhaving, etc.
	3.217,	Cobelens, P.W.C.M.
	3.221WTO,	Kuilwijk, K.J
	4.3,	Alfenaar, K.; Boeles, P.; Fernhout, R.; Guild, E.; Meulen, J.W. van der; Staples, H.
	4.64,	Integrale veiligheid, etc.; Op weg naar Tampere
	4.66,	Adviesraad Internationale, etc.
	4.7,	Bijsterveld, S.C. van; Schermers, H.G.
	6.224,	Boer, M. den; Corrado, L.
	16.112,	Colijn, K.; Rusman, P.
	16.5,	Heijden van der, P.F.; Sjers, C.M.
	16.726,	Corstens, G.J.M.
	16.8,	Staden, A. van; Vierhout, R.

— *Flexibiliteit en het Verdrag van Amsterdam* [Flexibility and the Amsterdam Treaty] (The Hague, T.M.C. Asser Press 1999) Asser Instituut Colloquium Europees Recht 96 pp. Twenty-eigth session, 4 September 1998 at the T.M.C. Asser Institute.

Barents, R.; Brinkhorst, L.J. — 'De toekomst van het Europees recht' [The future of European law], 48 *Ars Aequi* (1999) pp. 455-466.

Barents, R.; Brinkhorst, L.J. — *Grondlijnen van Europees recht* [Ground rules of European law] (Deventer, Kluwer 1999) 652 pp. Ninth totally revised edition.

Barents, R. — *Het Verdrag van Amsterdam in werking* [The Amsterdam treaty in practice] (Deventer, Kluwer 1999) 452 pp. Europese Monografieën 62.

Donner, J.P.H. — 'Het Verdrag van Amsterdam; Slotbeschouwing' [The treaty of Amsterdam; concluding observations], 74 *Nederlands Juristenblad* (1999) pp. 1233-1243.

Drijber, B.J. — 'De Europese instellingen na het Verdrag van Amsterdam: evenwicht zonder overzicht?' [The European institutions after the Treaty of Amsterdam: balance without clarity?], 74 *Nederlands Juristenblad* (1999) pp. 587-596.

Eijsbouts, W.T. — 'De Europese krachtmeting is pas begonnen; Beloften van de crisis van maart '99' [The European showdown has just begun; promises of the crisis of March '99], 74 *Nederlands Juristenblad* (1999) pp. 627-635.

Hoetjes, B.J.S. — 'Een Europees-bestuurlijke verdieping?; De Nederlandse provincies en de Europese Unie sinds het Verdrag van Maastricht' [An European-administrative deepening?; The Dutch provinces and the European Union after the Maastricht Treaty], 53 *Internationale Spectator* (1999) pp. 485-492.

Lauwaars, R.H.; Timmermans, C.W.A. — *Europees recht in kort bestek* [European law in brief] (Deventer, Tjeenk Willink 1999) 392 pp. Fifth revised version.

Rood, J.Q.T — 'Amsterdamse left-overs; De uitbreiding en hervorming van de Europese Unie' [The Amsterdam left-overs; the expansion and reform of the European Union], 53 *Internationale Spectator* (1999) pp. 635-639.

Schijndel, A.H.J.W. van — *Het Europese wiel. Opstellen over Nederland en Europa* [The European wheel. Texts on the Netherlands and Europe] (Assen, Van Gorcum 1999) 134 pp.

Vree, J.K. de; Jansen, M. — *The Ordeal of Unity. Integration and Desintegration in Europe* (Amsterdam, Instituut voor Internationaal Juridisch Onderzoek 1998) 604 pp.

Witte de, B.E.F.M. — 'Kroniek van het Europees recht' [Chronicle of European law], 74 *Nederlands Juristenblad* (1999) pp. 1480-1486.

Zwaan de, J.W. — 'Het Verdrag van Amsterdam: Etappe in het proces van Europese integratie' [The Treaty of Amsterdam; a step in the process of European integration], 74 *Nederlands Juristenblad* (1999) pp. 492-500.

3.224 OTHER TYPES OF ORGANIZATIONS

Nederlandse Organisatie voor Ontwikkelingssamenwerking (NOVIB)
See: 16.2, Kratzenberg, J.

3.3 OTHER SUBJECTS OF INTERNATIONAL LAW

Arts, B. — 'NGO's in de internationale milieudiplomatie; Toenemende invloed?' [NGO's in international environmental diplomacy; increasing influence?], 53 *Internationale Spectator* (1999) pp. 419-424.

Arts, B. — *The Political Influence of Global NGO's. Case Studies on the Climate and Biodiversity Conventions* (Utrecht, International Books 1998) 352 pp.

Schennink, B. — 'Vrede en mensenrechten; Burgerbewegingen in het buitenlands beleid' [Peace and human rights; civil movements in foreign policy], 53 *Internationale Spectator* (1999) pp. 81-85.

3.342 TRUST TERRITORIES
See also: 3.14, Dijkstra, G.S.A.

Pauwels, A. — 'Een VN-trustschap over Kosovo; Een andere kijk op de vredesregeling voor Kosovo' [A UN-trust over Kosovo; an other view on the peace agreement for Kosovo], *Jaarboek Vrede en Veiligheid* (1999) pp. 135-146.

3.344 SPECIAL REGIMES

Genugten, W.J.M. van — 'Jerusalem, city in need of a special regime?', in W.J.M. van Genugten, E.M.H. Hirsch Ballin, E.J. Janse de Jonge, P.H. Kooijmans, eds., *Realism and moralism in international relations; essays in honor of Frans, A.M. Alting von Geusau* (The Hague, Kluwer Law International 1999) pp. 107-128.

3.35 NATURAL PERSONS
See: 1., Realism and Moralism, etc.
11.216, Boven, T. van
12.273 ICC, Boven, T. van

3.362 INTERNATIONAL CORPORATIONS
See also: 11.243, Kamminga, M.

— *Multinationale ondernemingen en mensenrechten* [Multinationals and human rights] (Amsterdam, Amnesty International/Utrecht: Pax Christi 1999) 64 pp. This is a report of the Dutch departments of Amnesty International and Pax Christi International.

Wesselink, E. — 'Het bedrijfsleven en de rechten van de mens' [International corporations and human rights], *Jaarboek Vrede en Veiligheid* (1999) pp. 236-249.

4.1 NATIONALITY

Ahmad Ali, H. — *De toescheidingsovereenkomst inzake nationaliteit tussen Nederland en Suriname* [The assignment agreement on nationality between the Netherlands and Surinam] (The Hague, Sdu Uitgevers) 337 pp.

Beijen, K.H. — *Het Nederlanderschap in verband met het internationaal recht* [The Dutch nationality in relation with international law] (Utrecht, Van Huffel 1999) 195 pp. Dissertation at the University of Utrecht.

Groot, G.R. de — 'Verder op weg naar een hernieuwd nationaliteitsrecht; Bespreking wijzigingsnota Rijkswet Nederlanderschap' [On the road to a renewed law of citizenship; discussion on the note of amendment of the Kingdom Act on Dutch nationality], *Migrantenrecht* (1999) pp. 13-22.

Jessurun d'Oliveira, H.U. — 'Sociaal geslacht, huwelijk en nationaliteit' [Social gender, matrimony and nationality], *Nemesis* (1999) No. 6, pp. 65-80.

4.3 ALIENS OR NON-NATIONALS

See also:	1.203,	Kraus, S.
	4.73,	Goudsmit, S.; Lange, T. de
	6.224,	Boer, M. den; Corrado, L.
	11.3,	Verrijn Stuart, H.M.

— *Jaarverslag van de Permanente Commissie van deskundigen in internationaal vreemdelingen-, vluchtelingen- en strafrecht* [Annual report of the permanent commission of experts on international aliens-, refugees- and criminal law] (Utrecht, Permanente Commissie van deskundigen in internationaal vreemdelingen-, vluchtelingen- en strafrecht 1999) 10 pp.

Alfenaar, K. — 'De Nederlandse inbreng in de speciale Europese Raad in Tampere; Opinie' [The Dutch contribution to the special European council at Tampere; opinion], *Migrantenrecht* (1999) pp. 211-213.

Baudoin, P.J.A.M. — 'Detentie van vreemdelingen; Notitie vreemdelingenbewaring' [Detenion of aliens; notice of detention of aliens], *Migrantenrecht* (1999) pp. 39-43.

Boeles, P.; Fernhout, R. — 'Grondslagen voor een bindend Europees immigratie- en asielrecht' [Foundations for a binding European immigration- and asylum law], 20 *Nederlands Juristenblad* (1999) pp. 891-902.

Guild, E. — *European Community Law from a Migrant's Perspective* (The Hague, Kluwer Law International 1999) 341 pp.

Heijde, F.T.T. van der; Dijk, M. van — 'Schadevergoeding na onrechtmatige vreemdelingenbewaring; pleidooi voor nader onderscheid' [Compensation after an illegal detention of an alien; plea for further differentiation], *Migrantenrecht* (1999) pp. 119-125.

Holterman, T. — *Vreemdelingenrecht: toelating en verblijf van vreemdelingen in Nederland* [Law of aliens: admission and domicile of aliens in the Netherlands] (Deventer, Tjeenk Willink 1999) 248 pp. Totally revised fifth edition.

Kuijer, A.; Steenbergen, H.; Viering, M.L.W.M. — *Nederlands vreemdelingenrecht* [Dutch alien law] (Utrecht, Nederlands Centrum Buitenlanders 1999) 461 pp. Serie Migratierecht 2, fourth revised edition.

Meulen, J.W. van der — *Migratie en asiel in Centraal-Europa en de uitbreiding van de Europese Unie* [Migration and asylum in Central Europe and the expansion of the European Union] (Den Haag, Clingendael 1999) 37 pp.

Reurs, M.; Kroes, J.A. — 'Voortdurende perikelen rond legalistie en verificatie in de probleemlanden (deel II); Nederland als probleemland' [The continuous troubles concerning legalisation and verification in problem-countries (part II); The Netherlands as a problem-country], *Migrantenrecht* (1999) pp. 3-8.

Staples, H. — *The Legal Status of Third Country Nationals Resident in the European Union* (The Hague, Kluwer Law International 1999) 418 pp. European Monographs 22, edited version of the dissertation at the University of Utrecht.

4.36 RIGHTS AND DUTIES OF ALIENS

See also: 1.203, Pennings, F.J.L.

Bernini, P.; Engbersen G. — 'Koppeling en uitsluiting: over ongewenste en onbedoelde effecten van de Koppelingswet' [Linking and exclusion: the undesired and unintended effects of the linking act], 74 *Nederlands Juristenblad* (1999) pp. 65-71.

4.4 MINORITIES

See also:	1.15,	Internationale Organisatie, etc.
	4.7,	Law and Cultural Diversity
	13.22,	Bakker, E.

— *Minorities in Europe; Croatia, Estonia and Slovakia*, S. Trifunovska, ed. (The Hague, T.M.C. Asser Press 1999) 230 pp.

Bloed, A.; Dijk, P. van — Protection of Minority Rights through Bilateral Treaties: the Case of Central and Eastern Europe (The Hague, Kluwer Law International 1999) 451 pp.

Zaagman, R. — 'Conflict Prevention in the Baltic Area: The OSC High Commissioner on National Minorities in Estonia, 1993-1999', 10 *Helsinki Monitor* (1999) No. 3, pp. 30-44.

Zwart, T. — 'De juridische bescherming van minderheden door de Raad van Europa' [The legal protection of minorities by the Council of Europe], 24 *NJCM Bulletin* (1999) pp. 336-357.

4.41 GENOCIDE

See:	11.3,	McDonald, A.
	13.222,	Faber, M.J.

4.52 REFUGEES

See also: 4.66

Kuik, B. — 'Docudrama; Authenticiteitsonderzoek als middel in het ontmoedigingsbeleid van gezinshereniging bij A-statushouders' [Docudrama; authenticity research as means in the discourage policy of family reunion with holders of the permanent residence licence], *Nieuwsbrief Asiel- en Vluchtelingenrecht* (1999) pp. 444-456.

Lankers, F. — 'Diepgewortelde band met eigen volk; Dienstweigeraars met gewetensbezwaren door mogelijke inzet tegen de eigen bevolkingsgroep.' [A inherent tie with the own people; conscientious objectors with conscientious objection of possible military deployment against the own people], *Nieuwsbrief Asiel- en Vluchtelingenrecht* (1999) pp. 91-97.

4.63 EXTRADITION

Hattum, W.F. van — 'Ne bis in idem in de Nederlandse uitleveringsprocedure; Een verhaal over twee Grieken en een loden monster' [Ne bis in idem in the Dutch exdradition procedure; a story about two Greek and a lead monster], 29 *Delikt en Delinkwent* (1999) pp. 941-960.

Keijzer, N. — 'Uitlevering voor politieke delicten?' [Extradition for political offences?], 48 *Ars Aequi* (1999) pp. 239-243.

Wisse, C. — 'Staatsrechtelijke beschouwingen over het rechtskarakter van het Nederlands-Antilliaans Uitleveringsbesluit' [Constitutional remarks on the legal character of the Dutch-Antillian extradition resolution], *Tijdschrift voor Antilliaans Recht-Justicia*, No. 2 (1999) pp. 54-65.

4.64 OTHER ASSISTANCE IN CRIMINAL MATTERS

See also: 4.63, Hattum, W.F. van
12.273 ICC, Sluiter, G.; Swart, B.

— ***Integrale veiligheid in Europa: heden en toekomst*** [Integral security in Europe: present and future] (Den Haag, Nederlands Politie Instituut 1999) 90 pp.

— *Op weg naar Tampere* [On the road to Tampere], B.J.S. Hoetjes, ed. (The Hague, Clingendael 1999) 86 pp. Report of the conference held at Clingendael, The Hague, 27 September 1999.

Knoops, G.G.J. — 'Het EVRM en de internationale overdracht van gevonniste personen' [The ECHR and the international transfer of convicted persons], 79 *Advocatenblad* (1999) pp. 133-138.

Kruit, P.J.J. van der — 'Onze man in Barbados; Drugsbestrijding in het Caribisch gebied aangrenzend aan die van de Nederlandse Antillen en Aruba' [Our man in Barbados; drugs prevention in the Caribic region bordering to the Dutch Antilles], 109 *Marineblad* (1999) pp. 350-355.

Lamp, R. — 'Even kort: het internationaal strafrechtelijk verhaalsbeslag en de verbeurdverklaring' [Just in brief: the international criminal attachment of redress and confiscation], 29 *Delikt en Delinkwent* (1999) pp. 1016-1019.

Lamp, R. — 'Financiele informatie de grens over; De internationale uitwisseling van gegevens door het Meldpunt Ongebruikelijke Transacties' [Financial information across the border; the international exchange of data by the report centre of unusual transactions], 29 *Delikt en Delinkwent* (1999) pp. 41-53.

Mlicki, P.P.; Meulen, J.W. van der — 'Politiesamenwerking tussen de EU-landen en Midden-Europa; De Nederlandse ervaring' [Police cooperation between the EU-countries and Middle-Europe; the Dutch experience], 53 *Internationale Spectator* (1999) pp. 656-660.

4.65 EXPULSION

Dijk, P. van — 'Protection of "integrated" Aliens Against Expulsion under the European Convention on Human Rights', 1 *European Journal of Migration and Law* (1999) pp. 293-312.

4.66 ASYLUM

See also: 4.3, Jaarverslag; Alfenaar, K.; Boeles, P.; Fernhout, R.; Guild, E.; Meulen, J.W. van der
4.7, Vries, W. de

— *Adviesraad Internationale Vraagstukken – Asielformatie en de Europese Unie* [Asylum information and the European Union] (The Hague, Advisory Council on International Affairs 1999) Advisory Report No. 8, 21 pp. English translation avaiable.

Bergen, L. van — 'Bijzondere gevallen van humanitaire aard en de tenzij-clausule; Uitzonderingen op de verantwoordelijkheidsverdeling onder Dublin.' [Special cases of humanitarian kind and the unless-clause; exceptions on the division of responsablities under the rule of Dublin], *Nieuwsbrief Asiel- en Vluchtelingenrecht* (1999) pp. 265-270.

Bruin, R. — 'Discriminatie; Criteria in de Nederlandse asielprocedure' [Discrimination; criteria in the Dutch asylum procedure], *Nieuwsbrief Asiel- en Vluchtelingenrecht* (1999) pp. 538-534.

Bruin, R. — 'Kosovo: het vluchtelingenrecht in een crisis' [Kosovo: the law of refugees in a crisis], *Nieuwsbrief Asiel- en Vluchtelingenrecht* (1999) pp. 252-256.

Fleuren, J.; Zwaan, K. — '"Dublinclaimanten" en het recht op huisvesting van artikel 11 lid 1 IVESCR' [Refused asylum-seekers and their right to housing as mentioned in Article 11 paragraph 1 of the ICESCR], 74 *Nederlands Juristenblad* (1999) pp. 543-546.

Hoogenbeek, N.; Pastoors, K. — 'Pech onderweg; twee weken in een derde land als contra-indicatief voor de vvtv' [Bad luck on the road; two weeks in a third country as a contra-indicative for the conditional permission to stay], *Nieuwsbrief Asiel- en Vluchtelingenrecht* (1999) pp. 618-622.

— *Refugee Law in context: The exclusion clause*, P.J. van Krieken, ed., (The Hague, T.M.C. Asser Press 1999) 327 pp.

Rieter, E.; Boven, T. van; Flinterman, C. — 'Nederland wil asielzoeker uitzetten in strijd met een interim maatregel van het VN-comité tegen folteringen' [The Netherlands want to expulse an asylum-seeker in breach of an interim measure of the UN-committee against torture], 74 *Nederlands Juristenblad* (1999) pp. 908-909.

Soulje, N. — 'Rechtszekerheid voor asielzoekers; Europees, Nederlands en Italiaans asielbeleid' [Legal security for asylum-seekers; European, Dutch and Italian asylum policy], 53 *Internationale Spectator* (1999) pp. 661-665.

Spijkerboer, T. — *Gender and Refugee Status* (Aldershot, Ashgate 1999) 255 pp. Edited version of his dissertation at the University of Nijmegen.

Steenbergen, J.D.M. — 'All the King's Horses...; Probabilities and Possibilities for the Implementation of the New Title IV EC Treaty', 1 *European Journal of Migration and Law* (1999) pp. 29-60.

Wetten, J.W. van — *De positie van vrouwen in de asielprocedures* [The position of women in the asylum procedures] (Den Haag, Ministerie van Justitie, WODC 1998) Reeks Onderzoek en Beleid, Deel 172, 111 pp.

4.7 PROTECTION OF HUMAN RIGHTS AND FUNDAMENTAL FREEDOMS

See also:	1.11,	Cliteur, P.B.
	1.15,	Internationale Organisatie, etc.
	1.2,	Kambel, E.R.
	1.203,	Pennings, F.J.L.
	3.132,	Kelk, C.
	3.14,	Couwenberg, S.W.
	3.221 ICC,	Heijden, P.F. van der
	3.362,	Multinationale ondernemingen etc.; Wesselink, E.
	4.4,	Bloed, A.; Dijk, P. van
	4.66,	Boven, T. van; Bruin, R.; Flinterman, C.; Rieter, E.; Soulje, N.; Wetten, J.W. van
	4.73,	Heringa, A.W.
	4.742,	Arambulo, K.
	11.243,	Kamminga, M.
	12.273 ECJ,	Witte, J.B. de
	12.273 ICC,	Barkhuysen, T.; Kortmann, C.N.J.
	12.273 ICTR,	Wladimiroff, M.
	13.14,	Blockmans, S.
	13.22,	Genugten, W.J.M. van; Groot, G.A. de
	14.125,	Coolen, G.L.
	16.2,	Kratzenberg, J.
	16.51,	Dooren M.I. van

— *Globalization of Child Law; The Role of the Hague Conventions*, S. Detrick and P. Vlaardingerbroek, eds. (The Hague, Martinus Nijhoff Publishers 1999) 212 pp.

— *Human Rights and Ethnic Conflicts*, P.R. Baehr, F. Baudet and H. Werdmolder, eds., (Utrecht, Studie- en Informatiecentrum Mensenrechten 1999) 103 pp. SIM No. 24.

— *Human Rights: Maastricht Perspectives*, T. van Boven, C. Flinterman, I. Westendorp, eds., (Maastricht, Maastricht Centre for Human Rights, Maastricht University 1999) 51 pp.

— *Law and Cultural Diversity*, Y. Donders, K. Henrard, A. Meijknecht and S. Tempelman, eds., (Utrecht, Studie- en Informatiecentrum Mensenrechten 1999) 182 pp. SIM No. 25, Proceedings of a workshop organised by the working group 'Law and Cultural Diversity' in cooperation with the School of Human Rights Research.

— *Non-discrimination Law: Comparative Perspectives*, T. Loenen and P.R. Rodrigues, eds., (The Hague, Kluwer Law International 1999) 457 pp. Proceedings of the international conference on comparative non-discrimination law held in Utrecht, The Netherlands, June 1998.

Akkermans, P.C.W.; Bax, C.J.; Verhey, L.F.M. — *Grondrechten: grondrechten en grondrechtenbescherming in Nederland* [Basic civil rights: basic civil rights and basic civil rights protection in the Netherlands] (Deventer, Tjeenk Willink 1999) 239 pp. Third revised edition edited by C.J. Bax.

Baehr, P. — *Human Rights: Universality in Practice* (Basingstoke: MacMillan Press/New York: St. Martin's Press 1999) 178 pp.

— *'s Lands wijs, 's lands eer; Universaliteit van de mensenrechten* [When in Rome do as the Romans do; Universality of human rights] E. van de Berg, I. Boerefijn and J. Weerdenburg, eds., (Utrecht, Uitgeverij Prestige 1999) 160 pp.

Berkhout-Van Poelgeest, A.M.; Kelk, C. — 'Het bezoek van het European Committee for the Prevention of Torture and Inhumane or Degrading Treatment or Punishment (CPT) aan Nederland' [The visit of the European Committee for the Prevention of Torture and Inhumane or Degrading Treatment or Punishment (CPT) to the Netherlands], 24 *NJCM Bulletin* (1999) pp. 592-613.

Bijsterveld, S.C. van — *Godsdienstvrijheid in Europees perspectief* [Freedom of religion in European perspective] (Deventer, Tjeenk Willink 1999) 205 pp.

Bischoff-Heemskerck, S.C. van — *The UN-convention on the Rights of the Child: a Comparative Study* (Amsterdam, Free University of Amsterdam 1999) 274 pp.

Boersema, D.A.A. — *Mens mensura iuris: over rechtsbewustszijn, gelijkheid en mensenrechten* [Mens mensura iuris: on judicial conscience, equality and human rights] (Deventer, Kluwer 1998) 467 pp. Dissertation at the University of Groningen, with summary in English.

Bost, R. — RechtSpreken: mensenrechten in openbare orde [Administration of justice: human rights in public order] (Maastricht, Universitaire Pers Maastricht 1999) 192 pp. Dissertation at the University of Maastricht.

Bronkhorst, D. — Afgrond roept tot afgrond; Mensenrechten en religie [Abyss calls for an abyss; human rights and religion] (Amsterdam, Amnesty International/Uitgeverij Balans 1999) 127 pp.

Detrick, S. — A Commentary on the United Nations Convention on the Rights of the Child (The Hague, Kluwer Law 1999) 836 pp.

Genugten, W.J.M. van — Human Rights Reference Handbook (The Hague, Netherlands Ministry of Foreign Affairs, Human Rights, Good Governance and Democratisation Departement 1999) 203 pp. Second revised edition.

Gevers, J.K.M. — 'De wet medische keuringen in het perspectief van de mensenrechten' [The act of medical examination in the light of humanitarian law], 24 *NJCM Bulletin* (1999) pp. 442-452.

— *Mensenrechten in de politiek; fundament of bijzaak* [Human rights in politics; fundamental or side-issue] C. Huinder, ed., (Amsterdam, Stichting Bevordering Maatschappelijke Participatie 1998) 186 pp.

Ingelse, C. — 'Het VN-Comite tegen foltering: tien jaar achter het VN-mensenrechtencomite aan' [The UN-Committee against Torture: ten years behind the UN-Committee for Human Rights], 24 *NJCM Bulletin* (1999) pp. 1058-1071.

Ingelse, H.C. — De rol van het Comite in de ontwikkeling van het VN-verdrag tegen Foltering [The role of the Committee in the development of the UN-treaty against torture] (Maastricht, Thela Thesis) 405 pp. Dissertation at the University of Maastricht.

Kelk, C. — 'Wanneer behoren de gruwelijkheden in de gevangenis te Curaçao tot het verleden?' [When will the atrocities in the prison of Curaçao come to an end?], 74 *Nederlands Juristenblad* (1999) pp. 1-7.

— *De rechten van de mens – liberale beschouwingen* [The human rights – liberal observations] G.A. van der List, ed., (The Hague, Telderstichting 1998) 112 pp.

— *Grondrechten en wisselgeld. Aziatische en westerse visies op de waarde van de rechten van de mens* [Fundamental laws and bargaining counter. Asian and western views on the value of humanitarian rights) M. Meijer, ed., (Utrecht, Humanitair Overleg Mensenrechten 1998) 192 pp.

Mijnarends, E.M. — Richtlijnen voor een verdragsconforme jeugdstrafrechtspleging 'Gelijkwaardig maar minderjarig' [Directives for minor criminal law procedure in accordance with treaties 'Equal but underage'] (Deventer, Kluwer Rechtswetenschappelijke Publicaties 1999) 462 pp. Dissertation at the University of Leiden.

Morren, P. — *De rechten van de mens* [Human rights] (Apeldoorn, Garant 1999) 270 pp.

Munneke, H.F. — 'Gevangenen op de Nederlandse Antillen: Recht op geweldloze behandeling?; Beschouwingen naar aanleiding van bezoeken van het CPT aan Curaçao in 1994 en 1997' [Prisoners on the Dutch Antilles: right on a violence free treatment?; Considerations as a result of the visits of the CPT to Curaçao in 1994 and 1997], 24 *NJCM Bulletin* (1999) pp. 614-622.

Myjer, B.E.P. — 'Staat het OM voor mensenrechten?' [Does the public prosecutor protect the human rights?], *Trema* (1999) No. 6, pp. 198-202.

Schermers, H.G. — 'Acceptance of International Supervision of Human Rights', 12 *Leiden Journal of International Law* (1999) pp. 821-831.

Schermers, H.G. — 'Mensenrechten in het Verdrag van Amsterdam' [Human rights and the Treaty of Amsterdam], 74 *Nederlands Juristenblad* (1999) pp. 715-720.

Schillemans, A. — 'De toekomst van de mensenrechten: blijvend ideaal of echte erkenning en toepassing?' [The future of human rights: still an ideal or real recognition and application?], 12 *VN-Forum* (1999) No. 1, pp. 20-25.

Uildriks, N. — 'Police Torture in France', 17 *Netherlands Quarterly of Human Rights* (1999) pp. 411-423.

Vries, W. de — *Beyond All Bounds: Women about Their Active Role in Conflict Situations and as a Refugee* (Utrecht, Humanist Committee on Human Rights/Oegstgeest, Vrouwenberaad Ontwikkelingssamenwerking 1999) 64 pp.

Willems, J.C.M. — 'De internationale rechten van het kind en de voorkoming van opvoedingsproblemen, kindermishandeling en jeugdcriminaliteit' [The international rights of the child and the prevention of educational problems, child abuse and juvenil delinquency], 12 *VN-Forum* (1999) No. 3, pp. 34-46.

Willems, J.C.M. — 'Wie zal de opvoeders opvoeden?; Het mensenrechtelijke vereiste van een preventief systeem van opvoedingsondersteuning en kinderbescherming' [Who will educate the educators?; The humanitarian requirement of a preventive system of educational support and child protection], 24 *NJCM Bulletin* (1999) pp. 623-633.

Willems, J.C.M. -Wie zal de opvoeder opvoeden? Kindermishandeling en het Recht van het Kind op Persoonswording [Who will educate the educators? Child abuse and the rights of the child to personality formation], (The Hague, T.M.C. Asser Press 1999) 1185 pp.

Woltjer, A.J.T. — 'Verenigde Naties-Kroniek: Het internationaal verdrag inzake de uitbanning van alle vormen van discriminatie' [United Nations-chronicle: The international treaty concerning the expulsion of all forms of discrimination], 24 *NJCM Bulletin* (1999) pp. 407-418.

4.72 UNIVERSAL DECLARATION, 1948

— *Innovation and Inspiration: Fifty Years of the Universal Declaration of Human Rights*, P. Baehr, C. Flinterman, M. Senders, eds. (Amsterdam, Royal Netherlands Academy of Arts and Sciences 1999) 248 pp.

4.73 EUROPEAN CONVENTION, 1950

See also:	1.2,	Jessurun D'Oliveira, H.U.
	1.203,	Brouwer, J.G.; Franken, A.A.; Jurgens, M.; Graaff de, B.J.G.; Janse de Jonge, E.J.; Schilder, A.E.; Simon, H.J
	3.132,	Kelk, C.
	4.36,	Bernini, P.; Engbersen G.
	4.4,	Zwart, T.
	4.64,	Knoops, G.G.J.
	4.65,	Dijk, P. van
	4.7,	Akkermans, P.C.W.; Bax, C.J.; Verhey, L.F.M.
	6.12,	Velde, J. van der
	11.22,	Lawson, R.A.
	12.2704	
	12.273 ECHR,	Huussen, I.B.; Loof, J.P.; Velde, J. van der

— *The Right to Health Care in Several European Countries*, A den Exter, H. Hermans, eds. (The Hague, Kluwer Law International 1999) 208 pp.

Barkhuysen, T.; Emmerik, M.L. van — 'Legal Protection Against Violations of the European Convention on Human Rights: Improving (Co-)operation of Strasbourg and Domestic Institutions', 12 *Leiden Journal of International Law* (1999) pp. 833-845.

Boone, M. — 'De rol van de rechter bij de omzetting van vrijheidsbeperkende sancties getoetst aan artikel 5 en 6 EVRM' [The role of the judge in the conversion of freedom restricting sanctions tested against Article 5 and 6 of the ECHR], 74 *Nederlands Juristenblad* (1999) pp. 903-907.

Franken, A.A; Prakken, T. — 'Verdediging in strafzaken: oproep tot een grondslagen discussie; Bijdrage voor een congres' [The defence in criminal cases: an appeal for a fundamental discussion; contribution to a congress], 74 *Nederlands Juristenblad* (1999) pp. 1635-1639.

Goudsmit, S.; Lange, T. de — 'Kroniek vreemdelingenrecht; Eindelijk politieke aandacht voor immigrantenvrouwen?' [Chronicle on aliens law; finally political attention for female immigrants?], *Nemesis* (1999) No. 5, pp. 159-165.

Hartog, A. den — *De doorwerking van artikel 6 EVRM in het Antilliaanse en Arubaanse strafprocesrecht* [The effect of Article 6 of ECHR in the Antillian and Aruban criminal procedural law] (Deventer, Gouda Quint 1998) 100 pp.

Heringa, A.W. — *Het 'consensus principle': de rol van gemeenschappelijk recht in de jurisprudentie van het EVRM* [The consensus principle: the role of communal law in the jurisprudence of the ECHR], (Lelystad, Koninklijke Vermande 1999) 34 pp.

Hoitink, J.E.; Backes, C.W. — 'Eigendom van "milieuvervuilingsrechten"' [Property of environmental pollution rights], 74 *Nederlands Juristenblad* (1999) pp. 1759-1763.

Lanen, J.J.M. van — 'Mensenrechten en milieubescherming: Van een wankel evenwicht naar een sterk samenspel' [Human rights and environmental protection: from an unsteady balance to a strong ensemble], 24 *NJCM Bulletin* (1999) pp. 1038-1057.

Lenos, E.E.V. — 'Mensenrechtelijke en bestuursrechtelijke waarborgen bij handhaving van de sociale zekerheid' [Humanitarian and administrative guarantees for enforcement of social security], 24 *NJCM Bulletin* (1999) pp. 736-749.

Loenen, T. — 'Implementing Women's Human Rights under the European Convention of Human Rights: A Mixed Blessing', in E.A. Ankumah, E.K. Kwakwa, eds., *The legal profession and the protection of human rights in Africa* (Accra, Africa Legal Aid 1999) pp. 127-132. Special Series 1. Contains the result of a conference organized by Africa Legal Aid in November 1997 in Maastricht.

Loorbach, J.D. — 'Disciplinaire rechtspraak; proces leed (8)' [Disciplinary justice; process grief (8)], 74 *Nederlands Juristenblad* (1999) pp. 1730-1731.

Meer van der, I.; Klip, A. — 'Nederlanders in buitenlandse gevangenissen' [Dutch in foreign prisons], 74 *Nederlands Juristenblad* (1999) pp. 999-1000.

Plaisier, M.J.A. — *Het verstek in strafzaken* [Absence in criminal cases], (Tilburg, Het Schoordijk Instituut; Deventer, Tjeenk Willink 1999) 397 pp. Dissertation at the University of Brabant, summary in German.

Prakken, E. — 'De strafprocessuele Schutznormleer gerelativeerd?' [The criminal processual Schutznormdoctrine in perspective?], 74 *Nederlands Juristenblad* (1999) pp. 245-250.

Prakken, T. — 'Het proces Öcalan' [The Öcalan process], 48 *Ars Aequi* (1999) pp. 642-646.

Rozemond, K. — 'Stelselmatige observatie zonder wettelijke grondslag' [Systematic observation without legal basis], 74 *Nederlands Juristenblad* (1999) pp. 671-676. Reaction on this article by A. Beckers, and reply by K. Rozemond in *Nederlands Juristenblad* (1999) pp. 1158-1160.

Werd, M. de — 'Tijdigheid van rechtspraak en artikel 6 EVRM' [Timeliness of jurisdiction and Article 6 ECHR], *Trema* (1999) No.10a, pp. 19-25.

Wladimiroff, M. — 'Rechten van advocaten beknot; De zaak Öcalan' [The rights of lawyers restricted; The Öcalan case], 79 *Advocatenblad* (1999) pp. 726-728.

4.741 UN COVENANT ON CIVIL AND POLITICAL RIGHTS

See also: 3.221UNHRC,Boerefijn, I.
4.36, Bernini, P.; Engbersen G.

Roorda, C. — 'Trinidad loopt uit de pas – Nederland moet een signaal afgeven' [Trinidad is out of line – the Netherlands should make a signal], 74 *Nederlands Juristenblad* (1999) pp. 210-211.

4.742 UN COVENANT ON ECONOMIC AND SOCIAL RIGHTS

See also: 16.5, Toebes, B.C.A.

Arambulo, K. — *Strengthening the Supervision of the International Convenant on Economic, Social and Cultural Rights: Theoretical and Procedural Aspects* (Antwerpen, Intersentia; Oxford, Hart 1999) 449 pp. School of Human Rights Research series Vol. 3. Adaptation of dissertation at University of Utrecht.

5.11 HEAD OF STATE

See: 12.273ICTY, Sluiter, G.

5.210 DIPLOMATIC RELATIONS: RIGHT OF LEGATION, IN GENERAL

See: 14.129, Kooijmans, P.H.

5.365 CONSULAR PUBLIC FUNCTIONS IN THE FIELD OF PRIVATE LAW

Rutten, S. — 'Consulaire huwelijken: wijziging Wet conflictenrecht huwelijk' [Consular marriages: alteration of the conflict law on Marriages Act], 21 *Tijdschrift voor Familie- en Jeugdrecht* (1999) pp. 114-121.

6. THE LAW OF TREATIES

Brouwers, J.G. — *National Treaty Law and Practice: The Netherlands, Austria, Chile, Columbia, Japan, Netherlands, United States* (Washington, ASIL 1999) pp. 133-188. Studies in Transnational Legal Policy No. 30.

Klabbers, J. — 'Re-inventing the Law of Treaties: The Contribution of the EC-Courts', *Netherlands Yearbook of International Law* (1999) pp. 47-74.

6.12 RESERVATIONS TO MULTILATERAL TREATIES
See also: 4.741, Roorda, C.

Velde, J. van der — 'De toetsing van voorbehouden in Straatsburg; Kroniek van de EHRM-jurisprudentie over voorbehouden' [The test of reservations in Strassburg; chronicle of the ECHR-jurisprudence on reservations], 24 *NJCM Bulletin* (1999) pp. 205-218.

6.21 THE OBSERVANCE OF TREATIES
See: 4.7, Berkhout-Van Poelgeest, A.M.; Kelk, C.; Munneke, H.F.; Schermers, H.G.

6.224 CONFLICTS BETWEEN TREATIES

Boer, M. den; Corrado, L. — 'For the Record or Off the Record: Comments About the Incorporation of Schengen into the EU', 1 *European Journal of Migration and Law* (1999) pp. 397-418.

7.21 EXTRATERRITORIAL SCOPE OF LEGISLATIVE ACTS
See: 4.63, Hattum, W.F. van
11.21, Knoops, G.G.J.

8.2 TERRITORIAL JURISDICTION
See: 4.63, Hattum, W.F. van
16.726, Wolswijk H.D.

8.23 CONCURRENT TERRITORIAL JURISDICTION AND EXTRA-TERRITORIALITY

See: 1.203, Kortmann, C.A.J.M.
11.21, Knoops, G.G.J.
16.726, Wolswijk H.D.

9. SEAS, WATERWAYS IN GENERAL

See also: 9.92, Nollkaemper, A.

Schrijver, N.J. — 'De teloorgang van het Gemeenschappelijk Erfgoed der Mensheid' [The loss of the common heritage of mankind], 48 *Ars Aequi* (1999) pp. 405-412.

9.1 THE TERRITORIAL SEA

Hoeven, R. van der — 'De rechtsmacht van kust- en havenstaat' [The jurisdiction of coast- and harbour state], 48 *Ars Aequi* (1999) pp. 380-388.

9.11 ADMEASUREMENT OF THE TERRITORIAL SEA

Molenaar, E.J. — 'Het zeegat van Goeree. Rariteit binnen de Nederlandse visserijwetgeving' [The sea gate of Goeree. Curiosity in dutch fishing laws], 74 *Nederlands Juristenblad* (1999) pp. 550-553.

9.125 FISHERY IN THE TERRITORIAL SEA

See: 9.11, Molenaar, E.J.
9.612, Developments in international, etc.

9.6 THE HIGH SEAS

Kwiatkowska, B. — 'The law of the sea related cases in the International Court of Justice during the presidency of judge Mohammed Bedjaoui (1994-1997)', in *Liber Amicorum Judge Mohammed Bedjaoui*, E. Yapko and T. Boumedra, eds., (The Hague, Kluwer Law International 1999) pp. 399-447. Liber amicorum in honor of Judge Mohammed Bedjaoui.

9.612 FISHERY ON THE HIGH SEAS

— *Developments in International Fisheries Law*, Hey, E., ed. (The Hague, Kluwer Law International 1999) 632 pp.

9.619 EXCLUSIVE ECONOMIC ZONE

Entius, Y.H.M. — 'Gewapende conflicten in de Exclusieve Economische Zone (EEZ). De invloed op de visserijrechten en de jurisdictie van een neutrale staat' [Armed conflicts in the exclusive economic zone (EEZ). The influence on the rights of fishery and the jurisdiction of a neutral state], 92 *Militair Rechtelijk Tijdschrift* (1999) pp. 177-186.

9.63 JURISDICTION OF A STATE ON THE HIGH SEAS

See: 9.1, Hoeven, R. van der
9.619, Entius, Y.H.M.

9.634 ARTIFICIAL ISLANDS

Wassenbergh, H. — 'The Status and Use of an Airport on an Artificial Island', 24 *Air and Space Law* (1999) pp. 177-180.

9.65 POLLUTION OF THE HIGH SEAS

See also: 1.21, Brans, E.H.P.; Veen, G.A. van der
16.55, Borgers, H.C.

Boer, J.E. de — 'Internationale aansprakelijkheidsverdragen inzake olie verontreiniging en het zeevervoer van gevaarlijke stoffen' [International liability conventions on oil pollution and the carriage of hazardous and noxious substances by sea], *Tijdschrift voor Milieu-aansprakelijkheid* (1999) pp. 105-108.

Duursma, E.K. — *Dumped Chemical Weapons in the Sea-options* (Amsterdam, Dr. A.H. Heineken Foundation for the Environment 1999) 60 pp.

9.92 INTERNATIONAL RIVERS

Nollkaemper, A. — 'Beschermde rechtsbelangen in het internationale waterrecht' [Protected legal interests in international waterlaw], 48 *Ars Aequi* (1999) pp. 413-418.

9.922 SHIPPING

Hacksteiner, T.K. — 'Uniforme regels voor de Europese binnenvaart?' [Uniform rules for European inland shipping?], 48 *Ars Aequi* (1999) pp. 397-404.

10.1 SOVEREIGNTY OVER AIR SPACE

See also: 9.634, Wassenbergh, H.

Heere, W.P. — 'Problems of Jurisdiction in Air and Outer Space', 24 *Air and Space Law* (1999) pp. 70-83.

10.3 OUTER SPACE

See also: 3.222 ECSL, Dunk, F.G. van der
10.1, Heere, W.P.

Heere, W.P. — 'Vienna, Unispace III, 19-30 July 1999', 24 *Air and Space Law* (1999) pp. 268-272. Report of Conference.

11.21 RESPONSIBILITY OF STATES

Commissie van Advies inzake Volkenrechtelijke Vraagstukken — *Advies inzake: 'International liability for injurious consequences arising out of acts not prohibited by international law'* [Advisory committee on issues of public international law; advisory report on: 'International liability for injurious consequences arising out of acts not prohibited by international law'], (The Hague 2000) Jaarverslag 1999 van Commissie van Advies inzake Volkenrechtelijke Vraagstukken, annex 5, pp. 1-10.

Knoops, G.G.J. — 'De Lockerbie-affaire: Transponering van internationaalrechtelijke staatsaansprakelijkheid naar nationale jurisdictie. No hiding place for the State?' [The Lockerbie affair: the transponing of international legal state resposibility to national jurisidiction. no hiding place for the state?], 29 *Delikt en Delinkwent* (1999) pp. 601-613.

11.2111 ACTS OF PRIVATE PERSONS

See: 11.21, Knoops, G.G.J.

11.215 FACTORS EXCLUDING RESPONSIBILITY (SELF-DEFENCE, NECESSITY, REPRISALS)

Knoops, G.G.J. — 'Interstatelijk noodweerrecht: disculpatiegrond voor internationaalrechtelijke onrechtmatige daad' [Interstate right of self-defence: ground of justification for an international unlawful act?], 74 *Nederlands Juristenblad* (1999) pp. 2016-2021.

11.216 REPARATION (RESTITUTION IN INTEGRUM, DAMAGES, SATISFACTION, GUARANTEES)

Boven, T. van — 'Rendering justice to victims: a case for reparations', in *Realism and moralism in international relations; essays in honor of Frans A.M. Alting von Geusau*, W.J.M. van Genugten, E.M.H. Hirsch Ballin, E.J. Janse de Jonge and P.H. Kooijmans, eds., (The Hague, Kluwer Law International 1999) pp. 107-128.

11.22 RESPONSIBILITY OF INTERNATIONAL ORGANIZATIONS

Lawson, R.A. — *Het EVRM en de Europese Gemeenschappen; bouwstenen voor een aansprakelijkheidsregime voor het optreden van internationale organisaties* [The ECHR and the European Communities; building material for a liability regime for the actions of international organizations] (Deventer, Kluwer 1999) 568 pp. Europese Monografieen 61, edited version of the dissertation at the University of Leiden.

11.241 RESPONSIBILITY OF INDIVIDUALS

See: 11.3, Dugard, J.; McDonald, A.
12.273 ICTY, Sluiter, G.

11.243 RESPONSIBILITY OF CORPORATIONS

Kamminga, M. — 'Holding Multinational Corporations Accountable for Human Rights Abuses: A Challenge for the European Community', in *The EU and Human Rights* (Oxford, Oxford University Press 1999) pp. 553-570.

11.3 'INTERNATIONAL CRIMES', WAR CRIMES, CRIMES AGAINST PEACE, CRIMES AGAINST HUMANITY

Dugard, J. — 'Dealing With Crimes of a Past Regime. Is Amnesty Still an Option?', 12 *Leiden Journal of International Law* (1999) pp. 1001-1015.

McDonald, A. — 'Sex Crimes at the ad hoc Tribunals; The decisions in the cases of Akayesu, Čelebiči and Furundžija', 15 *Nemesis* (1999) No. 3, pp. 72-82.

11.31 TERRORISM

See also: 1.203, Kortmann, C.A.J.M.

Dugard, J. — 'Terrorism and international law: consensus at last?', in *Liber Amicorum Judge Mohammed Bedjaoui*, E. Yapko, T. Boumedra, eds. (The Hague, Kluwer Law International 1999) pp. 159-171. Liber amicorum in honor of Judge Mohammed Bedjaoui.

Leeuwen, M. van — 'Religieus terrorisme als "nieuwe dreiging": motieven, middelen, milieu' [Religious terrorism as a "new threat": motives, means, environment], 53 *Internationale Spectator* (1999) pp. 597-602.

Pronk, D. — 'Het tegengaan van ABC-terrorisme; een sleutelrol voor inlichtingendiensten' [The prevention of NBC-terrorism; a keyrole for intelligence services], 23 *Atlantisch Perspectief* (1999) No. 5, pp. 20-23.

12. PACIFIC SETTLEMENT OF DISPUTES

See also: 1.0, Kalshoven, F.
11.3, Dugard, J.
13.14, Waart, P. de
13.2, Cras, M.F.A.; Wecke, L.

Commissie van Advies inzake Volkenrechtelijke Vraagstukken — Commentaar inzake preadvies: "Peaceful settlement of disputes" van Fransisco Orreco Vicuña en Cristopher Pinto [Advisory Committee on issues of public international law; comments on the preliminary report: "peacefull settlement of disputes" of Fransisco Orreco Vicuña and Cristopher Pinto], in Jaarverslag 1999 van de Commissie van Advies inzake Volkenrechtelijke Vraagstukken (The Hague, 2000) annex 1, pp. 1-17.

12.211 NEGOTIATION, DIPLOMACY

See: 14.1293, Leurdijk, D.A.

12.262 THE PERMANENT COURT OF ARBITRATION

See: 1.0, Kalshoven, F.; Myjer, E.P.J.

12.270 GENERAL QUESTIONS OF JUDICIAL SETTLEMENT BY INTERNATIONAL COURTS

See: 12.273 ICC, Sluiter, G.; Swart, B.
12.272 ICJ, Werner, W.G.

12.2704 EXECUTION AND OTHER CONSEQUENCES OF THE JUDGMENT

See also: 3.221 WTO, Kuilwijk, K.J.
4.66, Boven, T. van; Flinterman, C.; Rieter, E.

— *The Execution of Strasbourg and Geneva Human Rights Decisions in the National Legal Order*, T. Barkhuysen, M. van Emmerik and P.H. van Kempen, eds. (The Hague, Martinus Nijhoff Publishers 1999) 416 pp.

Biesheuvel, M.B.W. — 'Europese rechtspraak in de Nederlandse rechtspleging. Impressie uit Den Haag en Luxemburg; Bespreking van het preadvies van mr A.W.H. Meij' [European jurisdiction in the Dutch administration of law. Impression of The Hague and Luxembourg; proceedings of the discussion of the preliminary report of A.W.H. Meij, LL M], 74 *Nederlands Juristenblad* (1999) pp. 987-989.

Bleichrodt, F.W. — 'Verslag van de vergadering van 20 november 1998 van de vereniging voor vergelijkende studie van het recht in Nederland en Belgie, afdeling strafrecht.' [Report of the meeting of 20 November 1998 of the society of comparative study on the law of the Netherlands and Belgium, department of criminal law], 74 *Nederlands Juristenblad* (1999) pp. 911-912.

Hirsch Ballin, E.M.H. — 'Vervlechting van rechtsordes; Bespreking van het preadvies van Dr. R.A. Lawson' [Interweaving of jurisdictions; comments on the preliminary report of Dr. R.A. Lawson], 22 *Nederlands Juristenblad* (1999) pp. 981-986.

Hoefer-van Dongen, P. — 'Interactieve rechters; De NJV-vergadering op 11 juni 1999 te 's-Hertogenbosch' [Interactive judges; the meeting of the Dutch laywer society on 11 June 1999 in 's-Hertogenbosch], 74 *Nederlands Juristenblad* (1999) pp. 1256-1258.

Kempen, P.H.P.H.M.C. van — 'De strafrechtelijke gevolgen binnen de Nederlandse rechtsorde van beslissingen van het Europees Hof voor de Rechten van de Mens' [The criminal consequences in the Dutch legal order of the decisions of the European Court of Human Rights], 29 *Delikt en Delinkwent* (1999) pp. 96-152.

Lawson, R.A.; Meij, A.W.H. — *Internationale rechtspraak in de Nederlandse rechtsorde: preadviezen* [International jurisdiction in the dutch legal order: preliminary reports] (Deventer, Tjeenk Willink 1999) 221 pp. Preliminary reports for the Meeting of the Dutch Laywer Society.

12.272 THE PERMANENT COURT OF INTERNATIONAL JUSTICE AND THE INTERNATIONAL COURT OF JUSTICE

International Court of Justice

See also: 9.6, Kwiatkowska, B.
12.2704, Lawson, R.A.; Meij, A.W.H.
12.273 ICC, Hebel, H.A.M. von; Lammers, J.G.; Schukking, J.
13.222, Dekker, G.R. den; Wessel, R.A.

Eyffinger, A. — *La Cour internationale de Justice 1946-1996* [The International Court of Justice 1946-1996] (The Hague, Kluwer Law International 1999) 444 pp.

Werner, W.G. — 'Rechterlijke controle op handelingen van de Veiligheidsraad' [Legal control on acts of the Security Council], 28 *Transaktie* (1999) pp. 336-359.

12.273 OTHER JUDICIAL TRIBUNALS

European Court of Human Rights

See also:	1.2,	Stroink, F.A.M.
	4.7,	Schermers, H.G.; Uildriks, N.
	4.73,	Barkhuysen, T.; Boone, M.; Emmerik, M.L. van; Franken, A.A; Prakken, T.
	6.12,	Velde, J. van der

Hoefer-van Dongen, P.T.C. — 'Op weg naar een Europees Constitutioneel Hof; interview met onze rechter in Straatsburg' [Towards a European Constitutional Court; interview with our judge in Strassburg], 74 *Nederlands Juristenblad* (1999) pp. 1025-1034.

Huussen, I.B.; Velde, J. van der — *EVRM: totstandkoming, toezichtmechanisme en procedure bij het Hof* [EVHR: establishment, supervision mechanism and procedure at the court] (Lelystad, Koninklijke Vermande 1999) 64 pp.

Loof, J.P. — 'Een nieuwe structuur voor het EVRM toezichtsmechanisme; Europees Hof Rechten van de Mens' [A new structure for ECHR supervision mechanism; European Court of Human Rights], *Migrantenrecht* (1999) pp. 9-12.

European Court of Justice

See also:	3.2112,	Ooik, R.H.
	6.,	Klabbers, J.
	12.2704,	Biesheuvel, M.B.W.; Hirsch Ballin, E.M.H.; Hoefer-van Dongen, P.; Lawson, R.; Meij A.W.H.

Curtin, D.M.; Ooik, R.H. van — 'Een Hof van Justitie van de Europese Unie?' [A Court of Justice of the European Union], 47 *Sociaal-Economische Wetgeving* (1999) pp. 24-38.

Witte, J.B. de — 'The Past and Future Role of the European Court of Justice in the Protection of Human Rights', in *The EU and Human Rights* (Oxford, University Press 1999) pp. 859-898

International Criminal Court

See also:	1.0,	Myjer, E.P.J.
	13.222,	Dekker, G.R. den; Wessel, R.A.

Barkhuysen, T.; Kortmann, C.N.J. — 'Oorlog en recht' [War and law], 79 *Advocatenblad* (1999) pp. 617-620.

Bos, A. — 'The International Criminal Court: recent developments', in *Reflections on the International Criminal Court*, H.A.M. von Hebel, J.G., Lammers and J. Schukking, eds. (The Hague, T.M.C. Asser Press 1999) pp. 39-46. Essays in honor of Adriaan Bos.

Boven, T. van — 'The position of the victim in the statute of the International Criminal Court', in *Reflections on the International Criminal Court*, H.A.M. von Hebel, J.G. Lammers and J. Schukking, eds. (The Hague, T.M.C. Asser Press 1999) pp. 77-89. Essays in honor of Adriaan Bos.

Boven, T. van; Hebel, H.A.M. von — 'De oprichting van een internationaal strafhof – Een echte stap voorwaarts?' [The realization of an international criminal – court a real step in the right direction?], 74 *Nederlands Juristenblad* (1999) pp. 759-764.

Hebel, H.A.M. von — 'An international criminal court; A historical perspective', in *Reflections on the International Criminal Court*, H.A.M. von Hebel, J.G. Lammers and J. Schukking, eds. (The Hague, T.M.C. Asser Press 1999) pp. 13-38. Essays in honor of Adriaan Bos.

— *Reflections on the International Criminal Court*, H.A.M. von Hebel, J.G. Lammers and J. Schukking, eds. (The Hague, T.M.C. Asser Press 1999) 211 pp. Essays in Honour of Adriaan Bos.

Henquet, T. — 'Mandatory Compliance Powers vis-a-vis States by the Ad Hoc Tribunals and the International Criminal Court: A Comparative Analysis', 12 *Leiden Journal of International Law* (1999) pp. 969-999.

Strijards, G.A.M. — 'De weergalm van een Romeins applaus; De totstandkoming van een internationaal strafhof' [The echo of a Roman applause; the realization of an International Criminal Court], 74 *Nederlands Juristenblad* (1999) pp. 765-771.

Strijards G.A.M. — 'Een internationaal strafhof. Jurisdictie en rechtshulpaspecten' [An International Criminal Court. Jurisdiction and aspects of legal aid], 29 *Delikt en Delinkwent* (1999) pp. 772-787.

Strijards, G.A.M. — 'Een internationaal strafhof. Strafvordelijke aspecten' [An International Criminal Court. Criminal procedural aspects], 29 *Delikt en Delinkwent* (1999) pp. 524-537.

Strijards, G.A.M. — 'The Institution of The International Criminal Court', 12 *Leiden Journal of International Law* (1999) pp. 671-681.

Swart, B.; Sluiter, G. — 'The International Criminal Court and international criminal co-operation', in *Reflections on the International Criminal Court,* H.A.M. von Hebel, J.G. Lammers and J. Schukking, eds. (The Hague, T.M.C. Asser Press 1999) pp. 91-127. Essays in honor of Adriaan Bos.

Wilt, H. van der — 'Rome aan de wieg van een onafhankelijk internationaal strafhof' [Rome at the cradle of an independent International Criminal Court], 24 *NJCM Bulletin* (1999) pp. 187-205.

Zwanenburg, M. — 'The Statute for an International Criminal Court and the United States: Peace Without Justice?', 12 *Leiden Journal of International Law* (1999) pp. 1-7.

International Criminal Tribunal for Rwanda

See also:	12.273 ICC,	Henquet, T.
	13.222,	Dekker, G.R. den; Wessel, R.A.

Wladimiroff, M. — 'The Assignment of the Defence Council Before the International Criminal Tribunal for Rwanda', 12 *Leiden Journal of International Law* (1999) pp. 957-968.

International Criminal Tribunal for the Former Yugoslavia

See also:	1.0,	Myjer, E.P.J.
	12.273 ICC,	Hebel, H.A.M. von; Henquet, T.; Lammers, J.G.; Schukking, J.
	13.221,	Kleffner, J.
	13.222,	Dekker, G.R. den; Wessel, R.A.

Sliedregt, E. van — 'First Lustrum for the Yugoslav Tribunal – A Reason to Celebrate?', 5 *International Peacekeeping* (1999) pp. 87-91.

Sluiter, G. — 'Enige volkenrechtelijke en strafrechtelijke kanttekeningen bij de vervolging van Slobodan Milosević door het Joegoslavie Tribunaal' [Some remarks of international law and criminal law on the prosecution of Slobodan Milosević by the Yugoslavia Tribunal], 92 *Militair Rechtelijk Tijdschrift* (1999) pp. 217-228.

Sluiter, G. — 'Vervolging van Milosević door het Joegoslaviё Tribunaal' [Prosecution of Milosevic by the Yugoslavia Tribunal], 74 *Nederlands Juristenblad* (1999) pp. 1198-1199.

12.28 SETTLEMENT WITHIN INTERNATIONAL ORGANIZATIONS

See: 3.221 WTO, Kuilwijk, K.J.

12.281 THE ROLE OF INTERNATIONAL ORGANIZATIONS IN THE MAINTENANCE OF PEACE
See: 3.222 OSCE, Cohen, J.

13.14 UNILATERAL INTERVENTION

Blockmans, S. — 'Moving Into Unchartered Waters: An Emerging Right of Unilateral Humanitarian Intervention?', 12 *Leiden Journal of International Law* (1999) pp. 759-786.

Dekker, G. den — 'De rechtsbasis voor militair ingrijpen in Irak (1998)' [The legal basis for military intervention in Iraq], 18 *Merkourios* (1999) No. 53, pp. 8-21.

Unck, M.B. — 'De Koerdische kwestie, een ommekeer?; Gedogen of legitimeren van humanitaire interventie' [The Kurdian matter, a change? Toleration or legitimation of humanitarian intervention], 109 *Marineblad* (1999) pp. 18-23 / 18 *Merkourios* (1999) No. 53, pp. 22-31.

13.2 COLLECTIVE MEASURES

Cras, M.F.A.; Wecke, L. — 'Conflictpreventie: meer dan een toverwoord?' [Conflict prevention: more than a magic word?], *Jaarboek Koninklijke Vereniging ter Beoefening van de Krijgswetenschap* (1998) pp. 242-259.

13.22 REGIME OF THE UNITED NATIONS
See also: 3.342, Pauwels, A.

Bakker, E. — 'Conflictpreventie door de Hoge Commissaris inzake nationale minderheden (1993-1994)' [Conflict prevention by the High Comissionair concerning national minorities (1993-1994)], *Jaarboek Vrede en Veiligheid* (1999) pp. 113-134.

Genugten, W.J.M. van; Groot, G.A. de — *United Nations Sanctions; Effectiveness and effects, especially in the field of human rights: A multi-disciplinary approach* (Antwerpen, Intersentia 1999) 161 pp.

13.221 PEACE-KEEPING OPERATIONS
See also: 13.222, Dekker, G.R. den; Wessel, R.A.

Kleffner, J.K. — 'SFOR's Half-hearted Compliance with its International Obligation to Arrest ICTY Indictees', 5 *International Peacekeeping* (1999) pp. 80-87

Walraven, K. van — *The Pretence of Peace-Keeping. ECOMOG, West-Africa and Liberia (1990-1998)*, (The Hague, Clingendael Notitie Reeks 1999) 131 pp. No. 10.

Zwanenburg, M. — 'Double Standards in Peacekeeping? Subcontracting Peacekeeping and International Humanitarian Law', 12 *Leiden Journal of International Law* (1999) pp. 753-757.

13.222 INTERVENTION

See also:	4.7,	Human Rights, etc.
	11.215,	Knoops, G.G.J.
	14.1293,	Leurdijk, D.A.

Faber, M.J. — 'Rechtvaardiging van de krijgsmacht; humanitaire interventie' [Justification of the armed forces; humanitarian intervention], 53 *Internationale Spectator* (1999) pp. 396-401.

Haandrikman, Y. — 'Mondiale interdependentie en militaire interventies' [Global interpendence and military interventions], 23 *Atlantisch Perspectief* (1999) No. 3, pp. 12-16.

Wessel, R.A.; Dekker, G.R. den — 'Veiligheid en volkenrecht: verval van het VN-systeem?' [Security and International law: decay of the UN-system?], *Jaarboek Vrede en Veiligheid* (1999) pp. 1-36.

13.224 UN FORCES; INTERNATIONAL POLICE-FORCE

See also:	13.221,	Kleffner, J.K.

Zwanenburg, M. — 'The Secretary-General's Bulletin on Observance by United Nations Forces of International Humanitarian Law: Some Preliminary Observations', 5 *International Peacekeeping* (1999) pp. 133-139.

13.23 REGIME OF OTHER INTERNATIONAL ORGANIZATIONS

See also:	3.222 NATO,	Duursma, J.
	11.215,	Knoops, G.G.J.
	13.222,	Faber, M.J.
	14.1121,	Aalbers, C.T.; Leurdijk, D.A.; Molier, G.; Myjer, E.P.J.

Bakker, E. — 'Kosovo conflict: who is to blame?', 24 *Jason Magazine* (1999) No. 1, pp. 16-20.

Blokker, N.M. — 'Kosovo, de NAVO en de Veiligheidsraad' [Kosovo, the NATO and the Security Council], 48 *Ars Aequi* (1999) pp. 467-471.

Daalder, I. H. — 'Nato, the UN and the Use of Force', 5 *International Peacekeeping* (1999) pp. 27-35.

Dekker, G. den; Wessel, R.A. — 'De NAVO in Kosovo; Toetssteen voor de militaire interventie?' [The NATO in Kosovo; touchstone for military intervention?], 53 *Internationale Spectator* (1999) pp. 358-367.

Leurdijk, D. A. — 'Kosovo: a Mandate for NATO?', 24 *Jason Magazine* (1999) No. 1, pp. 29-33.

Molier, G. — 'De Tachtigdaagse Oorlog: Kosovo, de NAVO-bombardementen en de doctrine van humanitaire interventie' [The eighty-days war: Kosovo, the NATO bombardments and the doctrine of humanitarian intervention], 12 *VN-Forum* (1999) No. 3, pp. 20-33.

Waart, P. de — 'Kosovo, Nederland en de VN' [Kosovo, the Netherlands and the UN], 12 *VN-Forum* (1999) No.2, pp. 3-4.

14.1121 JUS AD BELLUM, JUST WAR

See also:

3.222 NATO,	Duursma, J.
4.7,	Human Rights, etc.
11.215,	Knoops, G.G.J.
12.273 ICC,	Barkhuysen, T.; Kortmann, C.N.J.
14.1293,	Leurdijk, D.A.

Aalbers, C.T. — 'De legitimiteit van humanitaire interventies na de Koude Oorlog' [The legitimacy of humanitarian interventions after the cold war], 92 *Militair Rechtelijk Tijdschrift* (1999) pp. 141-152.

Gill, T. — 'The Nuclear Weapons Advisory Opinion of the International Court of Justice and the Fundamental Distinction Between the Jus ad Bellum and the Jus in Bello', 12 *Leiden Journal of International Law* (1999) pp. 61-124.

Molier, G. — 'Kosovo en het Internationaal Recht: de legaliteit van het gebruik van geweld' [Kosovo and international law: the legality of the use of force], 12 *VN-Forum* (1999) No. 1, pp. 1-15.

Myjer, E.P.J. — 'Internationaal recht naar de schroothoop?' [International law wind up on the scrapheap?], 74 *Nederlands Juristenblad* (1999) pp. 681-683.

14.113 LIMITATION AND REDUCTION OF ARMANENTS, DISARMAMENT

See:	1.15,	Internationale Organisatie, etc.
	11.31,	Pronk, D.

Commissie van Advies inzake Volkenrechtelijke Vraagstukken — 'Commentaar inzake preadvies: The development of international law relating to disarmament and arms control since the first Hague peace conference in 1899 van Hans Blix' [Advisory committee on issues of public international law; comments on the preliminary report: "The development of international law relating to disarmament and arms control since the first Hague peace conference in 1899" of Hans Blix], Jaarverslag van de Commissie van Advies inzake Volkenrechtelijke Vraagstukken, 1999, (The Hague, 2000) annex 3, pp. 1-7.

14.1133 LIMITATION AND CHEMICAL AND BIOLOGICAL WEAPONS

See:	9.65,	Duursma, E.K.

14.12 THE LAWS OF WAR

See:	1.0,	Kalshoven, F.
	14.125,	Commissie van Advies, etc.

14.125 HUMANITARIAN LAW

See also:	13.221,	Zwanenburg, M.
	13.224,	Zwanenburg, M.

Commissie van Advies inzake Volkenrechtelijke Vraagstukken — Commentaar inzake preadvies: International humanitarian law and the laws of war van Cristopher Greenwood [Advisory committee on issues of public international law; comments on the preliminary report: 'International humanitarian law and the laws of war' of Cristopher Greenwood], Jaarverslag 1999 van de Commissie van Advies inzake Volkenrechtelijke Vraagstukken (The Hague, 2000) annex 2, pp. 1-12.

Coolen, G.L. — 'De Balkanoorlog en het humanitaire oorlogsrecht' [The Balkan war and humanitarian laws of war], *Iust* (1999) pp. 33-40.

Coolen, G.L. — *Humanitair oorlogsrecht* [Humanitarian laws of war] (Deventer, Tjeenk Willink 1998) 211 pp.

14.1252 PRISONERS OF WAR

Roodt, E. de — 'Britse en Duitse krijgsgevangenen in Nederland; Uitwisseling en internering tijdens de Eerste Wereldoorlog' [British and German prisoners of war in the Netherlands; exchange and detention during World War I], 168 *Militaire Spectator* (1999) pp. 40-53.

14.1253 MERCENARIES

Mentjox, G.; Sandee, R. — 'De privatisering van oorlog; Het toenemende belang van Private Military Companies' [The privatization of war; the increasing interest of private military companies], 24 *Jason Magazine* (1999) No. 2, pp. 13-15.

14.129 TERMINATION OF WAR, TREATIES OF PEACE

Kooijmans, P.H. — 'De toekomst van de vrede' [The future of peace], 53 *Internationale Spectator* (1999) pp. 3-7.

14.1293 OTHER ARRANGEMENTS

See also:	3.14,	Dijkstra, G.S.A.
	3.342,	Pauwels, A

Leurdijk, D.A. — 'Kosovo: A Case of Coercive Diplomacy', 10 *Helsinki Monitor* (1999) No. 2, pp. 8-18.

14.21 RIGHTS AND DUTIES OF STATES IN A CIVIL WAR

See:	14.1121,	Molier, G.

15.12 SEA WARFARE

See:	9.619,	Entius, Y.H.M.

16.11 TRADE

See:	1.15,	Internationale Organisatie, etc.
	3.221 WTO,	Kuilwijk, K.J.
	16.55,	Wiers, J.

16.112 MEASURES RESULTING IN PROMOTION OR RESTRICTION OF TRADE AND OTHER TRAFFIC OF GOODS

Colijn, K.; Rusman, P. — 'Het beleid ten aanzien van de handel in strategische goederen' [The policy concerning the trade in strategic goods], *Jaarboek Vrede en Veiligheid* (1999) pp. 194-203.

16.164 PROTECTION OF PLANTS AND ANIMALS
See: 16.55, Wiers, J.

16.2 INTERNATIONAL LEGAL ASPECTS OF ECONOMIC DEVELOPMENT AND DEVELOPMENT CO-OPERATION (FOR INTERNATIONAL ORGANIZATIONS: SEE 3.22)

Berends, G. — 'Kleur bekennen; Tien jaar Nederlandse hulp aan Midden- en Oost-Europa' [Showing the colors; ten years of Dutch support to Middle- and Eastern Europe], 53 *Internationale Spectator* (1999) pp. 645-650.

Kratzenberg, J. — Mensenrechten in de ontwikkelingssamenwerking: een vergelijkende studie naar de ontwikkelingssamenwerking van de Nederlandse regering en NOVIB met Nicaragua 1979-1989 [Human rights in development cooperation: a comparative study on the development cooperation of the Dutch government and NOVIB with Nicaragua 1979-1989] (Rotterdam, Erasmus Universiteit 1999) 127 pp. Dissertation at the University of Rotterdam.

16.3 MONETARY MATTERS
See: 1.15, Internationale Organisatie, etc.
3.223 EMU, Amtenbrink, F.

16.441 SEA TRAFFIC (INCLUDING COLLISIONS, ASSISTANCE, SALVAGE)

Bom, C.W.D. — 'Berging onder 'No Cure - No Pay': Hoe lang nog?' [Salvage under 'no cure - no pay: how much longer?], *Tijdschrift voor Milieuaansprakelijkheid* (1999) pp. 75-76.

Ziel, G.J. van der — 'De milieufactor in het nieuwe hulp- en bergingsverdrag' [The environmental issue in the international convention on salvage, 1989], *Tijdschrift voor Milieuaansprakelijkheid* (1999) pp. 71-74.

16.442 MARITIME TRANSPORT

See: 9.65, Boer, J.E. de

16.5 SOCIAL AND HEALTH MATTERS (SEE 3.22)

See also: 3.221 ILO, Heijden, P.F. van der; Sybesma-Knol, R.G.
4.73, Lenos, E.E.V.

Heijden van der, P.F.; Sjers, C.M. — 'Het Verdrag van Amsterdam en een sociaal Europa' [The Treaty of Amsterdam and a social Europe], 74 *Nederlands Juristenblad* (1999) pp. 991-998.

Toebes, B.C.A. — 'Het recht op gezondheid: geen recht om gezond te zijn' [The right to health: not a right to be healthy], 48 *Ars Aequi* (1999) pp. 912-915.

Toebes, B.C.A. — *The Right to Health as a Human Right in International Law* (Antwerpen, Intersentia / Oxford, Hart 1999) 433 pp. Dissertation at the University of Utrecht.

16.51 LABOUR AND RELATED MATTERS

Dooren, M.I. van — 'Over de toepassing in Nederland van het internationaal recht met betrekking tot het recht op arbeid en het verbod van rassendiscriminatie' [The application in the Netherlands of international law concerning the right on labour and the prohibition of race discrimination], 24 *NJCM Bulletin* (1999) pp. 888-899.

Wentholt, K. — 'Effectuering van het recht op arbeid voor vrouwen: (inter)nationale ontwikkelingen met betrekking tot deeltijdarbeid' [The execution of the right on labour for women: (inter)national developments concerning partime labour], 24 *NJCM Bulletin* (1999) pp. 873-887.

16.55 ENVIRONMENTAL QUESTIONS

See also: 3.3, Arts, B.
4.73, Backes, C.W.; Hoitink, J.E.; Lanen, J.J.M. van
16.441, Ziel, G.J. van der

Borgers, H.C. — 'In dubio pro natura: het functionele perspectief van het voorzorgsbeginsel' [In dubio pro natura: the functional perspective of the precaution principle], 48 *Ars Aequi* (1999) pp. 431-441.

Kakebeeke, W.; Horvath, K.E. — 'Het verdrag van Arhus' [The Arhus Treaty], 26 *Tijdschrift voor Milieu en Recht* (1999) No. 4, pp. 98-102.

Koopmans, I.M. — 'Europa dwingt tot broodnodige aanpassing van het milieustrafrecht' [Europe forces to badly needed adaption of environmental criminal law], 74 *Nederlands Juristenblad* (1999) pp. 1308-1314.

Wiers, J. — 'Garnalen, schildpadden en de Wereldhandelsorganisatie' [Shrimps, turtles and the World Trade Organization], 26 *Tijdschrift voor Milieu en Recht* (1999) No. 4, pp. 103-107.

16.6 CULTURAL MATTERS (See 3.22)
See also: 4.7, Bronkhorst, D.; Law and Cultural Diversity

Albers, H.S.J. — *Europees Gemeenschapsrecht en cultuur: eenheid en verscheidenheid* [Law of the European community and culture: unity and diversity] (Deventer, Kluwer 1999) 461 pp. Europeese Monografieen 60. Dissertation at the University of Leiden.

Sjouke, P.S. — *Het behoud van cultuurgoederen, twee werelden, twee visies* (Nijmegen, Ars Aequi Libri 1999) 355 pp. Dissertation at the University of Rotterdam.

16.723 INTELLECTUAL PROPERTY

Bonofacio, M. — 'The Information Society and the Harmonisation of Copyright and Related Rights: (Over)stretching the Legal Basis of Article 95 (100A)?', 26 *Legal Issues of European Integration* (1999) pp. 1-90.

16.724 LAW OF CIVIL PROCEDURE

Berg, A.J. van den — '*Improving the Efficiency of Arbitration Agreements and Awards: 40 Years of Application of the New York Convention* (The Hague, Kluwer Law International 1999) 732 pp. International Arbitration Congress, Paris 3-6 May 1998. ICCA Congress Series No. 9

16.725 PRIVATE INTERNATIONAL LAW
See also: 5.365, Rutten, S.

Betlem, G.; Hondius, E.H. — 'Europees privaatrecht na Amsterdam' [European private law after Amsterdam], 74 *Nederlands Juristenblad* (1999) pp. 1137-1147.

Boer, T.M. de — 'Brussel II: een eerste stap naar een communautair IPR' [Brussels II: a first step towards a communitarian IPL], 21 *Tijdschrift voor Familie- en Jeugdrecht* (1999) pp. 244-250.

Galen, R.J. van; Apeldoorn, J.C. van; Berends, A.J. — *Grensoverschrijdende insolventieprocedures* [Border crossing insolvency procedures] (Deventer, Kluwer 1999) 47 pp. Report of the discussion of the annual meeting. Mededelingen [Proceedings] of the Netherlands Branch of the International Law Association 118

16.726 CRIMINAL LAW

See also: 4.6, Jaarverslag van de Permanente Commissie
16.55, Koopmans, I.M.

Corstens, G.J.M. — 'Strafrechtspleging na het Verdrag van Amsterdam' [The judicial procedure in criminal matters after the Treaty of Amsterdam], 74 *Nederlands Juristenblad* (1999) pp. 803-808. (In 28 *Nederlands Juristenblad* (1999) pp. 1323-1324 is a comment of R.H. Lauwaars on this article. This comment is replied by G.J.M. Corstens on the same page.

Spong, G.; Mols, G. — 'De zaak Bouterse; perikelen rond ne bis in idem en Mr. Haakmat' [The Bouterse case; perils on ne bis in idem and Haakmat LL M.], 79 *Advocatenblad* (1999) pp. 7-9. A reaction of Haakmat can be found at 79 *Advocatenblad* (1999) pp. 148-149.

Wolswijk, H.D. — 'Locus Delicti and Criminal Jurisdiction', 46 *Netherlands International Law Review* (1999) pp. 361-382.

Wolswijk, H. D. — *Locus delicti en rechtsmacht* [Locus delicti and jurisdiction], (Deventer, Gouda Quint1998) 353 pp. Pompe Reeks No. 24 Dissertation at the University of Utrecht.

16.8 MILITARY AND SECURITY MATTERS (SEE 3.22)

See also: 1., Realism and Moralism, etc.
1.15, Internationale Organisatie, etc.
3.222 NATO, Colijn, J.; Hirsch Ballin, E.M.H.; Rusman, P.; Wijk, R. de
13.2, Cras, M.F.A.; Wecke, L.

Adviesraad Internationale Vraagstukken — *De ontwikkelingen in de internationale veiligheidssituatie in de jaren negentig: van onveilige zekerheid naar onzekere veiligheid* [Developments in the International security situation in the 1990's: from unsafe security to unsecured safety] (The Hague, Advisory Council on International Affairs 1999) 71 pp. English translation available, 50 pp.

Staden, A. van — 'Mission impossible? Europe's role in diplomacy and international security', in W.J.M. van Genugten, E.M.H. Hirsch Ballin, E.J. Janse de Jonge and P.H. Kooijmans, eds., *Realism and Moralism in International Relations; Essays in Honor of Frans, A.M. Alting von Geusau* (The Hague, Kluwer Law International 1999) pp. 63-70.

Vierhout, R. — 'Het veiligheidsbeleid van de (West) Europese Unie: Kosovo als katalysator' [The security policy of the (western) European Union: Kosovo as a katalystor], *Jaarboek Vrede en Veiligheid* (1999) pp. 82-100.

Wurzner, H. — 'Van onveilige zekerheid naar onzekere veiligheid' [From an unsafe security to an unsecured safety], 23 *Atlantisch Perspectief* (1999) No. 5, pp. 4-8.

TABLE OF CASES*

INTERNATIONAL

* The cases marked by an asterisk are to be found in the section on 'Netherlands Judicial Decisions Involving Questions of Public International Law, 1998-1999'.

The table of cases was compiled by Mrs. B.M. Hall, Elie, UK.

INDEX*

* Multilateral agreements of all kinds (Acts, Conventions, Covenants, Protocols, Statutes, Treaties, etc.) are, for the most part, indexed under 'Agreements, multilateral'. Wherever possible, subheadings by topic have been introduced. Agreements concluded between the ECSC, EEC and Benelux Member States, and those concluded by the ECSC, EEC and Benelux with third countries are indexed under ECSC, EEC and Benelux and the name of the third country where appropriate.
The names of the authors appearing in the Literature section (pp. 381-419) have been indexed. The subject-matter referred to in the titles of the books or articles written by these authors, however, has not. Readers are requested to further consult the individual sub-headings contained in this section.

The index was compiled by Mrs. B.M. Hall, Elie, UK.

MIX
Papier aus verantwortungsvollen Quellen
Paper from responsible sources
FSC® C105338

If you have any concerns about our products,
you can contact us on
ProductSafety@springernature.com

In case Publisher is established outside the EU,
the EU authorized representative is:
Springer Nature Customer Service Center GmbH
Europaplatz 3, 69115 Heidelberg, Germany

Printed by Libri Plureos GmbH
in Hamburg, Germany